THE GIANT JOSHUA

THE
GIANT
JOSHUA

BY

MAURINE WHIPPLE

WESTERN EPICS, INC.
Salt Lake City, Utah 84101

ISBN 0–914740–17–2

Printed in the United States of America by
Publishers Press
Salt Lake City, Utah

TO

F. G.

WHO IS ON THE SIDE OF THE ANGELS

Publisher's Foreword

THIS is the new edition of one of the finest novels of Mormon history. *The Giant Joshua,* first printed in 1941, has over the years become known not only as a true picture of polygamy but as a celebration of the pioneer tradition and the women who lived it so bravely.

As a descendant of the real people on whom this story is based, Maureen Whipple has grown up in the surroundings and folklore of the area she writes about, and she has created with fidelity the characters we meet herein.

Because of continuing demand for the book, long out-of-print, Western Epics feels it is a pleasure and privilege to reissue this classic.

PREFACE

THE verses in this book are from the records of Mrs. Arthur F. Miles, whose father, Charles L. Walker, was poet laureate of early Dixie.

While much of the incident is true — that concerning the Virgin River and its dams having been gathered directly from United States Department of Agriculture Bulletin Number 124, and that concerning the starvation years, the plagues, Silver Reef, the polygamy raids having come down to me through diaries and by word of mouth — all the characters are fictitious except those relating directly to history. Erastus Snow is drawn from articles in Church magazines and from local memory. Brigham Young is, of course — always Brigham Young.

Most of the Mormon pioneers are gone now and much of the gallant courage, the unconquerable faith of the old West goes with them, but the spirit that lived in their hearts — as American as Plymouth Rock, as enduring as the Rocky Mountains — that can never die.

Perhaps therefore it is natural for our generation to deify them. Perhaps because of the abuse they suffered for over half a century, it is natural for us even now to carry a chip on our shoulder toward the world — to lack a sense of humor regarding those who could not have survived without humor.

But I believe we detract from their achievement when we paint them with too white a brush. These people of whom I write are my people and I love them, but I believe that what they did becomes even greater when we face the fact that they were human beings by birth and only saints by adoption.

M. W.

October, 1940

CHAPTER I

ALTHOUGH the surface of the rock was yet warm, its inner chill soon began to penetrate Clory's body. But it was such luxury to be free from the wagon's jolting for a second, or the bite of stones through worn shoe leather. Besides, they'd call her soon enough.

She moved her hand over the rock. It was hard and very black, and the surface was gleaming as if it had been rubbed for years with stove polish. This ridge they had just crossed was of the same black metallic formation; Uncle Abijah said it was volcanic and one of the hardest substances known. They had cause to respect its hardness, Clory reflected; they'd been stuck here two days hacking and hewing a dugway so the wagons could inch their painful way up its steep side. Uncle Abijah said gentiles made fun of Mormon dugways, but that a dugway like this, with its ruts cut so deep that a wagon wheel once in the slot never bounced out, could be built up a mountain-side steep enough to make a regular road turn tail and run. But now, facing the more arduous job of descent, she remembered he had said, too, that dugway builders offered no guaranty that all of the fit-out, including wagon, oxen, grub, and humans, would reach bottom at the same point. Two weeks ago just as they were leaving Beaver settlement she had seen a wagon gathering momentum run away with the oxen and end up at the bottom of the hill in splinters.

Now, besides chaining the hind wheels with a 'rough-lock,' the men were carrying out Abijah's suggestion to gather rocks and make drags for the backs of the wagons. She sighed with relief.

For seven days, ever since they had left ice-locked Cedar Fort, they had been continually conquering such hills as this — urging weary oxen up tall pathways and restraining them down almost vertical slopes. Below the rim of the Great Basin — Cedar Fort had marked the rim — such trails as they could make had seemed to take a fiendish glee in harboring concealed chuck holes, ruts, and wagon-splintering rocks. Seven days of trail-building around spiraling, doubling, vividly colored ridges, and through valleys treacherous with sand. Seven days of steadily replacing the black loam of the North with this fine red sand of Dixie.

She wondered where in all these sandy wastes they'd find clay for adobes, and then remembered the river toward which they were traveling. That famous Virgin River (called by the Indians 'Pah-Roosh' or 'Muddy Water') about which she'd heard so much and on whose banks they'd soon all be raising cotton and growing rich just as people did in the real Dixie in the States. She'd glimpsed the river for the first time this morning between a gap in a cracked red mountain — the Rio Virgin, a distant silver shimmer far to the south, faintly outlined with green and set against a misty background of blue mountains merging into sky.

Opposite this range a nearer neighbor gave the north a fanged and scalloped horizon; Abijah said President Young on his exploring trip to this country last spring had named this northern mountain Pine Valley and had suggested they might be able to get lumber from it. Now, snow-patched, shadows like cold blue flesh clinging to the barren bones of its sharp ridges, Pine Valley looked gaunt and forbidding.

White and crimson, or black and yellow and blue — behind her and ahead and around her — spewed in fantastic violence, in every shade and nuance, the colors of this unreal landscape glittered with such intensity that she closed her eyes and for a moment her breath clung in her throat. She felt hemmed in with untamed, imponderable forces. This land was as different from the gentle valleys of the North as she imagined hell would be from heaven. There was only one thing she liked about it. For seven days in spite of all their climbing they had been steadily bumping downward, and now in place of the shivering daylight of Cedar Fort this sun was soft on her cheek and the air just pleasantly biting.

Almost, lifting her face to the warmth, she could forget the hostility of the land; especially if she shut out the mountains and concentrated on the narrow strip of green below her. That was Washington Settlement, where they were going to camp tonight. She thought the handful of homes pretty, and the willow-banked stream reminded her a little of City Creek at home in the Great Salt Lake Valley. But even here lurked a threat: Apostle Snow had been worried about chills and fever along these streams.

It seemed there was no escaping the price this land exacted. Shivering, she lifted her gaze beyond the valley to the west. There, continuing their mad dance, the ridges behind her joined hands with others and circling, tier on tier, concentric rings of color, vermilion, scarlet, maroon, or striped white and pink and gray — pirouetting, gyrating out and down, like a congealed whirlpool — somewhere out there to the west brought their rioting to an end. At the very vortex of this tangled network of canyons there was a long black hill standing smoothly and soberly in the midst of the frenzy about it. Uncle Abijah said that a similar black ridge faced it, although she could only see its crest from here, and that between the two black ridges lay the valley, the valley of sagebrush where she was going to spend all the rest of her life — the valley that was already named, President Young had told them, the city of St. George.

Clory sighed; settling new places was fun, of course, but this place was different. She rubbed her eyes; they ached from too much brilliant light on too many shimmering surfaces. A regular crazy-quilt of a country; a savage, brutal country. Repellent, challenging, wildly beautiful.

Clory shivered and hugged into her shawl, and once more was conscious of the shouting and confusion back of her. Gathering up her skirts, shaking out the crinoline, thinking how glad she'd be to quit all this wagon-climbing and put on real hoops again, she picked her way back to the company.

2

'Clorinda! Clorinda Agatha! We're ready! Ain't no time fer moonin'!'

Running lightly, Clory thought Aunt 'Sheba must surely be mad at her again to call her by her full name like that. She didn't seem able to please Aunt 'Sheba any more. Standing there by the wagon with her hands on her hips, her broad calicoed bosom implacable and her face weathered into a sort of relentlessness, Bathsheba seemed to fit this country. There was a black mole on her chin, and now the black hairs sticking out of it quivered angrily.

'I was only gone a minute, wasn't I, Aunt 'Sheba?'

Even with her panting like that, Bathsheba was thinking grimly, there was something like bells in Clory's voice: a lovely warmth and roundness; a smoothness — like fresh-churned butter after you've worked it awhile with your hands. She hated herself instantly for letting the thought be born, but there it was — the truth.

Well, the girl'd never be able to stand this rough life. Her puniness and small bones and little helpless ways might seem cute to Abijah now, but he'd sing a different tune when he tried to fit them into child-raisin' and hoein' in the fields and all the million-'n'-one chores a pioneer wife had to do in a new country. Clory'd have to fend for herself, too. Abijah couldn't expect the first wife to look out for his other wives; that wasn't her duty. Goodness knows she had done plenty for the girl, mothering her for fifteen years — and this was the thanks she got! Still, she'd go on doing her duty. But not one whit more, even if he did lose his head over a pair of red cheeks! (*He*, too, knew Clory rubbed 'em with her handkerchief!) It was all very well for Abijah to talk about the counsels of Brother Brigham and to remind her that polygamy was holy. That might well be, but the light in Abijah's eyes was sometimes far from holy. She'd had her seven boys by Abijah (goodness knows how many more the Lord had in store for them) and there just wasn't much he could fool her about. Neither Abijah *nor* the Lord.

Well, she, Bathsheba, had warned Abijah that the girl was nothing but a little flibbertigibbet and so washed her hands of the mess. . . .

Clory, clambering up on the wagon tongue, smiled uncertainly at Bathsheba and wondered yet again why Aunt 'Sheba had changed so much since they had started on this Call to the Dixie Mission. Before, during the years in Great Salt Lake, and especially before that, during the long months crossing the plains and when her brother, Will, had died and after her father had joined the Battalion (knowledge part vague impression of early memories, part hearsay), no one could have been better to her than Aunt Bathsheba. Of course her tongue was sharp at times, but you got to know that was just her way. Surely, *surely* Aunt 'Sheba didn't think she *wanted* to be married to Uncle Abijah, or that she *liked* him — like *that?*

Curling the long whip over the backs of the oxen, Clory stole a glance around the side of her wagon, but Bathsheba was admon-

ishing her boys, Samuel and Abraham, who were driving Abijah's
two hundred and fifty head of precious sheep, not to get too far
ahead of the caravan. She had not looked back — she had not
answered Clory's smile.

'Giddup, Bluchy!' coaxed the girl, starting the oxen expertly
down the long rough decline; 'Haw, Whitey!'

Whitey, the left ox, stamped and tossed at the pull of the yoke.
Clory remembered guiltily that she hadn't yet told Abijah about
that yoke gall; he'd sure be angry with her for forgetting. Abijah
loved his animals; they were not dumb beasts to him, but friends,
and it seemed sometimes as if he worried a lot more about them
than about his family — than about this hateful thing growing
up between her and Aunt 'Sheba, two women who probably
would have to spend the rest of their lives together, maybe in
the same house.

Aunt Willie, clambering into the seat beside Clory, brought
back the girl's smile again. Clory liked Aunt Willie. Especially
her eyes. They were pale eyes rimmed with stubby, colorless
lashes, but they were wise and serene and curiously deep. There
was something ... Once, long before, when Willie was the hired
girl in Uncle Abijah's house, Clory had tried to question her, but
Willie had only smiled and cut her out some paper dolls.

Later, when President Young had kept after Uncle Abijah to
take another wife, he had married Aunt Willie; mainly, it is true,
because she had no home of her own and was right there in the
house. Afterward nothing changed much; Aunt Willie went right
on helping with the housework and kept up her old-maid silliness
and the foolish flutterings of her hands. Only now she had a bedroom of her own instead of sleeping with one of the little boys.
She still stayed drab and unbelievably homely, but Clory thought
that sometimes, when pity or love kindled the hidden depths in
her eyes, her face was gently beautiful.

Once on this trip Clory had asked her why Aunt Bathsheba
hadn't seemed to mind when she, Willie, had married Abijah,

but Willie had only laughed and told her that the next time they camped beside some water clear enough to mirror their two faces she'd show her the reason.

Now, thinking some day she'd see what sage tea could do for Aunt Willie's mousy locks and beginning grayness — such plain hair with its double parts, the middle section drawn straight back, the two sides brought severely down over the ears — Clory put her hand over the older woman's. Aunt Willie hadn't been feeling so good.

'We're almost there, Aunt Willie. Pretty soon an' it'll be "Hard Times Come Again No More" fer us for sure.'

'Law,' said Willie, 'I want you should be right the worst way, child, but I'm afeared an' else the scouts finds more water, it's gonna be, "Give Me Three Grains of Corn, Mother, Honly Three Grains of Corn!"'

Clory threw back her head and hooted, and squeezed an appreciative arm around Wilhelmina, whose shy humor always hid its head before the others.

' . . . Only three grains of corn,' sang the girl, until the hills answered; and then changed to alto as Willie took up the air (Willie, who could not carry a tune):

> 'It will keep the little life I have
> Till the coming of the morn!
> I am dying of hunger and cold, Mother,
> Dying of hunger and cold . . .'

'All right!' From his post beside his wagon at the head of the company, Abijah called back exasperatedly above the noise, 'Let's get a-goin', get a-goin'!'

Singing, he thought, always singing. Those two women had kept that up every minute of the entire four weeks of the journey. He liked to sing, too, but there was a time and a place. A man's wives ought to practice quiet and prudence instead of bawling out like giddy young girls. Here Clory was, seventeen and a woman grown; while Wilhelmina at thirty-six was still silly and didn't seem to have improved much for all he had married her. But Clory — Brother Brigham had wished a job on him, for sure; it was enough to have to raise her without having to marry her. But at that thought and the sudden remembrance of her white skin and the scolding-locks of her black hair crisping on her soft neck below her bob, a familiar compulsion gripped Abijah's loins. He repressed it sternly as befitted a secret weakness. There was a time and a place.

Bathsheba heaved up to the wagon seat, looked to the back to shush the squabbling of the twins, Lehi and Nephi, and called to the baby, Isaiah, to come sit on her lap until they reached the bottom of the dugway. Abijah goaded the oxen to begin their slow forward plodding.

3

Suddenly there was a shout. Abijah looked back, and there at the end of the line of five wagons Brother Tuckett's off ox lay in the dust with Brother Tuckett wildly waving his hands over it. Brother Tuckett was being called to the Dixie Mission because he was a good tailor, but, my conscience, thought Abijah, sometimes he didn't seem to have sense enough to pound sand in a rat hole.

'I'll be go-to-hell!' shouted Brother Tuckett. 'I vum he's deader'n a doornail!'

'You stay here,' said Clory to Aunt Willie. 'You shouldn't be climbing in and out so much; you'll get the pains again.'

By the time Clory got there, all the wagons were emptied and the shouting children in the group around the unconcerned ox were gleefully suggesting remedies to pry it to its feet. Betsy Tuckett, a buxom German girl who had left all her own people in the Old Country to marry Lon, the missionary, and come to Deseret, stood coaxing the beast softly. She was almost in tears. Lon, short and cocky, a bantam rooster of a man in the brass-buttoned blue of a Johnston Army suit, turned from the ox to look up at Betsy, big and forlorn beside him.

'I reckon ole Bally, here, quit just so's I could tell you folks my new poem before I fergits it.'

Someone in the group chuckled. They knew Lon's poetry.

'It goes this-a-way,' said Lon, eyes on Betsy:

> Oh, once I lived in 'Cottonwood' and owned a little farm,
> But I was called to 'Dixie,' which gave me much alarm.
> To raise the cane and cotton I right away must go,
> But the reason why they sent me I'm sure I do not know.
> I yoked old Jim and Bally up, all for to make a start;
> To leave my house and garden it almost broke my heart;
> We moved along quite slowly and often looked behind,
> For the sand and rocks of 'Dixie' kept running through my mind.
> But when we reached the Black Ridge, we could not move at all,
> For poor old Jim and Bally began to puff and lawl:
> I whipped and swore a little, but could not make the route,
> For myself, the team and Betsy, were all of us give out.

Lon paused for breath and his blue glance brushed the others laughingly, half defiantly.

'Go on, Lon,' applauded Benjamin Jarvis, the school-teacher.

Chuckles ran through the group. But Betsy was smiling, now, so Lon did a little shuffle, laughed his gay cackle, and answered: 'Give me a chanct! Got to make up the rest!'

Meanwhile, Abijah, vowing that Lon Tuckett would have to stop his swearing and foolishness, prodded apprehensively at the red ox. Abijah had always been a good bullwhacker, and experience had taught him that when an ox says no it means no. A mule will work until it dies in its tracks, but an ox when weary simply lies down in its yoke and nothing short of dynamite can get it back on its feet. Sometimes you had to hitch a fresher team to the wagon and let the tired ox follow at its leisure. He hoped that wouldn't be necessary now; the sun would soon be down.

He eased the heavy yoke off the animal's neck and rubbed the places where the pressure had been the worst. He fed the ox a little grain and talked to it soothingly. He was thinking that Brother Tuckett was a mite careless. At Cedar Fort they'd had

to spend a day digging a coal pit and making a furnace and fixing
the tires and axles on this same wagon, and today they'd had to
stop long enough to shoe this same ox. It wasn't as if Melancthon
Tuckett hadn't known President Brigham's orders.

Abijah remembered Lon Tuckett's being in priesthood meeting
the Sunday afternoon Brother Brigham had given them all their
strict directions, the same directions prepared by Apostle
Parley P. Pratt for the exodus of the Saints from Nauvoo in '46.
The estimated essentials for a family of five were ammunition and
one good rifle (if a caplock, the cap should be replaced by a piece
of leather to exclude moisture and dirt; if a flintlock, the priming
must be removed and the pan filled with tow or cotton), 1 good
wagon, 3 yoke of cattle, 2 cows, 2 beef cattle, 3 sheep, 1000 pounds
of flour, 20 pounds of sugar, a tent and tent poles, 10 to 20 pounds
of seed, 25 to 100 pounds of tools for farming, and bedding and
cooking utensils; cost, exclusive of the last, about $250. These had
been minimum requirements for the first great crossing of the
plains, and now, in '61, fifteen years after the original emigrants
had taken root in the Great Salt Lake Valley, were minimum requirements for those called to colonize the Dixie Mission, three
hundred miles to the south.

Of course, Abijah knew that some families had more worldly
goods than this specified amount, but he was also uneasily
aware that others had much less. In spite of the fact that Brother
Brigham had quietly and carefully investigated the resources,
both physical and spiritual, of every man he called to this, the
most difficult of all the missions, it was conceivable that even
Brother Brigham might have made mistakes, although he was
irrevocably the vicegerent and mouthpiece of God on earth.
Abijah knew positively that some men had been chosen who were
really poor; Brother Brigham had designated them because they
could bring some skill, artisanship, or unusually courageous faith
invaluable to the new colony. Certainly it would never have occurred to any man, poor as well as rich, to refuse the Call, for did

it not come from God? And God would watch over those doing
His work. But Abijah secretly thought a man was a fool to put
God to the test too often.

Abijah wondered if Lon Tuckett had expected God to feed
this ox.

'When did you feed this animal last?' he called peremptorily.
But just as Brother Tuckett, helping Betsy into the wagon, turned
his head to answer, the ox, as if ashamed of all the trouble it had
caused, got heavily to its feet, swinging its head from side to side
and bawling resentfully.

Amid the general scrambling for the wagons, Abijah reflected
crossly that Apostle Snow and the fast mule teams and skinners
of the other half of the company might even have made the St.
George Valley by this time. He, Abijah, had a hard job with these
five wagons of younger people, the slowest of the bullwhackers.
The rest of his company of ten, over which he had been appointed
captain at the outset of the journey, had followed this morning
after the first of the caravan, but he had had to stay behind with
these stragglers. Men like Tuckett, the tailor; Jarvis, the school-
teacher; Miles, who played the fiddle; Peabody, the tanner; and
Hichinoper, who was being called to raise castor beans for the
making of castor oil, all young men; no responsibility, and their
wives just like 'em. Always wasted hours like today with sick
young ones or something. Appreciated a joke more than a good
camping spot. Didn't realize the seriousness of bedding down
before it was dark, for instance. And Betsy Tuckett in her condition. It did seem as if women picked on the unlikeliest times to get
in the family way ... Abijah mentally rehearsed the phrases with
which he'd pillory these backsliders in his diary, a great comfort
to him at times.

Slipping, sliding, anchored by the heavy drags and the protesting chains on the hind wheels, the wagons jolted painfully down the
slope. Folks were tired, heads drooped wearily; lucky persons,
riding, fitted familiar aches into the sway; gritty pink sand

elusively tortured eyeballs, rimed around lips, and stuck in sweat-encrusted wrinkles; a hen clucked irritatedly and a puppy whined; children, usually running ahead, throwing rocks out of the road, were either trudging soberly by the oxen or were querulous in the wagon boxes. Abijah, plodding carefully beside his, the leading outfit — a double span of four oxen — felt that his feet were weighted.

The Hichinoper infant wailed fitfully. Eliza Hichinoper, stumbling with fatigue beside her husband's wagon, carried her ailing seven-weeks-old baby on a pillow; the child wouldn't go to anyone else and was too ill to stand the wagon's jolt. The thing that Abijah couldn't understand was that although Eliza and Charles, her husband, had for the entire month of the journey been sleepless with worry over this, their first child, and Eliza herself just out of bed from having it, you might say, when they started — and although between the two of them they had walked with that child on a pillow for every step of the three hundred and fifty miles over deserts and rivers and mountains, ice and snow and bitter sleet, and now, clogging sand — although they had done all this, they still had time to dally and joke. You would have thought they'd be sobered by now, as became those whom the Lord chasteneth. Not that Abijah didn't believe in shouting hosannas before the Lord for the deliverance of Israel into these valleys of the mountains; he always included in family prayer gratitude to God for deliverance from the mobocrats and rejoicing before the Lord for the raising-up of Zion. But there was a time and a place. Anyway, too much laughter was not rejoicing, but unseemly levity, and he had heard Brother Brigham exhort against it. There was always a time and a place.

But at this thought the picture of Clory's dancing eyes rose up before him again, and because he was so angry at himself he curled the lash smartly around his oxen and threatened to use it on the children in the wagon box. After that he felt better.

4

On their horses the scouts, impervious alike to crying babies or squeaking chains or Abijah's shouts, gazed ahead desultorily and forgot for a moment that there were such things as Indians. Abijah's boy, Freeborn, bringing up the rear of the caravan, almost lost his seat on a suddenly plunging horse. Even while he looked about for the disturbance, he soothed the animal with a gentle hand. Above all earthly creatures, save one, he loved his mare, Nellie. He had bred her himself, back at his father's farm in Great Salt Lake, and sired by a piebald Indian pony she combined the fleet endurance of the plains horse with the intelligence of blooded eastern stock.

In the mornings when she galloped to answer Free's call, she was beautiful to see with her white-flecked red coat burnished and her dainty hoofs high-stepping.

Now at the boy's touch she quieted and rolled the whites of her eyes at him, but still shied from the object in the road. He jerked for his gun and his reins: a tarantula? But the season was a little late for that, wasn't it? An Indian . . . and then he saw it, Clory's red sunbonnet. She'd forgotten it. He spurred the filly and swooped it up with one hand. He shook it free of dust and furtively put it to his nose. She always smelled so sweet of bergamot. He'd helped her raise it back home in her garden in Great Salt Lake so she could keep it in her drawer among her things.

He thought the sunbonnet very pretty, all fluted around the edge like that. He knew his mother always made her sunbonnets dark-colored so they wouldn't show the dirt so quick, and that she'd been angry when Clory traded her music box to one of President Brigham's daughters for this red sunbonnet. Clory had loved the music box, too, for it had belonged to her mother in Philadelphia — it was the dangdest thing, a china lid with ladies in powdered hair and men in knee breeches, and when you opened the lid to a perfectly empty box inside, a little tune chimed out;

she must have wanted the bonnet a lot to give the music box away, but he didn't blame her. Nobody could who once saw her cheeks and black eyes and black curls framed in that red color.

He eased his horse along the bank to Clory, who was concentrating on her oxen and the slope ahead. Seeing her quick smile, he blushed and held up the bonnet.

'Oh, Free,' she cried. 'My sunbonnet! My lovely sunbonnet!'

He wet his lips and stammered, 'It was back there in the road.'

'I know! I'd forget my head if it warn't fastened on. But I'd have just been sick if I'd lost my precious bonnet!'

Passing the whip to Willie, she put the sunbonnet on and twinkled from the hood at the boy. She had a way of clasping her hands under her cheek when excited. Free's defenses fell without a struggle. He thought she was the prettiest thing he had ever seen, in her sheep's-gray linsey-woolsey and that red bonnet.

'Thank you, Free,' Clory murmured with the little flute-notes in her voice. 'But where was it? How ——'

Freeborn suddenly wished a dozen Indians would molest her so he could shoot them all. He wished she could have seen him from the back of his plunging horse rescuing the bonnet. But all he could say was, 'It — was — was there, an' I jest picked it — up.'

'My, you *are* strong,' admired Clory, and blinked her lashes at him.

But at that, his gaze was so utterly bemused that she hastily snatched the whip again and kept her eyes ahead.

'Is everybody very gloomy, Free? Shall we sing?'

Throwing back her head, the girl sang, and instantly the world became a better place in which to live.

> Hey the merry, aye the merry,
> Hey the happy Mormon!

The boy's voice, strong and true, although still cracking a little, joined her; soon the whole wagon-train was singing lustily.

> I never knew what joy was
> Till I became a Mormon!

As soon as one song was finished, Clory took up another:

> Wait for the wagon, wait for the wagon,
> Wait for the wagon, and we'll all take a ride!

The oxen twitched their ears, the horses their tails, dogs bayed, contentment came back to weary faces, and the caravan reached the sagebrush of the plain intact and alert.

Clory loved to sing; her voice was warm and very sweet, and there was nothing she liked better on the journey than to lift her song pure and clear above the bawling of the oxen, the whining of children puny from insufficient food, the disheartened voices of men and women who, having already pioneered once, had sold dearly built homes to answer the Call for a second pioneering in a country whose reputation, to begin with, was none too good. There was nothing she liked better than to pour out that something in her heart which expressed itself in her voice — which never failed her, but always lifted her to a region so flooded with joy that sometimes she felt as if one small body could not contain it all but must burst — and then to watch dull eyes come to life, tired heads lift, and the miracle of melody once more transmute out of pain courage to do the impossible.

Abijah smiled and lifted his thundering bass in the song. In spite of her giddiness, Clory was a little soldier; and, of course, being married to him was going to make a lot of improvement in her. Looking back then, he saw Freeborn, lanky, sixteen, moon-calf eyes, but handsome in his fringed buckskin suit with the brown of his good straight features startling beneath his shock of blond hair; and Freeborn's father sighed, frowned, and determined on a future course of action. He was thinking that Clory was only a year older than the boy — they were so nearly of an age . . .

5

At the fringe of Washington's willow-built dwellings, John D. Lee, huge and jovial, led the rest of the settlement in meeting the emigrants. Behind him were grouped his wives and children and the other families. Looking at these people, now, Clory couldn't believe what she knew to be true about them. Five years ago, in '56, when they had been called to colonize Washington, they had been well-to-do converts fresh from the Southern States, Alabama, Georgia, Tennessee; and here in this southern portion of Brother Brigham's vast empire they had set out to build another Confederacy with their colored servants, their traditions, their pride and worldly goods. Now they stood before her, a dispirited, shiftless bunch, most of them barefooted, and this nearly December, too. The men's shirts, the women's and children's dresses and sunbonnets were all made of the same piece of homespun cloth, and Clory thought their clothes and faces were all of a color, being blue with chills.

She was thinking that John D., alone, in spite of the fact that his hairless features in contrast to the bearded faces about him gave him a singularly childlike appearance, still looked the part of the conqueror; Abijah, shaking hands, was certainly putting on his 'go-to-meeting' manner.

'Well, Bishop Lee, and how are the Saints in this part of the Lord's vineyard?'

'Still full of hosannas before the Lord, Brother ——'

(Clory, her eyes on the sickly-looking women and children, thought it unlikely they were full of anything, least of all hosannas.)

'Brother Abijah N. MacIntyre,' supplied Abijah, clearing his throat importantly. 'I was President of the First Quorum of Seventies in the Nineteenth Ward in the City, Brother Lee.'

(*I knew he'd put that in as soon as possible.* Clory's fingers gripped the whipstock. *He never can stand for anybody to seem better'n him.*)

'I hae had the honor and the pleasure of making your acquaintance before, Brother Lee, at a priesthood meeting in the ould Tabernacle just before you were called down here. Brother Brigham had you give us some exhortation that was verra fine, verra fine, indeed.'

Abijah's stance — feet wide apart, fingertips together — bristled with unction and authority. Contrary to most of the men, who wore waist overalls — always, however, decorously outside of their boots — and vests over their homespun shirts, Abijah, as befitted his superior dignity, clung to his black barn-door trousers (he considered the front closing immodest) and cloth frock coat, his black string tie, and his wide-brimmed 'missionary' hat. (In the City he had always worn a shiny stovepipe hat, but upon answering the Call he had changed to this hard-crowned, wide, rolled-brimmed headgear as being slightly less formal and more suitable to a new country.) Full-bearded, the dark brown hair crisply curling around his chin to his ears, his brown eyes crinkling their laugh-wrinkles at the corners, Clory decided he was unmistakably good to look at; he'd been called 'Handsome Mac' all his life. And as a child she had certainly adored him enough.

Her thoughts were just then interrupted by the realization that John D.'s eyes had suddenly grown cold and wary over some remark of Abijah's. Wondering why, she tried to remember . . . there had been something. Then the pieces fell into place and she clapped her hand over her mouth. Of course! This was the John D. Lee of that Mountain Meadow Massacre story! The authorities had hushed it up and Abijah had been unwilling to discuss it, but there had been plenty of talk about it at the time. That had been three years ago, just before Johnston's Army came. A wagon-train of Missourians had gone through the country poisoning the springs and upsetting the Indians and threatening the people with an army from the States, and John D. Lee, leading a band of Indians, had killed the whole company. Well, the Missourians had been part of the mobocrats who had driven the Saints out of Caldwell County and Nauvoo, and had probably deserved what they got, but, after all . . . She remembered Abijah's saying Brother Brigham was horrified because he'd always prided himself that human life was safer among the Latter-Day Saints than anywhere else in the world. Anyway, the authorities had hushed it up. There was something funny about it. Brother Lee didn't look like a killer; he looked untroubled and kindly. She resolved to question Abijah.

Abijah shook her arm gently. 'Come out of the dream, young lady, and meet these folks.'

He helped her and Willie out of the wagon and introduced them to Brother Lee and his wives. She saw that Bathsheba was primly discussing with one of the Lee women the possibility of raising indigo in this soil.

'It's good ground ——' the woman quavered.

'Good!' boomed Brother Lee. 'It's Canaan, that's what! Talk about "milk and honey" — why, in September at our Fair a man from down the crick at Seldom Stop brung up a cotton stalk with seven bolls, and a sunflower head three feet around! An' over on the Santa Clary I seen squash vines climbin' fifteen feet up a tree an' loaded with squashes like coconuts! I tell you I *seen* it!'

The little yellow flecks in Abijah's brown eyes were glowing like tiny lamps with his excitement.

But Brother Lee interrupted himself. 'Howsomever, come in an' set a spell! We kin talk later. You womenfolks come on in, Sister MacIntyre! We ain't got only "bread-and-with it," but ——'

Bishop Lee's invitation was for them all, but his eyes were on Clory. *No, thank you,* she thought; *your bread would be corn pone and your 'with-it' salt pork . . .*

As she opened her mouth to speak, Abijah answered for her: 'Thank you! Thank you! But we're making camp on the other side of your town tonight, and we're almost there.'

Thank Heaven! I wouldn't want to go in their ole houses! Old John D.'s the only one who ain't sick besides half-starved!

Looking at the women and children, Clory suddenly felt glowing with health. One ragged little girl, too listless for tears, returned Clory's stare until she shuddered and flashed an urgent prayer. The child tugged at her skirts.

'My name's Confederate America Jones, but they calls me "Mec" for short.'

The child's nose was running down over her upper lip, and she gave the discharge a tentative lick with her tongue. The taut skin of her face had the sickly whitish-blue color of skimmed milk.

'Pa would whup me fer sure if he seen me a-botherin' you.'

Clory managed to smile.

'Not if I *liked* you to bother me ——'

That surely was the worst of all — to succumb until you let your children get like little animals and your own hair stringy and dull, your dresses bedraggled and your face streaked with neglect.

It ain't necessary! Not if a person's able-bodied and willin' to work! ...

Clory was shaking when she reached the wagon. Willie got in beside her and put her arms around her.

'It's their victuals, mostly,' said Willie. 'Pigweed greens. They git the scours hand hit dries up their blood ...'

John D. Lee was telling Abijah good-bye as he started for his wagon. 'Heap Tickaboo!' called Brother Lee jovially. 'Heap Tickaboo!'

'That's Paiute fer "friend," I think,' said Willie; '"'Eap" friend.'

He *couldn't* be all bad; Clory resolved more than ever to find out all she could about John D. Lee.

6

On the other side of Washington a creek glanced and jabbered, here Abijah called camp. Clory sniffed hungrily: in spite of the acrid odor of wet salt grass, the smell was damp and fresh and green. As usual, the only meadowgrass hugged the stream in meager tufts, but the stunted cottonwoods chattered their leaves in welcome. Clory was entranced at this. She threw wide her arms and ran down to the water and looked up at the yellow leaves. Many, bright gold, were still on the trees, and as is the habit of cottonwoods at the faintest suggestion of a breeze, were prattling busily. She thought this rattle of leaves had the sound of rain, as if these trees of the desert country were trying to invoke it.

On the other side of the stream was a red knoll; Clory glanced back at the others making camp, hesitated guiltily, and then, jumping from stone to stone across the water, scrambled up the side of the knoll. Maybe there was a meadow on the other side. She was so starved to see a meadow.

The sun had just set, but there were whispers of color still left in the sky. She had never missed a twilight: down here, especially, they were so lovely and lingering. The translucent sky deepening to green above the horizon was so clear that sometimes she imagined if she looked long enough she could surely see right through it and maybe surprise an angel.

Before her to the west a dry gully stretched upward for a mile or two to another red mountain which seemed to elbow after a while and link arms with a long, low black hill sloping away to the south as far as she could see.

This chaotic red mountain now lay scarred and carved against the sky in fantastic figures and fanciful shapes. Clory could make out a rabbit, ears cocked, and a squirrel on its haunches. The tip of the squirrel's tail and the rabbit's ears were bright pink, but the rest of their bodies were dissolving with the lower part of the cliff in maroon shadow.   All the brightness going ... and the sky, with the glow gone, faint, somehow, and unfriendly, and naked without any trees against it.   The shadows might mask with velvet fingers the sagebrush in the gully, but it would still be sagebrush.   They had left all the greenness behind, all the moss and grass, all the fruit trees that had blossomed on their lot for the first time last spring.   Rolph, himself, had said if she'd only wait he'd shower her with blossoms ... but what could a girl do when President Brigham Young singled her out for the Call?   And now she would be in Abijah's kingdom for ever and ever, even unto the Celestial Glory, sealed unto him for Time and Eternity.   Since Uncle Abijah was a righteous man, that fact should make her happy, she knew; but it didn't seem to help her to forget the feel of Rolph's smooth young lips.

Clory put her hand to her throat as if to assuage the ache. Neither the twilights and the beauty nor excitement nor singing nor even flirting could make up for lost hopes and banished dreams, and the Lord seemed sort of slack, in spite of President Brigham and the promises in her patriarchal blessing.

Make me quit thinking about it, please, Lord; I know it's bad now that I'm married. Married to Uncle Abijah. And please, please help me to remember to quit calling him 'Uncle' so that he won't be cross with me again ...

'Hawckk!'

Even as she jumped, Clory reflected that Uncle Abijah's most nerve-racking mannerism was this habit of decorously prefacing every sermon, bit of advice, or reprimand with that hacking of his throat.

'Some day there'll be a tunnel where that red hill joins that black one, and the road to St. George'll cut clean straight across this gully and through these mountains instid of away around the point of the black hill, where we have to go now.

He checked his speech and stared at her.

'Clorinda, bairn, is some'at wrong?'

She hadn't been conscious of the tears on her lashes and now blinked them away hurriedly, realizing the while that Abijah never dropped into his native brogue unless he was deeply moved.

'It's nothing — really — Uncle Abijah.'

'"Uncle" again? Can't ye ——'

'I know! I'm sorry!'

Clory bit her lips in vexation. She knew that note of patient exasperation in Abijah's voice.

'I want ye should be happy, Clor-rinda Agatha. I maun be sad tae see th' glunch on yer bonny face. . . . Hae ye no thocht o' the promise o' Brother Brigham?'

'I'm — I'm all right, truly, A — Abijah.'

'Ye hae muckle need ——'

Wishing he'd not talk about it, Clory turned and started down the hill. She was always embarrassed when he tried to talk to her like this. She didn't know what to say to him. Certainly she couldn't use the banter she tried on most young men nor the coquetry with which she delighted to confuse poor Freeborn. And when Abijah began to get tender, she wanted to scream. She didn't mind his crossness; she knew how to act with that. But when he spoke softly and touched her in that caressing way (and he had a habit when fondling of gritting his teeth), something desperate rose up in her throat.

She knew vaguely what marriage meant; Aunt Bathsheba and Aunt Willie had both circuitously attempted her enlightenment. But Abijah had as yet not approached her, mainly because Brother Brigham so energetically advised continence and caution (although Clory in her curiosity and suspense had concluded grimly it was for lack of a chance). Whenever her thoughts strayed to what would happen when he *did* have a chance, little jabbings of excited terror broke out all over her body. But mostly she lived in the present. She always arranged things for gaiety if she possibly could.

So now, kicking a rock jangling before her, 'Isn't the air soft, Abijah?' And the flute notes were back in her voice.

Abijah, troubled, merely grunted. Picking his way down the hill beside her, determinedly holding her arm linked in his, he was thinking that he'd be glad when she had her first child. That always calmed women down. Meanwhile, although he'd try to be patient with her, he must, above all, insist that she retrench, as Brother Brigham would say to a wayward wife, and strive to walk in the paths of rectitude and ladylikeness. Fooling with Freeborn! He never knew what she'd do next. Polygamy was a holy principle, but it certainly had its drawbacks! . . .

CHAPTER II

O N THE other side of the stream, supper fires were being lighted with dry cottonwood limbs or greasewood or mesquite bush. Campfire smoke hung in the air like incense. The wild, keen fragrance of burning sagebrush plucked at Clory's empty stomach.

The fitful flames threw into relief the white-topped wagons drawn up in more or less the traditional circle with the tents at intervals. Quilts were being rolled down in wagon boxes and underneath on tarpaulin-covered ground for the boys of a family. Abijah had plenty of room with his two tents (the large Sibley tent was never used for one-night camping), his government wagon with its bed at each end, stove in the middle, its chair, door, and ladder down the side. This wagon was so large that it had to be drawn by a double yoke of oxen, but Abijah had selected the animals well, and as Lon Tuckett once said, they were 'stout enough to pull anything that had two ends.'

Usually, if they camped late, Abijah and Bathsheba slept in one end of this wagon with the twins and the baby at the other end, and Free and two of the three older boys (it was the duty of Abraham and Samuel to take turns guarding the sheep) on the ground underneath. Clory and Willie occupied the other wagon except when occasionally Abijah ordered the tent put up, and then Willie slept there alone.

Other people were not so fortunate as Abijah; the Peabodys owned but the one wagon, and bedding-down presented rather an involved process with the parents at one end, the three girls at the other, and the six boys underneath.

Many of the wagons had hencoops attached to the ends; other coops housed young pigs, and there were dogs and a cat or two. These animals, as well as the oxen and the loose stock, all had to be cared for before the caravan could eat, but, since the work was so well apportioned even to the baby of the family, and discipline so exact, Abijah's company were able to pattern after the Saints crossing the plains in that they could sometimes make camp and have supper prepared in half an hour.

Most of the cattle belonging to these families had been driven on ahead with the general herd by two young girls preceding Apostle Snow's caravan, but several of the wagons still housed bottle-fed babies.

One of these, a lamb owned by the MacIntyre twins, was bleating for its supper.   Lehi, whose evening job was to feed the lamb, patiently followed Bathsheba, getting supper, from fire to wagon box and back again, and repeated monotonously: 'What'll I do fer Blackie's milk, Mamma?   What'll I do fer Blackie's milk?' Fixing her with the unwinking stare of childhood, he made a dirge out of his plaint (knowing from experience that this always made a grown-up answer). 'What'll I do fer Blackie's milk?'

His voice was as insistent as a mosquito's buzz above the bawling of the oxen, the lowing of village cattle, home-bound, the crackle of fires, cries of men to their animals, cross voices of hungry children, coaxing animal voices of hungry sheep and pigs, the mewing of a kitten, the staccato barking of a dog, and the far-off, eerie howling of coyotes.

Bathsheba, blinking away the smoke-tears from her smarting eyes, carefully put down the stone crock of 'sarvice'-berry preserve and the sack of jerky she had just brought from the wagon, and turned on the boy with such sudden wrath that he gaped and paled.

'You little stew-bum! You know's well's I do we ain't had no milk since the cows went with the other herd yistiddy!'

The hairs in her mole wiggled angrily. She slapped some of the jerky on a smooth stone, picked up a rock and began to pound it.

'I ain't even got any milk fer supper! An' you ain't a-gonna have none of the buttermilk till I kin 'tend to the churnin', neither!'

Lehi stuck out his underlip and began to cry. Bathsheba shook him.

'Now, fer the Lord's sake ——' she began, and looked up to find Clory and Abijah, returning from their walk, directly in front of her.

Clory secretly gloated over the fact that then even Bathsheba was momentarily disconcerted. For Abijah saw to it that in his household the Lord's name was never taken in vain. Shocked at Bathsheba's wanton flouting of his orders, he gathered his righteous anger, but 'Sheba, rallying, forestalled him.

'So! 'S funny to me how some folks have time to lallygag around with supper to git!' And, as Abijah tried again to speak, 'Or is it you're afraid she'll soil her lily-white hands, this Miss High-an'-Mighty!'

Abijah, to escape this domestic crisis, was only too glad to forget Bathsheba's fall from grace and retreat to help Freeborn with the oxen.

'No call to make such a rowte,' he mumbled as he stalked off.

Thin-lipped with satisfaction, 'Sheba went back to pounding the long black strips of smoked salted beef, scooped the mass into the frying-pan, and then stooped to gather the chip-like fragments that had fallen to the ground. One jerky-sliver would flavor a whole pan of gravy, another make an hour-long chew for a hungry boy.... Abijah'd soon find out which wore the longest — the wife who was merely pretty or the one who knew how to make ends meet!

Clory, eyes downcast, cheeks burning, hurried to her wagon and tied a calico waist apron over her crinoline. Willie, bending over the grub box, was filling a pan from a huge sack of 'crackers' (oven-dried bread slices); silently the girl clambered past her to the churn, which, hanging from the bows, had been churning the milk all day with the jolting of the wagon. The butter having not yet come, she took the churn to a stump outside and began to work the dasher up and down viciously.

Willie, with the pan of crackers in her hand, stood watching her anxiously, half-teasingly.

'Did you see the look on Aunt 'Sheba's face?' she whispered.

But Clory burst out mutinously, 'He'd have killed either uv us 'f we'd said it!'

''E don't know it, maybe, but, hanyways, Aunt Bathsheba wears the pants,' observed Willie grimly.

2

Apostle Snow had been wont to decree a dance around the campfires at night. Supper over, the whole company joined lustily in a hymn; then a space was cleared and to the jolly notes of a fiddle, booted men swung full-skirted girls in the quadrille or 'Six Nations' until the dust arose and the dancers stopped for breath.

Abijah knew that Brother Miles was as always ready with his fiddle, and he was aware that his people would have welcomed some gaiety. But Abijah believed rather more in the efficacy of prayer. Usually evening prayers were not said until after the festivities, just before bedtime. But tonight Abijah decided to call the whole caravan together and combine evening prayers and the blessing on the food in one long supplication just before they ate. He wanted a very early rising in the morning; they had a long day ahead. He'd send them all to bed directly after supper.

Abijah knew a great many of President Brigham's speeches by heart as well as some of the Prophet Joseph's; and sometimes in his prayers his borrowed phrases became so telling that he could not seem to stop.

Now, with the meal ready to be dished up, he knelt in the midst of his kneeling people and pled with the Lord to keep their hearts from sin: 'And Thy sacred name, O Lord, save us from profaning it, as is the unholy habit of the gentiles. Knowing as Thou dost, O Lord, that most of the trouble of this world is of a woman's spawning, keep these dear sisters of this, Thy chosen people, in the paths of uprightness and virtue. And give thy daughters of Zion strength to dwell amicably together as sisters according to Thy latest commandment...'

Clory, kneeling beside Willie, nudged her and surreptitiously removed a tiny rock from under one cramped knee.

Lon Tuckett, shifting uneasily beside Betsy, prayed to himself rebelliously, 'Let's get it done with, Lord; hell, I'm starved!'

Abijah's voice went on and on, crowding the evening hush with great blobs of sound, subduing even the fretful cries of the Hichinoper baby.

'We thank Thee, O Lord, for this sumptuous repast which Thy bounteous hand hath spread before us; we thank Thee for the food, the implements and utensils with which we eat, the pure air we breathe, the clear water Thou hast provided for our thirst, the ground upon which we rest our bodies, the fertile soil upon the ground...'

'He forgot this pebble,' whispered Clory to Willie.

Abijah finished amid a chorus of 'Amens,' but while he poured the browned-flour-and-jerky gravy over his crackers, his glance from under his bushy brows shot indignantly at the girl. He'd teach her to poke fun!

Abijah ate with great gusto, smacking his lips and enjoying to the full his meal. Bathsheba, spooning food into the young Isaiah's mouth, watched her husband fondly. She liked a man who relished his victuals. Clory, eating daintily in spite of her youthful hunger, would have preferred less noise. Willie, swallowing primly, ministered to the needs of the twins beside her, and wondered if Bathsheba could be right about these fitful attacks of nausea. Freeborn, between Abraham (who was hurrying to relieve Samuel with the sheep) on one side and Joseph, fifteen and next-to-the-oldest, on the other, gulped his food dreamily and pondered Clory's beauty in the firelight.

Seeing Bathsheba's cup empty, Clory arose and, taking the coffee-pot from the fire, filled the cup with the dark, odorous liquid made of roasted whole barley grains steeped in boiling water.

Bathsheba said shortly, 'When I can't wait on myself any longer, I want to die.'

They all liked barley coffee, even without cream or milk, except Free, who preferred 'crust' coffee; so, after handing her cup to Bathsheba, the girl browned a piece of bread on a fork over the coals. Free's eyes worshiped her while she crumbled the toasted crusts into a tin cup which, filled with water, she put to boil on the heated rock.

'Uncle Abijah,' she called suddenly, 'would you rather have Brigham tea?'

Abijah in spite of himself had to smile; she looked so sweet. And how could you punish a woman who remembered your preferences like that!

Clory over at the wagon rummaged for the sack of tiny, yellow-green, jointed stocks of mountain rush, whose brew Brigham Young had so popularized that it retained his name. The brew had a pleasant, slightly bitter flavor and was much in favor as a blood-purifier and tonic. Abijah thought it helped his occasional spells of dyspepsia.

When Clory brought him the steaming drink, he found it so appetizing that he took another helping of jerky gravy. But his pleasure in the food was interrupted by the sound of singing. He frowned at the firelighted groups and saw that Lon Tuckett was indulging in another of his home-made ballads. It wasn't the fact that Lon Tuckett's cracked voice couldn't carry a tune — but the idea of singing at a meal!

Getting to his feet, Abijah prepared to call out a reproof when his eyes fell on Freeborn's plate, just filled with the stealthily emptied 'sarvice'-berry dish. Abijah, choosing his first duty, cleared his throat and launched a denunciation of the sin of gluttony.

'That's why the Lord revealed to His Prophet the Word of Wisdom! You have never tasted tea or coffee or liquor or tobacco in my household, but, by the eternal heavens, gluttony is just as much an abomination in the eyes of the Lord!'

Free, the scarlet-cheeked culprit, choked on the preserves; for to have wasted any would have been a worse sin than taking the food in the first place.

Clory, watching Abijah, towering, dark-browed, wrathful in the firelight, thought he looked like Moses denouncing the Egyptians. She sighed. *Oh, dear, just when everything was about to be pleasant!*

Abijah paused for breath. She seized the opportunity.

'Shall I brown some flour for your box, Uncle Abijah?'

He stopped, lost the thread of his speech, nodded uncertainly, and sat down. From his inner vest pocket he produced a small round tin box which he handed to the girl. As long as Clory could remember, one of Abijah's habits had been to carry with him constantly a bit of scorched flour for chafed wrists and hands exposed to bad weather. As a result his big-knuckled, well-shaped hands were always smooth instead of horny and cracked like the other men's. She thought he had probably picked up the habit from watching Bathsheba sprinkle browned flour over a baby's diaper and in the tender crevices of its body.

She held the frying-pan over the coals until the flour began to change color, filled the small box, and handed it to Abijah.

Bathsheba got to her feet, gave her bold nose a vigorous wipe with her finger, began to scrape the tin plates, and looked meaningly at Clory and Willie, who was at the moment having an attack of nausea.

'Regularity never missed a meeting,' said Bathsheba.

But when Clory began to help, Abijah called her to accompany him. Lehi was still beseeching his mother for milk for Blackie, and Bathsheba remarked that milk would also go well with the corn-meal mush for breakfast. There was no sugar except a precious lump Bathsheba kept wrapped in a handkerchief in the bottom of her trunk and only to be used in case of sickness, but honey would do for sweetening. Bathsheba with her corn meal and her honey and her preserves was able to set a much richer table than the other housewives in the caravan. Abijah always ate well, come what might.

Now he got a tin pail from the wagon, said to Lehi, 'I'll fetch the milk, but when I get back see that you have your kindlin' gathered,' and took hold of Clory's arm. The walk would give him a chance for that talk with Clorinda.

Abijah had a pocket in the right-hand tail of his frock coat, where he was fussy about keeping a fresh handkerchief daily. His wives might wear undergarments harsh to the skin, but Abijah's handkerchief had to be soft and white. Now, in that gesture so familiar to Clory, he reached for the still neatly folded square, shook it out, and trumpeted his nose.

Away from the camp the night was still and star-filled. The rutty road was very dark, and blackly outlined shrubs crouched close. To the right, in a little meadow, the sheep made a white blur. Coyotes were not far away. Abijah, again taking

Clory's arm in his, headed for one of the window squares of candlelight breaking the gloom.

'Brother Lee will provide us with our breakfast beverage.'

Clory wriggled in irritation at Abijah's heavy humor. He was always calling water 'Adam's ale,' and expecting you to second his chuckling self-appreciation. Once, when she had eaten rather heartily and sighed that she was 'as full as a tick,' he had instantly said, 'Well, you look like one,' and roared until the tears trickled into his beard.

Perceiving her withdrawal, Abijah began to stroke the girl's arm with his fingers, and gritted his teeth. He cleared his throat and lapsed into his native brogue.

'Clorinda, bairn, ye hae muckle need tae repent...'

Clory had found through much experience that the easiest way to get through Abijah's lectures was to crowd down her rebellion and think of something else — Rolph, who had kissed her good-bye with tears in his eyes. But tonight Abijah was particularly vehement.

'I hae no wish to be harsh with ye, my child, but I'm afeard ye're some'at light and foolish and not as serious-minded as I might wish. Ye'll remember' (he was always quoting), 'I hae read it to ye many times, Apostle Orson Pratt's words in the Nauvoo *Seer*: "Harsh expressions against your wife, used in the hearing of others, will more deeply wound her feelings than if she alone heard them.... Reproofs timely and otherwise good may lose their good effect by being administered in the wrong spirit..."'

Clory, ready for once, interrupted him sweetly, 'But you'll remember, too, Abijah (you've read it to me so many times), the *first* part of that same advice: "Do not find fault with every trifling error that you may see, for this will discourage your family and they will begin to think it impossible to please you ——"'

Wrath gathered upon Abijah's brow. She always wriggled out

of just chastisement this way. But they had arrived at Brother Lee's home, now, and he would have to postpone the rest of the lecture.

The rock house, built from native red sandstone quarried with undreamed-of toil from the hills miles away, loomed tall and square before them. It was famous for its two stories, fireplace in every room, and windows 'glassed' with pigs' bladders stretched and dried on wooden frames. It was the richest house in the southern country; most of the other houses in Washington were willow-topped earthen dugouts; a window was a rarity and, if one existed, was open to the elements.

The heavy door opened to Abijah's knock and Clory found herself in a kitchen where a gaunt, bony woman was cleaning out the kettle hanging on the crane of the fireplace. Wiping her hands on her apron and hushing her brood of children, the woman took her visitors through a doorway into an inner sitting-room furnished with a crude, home-made table, a rawhide-bottomed rocking-chair, and a long bench. Cottonwood logs burned briskly on the hearth, but there was a chill in the room. The floor was of boards, scrubbed white, and in passing through the doorway Clory saw that, its walls being about three feet thick and of solid rock, this house must have been built as a sort of fort against the Indians.

The place was lighted by a bit of burning rag tied around a button in a dish of tallow. Seeing the direction of Clory's gaze the woman said deprecatingly, 'Hit be too hot here in the summers fer candlemakin'; agin I git a new batch done, we gits along with a "bitch."'

She offered the girl the rocking-chair politely.

'Won't you set? Brother Lee's out chorin', now. I'll go call him.'

She went to the stairway leading to the floor above and called: 'Sary Ann! Brother and Sister MacIntyre 'r here!' and then disappeared into the kitchen.

The quarters above must be another wife's, Clory surmised. She could hear the soft, coaxing voice of a Negro slave and a harsher voice issuing orders. Soon the second woman came down the stairs. She was a scrawny woman with the pinched, blue look of an ague-sufferer. While they waited for Brother Lee, she told them of Brother Brigham's visits to this house and how he had honored them by spending the night here on his last visit.

When Brother Lee finally stamped into the kitchen followed by one of his sons carrying the milk, he beamed until he filled the house with his geniality. But Clory remembered people had said of him in Salt Lake that he sometimes made his women take the wagon and go to the hills for wood.

Abijah had brought a little flour to pay for the milk, but this John D. proudly refused. 'Heap tickaboo!' he said. 'Heap tickaboo!'

3

Once outside, Clory turned to Abijah suddenly.

'Ain't Brother Lee the man who led the Indians in killing all those Missourian emigrants up at the Mountain Meadows? And ain't that why Brother Brigham wouldn't let him be bishop at Harmony Settlement any longer, and so Brother Lee had to move down here? He must be an awful man!'

Abijah, off guard, turned on her vehemently.

'He's so easy-goin' and chicken-hearted that the Indians call him "Yaugauts" or "cry-baby"! That's how awful he is!'

Clory was thrilled.

'Then he *didn't* do the massacre?'

But Abijah's face had closed with wariness and he said crossly, 'Brother Brigham has asked us not to discuss the subject; you know that's well's I do.'

'But why? If Brother Lee ain't guilty ——'

'That will do, Clorinda Agatha!'

And Clory had to be content.

Abijah cleared his throat and, holding the milk with one hand, took the girl's arm with the other. His voice softened and blurred with tenderness as if to make up for his harshness.

'Ye are muckle young, child; and although we are one in the sight o' God and man I hae not wished to bother ye during the journey.'

He paused and cleared his throat again.

'But noo we are nearing our new home and I can set ye up in a place o' yer own, I shall come to your bed, my child . . . The Lord God commands that his servants shall multiply and replenish the earth . . . It is our dooty to give all the waiting spirits in heaven a chance to inhabit earthly bodies . . .'

Clory was silent. This was a subject which left her trembling and speechless.

Back at camp Abijah gathered his flock about him preparatory for the nightly Scriptural reading. Sometimes he chose the Book of Mormon, but tonight he got his Bible.

But since Bathsheba had gone to the Jarvis wagon to borrow some emptings with which to start a batch of salt-rising bread, Clory sat down on the wagon tongue beside Willie, and absently taking down her thick, black hair began to brush its shining length. Bathsheba, returning, called to the girl, 'Comb your hair after dark and you comb sorrow into your heart!' Clory laughed. 'Sheba looked at Abijah as if to say, 'You see?'

'The girl who pokes fun at her elders comes to no good end,' she pronounced.

Thinking 'Sheba might be more than half right, Abijah, when his people were about him, chose his passages with care:

' . . . And Michal, the daughter of Saul, came out to meet David, and said, "How glorious was the King of Israel today, who uncovered himself today in the eyes of the handmaids of his servants, as one of the vain fellows shamelessly uncovereth himself!" And David said unto Michal, "It was before the Lord . . .

to appoint me ruler over the people of the Lord, over Israel: therefore will I play before the Lord." ... Therefore Michal, the daughter of Saul, *had no child unto the day of her death.* ... Thou shalt
not take the name of the Lord thy God in vain; for the Lord
will not hold him guiltless that taketh his name in vain. ...
Now these are the commandments ... which the Lord your God
commanded to teach you. ... Hear, therefore, O Israel, and observe to do it; that it may be well with thee, and that ye may
increase mightily, as the Lord God of thy fathers hath promised
thee, in the land that floweth with milk and honey ...'

Clory, wakefully listening to the mournful howling of the
coyotes, the singing of the creek, so different at night from that
in the day, and the gentle sibilance of Willie's breath, wondered
again why Abijah had compared her to Michal, who had made
fun of David for being humble before the Lord; Michal, whom,
therefore, the Lord made barren. Clory thought passionately
that *she* wanted children, lots of them!

Abijah, having bedded his flock, sat by the fire and wrote in his
diary. Brother Brigham liked his leaders to keep diaries. Dipping
his quill pen, with fine lettering and extravagant flourishes he
wrote in his big red-backed ledger — the tenth such volume he'd
filled since Nauvoo days:

Dec. 2, 1861

Made four miles. Reproved Brother Tuckett for saying 'Hell.'
Some trouble with the womenfolks. Must counsel more with
Clorinda Agatha.

Bishop John D. Lee gave us a royal welcome into Washington. I wonder —— (This last sentence was crossed out. There
were some subjects about which Brother Brigham did not like his
Saints to wonder. Abijah dipped his pen and began again.) I
wonder how it would feel to have a city named after you as
Brother Brigham named St. George after Apostle George A.
Smith ...

Bathsheba, awake long after Abijah had come to bed and dropped into snoring slumber, admitted in her heart that she had taken the Lord's name in vain and prayed for deliverance from her sin. Then, just before sleep came, she remembered Willie's nausea. Getting quietly out of bed, she rummaged in the grub box for a salt shaker, and, first making sure that the Peabody youth on guard tonight was over at the other end of the camp, she tiptoed down the ladder and over the damp, rough ground to the other wagon. She poked her head under the canvas and carefully slipped the shaker under the sleeping Willie's pillow. Clory, eyes shut, stifled a giggle, but Bathsheba heaved a sigh of relief. There! If Willie was having a worm-fit, that would cure it, and if she was really in the family way, 'twould do no harm.

Back at her own wagon, her big, shivering body grotesque under the starlight in its long-sleeved, ankle-length 'garments' protruding beneath the flannel nightgown, and her loose belly, uncorseted, quivering as if with a life of its own, she stooped clumsily under the wagon to look at her boys. Abraham, mouth open, lay sprawled on his back with one hand flung outside the covers. Bathsheba, seeing the cracked flesh of the knuckles, remembered guiltily that the boy had complained of chappy hands that day. Chamber lye, she decided; there was nothing better for chapped skin. If she could just get the pot out from under the bed without waking Abijah . . . Back to her son, wrapping the sore hand in the reeking, dripping bandages, she held her breath, but although the boy stirred uneasily he did not waken. She was relieved, since she knew he would have to get up soon to 'spell' Samuel off with the sheep. Once back at her bed, she relaxed with satisfaction. Chamber lye was a sure cure for so many things from croup to proud flesh.

Just before she crawled in beside Abijah, she spit on her finger and made a cross on her corns; only because of negligence in such matters were the corns still there.

Drowsiness finally claiming her, she smiled contentedly. She had propitiated all her gods. She was ready for another day.

But her visit had awakened Freeborn. He had been restless, anyway. Feeling the ground's chill creep through his quilts, he wondered how a man could help coveting another's wife if she was like Clory.

4

The caravan's most persistent habit was early rising. Shortly before sunup, Abijah called his boys, from the oldest to the youngest: 'Freeborn, Joseph, Samuel, Lehi, Nephi, Isaiah!... Sam'l, eat and go to the sheep so that Abraham c'n eat!'

If they got up instantly, all was well, but if they dallied, Abijah was ready with a little willow switch. And having got his own brood under way, he was quite capable of dealing with another man's offspring. As a result, prayers were over, and the sun usually surprised the caravan at a shivering breakfast.

This morning, Abijah finished his steaming porridge, dipped his 'dough-god' in his salt-pork grease, and looked northward at the purple mists drifting over the broad flanks of Pine Valley; he saw relievedly that the day would be fine. He was worried. They had six miles yet to go before they rounded the southern point of the long, low, black hill stretching to their left far in front of them, and came into the St. George Valley. Six miles of brush-grubbing — for it seemed no matter how many wagons had gone before, there was always more brush to grub — six miles of brush-grubbing and deep sand.

He hoped Betsy Tuckett would hold off until they got there. Not that he was worried about Betsy — Bathsheba was a trained midwife — but a confinement would take time. Being already a day behind Apostle Snow, he was afraid if he had to make camp again before joining the others, Brother Snow would accuse him of laxity.

Bathsheba, feeling his impatience, urged the boys to hurry.

Lehi and Nephi, in a rush to finish eating, clanged their knives
together, and 'Sheba exclaimed in horror.

'Don't you know that crossed knives means you'll sure quarrel?
Your father's got enough to put up with, without that!'

The twins, promising to try to ward off the quarrel, each
grabbing a last piece of hot bread, rushed off to feed the lambs.
The women got after the dishes, while Freeborn and Joseph and
the older boys saw to the stock.

There was a noisy rushing to and fro at all the campfires; the
shrill voices of the women mingled with the rattle of dishes being
washed. Men and boys were driving bawling cattle to drink up
and down the creek. Babies cried. Sheep 'ba-a'd' protestingly
as the dogs got them under way for the new day's journey.

At last the water bags were filled, the wagons packed, the
caravan ready to start. The stream had changed to its day-time
tune again and the birds in the willows along the bank were just
beginning to chirp. Clory, in her wagon behind Abijah's, watched
a lizard scurry out into the sun and lift its green head to the
warmth.

Abijah called to Freeborn, flexing for the spring on his horse.

'Dout the fires thoroughly and see that none of the children
lag behind.'

He cleared his throat, sang out, 'All r-ready-y!'

Whips popped, oxen grunted and heaved forward against the
heavy yokes. The queue of white-tops headed south for Cooper
Bottoms, past the red mountain which had loomed over them all
night, past the gaily colored knolls sprinkled like pimples on the
broad, pink flesh of the land, even past the long, black hill which
some distance beyond them left its red companion and alone
stretched away into nothingness.

By noon the character of the land had changed. They had left
the red hill behind; and the hard, harsh alkali trail, from which
all morning the boys had grubbed mesquite, greasewood, sagebrush, and tumbleweeds had given way to soft, insidious pink

sand which clung halfway to the hubs of the wheels. Lon
Tuckett's wagon had been stuck once and they had had to provide traction with packed weeds. The stream had long ago
wandered off to the left. Abijah could see that the black hill to
the west was tapering, but its southern point was still too far off
to be seen.

Clory, letting the oxen have their way, listened to the sibilant
sigh of the sand as their hoofs went in, and the sucking gulp as
the beasts pulled them out. The long sigh — the gulp. She
stretched her arms and began to sing:

> Come, brethren, listen to my song;
>> Doodah, doodah.
> I don't intend to keep you long.
>> Doodah, doodah day.
> 'Bout Uncle Sam I'm going to sing;
>> Doodah, doodah.
> He swears destruction on us he'll bring;
>> Doodah, doodah day ...

Free, smiling at her, galloped past to Abijah's wagon, and
Abijah leaned out and called a halt. In a moment Bathsheba was
plodding through the sand to Betsy Tuckett's wagon. Willie
looked at Clory and clicked her teeth.

'I 'ope she hain't took bad here.'

Soon Bathsheba was back. She stopped at Willie's questioning
glance.

'Sister Tuckett's having a pain or two,' she said, 'but I taken
her some peppermint and horehound and made her a toddy.'

'That hought to backen 'em,' said Willie.

Bathsheba nodded, trudged ahead, and the caravan toiled
onward.

In Lon Tuckett's wagon, Betsy, biting her lip over the occasional pain, tried to fit her cumbersome body into the sway of the
jolting as she sipped Bathsheba's brew. Lon called back to her
aaxiously. She smiled at him. 'Ach, don't worry. I'll be fine.'

She sipped meditatively, her mouth puckering over the potion's bitter flavor.

'If it's a Liebchen we'll call her "Deseret" shust like dis state we help to build, *ja*?'

'Or if it's a boy,' said Lon, 'we'll call the little feller "Saint George" after the new town we're goin' to help build.'

'*Ja, ja*, you mean if he holds off long enough to get hisself born in St. George.'

'Well, if he don't, we kin call him "Millennium" and be safe!'

Lon had wanted a son for so long. Their first child, a girl, had died at birth. It had been a breech presentation and Betsy had almost gone. Lon's stout heart quickened now with fear. If only they could reach the valley in time!

Clory's voice came back to them, clear and gay.

> Doodah, doodah.
> Then let us be on hand
> By Brigham Young to stand,
> And if our enemies do appear...

Lon lifted his head and found a grin for Betsy.

In Clory's wagon, Willie was laughing at the girl. Pink sand had settled in the wrinkles of their dresses, was graying their hair, and outlining the fluting of Clory's red bonnet. Clory wiped a gritty bit from her tongue and complained, 'My land, I can't sing without choking on sand and I can't open my eyes without being blinded by it!'

5

The noon meal was eaten in haste and silence. Abijah even made the blessing on the food short and pithy. Everyone felt the suspense and the need for getting to the end of the journey. They ate beside a pink-and-lavender knoll shaped and fluted like a Christmas bell, each fluting striped in white. Although the river was plainer now, it was still nothing but a distant narrow gleam. Their way lay through a wasteland, through deeper, heavier sand.

Shortly after they had started up again, Abijah's heavy wagon mired, and no matter how he coaxed and whipped the oxen, no matter how his team tugged, the wheels stuck. By the time they had filled the loose ruts with brush, and dug around the wheels with their shovels, and the oxen had finally heaved the wagon to firmer ground, one more hour had passed. Abijah, irritated because he had not been able to control the swearing of the men, disheveled from the exertion, grimy with gravel particles and worried over the delay, stared ahead of him at the country. Three more miles like this to the point, and on the other side of the mountain at least another mile back up to the camp.

He whipped out his handkerchief from his tail-coat pocket, wiped sand from his beard, and sent Bathsheba back to the Tuckett wagon. She reported presently that Betsy's labor was more regular now and she was groaning a little with each pain. Abijah came to a daring decision.

He called the drivers of the company to him.

'We've got to reach St. George this night. The camp's on the other side of that black ridge. I figure we're just about even with it now. The hill's about half a mile straight across from us.'

They could see its volcanic rocks gleaming in the sunlight.

'We'll head straight for it, make a dugway up this side, an' if necessary lower our fit-outs down the other. We'll save four miles and get Sister Tuckett to where she'll be safe.'

The other drivers looked askance at the black berg looming formidably before them, but Lon, his face drawn with worry and fatigue, rushed thankfully back to tell Betsy.

'We'll git there, now, maybe. Abijah won't stop anywheres else fer hell ner high water.'

'He'll stop, all right, when dis baby de mind makes up to come!'

Betsy gasped with a pain and wiped the perspiration from her face.

'*Ach, ja, ja, ja!* An' de permission it ain't a-beggin' from dot Abijah MacIntyre ner any other.'

By the time they reached the foot of the hill, Betsy was writhing with pain. Bathsheba never left her now. She fed her lobelia until Betsy gagged.

'Even if you do puke,' said Bathsheba, 'the strainin' is good fer you.' And when Betsy doubled with another paroxysm, the older woman cried, 'Break the pains! Break the pains!' and forced her to stretch out full length.

Abijah, standing beside his oxen, chewed thoughtfully on a piece of jerky and stared up at the hostile black escarpment. The steep slope was scrambled with weirdly shaped boulders of lava rock of adamantine hardness. It was as if some giant had crumbled a mountain and thrown the fragments playfully into the air. Among the ebony rocks the sheep, already halfway up the hillside, looked like moving white stones, and the boys, herding them, like pygmy men.

Soon the whole caravan was helping to drive sheep, as boys and men, women and girls, attacked the rocky confusion; away from the trail Abijah outlined, they pitched rocks in all directions. There was a great smashing and crashing, shouts of 'Get the hell outa the way down there'; the instant of suspense while a chunk of lava as big as a house tottered on its edge and then the release as it roared down.

Bathsheba, in the wagon with Betsy, thought the people looked like ants assaulting that black citadel, but that nevertheless like ants they were clearing a space.

The children shouted with glee among the huge stones, much to the anxiety of their elders. Dogs barked hysterically. The deep, organ-like voices of the men echoed against the cliff as they sang while they labored. Clory's soprano shot pure and clear above the bass.

For had they not almost arrived at the promised land?

In an incredibly short time a pathway was comparatively clear, and picks and shovels, knives, even spoons in childish hands were hacking the lava coating, scooping out of the underlying soft sandstone two ruts diagonally across the face of the cliff. It was a back-breaking job, normally taking a day, two days. But Abijah was not only a slave-driver; he was a man of faith. He needed a miracle — let the Lord see to it. Nevertheless, hours later, it was with misgiving that he again faced the steep angle, and lowering into the climb and puffing beside the beasts, headed his oxen for the naked red ruts. Slipping, tugging, grunting — and it seemed to those watching, inevitably doomed to crash back down — Abijah's two stout teams made the summit. Abijah, panting, stroked their heaving flanks, darkly maroon with the sweat of the effort. A great shout went up.

'Hosanna! Hosanna to the Lord!'

Willie, breathless with excitement and fear, headed the second wagon for the ruts. Clory walked along beside the oxen and coaxed them to pull. 'Gee, Whitey! Come on, Bluchy!'

When finally the outfit was safe at the top, Clory's trembling knees gave way.

From where she rested on the summit she gazed back at the country they had just conquered; at the pink wastes and the lavender-skirted knoll, the stream, glimmering like a dinner knife to the south, the faint green of Washington to the north and the red mountain by it, the black ridge over which they had come yesterday, and beyond that, the series of brightly piled ranges ending in a square-topped, orchid mountain directly against the eastern skyline.

Abijah followed her gaze.

'That's Steamboat Mountain,' he said, 'called by the Indians Mukuntuweap or Home of the Great Spirit. It's the country where Apostle Orson Pratt took his company when we parted from them at Grapevine Springs, remember?'

The sun, an incandescent ball just above the hill behind them, suddenly flamed the paleness of Steamboat Mountain into iridescence. Pine Valley's purple shadows glowed redly.

Clory sighed with sheer joy, but an exclamation from Abijah brought her back to earth.

'Tuckett's ox! He's down agin!'

Leaving Willie to watch the outfit, Clory scrambled with Abijah back down the hill.

The ox seemed to have definitely made up its mind. It lay in the yoke with its eyes closed and its jaw working feebly, twitching its rump now and again at the flies. Abijah thought of a bolus of tobacco and cayenne, but dosing took too much time.

Lon Tuckett was incoherent with anxiety; he patted the ox and pled with it.

'Now, don't git my dander up — Bally, good ol' Bally.'

Clory thought how often she had seen him shaking with laughter, sandy chin-whiskers quivering, biting his lower lip until it bunged out as if to keep back a whole flock of swear words. His chin-whiskers quivered now, but not with mirth.

Betsy groaned inside the wagon. At every groan Lon gave the beast another frantic pat.

Miles and Jarvis and Peabody and Hichinoper all came to stand awkwardly over the animal; they sympathized with Brother Tuckett and offered their advice. Ringed about the beast, the curious children stared with big eyes. But gradually the men called to their families, and one by one pulled and heaved their outfits to the top of the hill, where they waited. Charles Hichinoper, carrying his wailing baby on its pillow, following beside his wagon driven by Eliza, was the last to reach the summit.

Clory, down below, thought the white-tops on the black lava rock looked as if the sober old hill had suddenly taken on a spurious gaiety and trimmed itself with a row of giant toadstools.

Abijah had exhausted his resources with the ox. He felt like swearing. He could never get his people to the valley without that animal. And Lon put his greatest fear into words: 'Betsy *can't* have her baby here!'

Abijah tried to think what President Brigham Young would have done. For Brother Brigham had not been an old man (he'd been in his forties) when he had led the Saints across the plains; surely Brother Brigham must have met similar situations. Or what would Apostle Snow do? He must surely have solved harder difficulties than this, and he was even now only in his forties. Abijah felt a glow of returning confidence. He was forty-one, almost as old as Brigham had been, almost as old as Apostle Snow was now. He was no unseasoned youth. He could and would handle this. For, after all, were they not God's chosen people? For a moment Abijah felt stunned; in this, his first real emergency, he had almost forgotten God!

He turned to Brother Tuckett.

Clory, sitting on a boulder near-by, wondered at the sudden purpose in Brother Tuckett's movements. What were they going to do? And then she saw Brother Tuckett appear with the bottle of consecrated sweet oil. She heard Lon say, 'You be "Mouth," Brother Abijah,' and the full significance of the scene burst upon her. Why, they were preparing for 'the laying on of hands'! For Abijah would have to be 'Mouth' since he held the higher priesthood! She sat up in horror. Administering to an ox!

She saw Melancthon Tuckett rub the oil between the animal's red ears and then both he and Abijah rest their hands, one over the other, on its head.

'We unitedly lay our hands upon thy head, O ox ... this oil which has been dedicated and consecrated and set apart for the healing of the sick in the household of faith ...'

Bewilderedly Clory grasped the fact that this prayer had all the earnest supplication of the ceremony performed for any ailing human being.

' ... We seal upon thee blessings of life, health, strength, and

vigor. . . . We do this by virtue of the holy priesthood in us
vested. . . .'

Suddenly Clory shared Lon Tuckett's childlike belief in Abijah;
it came to her that Abijah was in many ways a great man. He
was ruthless, fanatical, bigoted — a man more capable of winning
respect than affection — but a man to be depended on when you
needed him, a man who got things done.

Clory watched him calmly speak to the ox. Opening its eyes,
it stared at the men with its gentle, liquid gaze. She was not
greatly surprised when it scrambled to its feet.

Abijah felt that the Lord had proved Himself yet again; for
was not this a latter-day miracle? Beside Abijah, following
Brother Tuckett's wagon as it pulled up the slope, Clory decided
that there were many things about her husband she did not
know. . . . For truly he had saved a woman through an ox. '"God
moves in a mysterious way . . ."' she said softly.

6

At last, with all his people at the top of the summit, Abijah
dared to take stock of the other side. His heart sank at the
prospect. This downward grade was almost perpendicular.
They could never make a dugway across its face. They'd have
to get the biggest boulders out of the way, empty the wagons, and
lower them by chains. But God was with him.

He unfolded his plans to the men, and soon the whole company
was out rolling rocks. Clory, Willie, and Bathsheba emptied the
wagons. The girl's back ached from carrying bags of seed, flour,
clothes. She started to sing.

> Put yer shoulder to the wheel;
> Push a-lo-ong!

The other women picked up the refrain, and soon the men
joined in as they stooped to the stubborn stones.

Abijah drove them all relentlessly. The sun was low.

Clory, carrying Abijah's armchair down the footpath to the bottom, permitted herself only a glimpse of the valley as she eased herself from rock to rock. She could not see the upper part of the valley from here nor the camp, but she could see through the high brush the green banks of a stream, and nibbling through the brush, the herd of sheep. She envied Samuel and Abraham and the other boys for being the first to reach the camp. Directly in front of her, flanking the western end of the valley, just now casting its shadow before it, was the long black hill that Abijah had said would be there.

As Clory climbed back up the slope, thinking how good it would seem to be settled, she was startled by a scream. Seeing 'Sheba rush to the Tuckett wagon, she paled and ran to Willie.

'I guess poor Betsy's time's came,' said Willie, 'h'after all, in spite of everythin'.'

Clory wanted to go with Willie to the wagon to help, but Willie pushed her back.

'You'll 'ave yer turn soon enough, child, without seein' this.'

Clory stood uneasily about, wishing there was something she could do.

Betsy was shouting with anguish, now. Clory thought she had never dreamed having a baby could hurt that bad.

Lon was standing by the wagon tongue peering inside at the women ministering to his screaming wife.

'She'll die,' he whimpered, wringing his hands. 'O Lord, don't let her die — I'll quit m' swearin', Lord, an' chewin' terbaccer —'

Clory could hear Bathsheba shooing him out.

'Poor people have poor ways, Lon Tuckett. Now you git out an' don't bother me.'

Abijah came and got hold of Lon's arm, and the two of them walked off to find brush for a fire. There wasn't much growing among the lava rocks except the sticky 'evergreen' shrub.

While he poked among the stones for dry sticks, Abijah re-

flected bitterly that Betsy might die, anyway. He was a little
put out at the Lord. The Lord had saved the ox, but He hadn't
got Betsy there in time. And he, Abijah, would get the blame.
Still, he reproved himself, '— even as a grain of mustard seed . . .'

Abijah turned to Lon.

'He who sees the sparrows fall, Brother Tuckett . . .'

They walked silently back to the wagons with the fuel, their
attenuated shadows in the dying sun stalking before them.

Abijah was afraid one of their meager store of clumsy matches,
which failed to strike half the time, would never light a blaze.
Clory rummaged in her wagon and produced a torn piece of an
old newspaper (books and papers were so precious that even
scraps were saved), and crumpled it under the twigs. Getting his
gun, Abijah fired twice before the kindling finally burst into flame.
Blowing at the feeble tongue licking at the paper and brushing
the smoke from their eyes, the two men finally got a small fire
started, rank with the fumes of the resinous evergreen. While
Clory ran to find two rocks, Willie filled a kettle from the water
barrel to put over the blaze and reflected that the way of a woman
was hard. Lon kept running from the wagon to the fire and back
to the wagon again.

Some of the other members of the caravan sat silently on rocks
a respectful distance away; but Clory, taking Isaiah jiggling up
and down on his two chubby legs out behind a boulder, could see
most of the emigrants still toiling down and back up the hill with
the burdens of their earthly goods.

As she went back to camp, Willie poked her head out of the
Tuckett wagon and called to her.

'Run to Sister Peabody, Clorinda, an' see if she hain't got some
dried yarrow. 'Sheba says Betsy's kidneys are real bad.'

But when Clory returned, empty-handed, Willie met her hurriedly. She was fluttering her foolish, long hands.

'Never mind, child. Aunt 'Sheba's found her'n. Run git
Abijah's sweet oil and his box o' browned flour — 'urry!'

She waited until the girl returned, panting, with the things, and then handed her a large piece of white flannel.

'Scorch it good over the blaze,' she ordered.

'Scorch it?'

'Yes, good on both sides — and 'urry! Aunt 'Sheba says wool over a newborn babe keeps it from 'avin' colic.'

The suffering in the wagon grew more vociferous. Clory could hear between the screams the tense voice of Bathsheba.

'Bear down harder, Betsy!'

When Clory took the cloth back to Willie, the older woman smiled briefly at the girl.

'She's 'avin' a long labor, but Aunt 'Sheba'll pull her through.'

Suddenly Bathsheba came out of the wagon and, stalking intently all around it, peered under the wheels and the body. At the back she triumphantly pulled out an axe from under the canvas and threw it on the ground.

'There!' she said. 'I knew there was some'at wrong! No wonder she's havin' a bad time. If Lon had his way, carryin' that axe inside the wagon like that, she'd be dead!'

Clory wandered over and sat beside Abijah by the fire. He smiled at her, fingered the shrub-scratches on his hands, and reached into his inside pocket; then, remembering the browned flour wasn't there, spit on the scuffed and bleeding skin.

Near-by grew a stunted, cactus-like tree with spiny branches; it looked like a gnarled dwarf with weird, extended arms.

'That's a Joshua tree,' explained Abijah. 'When Brother Brigham called the Saints who were colonizin' San Bernardino back to Salt Lake at the time of Johnston's Army, they had to cross a big desert which stretches many miles to the south and west of where we be now.'

Clory forgot all about Betsy Tuckett, and Abijah, seeing this, warmed to his story. 'Twas good, he thought. She was muckle young. Even with the relaxation of his story-telling, Abijah's face never lost its sternness. Beneath the heavy beard, in the fleshy bulge of his chin, lurked a dimple, but the beard kept its betraying tenderness well hidden just as his life had rebuked and hidden the softness in his heart. His years had already carved their pattern in his face. But Clory's youthful prettiness was still vague, a story all yet to be told.

'Just at the beginning of the desert they ran into whole forests of these trees,' continued Abijah. 'Only on the desert they grow to be giants. Giant Joshuas. The Saints called 'em that because their twisted branches made 'em look like Joshua with his arms outstretched pointing the Israelites toward the Promised Land.'

Clory was absorbed. Eyes shining, she folded her two hands under her cheek and listened with her head on one side.

' ... They were some of 'em thirty feet tall, with huge trunks. Kinda scales on the trunks. 'Tis said they grow only three inches in ten years and ——'

Clory wasn't aware that the horrible screams had stopped until Bathsheba came toward them. Sweat was running down her face, but she was serene.

'A boy,' she announced. 'A crooked delivery an' Betsy's wore out, of course. But she'll be all right now.'

'Thank God,' murmured Abijah. He need have had no fear. The Lord was still taking care of His own, on a mountaintop or in a manger.

Lon, all smiles, called out to them from his wagon.

'Some punkins!' he cried. 'His name's "Millennium"! We're a-gonna call him "Len" fer short!'

He smacked his palms together and shuffled his feet.

'Got to celebrate! This pert night calls for a toot!'

And he chanted at the top of his voice:

> And when I reached the 'Black Ridge'
> And must slide my fit-out down,
> My Betsy had 'Millennium' —
> We were many miles from town;
> But with a clumsy chain and rope

> I got her to the bottom,
> For though the things began to slide,
> The chain and rope, they caught 'em!

Lon stopped for breath. Benjamin Jarvis shouted, 'Hooray!'
Amid the general laughter Abijah put a hand in an unaccustomed gesture of affection on Bathsheba's shoulder.

'You're a good woman, 'Sheba. A good woman.'

Bathsheba answered righteously, 'I'm willin' to work my
fingers to the bone for them that appreciates me.'

7

Now that Sister Tuckett's crisis was passed, the men set to work
to get the schooners down the slope. They uncoupled Abijah's
heavy outfit and attached chains and lariats to the wagon box.
The five men held back tightly on the ropes and chains until their
bodies bent double under the strain, while Free and the older
youths, digging their heels into the gravel, eased the box carefully
to the level ground below the hill. Joseph and a Miles boy dragged
the heavy doubletrees while Lehi and Nephi carried down the
tongue. They waited at the bottom while the men drew back up
the chains and ropes, sent sliding to them first the long reach, and
then, holding to the chains attached to the hounds, in turn rolled
down the two sets of wheels. At last the oxen, still yoked, were
persuaded down the steep path, and the job was almost done.

People sang while they labored.

> We all have work,
> Let no one shirk,
> Put your shoulder to the wheel!

Clory's voice rose like a bell over the others'.

'Careful,' called Abijah above the noise. 'It takes a long time
to make a wagon in a wilderness!'

The womenfolk finished carrying down the provisions; and
now Clory waited with the others at the foot of the ridge for the

men to put the wagon together again so that she might help repack it tightly with the precious articles. It was more important than anything in the world to handle carefully the seed — their very life's blood — so as not to spill a particle; but it was even more important to handle gently the sacks of flour which meant bread, now, today. The memory of starvation dies hard.

At last Abijah heaved a long sigh of relief. All but one of the wagons and their contents were safe at the bottom of the hill, and most of them assembled and ready to go. Only Melancthon Tuckett's still waited at the top. Abijah had left that until the last because it was going to be his hardest job, getting Betsy down.

Abijah watched patient Eliza Hichinoper, holding the pillowed child, finally reach her wagon. He saw Brother Hichinoper spread a quilt on the ground and Eliza sink onto it gratefully.

Freeborn was having trouble leading his red mare down the grade. She lifted her head skittishly, her ears back, and, sinking her hind hoofs into the rubble, gingerly felt out each step. The other horses at the foot neighed encouragingly to her.

'Shall I lend yu' my chariot, Free?' Clory sang out with the tiny flute-notes in her voice.

Her chariot. Abijah frowned. He couldn't understand Clory's 'pretends.' Once when she had called him 'Old Chief Sock-in-the-Wash' he had been disgusted. He mistrusted this habit she had of poking fun.

Voices came up to him. His people, in sight of the Promised Land, sang with joy.

> This life is a difficult riddle,
> For how many people we see
> With faces as long as a fiddle
> That ought to look shining with glee...

Abijah walked to the Tuckett wagon.

'Brother Tuckett,' he called inside, 'what's the best way to git

yer fit-out to the bottom?' Not that he expected Lon Tuckett
to provide any workable solution.

Lon spoke to Betsy. Her jaw was quivering with nervous exhaustion, but she drew the infant closer to her breast and smiled
at Abijah.

'Why, I'll shust stay on my bed while de wagon you lower.'

8

In the early darkness the valley stretched away before the
caravan to the jagged northern skyline. Brush had been cleared
by the preceding company and the road was plainly marked, so
that even the oxen, sensing that they were almost home, quickened their plodding. The wagons rolled along beside a clear,
energetic stream (on her stomach, drinking with her cupped
hands, Clory thought its brackish waters nectar), but on either
side of the line of schooners bushes loomed higher than a man's
shoulders from black ridge to black ridge throughout the valley.
Miles below them lay the Rio Virgin, Pah Roosh, which would in
time water their fields. Ahead gleamed the campfires of their new
homes.

Abijah, leading his oxen, looked to the beckoning flares. He
prayed in gratitude and satisfaction. True, it was late, and he
knew as a leader that he should never make camp after dark.
And even now there might be Indians in the brush. But the child
was safe, he had done his best, and he felt the Lord was pleased
with His servant. For the valley was just as he had been told it
would be. St. George. The Dixie Mission. The Promised Land.

He halted the wagons and led a cheer: 'Hooray! Hooray! Hooray for St. George and the Governor of Deseret!'

In May of last spring Brigham Young, standing at this same
end of the valley, had uttered his famous prophecy; afterward,
in the Tabernacle in the City he had preached to his new recruits;
Abijah remembered almost the very words: 'I looked northward

up a gently sloping valley about two and three miles in extent between the banks of the Rio Virgin, the valley being formed by projecting ridges of two spurs of Pine Valley Mountain opening and expanding toward the river skirting it on the south. I was moved to prophesy then the words I now repeat to you whom the Lord has called to settle the Dixie Mission: "There will yet be built between these volcanic ridges a city with spires, towers, and steeples, with homes containing many inhabitants."'

Abijah seemed to see the spires and towers ahead in the gloom. He ached to get at their building. For the Lord had promised him that the fruit of his loins, as numerous as the sands of the sea, would some day dwell upon this land.

Bathsheba, in the wagon, was thinking how glad she would be to see Hannah Merinda Lowgie's kindly face and discuss with her the technical details of Betsy's confinement.

Freeborn, riding ahead, wondered if he might find in the new settlement a girl who could make him forget Clory.

Willie thought about the two women who had been in the handcart company with her. They were at the camp. They'd remember about Joe and the children . . . She hoped Bathsheba was right about this nausea. She'd be happier with a baby of her own again.

Clory, so tired that it seemed her weariness was like a presence riding with her in the wagon, gripped the whipstock and hoped fervently that Palmyra Wight would walk a way to meet her. Pal was her best friend. *She* would understand about Abijah — and what he had said about coming to her bed. Her heart beat with excitement. She could talk about Rolph to Pal.

Lon Tuckett was thinking that when his son grew up there would be a city ready-made for him.

Eliza Hichinoper, driving her stiffened muscles to one last effort and, still with her pillowed infant in her arms, walked toward the welcoming gleam and voiced her wish to Charles. If only Brother Steadfast Weeks, who knew much of the mysterious ways of medicine and herbs, would come out to meet them!

The campfires grew closer. Faint noises drifted to the tired travelers. Under the friendly starlight, advancing to meet them beyond the flare of the flames and the protecting white-topped circle, marched a group of shouting, singing people.

Clory felt as if her heart would break with joy. Song spontaneously burst forth from all the weary caravan.

> Come, come, ye Saints — no toil nor labor fear,
> But with joy — wend your way!
> Though hard to you — this journey may appear,
> Grace shall be — as your day!
> Gird up your loins, fresh courage take;
> Our God will ne-ever us forsake . . .

CHAPTER III

APOSTLE ERASTUS SNOW sat his horse with a
faint air of distaste, his long black coat-tails parted over the horse's
rump, his booted feet awkward in the stirrups. To him a horse was
never more than a horse and, indeed, he would much have preferred walking. He was thinking that when they got the town
built, the trip to the Red Hill would be a pleasant Sunday afternoon's stroll instead of this grueling ride across half of the valley
floor and then the mile or two of climbing to the pinnacle itself.

With the characteristic writhing of his lips back from his teeth
and the following smack which prefaced most of his slow, quiet
speech, he turned to the man riding beside him.

'Funny to me ... Shadrach Gaunt ...' ptsahh, ptsahh ...
'funny ... to me, how the minute you get on that pony of yours
... you manage to seem so ... *wedded* to him ... Now take me
and *my* cayuse ...'

His full, mobile, clean-shaven mouth widened in silent amusement, and he reached up a hand to the pepper-and-salt ruffle
fringing his chin.

Shadrach Gaunt was a man of few words.

'Takes all kinds,' he said.

'Yes, it takes all kinds ... each one doing his bit ... each one working ... for the good of the whole ...' ptsahh.

Shadrach Gaunt, who had sacrificed his tobacco for the Word of Wisdom, went on chewing his squawbush gum. Theories were not for him, neither waste motion. His eyes beneath their tufted brows had the shrunk pupils, the concentrated focus of a man who has regarded distances all his life. In his Indian-cured buckskins, grayed and softened by time into a sort of second epidermis, he rode easily, his long braids of black hair looped beneath his rabbit's-fur cap, hands quiet on the reins, pistol butts curving casually at hand.

The two horses picked a careful way through the dense, shoulder-high brush, tempted now and then by the dried mesquite pods still outliving the season. The leaves had fallen, and the brown thorns of the mesquite, the black talons of the grotesque mescrew or cat's-claw, the gray branches of the 'old-man' sage, the feathery, powdered rabbit brush, rubbed at Apostle Snow's trousers, poked inquisitive tendrils beneath his wide hat, gave off the dry, sweet scent of the desert.

Occasional puffs of white dust from the crusted alkali beneath the horses' hooves hung in the crystalline air.

Coming out of the brush the faint path began to climb. Sudden brackish odor of salt grass and bad water, rustling yellowed reeds rising into blunt cattail fingers. Many of the fat brown bodies violated already, oozing white fluff seeds.

'People will love this hill ... Sweethearts ... girl-and-boy gangs ... Picnics ...'

Ptsahh.

'Mount Hope, that's it. Mount Hope and the Sugar Loaf on top!'

Bright red boulders began to jut through the brush. The path turned a corner. Another dank breath from the left; more reeds there in a tan pool, the stark branches of a cottonwood or two, tall gray arrowweeds, giving off their clean, astringent smell. The path turned ahead once more beside a murmur of water deep among rocks laced with reticent maidenhair. Another climbing corner. More red, jutting boulders.

Rounding a last turn, Apostle Snow drew up his horse. At his feet the red precipice flung itself downward in careless, stony abandon. At his back rose the face of the gigantic pink sandstone boulder, smooth-walled and four-square, dominating all the stretching distance below.

Tethering their horses, the two men scrambled around to the right of the giant; Apostle Snow's booted feet rang on the stones, the rawhide soles of Shadrach's moccasins slipped surely and silently. Ahead and beyond them the red stones sported like the vomit of some tipsy god.

Here in its right side the giant boulder gaped. Stooping through the opening, the two men found themselves standing in a lofty cave, light dripping through a crack in the vaulted ceiling. Bats burst out at them.

Sniffing the musty air, Erastus walked across the thick sand of the floor and kicked at the blackened embers of an Indian fire. He ran a hand over the cool pocked surface of the rock.

'Must scoop out ... steps here ... some day ... mebbe get through that crack to the top; ... fine view from there.'

Turning, he climbed back through the opening and over the rocks outside to the precipice from where he could see all the valley: the two black ridges like encircling arms, the brush stretching away to the south to the river, and the chameleon-like mountains beyond. Far over to his left, directly beneath the eastern ridge, cowered the white tops and the Osnaburg covers of ninety tents and several hundred wagons making up the two parallel quarter-mile lines of the encampment. There were willow sheds over some of the wagon boxes, and beside the green-bordered stream a long plowed drain furrow that you couldn't see from here.

He writhed his lips in affectionate amusement at the thought of Shadrach, towering quiet but relentless beside him. It was really the limit not being able to go for a bit of Sunday morning meditation without this looming shadow. But Brother Brigham had commissioned Shadrach to watch out for Apostle Snow, and from that time on the Indian fighter had been a second self, quite in the manner of Porter Rockwell, who had guarded the Prophet in Nauvoo so many years. As a matter of fact, Shadrach rather echoed Porter with his braids, his deerskins, marksmanship, ruthlessness. Except, of course, that Porter's crowning glory was the result of the Prophet's rumored promise that as long as his hair went uncut he would be invulnerable — quite an item to a 'two-gun' man. Erastus remembered him riding wildly up and down Salt Lake's muddy main street when it was taken over in '58 and filled with saloons and disorderly houses by the camp followers of General Johnston's 'blue jackets' (Brother Brigham had prevented the soldiers from entering the city, but he could not prevent pollution at the hands of the inevitable hangers-on) — both Shadrach and Porter, angered at this sore in Zion, yelling like Navajos and lassoing store-front signs and gateposts.

There was the story of Porter highwaying the Prophet, who turned the holdup into a conversion; the story of Shadrach shooting from a hundred paces squarely between the eyes each one of fifty stolen mules being driven out of his corral gate by the irate owner. Illiterate, lawless, loyal, Porter Rockwell and Shadrach Gaunt belonged to a fast-dwindling type of man whose home was his saddle, whose God his trigger-finger.

Shadrach was six and a half feet tall (dwarfing Erastus' stocky five feet eight), powerfully built, lived on the finest horse he could get. He believed that 'horses are not *raised* but *born*, like cowboys.' He hated Indians (call them 'red brothers' or 'Laman-ites,' they were still gun-fodder to him), and it was said of him that he could sniff their presence in a strange country as a dog sniffs out a rabbit.

In fact, it was this very quality that might counteract all his usefulness, Erastus was thinking. He, Erastus, believed rather more in Brother Brigham's admonition that it was 'cheaper to feed 'em than to fight 'em.' Besides, it was unthinkable that anything should disturb the work that was being done in Santa Clara by Jacob Hamblin, Brother Brigham's famous missionary to the Lamanites, who had been laboring among them since '54, converting them to the Gospel, teaching them to build houses and raise grain.

This whole land, over which he was in charge, should be like that, a land of co-operation, of peace and brotherly love. As he stood there, visualizing the city to be built, his soul swelled with the creative ardor that is always the driving force of the true pioneer. This was all his, his, to do with as he pleased. He felt suddenly as if he were holding in his two hands a lump of clay which would carry forever the imprint of his own personal molding. He thought of the heterogeneous mixture of his people — the colony of Swiss emigrants who had preceded his group by a day, called to swell the little town on the Santa Clara; he thought of the Norwegian, the Dutch, the Spaniard, the English, the Jew, the Indian, even the Negro, fifty different nationalities within the radius of fifty miles, all to be welded into one whole. Here was the land, untouched, primeval — surely the world had never seen anything like it before, human atoms from every country, 'having heard the word,' deliberately going forth into the wilderness to 'keep it fast and bring forth good fruit.' Offshoots from every racial antagonism with but one unifying thought, the Good of the Whole.

Each of the colonies spawned by Brother Brigham would yet have to find its own legs, work out its own particular interpretation of Mormonism. And *his* interpretation of Mormonism was very simple: here there would be brotherly love. In his enthusiasm he spoke aloud, and his words under the impact of his will-to-do sounded almost like a threat:

'Here every man *will love his neighbor* ...'
Shadrach Gaunt stirred, and spat.
'Or else, by gadder, we'll shoot him!' he finished happily.

2

Clory jack-knifed her legs into the round wooden tub and giggled suddenly at the thought of Bathsheba's contortions. Of course Bathsheba belonged to the old-fashioned one-limb-at-a-time folks, anyway; those who believed that if the garments were never entirely shed, even during a bath, they armored the body against enemy bullet and Indian arrow, as well as temptations. But recalling her own recent introduction to garments during the endowment ceremony, Clory decided that nevertheless there were some things she didn't believe ... and giggled again at the thought of 'Sheba scrubbing herself in relays.

There was just room for the tub in the middle of the wagon floor. Clory stepped out onto the rag rug, retrieved the piece of yellow squshy home-made soap with its honest smell, and reached to the bedpost for her towel. Although the winter sun was warm outside, she was blue and shivering in the cold air, and the square of harsh unbleach left her skin almost raw.

Now for her underwear, which, as was proper, had been carefully dried under a sheet to preserve its intimacies from masculine eyes. Her fingers tied the strings of the stiff, home-bleached garments into neat bows marching down the front. Now the chaste 'shimmy,' with her own crocheted edging, then the heavily boned corset, which constricted her exuberant spirits, but lifted her little breasts into pointed cups for the basque; the scalloped and boned corset cover and the drawers buttoned at the waist and blooming to the knee, where a gathered and embroidered ruffle fell below; finally her hoops. As she stepped into the cagelike frame she strutted with pride. A gift from her mother in Philadelphia, they were undoubtedly the most fashionable in the whole terri-

tory. Other women were still wearing the whalebone skirt or
horsehair flounces or crinolined tucks like those swinging her
everyday linsey-woolsey. At last over the hoops the four starched,
embroidered, and ruffled petticoats; shaking out the dried
bergamot leaves, she wished she could afford six Sunday petticoats. Then the black-ribbed home-knitted stockings (thank
heavens these had taken a good dye and were not mottled), and
the many-buttoned kid boots (freshly blackened with stove soot
and vinegar) Abijah had got for her in Salt Lake by trading a milk
pan of flour to a passing emigrant. They were much too large for
her, but she thought them elegant with their pointed toes and
tiny curved heels.

Her best dress was soft, dark red cassimere; it had been an old
one of Bathsheba's, made over and cut down, and only in one
or two places was the cloth worn. It had, in fact, been her wedding dress, since she had worn it to the Endowment House that
day — there had been no time to think of new finery. Both the
skirt and bodice were gored and fully lined with coarse brown
cloth; the basque was fitted around two stays that supported her
breasts like stems topheavy with bloom. Glittering jet buttons
trimmed the back fastening and the long tight lined sleeves.
Fancy beaded braid circled the peplum with its postillion back,
and flounced three deep around the skirt. She had wanted black
lace, but Abijah said lace was Babylon, and for the same reason
she had had to be contented with a simple crocheted collar instead of the more fashionable lace undersleeves and chemisettes.

Clory had of late been wearing her hair in the new 'waterfall'
style. Although she did not have the horsehair frame, she found
that her own hair was thick enough when gathered into a net to
make the same huge loop on her neck. Center-parted, brushed
in two black wings from her temples, the style pleased Abijah, but
she could not prevent the tendrils that continually frothed away
from her hairpins.

Now her mother's cameo brooch, pinning a black velvet bow at her throat; matching earrings already dangled at her ears (thank goodness, Aunt 'Sheba had finally relented about the piercing); her precious hair bracelet, intricately woven and braided from Will's childish tow-colored locks; finally the bead-embroidered plush cape, badly crocked, but with a deep collar to be turned up around the ears.

Wishing she had one of those new chenille snoods, she picked up her red plush bonnet with a little frown of distaste. Heaven knew how many heads had worn it before it finally appeared in the stock of Gilbert and Parrish's General Store last spring. She had worked to pay for it by sewing pieces of heavy canvas cut from cast-off army tents and wagon covers into sacks, which were scarce in the territory and would therefore retail at a high price. She would never forget how her hands had ached from pushing those heavy sacking needles through that material. (Abijah said it served her right for being so weak in the faith as to prefer States' goods in the first place.) And now, after all that, bonnets were going out, anyway, in favor of pork-pie hats and mushrooms — she had read it only last summer in a *Harper's New Monthly Magazine*, accidentally strayed among the stacks of *Peterson's*, *Bow Bells*, and *Woman's Exponents* on the shelves of the old Council House library.

She tossed her head, longed briefly for some mitts (which, after all, would only accentuate the splintered brittleness of her fingernails, which much tallow-salve did not seem to help), stepped around the tub (one of the boys would have to empty it), and climbed out of the wagon and down the ladder, looking in her dipping crinoline like a glorified hollyhock.

3

Walking sedately between Abijah and Willie (Bathsheba always had to have one side of Abijah to herself), Clory shot a demure glance at her husband's Sunday garniture. He was

groomed and polished black and white from his congress gaiters
to the stand-up wing collar above the gleaming shirt-bosom that
was such a chore to the wife who had to do it up. Black circular
cape with the shoulder cape lined with red flannel. Crisp white
lawn necktie he wore for best almost hidden by the springing
beard, but which nevertheless had always to be tied with such
precision. Watching the erect swing of his broad shoulders, the
way he carried his big, narrow-hipped body, the lightness of his
tread, she could not imagine him ever stooping, literally or
figuratively. Even the flintlock in the crook of his arm he carried
like a soldier.

This was the first meeting to be held in the bowery just now
completed one week after the Saints had entered the valley.
Although Abijah's Sibley tent was only a few steps away, he and
his wives made out of the walk a triumphal procession.

The bowery was set some distance from the double row of tents.
The ground had been well cleared and the earth raked over and
wet. Although the brush had been grubbed for yards all around,
Clory thought it strange to gaze through the interstices of the
woven willow walls and watch a rabbit poised at the edge of the
thick cover, or blackbirds whee-ee-ing in the mesquite trees, or,
maybe for a second, a skulking Lamanite.

Since they were early, she and Bathsheba and Willie had found
a bench well to the front. Abijah, being a Seventy, had stacked
his gun with the others and gone directly to the stand, where he
sat beside Brother Orson Pratt, Junior, and put his Bible and
Book of Mormon over the vacant place on his right to hold it
for Apostle Snow, just now coming tardily up the aisle. Clory
was thinking Abijah and Brother Erastus wore their hair somewhat alike, side-parted, brushed back in a wave from high fore-
heads, and the ends turned up in a slight curl at the back. But
Apostle Snow's hair was light, graying and slightly thinning on
top, while Abijah's dark brown silken thatch fairly lifted with life.

She craned her neck to watch the people filing in, noting with satisfaction that so far she was the best-dressed woman there. Such a mixture! Men in dressed deerskins or old tow breeches, flannel or linsey shirts and cowhide boots, calfskin vests and blanket coats. Here was one wearing leather leggings like a savage; there that scout she had often noticed on Salt Lake streets who dressed in the curly hair of his dog, sheared annually. Here came Freeborn, cheeks scrubbed to rosiness, light unruly hair darkened and subdued with goose grease, big hands that always seemed to hang on his wrists like an afterthought, jammed into the high pockets of his best jeans. More men in sober gray homespun carrying wide soft hats. A few like the dignitaries on the stand in the longer full-skirted coats of black broadcloth.

Among the women she saw here and there red flannels, calicoes, the blowzy Eardley girls in the extremity of black sateen, even the gracelessness of blue denim on Sister Oleson, whose husband Clory thought the ugliest man she had ever seen, but for the most part homespun checks such as Sister Jarvis's red madder and sheep's gray, Sister Miles's and Sister Peabody's indigo blue, or that German woman's sloppy yellow-and-brown plaid, home-made shoepacks on their feet. Calico was fifty cents a yard in the City, and most of the sunbonnets, plain or slatted, were made from hand-me-downs, while some of the men and boys carried caps cut from an old shirt or vest, with a piece of bootleg for a visor.

Here came Eliza Hichinoper, earnest and anxious-eyed in her plum-colored silk wedding dress, Betsy Tuckett carrying Millennium and stretching the seams of her brown kersey and towering ahead of Lon, sprightly on his bandy legs, carrot-hair standing stiffly at attention, apologetic in his uniform and caped government overcoat sweeping his boot-tops, so obviously made for some six-footer. (At the time of the recall of the army the summer before — at 'Uncle Sam's auction' — surplus uniforms were sold for about the price of wool to make the cloth, and for years thereafter every homespun gathering of Saints was incongruously spiced with the blue of those they had fought.)

Clory was suddenly proud of Abijah and his wives. Even Willie, timid in her gray silk-and-mohair, boasted a new dickey of black beaded net and a new crocheted fascinator over her hair. Bathsheba, of course, was majestic in her flounced black taffeta glittering with jet and lace (evidently Bathsheba even in lace was above Babylon).

Then Clory's wandering eye caught sight of Palmyra Wight preceding David up the aisle; at the same time she shoved the other two women over on the bench and beckoned frantically, her heart sank. She brushed at her cassimere spitefully. For here was Pal, buxom in a new blue merino pelisse and a black beaver hat with ostrich plumes — *brand-new!* And, yes, the sway of the blue delaine underneath was much wider, much more stylish than her own. Clory burned with envy. Pal could hardly negotiate her square circumference up the aisle.

She sank down beside her friend with a squeeze and the two girls dissolved into excited murmurings, Clory drowning Pal in extravagant compliments.

Bathsheba drew out her gold watch from its nest over her left taffeta bosom and frowned heavily.

David, on the other side of Pal, looked on in amusement. He was a large young man with a mane of sun-streaked hair waving back from his forehead and curling over his collar, and gray eyes that could be blue and direct or dream-filled and almost black. David Wight was a sheepman (and a good one, too), and the thing you remembered about him was his clean smile streaking across a sensitive brown face that humans as well as animals trusted. He liked to make up poetry on the sly, but hated to be teased about it. His smooth-shaven cheeks were lean and handsome, but Clory thought he couldn't be much fun to be married to, except, of course, that he was young. For wasn't it one of Brother Brigham's daughters who said 'kissing a man without a mustache was like eating an egg without salt'?

There was a rustling on the stand and Brother Wheelock lifted an improvised baton. It was during the opening hymn that Clory first caught sight of Marianne Snow, Apostle Snow's youngest wife, up at the front between the first and second wives, Keturah and Martha, and the Snow boys and girls. Aunt Ket's Lucy was about the same age as Marianne and Clory and Pal, but it was Marianne who drew their eyes — she certainly must be the favorite wife! There the hussy strutted in one of those new Garibaldi blouses of foulard silk in the latest Solferino shade and a *plissé*-shirred hood and cape to match! Clory nudged Pal.

'Well, the cape isn't so much,' whispered Pal above Bathsheba's indefatigable soprano; 'I'd rather have a dolman any day; and a hood — imagine wearing a hood!'

Lucy turned and waved, but Marianne was too hoity-toity.

The congregation subsided onto its seats and Clory's fascinated eye caught just the suggestion of a laced boot below the cape, the tease of an intriguing tassel. 'Balmoral boots!' she hissed to Pal. 'The latest thing for croquet!'

Pal grinned maliciously.

'A lot of croquet she'll play around here!'

Bathsheba's patience was thinning. '"Whisper in church and your soul's in the lurch." Quit flouncing around and sit up like a lady. My laws, you've been showing your ankles to every man on the stand!'

Abijah got up to open. 'Hawckk!' He gazed the people into silence, lowered his eyes, and bowed his head. His watch chain was a reproving diagonal gleam across the virtuous expanse of his vest. Like some bearded Elijah he rolled out the sonorous phrases of his prayer, spiced with the Scotch burr.

Clory couldn't stand it any longer.

'How wide is your dress?'

'Six widths in the waist,' whispered Pal, mouth and shielding palm to Clory's ear; 'and I can raise the hem of the skirt to the top of my head. David traded five bushel of beets...'

'Sh-h!' frowned David, finger to lip.

You'll suffer for this, young lady, silently vowed Bathsheba.

Clory wriggled on the seat. Today, being the first Sunday in the month, was fast day and her stomach growled rebelliously. Saliva started running even at the thought of the Sacrament. No silver goblets and plates for the bread and wine down here... She had a sudden memory of donating her father's watch toward a Sacrament service after general conference in '52, and vowed nobody should get any keepsake out of her a second time! She itched in various places where the harsh cloth of her garments scratched her skin, and the narrow uneven benches (mostly willows roped together) bit into her soft flesh.

Abijah's 'Amen' rolled out just as she palmed a yawn, and she thought his gaze as he sat down seemed too intent in her direction.

Apostle Snow introduced as the first speaker a newly returned missionary from Paddington Branch, London Conference — Elder Orson Pratt, Junior, whose father, Apostle Orson Pratt, the famous philosopher and mathematician, was colonizing up the river toward Mukuntuweap. His plain brown beard, sparse on the upper chin, and tufted sideburns gave him a scalloped profile.

'I am glad to see here today — so many brethren and sisters from across the seas.' He hesitated and scowled earnestly at the congregation. 'The divine "Spirit of Gathering" is indeed upon us ——'

Pal was at Clory's ear again.

'Did you know he's being talked about?'

'What for?'

David with his arm through his wife's brought her firmly back to attention.

Clory dreamily watched a fly annoy Bathsheba. The speaker's words fell around her like a soft mist. Fast-day meetings, turned over to the congregation for the bearing of testimonies, always dragged.

The audience stared at the dignitaries on the stand, the dignitaries stared back. Stern, close-lipped faces — hard-driven, indomitable.

4

Abijah's brown eyes, normally hazel-flecked and soft, were coldly gray, the pupils gorged and black with his anger. Gritting his teeth, he stared in helpless exasperation at Clory on the bed. It was all he could do to keep from grabbing her and — and — ou aigh, Lord! *kissing* her. He ached with the longing to crush that provocative mouth into quivering submission. He wanted her soft hands in his hair, her gay lips tender in caresses, her voice broken in endearments — but a man had to be master in his own household. Sometimes he suspected she knew how he felt and deliberately tantalized him. Ech, why, now that he had married her, couldn't she conform to the pattern he laid down for his wives! Was that too much to ask?

He cleared his throat uneasily. She had such a habit of reading his thoughts. Around her he was never so sure that he *was* great and wise and God's anointed.

'Clor-rinda Agatha, I ne'er thoct I'd ken the day t' see ye makin' light in the Lord's ain house! An' before a' the unco folk ——'

'We weren't talking about you, Abijah. I just asked Pal about her new dress.'

'It's no the day to be speering sic things!'

Ech, to be able to curse a fyllie...!

That dimple that came and went; the long lashes on her cheek — she probably lowered them to hide the imp in her eyes instead of from any sense of proper female modesty.

'It was only that Pal and I were gettin' the "Spirit of the Gathering," Abijah!'

'Eneuch! Kape yer fulish tongue off the words of the Lord!' he stood irresolute, the fierce color coming and going in his cheeks. Swearing was wrong, but he could see the hot words forming on tonight's page in his diary...

How could she luk sae gash! 'n Sunday, too, looking as happy

as if it was ta middle o' ta week. A man could pandy a bairn an'
be done with it, but a wife ... Weel, he wasna gaeing to hae this
evil gyre in his hoosehold, the deil take it.

'Clor-rinda, I prefare ye shud stay home the rest o' the day an'
study the gude Scriptures. Get yer mind off frae claes. Humble
yersel' in prayer before the Lord. My heart is sair troubled about
ye, Clor-rinda.'

He handed her the Book of Mormon he had carried with him
to the meeting, and the touch of her hand made him shiver. He
maun be gaeing daft.

'Premeese yersel' tae see to it, Clor-rinda!' he thundered as he
climbed out between the wagon bows.

Clorinda, still sitting in her cape and bonnet as he had left
her, was reflecting how much Abijah disliked noise unless he made
it himself.

She got out of her dress, loosened her stays, propped herself
up on the bed, and opened the Book of Mormon. She supposed
she must be very wicked, but really she could never get interested
in the story. She thought it dull as dishwater. People seemed to
spend all their time begetting.

Clory lifted her head.

There was a scratch on the canvas cover.

'Clory? ... It's me, Pal.'

Palmyra, finger to lip, poked her cheerful, freckled face between the flaps.

'Sh! I sneaked around the back way. Brother Mac's with
Aunt 'Sheba. I could hear them jawing.'

'About me, I guess. I'm stuck here for the day, you know.'

Pal nodded her head and giggled. 'David said he supposed as
much!'

The two girls fell on the bed with hushed squeals of delight.

Clory sat up, stroked an imaginary beard, and pulled down her
brows in Abijah's frown. Her voice, that shaded so richly to suit
the meaning of each word, took on the exact tongueing of Abijah's
burr.

'Ou the puir body! Someone shud tak an awl an' prod him weel and let the wind out o' him!'

Pal howled with joy. Inclined toward dumpiness herself, she felt a little envious of Clory's fashionable fragility. When she caught her breath she reached up a hand to the other's shining hair.

'Let's do hair, kid!'

But Pal's mild locks, crimped and pushed below the tortoise-shell comb in front for bangs, still could not do much for her flat face.

'Do you suppose curls behind would help? David (poor David — he'd do anything to make me like this awful country!) says I can have 'em if I like.'

Clory snorted.

'Abijah thinks even bangs are sinful.'

Pal sighed.

'Just think, you might be married to Rolph by now and living in the States.' She who was herself so placid reveled vicariously in Clory's stormy passions.

Clory's face glowed. She fluttered to the chair and clasped her hands under her cheek, and gazed dramatically into space. Why, who knew, Rolph might keep her in his heart forever, never get over her — he might even pine away for her!

'You know, I'm getting so that I can't remember his face so clearly, no matter how I try. I say what he's like to myself over and over, but ——'

And she was off, mentally tracing each dear feature with the minute precision of one who is forever confirming each precious detail of remembered happiness. The blond mustache that drooped so enticingly, the merry eyes under the visored cap, the dust-stained uniform. The youth of him. He had swung off his horse at the gate (the other soldiers waited, feet firm in hooded stirrups, poised to gallop) and stood at the door, cap in hand, and asked to buy the fresh butter and milk. Hesitantly, because

after all he *was* a member of Johnston's Army sent by President
Buchanan against the Saints. (She remembered her scared excitement over seeing a gentile, a *real* gentile, and her twinge of disappointment because he appeared, after all, so much like other men.)
But even that first day there had been an infection about his smile.

After that, Free had had to deliver the eggs and butter regularly to Camp Floyd in Cedar Valley. He and Rolph, so nearly
of an age, became friends. She used to get angry because they
always had to sneak about it. But Free was a dear and from the
first he had understood, always patiently answering her rush of
questions after each visit. He even brought Rolph to one of the
ward picnics in the Old Social Hall and they had managed a walk
in the moonlight. Those wildflowers he brought her ... She had
crawled out of the window to meet him several times in the evening in the ravine back of the farm.

'You are like a saucy angel,' he said, 'and I love you. If I
thought I could satisfy your Mormon God I'd ask you to marry
me.'

But she couldn't tell even Pal how it had felt when he kissed
her. His lips suddenly forgot to be gentle, and her body dissolved
into a thousand premonitory tingles of delight.

Then there was Uncle Abijah telling her that girls who married
gentiles suffered for all eternity; and Brother Brigham seducing
her young romance with fine words.

Even then, even with knowing that Rolph was going back to
the States with the rest of the troops in July, she had held out
against them.

'I won't marry Abijah,' she had stormed at Willie — Willie
with her patient bowing of the neck to the yoke. 'Not if Brother
Brigham in all his robes commands me! I'll *spit* in his face,
I'll ...'

But Brother Brigham was the Prophet of the Lord. And she
had come away from her talk with him trailing glory, meek as
became a handmaid of the one true God.

The only trouble was that the glory hadn't lasted. And although she knew it would be nice, of course, to be saved in heaven, Rolph's kisses were sweet to be tasted now.

Just with thinking about it, she still blinked at tears.

'Imagine having a husband all to yourself, Pal! And one who jokes and laughs — *and laughs!* I do try hard with Abijah, but he — he ——'

'Hush!' Pal gestured. 'Sh! Listen!'

But Abijah's presaging 'hawckk!' and her warning were too late. This time, his angry tread quaking the canvas, he might have been scourging the money-changers. Clory, drugged with memory, could only sit stricken. He was bitter with Pal.

'Ye lure her tae blasphemy, Sister Wight. Gang yer waas.'

Pal, freckled cheeks flushed, pecked Clory on the forehead and hastily gathered up her things. Abijah watched her go and turned to his wife with obdurate eyes.

'Dinna forget we're cleeked, Clor-rinda Agatha. Ye've cam tae the end o' my patience. I ken this is a matter for the Pr-riesthood.'

The girl could not lift her gaze from the black hairs springing out of the soft white flesh of his pointing hand.

When he had gone she stood a moment panting with rage and tears, picked up the Book of Mormon, pitched it headlong, and flung herself across the bed.

5

When Clory woke, dusk had filtered into the wagon box. Her breath still came in little gasps like a punished child's. She lay there listening to the nightly far-off barking of the coyotes, then the gathering voices outside, the crackling of a campfire. She had never before been conscious of the mixture of dialects and brogues in the camp. Even some out there who could not speak English, chattering in Swedish or Welsh or German.

Oh, yes, the Sunday evening sing-and-story-tell. (The amusement hall, an open space encircled with banks of rabbit brush,
was just beyond her wagon.) She got up automatically, then remembered her stormy, swollen eyes. She could hear Apostle
Erastus drawling: 'All those here ... hold up their hands ... who
saw and knew ... the Prophet Joseph! ...' Ptsahh. Ptsahh.

It was cold in the wagon box. Clory got into the bed and
pulled around her shoulders the scratchy blanket woven from the
buffalo and cow hair her childish hands had helped to pick from
the sagebrush on that first big trek across the plains. She dropped
her head in her palms.

It was harder than anything — this having to please Abijah.

But the sound of Erastus' drawl tugged at her mood. Like
Brigham he was given to jawing his people into order, but unless
really angry, his low tones never lost their hint of good humor.

'How many?' The slow voice was continuing. 'How many
hands? ... Ten? ... Ten people in our own little community have
seen and known the Prophet Joseph!'

He sounded like a benevolent school-teacher.

'Who remembers what he looked like?'

The creaking of benches, eager rustlings...

Ptsahh. Ptsahh ... 'Ah ... very good ... Sister Perkins?'

The catechism was familiar as habit to Clory, but always before
she had been part of it, busily craning her neck to get the tilt of
a hat, or provoking the Sabbath piety of youths into half-glances
of exasperated homage.

Now that she could do nothing but listen, the litany took on
new meaning, and pictures began to form before her closed eyes.
The crowded, legendary years, the tales, the folklore of her people
which she had absorbed at Bathsheba's knee along with her
'lumpy dick.'

'The Prophet Joseph,' quavered Sister Eardley's nasal voice,
'warn't like no ordinary man. There allus seemed to be a light
somewheres inside of him — like a candle behind his eyes. But

he warn't no mealy-mouthed preacher, neither; I can see him
pitchin' quoits...'

Clory was seeing him as an ignorant, uncouth youth — tall,
handsome in spite of his beaklike nose — torn among the frenzied
'professors of religion' who cried to him 'Lo! here' and 'Lo! there.'

'How old was Joseph when he had his first vision?...' Ptsahh.

A man's reply this time: 'He was fifteen, and it was 1820, the
year of the great religious revival, and he read in the first chapter
of James, "If any of you lack wisdom let him ask of God that
giveth to all men liberally and upbraideth him not; and it shall
be given you..."'

'Where was this?...' Ptsahh.

'Manchester, New York — Joseph retired to the sacred grove
and kneeled down...'

The old, old story, but Clory was suddenly feeling the 'thick
darkness that gathered around,' and hearing the voice from out
the blinding light: 'This is my beloved Son. Hear Him...:
"They draw near me with their lips, but their hearts are far
from me ——"'

'When was his second vision?'

'Three years later. The angel Moroni appeared to him at the
Hill Cumorah and gave him the golden plates and the Urim and
Thummim ——'

'*Two stones in silver bows for translating*' — Clory's mind took
up the chant — '*To be for good or evil among all nations.*'

'And what was the record on these plates?'

A child's voice: 'Book of Mormon!'

*A record of the people of Nephi and also of the Lamanites, their
brethren, and also the people of Jared who came from the Tower of
Babel ——*

Her thoughts retreated before sonorous bearded words:

'Jaredites destroyed by the Israelites, descendants of Joseph
from Jerusalem ... Nephites, principal nation of the Israelites,
fell in battle before their brethren, the Lamanites, whose descend-

ants are the Indians inhabiting this continent... who forgot
the God of their fathers and were cursed with dark skins... The
Nephites, cut off in consequence of their transgressions, commanded to write an abridgment of their history... The last of
their prophets, Mormon and his son, Moroni, hid it up in the
earth so that it should come forth to be united with the Bible
for the accomplishment of the purposes of God in the last days...'

The kindly drawl: 'And how do we know... the Book of
Mormon is true?...' Ptsahh.

Chorus: 'Testimony of the three witnesses and the eight witnesses!'

*And we also know that they have been translated by the gift and
the power of God... and we declare with words of soberness that an
angel of God came down from Heaven...*

'Did any of the three or the eight signers ever go back on his
testimony?'

Chorus that shook the wagon box: 'No!'

'Did Joseph ever have any other heavenly visitants?'

'Yes! John the Baptist came to him as he walked on the banks
of the Susquehanna River and baptized him as First Elder of the
Church! And later Peter, James, and John imparted to him the
keys of the priesthood of Melchizedek!'

'When... was the Church of Jesus Christ of Latter-Day
Saints... organized?'

Chorus: 'April 6, 1830, in Palmyra, New York!'... *First
gathering!*

Then the tempo began to gentle, the long, sad legend welling
like the resigned complaint of rain. The pictures formed and dissolved and formed again behind Clory's closed eyes.

The *second gathering* in Kirtland, Ohio. The Prophet making
of the frontier colony a thriving town with a store, a mill, a bank,
a tannery, a temple. The eventual dedication of the temple. The
awe of the watching gentiles, the angels, the favored of the Lord
who chanted in unknown tongues, the presence of the Holy Ghost

with a sound 'like the sound of a mighty rushing.' ... Persecution. Violent hands, a tar bucket in the night.

The financial panic over the government's Specie Circular of 1837, Church bankrupt, Joseph jailed. Flight from Kirtland.

The Lord reveals that Missouri is Zion, the Promised Land! Building Independence. The *third gathering* ...

Persecution. Driven. Bloody footprints on sleeted crust across the river to Clay County. Wigwams of brush. Heavens streaking fire! A sign from God. Down on weary knees, hands upraised in supplication ... 'In the day of peace you esteem lightly the counsel of God; but in the day of your trouble you feel after Him.'

From Clay County to Caldwell County, primeval wilderness. We'll try again. We'll build another city and call it Far West. We'll triumph over the spirit of 'apostate mobocracy!' *Zion shall not be moved out of her place, notwithstanding that her children are scattered.* Once more a timid contentment, food for our bellies, good preach for our hearts. Missionaries sent out; Joseph organizes the Twelve Apostles.

Puling whinings, naggings: *You grow too fast. Your town's too prosperous. You're too powerful. Are you trying to swallow our whole state? You pretend you're so God-damned holy!*

The tar is scalding, neighbor; it's like being fried alive; they're sticking the pointed ends of the feathers under the blistered skin.

We'll fight this time ... Breastworks at Far West.

Governor Boggs and his Order of Extermination: 'The Mormons must be treated as enemies ... and driven from the state.'

Surrender your arms, neighbor, the Prophet is condemned to be shot at sunrise. Look to your lives! Massacre at Haughn's Mill ...

Audible syllables seeped into the picture, scattered it. Hannah Merinda Lowgie, the midwife, thought Clory; she was at Haughn's Mill.

'We women ran; ... our men, mostly unarmed, crowded into the blacksmith shop. The mob spit on our white flag and shot through the crevices between the logs, and with every shot they laughed like painted devils. My Johnny — he was just seven then — saw it all. One ruffian cornered my boy and blew his entire hip joint, flesh and bone and gristle, right out of the socket. And when his father threw up his hands for mercy another fiend split each palm down through with a corn cutter.'

The voice was hollow as if it had long been sucked dry of all emotion. Clory could hear Apostle Snow's nervous 'ptsahh' as if he'd like to interrupt, but the toneless voice seemed driven.

'One mobber put his gun at the head of my baby — he was only five and just would tag after his daddy — and scattered his brains and hair all over the floor and walls and left the skull empty and dry.

'Another mobber said, "Damn shame to kill those little boys!" But the first mobber only wiped off his gun muzzle and laughed, "Nits make lice!"

'When we darst to come out, I found my oldest unburied in the sun and the flies at him. We darsn't hold no funeral. We threw the bodies into a deep, dry well, but when the devils come back they built a privy over the well and every time they used it we could hear 'em hootin' with delight.

'They was us women prayin' aloud and the howlin' of the dogs and cattle mad from the scent of the blood. The mobbers said they'd kill us, too, if we didn't shut up, so we crawled to a stout of corn and started prayin' all over again, because prayin' was all that was left to us. The Lord answered our prayers, too. He told me to make a lye out of the shagbark hickory you burn in the fireplace and put a pack of the lye into my Johnny's wound. Mashed flesh and splinters of bone come away, but the Lord grew flexible gristle instead, and after five weeks on his face my boy walked.'

Murmurs from the audience — 'Hosanna!'

'And then we was all driv before bayonets barefoot across the frozen prairie . . .'

Clory began to sing under her breath,

Missouri
Like a whirlwind in its fury
And without a judge or jury
Drove the Saints and spilled their blood.

Apostle Snow's drawl: 'But Sister Lowgie, we must remember ... our blessings, too; you lived through it, you helped build up Nauvoo the Beautiful...'

A diapason of anecdotes... Clory's inward eye translated the kaleidoscopic voices...

Commerce, Illinois, a death-hole, a malarial swamp, to be converted into Nauvoo the Beautiful. A gaunt, tight-lipped, mosquito-crazed Mormon elder shoulders his aching spirit under the burden. He has put down roots and torn them up in three states within ten years, his trail is blazed with the blood of his wounds and the graves of his children, and now he gazes at his wife huddled under a torn kiver-lid on branches that fail to bridge the stinking ooze, and listens to the death-wagons slush through the mud past her door.

The Prophet's lopsided, dirt-covered, one-roomed cabin packed with the homeless sick... 'After much tribulation cometh the blessing,' he is saying; 'let your sufferings be what they may, it is better in the eyes of God that you should die than that you should give up the land of Zion.'

And so the Saints are persuaded to their *fourth gathering*.

The Prophet tries to get redress from Missouri through Washington. 'Your cause is just, but we can do nothing for you,' says President Van Buren.

But miraculously Nauvoo is suddenly a shining city with fourteen thousand souls, ten wards and ten bishops, and the Prophet is courted by the elect of the land, fêted by magistrates and rulers. Colleges, stores, churches, fine brick, lawn-grassed homes with a fireplace in every room, steamboats at the wharves, a Mansion House for the Prophet with marble-topped tables

and walnut commodes, a Nauvoo House for his distinguished
guests with red carpet brought clear from St. Louis, a gorgeous
ceiling lamp with prisms like icicles, prairie chickens, pumpkin
pies, wild honey, cider, God's own Temple being built — the
Prophet in black swallowtail and ruffled stock leading lovely
ladies in the quadrille, the Prophet in long seersucker pulpit coat,
the Prophet in blue satin and sweeping plumes on his white
charger reviewing the Nauvoo Legion, the Prophet running for
President of the United States — 'Resolved: whether we view
him as a Prophet at the head of the Church, a General at the
head of the Legion, a Mayor at the head of the Council, or a
Landlord at the head of his table, he has few equals and no
superiors' — the Prophet toppling out of a second-story window
at Carthage jail with a bullet in his heart.

'... "Take care of yourselves.... I go like a lamb to the
slaughter." As far away as Nauvoo we could hear the pealin' of
them fiendish bells.'

Clory's thoughts took it up. *June 27, 1844* ——

'Woe to Israel! When the time comes that the kings of this
earth become nursing fathers and the queens nursing mothers in
the habitations of the righteous in Zion, the whole world will
regret...'

*That was the exact moment her father was being baptized in the
old bath-house on Walnut Street, Philadelphia, by the stern, dark-
browed young man who was Abijah McIntyre...*

She smiled to think of Abijah dandling her on his knee. She
had been just nine months old. And her mother's darling.
Nothing could change her mind about that. And there were the
gifts to prove she was right, the earrings and brooch made long
ago by her father, jeweler and wealthy merchant who delighted
to lead out his beautiful wife in the meticulous measures of the
cotillion (Clory loved to taste the word on her lips); there were the
music box, the hoops — even, she could remember, red satin
slippers with stiff gold bows that somehow found their way to the

pioneer community in Great Salt Lake Valley when she was five. She could still remember her bewilderment looking from the slippers to the endless mud outside and then her own feet with the lacerated calluses, wrapped in gunny-sacks. Hugging the slippers to her heart, she yet wondered humbly why they couldn't have been shoes with thick soles; but Aunt Bathsheba only snorted.

It was the same with the note. Even now she was convinced her mother would have *wanted* to help. Just after the slippers had come, Will, her big brother, going on ten, had the beautiful plan. Aunt 'Sheba was boiling up the last strips of rawhide from an old boot, and it made you puke the way your insides coveted the mess. Will hunted bulbs along the ditch in spite of Abijah's admonitions. Then he found the piece of foolscap. They had printed the note with such ardor and hidden it up among the rafters of the cabin until they could get hold of the money to send it. But Aunt 'Sheba found it and tore it up. They wouldn't understand, she said.

After that, desperate with his own need and his little sister's tears, Will did go to dig roots. Wild parsnip roots ——

'I'll eat it first,' he said, 'and if it don't hurt me...' He wasn't long in dying, but she never forgot how he looked with his stomach puckered double.

Nor could she forget her own terror of this thing they called Death. Papa was dead — but she could not remember Papa, anyway. But Will was part of her very self. Grown-ups looked at his damp towhead and at the stilled grimace on his face and then retreated into a secret world of their own: looked out at her with an understanding she could not share, shook their heads and said — and took the momentous saying for granted — 'He is dead.' When her spirit tried to comprehend, to reach him through those words, that barrier, it was like banging up against a closed door. Will was gone and the familiar world became fraught with horror. Dead? Did that mean his voice might lie on the edge of the wolves' howl as they prowled the streets at night?

They put him in a box and she watched them clunk frozen clods on the box. All the earth lay shivering, listening to the bitter and final clunk of the clods. How Will would hate it down there in the dark! 'Heaven' and 'angels' were just words grown-ups used ... Familiarity splintered into a thousand abysses, and for weeks she lived on the edge of disaster.

For if they had sent the letter ...

Of course Aunt 'Sheba wasn't to blame for Will's death, and of course now that Clory was grown up she did understand better about that early bitterness, but even at that she was not convinced her mother wouldn't have *wanted* to help. Her lovely, willful mother, aghast at her husband's preoccupation with the strange new life, shuddering at the idea of replacing her silken sheets for a bed in a wagon box, of replacing her own fastidious intimacies with the somber garments of the Saints — 'Good-bye while you're handy,' she said to the harassed young man she had married, and nodded a pretty assent to an importunate admirer.

But never easily, Clory insisted, never happily. Sometimes, fondling the slippers or the jewelry, she imagined she caught an elusive fragrance, a dim, sweet echo of that gay and buoyant spirit. Sometimes, out here in this wild land of sagebrush and war whoops, it seemed to her that if she could just be quiet enough she might hear above the coyote's howl the lilt of such charming laughter, or over in the shadows there surprise the startled rustle of sprigged muslin.

And that feeling was all mixed up with the new idea she began to get about Will. At such times she would sit very still, hands clasped in her lap, not moving, and close her eyes and hold her breath and wait for the Great Smile to come, the Door to creep open ... And Something like the brush of a butterfly's wing, the touch of mist on her cheek — something gone before she knew it was even there, but something so real and live and vast that it fitted all the splintered fragments back into place and blotted out the dark abysses with security again and sent her to sleep with

her hand contentedly curling on the pillow as if it lay clasped in
a warm and loving palm...

Voices from the campfire: 'They stoned our little children in
the streets...'

'We rigged up a cannon from a steamboat shaft...'

'Brother Brigham said we'd leave soon's water run and grass
grew in the spring...'

'We got nothing for our lands, not even chips and whetstones.'

'It was the time of the "burnings," "fire-and-sword" parties,
"Mormon-baiting"...'

(*Be still and know that God reigns... I have pledged my word the
violence will be on their part... I say to my brethren in Nauvoo in
the name of the Lord, Be still, be patient.*)

'We ran for our lives, but it was hard to pull the door latchet
to with the coals on your hearth still warm, the new Haviland
plates gleamin' through the cupboard doors, the geranium a-goin'
unwatered, and the old clock tickin'; tickin' same as always.'

'Some of us got our endowments, but even before we left, the
militia defiled the baptismal font, scrawled filth on the shrines...'

'But our Temple had "more revelation," more splendor, and
more God than all the rest of the world...'

'Whittling Deacons with long bowie knives...'

'Four hundred wagons clunking across the ice of the Mississippi — one exile harnessed between the shafts of his own cart...'

'The fiends ducking one elder in the icy water: "God damn you,
the Commandments must be fulfilled and we baptize you!"'

'... Always looking back from the top of every hill to this city
we loved so much, heavy-headed yellow grain rotting ungathered
in field after field, our homes under a kind of enchantment, waiting there ready to be lived in, waiting till Judgment Day.'

'Finally, squint as we would into the blue distance, the last we
could see was the Temple spire pointin' like the finger of God, and
all we had left of our Temple to carry away was its motto, "Holiness to the Lord"...'

Poor Camp, Misery Bottoms, dysentery, cholera — gruel of parched corn and the pounded bark of slippery elm. Little Butterfly River like an open cesspool crawling sluggishly through slime; steaming yellow ponds — 'Oh, goody, Mamma, that's frogs' spawn!' Cows unmilked. Corpses loathsome before men can bury them. The look a woman has who squats hour after hour brushing the flies from her dead child's face. ('Where much is given, sister, much is required.')

Winter Quarters four hundred miles away. A city of mud and logs covered with puncheon, straw, or willows. Houses like heaps of earth piled up over potatoes to shield them from the frost. Black canker, blackleg scurvy, cold and hunger.

'But Mormons could always find a little honey to suck...'

A party with sheets hung over the walls, hollowed turnips for candles. Brigham leading out 'in an acceptable manner before the Lord, among the "Silver Grays" and spectacled dames, dancing like ancient Israel.'

Clory's mind on another tangent. That had been the spring of 1846. She was just toddling about, Will was six. Her father had taken his two children and joined the outcasts at Winter Quarters.

Dashing Captain James Allen of the First Dragoons rides into camp. President Polk of the United States wants five hundred men to fight against Mexico.

'It was a feelin' time for us Mormons. We was rememberin' Brother Brigham's revelation: "Thy brethren have rejected you and your testimony; even the nation has driven you out."... Why should we fight their battles?'

'You go,' Abijah is saying to the young man from Philadelphia; 'you're younger and freer. Bathsheba and I will care for the two children until your enlistment is up and you can meet us in the new Zion.'

And the Mormon Battalion marches two thousand miles to California, while two thousand Saints and eight hundred white-

tops string out like a meandering chalk mark across the plains —
'in the way the spirit of the Lord shall direct us.'

(*Why are you going, Brother Brigham?*
Morman exodus or Mormon massacre.
Where are you going, Brother Brigham?
Anywhere to get away from Christians.)

'We met Jim Bridger near South Pass.

'"You can't do it," he said. "The soil is too dry to produce.
I'll give you one thousand dollars for the first bushel of wheat or
ear of corn grown in that salt basin."

'"We will show you," says Brother Brigham.'

Flimsy wooden-bowed wagons; greasing the wheels with wolf
fat; unbroken cows in place of exhausted oxen; emergency
teamsters, women and little boys, buffalo-skull headstone-
postoffices. . . .

'William Pitt's Nauvoo Band had followed after the camp of
Israel. How far you could hear those trumpets, drums, and
hautboys in that thin dry air; hunting a ford over the wild Platte,
perplexed among the far-reaching sand bars; how strange to hear
sweet Mendelssohn drifting away there in the Indian Marches...'

(*I do not mean on this journey to bow down to the spirit which
causes the brethren to quarrel ... Joking, profane language, and loud
laughter do not belong to us ... You do read of praising the Lord in
the dance, but who ever read of praising the Lord in a game of
cards? ...*)

The rumbling of the caravan as it comes picking its way down a
dark ravine, grinding of wheels among rocks as they plunge down
one bank and climb another, or thread their way along the narrow
ledge overhanging a chasm; the cracking of whips, Israel's songs
— 'Now let us rejoice in the day of salvation...' 'Nay the
journey is not so hard, Bonnie Lassie O ...' 'Hosanna, hosanna
to God! He has broke from off our necks the gentile yoke...'
The struggle through the underbrush choking the mouth of the
canyon, the abrupt emergence upon the terrace, the shocked

silence, the gasp of disbelief before that valley hanging like a
jewel in the still, luminous air. Mountains eating away at all the
horizons, the glistening, salt sea, the winding river, the creek
banked with green cane like waving corn, the omnipresent gray
sagebrush, the Promised Land. Down on your knees, O Israel.
Down on your knees!

Who knows what Brother Brigham saw? Did he see the stately
thoroughfares, the homes? Did he see Moroni flash goldenly atop
the temple spire? Or did he see how the roses would terrace the
capitol in June?

(*Behold, I send an Angel before thee, to keep thee in the way, and
to bring thee into the place which I have prepared . . .*)

'What shall we do?' they said to him.

'*It is enough*,' he answered. '*This is the place. Drive on.*'

Peace now, entreated Clory, her very flesh protesting . . . *O
Lord, they have suffered enough! . . .*

But even yet her most vivid recollection was the hunger. Hunger that had persisted in spite of Brother Brigham's defiance —
'Until we eat up the last mule from the tip of its ear to the end of
the fly-whipper, I am not afraid of starving to death!' There had
been a man sitting on a wagon tongue slicing mouthfuls from a
loaf of bread with a pocket knife, and she and Will, coming upon
him unexpectedly, had stood transfixed. 'You don't need to
think you're going to get any,' he said.

Her unfilial memory held on to that childish pain and forgot
the soldier in the battered uniform who had such trouble telling
Abijah why her father could not meet him, after all, in the new
Zion. Her father had been one of three scouting the trail for
members of the home-coming Mormon Battalion, taking the
shortest cut from San Diego over the Sierra Nevada mountains.
The three camped one night near the Carson River, so green after
the Nevada deserts. The Indians must have come upon them
entirely without warning. When the rest of the company caught
up with what was left, they carved an inscription on a near-by
tree and named the spot Tragedy Springs.

Clory could certainly remember the terror of that child, used to playing around Abijah's feet, when suddenly boosted up in his arms after the soldier had gone, and for the first time coming on a level with the fierce brown bush of his face through which the tears were trickling.

There were other memories. Putting out the arsenic bait at night and the pile of timber wolves on the doorstep in the mornings. The first crop of green grain, thanksgiving, and the goggle-eyed crickets with clock-spring legs.

'We can hit men,' said Brigham, 'but if you kill a cricket, two come to bury him.'

Kneeling men, suppliant among the crunching hordes, weep like Job at the circling zoom of the gulls — only to stand awe-struck before the Lord's own miracle among the wheat stalks. . . .

The year of '49 fulfilling Brother Kimball's early promise that one day the Saints would be able to buy necessities in the valley cheaper than in the States. The gold-seekers, mad with the fever, dropping excess baggage on the way — Abijah bought tools, costing one hundred dollars in the East, for twenty-five cents. But the fever was catching and the Saints 'lusted after the whoredoms of Babylon.' . . . 'Every man that stays here and pays attention to his business,' pledged Brother Brigham, 'will be able within ten years to buy out four of those who leave for the gold mines.'

But Israel needed to be humbled and the Lord sent another famine in '56. The great Reformation swept all of Zion. But although little children made up sins that they might have something to confess, and men promised to reform, 'there has been more confessing than forsaking,' said Brother Brigham . . .

Sudden shout from the campfire:

'Judgment must be laid to the line and righteousness to the plummet!'

Erastus interrupting: 'Now, now, Brother Zebedee Trupp, those days are over with' . . . ptsahh. 'Saints improve right along,

I think. Just take plenty of time . . . for family prayers . . . see to
our tithes and fast offerings . . .'

There was a moment crowded with the silence of those, like
Willie, whose secrets remained always unshared.

The long lament was drawing to a close. Clory knew by heart
the final chapter.

She was just beginning to put her hair up, just beginning to
be aware of the boys.

Silver Lake Valley, poised in the very tops of the Wasatch,
meadowed with bluebells and columbines, haloed with snow-
crested, pine-flanked cliffs. You climbed twenty miles from the
canyon mouth, you mounted a rim, and there you were — back-
ward-straining to see the tops of a quaking aspen, watching the
play of the mirrored trout. Tents and wagon boxes of three thousand people. A great flag with the legend, 'The Pioneers of 1847
at the Upper Crossing of the Platte, in Pursuit of the Valleys of
the Mountains,' and another with the motto, 'Peace Reigns
Here.' Swings and rafts and boweries for dancing, a pavilion for
the speakers, a martial band fifing 'The Girl I Left Behind Me,'
and Professor Ballo's trumpets flaring the 'Overture to Tancreda'
to the counterpointing echoes.

Brother Brigham's quiet words: 'July twenty-fourth, Utah's
annual holiday in honor of the Pioneers entering the valley . . .
what do you think the Prophet Joseph would have given to see
this day in the flesh? We are hid up in the Lord's secret cham-
bers, according to His promise, where none can molest us, or
make us afraid.'

The clunk of a horse's hoofs on the stones of the trail. Porter
Rockwell bearing news, grim and travel-stained. Brother
Brigham, in '47, had asked for ten years 'and we will ask no odds
of the United States.' It had been exactly ten years.

The United States is sending an army to destroy us.

*Well, if there really is an army, they will forever be en route either
to Utah or to hell; there is only one entrance into this valley, through
the canyon . .*

'We have burned no territorial records, we are not treasonous toward the government. But we are tired of your armed minions of the mobocrats, of your "runaway" judges who bring their strumpets to sit beside them on the judicial bench. You gentiles think there is no civilization in Utah because, forsooth, there are no gambling hells or houses of prostitution. . . . I tell you, if the United States forces the issue, I will no longer hold the Indians by the wrist for white men to shoot at. . . . I have broken no law . . . and I will not suffer this people to be taken by any United States officer to be butchered as they butchered Joseph Smith. God Almighty will give the United States a pill that will puke them to death and that is worse than lobelia. When these troops arrive . . . they will find Utah a desert; every house burned to the ground . . .'

Clory remembered the battle song:

> If what they now propose to do
> Should ever come to pass
> We'll burn up every inch of wood
> And every blade of grass . . .

The Echo Canyon War, scythes into bayonets, Uncle Sam's 'Jackass' Cavalry, burning the supply trains.

Say your prayers and keep your powder dry!

The Move, straw piled in a city of empty houses ready for the torch, thirty thousand people whose altars were their hearthstones once more on the march. 'To your tents, O Israel!' . . .

Apostle Snow's drawl scattered defiance.

Swept back to the present by his quiet tones, Clory wondered not for the first time what there was about this mild man of very ordinary appearance that could so instantly subdue the nostalgic frenzy outside.

'But that has already gone down in history as "Buchanan's blunder"! *Zion's tears are dried at last* . . .'

She could see his kind gray eyes wise with common sense.

'Right now in the States there is a civil war — business of States' Rights and Nullification and the Union and Secession —

but we in Zion are at peace. Israel, rejoice in your *final gathering!* '
(A dim foreboding clutched at Clory, a sense of hidden futures.)

'I remember in '47, Sam Brannan fresh from California's sunshine and flowers, saying to Brother Brigham, "For heaven's sake, don't stop in this God-forsaken land. Nobody on earth wants it!" And Brother Brigham answering him, "Brannan, if there is a place on this earth that *nobody else wants*, that's the place I am hunting for." ... Well, folks, *only the lizards want Dixie.* But think what that means!... We've got tested men here, hand-picked for endurance, to wrest out of hell a cotton supply. But we'll wrest out of hell a great deal more ... Long after the gentiles have invaded the North, they'll let us alone ... Forever alone, folks, to tame the lizards, to sink roots we'll never have to tear back up, to actually build the Land-of-the-Unlocked-Door!' Ptsahh!

When Willie clambered into the wagon box with a smuggled sandwich for the culprit, she found Clory motionless as one under a spell, chin on her knees, eyes tranced and shining.

'Aunt Willie,' she said softly, 'things ain't stopped happenin' to us by a long shot. But I thank God I'm right in the thick of it.'

The dimple came and went.

'We call ourselves Latter-Day Saints, and the gentiles call us Latter-Day Fools. But I'm a-sayin' to you, Saints or Fools, in a hundred years from now it's folks like us that'll be fillin' up the history books!'

CHAPTER IV

I N THE first place, Abijah had been mild with the Lord at family prayers this morning. On top of that, his announcement that *she* was to accompany him on the ride to the river so shocked her that she choked on her dough-god.

'I want to look at some land,' he had said. 'Would ye like to go with me, Clor-rinda?' Just like that. Other women went with their husbands and stayed all day, but she had never dreamed of going with Abijah. He even planned to borrow Apostle Snow's team of horses.

It was distinctly an occasion. In honor she passed up the gum myrrh in its corner of the grub box, sacred likewise to asafetida and turkey rhubarb and chlor-alum, and rummaged in her carpet-bag instead for the toothbrush inherited from Will. The bristles were shedding, but she brushed her teeth reverently, spewed out the salt water and folded the brush back into the little tin container that was its handle.

Her skin felt fresh and glowing, her bran porridge lay sweet on her tongue, she had prepared their lunch, and when Abijah called to her she crowed with pleasure at the sight of the wagon stripped

of its top and the sassy bays. That eager tilt of her head — such
an uplifted laughing face! Abijah reached down a hand to her.
All the women and girls were peeking out of tents and wagon
boxes to see her off — Marianne Snow, Aunt Ket's daughters, the
Eardley girls . . .

For some reason a fragment of music sang in her brain, and
twinkling at Abijah from out the red sunbonnet she hummed
under her breath: 'Um *um*, um *um*, um *um!* u-u-*um* . . .'

Her thoughts fitted themselves to the tune: 'I'm *hap*-py,
hap-py, haa-*ap*-py . . .'

The horses trotted to the refrain.

She threw off her bonnet and laughed aloud.

'Abijah! Listen! The world is singing! *This* world is singing!
Hear the blackbirds? . . . They're singing because of the sky and
the sun!'

Abijah frowned and clucked to the horses, keeping a smart pace
down the half-cleared roadway between the banks of tall brush.
There were usually Indians lurking about here and it was better
not to loiter. These strange, wild moods of hers were what he
most mistrusted. Such joy was . . . it was . . . well, it wasna
seemly! He couldn't see anything to make such a fuss over.

'Tra la la *la!* la la-la-la la *la!*' sang Clorinda. The sky and the
sun and the stretching brush and the river burst into a thousand
pieces of light whirling about her head. Her heart swelled and
her throat ached and even her fingertips tingled. Her foot
tapped, her hands beat the rhythm, her head was flung back
against the seat, her eyes were haunting, dusky slits of laughter,
the pulse in her white throat throbbed crazily, her open lips were
ripe, like fruit, and Abijah could see the gleam of her pretty teeth
and the flutter of her tongue as she sang.

'Tra *la*, la *la* . . .'

Abijah thought he had never seen anything so young, so alive.
Suddenly he forgot that he was a servant of the Lord.

'Tra la *la*, la *la*, la *la!*' he joined her rhythm, and ducked his chin lower and sucked in his belly so that the notes would come out rounded and full. There was a subtle kinship between the two when they sang that manifested itself even in church; no matter how displeased he might be toward her, Abijah involuntarily sought out her eyes on every hymn. Always their two voices rose above the others, his as dark and rumbling as summer thunder, hers as brilliant and free as summer lightning that frolics around the edges of the cloud.

She sang with such an ease, dropping her jaw, biting off her words in that clean-cut way, everything about her keeping time to the tune.

The river was closer now, glinting between its red shelving abutments and the copses of cottonwoods and fringing willow trees. The landscape down here was spotted with reedy swamps where the blackbirds hung on the bulrushes like overripe fruit; and there were whole acres of arid mesas transformed by the late golden flowering of the heavy-scented rabbit brush.

Clory held the last note like a bell above Abijah's bass, lifting her arms wide to sustain it, finished on a proper flourish, and dropped her arms around his neck in a very abandon of pleasure.

'Don't you *love* it, Un ... Abijah! The morning, and ...'

But that broke the spell.

'"Man is that he might have joy," ' pronounced Abijah.

The girl's smile shrank. What on earth was the matter now, Abijah wondered. My conscience, women!

He pointed to the cattle of the community herd roaming through the brush, disdaining the wild taste of the rabbit-brush, but reaching for the yellow clusters of honey-mesquite pods or the twisted brown spirals of the screw-bean mesquite — bushes in the valley, but here, where the roots more quickly tapped moisture, growing sometimes to twenty feet.

There was a cow sampling the saltbush, there another munching on the humble burrow-weed — they were even nibbling the silvery-filmed greasewood.

Every man had to furnish one hour of herding a day for each cow he owned, vigilant herding because of the Indians. Now Abijah's Abraham and the other boys caught sight of the visitors and waved.

But Abijah's eyes were still on the careless cattle.

'Ye see, Clor-rinda,' he said, 'even the cattle learn to adapt themselves to a strange country, strange foods . . . and different ways . . .'

The land Abijah wanted was on this side of the river. He handed the reins to Clory and got out for a moment to investigate. Healthy growth of 'old man' sage, always a sign of good land. He chewed one of the threadlike leaves, puckered over the bitter flavor, but nodded his head. Nice and juicy — moisture here; and, of course, bordering the river, the strip would be easy to irrigate when they got the canal built. A sprinkling of creosote bush with its pungent aroma and resinous-covered leaves, always so green against the universal drabness of winter: creosote seldom grew where there was alkali. And none of the alkali-loving grease-wood. That sand hollow might do well in white flint corn, mastodon corn . . . Yesterday in priesthood meeting Apostle Snow had suggested they farm at first on the joint enclosure system, and Abijah's two older boys had been out since dawn helping to grub brush farther up the river — the canal would probably not reach this far the first year. Meanwhile Abijah meant to see about the title to this piece.

'I was right,' he said when he came back to Clory; 'it's a fine strip.' He was thinking of fall wheat on the upland section, maybe the rabbit-brush land in cotton and lucerne and fruit trees on the wire-grass bottom, protected from the frost, roots nearer water; but Clory saw only the darting lizards and the bleak country with the muddy river creeping between its scarred banks. Farther down by the water she could see a stunted cottonwood and some willows.

'I'm going down there,' she said to Abijah.

He nodded and began to unhitch the horses.

Clory picked a wary way over the ground where the shad scale and cactus and devil's-claw pods with their hooked horns caught at her skirts. But when she reached the open space around the trees the sand was soft and sunwarmed.

Abijah, having watered the horses, brought them up along the bank, tethered them among the willows where they could nibble on the bunch grass, and came over to the girl. He had meant to explore a little farther; also, he had to get back in time for the meeting this afternoon to appoint permanent officers of the camp; but the riddle of Clory nagged at him. There she lay, propped up on an elbow, digging into the sand and lazily smiling. He could see where her breast leaned against the basque and how the sun brought out copper lights in her black hair and touched the transparency of her cheeks to rose. Even her eyebrows had a delicate perfection, trailing quite to the outer edge of the eye-socket without that unfinished look so common to most female eyebrows.

He meant to do his duty by her, God knows; that was one reason for Brother Brigham's constant urging for young girls to enter the covenant with older men — the safety involved. An older man was so much less likely to lead his wives to apostasy. He was always exhorting her to greater righteousness; and he had tried to be patient, had not rushed her ... of course, it was just possible she might have rather married someone her own age; still ...

He sat down beside her and cleared his throat and shot her a glance from under his brows, and brought out his small box of brown flour.

'Rub some on mine,' Clory said, and held out her hand to him. Brushing the flour over the small, calloused palm Abijah was unexpectedly conscious of how fragile she was, how lonely she must sometimes be in the long evenings in her wagon box listening to the coyote chorus.

Dropping the box, spilling the flour across the sand, he leaned over and kissed her.

'Clor-rinda, bairn,' he breathed, gritting his teeth, his nostrils flaring, 'Clor-rinda, Clor-rinda ——'

Clory struggled up from under that embrace with a look in her eyes like a wild thing's startled wonder just before the instant of its flight. But Abijah was abruptly a man surrendering to a long want, and his lips were greedy.

The girl, drowned in his urgency, could only push futilely at his strength, turn her head away from the masculine sweat-odor of his armpits — she who so disliked smells. His fumbling hand inside her bodice filled her with an ancient clamor that left her panic-stricken.

This is it, thought Clory; this is what it's all about. Where were the stars Rolph had exploded in her heart? Where the ecstatic pother one read about in all the stories? Just Abijah suddenly like a man gone mad and her own wild alarm at the touch of his hot flesh. This, she thought, is what they meant by obedience . . .

When it was over, the girl lay staring at the blue sky with the tears slipping silently down her cheeks. Abijah was willing now to be tender, but she eluded his outstretched hand and jumped to her feet and backed away from him . . . There she was again with that same questioning high-held look, that same tremulous valiancy, that something about her which forever eluded him — like a yearling colt still unbroken to the harness, fearless and gay and shyly proud.

Abijah stooped to pick up the spilled tin box.

'Remember,' he said, avoiding her eyes, 'remember our union is sacred in the eyes of God; He decrees ye shall replenish the earth . . . woman is a vessel of His will . . .'

Clory turned and started back to the buggy. Well, there's one thing he won't have to worry about any more, she said fiercely to herself; I'll never think of him as an uncle again!

2

There had never been more than a few matches in the camp, and flint rocks and steel were difficult. As a result people tried not to let their fires die out, but if one's coals should be dead in the morning, it was customary to borrow. One peered through the frosty half-light, located smoke coming from tent or open campfire, and took one's shovel to that place.

Clory usually breakfasted with the others in the Sibley tent, and thus had not needed a fire of her own. But since Abijah had been spending his nights with her, he had brought over Bathsheba's little tin step-stove. Perhaps that was why so many of her neighbors had been paying her early-morning visits.

'We saw your smoke,' they would say; and after she had supplied them with coals, they would stand about like inquisitive birds, darting surreptitious glances toward the unmade bed where Abijah's night garments lay in a careless heap, and back to her face again.

Sometimes these strange nights, filled with such breathless flutterings and mute terrors, left her so weary that her ubiquitous callers found her still in bed. Then, indeed, they were apt to click their tongues, their eyes gleaming with a curious half-veiled eagerness, and fairly itch to be off.

Pal met a group of them one early morning. They ducked their sunbonneted heads and scurried away between the tent and wagon rows like startled rabbits. Her freckles flamed with indignation.

'I think it's a shame,' she said to Clory, 'Abijah making you the subject of everybody's gossip! Why, the whole camp's in a to-do about it! How much does he think a woman can ——'

Clory blushed furiously and turned her eyes away.

'Please don't pay any mind, it'll all come out. Please, I can't talk about it ... I just can't ...'

Pal, miserable with her inability to help matters, offered to

take the step-stove in its daily jaunt back to the Sibley
tent.

Abijah's Sibley tent was the only comfortable shelter in the
northern end of the camp. The cone-shaped canvas hanging from
the iron hoops, somewhat in the manner of an Indian wigwam,
provided through the opening at the top a very good draft for a
fire; elsewhere the fires had to be built outside. The little step-
stove, fed with coals and cradled among coals, baked innumerable
loaves of bread, helped to cook the family dinner, and radiated a
circle of warmth within which every morning it was customary for
neighboring young mothers to take turns bathing their babies.

When Pal entered the tent she found quite a group already
there. Isaiah and the twins were underfoot, and a setting hen in
the corner was doing some irritated clucking. Bathsheba plied an
after-breakfast bustle between crane and corner table. Hannah
Merinda Lowgie was rubbing oil over Eliza Hichinoper's howling
infant. She hefted the child critically, grunted with satisfaction,
and looked up at Eliza's thin, anxious face.

'The little shitepoke,' she cried, hushing the baby against her
shoulder, 'the little shitepoke! Did him t'ink everybody's so
mean to hims . . . I think he'll do, now, if he don't have no trouble
with his teeth.'

'Rub some freshly killed rabbit's brains on his gums,' Bathsheba commanded.

At that moment she caught sight of Pal, her arm crooked
around the step-stove, standing just within the flaps, and with an
exclamation of pleasure went over to meet her.

Judging from Bathsheba's rigorous dignity and her proportions — she was nearly six feet tall, broad of bosom and hip,
strong and tireless as a good horse — one would expect her
to boom, but instead she had a quavery soprano voice that
'teehee-ed' when she laughed.

'Land sakes alive,' she trebled, taking the step-stove from
Pal. '"Dream of shrouds, you'll entertain crowds!" I used to

say, "Keep your dooryards clean, more people pass by than come in," but I ain't so sure this morning, I ain't so sure!'

'Shucks,' said Hannah Merinda, folding a paper funnel for blowing smoke into another baby's aching ear, 'you know's well's we do why we're here, 'Sheba. The whole camp's in a stink about it. If us women don't stand together, we can't expect nothin' from the men. Two weeks straight-hand-runnin' is goin' too far. I ain't a tonguey woman and I never talk and it's none of my business, but...' Head on one side like a garrulous hen, she leaned toward Bathsheba, crouching near her, shoving the stove among the coals, and Pal did not hear the rest.

Bathsheba got to her feet, spatted the soot from her hands, and smiled grimly at the midwife.

'Men's men,' she stated, 'just like piss-ants is piss-ants. And if any man of mine wants to wet his pants over a pair of lily-white hands that shrink from a cow teat...'

Pal ducked hastily between the flaps and walked down to her own domestic peace with a burning heart.

The old blathergabs, she thought. It ain't *Clory's* fault!

For days the camp seethed with speculation. Waiting in line with Clory at the cottonwood-stump corn mill, watching the precious kernels pounded between the heavy lever rock and the smaller one fitted down into the thick base of the wood, Pal was painfully conscious of the comments, the jokes. Men slapping each other, breaking into broad laughter. Women nudging each other.

'Ho, there, slowpoke,' to the man working the mill, 'you can't take forever! Who d'you think you are, "Handsome Mac"?'

Erastus dreaded the job before him. Abijah was one of his own High Council, one of his right-hand men. He looked at the earnest bearded faces of his High Priests — he had called together all the Melchizedek quorum, to which Abijah belonged — and wondered how to begin. 'Ptsahh.'

'... Remember what the Prophet, Joseph, said: "If we seek first the kingdom of God, all good things will be added." ... Satan is always around to kick up a broil — he will drive you to desperation until you become careless and indifferent and forget to pray ...

'Brother Brigham says, "When a man sins" ... ptsahh ... "with his eyes open he cuts the thread of the priesthood through which Eternal Lives are given."

'You know ... polygamy is simply a means whereby a man might inherit a higher degree of glory in the next life ... it is not a call to pleasure, but to' ... ptsahh ... 'religious duty. Its purpose is not earth-happiness but earth-life discipline ... To give succeeding generations a superior fatherhood and motherhood ... by' ... ptsahh ... 'enlarging opportunities of men of high character to become ... the progenitors of the race ... Must apportion your time among your wives ... be strictly fair ... a week with each one, no more, no less ...

'If our women are willing to consecrate their lives to the duty of motherhood, to this end sacrificing earthly pleasures ... the least a man can do is' ... ptsahh ... 'be temperate in his habits.'

(He regretted the slow red creeping up Abijah's cheeks.)

'If a man can't control himself he has no right to hold the priesthood. Don't force yourself on a woman. Always be sure she' ... ptsahh ... 'wants you. Never go near her when she's in a delicate condition' ... ptsahh! ... 'The act should take place rarely, do not make it a common thing; hold it as something' ... ptsahh ... 'sacred. You are not beasts but men created in the image of God ... Remember that these things are *naturally* distasteful to the sensitive nature of woman; just because marriage gives you the right to her bed, do not' ... ptsahh! ... '*victimize* your wife!'

Erastus walked home with his arm in a brotherly link with Abijah's.

'Women are ... *women*, Brother Mac: any kind of' ... ptsahh!

... 'favoritism may cause backbiting and evil speaking ... Besides, you've got *three* wives, man! You're acting like Thompson's colt who swum the river to get a drink!'

Abijah was like a small boy caught stealing apples, but stubborn, too — he'd be damned if anybody 'ud stop him as long as the apples were sweet to his palate! But walking to Clory's wagon box that night, darting defiant glances right and left at the innocent sagebrush, he was nevertheless wondering uneasily if anything he enjoyed so much as sleeping with Clory *could* be right. He resented women, anyway, because he thought in his heart they were the one means of keeping him from being absolutely pure. Women couldn't quite belong to the Kingdom. He felt that Brother Brigham and he saw eye to eye in that. But since they seemed to be inevitable one might as well get what one could out of them, always remembering to keep them in their place. His favorite sermon was on the theory that behind every sin man ever committed you could find a woman ...

Clory, subject to be seized any moment these days by breathless wonders and awakenings in the soft, young-girlish core of her, was thinking that she *wanted* to be a good wife to Abijah ... If only he'd not be so scary and stern ... maybe she *was* bad for thinking anything so sacred might also be fun ... but if only he'd *play* a little ...

When Abijah stamped over to the bed, she raised herself up on one elbow and twinkled at him.

'Well!' she cried, the little flute notes in her voice, 'Well, my dear! I've put on the pink satin sheets for us tonight!'

Abijah merely glowered at her and went on struggling with his boots. She looked a good pattern to make a wife out of, but even the young curve of her breast couldn't compensate him for the fact that now she was making fun of him. He ground his teeth. She was like a drug in his veins, and he hated her.

3

Christmas was near. There were meetings and more meetings to decide on the festivities, to decide about schools, to choose trustees. (Taking a census of prospective scholars, a committee reported as many as one hundred and three for day school and forty-eight for adult evening school.) Erastus appointed Brother Benjamin Jarvis to give daily lectures on grammar. Bathsheba was out of patience with the men because they wouldn't also hold a meeting to cope with the coming bad weather. Willie's rheumatics had been bad for weeks, and she herself had been prophesying rain ever since the cat started lying on its crown and her big toe began to jump. This wire-grass bottom with its clayey soil would be a pigpen when wet.

With Abijah away all night and Freeborn usually at a meeting with his father, and Joseph so often taking his turn as camp-guard, Bathsheba sometimes these days was forced to admit an unwilling loneliness. Willie, being temporarily 'subject to vomit all her food up,' could not be much company; and Bathsheba had made it painfully clear to Clorinda, who used to be such a help with the little boys, that her presence was no longer welcome in the Sibley tent. Feeling that Abijah's dereliction was clearly Clorinda's fault, Bathsheba tolerated no halfway amenities except when Abijah was around. (Even 'Sheba dared not stir up Abijah's well-known impatience with feminine disputes.) 'You might as well drink the Devil as sip his broth,' she said to Willie.

No one colonizes without a heartbreak. The old easy world of 'Sheba's childhood was forever gone and the new stood stark about her: a queer brute of a world where the bright bodies of lizards glanced in the sunlight, hid between the quilts, plopped into the hanging pots of soup; where the coyotes' hungry yowling rode on the echoes and haunted every twilight; where savage eyes came and went in the deep brush, watching, watching, and men and women settled and quarreled and prayed and begot and never for a moment ignored those watching eyes.

Bathsheba hugged Isaiah to her and brought out a piece of bread for the naked Indian mumbling on the step. She shrank from his vermilion-streaked cheeks, his matted locks, his fierce, insolent eyes.

He grabbed the flapjack.

'*Ta-wi-cha shet-cup! Ta-wi-cha!*'

Bathsheba shook her head.

'No, no more "breat." Go away.'

The gutturals rose.

'*Yaw qui! Yaw qui!*'

'You red devil, there *isn't* any more! Now you git ——'

The copper face broke into demoniacal glee.

'*Squaw scharee! Squaw scharee!*'

'I am *not* scared! You, you *filthy* . . . you ——'

Bathsheba's wrath suddenly consumed her fear and she raised her free hand and slapped him. For a moment the Indian stood his ground, but his stare wavered before the woman's omnipotent indignation and he shuffled off down the path.

Isaiah, surprised into a wail by his mother's unaccustomed violent caress, could not know she was suddenly most afraid for him whom she most greatly loved; calling back the Indian with the rest of the flapjacks in her outstretched hand, she offered up a sacrifice to those more indifferent, ageless, unadmitted gods.

Long winter sunsets with the sky on fire above the lava hulk to the west. Bathsheba would sit in the tent door, her towheaded child in her arms, and watch the splendor modulate and the forbidding hill breed a creeping triumphant shadow. As if at a signal with the gloom the coyotes would begin. A staccato yarring stretching into a prolonged wail that seemed the very spirit of prowling hunger, desolate reaches.

Suddenly the years retreated and she might have been crooning to an alien black-haired waif. What kind of God was it who could betray such long generous mothering with that scene at the Endowment House? *Are you willing to give this woman to your husband to be his lawful, wedded wife through time and all eternity?* And blind with suffering she had placed that child's hand in his and waited for his *second kiss*. She, too, had been young and eager once in ruffled muslins and black velvet ribbons — several lifetimes ago. But all that lay between, paled before the anguish of that one moment.

'Why must I marry him?' the child had asked.

And she herself had answered, *'Because it's better to have one third of a good man than the whole of a bad.'* ...

Isaiah slipped from her brooding embrace and jumped excitedly up and down.

'Doggie! doggie! doggie!' he cried, pointing.

Bathsheba blinked unbelievingly at the gaunt head between the tent flaps; the rapacious furtive stare, the slobbering jaw. The coyote yelped and fixed yellow eyes on the broody hen ruffling angrily over her eggs in the corner. In one instinctive movement Bathsheba shoved her chair in the animal's face and stacked the dry-goods-box seats up on the barricade, and knocked desperately on the wood of a chair rung.

She threw brush on the fire and gathered her big-eyed children behind the flames. But all the night, long after the supply of brush was gone and her limbs were stiff with vigilance, the beast's head poked between the chair rungs like the evil genie of this land materialized. She reflected bitterly that only daylight could succor *her* with a husband!

4

Erastus owned a large military marquee (for school and social purposes), bequeathed by Johnston's Army; in this and the outside 'amusement hall' he planned to hold the Christmas festivities.

The morning dawned dark and forbidding. Santa Claus brought each of the MacIntyre boys a small lump of Bathsheba's brown sugar, some roasted pine-nuts bartered from the Indians, and a very few home-dried seedless raisins from the Santa Clara settlers.

'What can you expect without a chimney?' stoutly defended one of the twins. 'Santa would have a hard time trying to come down a wagon box or tent!'

But Abijah was unhappy at breakfast, not because the gifts were meager — that could not be helped — but because Freeborn still avoided his eyes.

For the morning program the willow benches from the bowery were moved into the marquee, but even the canvas could not mitigate the cold. The audience, swelled by Saints from the little settlements on the Santa Clara creek-bottoms, overflowed the benches and crouched in corners or huddled together for warmth.

Young Benjamin Jarvis, the school-teacher, delivered a lecture on English grammar; Brother Orson Pratt, Junior, read from the *Pickwick Papers*; Grandpa Slegosky, of the new Swiss colony, did a step dance accompanied by his wife on a 'mouth swab,' with much clapping of hands and stamping of feet by the onlookers (afterward Grandma, remembering fragrant giant linden trees of her native land and the holiday warmth of the heavy slabs of the big stone oven in one corner of her mother's scrubbed kitchen, bobbed her head and breathlessly demanded, 'Dot vas purty goot, hain't it?'); and Lon Tuckett, cackling with cheer, delivered a Christmas song with the somewhat lugubrious refrain,

The land it is no good and the water is no gooder
And the bare idea of living here's enough to make men shudder.

Mirthful over Tuckett's high nasal singsong, everybody joined lustily in the closing anthem.

The rain began before the celebrants had reached home. Christmas dinners prepared over open campfires were well watered and only half-cooked. A few families had piles of dried brush ricked up; these and other exposed supplies were hastily rushed to shelter. Boys ran shouting out into the downpour to cut great armloads of the greasewood, which would burn even when wet. But the flood ran in streams under tents and beds, and although brush was piled over mud floors to form some slight protection against the dampness and cold, canvas coverings soon dripped soddenly, bedclothing grew clammy, and food mildewed.

The MacIntyres rejoiced in warmth and a Christmas dinner augmented by potatoes saved over from last year's crop (the goodness of each mealy mouthful!) and the rarer treat of a pumpkin from Santa Clara. Only Willie — gaunt in the traditional 'Mother Hubbard,' liver spots stark on her pasty skin, silly hands picking at her puffy lips — lagged in appetite. The younger boys were in a sweat to be off to the foot races planned for the afternoon, but Free remained locked in a dark world of his own devising. Only once did he glance at Clory — herself silent, brooding gaze on her plate — and that was to reassure himself that she had undergone no monstrous transformation because of this thing that gripped his thoughts.

The day dripped on. The Peabodys sent their children around to ask Christmas Day forgiveness for recent mischief — tipped-over brush piles, stolen willow brooms, tormented cats. Oldsters watched the driving wall of rain.

The Christmas dance was slated for early candlelight. But long before supper-time Erastus held a coal to the damp wicks, which hissed, died out, and finally stretched themselves into half-hearted slivers of flame. Boys and girls ran soaked from the races to the dance; there was nothing else for them to do. Room was scarce in the wagon boxes, and unless they were in bed they had to be out in the rain.

The marquee was large, but only those actually incapacitated sat around on the willow benches lining the walls. The musicians (paid in squash, flour, cedar posts) occupied three chairs beside the pole in the center of the tent: Miles, the fiddler from Abijah's company; Ferrano, an Italian cooper and fiddler from Erastus' group, and a man from the Swiss colony with that most beloved instrument, a banjo. Relief volunteers with 'mouth swabs' contributed ear-splitting obbligatos during the evening. At times when spirits rose high, the dancers themselves clapped the lively rhythms and whistled accompaniments.

Old Dan Tucker, he's a fine old ma-a-n . . .

The wet clay stuck to shoes and the hems of swaying crinolines. Couples overflowed the tent and promenaded and 'do-ce-do-ed' on the slick salt grass outside. Buckskins shrank and stiffened, darker trappings of the men wove among the bright calicoes of girls, the dyed homespuns streaking into Joseph's coats. Soaked bodices revealed figures, soaked skirts revealed hoops, wet palms clutched, coiffures straggled, young men twirled limp mustaches and complimented girls on the effect of moist complexions — squelch of booted feet languorous in the Spanish waltz, heavily flirtatious in the Varsoviana, frankly flicking gobbets of mud in the polka. Mouldy smell of damp cloth, human sweat; steam rising upward, yellow candles blinking through the mist. Hands clapping, feet stamping, slushing of soaked garments, music threading shrilly in and out, a word now and then caught above the babel, bursts of laughter, steady beat of the storm.

Fiddlestrings pop; here's a sister who finds among her treasures from the Old World a spool of silk thread — twisted, stretched, it works!

Cotillions, schottische, Virginia reels, Six Nations, two-step, snap waltz, spat waltz (*Here, there, young feller, daylight between!*); frisky tunes: 'Pop Goes the Weasel,' 'Row, Boat, Row,' 'Turkey in the Straw.'

Swing your partners!
Shuffle all!

Alleman left! ...

Swing your partners!

The floor manager's roguish anxiety ... 'Look here, Brother Freeborn, can't you swing her without putting your arm all the way around?'

The stately Spanish waltz, the couples side by side, circling precisely about the tent.

'You're out of step, Brother Freeborn!' The waggle of a peremptory finger.

Abijah, usually leading every set, tonight stood apart, with clenched fists. *To be humiliated like that by his wife and his own son!*

Free, dipping, swaying with Clory in his arms, lost in her dark gaze, tangled in the curls which the rain only aggravated, felt his muscles twitch as though they longed to grip something, shake it, throttle it. His unruly hair matted boyishly at his temples, his too-long sideburns stood on end, his protuberant light eyes were haunted and staring. One moment he was bogged in the nauseous visions he had been conjuring for the past three weeks, the next he schemed wildly to snatch her away from all their clutching old men's hands. This new tenderness replacing her old coquetry stormed at him until he broke into goose pimples. He wanted to prostrate himself at her altar, to cut his flesh with sacrificial knives. He shuddered to remember that he used to pinch her legs and pull her braids when they were children together, and he prayed Jesus not to smite him dead for his irreverence. He shut his eyes thinking of Clory's legs, and the mustache he had been coaxing stood out valiantly above suddenly quivering lips.

5

Long afterward, lying beside Abijah in her wagon box and listening to his snoring above the insistence of the rain, Clory reflected that there was something terribly unfair about being a woman. Abijah liked to think of her as a frail, spiritual creature submitting to duty, but she knew she loved to eat and drink; she loved kisses and she could love ... she could love all of life. She squirmed at the shamelessness of her own thoughts ...

What was that? A horse's pounding hoofs splashing between the wagon rows! Hoarse voices shouting.

'Help! The Clary Crick is flooding! Help!'

Lick Skillet, Never Sweat, Munkey Rench, the defiant little settlements on the creek-bottoms, the Indian mission, the fort ——!

Clory was half-dressed by the time Abijah, drunk with sleep, reached for his trousers.

She shook him.

'Men and teams — there'll be people hurt — I can help — let me go!'

Blinking in astonishment, he flicked away her words as he would have done the babblings of a child. But when Bathsheba appeared, cloaked and bonneted, awesome and forbidding in the upflung rays of the lantern she carried, he threw on his cape and followed her out without a word.

Clory spent the night huddled beside Willie in her tent. Sleepless hours in the humid darkness now suddenly prescient with dread, waiting for the morning, for news, listening to the Virgin's growing bellow, to the water seeping through the canvas, gurgling around the bedposts. Now and then, above the clamor of voices and the downpour outside, sentences drifted in to them. The settlements on the creek-bottoms were all under water, the refugees fled to the hills. The dam had gone out, most of the farming lands washed away. The Virgin was, unbelievably, a quarter of a mile wide! Former narrow channels were torn and widened, and great cottonwood trees rode on the flood, a large anvil, pieces of Hamblin's gristmill.

A wall of water fifteen feet high struck the fort, but the solid rock rectangle stood like a dam, forcing the stream to divide

around it. Neighbors tied ropes to fence posts to rescue children
marooned on the tops of houses. One woman watched her home
go by, her cookstove bobbing like a toy.

The new Swiss colony, the settlers just preceding Apostle
Snow's group, suffered the most. Their campground at the point
of the hill was soon inundated, and they spent the night on the
Black Ridge exposed to the drenching skies.

Jacob Hamblin himself (Clory could see the Indian missionary
with his black chin-beard and long, loose hair) had fallen from a
caving bank twenty feet deep into the racing waters and been
pulled out by one of his own Indians.

With the coming of daylight Clory and the boys succeeded in
getting a fire started, the Sibley tent warmed, damp blankets
heated, barley coffee and Brigham tea steaming.

'We'll need 'ot water, too, agin they gits back,' said Willie,
crippling around to help. 'They'll want to rench off their mud-
died faces and clothes. Laws, they'll more'n likely not 'ave a dry
stitch atween 'em! 'Sheba'll feel like a stewed witch.'

But when the big woman and Abijah finally appeared, mired
to the knees, no less a person than Apostle Snow accompanied
them, and Bathsheba strode ahead exuding mud and energy.

'Well, we had a precious time of it!' she shrilled, aggressive and
efficient as a good sheep dog that has just barked all its charges
back into line.

Brother Snow, his gray eyes wrinkled pools of worry and
fatigue, beamed at Bathsheba in frank congratulation.

'She carried a brand-new mother with her child in her arms...
right through the flood,' he explained, peeling mud from his chin
whiskers. Ptsahh! 'You never saw such a woman!'

He turned to Abijah and shook his hand.

'You should be proud of her, Brother Mac, proud of her!'

Abijah for the first time in many weeks really saw this wife of
his youth, whose eyes were so disconcertingly on a level with his
own; beside her, Clorinda looked like a little girl. Bathsheba,

taking the coffee-pot from Clory's hand, could afford a smile.

'I always say, "It isn't enough just to be good, you have to be good for something,"' she said, the hairs in her mole tremulous with virtue.

'Land sakes, Brother Snow, I was just a-thinkin' we might spare our little tent when you take the big marquee down to the flood victims; I was just a-thinkin' Sister Clory won't mind havin' Aunt Willie double up with her for a while...'

No, I won't mind, Clory's thoughts ran on; *you win; but isn't it funny: here we are, three women married to one man and to only 'Sheba is he 'my husband'; to Willie and me he'll never be anything more than 'Brother Mac.'*

CHAPTER V

THE rain fell steadily for forty days and nights and reduced food supplies to a grim margin. Sickness ran riot and there was one burial beneath the sodden salt grass in spite of all Sister Lowgie's cayenne pepper and the laying on of hands. 'Sheba, laying out the body, thought the burial-clothes would mold before she could get them ready. But the rain at least soaked the ground, and the settlers were doubly anxious to get about the business of real living, making gardens, growing green things once again.

In March, Brother Orson Pratt, Junior (whose craggy, earnest person, no matter how unselfishly he labored, seemed never quite one with his neighbors), surveyed the city and laid it out into thirty-six blocks, each block having eight one-acre lots. There was a public square, with the three blocks around the square reserved for school purposes. The site for the new city was chosen, with an eye to future floods in the northwest corner of the valley, on as high ground as could be watered by the springs tumbling from the slope of the Red Hill — near the Upper Gap, through which wound the road to Santa Clara, where the northern red mountain eased to a scarlet streak that merged with the scattered beginnings of the abruptly climbing western Black Ridge.

The city plots were laid out foursquare with the horizons. Helping Brother Orson with transit or chain, observing his mathematical genius, Erastus was reminded again and again of his fellow apostle in this Dixie Call, the elder Pratt, he who in 1854 had startled even Brother Brigham with his great discovery of a 'new and easy method of solution of the cubic and biquadratic equations.' Brother Orson, carrying on his illustrious father's tradition, was such a good man; if what his own wife had been saying should be true, it seemed a shame...

After the survey was completed, Apostle Snow's first concern was for a schoolhouse. During the three months on the Campground school had been taught privately in wagon box and tent, but the scholars were only those who could pay, and even they were likely to sneak out of the back end of the wagon and play hooky outside, and more often than not young Jarvis, the teacher, was glad to see them go. Now Erastus planned to have a public school whose expenses would be met in part by the proceeds from the stray pen — every month all stray stock were to be sold at auction. He would have a building for educational and religious purposes before there were even homes. Accordingly he called a mass-meeting and proposed to the brethren that they should 'unite their labor and means... voluntary contributions to begin at once.'

Three days later, when the citizens reassembled, the committee reported that the structure would be forty feet long and twenty-one feet wide, to be built of native red sandstone rock, and that its estimated cost would be three thousand to thirty-five hundred dollars. It should be called the 'St. George Hall.' At this meeting the total subscription consisted of one hundred and twenty names — $2974 donated in materials and labor — and not a subscriber had a roof over his own head as yet.

Sitting there in the old bowery, listening to the chairman read-

ing his report, Clory thought such a display of civic pride too much
like counting your chickens before they were hatched. Besides,
men were such fools. Didn't they know homes came first, any
time, anywhere? A new country wouldn't be much good without
its homes!

For the last month becoming daily more certain of the hope
groping beneath her heart, welcoming even the morning sickness,
she planned away the hours. A home for her child. She looked
with affection upon even Abijah, since he had helped her work this
miracle. A home of her own. Of course Abijah would want to
house his three wives under one large roof, but Clory wanted none
of that. Bathsheba should have no hand in raising this child.
Clory would have her own baby in her own house if she had to
build it with her two hands . . .

The city lots had been numbered, and now Apostle Snow put all
the strips of paper bearing the numbers in an old hat, clutched the
brim together, and shook the hat. One by one each solemn
elder walked up the aisle, shut his eyes, and drew out a number.
The moment was hushed with significance. There was no sound
except the chirp of a cricket under a bench; and then decisive
on the packed earth floor the footsteps of a man awestruck with
a sudden sense of history-making.

Bathsheba watching Abijah returning down the aisle, frowning over the number he had just drawn, waited until he sat down
and took the piece of paper from his hand. Southeast corner of
block 9, plat C. One of the lots on the southernmost fringe of the
survey. He had wanted land under the brow of the Red Hill,
near a spring. Still, the piece was a corner lot; one could irrigate.
She was seeing new pea blossoms . . . What a triumph to have the
first green peas in town! She would just get Abijah to show her
the cornerpost of their lot . . .

Apostle Snow was speaking. The settlers were to have three
days in which to pack their belongings and clean up the débris of
the camp. Early on the morning of the fourth day at a given

signal the wagons were to move over onto the lots, and the City
of St. George would officially begin.

During those three days Clory packed and repacked and
planned. But Bathsheba, while Abijah was in the fields, walked
the two miles over to their lot every day and grubbed sagebrush
from her new garden. She meant to surprise him.

Those three days seemed endless to Clory. When the big bass
drum beat out the signal at six o'clock on the morning of the
fourth, she had her oxen yoked and had been ready at her post
for a good hour.

2

Once more — did they dare believe this time was the last? —
the white-tops took up the march. Shadrach Gaunt, gun in crook
of arm, rode beside Erastus in the lead. A makeshift road had
been cleared through the hub-deep brush, but it was odd to go
jolting over the ruts, in single file, hemmed in by the tall bushes,
the smoke of an Indian fire wisping across the sky, and to know
that when you reached your home there would be nothing to
distinguish it from the rest of this land of alkali and cactus except
a post. But the sun was warm and the air soft with the coming
spring, and there were shoots of green at the roots of the brush.
Clory spied even a wildflower with a tiny pink cup — Willie
thought it was an Indian red bell. And above all, if you lifted
your head, there to the north, growing constantly more commanding as the caravan approached, reared the Red Hill and its Sugar
Loaf. That gigantic sandstone slab, flung like congealed fire
against the horizon and crimsoning now with the rising sun, sang
out against a sky of contrasting blueness like sudden band
music.

At the edge of the surveyed plots the citizens stopped for instructions. They were to continue along this road which led to
the public square in the center of the town (not a citizen smiled —

houses and streets and schools were more real to them at the moment than the brush), and then each man was to proceed as best he could to his own lot.

At the square you were directly facing the Sugar Loaf. In the changing light, enduring and warm and friendly, it dominated the valley.

Abijah called out 'Giddup!' and 'Haw!' to his oxen, turned them to the left, and broke a trail due south for about a mile. Bathsheba had a hard time keeping the boys in the back of the wagon from scampering ahead, but even this early in the season there might be rattlesnakes, and always there were the Indians. She shut her eyes against the thought of all the inevitable future scamperings of those bare young feet through the trails of this new country.

Clory and Willie were directly behind Abijah in the other wagon. Free trailed alongside on his pony.

Finally they reached the lot — there, away from all the spring-watered northern land, lay Abijah's alkali-crusted ground. Seeing it, Clory's heart sank. Prickly greasewood, gnarled cat's-claw and sand burs here and there above white, sterile patches ... One corner had been grubbed clean, the earth freshly turned.

Clory climbed down and walked up to the front wagon. The lot was plenty large enough for two houses, a big one and a tiny one.

Bathsheba was staring expectantly at Abijah, whose eyes were fixed in bewilderment on the grubbed space. Then the brown, furry bearskin of his face parted in a grin.

Something was happening to 'Sheba's triumph. 'Aren't you surprised?' she queried uncertainly. 'I'll be the *first* to have green peas in blossom!'

'Hawckk!' said Abijah, and then his rare laugh boomed out. 'Ye've grubbed the wrong side o' the corner-post!' he shouted. 'Ye've grubbed the *sidewalk!*'

Clory thoroughly enjoyed Bathsheba's discomfiture. Then the

older woman threw back her head like a horse accepting a strange bit.

'Well, anyway,' she shrilled, 'I'll be the *first* to work out my poll tax!'

Abijah chuckled and gave the big woman's hand an unexpected squeeze.

'Ye micht be able t' have the first pea blossoms at that,' he said, studying the layout of the land through half-closed eyes. In the southeast corner grew a few scrubby bushes of 'old man' sage. He indicated them.

'We'll try making a garden there first,' he said. 'Haul some r-rich loam from the river ... manure it well ... several rows of good cotton ...

'The path we've just come down will be a main road leading from town,' he said, half to himself, 'and it will turn this corner and go there' — cutting an angle in the air with his finger and tracing a straight line toward the west — 'along the southern boundary of our place. That's where we'd better have the gate and a nice white picket fence and the front lawns. A big house with three stories facing the south and the road ... barns and corrals at the back, maybe grapevines, fruit trees ... vegetables, as I said, right here, and flowers along the front of the house ...'

Somehow the moment didn't seem auspicious. Clory stooped to break a twig of the sage, so good for the gripes, hesitated, and went back to her own wagon and climbed in beside Willie.

'Wouldn't you rather have a little house of your own, Aunt Willie?' she demanded, handing her the sage.

Willie raised her head, belched, and shuddered weakly.

'Laws, child,' she said, 'it makes no never minds to me. All I ask is a place to lay my 'ead, right now ...'

Clory stared a moment, and patted Willie's hand. But her heart was hot within her. You'd never catch *her* giving in weakly like that! She'd just wait until Abijah had gone one day and take matters into her own hands. She was young, strong. She'd just start digging her own dugout that might some day be a basement, gathering her own willows for a roof that might some day be of real shingles, and if Abijah didn't like it, he could lump it!

By nightfall the tents were pitched, a temporary corral built for the stock, and the desolate piece of ground began to look domesticated. The boys shouted to each other as they stacked their loads of chopped greasewood and turpentine brush against the tents; Bathsheba scolded Isaiah for always getting underfoot as she rushed busily about superintending the last details of making camp.

'Well, I'm tired, too,' she burst out at Clory and Willie, who were helping prepare the meal, 'but you never hear me complain! I always say, "Never leave today's work for tomorrow; tomorrow will have enough of its own!"'

Freeborn and his father, having doled the stock their rations, sniffed the good smell of frying salt bacon, and walked through the gathering dusk toward the Sibley tent, whose spreading canvas walls glowed warmly in the gloom. Abijah was holding forth: 'Remember, my son, the Prophet's advice: "Grain for man, corn for the ox, oats for the horse, rye for fowls and swine, barley for mild drinks — always keep the Word of Wisdom; strong drinks are not for the belly, but for the washing of your bodies... Tobacco is not for the body, neither for the belly, but is an herb for bruises and all sick cattle." Beware of eating too much meat. Pay your tithes and fast offerings, tend to your secret prayers, never profane the name of Deity. If any man do these things he shall have "health to his navel and marrow to his bones... run and not be weary, walk and not faint..."'

All over the valley echoed the sounds of people taking up the new life, children playing, mothers calling them frantically... 'Le-H-I-I-I! Ne-P-H-I-I-I! If you don't hurry I'll blister your behinds!' Rhythmic thud of an axe on brush roots, lowing of hungry cattle, always and forever the howling of the coyotes.

3

The next day Abijah left early with Apostle Snow for the fields.
The trip to the site of the new dam took over an hour with oxen,
across the valley to the east, a jog south on the Old Campground
road, up along the river. Work on the dam and the canal must
be pushed, they would soon be wanting water for crops. The
canal was planned to be six miles long, three feet deep, six
feet wide, but the country through which the Virgin flowed
was so chopped up and inaccessible that even with the canal
they could never get water to some of the most fertile ground
unless they also built a tunnel through the very tip of the jutting Black Ridge point. And such a tunnel would have to be
at least nine hundred feet long, hewed out by hand from the
solid clay under the lava rock . . .

As soon as Abijah was gone, Clory investigated her situation.
The tents and wagon boxes were strung out much as they had
been at the Old Campground. The Sibley tent stood in the south-
west corner where Abijah wanted his house, then parallel to it
Willie's tent (long since recovered from the flood victims), and
then Clory's wagon box, stripped of its wheels and squatting like
an inflated turtle not far from the fertile spot where 'Sheba wanted
her garden. The big wagon box where the boys slept was behind
the Sibley tent near the corral. Clory decided that just back of
her own wagon box would be the best possible place for her
house.

After the morning work was done and Bathsheba safely knitting a sock in the big tent, Clory put on her sunbonnet and got
the shovel. The older boys were all either at work in the fields
or herding the cattle, and the twins were playing Injun in the
near-by brush. She'd better 'make hay while the sun shone,' as
'Sheba would say.

A few paces north from her wagon box she traced with the
edge of her shovel the four sides of a large square. She thrust

the heavy blade into the soil. But in spite of the recent rains the ground seemed like rock.

The sun was warm for March. She mopped continually at the sweat dripping from under her bonnet into her eyes. Recurrent giddiness seized her. The twins came and stared. 'What ya doin', Aunt Clory? What ya doin'?' Once she froze at the intrusion of a familiar stalwart shadow, and looked up to encounter Bathsheba's ironic eye. But the big woman merely stood there for a moment, one finger absently worrying the mole on her chin, grinned to herself, and strode away without a word.

By the time Clory had scooped two rows completely around the circumference of the square, her back was so brittle with soreness that she felt another effort might snap it like a dry twig, and all she could think about was that Clary Dutchman who was grubbing lots for other polygamous wives, walking over barefoot in the morning, working all day, and walking back at night to earn provisions and clothing for his family. Now, if Abijah was like some men who'd hire a little help . . .

Never mind, her thought insisted, if she couldn't do the job herself, one of the boys must. She'd have a path to the street and a gate of her own, too. Abijah would get over being mad in time. At first his eyes would flash, his voice would boom and burr, the little vein in his forehead would swell and throb, and he'd denounce her and throw out his chest (and how he would enjoy himself!) like one of those crusading prophets in the Bible. But she knew now in time he'd be a little ashamed, a little sorry, as he always was, and he'd feel sure he was making amends by coming to her bed two nights in a row. Always, after punishing one of his sons, he'd make it up to the boy by being nice to Bathsheba! And yet, when anyone reproached him for his bitter tongue, he was always astonished. He never could understand why folks made such a fuss over something that to him was so soon forgotten. Clory had come to believe he really was the most tender-hearted of men underneath — like a coconut a missionary had

brought back once from the Sandwich Islands, tough and hairy
outside and needing a lot of opening up before one could get at
the sweet good core...

Meanwhile, there were the willows to be gathered for the walls
and roof. Starting off in the early afternoon, armed with her
butcher knife, eluding even the little boys, she felt her feet winged
with adventure. There was no one to stop her. Abijah was in the
fields near the place where he had taken her on that first day —
her thought shied from that day and concentrated on the path
before her. Down the two ruts that led straight from the center
of town toward the river, the brush loomed denser and higher
than she had ever dreamed riding through it in a wagon. But she
stared boldly at the shadows and hummed and hugged her giddy
sense of exhilaration. This is it, she thought, this doing things
really all on your own, this is *really* being a pioneer!

As she walked, swinging her bonnet in one hand, the knife
clutched in the other, her thought took to its heels and tilted at
obstacles. The walls were woven, Abijah liked her house so
much he spent all his nights there — well, nearly all — and forgot
to be stern; the floor was clean and hard with many dampenings
and much sweeping with sand, there was her bed such as she
remembered from her childhood in Great Salt Lake snugly built
into a corner which formed two of its sides, rails or poles forming
the opposite sides — pegs driven into the walls and rails and the
good bed-cord woven tightly between the pegs for springs, and a
mattress filled with the soft and faintly scented cattail fluff or
the rustly rabbit-brush blossoms...

An arrow would probably have frightened her less than the
Indian's surprised grunt stopping her headlong, and that instant's
horrified glimpse of the painted face framed between parted
branches and so instantly gone she had only her hammering heart
to verify what her eyes had seen. She was struck motionless,
and then her knees shook with the effort not to run. Even as her
mind churned with a thousand remembered tales, she forced herself to go forward unhurriedly.

Of course she had been a fool to come alone ... Free was grubbing land down here somewhere today ... on the Clara Creek — for some man at Santa Clara ... Those Navajos who shot a sheepherder in the legs, made a fire in his stove, laid him across the stove, and roasted him to death. Those Pavants who caught an outlying ranch unguarded, stripped an eight-year-old boy, tied a rawhide rope under his arms, and dragged him behind a horse up and down past the house where his mother watched. What happened to a captured white woman at the hands of any tribe —!

'*Tucuben noonie! Tucuben noonie!*'

There the face was again, barely ahead of her, peering from behind a mesquite bush. For just a moment her scared glance caught a disconcerting gleam in the savage eyes.

Holding her butcher knife stiffly in front of her she marched ahead. How did one blaze a trail —?

'*Tucuben noonie! Tucuben noonie!*'

This time the face, darting around chaparral, wore an unmistakable soundless grin. Why didn't he start, she wondered, brandishing the knife; she'd make a fight of it ——

'*Tucuben noonie! Tucuben noonie!*'

Peering briefly out at her from one bush after another, keeping always in front of her like a small boy saying 'Boo.' It was too much. She dropped the knife and her bonnet, surrendered to panic, and ran. Did she hear a yell behind her or was it merely a derisive 'ugh'?

The narrow path widened out near the river where reedy marshes and squawbush copses interspersed a grassy space. Once clearing the shadowy aisle, Clory threw herself down, sobbing with exhaustion. After a time, when her lungs burned less, she sat up and gingerly touched a finger to her lips and eyes and breast; it seemed miraculous that she should find her body still intact, alive. Impossible to go back over that same way — she shuddered and resolutely reined in her thought. From where she sat she could see a cut of the land sloping down to the water and the fragile green of new willow leaves. Perhaps she could break the stalks with her hands.

The hem of her linsey-woolsey was bedraggled, her hair rioting over her shoulders, and her cheeks flushed with exertion by the time she first heard the voices. It was just a moment then, after her call and her eager rush, until Free was beside her holding her hands, his boyish face strained with concern. Only then, when she dared lift the clamps from the timid, foolish core of her, did the tears come. Such relief to let oneself go weak and feminine again, to feel protected and safe (she peered out from her tears to make sure Free's concern was still there), to be petted.

Free turned to the other boys in the buckboard with their hoes and shovels and waved them back to town, looped the rope over Nellie's neck, and pulled Clory down to the grass beside him. Thinking she really needed a good shot of whiskey, he snapped in two the piece of jerky he had saved from his lunch and gave her half. He was so full of anxiety he forgot to be shy.

'Now tell me, Clorinda,' he said, settling at hand the brass powder pouch slung over his shoulder and keeping the flintlock handy.

Chewing hungrily on the salty meat, she sat for a moment savoring the good presence of him — his clear eyes that were the color of mountain water running over stones, his blond hair, sun-bleached into white streaks that waved back from the high brown forehead and curled lightly above the ears; the soft buckskin hunting-coat hanging loosely above a red-and-brown-checked flannel shirt, open at the neck where golden fuzz filled in the V; the bronzed, strong cords of his neck; the firm chin with the front dimple like his father's; the clean long length of him, his copper-studded belt with its bowie knife and bullet pouch above deerskin trousers, creeping up a bit on still-growing legs and wrinkled like old flesh on the inside of his thighs from long gripping a horse, the gay line of fringe on the outside wearing thin . . .

She told him about the Indian. He looked puzzled.

'Are you *sure* he said "*Tucuben*"?'

'Oh, yes' — Clory nodded emphatically. She sat facing him with her legs folded under her spreading skirt, propping herself with one hand, looking at him as if she expected him to dispel all Indians with a single arm-sweep.

'Oh, yes, something like "*Tucuben noonie.*" He was a bad Injun, I know' — she could afford to be indignant, now.

But suddenly Free began to snicker, flung himself backward on the grass, and laughed until the tears stood in his eyes.

Clory was insulted.

'You see,' he spluttered when he could talk, 'the cusses like to joke. Most folks don't realize that. He was plaguing you!'

The boy went off into spasms again.

'Don't you see, when you stampeded you played right into his hands! You with your butcher knife! Oh, shucks —!'

He convulsed at the thought, and Clory's sooty gaze shot danger signals.

'"*Tucuben noonie*" means "We are friends" — it's the Indian way of saying "Howdy" ——'

Clorinda got to her feet.

'Well, I don't care! I think you might ——'

He was instantly contrite and scrambled after her, staring down at her gravely, the grin still twitching at his mouth.

'Don't be mad, Clory; shucks, why, if one o' them varmints harmed you I'd — I'd ——'

He felt infinitely wise and masculine and indulgent.

Clory relented suddenly and dimpled, clasping her hands beneath her cheek and laughing with him at herself.

His eyes sang with tenderness.

'Come on,' he said, afraid of himself. 'I'll help you cut your willows.'

He caught her hand and they raced down the grass.

Time passes so quickly when two are young and love to laugh

together, when two can chatter carelessly, sure of understanding, when the casual touch of another's flesh is like a sharp thrust of delight.

The pile of branches spilled over itself when Free finally straightened.

'We have to go.'

Clory threw down her last load, smacked her palms together, and beamed and glowed at him like a crimson cactus flower.

'See,' he said, pointing toward the western Black Ridge. 'Your Injun would say "*Tabby yike wa*" — "Sun dies."'

Nellie came at his whistle and nuzzled his shoulder. He boosted Clory (such a featherweight!) so that she sat sideways in front of him on the blanketed horse. Dizzy from the touch of her body, he heaped her arms with the willows and swung himself up behind her. His arms around her to hold the guide rope, his hands lying loosely above the willows on her lap, he trembled at her nearness and the blood throbbed in his temples.

The long, brush-enclosed aisle and the shadows swallowing the slanting shafts of sunlight gave them a feeling of security and peace and rightful privacy. Once Free leaned from his horse to swoop up her bonnet.

'I seem to be always doing that,' he said, and lifted the red calico for its haunting whiff of bergamot.

Clory's smile remembered, and thanked him.

They sang, one song after another, and their voices seemed to grow stronger and truer as they sang, seemed to ride out to the hills through the silence and come back to them transfigured on the echoes. By the time they reached the clearing, they were so filled with the communion of their shared laughter, their common labor, their long ride together through the mystery of the brush and the twilight, that they were beyond songs or words. Like figures locked in a spell they rode soundlessly, almost motion-lessly, as if the contentment between them were something so precious it might be shattered by a breath. Deep in enchantment,

Clory cupped her palms around the moment as if to preserve its quicksilver iridescence against life itself. When Abijah on his way to council meeting met them at the edge of the clearing, she could almost see the mood spurt apart like a dissolving soap bubble.

4

Abijah got them before him in the Sibley tent. Afterward he could never clearly remember what happened except that there was this soreness bunched inside of him and he wanted to strike out at something, peel from their two young faces that remote look shutting them in together, convicting him of trespassing. He wanted to bore behind the wonder in their clear, unaware eyes and discover a hidden guilt that would justify and assuage his own misery.

He shouted and did not dare to stop shouting: he built up a wall of words against his own sick apprehension that there was nothing he could do about these two. He wanted to bring them to their knees, to tears, as if, by resolving the intangible radiance between them into an ugly thing with a name and a form, he could lunge against it and stamp it out. They were so clearly united, and their union was so clearly beyond their power and his, that he longed to pull them bodily apart, break them up into two alien beings once more and so bring back to him his love and his son.

Surrounding him in the tent were his whole family like a jury. The coals popped and sighed under the crane, and the candles cast giant shadows. His brood of dark boys were there, squatting against a wall, the older brothers staring painfully away from Free as if to leave him at least a spiritual privacy, the twins bewildered and scared, puckering up their faces and crying silently. Bathsheba knitted placidly, the clicking needles never dropping a stitch, squeaking back and forth in the little rocker, only now and then lifting her lip away from her strong yellow teeth like a horse getting ready to bite. Over on the bed in a far corner where the sleeping, pink-cheeked Isaiah lay curled, Willie wrung her futile hands.

Abijah whipped out his handkerchief from his tail-coat pocket and mopped his trembling beard. Silly to keep those two standing there, and yet he couldn't seem to let go. He was like a man pressing a sore tooth.

'Ech, I dinna ken ye're thoct at all, Clorinda Agatha,' he said in a held-in voice, as one would reason with a child, 'ridin' a horse with a man for a' the worrld t' see like any shameless gentile hussy! Gin ye dinna hae no respect for yersel, ye micht remember ye're a handmaid o' the Prophet o' the one true God! — And I might add, wife to one of his apostles.'

'You're only a Seventy, Abijah.' Clory couldn't believe the sting spitting out of her own mouth.

The pounding began again in Abijah's ears. 'Hawckk!' Just because his abilities hadn't been fully recognized yet was no reason to — to —— Why, they were trying to make *him* the one on trial! His bass rumble sputtered up from his chest.

Free's voice stopping him, championing the girl, breaking through into a valiant falsetto:

'You got her in the family way and now you'd make her walk all those miles alone, in the dark ...'

Abijah's hand seemed to leap out of its own accord, and the palm flattened against his son's cheekbone with a sharp and staggering smack. He almost hoped for a moment the boy would break through the habit of filial respect and take his shaking hand away from the welts reddening the pallor of his cheek, and hit back. Another move and he'd really pound some sense into him. Needed a good walloping. Thought he was all grown up, did he? A ladies' man? Why, he couldn't even grow a decent mustache. Why, that great, big, green gosling of a fellow, presuming to criticize, he wasn't dry behind the ears yet, he didn't know

sickom. Why, my conscience, he didn't *know* enough to —
to ——

Abijah shrugged. He couldn't handle the pair. This was a
matter for Apostle Snow and the High Council. He set his jaw.
It was council meeting tonight. He'd almost forgotten. He was
late already, but then Apostle Snow had never been known to be
on time himself. He'd march these two up there with him. He'd
teach them decency. They'd find out who was boss! The High
Council might be the court of last resort, but he was in no mood
to palaver with Bishops' Courts. He'd disregard the customary
written summons, he'd ——

'Pa,' said Bathsheba, lifting her eyes from her flying fingers as
if she read his thoughts, 'forget about it, Pa. It ain't the boy's
fault. I says to myself when I dropped my dishrag this morning,
"It's a sure sign, 'Sheba, a bigger slut than you is coming to visit
you," and she's here.'

For a moment her glance rested on Clory's bowed head. Her
hate was bloated and unwholesome, growing in the dark like a
toadstool. 'But you're being a fool, Pa — no use punishing the
boy; and you're goin' against authority when you forget Brother
Brigham's rules to them livin' in the covenant: *Never reprove one
wife in the presence of the others.* . . . Besides, it won't do your standing in the church no good to have the Priesthood find out you
ain't master enough to control whoredoms in your own household . . .'

Her lip lifted and she spat out the word as if it were a piece of
dung.

'Better to wash your dirty clothes at home even if the stink's
as sour as swill — it'll be sourer still in other folks' noses . . .'

Willie's quavering voice piling up the argument: '"Judge
not . . ."'

In the dark outside, walking up the rutty pathway between the
two culprits, Abijah girded his loins against them all. Like
Brother Brigham he'd say to wives who got above themselves,

'Get out of my path, for I am going yonder, and you may whistle at my coat-tail until you are tired of it!' There came a time when a man had to make his own judgments — 'Let our wives be the weaker vessels and the men be men ——' He hated Clory for making his conscience this tormenting goad. Her resentment was about him like a mist, but he was justified, he had to be. These two bearing his name had dared to sin, or at least to permit the appearance of sin, and they must be punished. He had thought of himself as God's mouthpiece too long (at least a minor mouthpiece), and one couldn't have God confessing to mistakes.

He hoarded his grievances. Clory refusing to live with his other wives; the unseemly loudness of her laughter he'd failed to tame — the special glance that spoke to his son even across a room; her tomboy ways. He had a sudden memory out of the disciplines of those first ruthless years in the new territory. The whipping post with its bell to assemble the people. A man convicted of adultery. And among the watchers a frightened young fellow and a girl accused of riding together on horseback. Reprimanded for such abominations before the Lord by the Public Complainer, they had been sent to witness execution of proper punishment. For the law also read, '*Adultery or fornication: 39 lashes on the bare back...*'

Punishment — the Great Reformation of '56–'57. Saints were fleeing famine and hard times by way of apostasy and the gold fields, Saints were refusing to obey counsel, laboring on the Sabbath, coveting a neighbor's ox and his wife, and Zion had to be humbled, purified, and rebaptized. Every man must confess his sins publicly and repent or forfeit his good standing. The sword to be unsheathed, 'judgment to be laid to the line and righteousness to the plummet'; Brother Brigham facing his priesthood members and demanding, 'All you who have been guilty of adultery, *stand up!*'

It was an awful thing to disfellowship a boy and give over his soul to the buffetings of Satan ... (*If a man have a stubborn and rebellious son which will not obey the voice of his father ... then shall his father lay hold on him and bring him out unto the elders of his city ...*) But it was a far worse thing to let one you loved lose eternal salvation. Brother Brigham himself had put the question, 'Will you love your neighbor well enough to shed his blood? ... There are sins such as apostasy and a woman's transgression of her marriage vows ... sins for which they cannot receive forgiveness ... unless their blood be spilt upon the ground that the smoke thereof might ascend to heaven as an offering, as a smoking incense to the Almighty ... As it was in ancient days, so it is in our day — the doctrine of salvation, the doctrine of *Blood Atonement* ...'

5

Erastus looked down the long table at eleven of his counselors. He was too heavy of spirit to wonder at Abijah's absence; they had had to go ahead with the case without him. These court proceedings, this putting himself up as a Solomon knowing so surely wrong from right, this presuming to sit in judgment on a fellow being, this damning a man and praying for him as you damn him — these things were what withered his spirit, not the bitterness of the land, nor privation. The evidence was all in; the man's own wife had testified against him; Brother Orson, Junior, had himself admitted his doubt concerning Joseph Smith, and had resigned his job as ward teacher. There was nothing left to do but cut him off. Just the formal vote. And yet Erastus could not bring himself to speak.

Orson sat there now at the foot of the table, flanked by the jury of his fellows, his shoulders hunched, his gaze fixed straight ahead, the long furrows from brow to chin carved and deepened, his sparse brown beard and sideburns disheveled, his mouth thinned in an unwonted bitter line. And he had a right to his own beliefs. 'Where every man shall worship God according to the dictates of his own conscience...'

But *togetherness* — you couldn't whip the desert without *togetherness*. The Group Faith — the ability to live outside oneself, for something greater than oneself, to sacrifice oneself for the Common Good. Some day they would be strong enough to afford dissenters — now salvation lay only in complete and disciplined togetherness. *Except ye are one, ye are not mine.*

Erastus had a sudden clear insight into past doubts — Brother Brigham pushing men about, as if they were wooden figures on a checkerboard, and being called heartless by even his own people; but holding them together like a wedge against disintegration from within, Indians, starvation, the wilderness from without, and never for a moment faltering before the Vision. You had to be ruthless to colonize...

Erastus pushed back his chair, but before he could speak Brother Orson was abruptly on his feet, commanding them to attention with his eyes. His mouth opened and shut and no words came, and then his voice grew resolute. He had always had the finest Adam's apple in the country, and now it acted as if it were trying to escape.

'Brethren — for I suppose I may still continue to call you so, as we are all the children of one Father in spite of ourselves — and notwithstanding action may be taken today which will sever me from the Church, I shall continue to look upon you as brethren...

'Although I am not in the habit of saying anything in self-justification, I wish to state (and you will bear me out) that ever since I have been in this Church I have led a godly and upright life. In regard to my faith it is true I have long since seen differently from this people and I could not betray my own conscience — there was much said about the receiving of a testimony, that unless one had the testimony that Mormonism is true, he was in some way deficient. I asked myself the question if I had it, even whilst on my mission, but was sensible I had not...'

Erastus had a hand to the pepper-and-salt ruffle on his chin to keep it from quivering. Maybe the fault was his. Maybe if he had counseled with him more, the testimony would have come.

'... I have reached the conclusion that Joseph Smith was not specially sent by the Lord to establish this work. I could not believe otherwise even if I knew I should go to hell tomorrow. But is this a sin, to believe as I must? For this you will drop me off, send me down to disgrace...'

The voice broke, faltered, and steadied.

'Though a man be guilty of ever so heinous a crime, if he can stand up and say that he believes the same as you do, you will hold to him and keep him in fellowship! If a man has not sinned against his heavenly Father...'

Erastus tried to smile a plea for understanding at Brother Orson fumbling for his chair. And momentarily his suffering eyes dodged the group about the table, ranged the candlelit marquee as if trying a last escape from the thing he was about to do. Only then did he become aware that Abijah MacIntyre was in his seat, and behind him, ranged like prisoners before the bar, his wife and his son. The sore place in his heart quivered in angry recognition. But that was what he, Erastus, was for, hearing and counseling.

6

Erastus turned from Abijah and, cupping Clory's chin in his hand, tilted her face. *Your love is like a stranger standing just outside your heart,* his thought spoke to her gently, *but I have to send him packing before you even know he's there.* And yet, looking deep into her eyes, he comforted himself that she was strong enough to bear up. It was the boy he was worried about. But the thing between them must go down, even as Orson, before the Vision. There was no other way...

'There's no sin in her,' he said, shaking his head at Abijah; 'they're just young.'

He smiled at the boy and girl sitting white-faced before him, convicted of their youth; and wrapped his counsel into neat little bundles and parceled it out.

'Sister Clorinda, beware of giddiness ... carelessness.'

She nodded gratefully. *They always did say of him, 'his plaster's bigger than the wound.'*

'Brother Freeborn ... it's time you found yourself a wife of your own, went through the Endowment House, clothed yourself with the priesthood.'

The boy's strange, light eyes, refusing to shed their mutiny, rested sullenly on Abijah.

'And Brother Mac' — Erastus sighed in spite of himself. Ptsahh! There was such a thing as over-righteousness. 'Brother Mac, you're like the butterfly who passed up all the flowers in the garden to light on the manure in the barnyard ...'

CHAPTER VI

AT LAST civilization was timidly abroad over the land. Across scatterings of stone arrowheads of lava or pale flintrock, pieces of traced pottery, and hidden graves with their baskets, beads, and swathed bones, settlers were plowing — always with the cautious gun on the beam.

Fields planted to cotton, to corn and grain and sugar cane, soon wore a faint dusting of green. Step by step this fierce and ancient land, so old it was new and virgin, grudgingly acknowledged its latest conquerors.

For it was not to be thought that this land, so vast and bitter and brooding, would be easy to subjugate, would ever be taken without a struggle. Sometimes at night when the sod turned surprised red bellies up to a wide and glittering sky, a defiant spirit seemed to ride the echoes with the coyote chorus:

'Yah! Yah! *You* there, *you* man, who planned to tame the Great Basin of North America! I am the very rim of the Basin; nothing has ever prepared you for the life I'll lead you! Keep on your guard, keep your eyes open; I'll fight you with heat and cold and drought and pestilence, rattlesnakes and scorpions and gila monsters! If you think you have me beat on your right hand, look out for your left. I have no sense of honor, I strike in the dark, behind your back . . .'

2

Zadoc Hunt, a well-to-do brother whose lot was in the northern end of the town, had opened up a stone quarry in the Upper Gap where the Red Hill sloped to meet the Black, and was building him a red stone house, much to the horror of the more orthodox. A fine house finished *before* the church building done! And donating money toward the Social Hall instead of actual labor, which somehow would seem more honestly to testify before God and one's neighbors that a man was doing his share. Watching his wagons drag out the big red stones from his private, unapproved quarry, citizens delivered dire prophecies.

But Abijah, unabashed, saw a chance to get some foundation rock cheaply and made a dicker with Zadoc. And for a few weeks Free quit making ditch and was put to hauling rock. Abijah suggested the boy might keep his eyes open and learn something at the same time, as Zadoc was an excellent stonecutter.

Free thought, of course, some of the stones would be for Clory's house, but Abijah had not yet forgiven his youngest wife, and while Clory's wagon box still squatted on its bottom more than ever like a turtle with an inflated canvas back, Bathsheba's dwelling grew in arrogance.

'Sheba herself mixed the clay (only for the Social Hall could anyone afford lime plaster) and daubed the rough red rocks. Watching 'Sheba's face, intent in lines of strength and satisfaction and her big muscles swell below the rolled-up sleeves, Clory thought the other woman better at such a job than any of her sons, and held up her own still childish arms and bit her lip in vexation.

One morning Clory and Willie sat apart and watched the

Sibley tent struck and repitched squarely over the foundation and its voluminous wings stretched into place. (Even with the North Star as the authorities recommended.) This tent was sixty feet long and twenty feet wide, and Abijah with an eye to permanency put up three poles on the outside and suspended the tent to the apex by ropes. Divided by a canvas partition into a dining-room and bedroom, it became a home. Willie accepted it as such, and lowered her pendulous body into one of 'Sheba's little rockers with a sigh of pleasure, but Clory went back to her own unfinished dugout with bitter eyes.

Free, whose glance shied away from her these days, had nevertheless hauled her a load of the grass sods drying out as the Old Campground springs were diverted into ditches. These grass sods, one by two feet, ricked up in rows like regular adobes, would make with the woven willows a fairly snug wall. The basement was all dug now — six by eight feet around and about three feet deep; but when she watched the long wet worms wriggle out of the raw earth and slither over projecting roots, and whenever she turned over one of the grass sods and the slimy sow-bugs or slim gray centipedes scuttled away from the sunlight, something inside of her quivered like jelly.

The walls were halfway up; four posts outlined the corners, and the stems of the strong, limber water willows, that grew eight straight feet before branching out, were stuck upright thickly in the ground between the posts. In and out between these upright willows, slenderer ones were woven halfway to the top of the poles, where Clory planned to thatch the roof, mat it thickly with leaves, and then cover it finally with dirt. She would have a house as snug as a squaw's basket. As she went on with the work, winding the branches, still pliable with sap, around and around the four sides of the square, and the walls crept up another inch, peace came back to her with the rhythm of her steps. She would plant her bergamot seeds on each side of the step . . .

All over the flat little valley women were home-making. Wo-

men of the West, who had borne children on the jolting floors of
wagons and knelt by icy streams to scrub clothes stinking from a
week in oiled saddles, now left their husbands free to plant crops,
and molded their own adobe, mixed their own mortar, laid their
own walls, and before long would tongue-and-groove their own
doors.

Apostle Erastus came home unexpectedly one morning to find
Marianne, his youngest wife, three months gone with child,
crawling up the gable end of her new house and tugging at the
heavy roof beam. When he called to her in anger, 'There are
men to do that!' she only set her lips and shook her pretty head
at him. The women, he brooded — pioneering was always hardest
on the women. Would they pay with their unborn children?

And suddenly he saw as if on a scroll all those hordes of grim-
faced women obediently making merry at a command from their
Prophet, with hunger and fear in their vitals but courage on their
lips; hordes of singing wives and mothers clinging, with the desperation known only in women, to their household gods: heavy
one-piece smoothing irons from family estates in the South and
East, silver sugar tongs from England, huge wooden stirring
spoons from Sweden, carved and decorated wooden foot-length
measuring sticks from Germany, brass preserving pans and crimp-
ing irons, the samplers and tester beds, Spode and Haviland, the
Chippendales and ornate mahogany pieces; hordes of women
desperately carrying loved familiarity into a wilderness — and
keepsake after keepsake, each like a drop of heart's blood, strew-
ing the thousand miles of plain as the oxen gave out and the load
had to be lightened.

Erastus, who loved Brother Brigham with all his soul and
would obey him without question to his death, thought of the
President's way with women and considered in spite of himself
that that way was hard. He had heard him thunder from the
pulpit: 'My wives have got to do one of two things: either round
up their shoulders to endure the afflictions of this world and live

their religion, or they may leave, for I will not have them about me. I will go into heaven alone rather than have scratching and fighting about me.... If you stay with me you shall comply with the law of God in every respect and walk up to the mark without grunting ... I do know there is no cessation to the everlasting whining of many of the women in this territory ... "Give us a little gentileism, for Heaven's sake," you say. "Let us wear hoops because the whores wear them."... If a whore comes along and turns up her clothes, don't turn up yours and go through the streets;... break off from your sins by righteousness ... "But," says one of you, "I want to have my paradise now!"'

And that was the trouble, thought Erastus; that was the trouble. It was natural for a woman to want her paradise now, and there was too much preoccupation with her petty bickerings, too little recognition of her gallantry when she did not get it. Polygamy was infinitely harder for a woman; Erastus marveled at the evidences of goodwill he saw every day in his own home. For a woman was not like a man — a woman since time began craved just one man, all to herself, and the secure possession of one man's love. No gospel could ever mean so much to any woman as her own home, her own mate, and a little sucking mouth at her breast.

Erastus, trying to handle the problems of these days, was like a man driving a twenty-mule team. He had too much on his hands. Sometimes the dust of the journey swallowed up the temper of the beasts, and sometimes the braying of the beasts made him overlook the details of the wayside; but never did he lose track of his destination or falter in the going.

There was his duty to his people (his family claimed he was always neglecting them for their neighbors), but he felt he belonged to his flock first of all. Wishing to keep close to them he devised the red-flag signals. And on his rounds of the village in the early dusk if there was a red flag sticking up at the turn of the road he took that turning, no matter how many irate brethren waited for him in council meeting. Sometimes to administer to the sick, sometimes to marry the young, sometimes just because folks were blue. By the time he had disposed of several red flags, the meeting would be almost out, and it was true that when he did get there he usually made his counselors revise the whole course of procedure. He knew he was a thorn in the flesh of the up-and-coming youngsters who wanted all things right on the dot. But he would think of calm, chewing Shadrach Gaunt, who usually insisted on accompanying him on these midnight forays, waiting patiently outside a lonely house, always there after council meeting to see him home — he would think of Shadrach's vast indifference to public opinion and be comforted; for the world would wag a long time after they were all dead, and he believed in taking his time and letting the answers to his problems just come around. Men didn't colonize in a hurry — you had to sink into the feeling of a country; win acceptance, not demand it.

He had quite a time being a nurse, counselor, and miracle-worker all in one. He was reminded of Brother Brigham when a one-legged man came to him demanding to be healed. 'What!' said Brother Brigham. 'Would you have three legs in eternity!' But he felt if he could just never forget to laugh at the idea of *himself* ordering other people's lives, his vision would keep clear and his faith not bog down. As for the grumblers — well, there'd always be some folks who wouldn't understand.

This problem of the alkali, for instance, so foreign to anyone's experience that they had called it snow at first. Now these early spring mornings the children all over town crouched among the immaculate garden rows, scraping off the crust of white mineral formed during the night. There were diseased strips even among the fertile Virgin and Santa Clara bottom-lands.

He was responsible for several hundred families in a hostile country, six bitter weeks from help — even if the half-fed oxen could have held up for six weeks. Thank God for alfilaria and bunch grass; he smiled when he remembered how every one of the early pioneers, from Brother Brigham on down, had disdained those clumps, yellow and summer-dried, when they had first seen them on the Plains, and how the cattle and sheep had been unhesitatingly wiser. Bunch grass would grow on barren hills, and although the clumps were green now in the early spring, even when strawlike with the heat of August they were still nutritious; and well he knew how the autumn rains would bring forth, amazingly, a new green shoot within each withered stalk.

But there were no kindly clumps for humans. Of the seeds his people brought with them — cottonseed and cane seed and flax seed, bran and barley — he knew that even now some of the poorer families were making mush for food. Others were sending their sons to hunt quail and rabbits and sage hens. He had visited one family dining on an owl. More and more the brothers were borrowing from their medicine chests asafetida to rub fishhooks with which to catch chub and carp and suckers, and, very rarely, an alien salmon bucking the turgid currents of the Virgin.

The problem of drinking water was almost as bad as that of food. There was talk of sinking an artesian well. Meanwhile, the springs gushing from the sides of the Red Hill were strong with alkali salts, and the river water was so thick with red mud and had such a disastrous effect on those who drank it that already settlers spoke of it as 'Virgin bloat.' Many a time Erastus had rested on a ditch bank beside a man who stoked himself for another six hours of bucking a breaking plow through the cooked topsoil with a solitary chunk of bread dipped in 'Virgin bloat.' Crops bought at such a price *had* to bring a harvest.

He was glad most of those shadowed-green squares he could see were in corn; fall wheat would take another year and a half. Besides, it was surprising how much more corn than wheat a man could get out of an acre of ground. Four months to wait for your own corn meal, hand-ground and baked with sour milk on a johnnyboard before an open fire!

But right now food was not to be bought. Flour was twenty-five dollars per hundred — many a man would have mortgaged an acre of land for a sack of flour. Sugar was one dollar a pound, molasses four dollars a gallon; one hundred dollars for a thousand feet of lumber less than fifty miles away; a sheep for a pound of tea was a common bargain, or a pound of tea for two weeks' service of mules. Tobacco was the worst. Brother Brigham said that 'as Latter-Day-Saints we are against tobacco, but as Mormons we use quite a bit!' And Erastus found the old-timers smoking Indian *toquap*, or red willow bark roasted and pulverized, or trading a passing freighter half a crop of cotton for a caddy of tobacco.

Usually he was amazed at the variety of substitutes his people were continually finding here in the wilderness, a unique land calling forth unique ways of living. Housewives utilizing even the hated 'saleratus,' the white alkali, in place of baking soda; hunting in mica deposits for the alum-bearing rock, the alum for canker; making 'coal' from green weeds piled and packed with dirt, a fire started in some loose bark underneath and enough air let in to char but not to burn — a 'coal' whose lasting heat surprised even Erastus.

Here was Steadfast Weeks, the doctor, setting a leg with the aid of the foul-smelling Jimson Weed or moonflower beloved of the Indian medicine-man who called it *nea-nump*, or crazy plant.

One night Erastus was called to administer to a family who had eaten mesquite bread, made Indian fashion — the sweetish mesquite beans ground in a coffee mill and mixed half-and-half with flour. The father had soberly taken Erastus to one side: 'I don't see how them danged Injuns get along! It bound *us* all so tight, I's afraid we'd have to have a midwife come deliver us!'

Always, after discovering a settler enthusiastic over some new idea, his spirit would soar with fresh confidence. What couldn't he accomplish with such a people?

Not slacking the work on the Social Hall (already there was a kiln, and they were burning lime over by the knoll someone had dubbed 'Molly's nipple'), they had at the same time built a temporary bowery, four hundred and fifty-eight by thirty-five feet, on the northeast quarter of the public square, with a wooden chandelier grooved for candles and the willow-twined benches from the old bowery in rows below the raised dirt pulpit. Pending the granting of the city charter, their first community act in the bowery had been to elect a mayor, two aldermen, and three councilors. Some trouble was had with disgruntled citizens like Zebedee Trupp (called by Brother Brigham because he was a chair-maker), who wanted an office, but in general proceedings were shipshape.

Laws were tentatively drawn up making it 'unlawful to use with disrespect the name of the Deity' and 'to become publicly intoxicated so as to endanger the peace and quiet of the community' — penalty, labor on the public highway. Erastus didn't believe much in the old whipping post of early Salt Lake days; the country needed roads (which were going to be difficult to build anyway in a land so chopped up), and he believed if a man transgressed against his fellows that he should pay with something they needed. But although he encouraged a heavy poll tax ('six days' labor be levied on all male persons over the age of sixteen years or the equivalent of two dollars per day in cash — and all persons owning slaves held accountable to pay the same amount for each slave'), he also strove to be scrupulously fair. 'Two dollars per day for faithful labor of able-bodied men, and *for boys or lazy men a proper and just deduction to be made.*'

And as he sat there in the pale March sunlight gazing out over the valley he could peer straight down the first road his poll tax had built — a road like a red gash directly bisecting the center of town all the way to the river. Bounding the cleared lots, his rock wall cut across the road and shut in the town from Black Ridge to Black Ridge, kept the cattle from their unfenced gardens and —

he hoped — Indians out and the settlers in. He thought of Brother Brigham, who had wanted 'a rock wall so high around the Territory it will be impossible for gentiles to get over it.' Where the road met the rock wall stood a big wooden gate. While there were still unclaimed lots high in brush above the wall, below it brush crowded the red gash of the road as thickly as bristles on a porcupine. About a mile beyond the gate, the red gash almost lost itself in the neat and furrowed acres of the community cotton field and lucerne patch. For that bit of lucerne seed tied up in a handkerchief and brought back from Australia by a missionary, Erastus had traded a whole sack of grain.

Yes — he packaged and tied the day's thoughts — it looked as if civilization was coming to stay. Of course, like death and taxes, there were always the Indians ...

He shivered suddenly in the wind that seldom slept up here on the Sugar Loaf, and peered out through the gathering dusk at the four pine poles, the tallest his men had been able to find, shooting upward in the yard of each most outlying home on the fringe of the settlement. He dreaded the day when someone would run to tell him that a pole fluttered its white-diaper danger signal. Indians! And then there would be the thud-thud of the old bass drum in the bowery, and white-faced citizens fleeing to the square. But perhaps that fear would never materialize, perhaps there never would be the jutting war smoke in the valleys, and only, as now, the tranquil ribbon that floated from the South Mountains, a sign of peace and token for friendship.

Erastus did not worry about the local Paiutes, timid root-diggers. Most of them were baptized into the Church. But the thieving Navajos from beyond the Colorado, like the Uintahs and Pavants of the North, plundered and pillaged any people, white or red. They were a constant menace to the community sheep herds and sometimes they tackled the cattle closer in. They hunted weaker tribes in the spring of the year when they were famished and helpless, and caught and fattened papooses to sell to Mexican slave-traders. A girl brought one hundred to two hundred dollars in her teens, a boy one hundred dollars. Sometimes even the starving Paiutes themselves traded a child for a horse — they could eat the horse. But Brother Hamblin could handle the Navajos, even if they wouldn't be baptized. And Erastus settled back once more to his contemplation.

There was a newly organized Citizens' Mail Service which brought letters from Cedar Fort and forwarded one's Salt Lake letters after they had waited there only nine days.

There was the Drinking Hour: every morning at five o'clock each house poured out a son or a father, bucket in hand, to go to the ditch flowing by the nearest sidewalk and carry water for the Drinking Barrel. Cows were corralled during this hour — and there was inexorably the stray pen for those who got out. Each householder carried twenty to thirty gallons to fill his gunny-sack-covered barrel with its tin cup; this had to last for all home use until the next day.

The Council, wishing they could corral children as well as cattle, searched all over to find the ugliest man in town for water master; the ugliest man so that he might scare the youngsters from piddling in the stream, and yet a responsible man because there were many troubles among water-users — in a desert country a man's watering turn was his most indispensable possession. The ugliest man was Ole Oleson, a Swedish convert, a friendly fellow with huge red ears, a bald head, and a turned-up nose, almost entirely flattened, so that his black nostrils were the focal part of his face. He had been wont to sell cheese from door to door, intoning, 'I'm both sheese-maka, a-sheese-peddla!' And folks had been wont to push up their noses and pull out their ears and mock him after he had passed by. But now little boys and girls regarded him with new wide-eyed respect and somehow began to get the Old Nick all mixed up with cheese.

There was the school, of course, the very nucleus of civilization. It was held in a willow house with a large flat rock in the center

for a desk when the pupils wished to write. Every week they
trekked to the hills to search for slate-rock. The teacher, young
Benjamin Jarvis, would have liked to equip the school with Wil-
son's Readers, 1 to 4, the Blue-Backed Speller, and a number
book on arithmetic, but the scholars came with anything from the
Book of Mormon to an old newspaper. So Benjamin taught his
classes to chant, since several classes could thus carry on in the
same room. And when Erastus visited, he was likely to hear the
Great Lakes and rivers being chanted in one corner and the multi-
plication tables being chanted in another, or the States and Terri-
tories and their capitals from 'Washington, Olympia,' to 'Maine,
Augusta,' being chanted all the way across the continent. And
when a child misspelled 'cow,' he was sent to water her; when he
misspelled 'weeds,' to pull them.

Every morning at four o'clock civilization began with the
pealing of Abijah MacIntyre's copper prayer bell with which he
routed out his flock. This had been given him by Brother Brigham, the wooden handle worn smooth by many graspings, the
iron knocker having a sweet but imperative summons which
echoed at the same moment daily, stirring all the sleeping valley.
Shortly after came the cowbells, and a blast from the herder's tin
horn as he drove the community cows down through Main Street
to the pasture near the river, shouting at his charges and throwing
his expert stones at the ugly ones, not killing the critter but stun-
ning and deflecting it. And then the school bell with a louder,
harsher tone.

But when occasionally gentile wagon trains would rumble
through the village on their way to California, Erastus was not so
sure civilization had come. For sometimes the bullwhackers had
named their oxen after the heads of the Church and considered
it a good joke to roll slowly along the street yelling, 'Giddap,
Brigham, damn your hide! Haw, there, Heber, you bastard!'
And the settlers would stand and stare with clenched fists.

3

'Sheba stumbled down the three shallow steps of the dugout,
ducked under the low roof whose still-green twigs projected from
the packed dirt and fringed all the eaves, and peered through the
smoke at the girl kneeling before the sod hearth.

'Oh, it's you, Aunt 'Sheba! I'm afraid it don't draw very
well ——'

'Your flue's probably stopped up,' said 'Sheba, clearing her
throat, anxious to conclude her errand and escape. 'But, land
sakes, you ain't ready to move in yet anyway! Why, you only
mudded your walls last week!'

She scratched a finger-nail along the still-damp earth of the
wall.

'They won't be dry for another couple days. . . . Bottom your
floor good now and you won't have so much dust later on.' And
remember' — she peered into the low, dark shadows — '"sweep
the corners and the middle of the floor will sweep itself." . . .
Land, it's black as pitch in here, I'll give you one of the candles
to use in place of that bitch; think me on it in the morning . . .
And a strip of carpet to put there in front of your fire. There's
those two big boxes at my house you can use for a table and a
cupboard . . .'

She cleared her throat again.

'But what I come to tell you was that . . . I guess I c'n loan you
one of the rockers.'

Clory was speechless. In her wildest dreams she had never
dared hope for one of the rockers.

'Thank you!' she cried in a put-on voice, and wondered yet
again why it was Aunt 'Sheba's kindness clogged in her throat.

Why should she resent 'Sheba's bossing so much? Someone had
to be boss. And it was right for the first wife to appoint who to do
what. . . . Clory usually said her prayers down under the covers in
bed, cheating the Lord, but tonight for punishment she knelt long
and earnestly on the cold boards of the wagon box.

When Abijah drove out of the big gates that morning, pulling his striped knitted wristlets on under his coat, three women followed him with their eyes. The curl of his brown hair brushing the collar of his homespun coat glinted in the early sun, and just as he turned and lifted his hat in a gay good-bye, his magnificent beard shone as if with a life of its own. The triangle of cheek not hidden by the springing hairs bunched with his smile, and his russet eyes narrowed with laughter.

They've all got that trick, thought Clory, watching him; every one of his children — that trick of half-shutting their eyes when laughing.

Until his wagon was swallowed by the brush, the three women did not move. There was something about having Brother Mac around — the very air seemed to crackle with his anger, sparkle with his gaiety, throb with his tenderness. His presence dwarfed the largest room, made the sickest woman reach for a looking-glass. Three women turned again to their tasks remembering the bigness of him — big chest, big voice; the way he smacked his lips over his food and his eyes darted and sparkled; the grace of him, slightly stocky with middle-age, but unstooping, never giving in; his verve, his zest for life.

But only one woman thought of him in complete surrender. One sighed with relief because his vitality wearied her. The other shrank from thinking of him at all, since she could not remember him without a sense of confusion, shame, and something else that was like the sensuous stroke of fingers over her skin.

Abijah himself was complacent as he threaded his wagon through the brush. The lot looked fine; this summer he'd put up a new stake-and-rider fence, a nice gate at the end of the path that led to the sidewalk from the Sibley tent, some day neat white pickets, and plant cottonwood saplings along the ditch bank. He was doing pretty well — a man could get along anywhere if he just used his head. 'The Lord helps those...' Everybody knew a pair of mules was worth four times as much as an ox team, and yet he had just yesterday wound up a shrewd dicker with Lars Hansen, his new neighbor on his right trading Bluchy and Whitey, his oldest steers, along with some seed and several sacks of grain (luckily his ranch had yielded an excellent harvest last year before they had left the City), for the finest span of matched mules he had ever seen in his life! He hummed with that sense of well-being that comes from getting the upper hand of someone in a bargain, and reflected that he still had the best of his oxen left; the couple plodding along ahead of him this morning were stout fellows — it took oxen to pull a breaking plow through new ground; mules or horses couldn't do it. But well-curried mules could certainly whizz a buggy up in front of church with a flourish! And if this next harvest amounted to anything he intended to get a new surrey, first thing; meanwhile Free was back at the lot patching up the old buckboard.

Abijah saw himself dashing along Main Street before all the Conference visitors with — say — Clorinda beside him. He flattered himself that at last he'd got his wives to behaving; they'd been harmony itself this morning. He hoped uneasily Clorinda Agatha had forgotten that business over Free by now. Abijah was ashamed of himself in his heart when he thought of that scene before the Council. But he'd been so damned mad. Since then he hadn't visited Clorinda much, but of course there was the rule about pregnancy. And it was hard on a man to stay away. A man like himself with plenty of red blood. Clorinda was the only one of his wives ... Bathsheba and Willie were both — well ... The little minx was probably tamed by now, he reassured himself for the thousandth time. But with a woman like Clorinda you never could tell. You never could tell.

Back at the house Bathsheba, looking up from the scrub-board to watch Clory take the clothespin from her mouth and clamp the wet woolen edge of Abijah's garment-leg expertly to the line, also reflected that you never could tell. In spite of the fact that she'd routed Clorinda out of bed at half-past four this morning, she still hadn't got much out of the girl. That Hansen woman next door had beat her getting her whites on the line.

Clory had worked almost to the end of the taut rope strung across the back dooryard nearly to the corral, where it was fastened to a pole; near the pole stood a weatherbeaten buckboard from under which protruded a man's long booted legs. The man lay on a tarpaulin underneath the buckboard tightening the bolts of the running gear and there was the sound of hammering; now and then the hammering stopped and the man would wriggle out his head bright as ripe wheat in the sun and squint up at the girl and grin lazily. Even as she whipped another dripping garment free of wrinkles and pinned it securely, she would droop one eyelid in reply and purse her lips in the most ridiculous fashion. They had a code of little winks and grimaces, and 'Sheba, who had seen the by-play before, thought if the Lord knew what she suspected between these two and let it run on, He wasn't as respectable as she'd always thought Him to be.

Joseph, fresh from his sheep for a day in town, squatting on his heels, lacing a new cinch ring on Free's saddle in the hope that Free would be more generous with Nellie, pinched the end of the thong between his teeth and enjoyed the little drama. He was vastly amused at his mother and the whole kit-and-boodle, but personally he considered Free a fool to court so much trouble over any bunch of petticoats.

Clory, serenely unconscious of anyone's speculations, carried the empty basket back for another filling. The wash-bench and the heavy iron kettle (it had been a hatter's dye pot someone had brought across the plains in '47), slung over the depression where the flames licked its black sides, were set some distance back from the Sibley tent. Abijah planned to shade the wash-bench; he had planted a budding cottonwood tree and tied it to the clothespole for support — the circle of damp earth at the roots was still loose from the transplanting — and he hoped before many years to shelter the whole washing apparatus with a grapevine arbor, but meanwhile the women worked stark to the sun. Clory found this pleasant; her only demand of life at the moment was that they might finish before Pal came. The sheets and pillowcases were already dry and in the house; as 'Sheba stirred the last batch of bubbling whites, Clory rinsed and wrung the few pieces left in the blueing water and carried them again to the far end of the line. There were only the coloreds left, she thought; then they were through.

She reeled suddenly from the constant bending.

Free called: 'Hey! Take it easy!'

Wrinkling her nose at him, she turned to the line with busy fingers. But her heart went out to the figure under the buckboard. It was getting so she was almost afraid to be around him any more. Abijah had made people think things — nasty things, so that they stared and whispered. There was a 'scalp-hunting' next week — all week the boys would hunt 'scalp,' and on Friday the side that had the fewest rabbits, squirrels, or quail would cook supper for the others. It would be fun, but they always managed to put her on Free's side ... And there was the dooryard dance afterward, with a member of the bishopric there to supervise. They were sure to play 'post-office' — Free always did call her out for a letter with a stamp on it, and she never could seem to act unconcerned after one of his hasty pecks in the dark of the woodshed. Lately once or twice at the table she had surprised desperation in his eyes; he was like a man going through life on a quest to which he could see no end. She knew he was increasingly reckless, putting Nellie at all the highest fences, daring the greater wrath of his father, forfeiting the community pleasures that should have been his. It was all her fault, but the knowledge was powerless against the soft bloom in her heart. Abijah's touch could make her shiver, but the feeling she had for Free was entirely precious, as glad as sunshine, as gentle as rain. She longed to cradle that stubborn, wayward head against her breast, to shield it from all the storms of life. She sang as she worked,

... put a kiss
Within the cu-up ...

But the tenderness that muted the flute-notes in her voice had
nothing to do with the song.

Free, hearing her, swung the hammer viciously. Even on a day
like today when he could glimpse her occasionally, when he could
hear her singing, when he could merge all his worries into work
with his hands — always he was happiest when his knowing
fingers were splicing, sawing — even today, spared those long
hours of brooding behind a slow ox team when his thoughts, unused to abstractions, galloped aimlessly around and around the
ugly thing squatting squarely in the middle of his brain, even
today when the ferment inside of him ran out into hammer blows,
he knew it was no use. He could not tear her out of his vitals.
They could cut him off from God and all His angels, but the passion that got him by the throat and shook him until he was weak
would still possess him utterly. He no longer believed he was bad
— he had prayed on his knees, and he did not believe God would
fill him so full of this senseless, lovely longing, if He did not know
what He was about; but it was no longer a question of wrong or
right.

Willie, whose job was the housework, hobbled around the tent
with some table-scraps for the swill barrel. Pregnancy had aggravated her rheumatism so that she walked more than ever like a
mechanical, jointed doll whose spring is never quite wound up,
and the shapeless black Mother Hubbard made her look like a
spare, stoop-shouldered scarecrow.

Clory, smiling at her, dreaded her own time for Mother Hubbards to begin. Already she had had to let out the basque seams
of the linsey-woolsey. She was a little amused at her growing
plumpness, she who had boasted of the tiniest waist in Salt Lake
City. But hoops were awfully good to hide growing bulges. She
wondered if she could get into the red cassimere for Conference.

Willie, bending over the swill, retched violently at the sour smell, and clutched at the barrel for support.

Angry rebellion surged up in Clory's throat against 'Sheba and her remorseless energy; 'Sheba, who despised all weakness, had borne all her children with the greatest of ease, up and doing her own housework on the fourth day, and expected other women to do likewise.

Willie ought to be in bed. But 'Sheba's caustic tongue would keep her on her feet until she dropped. There was no reason to crowd three days' work into one.

'She ought to see a doctor!'

'Nonsense,' snapped 'Sheba, straightening up from the washboard to flick a lock of hair out of her eyes. 'He'd only salivate her till she couldn't keep her teeth in her head! Besides, there ain't a doctor ——'

'Oh, yes, there is, Ma,' cried Joseph on his way to the barn with the mended harness — 'travelin' through, camped in the square. I seen him last night standin' in his wagon door with a big bright oil lamp behind him, makin' handkerchiefs disappear up his sleeve; honest, Ma! An' usin' fine words and passin' around big black bottles of medicine that would cure warts an' moles an', an'' — he suddenly began to quote in a mincing falsetto — '"late-discovered art of electricity especially good for female complaints!"'

'Why, you — you ——' 'Sheba spatted soapsuds from her hands and started after him, but the boy grinned back at her and dodged through the corral gate.

'Sheba plunged back to the washboard wrathfully. She couldn't think what the younger generation was coming to. He shouldn't have been listening to such talk in the first place. Seemed like she made out to do a day's work and trouble was all she got for her pains. Here she was, almost wore out with the fatigue, and all she asked of that trashy Willie was to redd up the table and take care of the victuals. Willie, always crippling around with her scrawny neck, her bosom flat as a squaw track ...

Pal came while they were in the midst of the coloreds. In her placid way she appraised the situation, gave 'Sheba a glance of distaste from her china-blue eyes, and was not a whit upset by Clory's apologetic flutterings. She merely took off her hoops, tied on one of 'Sheba's voluminous waist-aprons, and began to help rinse-and-hang-out. There was nothing mixed-up about Pal; she was as honest as well water. Clory thought, how different people were inside! There was Pal's open-hearted frankness — blurting the truth to everyone just as she thought it — her spurts of anger soon over and forgotten, never holding a grudge. Abijah blurted things out, too, but he did not always say exactly what he thought; his words were too tangled with his emotions — she gave him up; she never had been able to understand him.

Sloshing clear water around the black kettle, emptying it onto the red coals so that they hissed and shot up steam, Clory looked inside herself. She saw there a hidden shyness, a too-deep capacity for suffering, a tendency to lie to keep from hurting people's feelings, a soft, overgenerous self craving gaiety above righteousness ...

'You'd better fill up those tubs before you go,' admonished 'Sheba, carrying a basket fluffy with dried clothes into the tent. 'Do you want them to fall to staves?'

Pal started for the water barrel with a bucket, and Clory hastily turned the wooden tubs up on their bottoms again.

The two girls walked arm in arm toward the dugout. It was a good two hours until dinner-time.

'I'd like to have a vinegar pie,' said Clory, her mind busy with the thought that the usual washday dinner of beans and boiled pudding wouldn't be very tasty, and how she, Clory, would like to entertain her friend in her own house: the pie in the bake-skillet, coals heaped around it and on its head so that the filling, not too dry with flour, not too sweet with molasses, not too sour with vinegar, and the crust browned to a turn ...

'I might's well not have a house,' said Clory crossly; 'I have
to wash with her and spin with her and eat with her! I can't even
have a backhouse of my own!'

'Never mind,' Pal comforted; 'maybe it'll be different when
the baby comes.'

Clory shook her head and nursed her rebellious brooding. In
any other part of the land a girl her age would be learning to be a
lady like the ones in the Godey's magazines, working cross-stitch
samplers, making crazy-quilts, playing the harmonium with all
possible melancholy, and swooning comfortably in the direction
of every marriageable male ...

She giggled suddenly and looked at Pal, who squeezed her
and giggled back as if she knew exactly what she had been thinking.

Over at the dugout the two girls worked in happy absorption. There was the door to be hung — of cottonwood sticks
fastened together by pegs, and a linsey blanket over them.

('I know a new complexion pack — bran and vinegar, and the
beaten yolks of three eggs ...'

'Aunt 'Sheba says manure ...')

There were the dishes to be got out, the tin wash-basin and
pitcher made in the tin shop in the City ('Sheba had a blue china
set imported from the East!); the wooden buttermilk tub, with
its butter mold having the oak-leaf and acorn pattern.

('They're going to start baptizin' next Wednesday.'

'I know. Last time in the City Aunt 'Sheba went in sixty-five
times for the dead.')

Her heavy flatiron (Abijah had had some lighter ones made up
for 'Sheba out of old Johnston's Army wagon tires); her two jugs,
the shitbrindle-colored one, brought from England by Willie in
'57 and spurned by 'Sheba because it was too narrow-necked for
preserves; and the brown earthen one with ears, and on its side a
picture where the paint was beginning to peel at strategic points
in the lady's costume.

('I couldn't meet you last Sunday because Abijah made me read Scripture.'

'What'd you do?'

'I dug steps and broke the Sabbath. 'Sheba told on me.'

'He'd never punish her!'

'No, she'd scratch his eyes out. But see, that's it; I'm neither his child nor his wife ——')

Her tin tea-caddy, her nutmeg grater — and how she longed for a silver vinaigrette!

('I'm going to cut up my second-best petticoat for a window curtain . . .')

There was the mug bordered with '*Utah Pioneer Jubilee (1847)*' surrounded by oxen, handcarts, and Indians; there was the white china plate with the picture of the Nauvoo Temple in the center and '*Holiness to the Lord, the House of the Lord,*' scrolled beneath it, and the names of the Twelve — Brigham Young, Heber C. Kimball, Parley P. Pratt, and all the others — printed in gilt around the edge. (This had been given to her father in Winter Quarters by Brother Brigham himself.) Each dish Clory dusted lovingly, as a woman will who has dreamed all her life of a home of her own.

Finally, there was the little rosewood writing desk that had belonged to her mother. This, Clory had to show Pal — how it opened out like a book, and within, the phial with genuine ivory case studded with gold pins. Clory brooded over the tiny prism of hand-blown glass upon her palm.

'My uncle got them in a bazaar in Spain when he was a jack-tar under Lord Nelson — they were from India . . .'

She handed the little bottle to Pal, who wafted it beneath her turned-up nose and sniffed delightedly.

The musk odor still clung, breathing across the years of voluptuous luxury, of old, far-off romance.

'These,' said Clory, 'are the only things I have that I really want to preserve. The only things good enough for the world

we're making for our children. I can just see my daughter sitting
at the rosewood desk writing perfumed notes . . .'

Practical Pal laughed, and Clory grinned sheepishly and
turned to her prosaic gourd bowls. There was just room left in the
cupboard for them.

('Free says he'll put down flat rocks for me for a floor as
soon as he gets time — and maybe Abijah will let me have a walk
and a gate of my own . . .')

When the iron spider and patty-pans and 'Sheba's cast-off
brass bucket, worn so thin you could dent it with your fingernail,
were beside the hearth, Clory and Pal surveyed their handiwork
and broke into excited chatterings.

There was a picture for each wall. One, a gilt-framed embroidered motto on cross-stitch scrim, '*Welcome to All,*' in shaded
pink and green. The other was a wreath of shiny brown paper
cut in a pattern of pomegranate leaves and blossoms and gilt
doves; in the center of the wreath were two clasped hands, and
around the inside of the wreath ran wilted gilt words: '*In memory
of Will* —— *Born* —— *Died* —— *Rest in Peace.*'

'It isn't everybody whose pictures are all hand-made,' said Pal.
'Your red sunbonnet will look pretty on the mantel. We'd better
put *Child's History of England* and *Little Lily's Travels* there, too.'

'I wish I had cloth to cover the walls. Marianne Snow's house
is 'dobie with a horse block in the dooryard so ladies can enter a
wagon without climbing the wheel, and an iron foot-scraper at
the door. Real tony . . . I wish 'Sheba would give me the cathedral clock; she don't need it with the eight-day brass they brought
down. And the dulcimer — no one over there knows how to play
it . . . oh, yes, my memory gem!'

Clory had to run to the wagon for the postcard won for punctuality at the Washington Mousley School in the City:

> A kiss for a blow always bestow
> And angels will guard you
> Wherever you go.

And this had to be tacked below the wreath.

'You won that when you were in the Fourth Reader, didn't you? Pretty lucky, in lots of ways, Clory; not many girls get as many years of schooling ... Do you remember how we were taught to syllabicate? "Go into a room by yourself, stand as if facing the class, and read the lesson five times aloud" ...'

Clory nodded, her eyes suddenly dreamy.

'Do you remember our skating and dancing club? And bathing at Hot Springs?'

'And our house with its row of poplars, and rosebush at the doorway, and the creeper trellised on the porch ——'

'And do you remember how exciting it was around the Salt Lake House when the stagecoach came in — the yellow lanterns moving about the stable door and the fine ladies ——'

'And the little locust trees under buckets and the campers on Main Street, and Immigration Square with the wagon-trains stopping, and people coming out of the stores with packages ——'

Pal stopped for breath. Clory's eyes were shining.

'And that day we watched that man from Montana give two thousand dollars in gold for four bushels of wheat and how the gold dust ran out of his buckskin sack like coarse bran, and the cashier kept running his magnet through it to clean out the dirt — and how we went on down to the Fountain Shop afterwards for our drink of water-and-sugar-and-soda and we wouldn't wait for it to quit foaming and the waiter got disgusted!'

'And putting on *Moses in the Bulrushes* in the Social Hall and you were the princess —?'

'And I remember the times with Luna Young —— How thrilled we were when we first got permission to sit on the lion in front of the Lion House. ... I used to stand on one of those tiny balconies and gaze across at the Temple and wonder if it would be finished in time for me to go through it and do work for the dead and — and be married for time and all eternity ——'

Clory could not go on. How tell even Pal the longing that sometimes filled her heart for those carefree days?

Suddenly they were clinging to each other.

'I want to go back, Clory! I want to go back! Do you realize no mail's got through since we first come down? I haven't heard from my folks for nearly four whole months!'

'And I'll never hear from mine,' said Clory somberly.

'I'm sick of this place, Clory.'

'Yes,' said Clory slowly, 'so am I, but ——'

'I — I'm going to have a baby, too, Clory. I guess it's for true. And I'm afraid. I'm afraid with only midwives! You know David won't let me have Stiddy Weeks any more than Abijah'd let you, because it 'ud be going agin counsel! I want to go back to Mamma and Papa. David is tickled, but *he* isn't having it! And we're so poor I've got to cut up my lavender-gray alpaca for a layette — or else do like that woman in Washington who boiled down an old tent canvas ——' She giggled hysterically and wiped her eyes.

'Don't you love David, Pal?' Clory's voice was gentle. Seeing Pal get worked up was somehow alarming.

'Yes, of course I do! And David says I'm all he wants and if he has his way he never will take another wife ——'

Clory drew a long breath.

'*And he's young and all yours . . .*'

Clory laughed suddenly at her friend's woebegone face.

'Come on, I'll show you *my* layette!'

Out in the barn the broody hen slashing with angry beak at the girl's hand, and clucking with outraged indignation, finally waddled off the nest. Clory displayed proudly the dozen warm eggs.

'Free says, if Abijah will let us, he'll build me a pullet coop when they're hatched . . .'

Pal was all admiration.

'You're so brave, Clory!' Her eyes narrowed in unexpected shrewdness. 'And it's harder for you to be brave, too, because you've got so much imagination!'

Clory's gaze was abstracted, eager.

'No. I beller like a calf if I don't get my own way. But come on; I want to show you my cotton.'

Beyond the dugout the land was laid out in clean red humps.

'I was crazy to have flowers but I figgered they could wait, and so I shoveled and hoed that ground myself, early mornings before breakfast. I've got fourteen rows there, and Abijah says I should get three or four hundred pounds . . . See?'

She displayed her palms where fresh blisters had formed over the calluses.

'I guess I never will have decent-looking hands again. . . . But if only the alkali ain't too bad in that land I'll have a layette!'

Touching a sod with her toe, she almost stepped on the snake before she saw it. She shrieked and leaped back, clapping a hand to her mouth.

The rattler was coiling like a long gray bowel. Pal screamed. But Free was suddenly there, panting.

'What is it? Oh . . .' He ran to get the shovel.

The snake had its head raised now, mouth open, spitting tongue in action. Its angry, staccato rattle filled the air.

Free's first blow missed, but the second struck off the head neatly, and the mottled skin slipped down the body an inch or two. He put his foot on the bare neck and grabbed hold of the skin, peeling it off like the outside of a banana. The flesh was the salmon color of trout, and there was a fat-cushioned crease straight down the center of the back.

'Injuns would roast it and eat it,' said Free, strutting a little before the girls.

'Sheba had come up behind them and stood staring balefully at Clory's still-white face.

'This means your baby will be marked, young lady! I knew a woman once who seen a wasp beforehand, and ——'

Clory cried out as if someone had struck her.

'Serves you right for lallygaggin' around when you should have been in the house helpin' ready the eatables!'

4

One evening during the middle of the next week, when they were at dinner and Abijah, with much pushing aside of heavy beard and mustaches, had just placed the curved bar of his mustache cup against his mouth for a long drink of scalding Brigham tea, there was such a knocking at the door that the tent shook.

Abijah put down his cup.

'Come in,' he boomed, 'and stop that racket!'

It was one of Apostle Snow's boys.

'Dad says to tell you,' he panted, 'Porter Rockwell just got in with a packmule! He come a-bustin' into the yard where I was shootin' Chinies, and right while his horse was still a-gallopin', blowed off the head of one of our old hens and says to me, "Take that to your ma and tell her I'm here!"'

'Hawckk!'... Abijah was beaming. 'That means mail ——'

'Yes,' the boy nodded, his eyes big; 'letters to be cried off on the stand tomorrow morning; and Brother Orson Pratt's here, too — joined him at the Big Sand ——'

'— and Conference,' continued Abijah. 'You womenfolks had better get your duds ready. We won't wait for April now ... And Freeborn, you had better plan to go back with Brother Porter and collect the rent on the farm and see if you can pick up some flour ... Better take the buckboard ... And tell that Mart Tyler I want the rest of what he still owes me on them pigs!'

Abijah drew a long, pleased breath.

'My conscience,' he cried, 'it will seem good to see a newspaper!'

The men had banded together in clubs to subscribe for extras, so that they might get the latest news from the front; they planned to meet at one another's homes and have someone read the news aloud, and they had hoped before now to promote a pony express to the City. They were particularly anxious to get

Harper's Weekly and *Frank Leslie's Illustrated Weekly* with their line drawings of the war made by staff artists in the field, and the *New York Times*. Any sort of paper from the East cost one dollar just for the trip alone — which still wasn't much considering how transportation was looking up — one thousand miles through Indian country in ten days. There had been a pony express started from the Missouri to San Francisco last year, and now it seemed there was a new company called Wells Fargo taking over.

Although Apostle Erastus was late as usual the next morning, the congregation arrived early and stood about in clusters in front of the bowery. The talk churned on speculations about the war. Most of the Saints were not averse to the Union cause, even though they felt themselves to be apart from the quarrel. Brother Brigham, for his part, promised to keep the Indians quiet, which was quite a job over a thousand miles of plain. And last October, when the telegraph line was completed from Missouri to Salt Lake City, Brother Brigham sent as the first message to bridge the wastes, 'Utah has not seceded but is firm for the Constitution and the laws of our once happy country...'

Erastus finally came and strolled up to the stand, writhing his lips in affectionate greeting. Porter Rockwell, eyes as fierce as ever but long hair graying, opened the buckskin sack and took out the letters — foolscap or the coarse product of the paper mill in the City, unsealed, and tied with buckskin thongs; Erastus cried them off. There was one scribbled in the South's emergency ink, pokeberry juice, on the torn flyleaf of a book — Washington settlement was violently sympathetic to the Confederacy. A new gored skirt pattern for the ladies that every woman in town would borrow. A new war song — already feminine heads bunched over the tune:

> Must I be a soldier's daughter?
> Does that mean I must not cry ——

Erastus licked a shuffling thumb:

'Palmyra Wight!'

Watching Pal's David go radiantly up the aisle, Clory clenched her fists. This was the ceremony she had always dreaded ever since she could remember.

There were several communications of public interest, including messages from Brother Brigham.

The city charter had been granted with provisions for lighting the streets with gas. St. George had been made the county seat and the settlers must get at the building of a courthouse. The new Governor Dawson, President Lincoln's appointee, whose opening speech to a disgruntled people was an accusation of disloyalty, had attempted the seduction of a Mormon girl as his first act, tried to escape, but had been waylaid by her relatives at Mountain Dell and soundly beaten.

There was a murmur of approval throughout the congregation at this news; they had suffered at the hands of such a long line of scalawag federal officials. Abraham Lincoln had promised to let them alone if they'd let him alone, but he hadn't kept his word — and now there were more rumblings about polygamy. Whose business was it how many wives a man had?

Abijah MacIntyre got to his feet.

'Cur-rsed injustice! Ar-re we who have settled and developed the countr-ry at the risk o' our lives and the lives of our dear-r ones never to have any say in the gover-rnment of it? Are we to bow our necks for-rever to the foisting upon us o' the States' offscourings, to surrender into their-r wicked hands the very principle for which we came out here in the fir-rst place?'

There were sly grins at Abijah's rhetoric, but all over, heads were nodding agreement. He spoke truth. For five years the States had shouted from the housetops, 'Down with those twin relics of barbarism: polygamy and slavery!' Well, slavery was being taken care of. And when the war was over...

Erastus announced as the text of his sermon Doctrine and

Covenants, sec. xxx, xiii, verse 27: '*I say unto ye, be one; and if ye are not one, ye are not mine.*' He led off with a quotation from the Prophet's revelation of December 12, 1832, on the Civil War, and reminded the people of Brother Brigham's visit to the Indian Mission here in '54, when he had prophesied: 'If you are united you will be blest, but if you allow the spirit of strife and contention to enter your ranks this place will come to an end in a scene of bloodshed.' And when they assured him roads were impossible, 'A wagon road will be made over the Black Ridge and a temple built to which the Lamanites will come from the other side of the Colorado!'

After a lecture on the supreme rule of obedience — obedience of the authorities to the voice of God, unquestioning obedience of the rank-and-file to the authorities — Erastus got down to what was really on his mind: that they *must get their crops in.* Even if it meant going against Brother Brigham's counsel to grow cotton, they must grow *corn that made a quick harvest.* He wanted more careful scalding of milk buckets, pans, and churns, setting them to air in the sunlight.

Finally, lest they think him too autocratic, again he quoted the Prophet Joseph — 'I don't want you to think I am very righteous, for I am not. There was one good man and his name was Jesus' — and wound up by exhorting them to love one another. There was the story of that sign over the first hotel in Salt Lake: *If you have the money, you can eat.* A Mexican bought the place and added: *No got money, eat anyway!* 'Ptsahh!' That was the spirit!

Apostle Orson Pratt arose to say a few words. 'As Jefferson said,' he proceeded, '"Nature and Nature's God" will provide for us. Though they call us soggum-lappers or cane-seed-eaters, we will yet show them!'

Crops were slow and Indians fast in Mukuntuweap, and he had had a terrible time getting through the Big Sand at Grape Vine Springs . . .

As he talked, Erastus' heart grieved for this father whose son was too bitter to come even to church. Erastus was remembering that this writer, this 'Gauge of Philosophy' who had been Professor of Mathematics and English Literature in the University of the City of Nauvoo, had brought twenty-one thousand converts into the church during his mission to England, alone. Now here was his son, an apostate!

Before the meeting could conclude, there was some business that had to be attended to. Erastus and Orson were sustained as Presidents of the Southern Mission, corroborating word from Brother Brigham, and the town was officially divided into four wards and the subject of bishops approached. After which the congregation would adjourn to lay the cornerstones of the new Social Hall.

Erastus could see Zebedee Trupp with his childless, hard-lipped wife, sitting well toward the front, now lean forward with a gleam in his eye. Erastus hadn't forgotten Zebedee's old passion to be mayor. Now he probably wanted to be bishop. Brother Trupp was a squat man of about sixty-five with a bald head, side whiskers, and one arrogant yellow tooth in the right center of his upper jaw. (Folks said he was too stingy to buy false teeth, even when that immigrant dentist came through the City on his way to the gold fields.) He might be a good chair-maker, but his eyes were too close together, and anyway he beat his mules. Erastus had seen him using a heavy mule whip of braided rawhide strips and bury the knots in the flesh each time according to the approved style of whipping.

Brother Zebedee raised his hand, waddled up to the stand like a belligerent duck. He prayed the Lord might bless him to say a few words of benefit to his listeners (his listeners obviously doubted the benefit; there were whispers — 'Addlepated' ... 'He's only fifty cents on the dollar!'), and declared that he wished to unbosom his feelings. He rejoiced to see the females and childern about. He allowed that the previous speakers had both been full of good preach and had indeed given their hearers a feast of the bread of life; he himself always exhorted to meekness, and against theft, although some thought it not wrong to steal from gentiles. Then he got down to business.

He had sacrificed much for the Gospel, he said, having run away from Metelen in Prussia, Germany, at sixteen to escape having to go to military school, and having been a faithful convert ever since. He abominated gentile doctring and his faith was not rusting out. And although several brethering had criticized his desire to be mayor — 'I ain't disfected in my mind atall! Ask me any questions you amind to!'

He paused for a strategic moment, and then spoke slowly, patiently reasonable.

'It seems to me them that want to be bishop, shouldn't ought to be bishop ... And them that don't want to be bishop, ought to be bishop.'

He drew a long, triumphant breath.

'Now I,' he concluded, his neat gray side whiskers becoming quite agitated, *'don't want to be bishop!'*

Erastus hastily suggested they should decide the new bishopric in council meeting, and called for the closing hymn.

5

Clory stood about listlessly and watched the men get ready to lay the cornerstone. People poured out of the bowery and milled about the ungrubbed brush of the square, laughing, visiting, exchanging news.

New steam passenger cars in the States with two stovepipes sticking through the top. A man on Pike's Peak getting twenty-five dollars in dust from a pan of iron pyrites. Had they heard of that new machine that would both reap and mow, cutting a swath six feet wide? Queen Victoria's husband had died — someone said she ought to come to Utah, and they all whooped.

Dust stirred by gregarious feet rose like red steam. '... Kinda hard to leave the City now just's Utah's about to be connected with the outside by the Iron Way...'

'Weeks said my cow was possessed of devils, but we stuck her.'

Among the women the talk ran on whether yarrow was better for female troubles than camomile, the best way to make soap come, and was it five or six years you had to raise a child before it quit having worms?

Clory said to herself that they'd go on chewing the fat for hours; she'd just go on home. Her head ached from crying the night before, and although she stoutly refused to believe that babies could be marked, still ——

Opening wide the door of her dugout that was not yet quite a home, she flopped into the rocker, not caring that her earrings jerked at their moorings and her hoops ballooned over her head. The spring sun splashed in pools on the maroon-dirt floor, and somewhere a blowfly buzzed. Sabbath peace fell all about her, but she rocked back and forth, back and forth in quiet desperation.

Shouts wakened her. She started up in alarm at the squaw clutching at her shoulder. Phew! Indians never smelled very good in close quarters. Shouts and pounding hooves were coming closer. She got to her feet and tried to make out what this crazy savage was saying.

'*Co-quets, co-quets, co-quets,*' the squaw repeated over and over, pointing to the papoose clinging to her skirts.

Her eyes were frantic. Suddenly she thrust the shivering little boy at Clory and darted out the door. Clory could hear the patter of her swift moccasined feet.

Someone was galloping into the yard...

And then Clory had it. Slave-traders! There was no time to plan; she acted instinctively, popping the shuddering baby under her hoops. He was brave in his terror, standing on her toes so that he came just above her knees and clinging to her legs with both arms; although she could feel his tears soak through her best drawers there wasn't the sound of a whimper.

When the Indian rode up on his mustang he found a lady in a spreading dark red dress standing calmly in her doorway. They regarded each other haughtily for a moment. But the Lamanite's glance was like a live thing, darting from the girl to the dugout.

'Squaw? Squaw?'

His chiseled copper features were stern.

'No squaw here,' said Clory firmly. 'Go away! Vamoose!'

The Indian grunted, got down, brushed past her outstretched arm, and walked into the dugout. There was a piece of willow bark on his loin string that hung halfway to his knees and made a rattling noise when he moved. Unsatisfied, he explored the wagon box and even the Sibley tent. She watched him standing in the yard, glancing toward the corral.

The papoose trembled against her legs.

In spite of the terror churning in her vitals she almost giggled. There was something very funny about the situation. She had watched many a squaw snatch a playing papoose, hold him between her legs, paw through his head for a louse, crack it between her two thumbnails, and drop the carcass into her mouth . . .

At last! The rattle of the buckboard up the road. The Indian heard it, too, and came back to his pony. He shot her a look of puzzled resentment — grunted, and rode away, glancing reluctantly over his shoulder.

Clory did not move until the family had driven into the yard.

'Laws,' said Willie, holding her skirts as she climbed down over the wheel, 'did you see that Marianne Snow a-faunchin' around . . . ?'

She stopped at the look on Clory's face.

'Sheba stood in the dooryard, her black taffeta bosom glinting in the sunlight, her arms akimbo, and watched Clory lift her hoops and the child wriggle out.

Clory's knees were suddenly as weak as 'Sheba's vinegar-and-soggum lemonade, but she couldn't seem to move even after the squaw came and took the boy away.

'Well!' said 'Sheba, 'that's a fine way to observe the Sabbath, I must say!'

The muscles of Clory's face jerked uncontrollably. Sour ghosts of all the old hurts clamored up in her throat. She suddenly picked up her skirts and, like the squaw, ran for the willow fence, across the stubbly sidewalk to Main Street, and up to Pal's as fast as her feet and tight lacings would let her. Pal was right. Day after tomorrow Free was leaving for the North with the buckboard . . .

6

Not daring to light a candle, she fumbled with her dressing.

Clory laid her two starched petticoats and the remains of the one she had cut up for the window curtain at the bottom of the trunk; folded, they took up more than half the space. There wouldn't be room for anything more than her corset-cover and the red cassimere, but it couldn't be helped. The hoopskirt frame she would carry. She banged down the trunk's lid (Free said they hadn't better try taking any more than a trunk apiece), buckled the straps tightly around its middle, tied the red plush bonnet under her chin, and was ready.

Outside, the east was vaguely prophetic of day but the world was still hushed and gray and chill. Now that she had nothing to do but wait, thoughts stormed her resolve.

Her heart was pounding violently. If only they didn't get caught!

There were cautious footsteps outside. She lifted her skirts and stooped through the doorway.

Then her heart stopped. There were two people.

The other person was David, his face looming toward her out of the gloom. Pal gave her a small, apologetic smile.

'I've got something to show you girls,' David said, planting his big bulk firmly before her. 'I've left word for Free, Clory, but if you still want to go after I've had my say, I'll take you to Apostle Erastus myself.'

He didn't seem angry as Abijah would have been, but somehow understanding and yet determined.

Pal put out a hand toward her friend and then withdrew it.

'He guessed, Clory; and anyway, I —— '

'You see,' went on David, 'Pal loves me. And I love her ... But I know how you girls feel. You're sick of the loneliness and the flies and the bad water and the lack of lawns and trees —— But, great guns, we'll get those things! This isn't a woman's country yet, I admit, but give us time! I *can't* leave. A man whom Brother Brigham has trusted doesn't leave a mission *unless he's carried out feet first!'*

He was trembling and his voice rose, but he stopped and lowered it again to a whisper.

'So I've made a bargain with Pal. She said if I could show her one pretty thing in all this desert she'd stay. And I'll keep my word, too. If you don't like what I've got to show you, I'll help you both go north, only not like thieves in the night.'

He took hold of Pal's arm and started away.

'Go back to bed, Clory. I'll fix everything with Brother Mac, and we'll have a surprise for you when the sun warms up.'

But she didn't go back to bed. She couldn't. She sat in the doorway and watched the chill grayness lift and the breeze come up and the day awake behind Steamboat Mountain and drain the dregs of night clinging to the brush. She was so still that a jack rabbit sat up in front of her and lapped the fresh yellow sunshine as if it were honey.

Afterward she had no memory of breakfast or any of the things people said to her. And when David came to get her, the little procession waiting out at the gate didn't seem strange at all.

Tutsegabbett, chief of six hundred Paiutes, sat his horse in kingly dignity, keeping his gaze straight ahead. He wore a rabbit-skin loincloth and rabbit-skin leg-bands below his knees, and a cape of rabbit's fur about his shoulders. His moccasins were new and beaded. His hair was braided and hung down his back, and in a band about his forehead stood a lone eagle's feather. There was a quiver full of feather-tipped cane arrows slung under the cape. White and red and yellow stripes slanted across his high bronze cheekbones. His nose was arrogant and his liquid eyes expressionless. He smoked a pipe made of the small end of a cow's horn.

On the second pony sat Jacob Hamblin, dark and slender, quite self-possessed, as if this were an everyday occurrence. Pal and David rode behind and David was leading another horse by the bridle.

He caught Clory's heel and boosted her to the pony's blanketed back, and they were off without a word.

Tutsegabbett led the way south, down lower Main Street, and they rode silently until they came to the rock wall. David got down and opened the gate; they passed through to the deeper brush and Tutsegabbett spoke.

'He says,' interpreted Brother Hamblin in his soft voice, 'that the tale he is about to tell you is true, but it was *wetus* — long time ago — and has been told around the wickiup fires of his people ever since he can remember.'

He paused while the Indian's gutturals took up the story, and then he translated again.

'He says before the Mericats came, before his people were weakened with to-oopah, white man's crazy water, and the white man's customs, the Paiutes had a great chief, Peeup Neab, and this chief had a son, Neab.

'He says Neab, the son, fell in love with a maiden named Nannoo, or "little girl," and married her. He says they were very *ke-um-kie* — laughing, happy.'

The teller-of-tales and the interpreter were in such harmony, that Clory found herself forgetting the horses and the brush and the barren country, and living with Neab and Nannoo and their ancient story.

They had put the valley behind them and were rounding the southern slope of the Black Ridge. The horses felt their way through huge, fantastic ebony boulders, many of which bore weird picture-writings, the sign-language of Tutsegabbett's people.

The U-ano-its were a people who traveled from season to season. When Ye-ah-bun came and the sun left, they camped in the warm valley; when Tah-mum brought the heat they fled to the mountains. There were always among them people too old or sick to travel when the time came to take down the wickiups. And they had the custom of burying the weak ones in the caves of U-nav-ich to let them die.

Neab and his father tried to teach their people that this was an evil custom, and for many moons the people obeyed them and were gentle to the weak ones.

Then, one sleep in the late summer, Neab returned to his wickiup to find that Nannoo's 'other self' had left her body. Her skin was so hot he thought at first she had swallowed the coals of the fire. Neab called Medawin, dreamer-of-the-gods, who rattled his gourds and danced until the weasel skin leaped upon his breast, but Nannoo did not get well. And the trouble was that many others in the tribe became sick, too. Na Pau Mi — sick, sick. The U-ano-its were frightened and forgot their new teachings.

Neab cried many *to-paip*, but at dawn the burial ceremony began. The women went ahead, gashing themselves with flint knives and pulling their hair and wailing the chant of mourning. Nannoo, encased in blankets, was strapped to a pony. Across the plain and up on the gleaming rocks — across the heated base and at last up over the pointed bosom of U-nav-ich to the yawning cave of death. The shrieks and wails scattered themselves to every pinnacle and crevice.

When the black boulder was rolled away and the women shoved Nannoo through the dark, gaping mouth, Neab did not hesitate.

'What you are doing is evil,' he said; 'Ah-bat Moap, the great On-Top god, will take away the rain and the U-ano-its will die. You have not listened to Peeup Neab. I go to prove his words to you. I go to intercede for you. I go to coax the anger from Ah-bat Moap.'

His people begged him to come out, but when the women rolled the boulder back into place, Neab was there to keep Nannoo company . . .

The voice stopped. Clory was still in her dream, feeling the silence of the baleful lava rocks close in, the solitary protest of a mourning dove down among the reeds by the river . . .

The horses were rounding a queer, rock-piled formation, their shoes clinking against the stones. Suddenly Tutsegabbett pulled up his pony and waited for the others to catch up with him. He was staring straight across the valley with its brush sheds and tents to the mountains beyond and Steamboat on the horizon, iridescent as a bird's wing in the sunlight.

Tutsegabbett spread wide his arms and Jacob matched the solemnity of his intonation.

'Ah-bat Moap, pleased with his servant, set His footprint before the cave of Neab to show his stubborn people the way.'

The Indian pony took another dainty step or two. The others followed, the girls craning their necks to peer around the figures of the men. They lined up at the very lip of a huge basin scooped out in the solid rock.

'See-coe!' cried Tutsegabbett.

Clory sucked in her breath, transfixed in amazement and delight.

'David!' Pal gasped, and the two girls were on their knees among the stones of the lip.

There before them, carpeting the depression, were thousands of fairy bells with lavender hearts, tossing their lovely heads. Flowers wilting at a touch, so delicate as to be almost other-earthly there among the black rocks.

Sego lilies! Sown as thickly as a desert sky with stars. Poised like heavenly butterflies there on the grim lava surface as if they needed no roots, would float upward at a breath ...

' ... The U-ano-its resolved never to fight on a battlefield where sego lilies grew: thus the sego lily became an emblem of peace ... '

Ah-bat Moap and His mighty footstep before the cave of Neab. Neab, who did not run away.

Clory bent over and brushed her cheek against the blossoms. When she looked up, David mutely questioned her; and although her face was tremulous with tenderness, her smile flew banners.

CHAPTER VII

ONE morning toward the end of May, Clory shook up the last pillow on the last bed and herded Isaiah and the twins outdoors to the wash-bench. They babbled and frisked away from her like young calves, but the girl, shivering in the gray light still drowning the valley floor, was glad for a reprieve from those winter ablutions in the stuffy tent.

Isaiah screwed his eyes against the soapy washrag and bawled lustily so that he got his mouth full instead, but the little boys submitted their necks and ears with a wriggling fortitude.

'Aunt Clory! Aunt Clory! Watch me stand on my head!'

She jerked Nephi by the seat of the pants up to the bench in time to see Lehi dragging at Isaiah's forelock.

'Ugh! Me heap big chief! Me scalp um!'

Isaiah's cries split the air.

The twins were everywhere at once.

'Aunt Clory, Aunt Clory, what makes your stomach stick out?'

'Sh! You mustn't ask questions. Come on, now, let's play soldier, see who can stand the stillest ...'

Laughing, scolding, she got them scrubbed and combed, their

shirts buttoned in the proper buttonholes, and, now that spring had come and shoes were discarded, their bare feet doused in the water left in the basin.

'Just a lick and a promise,' she said; 'you have to be careful of toes that've been turned out to grass . . .'

She parted the baby's hair and slicked it back until it lay like wet straw. She buttoned a clean, sleeveless apron over his stout blue hickory dress, bathed his grubby knees and feet, and sent Nephi to the line for a fresh diaper. Isaiah's chunky body squirmed precariously on what was left of her lap, but she managed to pin his sturdy buttocks into the three-cornered fold.

'Shame on you,' she mumbled through the safety pins in her mouth, 'a big boy like Isy still having to wear didies! You bet I'll see that *my* baby's broke by the time she's *shortened* . . .'

'Didy, didy, didy!' squealed Isaiah, kicking his legs.

Abijah stood in the doorway and rang the bell for prayers, and Bathsheba came around the corner carrying a pail of frothy milk.

'Make tracks,' she ordered Clory; 'the Lord hates a dawdler!'

In the tent, where a single candle-flame guttered on the table and the morning poured through the open door to push back the gloom, Abijah's family knelt in prayer. His soft-boiled egg, the yellow corn-meal mush, crust coffee, and fried potatoes and mutton steamed upon the table. Each knelt by his place, Abijah like a bearded patriarch beside his chair at the head, Bathsheba at the foot, and the others ranged along the benches between. Abijah covered his face with his hands, propped his arms on the chair, and cleared his throat.

'Mother, will you offer prayer?'

Clorinda dug her elbows in the bench, rubbed her palms along her forehead, and sighed. When the boys had their turn, they skated through with a hasty crush of words as formless as bread sopped in gravy, 'nameofJesusamen,' and she and Willie were always to the point, but 'Sheba, like Abijah, made sure that the Lord understood his full duty.

' ... this food, that it may nourish and strengthen our bodies, that they may run and not be weary, walk and not faint, be lifted up in Thy service ... these clothes upon our backs, that they may shield us from harm, keep us in health and strength, and wear, O Lord, until we are able to replace them ... (Nephi, stop that wigglin'!) ... Bless this land Thou hast given us for an inheritance that it may prove fertile and yield sufficient crops for Thy children who love Thee. ... Bless that sore tit on my cow, Bessie, who's a-freshenin' up, that she won't have no trouble, O Lord, because we sure do need that milk and butter ...'

Willie, who had been increasingly uneasy, jumped to her feet with a wild cry.

'The dough-gods! They're burning in the skillet!'

The Lord hung in midair, so to speak, while 'Sheba muttered at Willie's poor management.

'Help us, O Lord' (she rescued Him), 'to remember that the little horn shall wear out the Saints until the Ancient of Days shall sit. Until the battle of Gog and Magog when the earth is sanctified and becomes like a sea of glass, like one great Urim and Thummim ...'

Clory rubbed hard on her stomach where the baby was kicking and decided she had never been so hungry. She was glad they weren't as religious as some families who knelt before every meal. God must be worn out listening. Wasn't it the Prophet Joseph who admonished a windy pray-er not to 'bray so much like a jackass'?

At last Abijah's bass and the treble of the others echoed 'Sheba's 'Amen,' Abijah cut short the daily Bible reading, and the MacIntyre family fell to upon the victuals.

After breakfast, 'Sheba, making out her daily schedule, called the others about her and outlined in detail each one's twenty-four hours.

2

Clory had sworn never to wear a Mother Hubbard in public, but this was singing practice night, and singing practice wasn't like Sunday meeting, where you had to be dressed up. When the chores were finished, Freeborn started off ahead, and she and Bathsheba and Abijah followed leisurely through the soft twilight. Until they reached the lighted bowery they would all walk barefooted to save shoe leather, and as Clory tramped along the road, swinging her shoes, foxtails caught at her skirt and snagged at her ankles, and ungrubbed mesquite and the stiff, wiry salt grass stung her flesh like tiny knife-blades. Occasionally she would have to drop behind to pull out a grass-burr, and as she stooped, rubbing spit on the place, the harsh, briny smell of the grass would come up to her, and the fecund earthiness of the spring, and the cool breath of the water ditches chuckling mysteriously along the sidewalks.

Dusk like the plush of a blackbird's wing seeped up from the floor of the valley; only above the shaved western horizon stood the day in a bar of clear, deep green. Below, here and there, scattered sequins of light strung the darkness. Front doors were open to the warmth, and folks sat upon their steps framed in their own candle-glow. There was an occasional whistle or the wheeze of an asthmatic accordion. Now and then Abijah called out a greeting . . .

The air moved with a faint, wayward sweetness as if it had brushed some far-off field of wildflowers. And Clory noticed as she had done before that the evenings seemed to bring windless currents in layers, cooling her cheek here, and a block farther on growing imperceptibly warm again.

Abijah filled his lungs and emptied them with a long, ecstatic sigh.

'Aigh, what a nicht! Tae think when I was ca'ed tae this countr-ry I said I wasna gaen! I must hae been daft!'

His voice rumbled with tenderness.

'I dinna ken it before, but I've had my eye on the hills ever since we've cam' along an' — hae ye noticed? — they seem tae come closer at nicht...'

Free picked up a stick and loitered behind and beat at the weeds, and Clory nervously edged ahead beside Bathsheba.

'And sic a routh o' gude things! Long, r-red r-radishes and lettuce in April, and green peas in May, all out o' the same garden rows; corn a foot high, cotton in blossom, spr-ring wheat in the dough, and the town patch of lucerne coming up a'ready... tomatoes by the Fourth o' July!...'

Abijah thought aloud as he walked on through the night.

'Aye, we're gettin' to be quite a town. I see Eardley straddlin' his grindstone t'other day with his daub o' clay on the spindle and him a-treadin' the lever an' whirlin' the clay, an' his fingers a-shapin' and a-shapin' it...'

His heavy laugh boomed.

'Ech, 'twon't be long now 'til you womenfolks can break a dish without breakin' yer hear-rts!'

'And Brother Mansfield's got a nail-machine. Handy one he is wi' an ox, too; has th' ould crosspatch harnessed up in the sling and half the shoe on an' the other half a-comin' before th' ox has time to beller!'

It was as if his words thrust out their chests and strutted.

For weeks the men had been boasting. Peabody hauling his great stacks of tanbark down from Pine Valley, Ferrano making his wooden churns, Lars Hansen his bedsteads, Robert Gardner (in charge of tithing over all the wards and newly appointed Bishop of the Fourth) setting up his sawmill in Pine Valley, Erastus Snow his grist mill, Lon Tuckett bouncing up in Sunday meeting to announce he was all ready to begin tailoring as soon as the wool-clip was washed and spun, Charley Hichinoper growing his beania bushes for the sweet oil to be consecrated and substituted for olive oil... Clory thought the community swaggered and sprawled until it was like to burst its seams.

Long before they reached the end of the last block and turned to cut kitty-cornered toward the square, they could see the bowery dripping candle-gleams through its leafy walls like an oasis of light.

There were greetings to be shouted before the choir-leader could distribute the hymn books and get his pupils seated in order on the willow benches — the baritones and sopranos in their respective places on each side of the aisle; and behind them, balancing each other, the tenors and basses opposite the second sopranos and altos.

As Clory and 'Sheba seated themselves among the sopranos, Eliza Hichinoper edged along the bench toward them. She carried her baby on her hip and he reared and squealed and grinned gummily at the women. It didn't seem possible he was the same human mite Eliza and Charles had carried on a pillow all those three hundred and fifty miles last fall.

'Eight months old today,' his mother declared proudly.

'Seems good to see you out,' said Clory, booing the delighted baby and bunting her head against his chest.

Eliza nodded and drew a long breath and looked about her with hungry eyes.

'The second time this winter,' she said; 'you can't go places when you have a baby. We were so scared we'd lose him that we named him "Marvelous," you know ... I shouldn't have brung him here tonight, but ...'

Bathsheba looked at Clory significantly. What then would become of her fussiness and her bergamot and her love for parties?

But Clory only nodded her head understandingly at Eliza in her soiled calico that clung to her figure, so immodest without hoops. Everything had a price, and if that was the price you paid for a baby, why, it was worth it.

Brother Wheelock rapped for order. He was a huge, bald-headed, red-faced man with long, sensitive hands and a voice that rolled out like the sound of a great bell. Brother Isaac was an

English convert, an excellent musician who knew well the fine old
anthems of that country. In '47, when President Young had pre-
sided over the first Sunday meeting in the Old Bowery in the
City, and had organized the 'Tabernacle Choir of Deseret,' he'd
said: 'We're just getting a choir ready for the Tabernacle that
we'll have some day. We cannot preach the Gospel unless we
have good music . . . we'll sing the Gospel into the hearts of the
people.' Brother Wheelock had been leader of that choir and he'd
never forgotten President Young's words. Now Brother Brigham
had called him to train the first choir in the Cotton Mission . . .
'to sing the Gospel into the hearts of the people.'

Brother Wheelock raised his stick.

'We'll work on some songs for the Fourth of July,' he said;
'turn to "What Shall the Harvest Be?" '

Bathsheba's voice had all the single-mindedness of a steam
calliope. Secretly convinced that she could sing higher than
Clory, she was always nettled that Brother Wheelock should go
on giving Clory the solo parts just the same.

'So-o-own in the dark—ness,' Clory's voice traced the quicksilver pinnacles of the fife, while 'sown-in-the-darkness-or-sown-
in-the-light' Abijah kept the steady undercurrent of the bass
drum. And as always with the communion of the music, his eyes
saluted hers across the room.

'Loosen up!' shouted Brother Wheelock. 'Chests up and dia-
phragms in! We'll do our exercises now, beginning with the
round. All right, sopranos, give each note its full value ——'

Every time, to start them off, he opened his big mouth earnestly and went on furiously pounding out the rhythm. Half-
moons of sweat darkened his shirt-sleeves above the armholes of
his waistcoat, and his arms and feet and body all swayed in unison.

'Do ra mi fa!' sang the sopranos with dignity, and 'do ra mi
fa!' affirmed the baritones; but meanwhile the sopranos had frol-
icked ahead,

> Hold your heads up in sol fa-ing
> Open wide your mouths while chawing . . .

So the baritones, not to be outdone, set off in hot pursuit, only to
find that the sopranos had changed their minds and retreated,
'Do ra mi fa.'

Faces relaxed, eyes took on a trustful peace, and the crazy-
quilt of sound overflowed into the night with a senseless kind of
harmony.

> Hold your heads up in sol fa-ing
> Open wide your mouths while chawing...

The basses finishing up in the sudden, shouting silence were as
substantial and self-respecting as the tail-end of one of 'Sheba's
snores.

3

Apostle Snow did not get there until Brother Wheelock was
gathering up the hymn books.

'News,' he drawled, strolling up the aisle. 'I was counseling...
in the Clary... and some folks going through... left... this
copy of the *News*...'

He held up a battered copy of the Saints' own organ, the
Deseret News, and watched them settle back quietly in their seats
and strain forward.

'It says,' he read, 'on Tuesday, May 8, Mr. Morrill of Vermont
... introduced a bill in the United States House of Representatives... to *punish and prevent the practice of bigamy in the Terri-
tories of the United States.*'

There was a dead silence and then bedlam broke out. Hinted
at before, here the thing was out in the open. Driven and
mobbed for their religion, they looked at each other with eyes
shadowed by remembered terrors. Would there never be an end?
If the government joined in —! According to the dictates of his
own conscience: for that right, guaranteed them by the constitution of a free land, they had fled for thirty years from Christians.

You couldn't love your neighbor if he carried a pitchfork in his hands. Besides, celestial marriage, a holy principle revealed to them by God, was certainly anything but bigamy! What now of President Lincoln's vaunted policy regarding the Mormons, '*Let them alone!*'

Aunt Keturah Snow jumped to her feet. She was a motherly woman with comfortable proportions, but now her gray hair was awry and her eyes shot sparks.

'Sisters,' she said, enlisting them all with her glance, 'I move we petition Congress about this. I have a hankering that the sisters up North have already done it. My gracious, this here bill's an insult to the women of Utah! Why don't the fools come out and *see* what polygamy's like! They'll judge us sight unseen again, just like Buchanan! Why, for gettin' along peaceable, I'd put our home up against any in the land!'

She looked down at Erastus' two younger wives on the bench beside her.

'Why, them women are just like my own sisters! I love each one of them and I know that all you living in the covenant could say the same thing! My children's their children and their children's my children — Why, that time when I was so sick in the City, Martha, here, practically raised my youngest boy!... You single wives'll never know the blessin' of bein' able to go to meetin' of a Sunday and know your young ones'll be cared for and dinner on the table agin you get back!'

Hannah Merinda Lowgie bubbled over. Raising the children of a second wife killed with Brother Lowgie at Haughn's Mill (and that while plural marriage still had to be practiced in secret), she had the right to stand proudly upon her feet; she looked as if she could mother the whole world into behaving. Mormonism was hard on widows, too, since, if a woman married again, children by the second husband would belong in eternity to the first.

'Look at the fine wives Sister Ket has given her husband, their posterity to be stars in his kingdom forever! It's the joy of her life to know those three who love each other more than sisters are laying the foundation of a life to come and will go hand in hand together down all eternity!'

Aunt Ket was not to be out-congratulated.

'My gracious,' she said, 'sometimes it's a downright relief to me to turn Erastus over to them girls!'

At this the audience forgot its indignation and howled.

Erastus flushed and writhed his lips and grinned.

'There's more news,' he answered the women mildly, glancing down at the paper. 'War news. The Union armies have lost again — seems that dumbhead Hooker with one hundred and thirty thousand men couldn't beat Lee's sixty thousand; but the South lost Stonewall Jackson ... At each other's throats like two mad dogs.... We're mighty lucky to be in Zion, folks....'

He stroked his ruffled beard. 'Mighty lucky ...'

'"Nearly fifteen hundred Scandinavian converts sailed from Hamburg, Germany, last month ... and 262 wagons, 293 men, 2880 oxen, and 143,315 pounds of flour have been shipped under the Perpetual Emigration Fund across the Plains to help them get to Zion." That doesn't look as if Zion had to worry, does it? ... Our job's to build up Dixie so we can help the P.E.F. next time, have cotton to send ...'

He consulted the paper again.

'Josiah Evans and Martin Penrose have been sent to Italy to study art under the great masters, so we can have the best paintings there are, in the Temple ...

'Thursday, March 6, the Salt Lake Theater was dedicated ...'

Instantly the hubbub faded for Clory. She could smell the smoke from the massive oil lamps, see the orchestra in the pit ...

'Colonel Patrick Edward Connor marching to Utah with California volunteers ...'

What have we done now! We've just got rid of one army stuck under our noses for four long years!

'They say the army's to protect the mail route and telegraph lines from the Indians, but that can't be true, since Brother Brigham responded to the call of the War Department for this service just last month with one hundred special men ... I'm afraid, brothers and sisters, Colonel Connor will watch more Mormons than Indians ... With the country legislating against us and refusing for the third time to make us a state ...'

Erastus did not blame his people for being bitter. Some of them were on their feet.

'What folks were the first to petition Congress for a telegraph line across the continent?'

'Who first memorialized Congress for a Great National Central Railroad from the Missouri River to the Pacific Coast?'

'And yet they accuse us of disloyalty!'

Erastus raised a hand.

'This ... won't get us ... anywhere,' he said. 'Like Brother Brigham ... we "love the government ... but we do not love the damned rascals ... who administer ... the government"!... Remember, the Constitution is a document inspired of the Lord; go read your Doctrine and Covenants ... Remember the circular the High Council issued in '46? "*Our patriotism has not been overcome by fire, by sword, nor by midnight assassinations which we have endured.*" ... Now, then, what about the Fourth of July? ... I have in my veins the blood of America for eight generations and I'm not going to forget about her no matter how she acts ... Now, then, what about a flag?'

His listeners stirred uneasily, loath to relinquish their sense of injustice.

'We'll have to have a flag, anyway,' Erastus went on, 'when Brother Brigham gets here.'

Ears pricked up at that. Was Brother Brigham coming?

'I think so,' said Erastus, 'in the fall ... That makes you happy, don't it? But you can't celebrate for him without a flag.'

Then Pal got up, in the back of the bowery. Her freckled cheeks were pink.

'I — I have a spare white cambric petticoat...'

Erastus ignored the titters and beamed at her.

Marianne Snow was bolder.

'My old blue taffeta is just the right color for a flag.'

Clory didn't recognize her own voice. Maybe after the baby the red cassimere wouldn't fit, anyway...

'I have a red dress...'

A sacrifice to those ancient, unknown gods. So much for vanity. Thinking of the new theater, she had, for one blinding, homesick moment, almost hated the baby in her womb.

Erastus' gray eyes were tender. Ptsahh!

'A wonderful flag!... Every thread in it... brought a thousand miles across the Plains. Let us sing, my brethren.'

4

The spring went by in a sunny enchantment. The days were like polished gems, each more perfect than the last, strung on a thread of warm, sweet darkness. Slim waterfalls and the new green of cottonwood leaves suddenly splashed the little canyons gashing the flank of the crimson hill. Against the tumultuous edge of that color, so orange in the morning and mauve at night, the sky fitted like a cloudless turquoise bowl. Sometimes Clory, getting up in the morning to scrape alkali from the bad spots among her cotton plants, longed to stretch out her hands and snatch forever some of that calm beauty.

On the last Sunday in May, Abijah ushered his whole family to Sunday school. Even Willie, who was feeling better just then, and Joseph, up from the sheep-herd. It was too nice a day to take the buckboard. Clory never forgot that day. The intense light, the sunflowers that seemed to catch and distill the sun, sky-colored morning-glories opening their creamy throats. There was such a peace about the morning and the fresh green of the crops.

Abijah linked his arm companionably in Freeborn's. Handsome Mac was starched and brushed and polished, and Free had on a clean white shirt with his buckskins.

'But, my boy,' said Abijah reasonably, 'ye were makin' sae much noise Brother Peabody had to stop talkin'. Besides, the ithers hae all confessed and are willin' tae make things r-right...'

Free scuffed a rock with his boot.

'I can't get up and ask forgiveness for doing something wrong when I can't think it's wrong. We were only comin' down the street singin'. We didn't know you was havin' theology class——'

'But you boys belonged inside, yoursel's,' said Abijah. 'It's the example...'

Free looked at Clory walking in front of him, moving with her own grace that not all the Mother Hubbards could conceal. His eyes lost some of their torment.

Abijah cleared his throat.

'It's natural when ye're young; aye, when I was young...'

Free stared. He had never thought of his father as being young once, and human and vulnerable.

'All right, Pa,' he said, 'if it'll make you feel better, I'll do it.'

It was as if they were all under a spell. Dinner was gayer than Clory had ever remembered, with Free forgetting to sulk and even 'Sheba exuding a forceful goodwill. The meal was a good one, spiced with watercress and the dark green of leaf-lettuce.

In the middle of it, Tutsegabbett in his rabbit-skin loincloth stood in the open door of the tent. When they all looked up at him, forks poised in midair, he raised his right arm and grunted 'How!' Beside him was his fat squaw, her neck draped with the customary sack yawning for bread.

Abijah had a way with the Lamanites. He was always quoting — 'Shoot them with tobacco and bread and biscuits rather than with powder and lead' — but 'Sheba couldn't 'abide the dirty varmints.'

Clory expected her to shoo the tall, silent Indian away, but 'Sheba grumbled and found some scraps of bread. Abijah expanded, and tried out the Paiute he was learning to speak on the chief. Tutsegabbett broke into voluble gutturals.

Abijah listened, questioned, and his brown bush parted in a grin like a pleased child's when Tutsegabbett understood his halting syllables.

'He says,' Abijah translated, 'the Paiutes are starving more than ever this year because the irrigation ditch they built in the Clara bottomlands went out in the flood last fall.

'He says the Paiutes used to dig ditch with a wooden spade cut with knife from a cottonwood. He says all that changed now with white man's shovel — new irrigation ditch this spring — soon no more starve.'

The chief grew vociferous. '*Suttickie! Suttickie!*'

Abijah's brown eyes twinkled.

'*Suttickie* means "White Friend."' ... He says in pay for help, he has come to warn us to watch our own ditch — big flood two moons away ——'

Abijah broke into a chuckle and flipped a marauding black ant from the table.

'Ye're a sly fox,' he said to the chief in English. 'Ye can't *scare* us into giving you any more bread. We ain't scared of Pah Roosh; we've got that old river tamed!'

Tutsegabbett stalked out in affront.

After meeting, during which Free and the other shamefaced youths admitted they were sorry, and the indulgent audience voted them to full fellowship again, Abijah started his flock westward toward the Black Hill dozing in the yellow sunshine. He said to himself that he had never been so saturated with contentment. His pride in his son brought tears to his eyes. That was the way to handle a stiff-necked youth: teach him to be humble, and he'd get the Lord back in his heart soon enough. And when he was properly repentant, send him on a mission. Abijah dreamed of his boy full of good preach before some foreign congregation, perhaps on a street corner, fearlessly singing Zion's hymns among the discordant gentile traffic; or perhaps in a den of Methodists, unraveling their lying beliefs before their astonished eyes as 'Sheba unraveled a sock, and then offering them the Gospel out of whole cloth, and so bringing converts home to the fat valleys of Ephraim. Perhaps now, as he strolled along, Free was deep in contemplation of some phase of doctrine . . .

Freeborn stooped to pick the little flower, and smiled at his own fancy. He was a fool, but the Injuns claimed it worked. He ambled over to Clorinda, hesitant among the black stones. The burden she carried was heavier, now, and she often had to rest. She couldn't get used to her clumsy self. But Free, squatting beside her, thought only that her eyes seemed deeper lately. He brushed the flower with its fuzzy flame against her cheek.

'An Indian paintbrush!' she cried.

Free worried a pebble between his fingers and gulped.

'Yawp; the Injuns say if you rub some on a person you — you like, why, she will, she will . . . like you; it's a love-charm, sorta . . .'

'Why, Free, what a pretty thought!'

The boy's eyes sought hers.

Was that all it was, just a pretty thought?

Clory avoided his gaze and jumped to her feet.

'Come on, let's hunt wildflowers!'

The hill was spotted with clumps of yellow daisies and buttercups, fragrant wild candytuft, and myriads of cactus blooms, red and yellow and pink and mauve, secret and still among their spines like congealed and scented flames. There was the barrel cactus with its stout, flower-crowned body and its wicked bristles with their musical twang. The prickly pear with its blossoms like full-blown roses. The niggerhead cactus pushing golden cups out of every rock crevice. The old hen-and-chickens, the beaver-tail, clumps of tall cactus like vicious shocks of wheat, yellow spines flung like blobs of sunlight on the gray desert floor.

All desert plants are emphatic; it is as if by sight or smell they must impress the visitor instantly, since they have their own way to make in the world and cannot depend on man to nurture and preserve them.

'They have to lead with their chins, you see,' Free explained seriously.

Perhaps he failed to make a showing when it came to the Scriptures, but up here he was at home. And pointing out this world to Clory, he was like a man who takes a woman sight-seeing around the inside of his heart.

While Bathsheba and Willie and Abijah soaked up sun on the rocks, and the younger boys scattered like sheep (only Joseph tossing his older brother a mocking over-the-shoulder glance), it seemed natural for Free to load this girl with sego lilies and red bells and tell her about his world. Words could do no harm. And so he told her of the hesitant, spicy smell of the wild-rose hedges along the creek at the far foot of this hill; how one could catch the perfume of the willow trees in bloom on the riverbanks a mile away; there were even weeds he loved, such as the star-shaped milkweed flowers and the sand verbena which embroidered the ground of mesquite hummocks like a Paisley shawl.

There were wonders he had seen, such as the drops of honey sparkling on the ends of rabbit-brush — Jacob Hamblin said that aphids sucked the sap and left the drops behind, and that the early Santa Clara settlers broke off the sweet twigs and washed them and boiled down the water to a syrup that was mighty tasty on morning dough-gods.

He found a blossoming oose for her — a panicle of creamy blooms that shot out of its nest of dark green swords a dozen feet into the air. The flowers were like bells with petals of malleable ivory.

'Why, it's what I wash my hair with!' she cried, breaking off a cup to sniff the wistful perfume. 'I used to wonder how such tough, brown roots could make such fluffy shampoo, but I never dreamed those ugly spikes knew about anything like this! Why, I think — I think it must make the meanest Injun fall down and pray.'

For a second they were both silent, and the shrill sibilance of the day closed in upon them.

'Listen!' said Clory. 'Listen!'

The air was suddenly filled with a plaintive, tender song.

'It's a desert sage thrasher,' explained Free, 'over there in that greasewood ... He's got a nice tune, all right, but you ought to hear a meadowlark!'

He cocked his sunny head and seemed to forget momentarily that the girl was there. His voice deepened:

> ... Sings each song twice over,
> Lest you should think he never could recapture
> That first fine careless rapture ——

At her startled stare, he dropped his head, abashed.

'I — I learned it from David Wight ——'

For the first time he had let someone all the way inside that secret place where he hid his dreams, and he did not quite know what to make of himself. But Clory tiptoed reverently — this was hallowed ground. And when he looked up, he found the irises of her dusky eyes so clear, so open with admiration, that his own image was mirrored there.

She was staring as if she had never seen him before. Free, with whom she had used to flirt! Free with his bashfulness, his awkwardness, his cracking voice. This was no gangling boy; this was a man ...

The spell still held as the day died. It had been one of those days when time hushes and heaven bends closer to earth. As soon as the children were in bed, Clory went out and sat beside Abijah on the step. Because once again she'd forgotten things as they were, she felt guilty and wanted to make amends, but Abijah patted her hand and watched the cumuli ride east and the blaze come up in the west.

'Does the bairn fret ye much, Clor-rinda Agathy?'

'She — she kicks, sometimes,' said Clory shyly.

Abijah's eyes crinkled and he leaned over and brushed her cheek in an unexpected caress.

'Ye're sure, then, 'twill be a girl?'

At the quiet conviction in her face, affectionate laughter rumbled up from his chest.

'Weell, then, we'll hope she's bonny!'

Clory thought of David's prancing delight over Pal's new pregnancy, and how he called her 'Ma' and teased her with a kind of sweet horseplay. David spoke jocularly of their baby as 'Butch.'

'Well, how's Butch today? . . . How's he like the victuals down there?'

As soon as Pal told him, he had brought up a leppy-lamb from the herd to raise for a playmate for 'Butch.' ('Just as if it wouldn't be a full-grown sheep by the time the baby gets here!' Pal giggled to Clory afterward.)

Remembering Pal and David, Clory hugged the thought of her own baby fiercely to her breast. She felt more than ever that her baby was *hers, alone;* she felt that, just as surely as she felt her baby would be a girl. Somehow, she knew it . . .

Abijah stretched his arms and sighed.

'Aye, it's a nicht for singing,' he cried. 'I remember ——'

Clory knew what he remembered. The old days on the ranch at Cottonwood before he had taken other wives and polygamy had fermented his household, simple days of harmony and peace when evening 'sings' were as natural as laughter. Scotch dances in the South Fort with the frolic of the fiddle and the wild, haunting skirling of the bagpipes, 'Leard o' Cockpen,' and 'Jeoke Tar' . . .

By the time the moon came up they were all singing with such an abandon of pleasure it was half pain. Clory's fingers nimble on the dulcimer. Rollicking melodies that tapped the foot and swung the shoulder —

Oh, where and oh, where is your highland laddie gone?

Martial melodies, proud and gay, the colors of the clan marching to war, kilted courage —

> Scots wha hae wi' Wallace bled...

Pensive melodies that turned Free's eyes to Clory —

> What's this dull town to me?
> Ro-o-bin's not here...

Clory's voice touched with heartbreak, silver as flute-music in
the night, jetting like a fountain above Abijah's dark bass —

> Kathleen Mavourneen, the gray dawn is breaking...
> Oh, why art thou silent, thou voice of my heart...
> It may be for years and — *it may be forever*...

Songs that softened 'Sheba's eyes and clasped Abijah's hand in
hers —

> John Anderson, my jo, John...

Free's tenor took on warmth and roundness, 'Sheba's neighing
softened, the boys' young voices blended, a chorus of voices,
united, freed, pouring out grief and fear and hope to the
stars.

When the last song had washed away pretense and resentment,
Abijah bowed his head quite simply.

' ... For my soul delighteth in the song of the heart; yea, the
song of the righteous is a prayer unto me, and it shall be
answered with a blessing upon their heads.' And then, almost as
an afterthought:

' ... Be ye kind one to another, and tender-hearted.'

5

By the first of July the heat had struck. Nothing the settlers
had ever known before prepared them for it. Heat that shriveled
the skin and parched the tongue. Boys herding cattle took to

carrying boards on which to rest when stepping became intolerable. Since leather was long in tanning and new shoes future eventualities, women who had already formed the custom of going barefooted to the door of meeting or sociable began to wrap their feet in scraps of tenting, old cloth, or pieces of buckskin. The arm-tucked cushion with which to provide little oases of relief on a scorching walk came to be as common among visiting women as the sunbonnet. Lizards scooted for shade and watering troughs steamed and stank. And sometimes bare feet encountered churlish scorpions or centipedes or tarantulas, and always the beds of red ants.

There was something vulgar about the heat — it had no decent interval of relaxation as in other climes. The hills had turned to metal furnaces that steamed along the horizons, and at night reflected stored-up heat. The blue of the sky was washed white with brilliance, and dust-devils whirled in southward-sweeping clouds. The valley had become literally an oven from which there was no escape. Only now and then strolling in the evening did Clory encounter one of those mysterious air-currents like a cooling sigh and just as suddenly gone.

Abijah groaned over the wheat in the community field and rejoiced over the corn in the same breath. It did not seem to be a wheat country; indeed, if they could just get by this first season there was no reason why they could not trade their cotton and corn and molasses for northern wheat — but this first season was the stickler. Most of them had taken Apostle Snow's advice and planted a few rows of corn or sugar cane in their town lots, and so he supposed they wouldn't starve, but it would be hard to forego wheat flour a whole year.

By the end of June, Abijah was husking the pale wheat-grains on his palm. The hardened kernels were still smooth, standing the burning weather, but they were smaller than he had hoped, not quite filling out the husks to the blunted tips of the long heads. Neither would they have the yield he was used to from his northern land, where he had once gleaned one hundred and eighty bushels from three and a half acres of ground, and that from a single bushel of seed.

Worried, he would slip the yoke-ring from the pole and let his oxen stand to cool while he pondered the corn just silking out, the blossoming vines with the tiny melons and squashes squatting under their leaves. If only the rain would come!

The springs on the Red Hill shrank until the water became so strong in free iron and calcium that it was almost impossible to drink. There was the nagging threat of chills and fever. The cottonwood saplings set out along the ditch-banks with such anticipation in April drooped their dust-grayed leaves, and not all the water doled out in buckets could save them. At night Clory sneaked cups of water to the bergamot about her door.

One morning Jacob Hamblin had come from Santa Clara and proceeded to the square with Apostle Snow. He was holding a forked squaw-bush stick, the two ends grasped firmly in his hands with the palms upright, the point directed heavenward. All the small boys in town were out to see this 'water-witching.' Jacob paced over the hot ground, his dark face above the stick intent, absorbed; but the stick remained a stick. And then, with startling suddenness, the pointed end twisted, hung downward.

'There!' said Jacob. 'There is where you must dig!'

But by the end of July the well was still bone-dry.

For Clory the whole long summer was just a time of waiting. She begged some wool from Abijah's recent clip (his sheep were American Rambouillets, mostly 'run for wool'), and went out before sun-up to search among the hillside rocks for the sticky soapstone. And when this had been pounded and soaked until the water was sudsy enough, she spent days scrubbing the wool matted with cockle-burrs and sand-burrs and a year's accumulation of dirt, black-daubed with the nauseous sheep-dip. Making fresh suds daily, saving the frothy oose suds until the last — Abijah said because of this country's dirt she could expect washing to shrink the wool over half its weight. And when the wool was finally dried, and as white as the down of a newly burst milkweed pod, and her stomach retching from the long contact with the oily animal smell, her hands cracked and bleeding from the soapstone, she would spend another day dreading to ask 'Sheba for her cards and spinning wheel.

The dugout was stifling within, but during the afternoons a thin patch of shade would creep behind its eastern wall. And here the two girls, Clory and Pal, would beat at the flies, and push the little rawhide-bottomed rockers, and sweat, and while away the long hours.

Pal brought over her wool and wheel. All the long afternoon the two girls and their machines in pretty rhythm, each girl part of her machine, feet stepping off the even beat of the whirring yarn as it whizzed from the flying point beneath her nimble fingers into threads of a fineness for a baby. And finally, the whir of the skeining swift.

Pal always won each day's race, completing her four skeins a day; Clory's hands were too prone to linger while her mind dreamed ahead on the baby. She had enough wool to knit stockings, a cape; a hood, perhaps. If she could just raise the ten biddies she had hatched out of that setting of eggs... Every morning she hovered over the pregnant green bulbs on her cotton plants, figuring, planning. There was, of course, another of her precious petticoats. Though she supposed, if she ever did get dressed up again, folks would think her shameless, wearing only two petticoats.

'I think I'll name her "Calistra,"' she would say; 'don't you think that's sweet? Calistra. Kissy? Kissy!'

But Pal was more practical. Half of her skeins were going into a warm winter shirt for David, to be dyed reddish-brown with the sticky branches of the evergreen tree, to be woven on Aunt Ket Snow's big hand loom.

'I'm a-goin' to wait until *my* baby gets here,' she said, 'and I'm a-goin' to have Stiddy Weeks bring it, too!'

Clory spent most of her free hours unraveling the crocheting on the flounces of her petticoats, picking out the minute hand-stitch· ing of the tucks. Kissy's christening gown, at least, should be perfect — soft with the texture of old, much-laundered cloth, fashioned with all the grace of loving hands. The incredibly tiny stitches, the crocheted insertion between the rows of tucks on the long skirt, the fragile eyelet embroidery of the yoke. The matching slip beneath. Pinning-blankets, bellybands, the shirt she made out of an old piece of shawl Pal gave her, large enough to pin over and let out as the baby grew.

Her resentment mounted at 'Sheba for not lending Isaiah's layette to the other wives of the family, as was the custom. But 'Sheba still figured on having another baby; lots of women had babies until they were fifty; a baby girl would switch Abijah's attention back where it belonged.

And so Willie, too, ripped apart and cut and contrived with hand-me-downs — colored clothes would be better in this country, anyway; but Clory went on scheming for white. White for Kissy.

And the heat thickened until human flesh protested with a constant, nagging thirst — no amount of water could stop the craving. But Abijah still refused to be worried. The winter with its perplexities was past, the peace of the spring still held, and they had Pah Roosh by the tail.

A week before the Fourth of July, Clory and Pal and Marianne Snow met in the dugout to make the flag: Pal with her cambric petticoat, Marianne with her blue taffeta, Clory with her red cassimere. Clory's eyes were wet when she finally cut into the cassimere; this meant more her than to the others — they could get other dresses, but with a width out never again would her red skirt swing so stylishly.

There was a lot of argument about the stripes; Apostle Snow had to be called in before they got the number exactly right. Even then the stiff cambric and soft cassimere puckered; and even after Clory had gone next door and borrowed Sister Hansen's heavy smoothing-iron and they had removed the plug and stuffed its belly with hot coals and each taken turns pressing, the puckers still showed. But they had real trouble over the stars. The blue taffeta made a lovely background — the snag they struck was the State of Deseret. Pal said Clory and Marianne were both crazy: there wasn't any real State of Deseret; this was the Territory of Utah and had no place among the stars. But Marianne said Deseret ought to be a state if it wasn't, and darned if she was going to sweat all week over a flag to celebrate the nation's birthday when the very land she stood on had to be ruled out! But Erastus said truth was truth, and while he praised his youngest wife's spunk, he regretfully ripped the stitches from the last star.

All her life Clory had loved the Fourth over any other holiday. The local militia, branch of the Territory's Nauvoo Legion, had not yet been organized; but Shadrach Gaunt got the young men out drilling up and down Main Street in the evenings to the martial band — young Miles brooding above the fife, Eardley's agile wrists quick-stepping on the snaredrum, and Isaac Wheelock ponderous as time on the bass. The snare's gay tattoo like a cavalier off to the colors, cocking an eye at the ladies; the bass, a statesman with pompous belly and rounded phrases, roaring reasons for war; and the haunting, yearning, shrilling of the fife, the tears of those who wait at home. Watching Free, Clory thought her heart was like the crying of the fife.

The old world paused in its creaking.

'*Look at them!*' it cackled. '*Running away from Uncle Sam and planting the flag on Ensign Peak, drilling an army to fight the Union and parading on its birthday — the Spirit of '76 singing "My Country, 'Tis of Thee," to "God Save the King!"*'

On the morning of the Fourth, Clory was up before five o'clock, 'fanning the churn' so that the butter would come before the flies did. She listened for the cannon.

When Johnston's Army left in the summer they had burned their rifles and thrown their cannon into wells rather than play Santa Claus to the Saints, but Brother Brigham had ordered the cannon rescued and Erastus had trundled one of the big guns all the way down to Dixie last fall; and now, as Clory churned, its iron throat saluted the dawn and the colors on the Sugar Loaf (her colors!) and boomed away among the hills.

After the parade (the Indians had watched with noncommittal faces) there was a meeting in the bowery where Jarvis, the schoolteacher, read the Declaration of Independence, and Erastus reminded his people of Brother Brigham's words at Council Bluffs when the Mormon Battalion was being mustered: 'If there are not enough men ... we will take the women. I tell you in the name of Jesus Christ ... *magnify the laws!*'

Abijah, unsubdued by the sweat that wilted the freshness of his shirt, rallied his fellows with his own vitality.

' ... Ye know that since the soldiers came, gambling, theft, drunkenness pollutes our City of Grreat Salt Lake. Even now the r-rascals are shootin' each other to death on the streets. But most of ye here can remember that City before the gentiles came. D'ye remember Apostle Parley P. Pratt's words? "Our old firelocks have not been rubbed up or our swords unsheathed ... Oh, what a life we live! It is the dream of the poets actually fulfilled!"

'That's what we have here, my brethren, "the dream of the poets"! Now, then, up an' smile! Shame on ye for your long faces over some dried-up ditches! ...'

But all during the afternoon's races — potato races, three-legged races, chasing the greased pig — and even though there was a big gunny-sack-wrapped barrel of vinegar-and-soggum lemonade and a cup for all the free drinks a feller could hold, and kegs of sour soaproot beer and slices of molasses-covered bran bread for the older folks in the evening, and a sheep barbecued and story-telling and dancing to the fiddle in the sand — even though folks wore merry faces, through the smiles peered gloom.

6

From the first, the wheat was doomed. Heat too sudden, too intense, too lasting.

Clothes became unbearable, especially corsets. Only the hoops which held the half-dozen layers of skirts away from sticky bodies kept the women from suffocating. Skin weathered brown changed to bright red, and men who had worked in the fields all their lives pitched hay in that sun and keeled over with a shooting fever. There came a day when it seemed impossible to work. Even Bathsheba sat on her rocker inside the airy Sibley tent and fanned herself and panted. Clory, constantly wetting down the gunny-sack around the water-barrel, constantly going for another dipper-ful of the insipid stuff that only seemed to whet her thirst the more, dreamed of the cool well in the back dooryard of the ranch in the City and could have wept. The 'milk-house' — around the well Abijah had built a little board house with a hinged lid they could raise. The well was rocked up high, and underneath the lid, just above the surface of the water, were shelves — shelves stocked with wooden bowls of milk, eggs, butter. Raising the lid, you smelled the freshest smell. No day too hot for the buttermilk to be ice-cold.

Down here where there was little forage and the cows had to graze on salt grass, the milk was always weedy. And always sour. Even scalded, morning milk seldom kept until supper-time.

She hoped she would be able to nurse her baby. You couldn't raise a baby on a bottle with the heat and the crawling flies . . .

By mid-afternoon Abijah was standing up to his thighs in his wheat, a thick, flat mass of heads that rippled away from him like a solid sheet of silk. But the golden husks he shelled out on his palm were browned at the edges and the kernels shrunk and withered. Not quite ready to harvest — sun-parched. Scything took time; there had been no way he could have saved the crop, nothing to do now but turn the cows in, cut it for straw. . . . Well, he would have to give up buying the new surrey, 'Sheba's new Charter Oak stove.

But the corn and the sugar cane stood as high as his shoulder, green and moist and healthy. They would have the corn.

The end of July and no rain. Stifling days that melted into each other with a long, slow hush. The river crawled for cover under the mud. Nothing seemed to stir except the red dust.

There was no sleeping in wagon boxes and tents. People moved their beds out under the stars. In spite of Bathsheba's disgust, Willie took to spending most of her last hard month on the cool floor of Clory's dugout. Clory, assuming Willie's share of the housework, thought she could not drag through the summer with her body that seemed more and more like a foreign, misshapen barnacle.

Out in the brush, where the springs had once coursed through the Old Campground, Tutsegabbett and his naked savages drew a prayer-circle and made the nights and days hideous with their incantations. The tails of their coyote-skins dragging on the ground, they danced around the circle with high, curving steps. Three times and then the chief sprinkled each warrior with holy water on face and breast. Over and over to the keening of the Paiute Desert Song:

> Streams dry up, leaving dead fish festering in sun —
> Even the lizard is starving —
>
> *Tu-gwi-mi-rua-tu-wip*
> *Un-kar-ti-si-av-wi-mi-ni*

The first Sunday in August, Erastus dedicated as a day of fasting and prayer for rain. Family prayer, secret prayer, and in the afternoon meeting a fervent communal supplication. Furthermore, *rain would not fall on your lot if you did not attend!*

The bowery was stifling, but before Erastus had finished praying a subtle change moved the atmosphere. A quickening sense of expectancy. And even as he murmured the final 'Amen,' the first thunder rode the hills. People opened their eyes to an absence

of glare, a shadowed darkness as welcome as water to a thirsty
man. Gooseflesh stood out on their bodies and their eyes were
awed at this sudden proof of the Almighty's listening ear. They
sang the final hymn with an exultation that shook the heavens;
silly with relief, they tumbled out to the yard, to stand with upraised faces, open-mouthed to the drenching downpour.

There is nothing in the world like that first smell of rain on
parched earth. An excitement, a newness, an untouched feeling
that surely must have belonged to the first Creation.

Clory, home alone with Willie, hurrying to drag the bedding in
out of the storm — hers, and 'Sheba's-and-Abijah's beyond the
Sibley tent, the boys' out by the barn — longed to be an angle-
worm, to get down and burrow her body through the rich mud.
She could hear the water running in the sidewalk ditch, a howling
torrent. Thousands of red water gullies were streaming all over
the lot.

7

Abijah stretched his body luxuriantly between the sheets.
Only last night he couldn't have stood the touch of sheets. Above
the drumming of the rain on the canvas he could hear the far-off
roaring of Pah Roosh, swollen with the storm. But he wasn't
worried. That brush-and-rock-and-earth dam they had spent
all winter in building should withstand a deluge. And the tunnel
— about one and a half miles below the dam was the tunnel —
nine hundred feet of timbered tunnel driven through the clay
foundation of the eastern Black Ridge — through the southern
point which Erastus had rounded to first enter the valley, the
point like a long black finger poking the river, jack-knifing it.
The storm couldn't hurt the tunnel.

And leading through the tunnel the irrigation canal was deep
and broad and stout — head-gates solid and snug — watering
their fields for nearly six fertile miles, watering nearly four hun-

dred and twenty acres (their goal for the first year). What a job
that ditch had been! He had come home night after night,
plastered with mud, too tired to eat. But the ditch would hold.
Besides, that was the water-master's job.

He turned over by the snoring 'Sheba and slept.

Someone shaking his shoulder, hoarse, fear-ridden voices, lanterns like the yellow eyes of cats. A flood. The dam. Wake Free.
Harness the mules. Throw a blanket on Nellie.

There was a fury in the storm. It beat at the men, hunched
them over the wagon seat.

The ride to the dam would take more than an hour through the
black tumult. Abijah gave the mules their heads. Down the
road through the gate in the rock wall, across the floor of the
valley, the jog south on the Old Campground trail nearly to that
piece Abijah meant to farm next year, where he had taken Clory
that day — why did it seem so long ago? — then the turn east
again to the dam.

As they came nearer, the river boomed until the sound seemed
to fill the world.

Free jumped down from Nellie, tossed the bridle over her head,
patted her nuzzling nose. Abijah tied the reins to the brake
handle and yelled at him.

'We'll have to go on foot ——'

There was something — almost — indecent about Free's
answering laughter. Something Abijah did not like. A wild
exultation that died away on the wind. But perhaps it was only
his imagination in the night and the storm.

They blundered through the brush to the shelving bank. Pah
Roosh bellowed like a chained bull. Men were already there,
yelling, rushing frantically about. Abijah recognized voices —
Wheelock and Wight and Jarvis and Peabody and Hichinoper
and Tuckett: Hansen, his neighbor, Zebedee Trupp, Shadrach
Gaunt.

Lanterns pricked the night at their feet, and here and there along the shore; little circles of rain-bleared light that trans-figured for an instant spots of greasy muck, glistening drops on whipping brush-ends, but only deepened the terror in the void beyond.

The dam was still holding, the men cried. A few leaks here and there. More brush and rocks . . .

It was totally impossible to see. Abijah stood on the bank and tried to peer out into that welter of wind and rain and water. But there was only the tumult, the sense of cataclysm.

A cold hand grasped his wrist, and he looked up to see Apostle Snow, with Shadrach Gaunt looming beside him, carrying a lantern. Shadrach's long black braids had come loose and dangled wetly over his buckskin shoulders, but his bony face was calm, his eyes beneath their tufted brows quietly reflective, and his jaws moved with gentle rhythm on his Paiute gum. But Erastus' face was strained and haggard in the upward glow of the lantern, his full cheeks high-lighted, full lips writhing, drops clinging to his ruffle of beard.

'There's not much we can do!' Erastus shouted in Abijah's ear. 'If it holds till morning . . .'

The river bed was shifting quicksand that could swallow an ox at a gulp; how build a dam that would reach below the sand?

A familiar figure loomed up behind Erastus and Shadrach. It was Tutsegabbett, wrapped in his rabbit's-fur cape, his eagle feather undaunted by the onslaught, his dark features weird and primeval in the faint upward rays of the light.

'How!' he greeted Abijah. But there was no reproach in his eyes, nor did he remind Abijah of the special trip he had made to warn him last spring.

'Mormonie . . . help Tutsegabbett,' he intoned in his halting English; 'now Tutsegabbett . . . help Mormonie . . . Bring squaw. Strong . . . carry rocks!' He flexed his biceps to show them.

True enough, the white men could just make out his voluminous wife beside him, like a plump brown pudding in her rabbit's-skin shirt.

Erastus writhed his lips and laughed, lifting the lantern from Shadrach to see and thank the Indian. Ptsahh!

There was a sudden near splashing, and another face burst out of the darkness as if it had been running for miles without a body: Ole Oleson, the water-master, with his huge red ears and his yawning nostril holes. The water spurted on his bald head and ran in little rivulets down into his collar. He kept mopping his eyes with the back of his sleeve.

'She, bitch!' he yelled. 'Canal too much side-hill. Clay here, go out! Gravel there, go out! Why He not mix 'em, make 'em stick like hell, huh?'

Other feet slushing.

'Ole, Ole, she's going!'

'Bitch!' yelled Ole, and started off through the night, the others at his heels.

The river's pounding lessened as they ran, but the canal itself was a noisy bully, surging between its banks of brush.

The men jumped back just in time and held their lanterns high. The light struck four feet of bank crumbling before their eyes.

'Damn gopher,' sobbed Ole, and began futilely to scoop up mud with his hands.

Tutsegabbett clapped for service like the potentate he was. '*To-win-nee! To-win-nee!*'

There was a panting hail behind him.

'*A-mon-yaa!*'

Before their astonished eyes the fat squaw flung herself, back upstream, into the gap, her face expressionless as the water piled up and lashed at her neck and finally drizzled away in chagrin on either side of her broad hind-quarters.

Tutsegabbett gestured and folded his arms. There! Now you can shovel the mud where it will do some good. . . .

The ditch mended, Erastus and Shadrach and Abijah and Tutsegabbett slogged back to the dam. There was perhaps an hour left before daylight, but the night had seemed to drag forever, the world long since wiped out. There was only the blackness walling in these savage sheets of rain. Drenched, shivering, defeated, the little group of men stood beside Pah Roosh and watched the gray dawn lift.

It did not seem possible this was the same innocent stream they had known. Choked with mud, the thick water rolled along like molasses — mighty waves that churned themselves into whirlpools. Instead of their accustomed red, waves black with borrowed, up-country loam. Alien pine-nut burrs rode in the whirlpools, and looted haystacks and dead chickens.

The watchers marveled that the dam had held this long. Even now, waves licked greedily at the top layer of rocks, brimmed gently over.

'Look!' someone yelled.

'Mac! Mac! Isn't that your boy?'

Abijah lifted numbed eyes.

For at first the watchers saw only Free recklessly putting Nellie at the ugly water. Mad and futile bravado.

'Come back!' they screamed. 'You fool! You crazy damn fool!'

Only then were they aware of the figure ahead of Free, lashing out with cool courage, swept along like another pine-nut burr. Abijah saw Eardley start, transfixed. Shadrach grabbed him, held him back, gibbering with horror. His oldest boy. His fine grown boy who had just returned from a mission a year ago . . . Caught by a caving bank? Clutched by the flood, sucked under, helpless against the current.

'Come back!' they shouted again. 'You can't save him!'

But Free flung up an arm to them and threw back his head to the driving arrows of rain and laughed. The surging, crazy life in him, whetted by the excitement of the night and the turbulence, seemed to glory in the storm, a part of it, gay and unquenchable,

savage and splendid. They could see him talking to his horse.
Above the uproar they caught the faint, incongruous echo of
singing. He charged the waves like a knight with a lance and the
valiant little mare put back her ears and plunged.

The men on the bank waited, held their breaths, followed the
two bobbing figures with their eyes through the half-light. Now
horse and rider were swallowed, now they could see the tips of
Nellie's ears. They had lost entirely that other black, bobbing
head. Then they saw Free swoop with an arm. The current
whirled him like a cork, but Nellie righted him — his eyes searched
the waters, he swooped again. But the dam was going — going.

'You devil!' Eardley sobbed, shaking his fist at the river.

A sudden acceleration in the roar whipped their eyes above the
dam again. My God! here it came. A wave twice as big as the
Sugar Loaf. That bobbing head far down there was only halfway across, two thirds of the way . . . They watched, they waited
for the wave to strike, holding their breaths.

A whoosh, a boom, a shudder — a chaos of brush and logs and
water, boulders thrown high in the air like pebbles. Their
breaths went out on a long sigh. They watched Pah Roosh shake
herself free from the last of her tethers, leap jubilantly beyond
the banks — a year's work gone by. Ech, thought Abijah incon-
sistently, there goes my new stake-and-rider fence.

They stood there silently. No one spoke, even when Free
pulled himself up on the far shore, dragging a limp body . . .

There was nothing Erastus could do for the dead, and little
enough for the living. He stood with Abijah and Shadrach Gaunt,
David Wight and Ole Oleson, Hichinoper, Miles, Jarvis and Lon
Tuckett, and watched the Eardley wagon slush homeward
through the mud, Eardley hunched over his dead son in the back
and Free hunched over the reins. Nellie trailed alongside, her
gallant head lowered, her burnished coat scabbed with
mud.

Erastus started off through the rain for the fields. As Bathsheba MacIntyre would say of a cup as bitter as gall, or a dose of castor oil, 'The quicker it's down, the sooner it's over.'

Unbelievable that only yesterday these farms they had marked off and enclosed with such hope could have rippled with life. The grain was entirely buried under five inches of silt. The corn and sugar cane were whipped to the ground, stalks broken off and weighted with mud. The ruin was complete and devastating. Much of the land itself was gone — the river had taken some big bites. Well, maybe this was their punishment for going against counsel and raising grain instead of cotton in the first place.

Erastus made himself look at his men. There was fear in their eyes but no panic. They had faced too much for panic. The psychology of courage buckled them together like a visible bond.

He did not try to reassure them falsely. There was danger, plenty of it; they faced starvation. But there were worse things than starvation — there were mobs and rapings and the tar bucket. They had their freedom and their strong right arms — what more did any man need? Many of these men had been through Nauvoo with him.

Looks of recognition, of memory, flashed into their eyes for a moment. Erastus knew whereof he spoke — he himself had filled ten missions for the Church before he came to Dixie: he had been mobbed in Pennsylvania, pelted with rotten eggs in Kirtland, driven from Far West, scourged from Nauvoo, where he had given Abijah and Bathsheba MacIntyre their endowments in the Temple during those last frantic hours before the exodus. Named along with Orson Pratt in Brother Brigham's revelation of 1847 in Winter Quarters 'showing the mind and will of the Lord concerning the Camps of Israel,' he and Orson had organized the Saints into companies — Erastus looked at Abijah MacIntyre, president of one of his companies; Isaac Wheelock, captain of one of the Fifties; other faces remembered from buffalo hunts, Indian fights, the slow, hard toil of conquering a new country.

No, these men would never quit him now. After all, he re-

minded them, each town lot still had its tiny patch of grain or
corn or cotton . . . They would trust in the Lord — this was still
part of his vineyard — and turn the unused harvest hours into
extra opportunities for work on the Social Hall, into time for
building the tithing office, the cotton factory. . . .

The men were drenched, hungry, bone-tired. Shadrach Gaunt
stopped chewing, narrowed his eyes at Erastus reflectively. Lon
Tuckett lifted his carroty head and ventured a cackle.

'I vum, Brother Snow,' he said, 'when you was askin' the Lord
for rain, *why didn't you tell him how much!*'

8

Clory had never seen a baby born. She looked at Willie writhing with pain on her bed in the hot canvas cave of her tent, and
bit her lip. Willie's face was puffy and her legs and feet swollen to
twice their size.

Clory ran as hard as she could across the yard to the Sibley
tent, where 'Sheba was making the Eardley boy's burial clothes.

'Hurry, 'Sheba,' she panted, 'Willie's a-flooding and a-flooding!
Hurry ——'

'Sheba brushed away a fly and looked up from the garments
she was 'marking,' the significant small holes over each breast to
be embroidered with fine, even stitches. She had worked all the
day before and all last night with Hannah Merinda Lowgie and
Keturah Snow to weave enough wool for the garments and the
soft white trousers and the Temple apron — the creosote-bush
branches hadn't given a very clear green for the fig leaves, but it
couldn't be helped — they would use one of the young man's own
white shirts.

Her eyes were dark-circled with weariness.

'It's nothing,' she snapped at Clory. 'Willie's got about as
much sense as a piss-ant. Besides, I can't leave these now or I
won't get 'em done in time for the funeral.'

Back at the tent Willie was having one of her in-between times.

''Sheba'd rather lay out a dead body than save a live one, any day,' Clory said hotly, shooing out flies with a dishtowel.

Willie's pain-bitten lips smiled feebly.

'Well, I don't see 'ow's you can blame her. One more star in 'er crown. Laws, what's 'er record now?'

Clory recited as one does who has heard a thing many times: 'Five hundred bodies dressed and laid out since she was fifteen and first joined the church in Nauvoo ——'

'Agin she gits 'ere ——' began Willie, and doubled with another paroxysm.

Clory wrung her hands helplessly.

Willie's sallow flesh was ghastly, the liver-spots emphatic. The skin tightened across her sharp nose, her lips drew away from her teeth.

Clory flung herself down by the bed and grasped one of the bony, red wrists.

'I'm scared!' she cried. 'I'm scared, Aunt Willie!'

Willie waited a moment to be sure the pain had passed, and let out her breath.

'Laws, child ... all women folks 'as it ... like this. Birthin's the same whether y're rich or poor.'

She reached out a hand and patted the girl's dark hair. The summer's heat, the hard water had robbed it of some of its shine and curliness; Clory's face had thinned, lost its childish curve and lovely, wayward color. Even her voice had deepened, lost its light, faery tones. But the faint fragrance of bergamot still clung to her, and the same eager tilt to her head. She would get back her beauty when her child was born — yes, and something added.

Another pain came, and Clory wiped the sweat from the suffering woman's forehead, swatted a mud-dauber, and jabbered to divert her mind.

'I guess everybody's having to pinch. Abijah said Apostle Snow told the men in Council yesterday their wives had to start scrubbing all the clothes by hand. Washboards are too hard on calico at fifty cents a yard. And this morning' — she stopped to smile reminiscently — 'this morning I went to borrow something from Sister Hansen next door, and guess what she was doing?'

Willie blinked the tears of weakness from her eyes and shook her head obediently.

'Did you ever hear of a bum-rub? She was giving her clothes a *bum-rub!* She had all her dishtowels and sheets folded up and was sitting there on them, and when I asked her why, she said a bum-rub saved the wear and tear of so much ironing!'

The next pain was so bad that Clory begged Willie to let her go after 'Sheba again. If anything happened to Willie's baby it would be 'Sheba's fault. 'Sheba was a midwife before everything, and her first duty was to her own family.

The pains lengthened, grew in intensity.

Abijah and Bathsheba looked in on their way to the funeral. Bathsheba's hooped circumference almost swallowed the little tent. Abijah had to squeeze past her when he came over to pat Willie's hand. It hurt Clory, somehow, to see his shoulders stooped, his gusto blurred. Bathsheba had a steaming bowl of pennyroyal tea, another of slippery elm and horehound.

'Land sakes, you're beating the stork!' she shrilled comfortably, her black taffeta rustling. 'But it'll be hours yet. I'll bring Sister Lowgie home with me and you'll be snug as a bug in a rug. Just be sure you ain't got any double-bitted axes around so's you won't have twins!'

She handed Willie a leather strap.

'Put it on your wrist,' she ordered. 'It will hold the cramps till I get back.'

But neither the teas nor the strap worked. Clory tried to entertain Willie with tales of this and that — old Brother Hansen carving a bass fiddle out of hard wood he had found in the canyons up north, working by a pine knot in the fireplace, even on hot nights. He had the fiddle finished — so beautiful! — and the case for it halfway done. The wood whittled to an incredible delicacy, bent and curved to fit, and polished until the russet grain stood out like watered silk.

But Willie only grunted.

In the middle of the afternoon Clory went out to see what had become of the little boys. The weather was cooler since the storm, but the blistering dooryard sent her bare feet scuttling for shade.

A strangling animal shriek drove her back to the tent. There was a time of convulsive horror, Willie's body a possessed, contorting thing with a will of its own; Willie praying for 'Sheba while Clory helplessly shooed flies and hated 'Sheba for not being there. Willie's hands gripping Clory's, digging into her palms — Clory wondered why she had ever wanted to have a baby.

There hadn't been even time to borrow the Castile soap Sister Lowgie had brought across the plains and loaned out for birthings.

Clory held the blue, wrinkled, gnome-like creature in her hands and thought of an unfledged bird, still wet from birth. The misshapen head lolled on the spindling shoulders. There was a grimace of distaste on the blind, old-man face, a look of strain as if it had fought against giving up life. But a secretiveness, too, as if it had gained some ageless wisdom. Drowned newly born kittens looked like that — blindly struggling even with their heads under water.

Willie's lips moved feebly.

'Promise me,' she whispered, 'if I shouldn't come through this ... don't let 'Sheba lay me hout!'

Clory held the shrunken, fleshless feet in her palm and cried. What chance had Kissy! Hannah Merinda Lowgie might obey all the inspired rules for midwives laid down by Moses in Leviticus, but Clory would still see her with her head on one side, like a confiding hen — 'I never talk and it's none of my business, but ...'

She thought of 'Sheba's calm indifference. One of Abijah's

cows out in the barnyard got better care. This mustn't, mustn't happen to Kissy. O God, there ought to be some way for a woman caught in plurality!

9

The family were eating supper. Yant — 'squaw cabbage' — boiled up and salted. Last night it had been dandelion greens, and the night before pigweed greens. More corn-meal mush. It was a vicious circle — you ate and got the scours, which made you so weak and empty that you ate some more.

Bathsheba glanced at Clory speculatively, but made no comment as she slid into her place on the bench beside the twins. Free gave her a long look and went back to brooding over his plate.

Abijah, upset about Willie and the stillborn child, wanted to strike out at this tension at the table. Bathsheba, of course, was as stubborn as a mule — everybody knew that — but you could humor her. Trouble was, Clorinda didn't try to get along, took everything that happened so hard. And Free — aye, he could curse a fyllie. He had caught that sly look a moment ago. My conscience, was he never to have any peace? He remembered that one night last spring when they sang. There had been harmony among them all then, for the first time in a year. He had felt it. But he doubted if he'd ever feel it again. This goading hunger made things worse. He knew that for months 'Sheba had been saving a mess-pan of white flour and that bit of sugar in her trunk to make a cake for Brother Brigham when he came, and yet he had actually caught himself the other day sneaking after the sugar. When a man got that low...

Clory tried to eat some of the clabbered milk, but her stomach turned. President Snow said they must divide, and so their evening's milking went to the Hansens next door, but it was hard when your own mouth watered for the fresh, warm nourishment.

After the dishes were washed and the little boys in bed, Clory
wandered disconsolately out into the warm night, across the yard.
She peeped in at Willie, but Willie lay like one dead in the dim
candlelight, her hair a gray straggle on the pillow. Bathsheba
had taken away the baby, but there was something curiously
bereft in the curve of Willie's arm. As Clory turned to go,
Willie opened her eyes. They were red-rimmed from tears, but
that serenity Clory had come to trust, that look of peace and
infinite wisdom, still lived behind the grief. Clory flung her
troubled spirit on the broad, deep bosom of that peace. How
did one gain that wisdom? How did one get beyond the hurts
of life?

Always before, each day she lived had been a stair she climbed
to some radiant future, some future so spiced with hidden revela-
tions that her heart swung like a censer before each new dawn.
But now as the old world turned, she was conscious only of a bad
taste in her mouth. A nameless longing. A sense of time fleeting
by, too fast to catch, too precious to lose. She loved Kissy, but
there was something irrevocable about birth. Her girlhood would
go with Kissy, and all her bright young dreams. And she was
only seventeen ...

Willie's eyes were tender. Clory knelt by the bed and buried
her face in the quilt. There were no words for what she felt. How
find words to tell of Rolph's bringing her flowers, teasing her
about her 'Mormon God,' of Free with his love charm, his dare-
deviltry, his meadowlark that 'sings each song twice over'? Of
the child in her womb that had always seemed more Free's than
his father's? Polygamy was a prison with bars stronger than iron.

Willie put out a hand to touch the girl's bowed head.

'Remember,' her tired voice said, 'remember, "*where much is
given, much is required.*" ... Even the folks we envy 'aven't
everything. Nobody has *all* the things he wants in life ... And
we with the Gospel are so blessed. Think what it'll be like after
we die. The glory and the wonder ... And if God seems to give us

women a harder lot than men, at least He's given us the stren'th to bear it ... The back is suited to the burden ... Think of Abijah 'avin' to 'ave a baby!'

All the evening Clory sat in the doorway of her dugout, steeped in the fresh mint-smell of the bergamot at her feet, and watched the hills to the south creep closer in the twilight. She felt as lonely as the coyotes that howled out there, as forsaken as the solitary piping of the cricket under her step.

The light went out in the Sibley tent. The darkness closed in around her. Somewhere a frog croaked, and she thought of her cotton patch into which she had put so much time and hope and effort. Tonight was the watering-turn for their lot. Sometimes she had had to get out of bed and take the water herself, but tonight she could not stir, not even for Kissy's layette. Long after midnight she was still sitting there, a huddled little figure, chin on hand.

The sound of water running roused her, the 'ku-suck' of a lifted head-gate, the smack of a shovel. Small, wet sounds magnified in the night. One of the boys irrigating. Relieved, she heaved up her body and walked around the corner of the dugout. It was Free, tall against the starlight, hands idly clasping the handle of his shovel, one foot resting on its half-buried hilt. Preoccupied with the water flowing along each row of cotton plants, he did not see her at first. Then her foot snapped on a twig and he raised his head, but he did not speak as he watched her come toward him, the strong, healthy bushes brushing above her waist.

Over his undershirt Free had slipped a pair of waist-overalls, and the muscles of his hard young shoulders quivered under the bare skin. His body was bronzed by the summer. Clory had not noticed of late how mature his mustache was getting; nor how firmly his mouth closed below the line of blond hairs.

There was something so helpless about the little gesture with which she greeted him.

'Seems like I can't get around to it any more,' she said, indicating the cotton and trying to laugh.

'Judas priest!' he growled. 'You shouldn't have to! Judas priest!'

(Free with a new byword. A forbidden byword, making him more of a man. She regarded him tenderly.)

'But I'm a married woman, you know.'

Her voice was so low he could hardly hear her.

'I'm almost . . . a mother.'

She rested her cheek on her clasped hands as if her head would droop without support. There was nothing left in the little gesture of its old gay, flirtatious charm. His heart constricted. He would rather have had her making fun of him. Her voice had saddened, too; lost its flutelike notes. How often working late in the field he had listened to a mockingbird and thought it spiritless beside her voice. He caught a whiff of bergamot — that she would never lose; that clean, sweet smell was her very essence. It lifted her, a chaste goddess, above all these other sweating, earthy women.

'The water — it looks so cool. I . . .'

She wriggled her toes in the shallow stream at their feet. The dampness was delicious. But the mud was slick when she put her weight upon it, and she reeled suddenly and reached out blindly. Dreadful things happened to women who fell down when they were as far along as she. Free dropped the shovel and had an arm around her instantly. The solicitude in his face was balm to her sore heart. She clung to him and leaned her head against his breast. She could hear his heart lurch and then pound madly beneath the overalls.

The moon was just coming up and its silver shining caught her, spangled her dark hair, a fragrant cloud about her shoulders. He bent and kissed her head. He held her carefully, without pressure, as if she might break.

She raised her eyes and gazed at him lingeringly, with the concentration of one trying to memorize something. Her eyes were like velvet, deep and inscrutable as midnight.

'I get dizzy,' she confessed. 'I'm sorry, I ...'

He had never kissed her before, and now, trembling with re-straint, he suddenly became brusque, matter-of-fact, a man taking charge.

'You're hungry. I'm going to get you some milk ... Don't worry, Pa won't find out. Let Hansens go without for once.'

He made her sit on the steps of her dugout while he went inside and got the brass bucket from its shelf.

'Try to rest. I'll only be a minute.'

Comforted, she relaxed against the soft dried leaves of the wall and was half asleep when he came back.

He made her drink several bowls of the frothy milk, tipping each bowl to her mouth as she drank. When the bucket was empty, he returned it to the dugout and came back beside her on the step, held her hands, and regarded her seriously.

'Please take better care of yourself, Clory.'

She sighed with satisfaction.

'Oh, Free, I feel better than I have done for days!'

The moon was riding high and full — the unearthly brilliance of this country's summer moonlight, bright enough to read by — and she could see his full lips indented at the corners, the dimple in his chin, his strange, too-large eyes deep with unspoken thoughts. There was just a hint of quiver in the lips.

She leaned suddenly and kissed him. Beyond the guilty feeling in her heart was an older, headier clamor. But she hadn't ex-pected this wild, tumultuous bliss, this joy that struck her to the core. Her very flesh seemed to dissolve — a voice rode trium-phantly over the dark waves in her mind, 'I never knew kissing could be like this.' All the pent-up restraint of the last year re-leased, drowning them, blinding them. Free put his arms around her and kissed her violently, hungrily, as if he would never let her go. They looked at each other, half-laughing, half-crying, and then he kissed her some more. He kissed the red mouth cracked by the summer heat, and the blue pulse that throbbed where the riotous hair swept back from the temple. Her lips answered him, passionate, uncaring.

And then the words had to be said, out into the night, where they could take them apart and look at them without fear.

'You have to say it, Clory — that way we'll know we're not sneaking, it's not wrong ——'

Her head came up proudly, and she looked him in the eye.

'I do love you, Free,' she said steadily. 'I guess I've loved you for a long time and I just didn't know it. We shouldn't have ever let it happen, but now it has, I'm not ashamed. I'm glad.'

He gave a little choked cry at her courage and buried his head in her lap.

They sat through the long night among the crushed bergamot and made plans, quite as if they could make plans. Their happiness was so sudden, so overwhelming (nothing so right and safe could be wrong), that at first they would not believe it had to be denied.

One moment Free was the triumphant, conquering male — imperative and tender and rough, not an awkward boy but a man — begging her to run away with him.

But run where? There were deserts stretching endlessly on either side . . .

And the ugly facts would not be downed. Running away would justify all Abijah's suspicions. Blood atonement, and the transgressor's blood going up as an incense to the Lord in expiation. The law gave Abijah the right to do that to a wife who transgressed her marriage vows.

And gradually ecstasy paled before reality. There was no way out. But at least they had this night. They were tender with each other, prodigal of endearments, since they could never call each other 'darling' and 'dear' again.

When the moon began to go down and they awoke to a realization that dawn was almost here, Clory was lying in his lap, her head pillowed on his arm.

'Promise me . . . promise me . . .' he murmured inarticulately.

But she was stronger than he. She looked at him as she had done once before, as if she were memorizing each loved feature, and then she slowly drew herself away from his arms and sat up.

'No, Free,' she said softly, 'there's no use trying to hang on to it. Our lives were marked out by Somebody bigger than us and we've got to live them the way He's set us down. At least we know about our love and we can use it to make us stronger, finer. Every time I look at you I can say to myself, "There's the person who has made my life richer, who is always in my heart" — I'll look at you and know that as long as I live I'll never be lonely again ——'

Her voice broke, and for a moment she could not go on. His face was so young and piteous in the moonlight.

'Oh, Free, if we can build a world where girls like Kissy won't ever lose their dads and moms, nor see their brothers starve, what does it matter what happens to us?'

She was already a lost white blur to him, like last spring's apple blossoms in the moonlight, just a fragrant memory in this hot, hard country. He reached for her hand.

'Where men can marry the girls they like?'

'Oh, my darling'—she stumbled a little over the unaccustomed word, and then repeated it as if the taste were sweet upon her tongue — 'my darling, don't. It'll work out. You'll see. There are times when I know there's so much more to life than just this . . . this . . . When I feel close and safe beside Something so much bigger than any of us dream of . . . it takes my breath away! Times when there's a Hand laid soft over my heart . . . No, my darling, you have your job and I have mine. And all that counts is doing 'em . . .'

10

One day during the middle of August, Abijah took his lunch and left the house well before dawn. It wasn't that he didn't have

full confidence in President Snow's assurance that Brother Brig- .
ham would bring them help, nor was it that he had lost faith in
the Lord, but he was tired of seeing his family starve.

Besides, for some reason his oldest son was constantly at him
lately, begging him for permission to go to the California gold
mines, to join this or that wagon-train, to become a driver for the
new Wells-Fargo stage line he was told had started up across the
country. The authorities counseled that when there was no work
for young men the elders should construct more ditch and open up
new lands for them, and certainly he had been doing his share —
out every morning before daylight, helping to build a new dam,
clearing the flooded fields, mending and lengthening the ditch —
but Free seemed to take little interest in any of it. He was so restless lately. Abijah couldn't understand his indifference to the
games and sports of other boys his age. Abijah had even offered
to lend him his black broadcloth suit in which to go courting some
girl, if he was a-mind to; but nothing seemed to do any
good.

One day last winter, wandering by himself in the cut-up country far beyond the Sugar Loaf, he had come upon a ledge of
richly colored rocks. Sending a sample to a California assayer on
the next wagon-train, he had been delighted but not surprised to
find that the rock contained large amounts of gold. But that
night, the night he got the word, a strange old man had come to
his door for food and had told him to leave the mine alone, that
it would ruin his boys. Abijah, startled to learn that anyone else
knew his secret, had gone after the bread, but when he returned
the old man had vanished.

Abijah had ever since felt uneasily that the old man was one
of those Three Nephites in the Book of Mormon — those three
to whom the Lord had given the power to live on until the second
coming of Christ, after the rest of the Nephites had been wiped
out by the Lamanites; they were said to have the ability to become invisible at will. There were many instances where they

had refilled flour barrels, given warnings in the nick of time to the righteous, answered prayers.

But now Abijah did not care. Even though he knew he was going against counsel. Even though Brother Brigham had said they would stop up hog-holes in the fences with those who 'had a golden god in their hearts.' A mine would give his family food. A mine might save his boy.

All day Abijah wandered the hills. But the hills seemed changed. Even the very landmarks were unrecognizable. By mid-afternoon, weary and footsore, he had come to the conclusion that he could not find the place. A spine-tingling conclusion, since it meant only one thing — that the Three Nephites were determined to save him from himself. Brought face to face with that realization, he felt humbled and grateful that he hadn't been given over to the buffetings of Satan, and determined to make confession and bow his stiff-necked pride.

That night after prayers he told his family the whole story. Free, especially, seemed interested, making him recount every detail. Abijah went to bed easier in heart than he had been for some time.

It was only a day or two afterward that Apostle Snow's boy summoned Abijah to a hasty Council meeting.

Brother Erastus was on time for once. His pepper-and-salt chin-ruffle looked as if mice had been scampering through it.

He stared at his twelve right-hand men and writhed his lips.

'I ... don't know just what ... to believe,' he drawled, 'but ... it looks right enough. And ... if it's true ... it means we're having a visit ... by the Three Nephites!'

Brother Snow hitched his fast bay team to his wagon and they all sat on quilts in the box and drove across the valley to Washington. Brother John D. Lee wasn't there (Abijah heard that people in Washington were so critical of him over that Mountain Meadow business that he had taken to spending all his time at his

ranch near Cedar Fort), but the good Bishop Covington met
them and took them to see the footprints. They were just outside
of town on the south road leading to the fields (indeed, Erastus
had barely missed them at the turn), and were plainly visible.
The road had been flooded by the swollen stream that coursed
through town and on out into the flat, and there in the soft mud,
headed north in exact precision, were the marks of a gigantic bare
foot. The big toes themselves were six inches long, and the rest
of the foot in proportion.

The men examined the prints with awe and just a hint of fear.
But the people of Washington who had gathered about could
offer no clue. The boys herding the cows out this morning had
returned with the news — that was all anybody knew.

Finally Erastus suggested they all return to their homes and
assemble at the St. George Square in the morning. If the footprints came again during the night ...

Before sun-up the next day the big bass drum was booming.
All over town people left their homes and their work and flocked
to the square. The footprints had come back.

'We know they're not of this earth,' said Erastus, 'but ... just
what —? If it is the Nephites ... you'd think ... they would
come forward ——'

The faces of his people were grave. Were they to be harassed
by supernatural forces as well as material ones? They had been
hungry for a long time. Now they were frightened as well.
Erastus saw panic in their eyes.

'We have been ... in the main, righteous,' he reassured them.
'I cannot see ... God allowing ... Satan in this part of His vineyard; ... I move we go home ... to our work ... and say our
prayers, but send a rider to Brother Brigham ... as fast as possible. Brother Shadrach ——'

But when the square was cleared and he walked up the street
beside Shadrach Gaunt, he could not force himself to complete
acceptance of his own plan. The City was a good three hundred

and fifty miles away. It would take Shadrach a week to get there. Meanwhile, if anything was going to happen to them, it would be all over by the time he got back.

'Do you scare easy, Shadrach?' He asked, his gray eyes twinkling.

Shadrach spat.

'Who, me?'

They had waited in the clump of bushes for several hours. There was no moon, but they could see the road plainly. Erastus jumped every time he heard a twig snap or a sudden cheeping, but Shadrach chewed calmly. The prints were still entirely visible. Erastus had been sitting cramped for so long that he thought he would have to move in spite of all his caution, when they first heard the sound.

It came from the north, toward town. For all the world like someone, a very mortal someone, creeping through the brush across the road. Suppressed giggles, a whisper quickly cut off. Erastus relaxed, thinking another person had had his same idea, but some prudence kept him quiet. He put a restraining hand on Shadrach's arm.

Two figures on all fours crept out from the brush across the way. Erastus peered through the darkness. They were boys, all right, but they carried something with them. He watched them look guardedly about and then rise to their feet, the objects in their hands. One snickered and bumped into the other. 'Judas priest!' he hissed. Erastus knew that voice. Then the figures stooped again with the objects, and he suddenly knew what those objects were. Giant wooden feet!

Free was sullen and defiant before the Council. Erastus did not doubt the prank had started out as a joke, but he had to take it seriously now. A blasphemous joke, and furthermore people with empty stomachs would not relish the idea that they had been made to look foolish. The other boy — Gottlieb Uttley, the young Swiss — was willing enough to beg forgiveness in a public meeting, but Freeborn said he'd rather be disfellowshipped It had been a joke and he didn't see why all the fuss. Erastus watched Abijah's hazel eyes grow steel-gray with wrath, and wished that he could have this boy to himself a little while. Understanding and sympathy, but mostly just understanding, would get within that insolent armor.

Abijah was quivering with suppressed rage when he got Free out of the bowery and into the street. 'If a man have a stubborn and rebellious son which will not obey the voice of his father . . .' But even God couldn't tell the Israelites what to do about a son who blasphemed! To be humiliated like that before the Council! He gritted his teeth, so angry he could not speak. He held the boy by the arm and pushed him toward home as fast as he could walk.

When they turned in at the gate, he went straight to the barn.

'For a long time ye've been filled with the spirit of contention and trouble-making and evil,' he said, breathing heavily. 'I intend to put the spirit of the Lord in ye once and for all! And from noo on ye'll live as I say under my roof or else ye'll get out!'

He went into the stall where the harness was hung, and came out coiling the long braided rawhide mule-whip around his wrist.

Free stood his ground, but his voice trembled on the edge of hysteria.

'Judas priest, I'm not a child any longer! If you try to beat me, I'll fight you back!'

Clory sat on her bed in the dugout and stuffed her fingers in her ears. But even then she could hear the vicious pop of the whip and the cries and the gruntings and the feet thrashing about. She buried her head under the pillow and wept. This was all her fault. Free's waywardness, his contempt for authority. It seemed to her the sounds went on for hours, but at last the night was still.

With some notion of finding Free, she got up and put on her
Mother Hubbard. And then he lurched under the doorway. She
did not dare light a candle, but she made a soft little moan of sympathy and groped for him in the darkness. He was shaking and
gasping. Shamed, furious, bitter. She soothed him with little
murmurings as a mother would a child and led him over to her
bed. Her exploring fingers found a long welt clotted with blood
on his cheek; she clucked with distress and her caressing hand
pushed back the damp, disheveled hair.

'Why do you do it?' she mourned. 'Why do you drive your
father to it? You know how he is. *Promise* me you'll mind
him ——'

Suddenly Free flung himself at her feet and buried his face in
her lap and burst into long, pent-up, shuddering sobs.

11

Abijah stared at her with weary exasperation. As usual, he
dwarfed the dugout, but she thought she had never seen his
vitality so dimmed. His eyes, red-rimmed from sleeplessness, were
tired and sick with despair. Even the wave she had watched him
wet and press in his hair of a morning was flattened and dull.

She observed him with cool detachment as he hunted for the
right words to say to her. One hand fumbled with the buttons of
his vest (Abijah might be driven to take off his coat in the summer, but no amount of heat could make him take off his vest), and
the skin across the knuckles was rough and chapped. He'd had
to give up his browned flour lately.

'Come in to breakfast, Clorinda Agathy,' he pleaded patiently.
'Ye're only actin' fulish. Don't you think punishin' him touched
my tender spot, too? But he maun be humbled back to the Lord.
I hae longed many times to unbosom my feelin's to ye, Clorinda
Agathy, but...'

Her ankles were still pretty, anyway. She lifted her skirts, her eyes fixed innocently on his face, so that he could see her swinging pretty feet, toes pink, nails like white seashells. There was a devil in her. She wouldn't have admitted the ankle-showing was anything but an accident for worlds. She looked at him with wide-eyed, ingenuous innocence while she tempted him with the ankles swung back and forth. And reflected that she'd *dare* him to get his passions aroused. She saw by the way he gritted his teeth that he was fully aware of what she was doing.

'Eneuch!' he cried. 'Ye're shameless!'

He clenched his fists and started toward her, but then she backed away from him, eyes wide, knocking over the chair.

'Don't touch me! Don't dare touch me! — I'll run away!'

He was bewildered.

'But Clorinda Agathy, I'm your husband. I've only been waiting ——'

Bathsheba stood in the doorway, hands on hips.

'Land sakes,' she chortled, 'this is a pretty kettle of fish!'

Her eyes snapped with enjoyment.

'What'll you do with your baby if you run away?'

Clory's head went up. That woman should never have the satisfaction of knowing she'd got under her skin.

'Oh, if it's a girl, you can have it,' she said flippantly. 'If it's a girl I'll give it to you, since you ain't got any girls...'

Abijah was at his wits' end. His endurance blew up like a rocket.

'You'll keep that promise, young lady! I'll have no light-minded promise-breakers in my house!'

He had not meant it just like that, but a thing that was said, was said.

'Sheba watched Clory's face pale and her eyes widen. Abijah never joked. 'Sheba's smile was smug. 'You got caught in your own trap that time!'

Clory crouched against the wall and watched them go. She must have been out of her mind! But Abijah would never...

12

There were mornings during those last two weeks in August when Clory opened her eyes to another hot day and thought she could not possibly live through it.

Meal-times were an agony. There Free was just across the table, his eyes on his plate; dear God, let him keep them there, since if he looked up her own would answer like the willing slaves they were.

Flying from the strain of such concealment to her dugout, she would fall upon the bed with a sick reaction. She was not worthy of Kissy.

And at other times she was a miser hoarding her love, rushing from alien eyes to be alone, to take it out of its hiding-place and hold it in her hands, recount its splendors over and over, and lift its beauties to the light of day until it caught the celestial fire of all the suns.

In the reflection of such glory her remembered nights with Abijah became monstrous, against Nature. Who, then, had made the mistake? How were she and Free to blame? Had God given them their love and only Life meddled? And her brave words to Free were as dust in her mouth. Where, indeed, was the world where 'men could marry girls they liked'!

She was a prisoner in her body, her body that was chained to the dugout. And 'Sheba came and poked and turned her as impersonally as if she were an old cat about to have kittens. There was no use asking for Stiddy Weeks. Pal brought his Doctor Book, Doctor Chase's Prescription, and said that he advised the chewing of prickly pear — in fact, prickly pear for this whole town that was having trouble with the stoppage of its urine — and that he practiced the Thompsonian course of medicines. Clory could see him with his blown white hair and his round glass spectacles — 'cayenne pepper to give power to the blood, lobelia to physic and relax the system' — bitter root and wild milkweed and prickly pear.

But Abijah would quote the Prophet, 'trust in God and not in an arm of the flesh, live by faith and not by medicine,' and remind her that Bathsheba and Hannah Merinda had been set apart by Brother Brigham himself as 'midwives and nurses in Israel' — Brother Brigham who had once advised a wife, who thought she couldn't have her baby without a doctor, to 'go out under some sagebrush and see what happens!'

During those last endless days even books failed her. The books and papers hoarded through the years with all the tenacity of exiles: *Little Lily's Travels* and *Child's History of England* already worn threadbare with reading, Willie's *Fourth Reader* with its genteel chapters on 'Decisive Integrity' and 'Female Piety,' Abijah's *Book of Mormon* that she tried so hard to find interesting, David's dog-eared magazines he'd traded food for in the City — books that no longer spoke of far-off horizons, but only served to accentuate her prison bars.

Finally, as her hour drew near, she came to doubt that even Stiddy Weeks could have exorcised her own particular devil — it was something within yourself you had to tie to in the end.

Her time came on a night during the first week in September. The drought had broken and rain poured through the walls and the roof, streams of mud drizzled upon the bed. 'Sheba cursed futilely and held pans under the worst of the drizzles. Clory had been unshakable. Some ancient strength, built up by the weak hands of all those women gone before, had supported her spirit. She was going to have her baby on her own bed in her own house. That much, if no more.

And when the fumes of burning feathers brought her up from agony so that she might coax agony back again, she clung grimly to two resolves. In spite of all 'Sheba's tight-lipped disapproval, she intended to be washed with the scorched linen cloth dipped in beania oil. No world of smells for Kissy. And Willie was never to leave her, not for one minute. Willie would see that she got her rights. There were four days of grace before a woman had to be back on her feet. For that time, Kissy was hers ... When the darkness closed in around you and your head went under, like the kittens, the thing that counted was to keep on kicking, never to give up, even if you lost — then maybe you glimpsed that enduring wisdom ...

And finally there was a sharp smack and a thin, protesting cry, and the women busy with the dried malaga-grape raisin, boiled, opened, and the fleshy part bound over the newborn navel. Then a face like raw beef in the hollow of her arm. A small red *unmarked* face with eyes screwed shut and tiny hands under the chin. A face with a freshness, a newness she did not dare to touch. A mouth all gums, groping blindly like a kitten's.

And then one of those rare, stupendous moments when the old world bent his hoary head. She held her breath and waited, and all her being flowed into a vast acceptance, and in the acceptance there was victory. The thing she had tried to put into words for Free, the certain, living thing for which there were no words. If you lay still, unmoving, hardly breathing, the rim of the darkness might lift a little, a very little, and you might see the Smile, so easily startled, so soon gone. But you had glimpsed those aeons of triumphing laughter behind the closing rim, the warmth of the Smile was forever in your heart.

You had looked deep inside yourself and found Me, and that would never die.

Abijah blessed the baby to be a 'hand-maiden in the service of the Lord,' and Clory was glad. It was the priesthood she wanted — the channel through which it came did not matter.

Then suddenly she was forgiving Abijah, a helpless man. Pity lent her understanding. He was just another child, a man-child. Furthermore, he needed her. Already the child at her breast was giving her new eyes for seeing.

Abijah's beard was quivering. He stared at the baby.

'Right biddable little tyke... This is a feeling time for me, Clorinda...'

There was misery in his eyes, but ech! What could a man do who had never gone back on his word in all his life?

Clory smiled her slow, enigmatic smile and took the baby in her arms across the dooryard to the Sibley tent.

'Here she is' — she held out her arms to 'Sheba, fires smouldering in her black, unfathomable eyes — '*but there was a new moon at her birth and I made a wish — if you take her you'll have trouble all your life —* '

'Sheba shuddered away.

'She's put a hex on it!'

Abijah sighed with relief.

13

Since mid-morning the crowd had been waiting, two solid lines of men and women dressed in their Sunday best. Because the cortège would have to cross the Black Ridge dugway and come in from the south, they all faced down Main Street. Two lines, each four blocks long, on each side of the road. All the little girls in town, starched and curled, each clutching her wilting bouquet, formed a vanguard. The entire day before they had thronged the hills gathering the wildflowers that had sprung up after the rains — Indian pinks, red bells and paintbrushes, yellow buttercups and daisies, wild blue larkspur, armfuls of golden, sweet-smelling rabbit brush — flowers to strew the pathway of the great man.

Riding in wagons up and down between the lines, debouching on the square where curious Indians squatted under mesquite bushes waiting stolidly to see this Mormonie chieftain for whose religion they had gone-into-the-water, the Martial Band rata-planned and boomed the spirit of the day.

Behind the little girls, the Apostles, Erastus Snow and Orson

Pratt, together with the twelve members of the High Council, led
the solid citizenry. Tutsegabbett waited here with the authorities
as became a chief, sensible in his nakedness among the sweating
broadcloth-covered bodies of the white men. This celebration
seemed more like an ordeal of endurance to him, but he had cast in
his lot with the Mormonies and he was trying his long-suffering
best to live up to them.

Next came the mayor and his two aldermen and three councilors, and the visiting authorities such as Jacob Hamblin. Then
the bishopric, Robert Gardner, and his two subordinate bishops
and Bishop Covington from Washington. Then the high priests,
the Seventies, the elders, the Melchizedek priesthood and their
wives — Palmyra and David Wight, Eliza and Charles Hichinoper, Betsy and Lon Tuckett, Brother and Sister Hansen —
this division including those men with community jobs such as
Ole Oleson, the water-master. Finally the subordinate priesthood, the Aaronic — the priests, teachers, and deacons — all the
little boys in town, polished and scrubbed and brushed, forming
an eager, self-important climax to the Welcoming Parade.

Abijah's boys were all with this last group. The twins, pushing
and pulling with the other youngsters at the very tail-end, Samuel
and Abraham with the deacons, Joseph with the teachers, and
Free with the priests. Abijah, up at the front with the High
Council, wished, not for the first time, that Free could have been
old enough to go through the Endowment House and be ordained
an elder before they left the City (the garments were such an
armor against temptation), so that he now could be standing with
the Melchizedek quorums along with Apostle Snow's oldest boys,
instead of down at the foot with Gottlieb Uttley and other harum-
scarums.

Bathsheba, victorious over heat, tightly laced stays, and her
best black taffeta, clutched the whining Isaiah by the hand and
planted her feet firmly on the ground. Flanked by Willie, whose
gray silk-and-mohair hung on her wasted body in folds, and Clory

with her child in her arms (a plumper Clory whose old red cassimere's seams had luckily been wide enough to let out — but how
she missed that extra width in the skirt!), 'Sheba was an example
of rectitude to all as she waited with the other wives-of-the-
dignitaries among the elders.

Rumor ran through the lines like a flame. Everybody knew
that even with a fast team he couldn't get here before noon, but
still . . . And so they were in place by ten o'clock, content with the
long hours in the hot sun, the flies, the burning sand underfoot, the
cross, mischievous children, if only they could be there for the
first glimpse. Many had already walked from Washington and
Santa Clara.

Shadrach Gaunt, bony face unmoved, but showing his excitement in the way his hands gripped the reins, made cursory dashes
at intervals up and down the lines. Away he would gallop in a
cloud of dust, pell-mell across the valley, a speck attacking the
mighty ridge like a centaur, outlined against the top, dropped
over. They would wait for an hour. Here he comes back, hat
waving in air, cayuse pounding. They say at Washington Brother
Brigham's just left Harrisburg!

Dinner-time comes. Should we go home? Oh, no! Who minds
missing a little soggum and bran bread when we've waited for
this a whole year!

The women gossip among themselves. Winter coming on and
the crops almost all ruined, it was to be hoped Brother Brigham
would bring them help. Of course the Lord would provide, but
men were such impractical fools — you couldn't expect the Lord
to do it all.

'Sheba had had a mania for preserving. She searched among
the thrifty memories of her New England girlhood for ideas, forced
herself to learn what she could from Tutsegabbett's squaw.
Dogberries and pout berries grew wild, could be gathered by
spreading canvas under the bush and shaking the limbs, were
edible stewed or dried. Ground cherries preserved in sorghum

were nutritious, if insipid. She tried making jerky out of mutton.

Her cake made from molasses and the hoarded flour and sugar stood proudly crisp waiting for Brother Brigham in the Sibley tent. When it had first emerged from the bake-skillet this morning, the little boys had hung around its tantalizing fragrances in anguish, but 'Sheba had been adamant. She had been saving a whole year to make this cake for Brother Brigham!

Hannah Merinda Lowgie had made him some sour-cream-and-saleratus biscuits, and was preparing his favorite baked potatoes and buttermilk, which was bad enough, but that Keturah Snow had traded some whole spices from a passing emigrant — cinnamon sticks, whole cloves, pepper corns, oblong nutmegs — and these had gone into another cake for Brother Brigham — and they said he would eat his dinner at Aunt Keturah's that night! But still, 'Sheba only tossed her head at this information, as if to say she knew what she knew!

They said Brother Brigham would stay at Zadoc Hunt's — Zadoc Hunt, who had built his big, red-rock house last winter while other homeless settlers worked on the Social Hall; Zadoc, who had donated money instead of sweat. It wasn't fair, but since Erastus' 'dobe house wasn't finished yet, Zadoc's was still the finest in town and therefore the place for Brother Brigham. Of course, Zadoc's place was in 'sand town,' and they did say Zadoc's red stones that he had hauled from an unapproved quarry were beginning to weather in spots — his front doorstep already as hollowed as if feet had been tramping over it for a thousand years — and this was comforting, proving as it did that the Lord was still on the side of those who obeyed counsel.

Clory, half-listening to the talk around her, unhooked her bodice (she was having to wear it back to front), and bared her breast to the baby's puckered mouth. She watched the toothless gums fasten noisily and the tiny hands knead at her soft flesh. She smiled, thinking how often she had sickened at the sight of women placidly suckling their young ones in meeting — like —

like cows! — and sworn never to nurse a child of hers in public if it starved to death! Well, she reflected comfortably, she was now a matron with a year of marriage behind her and a baby on her hands, and the alarms and qualms of her girlhood looked foolish. All the doubts and confusions of the summer had vanished before the absorbing wonder of Kissy. She was amused at herself, now that strength was flowing back to her limbs; content to eat and sleep and care for Kissy, she could regard Free with impersonal friendliness (he was a nice boy), and go back to Kissy. She reveled in the ripe fruitfulness of her breasts, in the life which coursed through her, broad-bosomed and rich and deep.

Last week, on the twenty-fifth of September, she had been eighteen years old, and on that day she had finished picking the last of her cotton — three hundred and fifty pounds stored in the bins, ready to spin into yarn for hickory shirting, homespun trousers, and a dress for herself; ready to sell or trade for clothes for Kissy. She had watched so long for the miracle of the bursting pods that when it finally happened she was reluctant to confiscate the treasure; but those days of stooping along the rows under the hot sun were over, although she still had lacerated fingertips from the guarding prongs.

Next Sunday, being the first Sunday in the month, would be fast Sunday, and she would go with Abijah to meeting to have Kissy blessed. Calistra Agatha MacIntyre, dressed as she was today, in the eyelet-embroidered christening gown that would reach beyond Abijah's arms to the floor. Abijah said he thought the 'Agatha' would be nice, and she didn't mind. There was something settling about getting a baby blessed. The busy little mouth lost its grip for a moment and opened wide to protest, and Clory clucked and shifted the child to a better position.

The waiting had been so tedious that some of the boys had taken to running races. Free, dashing by, caught the intimacy of the suckling babe and involuntarily stopped, much to the loud disgust of the boys at the foot of the line. A spasm of pain flickered across his young face.

Clory beckoned to him to come and see the baby — she was hurt because he had seemed to avoid her since the baby was born — but at the look in his eyes her treacherous heart lurched in spite of herself and she was glad when he turned away...

At last, toward sunset, dust spurting from his horse's hoofs, Shadrach Gaunt came tearing across the valley. They knew before they heard his shout that the moment was at hand; and a hush fell upon the vigilant lines. For months women had been planning what to wear for the occasion; girls had hired out to do washings in order to save enough to get a calico dress woven for the Welcoming Parade. Little boys had worked in the hot sun day after day to pick every pebble out of the road over which the leader must pass.

At first they could see only the dust of his coming; then the scouts, their rifles over their shoulders; then the princely barouche, fringed and tasseled, and the high-stepping, milk-white horses. Finally the coachman, resplendent, high-hatted, on the driver's seat in front.

The dust clears, the carriage draws nearer until one hears the rhythmic clopping of the horses' hoofs, the rattle of the harness.

Look! There are figures on the two seats that face each other, women on one and a man in the seat turned toward us — that is his tall, steeple-crowned hat, his linen duster — it is! It is Brother Brigham!

A great shout goes up. Hosanna! Hosanna to God!

Isaac Wheelock steps out from the line, raises his hand, and the throng bursts into song.

'*Welcome to all! With joy we give you greeting...*'

As the carriage rounds the turn, the little girls get ready with their bouquets. The carriage rolls toward them, they scatter the flowers in the path of the high-stepping horses; the carriage rolls slowly between the singing ranks, hats come off, children curtsey, men and women bow and smile and weep. The figure in the coach doffs his tall, steeple-crowned hat, bows this way and that. The carriage rolls under the festive, green-leaved arch to the square and the bowery.

Brigham Young leaned slightly forward on both hands propped on the cloth-covered rostrum, and twinkled at his people — bulging the walls of the bowery, overflowing into the square. They gazed and gazed as if they could never get their fill of gazing.

The president's speech began slowly, hesitantly, hardly audible. Then his voice warmed and rose high and clear and sonorous. His words tumbled after each other in the animated manner his people remembered and loved. That gesture more familiar to them than the beating of their own hearts — the raised forefinger of his emphasizing . . .

He hadn't changed noticeably in a year. His gray-blue eyes nested in their smiling-lines were still steady and peaceful, still able to bore into a man's soul and pluck out the guilt. He was still magnetic and handsome — his light brown hair, parted at one side, sweeping back from his forehead, retained its shining curl just above the lobes of his ears. His long, streaked-brown beard still crisped around the line of his jaw — a little grayer, perhaps. His mouth still held its firm inflexible line, its humor and quiet strength, his bold, clean-cut nose its pride and spirit. His gray homespun clothes, loose and baggy, still became his stout figure. He still tied his dark silk cravat in a large bow beneath his turned-down starched white collar; he still wore his black satin waistcoat buttoned almost to his neck and the heavy gold watch chain across it, and his high polished Wellington boots under the trousers.

He was always and forever the leader, the commander whom they obeyed without question and loved without stint, whether he was autocratically refusing to see a stranger again because he had disliked him at the first interview, or violently jawing his people into order, or carrying his own sick child in his arms while

he shared his scant rations with hungry women and children holding out their hands for bread.

He stood there lifting his people up from the discouragement of
ruined crops, the goading of hunger, with the power of his words
and the magnetism of his presence.

'Mark my words. Write them down. This people as a Church
and kingdom will go from the west to the east ...

'If this work does not live, I do not want to live; for it is my
life, my joy, my all; and if it sinks, God knows I do not want to
swim ...

'Produce what you consume; draw from the native elements
the necessaries of life. ...

'Laws should be simple and plain, void of ambiguity and few
in number ...

'Responsibility develops men ... but give no man two offices ...

'Mothers, have children. Children are an heritage of the Lord.
You mothers are the hope of this land and the guarantors of its
future ...'

Tomorrow and in the days that followed Brother Brigham
would visit and inspect their homes, their shops, their industries.
Meanwhile — what had they done about schools?

He intended to open a free school in the City and pay teachers
from his own private means, and if the young men do not then
attend, he will *employ them to go, and pay them wages!*

The territorial superintendent of schools had recently reported
in nearly all the settlements log schoolhouses with slab seats,
some of which had very long legs doing double duty among the
rising and the risen generations!

'The glory of God is intelligence ...'

The government has given us a new mail route — there will be
a pony express from now on to St. George, regular letters, news-
papers. Goods from St. Louis in twenty-five days ... An overland
railroad soon, according to the prophecy — 'a highway cast up
that the eagle's eye had never seen, nor the lion's foot had ever trod.'

All these things are fine — we welcome progress; but 'watch out that gentile influences don't steal into your communities and corrupt them.'

The Social Hall was progressing — he was pleased with that — but more pleased with the one-room 'dobe Tithing House, their first public building. He was so pleased he could dance like a shaker to learn that the four wards had paid this first year the equivalent of $3201.61 in tithing.

He suggested they eat more fats with their food to overcome the alkali in the water; keep the rotten leaves cleaned out of their irrigation ditches so that the drinking water would be pure (if the water-master does not do this, he should be *made* to do it!); leave their windows open at night.

Produce was cheaper in the City — eggs eighteen cents a dozen, milk ten cents a quart, but tea was still sold by the ounce (which was a good thing; the human body didn't need stimulants); for a four-bit piece the storekeeper would let you have all the tea you could put on the coin, but he kept the coin!

How had they celebrated the Fourth of July? Oh . . . that flag over there — home-made? . . . He was pleased, and gave a special glance across the benches to Clory and Pal and Marianne. . . .

It was true President Lincoln had approved the anti-bigamy law in July, but even so he, Brother Brigham, would exhort them to be loyal to the Union.

Stephen Harding, Utah's fourth governor (Brother Brigham smiled a little at this), had arrived in the City in July. Yes, Colonel Conner was in the City and his government troops were on the way, but the Saints were not to worry — they had the Lord on their side. . . .

They must start to build as soon as possible a commodious, and well-finished meeting house or Tabernacle, large enough to seat at least two thousand persons, and one that would be an ornament to their city and a credit to their enterprise. The men who worked on it should be paid in scrip, and he would send down tithing flour from the City for them to redeem with the scrip.

Last summer he had made the Salt Lake Saints take out and re-lay the foundation for the Temple, that had been nine years in the building, because it was not solid or deep enough to last until the millennium.

And that is how they, the Dixie Saints, should build their Tabernacle. Co-operation is the thing — an individual would fail in trying to subdue this country.

He was sorry about the artesian well, but he could promise them plenty of water, the Lord would see to it...

He was pleased with the cotton crop — he could promise them Church funds for the erection of a cotton factory... Nearly one hundred thousand pounds of cotton had been raised in the country this first year...

Most of the faces looking at Brother Brigham are haggard from months of living on bran shorts and lucerne and pigweed greens. Hunger is so old it has become a habit. But joy shines in their eyes — no other year could be as hard as the first and they have lived through that, and Brother Brigham is pleased.

There have been two burials this first year in the new cemetery out by the Old Campground; two deaths, but many babies — and the deaths are hostages to the glorious future. Brother and Sister Eardley look shining-proud.

Brother Brigham blesses his people. The hush is so solemn one can hear the buzzing of a solitary fly.

'*Ye shall walk in all the ways which the Lord your God hath commanded you, that ye may live, and that it may be well with you, and that ye may prolong your days in the land which ye shall possess* ... and may the spirit of the Lord direct you and qualify you for every duty, is the prayer of your fellow-laborer in the gospel of salvation ...'

Amidst the concert of '*Amens*' like a great organ note, Brother Brigham sits down with the Apostles and High Council on the stand, and the shouts of 'Hosanna!' and the applause thunders on, until the bowery shakes as if in an earthquake.

It is time for Lon Tuckett to read his welcoming verses; he starts with the one about the Fourth of July, and his carrot-hair is on end with importance:

> A sumptuous feast was then prepared.
> All description it surpasses,
> Consisting of some burned bran bread
> Served up with scorched molasses;

Then, in case Brother Brigham doesn't fully comprehend about the damn dam:

> While repairing the dam and mending the ditches
> And soaking our flapjacks — the things wouldn't float —
> We ate them at the risk of splitting the stitches
> Of pants that grew tighter with 'Old Virgin Bloat'!

Brother Brigham smiles, and Lon gets a hearty lot of 'spats.'

The audience cinches up its belt (does a man good to 'gant' up now and then!), stands upon its shoeless feet, and sings with gusto:

> Hard times, hard times, come again no more...

CHAPTER VIII

(To *Abijah MacIntyre*)

HOMESPUN DRESS BALL

To be given in the St. George Bowery in honor of

PRESIDENT BRIGHAM YOUNG

Yourself and ladies are respectfully invited.

Committee { David Wight
Lucy Snow
Benjamin Jarvis

Nota Bene: Ladies are requested to attend the Ball attired in dresses of homespun. Tickets at the T.O., $1.00

.   .   .   .

BUT Clory, making starch out of the last of the Lars Hansen potatoes for her two remaining petticoats, offered to bet Willie Brother Brigham's ladies wouldn't be in homespun. Nor Apostle Snow's, especially Marianne. People living in Sand Town up around Zadoc Hunt's said Emmeline Free Young was even more genteel than Marianne Snow, if such a thing could be.

'Sis, that oldest Eardley girl's gone to work for Sister Young while she's here — like a servant,' said Clory, grating a peeled potato so that juice crisped from its white flesh and the raw, potato smell oozed up between her fingers. Willie's mouth watered for the starchy food that stuck to your ribs after so many weeks of greens, but she went on rocking languidly and smiled up from Kissy to Clory.

'Laws, what's the difference s'long as she gits a little something for it — pan of flour, dress to cut hover?'

'I know, but I don't see why Emmeline Free Young has to act so tony, especially with folks around her going hungry!'

Willie touched a finger to the soft down above the baby's ears. 'Little shite-poke,' she cried fondly. 'See her stretch! I think 'er eyes is goin' to be brown ... because folks is like that, child; it's human nature to put on airs if you've got the means; I only wish Abijah would let us go out to work!'

'Well, he never will. He'll let us go without things first ... Her eyes are blue! Don't all newborn babies have blue eyes? ... We'll have to *take in* work, so he won't be disgraced with folks' knowing he can't support his wives!'

'He does as well as he can,' said Willie gently.

Clory regarded Willie across 'Sheba's ruined milk-pan with the new grating holes in the bottom; she gave a little grunt of exasperation, and her round white arms with the rolled-up sleeves went back to slushing the potato. There Willie sat, her body still emaciated under its patched and faded homespun, her face thin and white beneath the liver spots, her baby gone — there she sat, unlovely and unloved, apologizing for living — at peace with the world. Now that returning strength had dissolved the morbid doubts of the summer, Clory again longed to batter life for her desires, and she wanted Willie to fight, too. That kind of good-natured giving up, that uncomplaining resignation, she thought the saddest thing on earth.

But Willie only turned from her absorption in the baby's red, unknowing face and twinkled at Clory.

'Laws, child, spuds bein' scarcer than 'ens' teeth, you can't blame 'Sheba for being a mite put out at the 'igh-'anded way you barged in on 'em and her milk-pans; and you can't blame her for going to Abijah, and you can't blame Abijah for bein' mad!'

Clory tossed her head and tipped up the brass bucket to pour more water over the glistening pulp. The milky potato-water trickled with little splashes into the kettle below.

'Well, I don't care,' she said, wondering how much starch would settle out of that milky water; 'you and I won't have any new homespuns, and how am I going to make my old cassimere stand out when I've only got two petticoats and they as limp as dishrags?'

She grinned and sucked a chapped, cracked knuckle.

'That ain't the only thing 'Sheba's mad about. She's always telling me' — her voice rose an octave to mimic 'Sheba's shrill admonitions — '"a thing well done is twice done" and making me French-seam everything and shorten my thread to sew with; but the other day she caught me cutting the baby's fingernails and says, horrified, "Don't do that! You'll make a thief out of her!" So I says, "All right, then I'll cut her toenails, too, so she can run good and fast!"'

Willie chuckled.

But Clory's busy thought ran on: it was true that the birth of her baby had given her a different status in the household; she was no longer a child, she was a woman, a woman who could have babies, and even 'Sheba had to respect her position. The realization after so many cramped months was a little heady — it compensated for many things, even the knowledge she kept buried below awareness that having a baby still couldn't quite root out the old craving for Free, as she had prayed it would.

Strangers remembered David Wight by his smile — his big, clean-toothed smile flashing so pleasantly across his brown face in that day of stained fangs. He stood, now, welcoming the women carrying the dishes for the dinner later on, and the menfolk crowding the door with their tickets and shoes (shoes that would change feet a dozen times tonight) under one arm, and their rifles crooked in the other. Those who hadn't bought tickets in advance from the Tithing Office were lugging live chickens, coyote pelts — here was an elder offering a lady's embroidered unmentionable, here another offering his bristling dog (which David declined) — but mainly they brought cotton and molasses, one quart of molasses being standard for one ticket (an extra quart for each extra wife), and dried peaches or apples, peddled in by 'them Dutchmen from the Clary.'

One corner of the bowery looked as if it had been dressed for a harvest ball — some small crops on the town gardens, at least. Tickets, one dollar, the program bragged, and there wasn't a money-dollar circulating in the whole town unless in Brother Brigham's pocket.

David figured Lon Tuckett's big pumpkin, and dug out a small squash for change.

Lon's sandy hair was slick with combings and his blue uniform slick with brushings. He cackled, shuffled a clog or two, and followed Betsy's imposing figure like a tugboat in the wake of a battleship.

Here came Abijah MacIntyre, big and handsome, with his freeswinging stride and his three wives. He handed David his pound of wool-batting sheepishly. David winked at Clory as she gathered up her skirts to sidle her hoops through the doorway.

At that moment Brother Brigham's hearty voice boomed out to them.

'Woe unto them that dance with guile and malice in their hearts toward their neighbors — if these shall go forth in the dance without confessing and forsaking their guilt, they seal their doom!'

Through the open door they could see him, virile and masterful in his homespun, his starched, ruffled, and embroidered shirt and flowing cravat, pronouncing a blessing upon them all with uplifted hands. They echoed his 'Amen,' he signaled to the orchestra, and led out Emmeline Free for the first cotillion. He had decreed in the meeting that all friends of society, all who remembered the needy though not members of the Church, all the Saints who had paid their tithing, all those who had not been excommunicated or disfellowshipped, or who had not sold liquor for gain, particularly to the Indians, and especially all who were not wearing silks and satins and gewgaws, could join in the festivities. And now here was Emmeline Free — Clory nudged Willie.

'There's ten yards in that skirt if there's an inch,' whispered Clory; 'look at her train, six or eight inches out behind, and all those buttons all the way down the front...'

'I 'eard Brother Brigham say once that there wa'nt "judgment, economy, and force enough in some women to knit their hown garters"; I wonder w'at he thinks now? That there dress haint 'omemade, it's States goods.'

'Sheba never could abide whispering. Her high, imperious voice cut in fiercely.

'"An idle tongue's the Devil's workshop!" — he's just a man, ain't he? Even a Prophet o' God can't boss some women!'

Abijah, hawckking with pleasure at sight of the dancers finding places on the hard-packed floor, the flaring candles, the musicians tuning up on the rude board platform at the opposite end of the bowery, crooked his arm for 'Sheba and led her out to a forming set, nodding and smiling to the other strolling couples, Bishop Gardner and his first wife, Doctor Weeks and his wife, Brother Eardley and his first wife.

Clory and Willie joined the women on the benches around the walls to wait their turn with Abijah. There was Pal, her pregnant body distorted in the new calico she'd worn to the Welcoming Parade, rising to dance with young Gottlieb Uttley squirming before her in the oldest Snow boy's shoes he'd just borrowed for the set. That Dutchman, thought Clory, he'll mash her feet, but how can she get out of it with David at the door?

The other extra women were here, Hannah Merinda Lowgie and Martha Snow, Brother Erastus' second — Marianne, his third, was too young and pretty to have to wait for any man — Isaac Wheelock's second, third, and fourth wives (his fifth, a young German immigrant girl, was staying on the farm in the City to see that the harvest was brought in, and eventually to drive a load of potatoes and flour down to St. George); the three Eardley women — Aunt Til, Aunt Zil, and the youngest, Sister Joe — Aunt Kate, the first wife, was dancing; here with their mothers were the growing girls of the town, sedate upon the benches, prim legs dangling in starched and ruffled pantalettes below smoothed-down skirts, as became children allowed out for once with their elders. How their eyes grew big with longing for the day when they could put up their hair and 'keep company'!

The marriageable young ladies clustered along a bench farther on — the oldest Eardley girls Sis and Miny (daughters of Aunt Kate and Aunt Til), who, everyone said, were too free; Lucy Snow, who *would* chum with them in spite of Aunt Ket; Stiddy Weeks's girl, Bella; Susan and Mercy Wheelock, Ole Oleson's two girls — giggling and whispering, stealing sly glances at the young men in the corner.

Free and the Wheelock boys, Hannah Merinda Lowgie's Johnny, who would have been married to Mercy Wheelock except he had been taking care of his mother, the Snow boys (Martha's and Keturah's oldest, both named after their father, but called 'Rastus' and 'Rassy' to tell them apart), youths from Washington and Santa Clara — young bucks milling about in the corner, slapping backs, guffawing.

Free caught Clory's idly roving glance. Her eyes like startled birds flew back to Willie, but there he was, serious and tall, bowing before her, fresh in his new blue hickory shirt and 'nappy yarn' jeans with the high pockets. How the blond grace of him got under a woman's guard!

The music had stopped with a shower of notes, a sprinkle of

applause, a rising tide of dust and laughter and conversation.
There was an interval of talk whirling brightly about the room,
feet seeking a lusty story, a pretty smile.

Brother Wheelock was calling tonight and his great voice ate up
the other noises; his bald head and full-moon face were beet-red
in the candlelight.

'One to twenty for a polka! Fill up the floor!'

Free led Clory to the forming line. Abijah, bowing before
Willie, saw them take their places; Clory ducked her head and
flushed with mute wrath at her own embarrassment. But it was
impossible not to sparkle with the rhythm, the exercise, the jol-
lity of the music. Brother Hansen had finished his bass fiddle,
and he was up there sawing away at its bowels with Miles and
Ferrano and the banjo-player from the Clara. He laughed all
over his kind old face at Clory as she swung by; Miles tapped his
foot and swayed his head and you couldn't tell where his hand left
off and the bow began, while Ferrano with true Italian vivacity
pranced around the platform as he pumped the accordion and
sang under his breath the chirruping two-four measures of the
polka:

> My mother *said* — that I never *should*
> *Play* with the gypsies *in-the-wood*.

Clory joined in, don't leave room for talking — swing the right
foot forward, swing the right foot back, hop-and-run-and-hop-
and-run-and . . . the long line jigged and circled around the room.
The bright, sharp bits of the music spun in the dusty air above
the stamping feet, the bobbing heads, the swaying skirts.

Brother Brigham liked the polka because it was lusty and vigorous, giving pleasure at the same time it preserved the propri-
eties. He did not approve of the languid pace then fashionable in
balls among the gentiles; he liked elaborately executed steps that
made a man work up a good sweat. That was why he also
frowned upon the waltz quadrille — too great a temptation to a

young man with his arm around a slender waist. But the polka —
ah, there was a dance! Who can make love while he hops?

Brother Brigham's dancing was always absolutely correct —
no floor manager ever had to tap him on the shoulder for being
out of time; he could prompt the caller himself on the cotillion
figures, and his feet were like two lively crickets in the 'break-
down' step at the end.

Brother Wheelock, patrolling the ordered ferment of the floor,
sharpened an austere and vigilant eye for out-of-steppers, out-of-
bounders.

Hop-and-run-and...

'Clory, Clory, Clory,' whispered Free, swinging her close for a
moment. Glancing frantically at Brother Wheelock, she sang the
louder. But Free's eyes were staring, intent, obsessed.

Horrified, sniffing, she wondered if he had been smoking. She
knew for a fact that Gottlieb Uttley smoked! How could Free be
so rash! Clory had heard so many times of Abijah's love for
tobacco before he joined the Church, and how he had lined all his
precious pipes and cigars on the mantel, and while he was trying
to break himself of the habit would file by and smell his craving
into temporary submission. He'd half-kill a son of his that broke
the Word of Wisdom.

Sis Eardley swung by with some strange man, and Clory saw
her bold eyes seeking out Free, claiming him... If Abijah ever
found out a son of his ran around with a girl like that...

The music rested for a moment, and the groups raveled and unraveled again while the floor was being swept.

Here came Ole Oleson and his wives through the cloud of dust
in the doorway. No doubt about it, the wives swayed more
stylishly than all the other women, but — heavens! — the first
wife was stuck in the doorway! Ole's big ears reminded Clory of
an embarrassed jackass's as he tugged at his giggling wife on one
side and David pushed on the other.

Hoops probably made out of barrel staves that clanked. Now

the lady was in, but one side of her skirt sashayed alarmingly —
Clory grinned and then sobered as Free squeezed her for the grin.
There were other homemade hoops here tonight — cat's-claw,
that dark, twisted wood like evil thoughts coming alive, fine for
singletrees and doubletrees but a mite too obstinate for hoops, and
unyielding canes in tucks that made a dreadful pouf! in front of a
lady sitting down. Clory thanked her lucky stars for her real
skeleton hoops from Philadelphia . . .

Free seated her with a too-confident flourish and stood about,
wishing to talk. But she stared at her lap and willed him to go
away. She had a dreadful surmise — what if he had been drinking? She wanted to enjoy this evening, she wanted to keep intact
the present household peace — she was afraid of Free and more
afraid of herself.

When she raised her eyes he had disappeared, and she sighed
with relief. It was only about eight o'clock, and the dance would
keep up until four or five in the morning in spite of all Apostle
Snow's agitation for a midnight closing. So long a time for Free
to maneuver stolen intimacies! The dinner, the community
'sings' throughout the long evening, the scarcity of partners that
would make it impossible not to dance with him . . .

Her thoughts flew off at a tangent to the last ball she had attended before she left the City. A Territorial and Civil Ball, with
elegant invitations on embroidered paper; Brother Brigham had
called for her in his own sleigh just as he occasionally called to
take her to his private school in the Beehive House. Clory remembered particularly that dinner and the menu — they had really
eaten the bear and beaver-tail dishes and enjoyed them, too, but
the 'slaw, mountain, pioneer, and snowball' items were Brother
Brigham's idea of poking fun at the fashionable gentiles.

How she worshiped him! She had gone into the Endowment
House that day ready to 'spit on his robes,' but she had come out
ready to walk over coals of fire for him. He had said, 'I am now
almost daily sealing young girls to men of age and experience.

Love your duties, sisters. What is your duty? It is for you to
bear children, in the name of the Lord, that are full of faith and
the power of God — that you may have the honor of being the
mothers of kings, princes, potentates — I would not care whether
my husband loved me or not, but I would cry out, like one of old,
in the joy of my heart, "I have got a man from the Lord! Halle-
lujah! I am a mother — I have borne an image of God!"'

Well, she had 'loved her duty'; but she was sure he had no idea
what a cross he had given her to bear. Yet even now, she would
gladly have married ten more Abijahs to win his word of
praise.

After the set Brother Brigham stood about a moment, fanning
himself, puffing a little; he caught her eye and came over and sat
down by her. Instantly she was the envy of every woman in the
room. Abijah, strolling off the floor with Willie, stared at her with
a new expression in his eyes. People thronged about Brother
Brigham like flies, but he brushed them away and took her hand
between his and beamed at her.

'We miss you in the City, Clorinda Agatha,' he said; 'we missed
your sweet songs at the opening of the Fun House last spring; and
there ain't a Desdemona who can equal you — last summer the
Dramatic Association put on the third act of Othello, but Desdemona was a tall masculine female with painted cheeks ——'

He shook his head at the memory but smiled down at Clory
again. 'But, sister, I am glad to see you building up this part of
the Lord's vineyard. That is a work for a daughter of Zion!'

Clory remembered the blessing he had given at the time of her
marriage — '*if she would be faithful the Lord would bring her every
desire of her heart . . .*'

'We are so privileged here in the Valleys of the Mountains' —
he looked about him at the people hanging on his every word —
'I see on your faces, peace. . . . And yet, some of you have complained there is too much sameness in Deseret; true, we do not
have the variety they do in the world, drinking, carousing, quar-

reling, and litigation. But if you want a change of this kind, you can get up a dog fight.'

He was so erect there on the bench, so unfaltering. Clory thought it would *take* a prophet of God to know so surely what was right from what was wrong, and she wondered if in all his life he had ever had any doubts or hesitations.

'Always there are a few skim-milk Saints,' he went on, 'to hearken after the gentiles; it has been said to me, "Yes, Brother Brigham, we have seen ladies go to parties in plain, homemade dresses, but every man was after the girls who had on a hundred dollars' worth of fol-de-rol!" Well, Clorinda Agatha hasn't lacked for partners' — he still had Clory's hand in his and he patted it and smiled down at her — 'and yet I know she has on her old dress, for I remember her wearing it when she sang to us in the City!'

Clory, conscious of Emmeline Free's eyes upon her and catching Abijah's stare, 'Sheba's disdainful profile, remembering the squandered potatoes, hung her head.

'It adds no beauty to a lady in my opinion to adorn her with fine feathers. If a woman is clean in person and has on a nice clean homemade, she looks a great deal better when washing her dishes or making her butter or dancing than those who, as I told them in Provo, walk the streets with their spanker jibs flying!'

He leaned forward and brought up that emphasizing forefinger in his old gesture.

'Why, the wickedness of the world is so great that in many places the gentiles would consider they had committed the sin of blasphemy if they heard a violin! If an old-fashioned Presbyterian even looked into a dance hall he would consider he had sinned against the Holy Ghost!'

Clory, cheeks burning, aware of eyes upon her, peeped from under her lashes at Brother Brigham's audience. The dancers, caught in the act of walking to the benches, talking, laughing, were stilled as suddenly as if struck by Gabriel's own trumpet. All except Willie. There she sat, indifferent as ever, over on the bench with the fourth Eardley wife, Sister Joe, and the Ferrano woman. Funny, thought Clory, she always sits by those two if she can — never says much, they just sit there somehow apart from the rest. They shared that secret world of Willie's where no one else ever intruded. But there was a sudden flirt of movement at the door. David, frantically shushing — Free and Gottlieb Uttley, grinning furtively, tiptoeing out under cover of Brother Brigham's talk.

Clory's heart gave a great leap. Had Abijah seen them?

Brother Brigham squeezed her hand and brought back her attention.

'I tell you if we keep ourselves unspotted from the sins of the world, not all the bigamy laws nor all O'Connor's armies can prevail against us! It reminds me of the company that crossed the plains in '49. Snowdrifts in the mountains seven feet deep beside their wagons. And when the others asked that leader what he'd do if they had to stay in the mountains all winter, they could hear him shout above the fury of the tempest, "Do? Why, we'll smooth down an icy even floor and take the skins of frozen cattle for roofing and walls for a dance hall and we'll merrily dance till spring opens!" . . .'

He signaled to the music and offered Clory his arm to lead out in the cotillion. She was delirious with pride . . .

The music, the laughter, the merry hum flooded out through the walls, into the empty streets, abroad through the lonely darkness to mingle with the coyotes' cry.

Free, hearing it in the barn, fumbled for the cottonwood stick whose glowing tip he applied to the Indian cow's-horn pipe.

'Judas priest!' he cried, taking great puffs and sinking weakly against the manger-railing, 'Judas priest, that's good!' He was glad the other boys couldn't see the sweat on his forehead.

He was sick of whining around a woman's skirts. A man had to be a *man*, didn't he? As for that pap-talk of Brigham's ——

'Silly olt jackass,' said Gottlieb, blowing smoke-rings' 'brophet, huh!'

He spat lustily, and it sounded so brave that Free spat, too,
only to clap a hasty hand over his mouth. It seemed you had to
pay for everything, even being a man.

Pung! One of the boys uncorked the keg of soap-root beer and
as the raw smell wafted upward, Free swallowed a convulsive
heave and wondered if Brother Brigham's heavenly allies would
crash the barn down on them.

'Um,' smacked Gottlieb. 'Vew swallows left; kill it, Vree!'

He gave Free a clap on the shoulder that set his insides to
churning.

'Trink to old pastard Prigham!'

He began to sing sloppily, 'Hoist yer leg oop! Hoist yer leg
oop!'

In the bowery the dancers were singing the Dixie cheer song
David Wight had written expressly for Brother Brigham's coming.

> The wind like fury here does blow,
> That when we plant or sow, sir,
> We place one foot upon the seed,
> And hold it till it grows, sir ...

> Mesquite, soaproot, prickly-pears and briars,
> St. George ere long will be a place that everyone admires ...

Faces alike in their patience, fortitude, and loyalty fixed upon
Brother Brigham, who listened and looked with softened eyes and
his quiet smile.

There was none more steadfast than Brigham, none in whom
success had developed so little of pride and vainglory. By his
foresight he had saved his people from dispersion, his faith from
destruction, led his followers through mobs, through savages,
founded them an abiding place in the wilderness, held off a United
States army, and built up Zion; he was a man they could lean
upon.

When they had finished he thanked them and spoke.

'There is not a hardship, there is not a disappointment, there is

not a trial that comes upon this people in this place but that I am
more thankful for than I am for full granaries. We spent twenty-
six years hunting for a place where we could raise *Saints*, not
merely wheat and cotton and corn. I care little about the cotton
and corn; *these things are not riches.* Hardship is a blessing, for
without it you can never know the value of ease.'

Brother Brigham pronounced the baked squash, the bran bread,
the molasses cakes, the baked potatoes furnished by Pine Valley
Ward, the watermelon-rind-and-molasses preserve from Washington, the peaches-and-molasses preserve and the grape wine from
Santa Clara, a sumptuous repast. And for once all stomachs
present were filled.

When dawn came and the company patted back yawns and
draggled out through the door, the last thing Clory could remember was Brother Wheelock holding aloft a pair of shoes that had
changed feet so many times the owner had lost track of them.

'Call for them in the T.O. window in the morning!' boomed
Brother Wheelock.

2

President Young's visit accelerated the whole tempo of life in
the Dixie Mission. He dined on 'lumpy dick' served from Spode
china hoarded through all the vicissitudes of the westward trek,
and ignored the china and praised the 'lumpy dick.' He approved
the slatted sunbonnets, the red-rock fence, the 'dobe yard, the
mesquite bread (would balance the greens!), Abijah's morning
prayer bell, the rabbit-brush-blossom bedticks, the newly made
candles. In poorer homes he pronounced first-rate the tallow-
bitch; in better homes he admired the dip candles and never
realized the sweating, flyblown hours housewives had endured
among the wreaths of fat steam, embalming the string folds in the
furious, rushing fat; dipping, cooling, dipping until the pale thin
wicks were tallow mummies. In Clory's dugout he pinched the

perfected flesh of her mold-candles, fingering up from their copper candlesticks, and never knew she had made Aunt Ket's entire batch in order to borrow the tin molds for her own.

Clory was glad, when he visited her, that she had hung the new curtains lacy with the shell-stitch pattern she had knitted from the homespun cotton yarn.

He pulled shut behind him the makeshift door with its linsey blanket and stood blinking gratefully in the shadowed coolness, so pleasant after the hot fall sunshine outside. Subduing the small room, he gazed about him with pleasure. The rosewood desk, the dry-goods-box cupboard leaning against one wall, and on its shelves the jugs filled with molasses-preserved ground cherries and cucumber-and-onion pickles. He fingered the 'Utah Pioneer Jubilee' mug and the 'Nauvoo Temple' china plate; he was interested in the 'Welcome to All' motto on the wall, and the wreath to Will's memory, with its bright tied-and-dyed picture-throw, and in the hearth with its crocheted lambrequin hanging from the mantel. He picked up her *Child's History of England* and *Little Lily's Travels*, read their titles, and nodded approvingly at her.

'I am glad you haven't taken up the gentile habit of novel-reading,' he said, the sound of his voice crowding the room.

Clory, standing by the rocker, one hand teetering it nervously, wondered why it was that forbidden things were always the sweetest.

The great man came over, lowered his body into the little rocker, twiddled his thumbs, leaned back against the tatted antimacassar, and smiled up at her lovely flushed face.

When Kissy whimpered, he followed her to the cradle in the corner, and she was glad Abijah had finally had Lars Hansen carpenter her up a decent one, and that Kissy was dressed in her christening gown. Brother Brigham chucked Kissy under the chin and she opened her unfathomable baby eyes, studied him, and after a moment gave him her enchanting gummy smile. Laughter rumbled in his chest at that.

'A biddable child, Sister Clorinda,' he said; 'a right biddable child. She'll keep you happy!'

He looked at Clory shrewdly.

'And I want you to have just as many more as the Lord lets you; that's the way to contentment!'

He turned to the baby again.

'Be careful how you wash her, Sister Clorinda; I would suggest warm water and soft flannel instead of hard cold water and rough cloth, and later on when she gets her teeth, instead of giving her pork for breakfast like some mothers, give her good wholesome bread and sweet milk, baked potatoes, and also buttermilk if she likes it, and a little fruit, and I would have no objection to her eating a little rice ... Do you talk baby-talk to her?'

The sudden sheepish quirk to the stern line of his lips was irresistible.

'*I* still do to *my* little ones, you know, but I'm trying to break myself of the habit. It can be done.'

His eyes twinkled.

'The Lord has given me fifty-two children to raise so far, Sister Clorinda, and that's a lot of experience!'

Before leaving he placed his hands upon Kissy's head and blessed her — 'May she live to be an instrument in the hands of God in doing much good, and a pleasing polished shaft in His quiver to assist in establishing the Kingdom of God on earth.'

Clory picked up the child and walked with Brother Brigham across the hot dooryard to where they could see 'Sheba's big rawboned figure bending over the black kettle making soap.

When 'Sheba saw them she was speechless for once. She sputtered, wiped her hands on her apron, and got out 'land's sakes,' but he held up a hand and stopped her.

'Go right ahead, Sister Mac; don't let me interrupt.'

'Sheba plunged her bared arms back into the stirring as if she would take out her flustration in physical exertion, but although her biceps stood in ridges as she pushed the stick around and around, Clory thought her quivering mole betrayed her; while there was Willie, carding quilt-bats on the back doorstep, acknowledging the great man's greeting with unruffled composure.

Brother Brigham's critical eye took in every aspect of 'Sheba's soap-making. It seemed that there was nothing a prophet of God didn't understand, reflected Clory. Peering into the leeching-box, now almost emptied of its wet cottonwood ashes, he tipped up the box and poked his head into the lye barrel beneath, but hastily jerked it out again as the fumes from the caustic yellow liquid at the bottom assailed his nostrils. In clutching the barrel one finger had found a daub of lye, and he ran to the wash bench and ducked it in the bucket of water there and grinned across ruefully at 'Sheba.

'Pretty stout stuff,' he said. 'Do you find it better than lime and saleratus?'

'Sheba had been surreptitiously mopping the sweat from her face with her apron and smoothing stray locks into the bun on the top of her head, but her brown eyes snapped at him from their wrinkle-nests and her strong yellow teeth smiled deferentially.

He came over and picked up a stick and scraped at the black kettle.

'Ought to be brass,' he said, and watched her soap-stick fold the thick white scum of the grease into the boiling lye-water.

Soap-making to 'Sheba was a ritual, and as she stood there, the strong, dominant lines of her face wreathed in the fumes and the raw odors, she looked like a high priestess of some sinister cult brewing up black magic. Clory thought that at any moment an evil genie might appear in the rank, plump steam.

Brother Brigham glanced at the bucket of hardened fat by the tub and wondered aloud if she had put in all the grease the lye would eat up; she nodded and dropped a bit of the thickening mess on a smooth board to show him. He watched the yellow stuff congeal.

'Soap's almost come, hasn't it?'

'Sheba smiled mystically, thinking of how this harsh liquid would cool overnight into a great smooth solid of soft soap that she would cut up into slippery yellow bars. She loved making soap.

'I hope you don't use lye-soap on your finer clothes,' Brother Brigham said. 'You'll have enough there to share with all your neighbors, won't you, Sister Mac?'

How he managed to strike at everyone's hidden depths! Clory marveled that he should guess at 'Sheba's close-fisted core, that so hated to share the results of her indefatigable energy with easy-going neighbors.

'You're a fine manager, Sister Mac, which gives you more to divide with others. I have no patience with the door that turns a hungry man away.'

The slow red crept up to the roots of 'Sheba's hair, but before she would let him go she had to take him down in the newly dug cellar pit to show him the great bunches of 'blow-horns' stacked in the corners, and how these dried hollow stems of seed onions made such good bellows — a few coals, a little dry cedar bark, a 'blow-horn,' and you had a fire!

Brother Brigham had a message for every member of the family. He praised Willie's uncomplaining spirit, and blessed her that she should yet raise up many children to the glory of God.

The twins came tumbling around the house with the youngest Eardley boys who lived up the street, Isaiah squalling in their wake; and Brother Brigham had to be told all their names, give them all peppermints from the inexhaustible store in his pocket, and lift up their tousled heads so that he might look into their grimy faces and remind them that in another two or three years they would be old enough to be baptized for their sins and take on the mantle of the Lord.

He strolled up by the barn to join Abijah, who was watering the young grapevines and peach trees in the back of the lot. Abijah was in his shirtsleeves, although he still wore his vest, and his trousers were tucked inside his boots because of the water. He hastily straightened them and ran his fingers through his great rumpled beard. Brother Brigham's homespun and flowing tie and the crisp hairs that rayed from his lips over his chin and along his jaw-line were always so immaculate. But the President reassured him, and the commanding lines of his face were relaxed and kindly.

'Just a friendly visit, Brother Mac.'

He stepped gingerly between the rows of tiny peach trees that had come up from the pits Abijah had got from the Clara last spring. He examined the shoots of the young grapevines, praised their weedless vitality, rubbed a pinch of the soft, tended soil between his fingers.

'Seedless grapes?' he wondered.

Abijah nodded.

'Well, they're mostly seedless — I've got a few "tough-skins" and "thin-skins" and some California gr-rapes for the wine——'

'Fine. The wine-grape is fine. But the seedless is good for Dixie, too, because they need so little water and can be dried into raisins and used all winter.'

Brother Brigham squinted against the sun.

'Your rows should be about fourteen feet apart — I think the vines themselves are a lee-tle too close together; about three feet apart is right. . . . Why don't you clean out your corrals and use the manure? Now is the time to put your land in condition to produce good crops. Cotton is the first consideration, of course, but I have no objection to your planting a little wheat and corn . . .'

Abijah, listening to Brother Brigham, was thinking he would always remember this moment as having a special quality all its own, a clear-cut crystal quality that intensified even details. He saw everything with a heightened consciousness: the steadfast clearness of Brother Brigham's level eyes, the touch of brown in the large, full irises, the clean whites slightly bloodshot from the dust of the trip, and the arch of the high broad brow to the hair-line — the strength, the human kindliness that emanated from his compact body.

Brother Brigham asked about Abijah's boys, and Abijah told him of Abraham and Samuel out herding, and Joseph out with the sheep. Yes, he answered, Samuel would be twelve in another year, old enough to be ordained a deacon and pass the Sacrament in meeting. Joseph was already a teacher. Yes, he sometimes went ward-teaching when he was in town, he and Free. Abijah stumbled somewhat over the latter name and Brother Brigham caught the stumble.

'Having a little trouble with the boy? We'll ordain him up in the Melchizedek priesthood before I leave; that will bring him around to the Lord.'

Ward-teaching needed a man's hand, anyway. Let's see, Abijah was first counselor to Bishop Gardner, was he not? And a member of Apostle Snow's High Council. Did he visit the members of his district in their homes often enough to understand their spiritual condition? To see that there was no backbiting or evil speaking?

And Abijah himself — he was a man of great strength and worth — wasn't it about time for him to go on another mission? Brother Brigham needs must go with him to the Sibley tent and re-read with him his patriarchal blessing given by the first Patriarch of the church, Joseph's father.

' ... of the House of Joseph, and thou hast a right by inheritance to the Holy Priesthood. Thou art called to go forth to the nations of the earth to hunt up the remnants of Jacob. Thou shalt have power to do many miracles when it is necessary to roll forward the great work of the Lord. Thou shalt have power over the elements of the winds, and the waves shall obey thy voice. Neither chains nor prison bars shall be able to hold thee ...'

When Brother Brigham went to go, Abijah walked with him to the gate and then up the dusty road a way. The salt grass and weeds and herbs along the ditch banks smelt harsh and clean and hot and Brother Brigham took his arm in a neighborly, intimate way and Abijah's heart swelled.

'See to bathing, Brother Mac,' he said. '"Cleanliness is next to godliness." I would advise a tub-bath once a week and a sponge bath oftener; clean children are healthier, and I want you to have more children. Children are our means of building up Zion and hastening the day when her enemies will be stamped out and their evil designs become as naught, when the blood of the prophets will be avenged and righteousness cover the earth as the waters the mighty deep . . . I would say to you always, Brother Mac — and you may teach your boys — pay your debts, keep your bowels open, walk uprightly before God and you will never have a care.'

True to his promise, in the next priesthood meeting Brother Brigham, with Erastus and Abijah, placed his hands upon Free's tow head and sealed the Melchizedek priesthood upon him and blessed him:

'If you will be faithful and follow the whispering of the Holy Spirit, you will never lack.'

In spite of the wagon covers Erastus had tacked during the day all over the outside of the bowery, the wind shook the flimsy structure until Brother Brigham's words were almost drowned. But even shouted words would have fallen back before the thin line of Free's lips; he walked down from the stand to his seat on the bench without a word. Abijah followed him with worried gaze; he had prayed so mightily that Brother Brigham might have the right utterance, the one touch to get through the mulishness.

Brother Brigham had three messages for the brethren — the vanity of attaching too much importance to material things, what to do about petty stealing, and the matter of taking more wives.

'There are hundreds of people in Deseret,' he said, 'who never owned a cow in the world until they came here, but now they have got a yoke of oxen and a horse to ride upon, they feel to be personages of far greater importance than Jesus Christ was, when he rode into Jerusalem upon an ass's colt!

'As for stealing' — his voice thundered through the room — 'if you want to know what to do with a thief that you may find stealing, *I say kill him on the spot!* A people that steal ought to have pitchforks rained upon them from the heavens, tines downward! If I caught a man stealing on my premises I should be very apt to send him *straight home*, and that is what I wish every man to do, to put a stop to this abominable practice!'

The faces before him were weatherbeaten, but lit with a rough beauty, mirroring hearts that had conquered space and time and blood for the hope of a brave, new world.

Polygamy was the hardest yoke many of them had to bear. The older men, seeing their children going hungry, rebelled against the idea of taking on another wife to raise more children, and the younger men, unable to support one wife properly, could not see the advantage in marrying more than one.

'God never introduced the patriarchal order of marriage with a view to please man in his carnal desires, but for the express purpose of raising up to His name a royal priesthood. Spirits must be born, even if they have to come to brothels for their fleshly coverings. I foresaw when Joseph first made known this doctrine that it would be a trial to the brethren, but what of it? We are to gird up our loins and fulfill this, just as we would any other duty. If any of you deny the plurality of wives, I promise that you will be damned, and as far as the women are concerned, they can never attain to the privileges of the celestial kingdom if they remain unmarried.

'Some stinking gentile curses say that we practice spiritual wifery for lust. Though I am now sixty-one years old, if I took another wife it would be for the same purpose, to bring forth noble children. Women were never meant to commit whoredoms with, as the gentiles do (and if they get in the family way to call for the evil midwife to get rid of it), but to raise up children.'

The silence rang when he stopped, and he brought up his fore-finger in that old gesture.

'But I tell you here, now, in the presence of the Almighty God, it is not the privilege of any elder to have even *one* wife, before he has honored his priesthood, before he has magnified his calling. If you obtain one wife it is by *mere permission*, to see *what you will do*, whether you will *conduct yourself in righteousness in that holy estate*.'

He leaned forward on the rostrum and his voice softened. His glance took in Free, Shadrach Gaunt, Charles Hichinoper, Benjamin Jarvis, and came to rest on David Wight, whose ascetic, clean-shaven face flushed under its brown.

'Now, young men, take to yourselves wives of the daughters of Zion, don't wait for us old men to take them all; go ahead upon the right principle, young gentlemen, and God bless you forever and make you fruitful, that we may fill up the mountains and then the earth with righteous inhabitants.'

After the meeting the brethren crowded about him, full of questions and explanations, wanting advice. Shadrach Gaunt stood there, talking to Free; his huge person, always more at home with sagebrush and skies than with a household, towered above his fellows. His sheepish grin sat incongruously upon his hawklike face.

'Women!' he said, and prepared to spit, and then remembered he was house-broken. 'The one I axed wouldn't wife me less'n I took her best friend, too, and I figgered a brace was more'n a man could stummick.'

Erastus, watching, was thinking there were others in the community who wouldn't enter plurality — Stiddy Weeks, for one; he was too sot in his own way.

Zebedee Trupp trotted up to the stand on his bandy legs, his single yellow tooth gleaming anxiously, his side whiskers agitated.

'Old Fifty-Cents-on-the-Dollar,' someone hissed, and Zebedee glared near-sightedly about.

The Lord had seen fit to keep Hepzibah childless, he told Brother Brigham — plainly the Lord had been absent-minded to let him marry such a woman in the first place — and he wanted to patch up the Lord's mistake with a fresh, young girl. Zebedee's little eyes were frantic with visions of himself abandoned to the sterile charms of Hepzibah through all eternity.

Although Zebedee was not many years older than Brigham, he looked twenty. Erastus, observing, remembered Brother Brigham's reiterated words that every new wife renews a man's age. Zebedee needed a harem.

Something must have tickled Brother Brigham's puckish humor. He put a hand over his mouth to hide his smile, but his chin-beard jutted like a fan.

'Well, I'll tell you, Brother Zebedee,' he said finally, 'you go ahead and take your young girl if you think you're man enough, but just let me warn you, she's a-going to need a lot more than the laying on of hands!'

3

Although Brother Brigham did not attend all the social functions, he visited with Erastus every home in the valley. Erastus was reminded of Winter Quarters when they were preparing for the trek, and people said of Brigham that he slept with 'one eye open and one foot out of bed.'

He watched Charley Hichinoper thresh and winnow the ripe seeds of the castor-bean plant, crush and steam and finally squeeze the hot bags of beans between the lengths of the heavy cottonwood press until the thick yellow oil dripped into the five-gallon cans beneath — sometimes as much as fifteen gallons in the day's run.

The indigo plants had not done as well, but the madder vines had climbed over their stakes and were feeling along the ground. Brother Brigham had to visit Eliza's dyeing-kettles in the house

where the madder-berry juice and sour bran water were being set
with cottonwood-ashes lye to make red, and the berry juice with
copperas or dock root to make brown. The dock root was especially good to dye leather. Pots of indigo were there, too, but the
blue color took ten days to dye, since it first had to be mixed with
aniline.

'We taken the yarn an' set the blue dye fast with chamber-lye
for a week,' explained Eliza, 'an' rench it out every day an' air it,
but the ammonia-stink of the chamber-lye gits so bad we have to
keep that pot outside ...'

Brother Brigham nodded — a long, unpleasant process, setting
dye with urine, but the dye stayed fast.

Eliza and Charles had to show him how the perfected blue-dyed
yarn could be colored green by scalding in yellow dye made out of
rabbit-brush blossoms or wild greasewood; black dye could be
made from logwood and copperas vitriol; dark brown from the
walnuts Brother Hamblin was raising in Santa Clara; olive green
from the creosote leaves, and 'shit-brindle' from wild sage.

Brother Brigham visited Brother Peabody, and rejoiced with
him that the hides soaking in the vats had only a little more than
another year to go before they could be made up into shoes and
harness tugs. Too bad timber was so scarce in Deseret — seems
that chestnut, hemlock, or sumac did not grow at all — and he
had to depend entirely on pine bark for his tanning. But Brother
Brigham was delighted with the idea of dyeing sheep pelts for
rugs, and promised him to help sell all he could tan.

He encouraged Benjamin Jarvis, busy in his willow schoolroom,
in his plan to get out a weekly news-sheet called *The Cactus*. He
consulted with Bishop Gardner, whose one-horse sawmill at the
foot of Pine Valley Mountain turned out a log a day. There was
chair-maker Trupp; Mansfield, the blacksmith; Eardley, the potter, whom he scolded for still grieving about his son, who was certainly in a better place than this world of fools.

He visited Erastus' own home, where the first community

molasses mill was operating in the back yard. Such a primitive affair that it had to be run night and day to care for the sugar cane from the town lots before the frosts came. Brother Brigham yelled above its squeak that he'd send down from the City some iron rollers. He chewed a joint of the sweet cane, watched the rich juice crush out as the faithful mule ambled around and around, licked a wary finger stuck into the green 'skimmings' rising to the top of the great kettle of boiling juice, and made Martha, the wife who was tending the molasses, promise to cook him up some 'skimmings' candy.

He could hardly make himself heard above the noise of Aunt Ket's big hand loom in the house. He followed Erastus into the room where Martha's five little ones and Aunt Ket's two youngest were sitting on the floor winding their daily stint of bobbins. The children stared at him with round eyes while he joked with them, produced peppermints, and learned each one's name — Brother Brigham always called everyone by name, even children. The huge, homemade loom, with its old-fashioned carpet-warp harness and four tall posts, almost filled the whole end of the room. When Aunt Ket started up again, her back muscles standing out as she treadled, threw the shuttle, and beat with the big beam to tauten the filling, the constant clatter of the treadles and the bang of the beam were deafening, but Brother Brigham, observing the twill she was weaving, seemed pleased.

Toward evening on Brother Brigham's last day, he went with Erastus on his favorite stroll up over Mount Hope to the Sugar Loaf.

There was something that had been bothering Erastus for a long time, and as they trudged along the dusty road west to Main Street and then up Main Street toward Mount Hope, he turned it over in his mind and finally decided to lay it bare.

'I'm worried — about this massacre business — up at the Meadows,' he said, coming right to the point. 'Bishop Lee ——'

Brigham turned his head and looked at him and his eyes were troubled. He hesitated.

'So am I,' he finally said. 'That dreadful business will be a blot on Deseret forever. That was the only wagon-train ever molested in this Territory, and yet history books will emphasize it so that the world will ignore the countless other times we've given freely of our substance.... But it's better to hush it up. It's better not to talk about it even among ourselves...'

But his thoughts would not be downed; they churned about in his heart... He would have given his life to prevent that butchery. Maybe some of those Missouri wildcats in the Fancher party *were* the mobbers who martyred Joseph, maybe they *did* carry the pistol that shot him, and maybe they *did* deserve killing, but he had always been against the taking of life — that was the Lord's business; and when he thought of the cold-blooded murder of innocent women and children...

He shuddered.

No, he said to himself, they'll say I have not wanted to bring the guilty parties to justice, but no organized body on earth is strong enough to guard against fanatics — and if I had punished the members of the priesthood who ordered the Mountain Meadows Massacre, I should have wrecked the entire Church organization down here; I'd have broken up colonization schemes in Dixie and pretty near killed Mormonism... Why, the president of Cedar Stake, Isaac Haight, himself, must have led that affair — and Higbee, his first counselor, and Klingensmith, Cedar's bishop, and Will Dame, the bishop of Parowan. — Brigham did not dare admit even in his heart that zealous John was only a tool ——

'The Saints were between — the anvil and the — hammer,' said Erastus, who refused to be hushed so easily — recalling the nervous fearfulness, of those days lest Nauvoo and Missouri be repeated, Brother Brigham martyred, and themselves caught between the United States Army coming upon them from the north and the army predicted by the Fancher party coming by way of the Gulf of Mexico and the Old Spanish Trail from the South — themselves, caught and crushed.

Martial law had been declared, Brigham's thought went on, and I wasn't governor at the time — my hands were tied. As soon as Governor Cummings and Judge Cradlebaugh got here I offered to help them investigate — but it took two whole years for Forney, that federal Indian agent, to gather up those children and send them back to the States and bury those poor stripped bodies rotting all that time in the sun . . .

Erastus nodded as if he had read Brigham's thoughts.

He had been up there. Bones and skulls — the wolves had gnawed — scattered half a mile up and down the valley. Someone — the gentiles accused the Saints and the Saints accused the gentiles — had knocked over the stone cairn and cross Forney put up. They say it's haunted now — spring's dried up — and on moonless nights you could hear the ghostly screams . . .

'It's bad for our people,' he said aloud.

Brigham struck his hands together.

'What could I have done!' he cried. He'd had the Move on his hands, evacuating a city of thirty thousand people, fleeing with them to the mountains —! Besides, at that time he'd believed John's story. Believed Indians were responsible. Only lately had he become convinced that Saints did it! Saints! the kind of saints who would sit up all night and ask the Lord whether it was *His* will to *butcher* or not! When Cradlebaugh got out that reward of five thousand dollars for Lee, John had written him that it was 'considerable for a man who had only been endeavoring to obey the Gospel requirements'! But the deed was done and he still thought it better to hush it up; the gentiles were just waiting to pounce on an excuse like that — no use bringing them on us like a pack of hellhounds to add to our other troubles . . .

Poor John; he brooded, his eyes on the thick red dust at his feet; he'd known he was too anxious always to be the big *It* in everything, but he hadn't thought he'd let himself be pushed into a murder. He'd been so faithful in Winter Quarters, keeping the Church records — he'd donated seventeen ox teams when they

started west. He was Brigham's own adopted son. Why, he'd
been a member of the legislature the year after the massacre!
He'd given him another wife then, too.

Brigham trudged along. He raised his head as if the gesture
hurt.

'Is John still in hiding?'

'No,' Erastus said. 'He came out when Cradlebaugh resigned.
He met our wagons at Washington a year ago. He spends his
time between here — and his ranch; I'm surprised he ain't here
now. But President Haight and the others are all in the hills —
one of them beat it to Mexico.'

'And John's left holding the bag.'

'And — stirring up a stink,' added Erastus. 'Some of the
Washington people told on him to Cradlebaugh, and now he
accuses *them* of apostasy.'

Erastus was suddenly filled with longing for his old dream of
perfection. A country where men should love each other. He
was thinking of Orson Pratt, Junior, whose excommunication
and bitterness had had the natural result of shutting him off
from his fellows. Neither he nor his family ever attended community gatherings any more (they had even shunned Brother
Brigham). He was afraid they were going hungry, but what could
you do with a man who slammed the door in your face? Orson lost
his team in the quicksand the other day simply because he
wouldn't ask for help.

'We can't fight among ourselves and lick the river — and the
government — and the country, too!'

'I know,' said Brigham, remembering the gossipers he'd reproved at Harrisburg, where sisters were accusing each other of
wearing breastpins and sunbonnets looted from the murdered
emigrants. Remembering that some of the Cedar brethren had
even tried to pay their tithing with the looted cattle!...

'The more you stir up a manure pile the worse it stinks!'

'Some of Brother Lee's wives are leaving him ——'

'Well, he won't miss one or two' — Brigham's sly humor crept around the corners of his mouth — 'out of nineteen.'

They had reached the top of Mount Hope — there where the road stretched before them over the plateau and elbowed to skirt the precipice and circle the flank of the Sugar Loaf — and they stopped to pant a moment and look about them. Erastus pointed out Steadfast Weeks's house beyond the road among the bushes.

Brigham shook his head.

'Brother Weeks is a smart man with herbs, Erastus, but I don't like all this hollerin' of our people after doctors. A surgeon is all right to set bones or cut off a limb, but all a man needs to do otherwise is to eat less, cleanse the stomach, bowels, and blood, *and call upon the Lord*, and if the man is not healed then, it is because the Lord does not will it. Doctors! They are like lawyers stirring up strife — or a judge, like a bean on the end of a pipestem, who would be flipped off if a grain of common sense happened to strike him!'

He shook his head again.

'A growing evil in our midst.'

At that moment the door of the dugout opened and John D. Lee stepped out, blinking in the sunlight.

Erastus gasped.

'Speak of the Devil and you'll see his horns.'

Brigham did not say a word, but John D. walked over to the two men, his eyes on the ground, and offered them his hand. Erastus, uncomfortably following the example of Brigham, merely stood. The President's eyes were hard.

'John,' he said, 'what made you lie to me about the Mountain Meadows Massacre?'

John's eyes wavered and fell before that cold stare.

'I never want to see you again,' said Brigham, and took Erastus' arm and turned and plodded on up the road.

4

Eliza Hichinoper never knew when she first missed her child, Marvelous. Just at the stage where he could toddle freely, he had got into the habit of running away. Toward evening some little boys out playing had seen two Indians with brush tied on their heads skulking through the bushes, but being only mildly alarmed they had run home and forgotten to mention the fact. But at dawn when the search-party came home, weary, bedraggled, and empty-handed, everyone believed the Indians had taken the child. But what Indians? Tutsegabbett assured Shadrach Gaunt that his own people were too fearful of being stolen themselves by the marauding Navajos ever to steal anyone else. But nevertheless, it was true that even the Paiutes were tired of being pushed back, back. They were faced now with another hungry winter, sleeping uncovered on the snow. Free, working on the ditch, was more and more pestered with young bucks who would stand and watch him shovel silently and then mutter 'My water! my land!' and stalk away.

Tutsegabbett and his braves helped with the search. But at the end of a week the settlers went back to their jobs and only Eliza was left roaming the underbrush, the empty, intricate hills, crying one name over and over. Erastus could not pacify her, and Charles was afraid she would lose her mind.

Clory, who had never liked her very well, left Kissy with Willie and went over and sat with Eliza. A sop to those blind, unfeeling gods. The naked, quivering torment in Eliza's eyes! Unspeaking, she would rock in the doorway, staring out across the valley, beyond brush and hills and deserts. After those visits, sick with the look on Eliza's peaked face, Clory would be wary of showing her love for Kissy, of saying it aloud for the jealous, listening gods to hear.

Erastus increased the guard over the community cattle, and saw that the danger signals were ready — the white diapers to be whisked up the four tall pine posts marking the most outlying lots on the fringe of the settlement, the ominous voice of the drum in the bowery.

The unrest spread to the local Indians. The squaws who were used to begging at Abijah's door took on a sly air of insolence.

Erastus called a public meeting in which he told the citizens that it was part of their religion to 'load fast and shoot straight.' And shortly thereafter Colonel William H. Dame of the Iron Military District at Cedar Fort came down with orders to organize the Washington County Militia.

The order was from Daniel H. Wells, lieutenant-general commanding the Nauvoo Legion:

' ... to hold muster and inspection of arms in your district. Keep a guard night and day. Have your places of rendezvous and arrangements made for a quick movement in any direction. Keep good horses, with the necessary equipment, wagons or carriages with teamsters and drivers selected — be minute men ...'

Erastus was made brigadier-general and Shadrach Gaunt his colonel, and drilling began at once.

Free seemed to take more of an interest in the drilling, Abijah thought, than in anything lately. Although by now he had worked on the Virgin ditch long enough to get himself a nice piece of land, he seemed lax about farming it. When the Salt Lake 'pony' had started up, Free had come to him with some wild talk of joining that — it seemed the boy longed to take harebrained risks, do spectacular deeds; he ranted about the old 'pony' across the plains when a rider was known by his dust in the daytime, at night by his lusty whoops; when Buffalo Bill was taking on the additional run of a scalped relief, making three hundred and twenty miles in twenty-one hours through country infested with savages and road agents.

Abijah had been short with him. Puzzled and troubled, he had

gone to Clory, who of course would not discuss Free with him
any more than she had ever done.

Abijah, trying to be diplomatic, seemed to her about as subtle
as a cow with a sore teat.

'I thoct,' he said, 'that I smelled tobacco on the boy. Dinna
ye ken aboot it?'

But she only shook her head at him, and went back to Kissy in
the cradle. There was a new softness about her; Abijah sighed
and took himself away — the softness was not for him. And that
night he wrote in his diary: 'Seeded my boy Freeborn's land with
the last of my Taos grain. Still stiff-necked. Would like to send
him on mission next month with young 'Rassy Snow, but...'

He had his hands too full these days, what with counseling
with Brother Eardley over his two girls who'd been walking with
young men unchaperoned (there was even talk about Free,
though he denied it), always making eyes at the boys, wearing
bangs, more free than ever now that their older brother was dead
and they were often unescorted — his hands too full to worry about
his own son. Abijah could not see why he should have a son who
drank and smoked; goodness knows he had never spared the
razor strap, but had always punished him regularly, had tried to
teach him right from wrong. He suspected uneasily that Clory
better understood the boy, but a long time ago she had closed
a door in his face — he had no idea when — and he could not
get beyond that sweet, vague smile of hers any more than he
could find out what lay behind Free's haunted eyes. Trouble
was, the baby would be old enough to wean in a few more months
and it would be his duty to visit Clory's bed again; the thought
gave him more distress than pleasure — how old did a man have
to get before he had a little peace!

Thwarted by the beam in his own eye, he plucked at the mote
in his neighbor's. On his rounds as ward teacher he found more
backbiting and evil-speaking than ever before. Unable to account for it, he counseled with redoubled zeal and could not

understand why so few were willing to repent, but greeted his
efforts in their behalf with tightened lips.

His diary began to bristle much as it had done on the trip from
the City —

'November 2, '62 — I told Bro. Eardley that unless he could
stamp out evil in his own family, he was not fit to administer such
holy ordinance as consecrating a bottle of oil, but he called me a
G. D. bastardly Son-of-a-B —— I told him he would have to
make that Right with me by a Public Confession or I will Prefer
Charges and write to the Church Patriarch...'

One day toward the end of the month Joseph rode in unexpectedly. He had just driven his sheep from the summer range
on Pine Valley Mountain to the warm flats below the river, and
he had a tale to tell. He was sparing of words in his usual laconic
fashion, but his eyes still glinted angrily. For a year he had been
saving up hairs from horses' tails to make a rope, hanging them on
the branch of a near-by tree. An Indian had sneaked up and cut
them off and run, and they were helpless because there were only
the two of them to fight. Joseph's dark eyes were furious as he
told the story — strong, pliable, waterproof hair ropes were not
easily come by.

The uprising seemed to be general. Gottlieb Uttley, freighting
to California for the new firm of Hunt, Wight, and Judd reported the massacre of an emigrant train, and further on in the
desert a family who had made themselves a temporary camp,
butchered around the willow half-faced tent, their naked, arrow-
pierced corpses rotting in the sun, the husband and father lying
in front of the tent which sheltered his family as if he had come
out to meet danger. One hand, both of his legs were cut off.
The mother, the bared bone of her skull still glistening, was
propped gruesomely against a tree. Gottlieb had to bury her three
times on his successive trips through the country before the
Indians would let her stay buried.

Free, especially, drank in Gottlieb's every word. Abijah did not like the growing intimacy between the two. Gottlieb was a big, rawboned, uncouth youth who laughed too loud; moreover, he was a mouther of oaths and a tippler of wine.

One day in early December a young gentile from those mysterious regions beyond the desert rode in on the seat of the high-piled freight wagon. Gottlieb, astride the near wheeler, proud of his skill with the twenty-mule team, proud of the music of the five graduated bells strapped over the withers of the lead mule, flourished the jerk-line and yipped all the way into town.

The young gentile, whose name, it seemed, was Cecil Davis, was as sleek and shining as a cat, in plaided trousers and a tall beaver hat. He and Gottlieb swallowed up Free under Abijah's very nose and prepared to swagger about town for three days. And when Gottlieb went back, this Cecil with the silken, curled mustache stayed behind. President Snow welcomed gentiles as long as they minded their own business, but before Abijah could say scat! there was this Cecil making eyes at Sis and Miny Eardley, and that girl of Stiddy Weeks's, and every other passing female. And tempting his own son. Abijah didn't like it; he didn't like it at all.

During these sunny fall days Erastus' precious Australian lucerne seed that he'd traded from the home-coming missionary last March was coming up for the third time in swaths of living green. He'd cut it the first time in June just after it had 'stooled out' and again in September for seed; now it had crowned again and the succulent knee-high bushes and purple blooms loaded their sweetness on every vagrant breeze. All the long, dry summer that bit of green had been a rendezvous; and doubly now, since the lucerne patch was the only growing thing in the midst of the surrounding brown, couples would stroll after Sunday meeting down the red road beyond the rock wall, lean over the brush fence, and gaze at that vivid square with hungry eyes. Lovers forsook the light cave at the Sugar Loaf and did their courting there. And so also did Cecil Davis. Stiddy Weeks and

Brother Eardley both had to hunt stray daughters there on more than one occasion ...

Abijah, worried about the lack of food in larder and barn, stroked the thin flanks of his animals, whose bones stuck up beneath their hides, and itched to take the scythe to that patch of feed. It hurt him to see his animals go hungry. He supposed he'd have to trade off the other pair of oxen — maybe send Free to Pine Valley or Cedar Fort to trade for potatoes — and that would leave him with just one pair. But he had to have those for the breaking plow. Mules weren't stout enough to work new ground.

But meanwhile he and Free used both pair of oxen for hauling rock for Brother Brigham's new cotton factory going up by the creek this side of Washington, and every Friday Abijah took the two slips of paper to the little adobe one-room Tithing and Post Office (known as the T.O.) alongside the bowery in the square, and redeemed them for the flour and wheat Brother Brigham had sent down. The wheat was cheaper (flour ran anywhere from ten to twenty-five dollars a hundred), but it had to be ground in Erastus' gristmill (a creaking old burr mill that crushed the wheat between two stones — Lon Tuckett declared it 'ground two kernels into one!'), and since there was no bolting cloth, the shorts and bran could not be separated, so the bread was as heavy as unleavened bread and so dark the children maintained it was made 'out of 'dobe dirt.' But, nevertheless, the whole family rejoiced over real wheat bread once more, and the twins quarreled over who should 'go after yeast.'

Sister Hansen ran the neighborhood yeast center; she had brought a start of flour yeast with her from the North and she kept a start on hand from which she made jars of yeast by stirring up flour and water and a little sugar or molasses; and for a cup of flour she would fill your quart bucket with yeast. She also kept on hand corn-meal 'rising' for salt-rising bread. The Yeast Lady was as important a cog in the community as the T.O.; children loved to go to her because she always smelled as if she had been

making spice cookies — and sometimes she had. On those occasions when the twins spilled the yeast, or drank it (which they
often did), 'Sheba found her more than generous — 'Sheba,
whose unneighborliness was well known. Starting your own
yeast was out of the question with wild Pine Valley hops at ten
dollars a pound.

As it happened, the Hansens saved Abijah from having to
trade in his second pair of oxen that fall. Lars had long had his
eye on one of Abijah's good States hoes, but Abijah felt that a
good hoe that had to be freighted at the rate of fifty dollars per
ton all the way from the Missouri was worth forty dollars. Lars,
who had just hauled in a load of potatoes from the North at
eighty dollars a hundred, came over one evening with an offer to
trade Abijah half a hundredweight of potatoes for the hoe, and
thus the deal was consummated.

Lars could play his bass fiddle, but that was unpaid community service, and as for his bedsteads and tables and chairs,
folks just did not seem able to buy furniture these days. He had
decided to go heavily into the cradle business, he told Abijah;
that was one market that never ran out in Zion.

Thus by dint of much scrambling the settlers got by. Abijah
traded four different times to get his winter's wood. He found
that Shadrach Gaunt in between spells of drilling was hauling
wood from the Pine Valley foothills. Abijah, wanting to trade
some wool he had on hand, discovered that Charley Hichinoper
would trade indigo-dye for wool. Abijah took the dye, part of
which his wives could use, and traded the rest to Hannah Merinda
Lowgie for butter and poultry which Shadrach could use, and for
which Shadrach hauled him the load of wood.

5

The winter went by with less actual want than Erastus had expected. The Indians gave little more trouble. In November, just

after the first scare, Jacob Hamblin led the first party of missionaries across the Colorado River to the Navajo and Moqui towns; he intended to baptize and bring back representatives of these tribes to counsel with Brigham, and meanwhile it was hoped his visit would have a quieting effect on the Paiutes.

Occasionally Tutsegabbett and his intimates conducted pow-wows out in the brush east of town, and papooses would be sent around to the homes of the Mormonies to gather bread for the rabbit-and-gopher-and-lizard-and-red-ant stew boiling in the large iron kettle hanging from the tripod around which sat the circle of smoking, gambling, cross-legged braves. The Indians had always been great teasers, delighting in taking advantage of the terror they inspired by peeking in windows and booing the children, or skulking behind a home-going child in the brush.

Abijah was able to keep his mischief-makers, the twins, and Abraham in school three months that winter — even Samuel part of the time — which was not only a record, but a great relief to 'Sheba, who was only too glad to help pay their tuition with eggs.

During the winter evenings, with a pine knot on the fire, Abijah conducted his 'sings' almost as much as he used to before they left the City. Clory practiced up on the dulcimer until her hands were lightning-quick with the little wooden paddles, and she could tap out the strains of 'Loch Lomond' and that new song, 'Massa's in the Cold, Cold Ground.' 'Sheba would sit, turfing yarn for Abijah's wristlets, and Willie would knit or sew carpet-rags, while Abijah's rich voice rolled out into the night and Clory accompanied him with the sweet, sentimental music of the dulcimer.

Clory asked for nothing better those days than the unceasing wonder of Kissy. As the baby began to notice things and crow at her mother, Clory wondered how she had ever filled up her life before.

'You funny little thingumabob!' she would cry fondly to the

baby, and Abijah, watching, thought he had never seen a human
face so naked and defenseless in its love.

Excitement came through simple things. Watching each man
take his turn digging away down in the funnel of the artesian
well — in December, when it was down four hundred feet and
had cost them five thousand dollars, the citizens gave it up. Wistfully estimating the snows of Pine Valley Mountain, rearing his
hoary winter head behind the Sugar Loaf, they went back to
'Virgin bloat.' 'Nothing will live, man nor beast, without more
water,' worried Erastus. 'Human beings ... don't stay human
very long if they have to drink "Virgin Bloat," and our women
get kidney trouble and the Big Neck from the mineral in the
springs ...' But some day Dixie *would* have good water!

There were Sunday visits to the new buildings going up — the
Social Hall, the Tithing Office, the projected cotton factory and
Erastus' Big House, even the first black foundation rocks in the
corner of the square Brigham had designated as the place for the
Tabernacle. Housewives proposed to aid the erection of public
buildings by donating all the eggs laid on Sunday.

Scrip was issued for these buildings — the people dealt in T.O.
coupons, city scrip, church scrip, factory scrip, Hunt-Wight-
and-Judd scrip. Bishop Gardner followed the example of the
bishopric in other communities and issued 'bishops' chips,'
eight-sided tin pieces with 'This amount good for ...' stamped
on them. The settlers joked about the lack of money — indeed,
the uselessness of money to them. They were likely to say offhand
to a trader, 'We'll pay you in chips and whetstones' — and then
when he looked blank: 'because a whetstone is a thing you
sharpen an axe with when you haven't got an axe.'

Free was perhaps the only one in the valley who took money
seriously. For almost a year he had been stealthily trading here
and there. From the City he had brought down a large copper
penny, star-ringed, inscribed with the Goddess of Liberty, whose
winged features he kept dangling on a string next to his heart.

And stuffed in the bottom of an old nosebag hanging in his wagon box were a Confederate bill, a gold eagle, and two of Lincoln's fifty-cent and five-dollar greenbacks. Of course, people said that the war had lowered the value of the paper money until the Confederate bill was worth one twentieth and the greenbacks about half, but at least the stuff was what people *used* back there in the States; a man couldn't buy a ticket on the steam cars for a *pumpkin* . . .

Always there was testimony-meeting to look forward to, held on the first Sunday in the month, when each family was supposed to fast one meal and give in the proceeds to the fund for the poor. These meetings, often attended by people from the surrounding towns, were turned over to the congregation for the blessing of babies and the bearing of testimonies as to the truth of the Gospel, and they invariably afforded a man an excellent chance to determine the state of his neighbor's soul, and at the same time obliquely air his own.

On the first Sunday in January, Marianne Snow and Palmyra Wight brought their new babies to be blessed. David proudly carried his child up the aisle between the craning necks. Pal had had the baby in December, and David, finally giving in to her wishes, had Stiddy Weeks deliver it. Clory had marveled at the serenity of Pal's freckled face under the sniffs of 'Sheba, Hannah Merinda Lowgie, and the other visiting sisters. But Pal had remained quite unmoved by censure; she had bargained with David — if she had her way with the baby, he could take another wife.

Now she sat beside Clory, calm and proud, as David on the stand gently teetered the child in his arms and Erastus and Abijah placed their hands upon it, blessing it and naming it Patience Elizabeth Wight.

Afterward, Erastus inquired if there were any present who had over-indulged in wine or tobacco during the week and wished to confess before partaking of the sacrament. Shadrach Gaunt stood up in the back of the room, and heads turned around.

His awkward hands plucked at the fringe down his buckskin trousers, fingered the strings of his hunting coat, clasped themselves behind his back.

'I reckon the "Devil" hankered a'ter me twicet last week,' he finally admitted.

'Brethren and sisters,' said Erastus, 'all in favor of forgiving Brother Gaunt his — ah, backsliding, raise their right hands . . .'

The sea of faces suddenly became a forest of hands.

There being no more confessions, the Sacrament was passed, the boys with their plates of broken bread and goblets of wine moving quietly between the rows.

There was silence then for a time, the congregation shifting uneasily in their seats.

Then Brother Eardley, who had been a member of the battalion, heaved himself to his feet. He was, he said, grateful for the knowledge he bore that this was the true Gospel of the Lord Jesus Christ revealed in these latter days. One reason why he knew it was true was that all of Joseph's destroyers were themselves killed. A colonel of the Missouri forces who had died in Sacramento in 1849 (and whom Brother Eardley had known) 'was eaten with large, black-headed maggots, seeming a half-pint at a time.' Brother Eardley would remind the Saints of the brother they had all known in Nauvoo who was baptized for his rheumatism and 'the ordinance over, he straightened and never used his crutches again.' Brother Eardley was 'thankful to bear his testimony and rejoice to God for the blessing we enjoy.'

Gottlieb Uttley's father arose next. A humble man, confused at the sudden focus of eyes, lost in the mazes of a new language, he scratched his ear a long time before the painful words came. He, too, was grateful for his knowledge that the Gospel was true. He was thankful for the opportunity to raise his children in the Gospel — 'My shildrens are all goot poys and girls,' he said. 'Yes, I got goot fambly. Of course, Gottlieb is not a very goot poy; he smokes and he trinks and svears . . . but t'ank God he's a goot Latter-Tay Saint!'

Sister Hansen's soul was full to bursting, but her heart quailed before all these people. She clung to the back of the bench and her old voice quavered, and her 'store' teeth clacked.

'I yoost vant to bear my testimony that the Gospel iss true,' she said, pushing her upper plate into place, 'that Yoseph Smith is a true prophet of Got. Ve try to obey the Gospel in our house and keep the Vord of Visdom. We don't haf the tea nor coffee nor vhiskey in our house, except maybe iss a leedle for Lars. But I somedimes vonder,' she said, her voice suddenly wistful, 'vhy it iss the Lord keeps all the good t'ings for the gentiles...'

Eliza Hichinoper was on her feet before the Yeast Lady had finished, her eyes wild and glaring. There was a hush; this looked like 'speaking-in-tongues.'

Her face was glistening, her hair disordered.

'La la la lelo,' she mumbled, a jumble of sounds strung together, and fell back on the bench as if she were lifeless.

Sister Weeks arose, her eyes awed. She declared that the Lord had inspired her with the power to interpret, that Eliza's message was to all parents who grieved for lost children, that the Lord was displeased with their grieving since the children were with the angels.

Clory, watching the faces about her, sincere, devoted, only a few like Marianne Snow's too high-nosed for simple folk, wondered about this thing called a testimony; this divine fire for which men would give up family and kindred rather than renounce. All about her tongues faltered, in an effort to express this gratitude of the heart. 'Where much is given, much is required' — the old, old saying of her people — housewives scooping the last cupful of flour, the last crust of bread to pay dues to this church they loved.

A testimony of the Gospel — not something one could smell or taste or weigh in the hands, or buy, or pick off a tree, but something so real and rapturous that with it all life became a song, all death an adventure. Either you had it or you didn't have it; no one seemed able to say exactly how it came. Shadow of dim mysteries, passionate gropings in the night — was it tinged with the earthy thing she had dreamed of with Rolph, guessed at with Abijah, touched with Free? All she knew was that with it, a man in rags was stronger than a king.

The old phrases were glib upon the tongue: *I know Joseph Smith to be a prophet of God!* But how, *how* did one know it? And you couldn't say it if you didn't know it... Clory wondered again if this dreadful lack in her soul would some day fester upon the surface for all men to see; she was like a person born with a hand missing, or an eye...

With the new year many of the brethren began acquiring new wives. As soon as Pal was quite well, she and David became very social, taking in all the dramatics and debates and house-raisings and barn-raisings and spelling bees. Pal made no bones about the fact that she was out courting another wife for David. 'For,' she said, 'if I've got to live with her, I might as well pick out someone I like.' She hoped in her heart when the time came for David to 'keep company,' she'd show more dignity than other first wives who chased long-winded husbands home from the chosen one's parlor.

One Sunday Shadrach Gaunt amazed everyone by coming to meeting with three new wives, two girls and their widowed mother from up the river. It seemed he had had to take a 'brace,' after all...

With the setting-in of the cold weather, mails from the north stopped altogether. But the Dixie settlers had not yet picked dry the bone of last fall's news. And as they worked on the canal and rebuilt the dam a few feet above the old one, they conjectured about where Brother Brigham would send the new European immigrants, over twenty-two thousand of whom had been brought across by the P.E.F. during the summer and fall.

The time had come when the Dixie Mission must assume its

share of this annual burden. In January Brother Brigham had written that Washington County would be expected to furnish 'fifty-five ox or mule teams (six mules or four yoke of oxen to each team), an equal amount of good and trusty teamsters, and four mounted guards armed and equipped for a five or six months journey with clothing, ammunition, ferryage means, ox shoes, spades, axes, picks, ropes ... and, since sacks and sacking are scarce you will have to make sufficient boxes for each team to carry at least one thousand pounds of flour with which to feed the saints on the road back.'

Erastus summoned the head of each St. George family, read the order, and requested each man to provide enough to bring one soul from the Old Country; he could choose his own soul.

There was always some grumbling about the P.E.F., particularly among the women who figured that a man had enough souls to provide for in his own family. The three English women, Keturah Snow, Hannah Merinda Lowgie, and Bathsheba Mac-Intyre, were thick as hops, as Willie put it. They were in the habit of meeting at each other's home once a week (on afternoons when the men were in the fields) to piece quilt blocks or sew carpet-rags. But because they were so secretive about these visits ('Sheba locked the door of the tent and never invited Clory or Willie), other women were very curious. Willie, English herself, was sure they drank tea, and Clory was equally sure they played euchre, for she had once come upon 'Sheba just in time to see her slide the cards into her apron pocket.

One afternoon when the three women were in the tent, Abijah came home unexpectedly, and, wondering at the expressions on the faces of Clory and Willie poking their heads through the dugout window, hesitated on 'Sheba's doorstep. Plainly through the walls of the tent he could hear voices and the slap of cards.

'We've just time for another drawin' of tea before Par gets home' — Aunt Ket's voice.

'Land sakes, don't care if I do,' said 'Sheba. 'I'm tired of bein' a man's footstool. I'd have a house by now if Brother Mac hadn't been so anxious to buy stock in that old Seventies' Hall of Science Brother Brigham built — twenty-four shares we took at twenty-five dollars a share ten year ago, and just try gittin' your money out of it now! Brother Mac tried to redeem them shares afore we come down here and Brigham says, "I'll take over your propity as trustee-in-trust of the Church — Dixie's your home now, stay there; don't keep an old sow t' suck up here!" Land sakes, I ain't like some folks who kiss a man's te-hinder like he's the Lord Himself!'

Hannah Merinda: 'Pooh, pooh. Brigham always did sit and wiggle his toe and give orders while the rest of us did the work and tolled unto him!'

But at that moment Abijah could stand it no longer. He pounded on the door, his face black with wrath.

'Let me in!' he sputtered. 'Ye'll keep yer fulish tongues off the authorities of this Church! You women know too dang much!'

The two faces in the dugout window licked their chops.

'Serves her right!' gloated Clory.

She was sick of 'Sheba telling her how to run her house and raise her baby. '"Always go to bed with a clean-swept hearth,"' 'Sheba would say, and '"A place for everything and everything in its place."' And whenever Clory went to kill a scuttling spider or a cockroach, '"If you want to live and thrive, let a spider run alive!"' As for Kissy —! 'Don't let her look in the mirror before she's a year old or she's apt to take sick and die.' Don't do this, don't do that —!

'I'd like to *see* 'Sheba right now,' said Clory, longing to be in at the kill.

6

One unexpectedly cold day in March, when the desert shivered like a gray ghost, Clory put on her old black plush cape, wrapped Kissy in a quilt, and started down the road to Stiddy Weeks's.

She didn't care if it was going agin counsel; Kissy picked her nose and chewed her tongue and had all the symptoms of worms...

There was a crowd milling about the square; she loitered, intending only to stop a moment. But when she saw the dust-stained figure in its rumpled chaps jump down from the cayuse, her heart gave a great leap. News! The first 'pony' from the North since spring opened up...

The winter's peace was torn. At the meeting that night when the mail was 'cried off,' the citizens were noisy with indignation. Congress had passed the Homestead Act throwing open all the public lands of the West. For years the Saints, feeling themselves merely squatters in Zion, had tried to buy Deseret from the government, but all they got for their pains were a lot of meaningless phrases about extinguishing the Indian title, pre-emption of the sections, and primary disposal of the soil. For years Congress had passed around slices of Deseret to new neighbors. And now Zion would be open to every land-jumper in the country! In fact, the Salt Lake brethren were already clashing with gentile squatters beyond the Jordan. Already Congress had taken away the Church's property, refused to compensate Brother Brigham for the three hundred thousand dollars he had spent on Indian troubles...

But that wasn't the worst news. Governor Harding's speech to the legislature in December — 'I am aware that there is a prevailing opinion that the bigamy act is unconstitutional and therefore recommended by those in high authority that no regard be paid ... *Warn you of dangerous and disloyal council* ...'

Mass-meeting in the Tabernacle! A petition for the governor's removal signed by thousands. Orson Pratt, newly elected speaker of the House, leads a committee to wait upon the governor — insults — 'Go back to Brigham, your master, that embodiment of sin and shame and disgust, and tell him that I neither fear him nor love him nor hate him — I utterly despise him!' Angry groups on street corners...

To make matters worse, Brother Brigham had just taken a new wife, Amelia Folsom, who was supplanting Emmeline Free in his favor, gossip said.... And now Brother Brigham is arrested under the new bigamy law! There is a frightened, angry buzz all through the bowery; but what can Brother Brigham do? He has just had three new children in February, all by different wives, and everybody in the City knows about Amelia! His case is dismissed this time, but ...

And the soldiers at Camp Douglas kidnap a Mormon girl, Colonel Connor stirs up the gentiles with tales of mining, bitterness swells between the troops and the citizens, it is rumored Connor intends to capture Brigham and take him to Washington — the signals are hoisted, the cannon loaded!

And the audience in the St. George Bowery are on pins with anxiety to know what is happening between those angry groups; they can hardly wait for April and Brother Brigham to come again. So great is their agitation that they completely ignore Lincoln's new draft law. Besides, the law was rather silly, since any man might obtain exemption on the payment of three hundred dollars. Just like those crazy gentiles to shout, 'Father Abraham, we're coming, three hundred thousand strong,' and then run around looking for exemptions.

But there is a boy with strange, light eyes in the far back of the room whose face begins to shine.

'Maybe it'll reach here and I'll go, I'll go!'

'Ech! Which side will you join?' laughs his father.

And at that, a shadow crosses the boy's face and he hangs his head.

'I wouldn't care,' he mutters, 'either side ...'

7

There were three of the varmints. Winter-starved, desperate, each with his quiver of cane arrows tipped with poison-smeared flint.

'Ta-wi-cha shet-cup!'

'Sheba had half a loaf of dark bread wrapped up in a dishtowel in the bottom of the cupboard, but it was all they had for dinner. She did not dare call for Clory — and what good would Willie be? The Indians pushed past her and began to ransack beds, knock over tables ... 'Sheba yelled and got the butcher knife ... one of the Indians tore it from her hands ... and Clory came running, and an Indian met her in the doorway, brandishing an arrow. 'Sheba was still fighting for the knife ... The crunch of popped chair-legs, ripping of rugs ... Suddenly Sister Hansen, her rosy old face alarmed, stood amongst the rumpus.

'Vat iss it?' she cried, her store teeth clacking.

And 'Sheba had an inspiration. She let go the knife and grabbed the savage by the naked flesh of his arm.

'Witch!' she shouted, pointing to Sister Hansen. 'She got devils!'

While the Indians stared, Sister Hansen thrust the teeth loose from her gums and dropped her upper plate in a ghastly misplaced grin ... What was this 'Mericat-medicine that could make a smile wander at will?

The bread was safe, but the three women, watching the Indians streak off through the brush, were weak with reaction. By nightfall when the men came home they had gathered all the women and children in town into the square ...

Erastus was in a quandary; he did not like to fort in until Brother Brigham came. Jacob Hamblin, crestfallen at the seeming results of his missionary trip, assured Erastus over and over that the Indians as a whole were quiet; he had Tutsegabbett there to prove it. But the settlers jostled about, afraid to go home. Would the warning drum thunder in the night?

In the midst of the confusion Free rode up on Nellie; an arrow stuck out of one satiny hind quarter. He flung himself off, half-sobbing, and took Nellie's head in his arms and crooned and petted her and turned back to the arrow. The men thronged about him, offering advice, but Free yelled at them to get away. He set his lips and grabbed the arrow with both hands; Nellie quivered but stood still.

'Don't stand there and gawp, you fools!' stormed Free, beside himself with watching the blood spurt. 'Go get me some Jimson weed to kill the poison!'

Tutsegabbett's eyes were distressed. He had tried his best to follow the 'Mericats' customs, he had even tried to understand them making medicine — their wamptun, many-wives, their poogi, praying words over people's heads, even the silly way they worshiped God instead of Winnopats, the Devil, when everyone knew Winnopats caused all the trouble and was therefore the one to please. But this last business — you gave full value for something stolen, two squaws for a horse, a life for a life. Then he caught Jacob's eye and his heart was water. More than anything in the world he valued Jacob's smile. For Jacob he'd even go-into-the-water again.

Suddenly he ran to Nellie, stooped over and put his mouth to the pony's wound, and began to suck the blood in great gulps, spewing it upon the ground. The crowd gasped. Jacob walked over and put a hand on his naked shoulder. Tutsegabbett looked up, and the lines of his face were harsh and proud in the dimming twilight.

'We cannot be good,' he said to this friend of his people; 'we just be Paiutes. We want you to be kind to us. It may be that some of our children will be good, but we want to follow our old customs...'

8

The town was ready for Brother Brigham when he came. Corrals were cleaned out, dooryards hoed and scraped, brush newly grubbed about the bowery, and 'dobe houses and dugouts freshly plastered (familiar, twice-yearly cleaning ritual) with the clay out at the Old Campground. Abijah himself had Free haul Clory's clay and with Willie's help she soon had her walls a glistening white instead of the dark red of the last year.

The minstrel show was ready for Brother Brigham; Sambo and Bones, David Wight and Lon Tuckett, burlesquing Governor Harding and Judge Waite. Brother Brigham rolled on his seat. Strange how the Indians no longer mattered, how *right* everything was, with him laughing there.

True enough, he had brought Amelia with him this time; there she sat on the front bench in all her splendor. Rumor had it he was going to build her another palace down here; they didn't care — he could bring down fifty wives as long as he brought himself!

'We're not husbands of more than one wife according to United States law,' he said, leaning on the rostrum; 'how can they arrest us?'

'Looks like you've got 'em by the seat of the pants!' shouted Lon Tuckett, irrepressible.

Here came that emphasizing forefinger:

'How will they get rid of this awful evil in Utah? They will have to expend about three hundred million dollars to build a prison large enough to hold us all. For the wives will follow the husbands! And after they've expended that amount for a prison and roofed it over from the summit of the Rocky Mountains to the summit of the Sierra Nevadas we will dig out and go preaching through the world!...'

It was the last day of Brother Brigham's visit. Crops were in, the warm sun was low in a clear sky, the world was good. Brother Brigham walked toward the spot he had selected three blocks north, one block west of the bowery. Here he would build his winter home and for a while each year spell himself of the cold and the fuss of the north.

All his duties were attended to. Jacob could handle the Indians... At the corner of the square he met John D. Lee. Anger wrung him. Why hadn't the fool gone away? *Hush this thing up!*

'*John*,' he said, '*my advice to you would be to take a rope and go to some remote part of the country where you will never be found, and there hang yourself to a tree, near enough to the ground so the coyotes can eat the flesh from your bones . . .*'

CHAPTER IX

KISSY was exactly a year and six months old. The wondering baby stare had almost given way to a little-girl awareness. Clory, fondly adding each new tooth, each smile, each new mannerism to the treasure of her love, tried hard to keep the child from being spoiled; but what could one do against a flock of adoring, sisterless brothers?

You would have thought the baby belonged to 'Sheba. Kissy's first hard winter the year before — she was a bright, forward child — Clory, hating to pin the active little feet in all those wadded yards of the long dresses, waited eagerly for the four-month shortening time, only to run up against 'Sheba's horror.

'What! In the middle of the winter! She'll catch her death of cold!'

But when the warm May days came and Clory again got out her scissors, 'Sheba was even more aghast. 'Shorten 'em in May,' she declared, 'you'll shorten 'em away!'

And although Clory waited until June, taking Kissy out for her first appearance in short dresses to celebrate the momentous occasion of the breaking of ground for the new Tabernacle that the Dixie settlers were building more of faith and prayers than funds — though Clory waited until then, 'Sheba still looked dubious.

During Kissy's first summer — that critical time when so many babies died — 'Sheba was over almost every day, criticizing, suggesting, interfering. Clory, frantic over a teething rash, colic, clung grimly to patience. It seemed impossible to raise a baby to be two years old — Marianne Snow's first baby had lived only a month. Of course, Marianne had been so determined to be sick on a wooden floor that she had helped put up her own house all the time she was pregnant, and of course every woman had to fight lack of food and overwork and bad water; but nothing seemed excuse enough for so many babies dying. Clory hoarded each day's miracle of Kissy with a cold hand at her heart.

Kissy first discovering her hands, twisting them admiringly on their dimpled wrists, Kissy discovering the solace of a thumb to suck — and 'Sheba striding in like a ship in full sail, bosom high and heaving from the tight, straight-fronted corsets, bold, hooked nose scenting Duty, forefinger waggling at sight of the baby.

'If she sucks her thumb she'll be addlepated!'

Clory had seen too much of 'Sheba's way with children. They had to ask questions, that was how they learned. And yet, when the twins pestered their mother, 'Who makes babies? What fur? What fur?' she'd turn on them viciously, 'Cat-fur-to-make-kitten-britches!' Only to about-face when Abijah was there and oh! so sweetly reprove Clory trying to teach Kissy not to spit.

'Birds in their little nests agree!'

It was unendurable. 'Sheba was so much harder to get along with since the baby came. Willie said it was because Abijah so worshiped his little daughter that 'Sheba was jealous, fearing in her heart her own child-bearing days were over and with them her charm for Abijah.

'Sheba haunted the dugout. Free might come on one of his rare visits to play peek-a-boo through the window with Kissy in her highchair, only to encounter 'Sheba's knowing eye that probed and speculated between Clory knitting in the little rocker and the boy's blond head outside the window.

'Never peek in at a window; if you cannot walk in at the door, stay away!' she snapped.

And Clory would lift imploring eyes to that face outside the window, that face flushing, closing against her, moving away.

Abijah spent hours playing with Kissy, teaching her to grab his great beard in her small hands ('when she's older and you punish her for that, remember who taught her to pull hair!' cried Clory, more free with Abijah now that she was a mother), teaching her to love him with slobbering kisses, laughing at her when she spat at him one day, so that thereafter she greeted everyone with spit.

It did no good to argue with Abijah. In his own mind he was still the Lord's servant who could do no wrong.

As for 'Sheba, that tonguey woman, Willie said Abijah had always been afraid of her tongue. And although now, during her turn with him, Clory had gained the right to feed Abijah in her own home and thus assuage her starved heart with a semblance of normal domesticity, 'Sheba was always there afterward, poking, prying into her housekeeping.

Learning for the baby's sake to control her old impetuosity, her old intolerance, Clory could meet most of 'Sheba's carping with calm. 'Funny,' she said to Willie, 'I don't belong to myself any more; by having Kissy I've given all of me that counts to the future. If I get angry, my milk curdles and Kissy gets the colic; if I'm upset, Kissy knows it and cries, no matter how quiet I am on the surface. And so for her sake I have to make myself over, learn to smile at things that used to make me mad...'

The only point she would not yield was in regard to Kissy, herself. When 'Sheba prescribed heavy blue denim for everyday wear, Clory rebelled at the thought of that harsh, ugly stuff, and cleaned house a whole week for Zadoc Hunt's first wife, to earn

ninety-five cents to pay for a yard of freighted-in nainsook —
hoighty-toighty Belinda Hunt, who, because Clory was temporarily the hired girl, made her eat black bread and tea in the lean-to
while the family dined on chicken inside; . . . and as if that weren't
price enough, Clory had to come home and endure Abijah's
stomping wrath at this spectacle of his own wife demeaning
his position in the eyes of the community ('the hold dog-in-
the-manger tightwad,' said Willie, who never judged anybody),
and 'Sheba's scorn — nainsook for every day, when 'A penny
saved . . .'

Clory hated 'Sheba for her duplicity. Watching her flatter
Abijah, Clory felt young and gauche beside such experienced
suavity. Blurting out her resentment to Abijah only convinced
him she was jealous.

''Sheba's a bright woman!' he would remind her. 'Ye shud
be gratefu' to live an' learn frae sic as she!'

And if the tension between the two women did finally vent
itself in words and Abijah ran away, as usual, 'Sheba's look
silently accused.

As if 'Sheba didn't know as well's I do, thought Clory, that
men are natural cowards, always running away from unpleasantness.

Willie was right. 'Sheba wore the pants. Bullied by his first
wife, Abijah in turn bullied his younger wives and found in that
his greatest reward for polygamy.

2

Other people's affairs were 'Sheba's very life. On an afternoon
in early May Clory rocked beside Willie in the doorway of the
Sibley tent, sewed on some shoes for Kissy, and watched 'Sheba
extract tidbits of gossip. Relief Society was a fertile field, even
the Fourth Ward Relief Society with its handful of sisters.

Fourteen women leaned over the taut rectangle of the quilt,

their needles busy weaving minute stitches around the basted quilt-blocks, the sharp colors of their dyed homespuns making a dappled border for the prismatic surface.

Lars Hansen had recently married the divorced seventeenth wife of John D. Lee — a gentle young girl who had been given to Bishop Lee by Brother Brigham just after the massacre — and she was there under the motherly wing of the first Sister Hansen, the rosy-cheeked Yeast Lady who always smelled faintly of cookies; gaunt Eliza Hichinoper, whom everyone said was a little off since the Indians had stolen the baby; bouncing Betsy Tuckett, still in her tight brown kersey; the two Oleson women, smelling sweaty as usual, but for once without their homemade hoops ('Sheba had simply sent word 'there ain't room in the Sibley tent for them barrel staves and the quilting-frames, too'); a new sister in the town — a Sister Couzzens; the four Eardley wives; and at the far end of the quilt, 'Sheba towering between Sis, the oldest Eardley girl, prim and prissy among her elders, and aristocratic Sister Miles, the fiddler's wife.

Sunbonnets hung upon the walls, and the drone of flies, the buzz of an errant bee cushioned the lazy sputter of their voices, their talk which nibbled at the conversational leavings of the men.

In April Brother Brigham had come and gone again. In spite of the fact that the Social Hall would be ready for dedication come October, he was still displeased with the progress of the Great Tabernacle in a year. He'd given his suggestions: he wanted a gigantic red-sandstone Tabernacle of true colonial architecture — timbers to be snaked down from the fastnesses of Pine Valley. He wanted seventeen or eighteen windows, eighty-four panes of glass to a window, and the men said the panes would probably cost eighty cents apiece after they'd been hauled around Cape Horn and across deserts — oh, he wanted a Tabernacle bell, to be cast in New York, and a Tabernacle organ from the City, and a Tabernacle town clock to be shipped from the Big Ben factory in London! Remembering, the women grunted with disgust. The men considered it an honor to skimp and sweat to build a Tabernacle in the desert but the women wondered what Brother Brigham thought they were made of, denying their children food, foregoing their own homes! Thank heavens, at a quilting they could grumble to their hearts' content without fear of censure from the men — unless that 'Sheba Mac tattled again.

You bet, Brother Brigham's own house was going up in great style, as well as Brother Snow's Big House!

Sis Eardley, bold eyes flashing with importance at having worked for Sister Emmeline Young, said that Brother Brigham was having real window-glass freighted in; and Clory, who had only just this winter succeeded in getting a pig bladder stretched and dried for the dugout, wondered why no one ever thought of being envious of Brother Brigham, and was promptly so shocked at herself that she complimented 'Sheba on her new dress.

Brother Brigham brought news of the States, as usual. This new Governor Doty, replacing that cowardly Harding last summer (didn't it beat the dickens the way Zion cleaned out the Federals?), was a welcome relief, but Conner's soldiers at Camp Douglas were still stirring up trouble, until Judge Kinney in desperation had rushed to Congress to plead for statehood again, for the fourth time. Brother Brigham was glad not one Mormon boy had gone to fight for the Union: 'If we cannot participate in the benefits of the Union, why should we share her burdens?' Betsy Tuckett said Lon said it was a shame Brother Brigham hadn't run far enough in the first place to get rid of the whole danged outfit — soldiers snooping, and all this fuss about a feller's own wives...

Clory never did like work-day much, anyway. They were doing a quilt for Big Tom, the Negro who had drifted away from Washington, and another for that destitute Mexican family in Pig-Dirt Patch... But there was some satisfaction in the thought that Pig-Dirt Patch, that place in the brush below the Rock Wall

where passing drifters camped, was on 'Sheba's Relief Society
beat and that she had to go poking about among all those unsa-
vory folks to make out her Report on the Needy.

'Brudder Snow, he sez,' said Betsy Tuckett, straightening the
kink in her plump back, 'dot dem dere folks'll either haf to clean
up and be one of us er git a move on ——'

'My foot!' snorted 'Sheba, 'who does he think he is, the Lord?
You can't make a town grow in rows like sugar cane; towns jest
happens like the five-legged calf. Didn't do much about Mineral
Park er Sand Town, did he? An' them names'll stick ——'

She interrupted herself to gaze upon Betsy's bent head, her
placidly moving fingers.

'Since when be you s' mealy-mouthed, Betsy Tuckett, that you
darsn't call a thing by its right name? Pig-Shit Patch!' she
shrilled across the quilt, and her mole twitched maliciously at the
sudden shocked glances, the faces hastily averted to the quilt-
blocks. 'I ain't like some folks who think one thing and say another!'

Biting off her thread, Clory sent her voice gaily out into the
acute discomfort of the silence... The fourth Sister Eardley,
Willie's friend, could be depended upon to keep the peace.

'Do you ever get homesick for Sweden, Sister Joe?'

The other woman's laugh rang out.

'Na, I never t'ink about homesick. Land o' mercy, I vass
about tw-anty ——' and she was off.

The needles wove as the cheerful voice flowed on; the women
were held by the gutturals, the slurred vowels of the dialect,
more than by the story, which they knew by heart. Clory was
reminded of the sings out at the Old Campground when the
medley of accents flashed and flew like the northern lights. Determined exiles, all of them, they nevertheless colored every spare
hour of the present with tales of the past, as wine colors water.

There were the Ferranos (the town cooper and his wife, with
their velvet-eyed children), their voices soft in an incredible tale

of conversion, deliverance, flight to Deseret. Not many Italians became Latter-Day Saints. There were the Guerreros, the Spanish family who lived up in Sand Town. There was Betsy Tuckett's German, Abijah's Scotch, and Ole Oleson's first wife's quick Irish tongue...

Clory stole a glance up at Maggie, the strapping Irish lass, quilting stolidly next to her, and skipped to dainty Sister Couzzens in the corner, poised beside the buxom figure of the second Sister Oleson like a wren in the wake of an owl. Directly kitty-cornered from Sister Couzzens was Sister Miles, and there seemed a strange affinity between these two women, calm-eyed, quiet-voiced, alike in the neat, folded wings of their hair, the round, white collar, and the fat breastpin at the throat — the length of the quilt between them, but a world apart in their memories. They weren't the kind who would talk about themselves, but Clory had heard their stories at other Relief Societies.

They said Sister Miles, the fiddler's wife, had been a great lady, her father a famous engineer who'd built the Croton locks in New York, and a colonel rich in slaves to tie even his daughter's shoestrings. She'd left all that to join the Church and marry Brother Miles. They said when she'd gone to meeting at Winter Quarters, wearing her lovely clothes, and had seen the other women in calicoes and cottons, she'd said, 'If I am to be one of these people, I'll *be* one of them,' and went home and took off her silk dresses and never put them on again ... Brother Miles was a handsome young man, a musician and a dreamer, and people were saying he was having a hard time to make a living; but she was the proud kind who would never say a word, never ask for help — finely tempered steel that would endure and endure and might one day snap...

Sister Couzzens, on the opposite side of the quilt, had been married to a French count, and to prove it she had a half-grown son named Jacques Giovanni—the MacIntyre twins said on his first day at school the other boys circled him as if he were a strange dog. They said she had dreamed of missionaries preaching on a street corner ... and when her husband had gone for a moment, she'd stolen the forbidden keys to the vault and filled her skirt with the high-piled coins ... Once in America and across the plains to Deseret, glad for any good Latter-Day Saint who would give her a home, she'd married Brother Couzzens, whose sole claim to distinction was the fact that he'd been a member of the Mormon Battalion and present when the first gold nugget was taken from Sutter's millrace ... 'Old '46,' he called himself, and Clory could not imagine such a woman the wife of 'Old '46' ...

'In Sveden I make the shoes of leather patent,' Sister Joe Eardley was continuing, 'but vhen I vork in The Big Boot in Salt La-ake City, my yob is to sew up the boot for the sole to make r-ready, and in the evenings the housework I do so the money I save all of him to send for my brudders, and vhen dey coom ve all vork to send for our parents ...'

'Tch, tch, you must have had it hard,' said Sister Miles pleasantly.

Sister Joe laughed.

'Na, na, ve have t' ta-ake it the vay it cooms ...'

But just the same, there were pages stuck together in Sister Joe's story, thought Clory, the same pages forever closed in Willie's and the second Ferrano woman's — she who was English, too, and had shared with Willie experiences too dreadful to be retold ...

'You've had a hard life, too, haven't you, Sister Hansen?' asked 'Sheba sweetly, jumping at the lull.

Oh dear! Clory jerked back to reality. 'Sheba at her old pastime of dragging out skeletons ... Clory quivered for the Yeast Lady. Everybody knew Brother Hansen had found his Julia in a house of ill-fame in Carthage and had dreamed if she were baptized she could live a clean life. Clory did not know exactly what a house of ill-fame was, except that people spoke of it in whispers and said that was why the Hansens were childless,

but she knew there was nothing but good in the Yeast Lady, with
her red cheeks and her cookies for children. Lars, worshiping
her, was always teasing her, at meeting or socials or cane-strip-
pings, and each fond quarrel ended the same way — Clory had
heard them a thousand times —

'Oh, vell, Yulia,' Lars would throw up his hands and the argument, 'vhere did I find you!'

And Julia would answer serenely, 'Oh, vell, Lars, vhat were you
doin' there!'

So now she merely smiled at 'Sheba's taunt, her eye alighting
on a new quilt pattern Sister Miles was studying.

'Oh, oh,' she cried, reaching in front of her husband's new bride,
'give him to me!... A new grapevine design, it is — I put him
in Yulia's Secret!'

They all laughed, watching her eyes sparkling mischievously,
her hand stuffing the quilt pattern inside the bosom of her dress.

I'll bet, thought Clory, she persuaded Brother Hansen to
marry that Serena Lee, since it was the only way she could give
the poor, lost thing a home. And now maybe she'll have some of
Lars's kids to love, even if they are another woman's ... Many
childless first wives gave their husbands children in that way ...

'I hear the rest of Bishop Lee's wives are divorcing him,' said
'Sheba, too-sweet again.

Serena paled and the Yeast Lady's eyes flashed fire at last.

In desperation Clory grasped at the stolid arm of the first Sister
Oleson who broke into pleased smiles at the chance to grab
attention.

'Sur-re an' it's the life I've led,' declared the Irish woman.

The second Sister Oleson, fuming beside the sudden importance
of the first, burst into the Emigration Welsh song that rang
through the steerage all the way to America —

Drou my gwrfus wedi bleno
Over there is my home forever...
Over there we'll get rest...

There was something in the plaintive syllables that silenced even 'Sheba, that invoked the past for all of them, stripped naked its shining hopes, laid bare its scuffed and battered dreams there upon the quilt.

'Time to roll again,' said Willie.

The spell broke; the ranks dissolved, and the women, glad for action, unscrewed the awkward quilting-frame clamps Abijah had made out of mesquite roots, pulled the wooden pins from the grooves, and rolled the quilt nearer toward the unquilted center...

Glumness was frowned upon by the authorities. 'Man is that he might have joy' was very much a working gospel, but even Brother Brigham could not stop the feminine love of tale-telling.

Hushed allusions to the Mountain Meadows Massacre, stolen glances toward the former Sister Lee, whisperings — them folks had it comin' to 'em! A hand poised with its needle in mid-air, lips frame the words — Destroying Angels! Furtive glances toward the doorway — even the walls have ears. They *Used Up* so-and-so! Well, he was a lying apostate, wasn't he?...

The women squabbled happily.

'Ach!' squealed Betsy Tuckett, 'dot calico piece is from the first leedle dress I made for Millennium out of Lon's old shirt...'

And this reminds me, they shouted, and that reminds me —! Where cloth must last so long, the scraps become a history of flesh and blood.

Eliza Hichinoper's thin hand was stretched toward a square of blue homespun.

'The first where the indigo took real good,' she said dreamily. '...I smocked the yoke...'

The women hushed; and Clory thought, how awful to meet constant reminders in carpet-rags and quilt-blocks — Eliza had given her one of the little dresses for Kissy, but she had had a nameless dread of using it; but, still, one could not afford to be sentimental, with calico at fifty cents a yard... They had never been able to get Eliza to speak her baby's name. 'If she'd only

call him Marvelous, natural-like,' said Charles. Looking at
Eliza's pale, brooding face, Clory thought that was one trial she
herself could never stand.

'Isn't that a piece of the shirt your boy was drowned in?'
'Sheba inquired casually of the silence.

Aunt Kate Eardley's heavy face darkened to purple, and the
resentment against 'Sheba mounted like thunder.

'Does anyone know when Marianne Snow's baby is due?'
Clory stirred herself in the interests of peace again, glad they
had only the once more to roll . . .

'Was born yoost yesterday,' spoke up the Yeast Lady, all
pleased eagerness at being able to help.

'Somebody hasked 'er was she goin' to name it 'Rassy,' said
Willie, 'like Ket and Martha did their first boys, but Marianne
says no, two hasses in the family's enough!'

The laughter cleared the air somewhat.

'Myself, I like a body with spunk like that, s'long as they got
sense, too.' When 'Sheba was out for blood there was no stopping
her. 'Now take that Lucy, Ket's youngwun, spunky but feather-
brained, allus chasin' after bad company . . .'

Oh dear! Remembering them as she'd so often seen them of a
Sunday afternoon, strolling down to the Lucerne Patch, Clory
thought of Sis Eardley and Gottlieb Uttley, and Miny and Cecil
Davis, and Free and Bella Weeks — or was it sometimes Miny?
And Lucy, always the extra girl, plucking at the gay fringe,
barred because the President's daughter could not be taken
lightly — Lucy with her eyes upon Free's reckless face . . . The
old pain twisted Clory's heart. She was suddenly shocked, realizing how long it was since he'd been willing to talk to her. If
only he'd get married . . . Am I just like all the rest, she wondered,
thinking marriage the cure-all? . . . But 'any boy who is not
married before he is twenty-five is a menace to the community!'
Apostle Snow continued to shout in meeting, which Free refused
to attend. . . . Lucy, now, or even Bella . . .

Clory looked up at Sis Eardley's bold-breasted figure, rigid under 'Sheba's taunt, and Aunt Kate's quivering jaw . . . Aunt Kate would hold her tongue under 'Sheba's own roof, but when she got out! She wouldn't care that a woman could be brought before the bishops for evil-speaking . . . Sis might be a bad influence on other girls, she might be a trial, but her mother'd let no other woman say so, particularly to her face.

The twinkle was back in 'Sheba's eye.

'If that Lucy was mine, I'd teach her to keep bad company, I'd larrup her good . . .'

'Don't she go around with Freeborn?' asked Eliza Hichinoper innocently, for the moment struggling up from the depths of her dark obsession.

'Sheba bridled and tossed her head.

'Oh, she makes eyes at him, but he won't have her . . . I hear Palmyra Wight's courtin' her up for David's second, and that Brother Snow's fosterin' the match . . . All I got to say is, she'd better grab him quick, she ain't a girl to get many chances, her a-chasin' around with Gottlieb Uttley an' them . . .'

3

Willie never remembered whose turn it was. But Clory, who always prepared Abijah's supper in her own home during her week with him, hung the dishpan on its nail, slipped into her shawl, and waited in the doorway of the Sibley tent while Willie performed her nightly query — Willie, who seemed to think like a mechanical, jointed doll, as well as to walk like one — 'Will you want me tonight, Brother Mac?' Sometimes Abijah lost patience and burred at her to remember that this week was Clory's week, or 'Sheba's, seven whole days of it, but Willie was back the next night, putting her question as usual, waiting politely for his gesture of dismissal before she retired to her tent.

Abijah, opening out his red-backed ledger on the table, shook

his head crossly without looking up, dipped his pen and wrote:
'Have not heard from Church Patriarch who is Lax in Duty.
Will Prefer Charges against Brother E. — and bring him into
Bishops Court, myself ——'

Clory nodded at 'Sheba darning socks opposite Abijah, took
Willie's arm, and went out into the murmurous May night.
Sometimes her heart was black with hate — this polygamy that
took all the romance out of marriage! Abijah used and discarded
his wives like old shoes.

'He'll ketch you at it,' said Willie.

'No, he won't,' said Clory, 'not if you mind Kissy so he won't
hear her cry ...'

Willie sighed. 'No good will come of it — what is to be, will
be ...'

'But I have to *try* ...' Clory strove to put into words the
sense of foreboding that had clung to her all the afternoon.

But once upon the hill, looking back at the huddled shadows
of the town, she was still at a loss for words. Brother and Sister
Weeks, sitting out upon their doorstep, visited and joked with
her, and Bella was ready enough to go for a stroll.

It was easier up among the looming red crags where she could
not read so plainly the anxiety-to-please on Bella's gopher face.

'Yes ... I do feel to want him,' the girl answered Clory's painful speech, her own words as hesitant. 'But you see, Sister Clory'
— the voice halted and then went on with a rush — 'he don't
feel to want me!'

'But surely,' said Clory, ' ... Miny ...?'

She could hear the girl swallow. Her voice came out of the
darkness, sad but resolute.

'He only goes with Miny because ... well, because ... Gottlieb
and Sis and Cecil Davis — they all get mushy ... but it ain't
because he's serious with her! He ain't serious with nobody!'

Clory was shocked.

'You — you mean he makes *free* with her?'

'I ain't that kind, Sister Clory!' Bella burst out, misery in her young voice. 'But with Pa like he is, the Authorities agin him for bein' a doctor and folks not payin' him — us not havin' a decent house nor me decent clothes, no nice boy would look at me! Already the bishops has been after me about Brother Trupp — they'll marry me off as third or fourth to some old man' — she caught herself — ' ... Oh, I'm sorry, Sister Mac! I didn't think!'

'It's all right,' said Clory grimly. 'I understand'... And wished she did, long after she was in bed.

4

I'm a darn fool, Clory berated herself, it ain't my fault if ... But the feeling of guilt persisted. She had tried to show him in a thousand different ways that she wanted to talk to him; at meals, at prayers, passing him in the yard, stretching her face until the muscles ached in the old code of grimaces and winks; no chance to get him alone long enough to come right out and ask him — not that it would have done any good; his lean, brown face was sullen, closed against her; his light eyes sought the ground, the sky, anything to avoid her gaze; even his mouth that used to give him away was completely hidden by the drooping blond mustache of which he took such tender care — Clory thought that Cecil Davis with his pomaded curls and his elegant waistcoats had something to do with that.

But it was funny — turning a deaf ear to Free's urgency so long, she had walled in her selfish heart with Kissy, only now to be herself shamelessly pursuing — still, there had been a day when her opinion counted with him. More than anything else she wanted him *safe* ... but that thought brought her up with a start. 'Safe!' That was the cant they'd fed her to get her married to Abijah. Was she, then, 'safe'? 'Safe' from what? They smothered your mind with words like cotton wool, anything to get you off their hands, into the chute with the others, forever robbed of the chance to explore the beckoning vistas, the shining trails of one's dreams. Marriage, the universal catch-all ... man, the sheep, and Life, the shearer ... We've got you in the pen, now, we'll prop you on your rump and shear you of your dreams, daub you with the muck of living, turn you down the chute nicked and scarred, stripped and shivering in the cold wind of reality ... Funny creatures, men and sheep, always tumbling after the fellow ahead ... blatting to get into the pen, blatting to get out, going down the chute, blatting, blatting ...

But there was one compensation — there was Kissy. Even going down the chute, dim eyes looked back at the Kissys of this world and called it worth the while. If Free only had a Kissy, then, indeed, he would be 'safe,' and they could all settle down until the years should suck the heat from the blood, the heat and the madness ...

David had been lucky enough to get a lot right up in town, across the road from the bowery, and he had just finished Pal her new house. A wonderful house with two rooms. Pal had only been moved in a day or two. She welcomed Clory in the doorway, with the candle held high above her head and her figure outlined against the firelighted room where David sat hunched at the table opposite his new hired man, a merchant from Montana who had been robbed on his way to the gold fields and was working for his board and room until he heard from home.

Clory could hear the voices of the men raised in some argument, and Pal smiled at her.

'You know how David loves to argue, about anything and everything — but come on in!'

Clory hadn't been in the house since it was finished and she must be shown the glistening walls Pal had plastered herself, and troweled by hand. It was the first house in town to be lathed and lime-plastered and have a shingle roof. For two summers with the sheep in Pine Valley David had cut rafters from every straight pole he found, and in between times split sheathing with a cleaver. He had even taken a trip to Cedar Ford to buy some iron ore which Brother Mansfield the blacksmith had heated and gripped in the jaws of his nail machine until square, blunt-pointed nails dribbled out, tenpenny to spike size. At first there had only been studding on the inside of the walls, made out of split timber, but as soon as he could, David put 'dobes between the studding to make the house warm. Pal had 'ricked' the 'dobes herself, and carried them to David while he laid them in the walls.

And now, beside the brick fireplace in the living-room, there were a table, some chairs, a chest, a cupboard, and David's desk, all of which he had ordered from Brother Hansen, and a bed with four posts, rawhide springs, and a corn-shuck mattress for David's second wife.

In Pal's room, the bed was built into a corner. And when the family got bigger, there was a trundle bed that could be pushed under the big bed, and one of Brother Hansen's cradles for the new baby Pal was expecting. During the winter David had rigged up some corn fodder into a cave-like sleeping place for the hired man, who said it was warmer than a wagon.

'And this summer,' said Pal, 'when David takes his second, he's going to dig me ... us ... a cellar for the milk, and build a shed on the north, there, with a slant roof where we can spread peaches to dry ...'

'Is it Lucy?' asked Clory too casually, trying out the bed.

Pal nodded.

'Yes, and tonight's his courting night — I always have to remind him ... I do wish he had a new suit for his marrying — they're going right after the shearing ...'

Clory gazed at her incredulously.

'Don't you *care?*' ... a question one simply did not ask, but she was past delicacy, tonight.

Pal hesitated, lifted honest blue eyes. Her freckled dish-face reddened.

'Of course I care! But there are the waiting spirits, and as
Brother Brigham says, Zion must be built up ... I wouldn't want
to find out, after I die, that I had kept David from any extra
glory because of my selfishness here on earth ... I want him to
have a large posterity ... Besides, I keep reminding myself it
ain't any worse for me than it is for the second wife, and I and
Lucy get along real well ... we've talked it all over ... You know,
Clory, there ain't so many single men for a girl to choose from ...'

Pal took David's black frock coat down from the peg and began
to shake it and pick off lint.

'Have you ever thought,' said Clory slowly, 'that Lucy might
be marryin' David because ... well, because ...'

Pal gave the coat a shake.

'David and I both know it's because she can't get Free, if that's
what you mean — she told us, herself; looks like Free ain't
marryin' nobody!'

It was Clory's turn to flush and bite her lip.

'Oh, Pal,' she cried, 'what'll I do? I know everybody thinks
it's my fault, but ... I was wondering if maybe I could persuade
him to take Bella Weeks and they could go along to the City to
get their endowments at the same time you and David ...'

Pal was still for a moment, hugging the coat to her breast.

'I ain't going,' she said slowly; and, at Clory's look — 'There's
the baby, and the new garden — Mr. Nelson'll have to be out to
the herd part of the time ... But I'm sure it 'ud be all right for
Free to go along ... Brother Zebedee Trupp's going along as
chaperon, to pick him out a wife from them new Liverpool
Saints ...'

She sighed, hung up the coat, and turned cheerfully to Clory.

'Come on, I'll show you Lucy's wedding dress. I been making
it for her ... I thought tatted lace about the neck and sleeves,
so much finer than crocheting ...'

In the other room, kneeling before the chest, looking at the
dress, and the clothes Pal was making for the new baby, Clory

could no longer swallow the lump of envy choking her at sight of Pal's house, David's love, the richness, the *peace* . . .

'Does he call the new one "Butch"?' she said under cover of the men's talk.

Pal laughed tenderly.

'Yes, and he's just as big a fool, bringing up another leppy lamb . . . he says he's going to see that his children each have enough sheep by the time they're grown to pay for an education . . . you know how David is, always reading his books and writing his rhymes . . .'

How very simple was Pal's life, thought Clory, with its values nicely pigeonholed, its two passions, family and religion, and its bedrock conviction of the part each should play. Pal loved her husband and her children, but her religion was her hope, her refuge — white was white and black was black with none of Clory's troubled grays between . . .

A sudden shout from the table made the girls look up.

Mr. Nelson was laughing.

'I agree with you,' he said; 'there has never been anything funnier in our history, dripping as it is with sentimental cant about religious freedom, than this furor over Mormonism. But you must admit that your President shows no signs of giving up his fight for independence — sending colonists who would never have gone of their own free will to every little water-hole from Mexico to Canada to forestall the gentiles ——'

He twinkled at David, tracing a finger around and around the newspaper he was leaning his elbows on.

'— and now, deprived of his seaboard, routing ships up the Colorado River! Oh, no, he hasn't given in!'

They were off again, but Pal and Clory were giggling over the little *Mineral Cactus* (two-column folio) Benjamin Jarvis was getting out with the aid of that journeyman printer wintering here.

'I can see David's hand in this,' snickered Pal — '*St. George*

*drinking water has more wrigglers per quart than a barrel of Salt
Lake irrigation water.* And this: *... difference between the rich
and the poor man: the poor man labors to get a dinner for his appetite, the rich man to get an appetite for his dinner ...'*

... A picnic, thought Clory. No one would think anything of
it if she chased Free about at a picnic.

But there were hollyhock and sunflower seeds to be planted
around the dugout, and morning-glories to cover the drab willow
walls ... Abijah, tired of fighting the alkali in his ground with
manure, had dug up the soil and substituted wagon-load after
wagon-load of rich loam from the river. It did seem as if the
only fertile spot on the whole lot was the cotton patch, where
the sagebrush had grown ... And Clory, helping him set out the
apricot and almond pits, and the little red Pottawatomie plums
he'd traded for, helping him transplant his seedling peach trees,
forgot the anxiety in her heart for a whole week.

She sat in Sunday School, hushing Kissy on her lap, Kissy
resplendent in knitted dress dyed pink with last summer's beet
juice. On the stand with the somnolent dignitaries (the new
Fourth Ward bowery was open to the heat and bees and flies),
Abijah, the chorister, Bishop Gardner, Hannah Merinda Lowgie's
boy, who'd just been made Superintendent, his counselors, and
the Secretary — with the dignitaries sat the elders to pass the
Sacrament, and Free's blond head shone among the others like a
blob of sunlight.

Love at home, sang Clory, catching Abijah's eye across the
room, her voice following his lifted stick — *Love a-at home ...*

The rustle as the crowd sat down, the benches of the kinder-
garten and primary classes streaks of color against the somber
tones of the parents' class, Free with uplifted hand kneeling
before the long white mound that was the tablecloth-draped
plates of bread and goblets of wine, his voice cool and clear

above the hum of insects and the subdued murmur of the children —

'... *to bless and sanctify this bread to the souls of all those who partake of it, that they may eat in remembrance of the body of Thy Son, and witness unto Thee ... and keep His commandments which He has given them, that they may always have His Spirit to be with them ...*'

Among the bowed heads Clory sat upright, staring, wishing His Spirit would be with Free. And when the Sacrament was passed, Clory found herself repeating her little-girl trick of watching where 'Sheba put her lips on the goblet — mouthing in 'Sheba's tracks would be almost like kissing her.

After the meeting was over and people were drifting out, visiting, shaking hands, she clutched Kissy and stood stubbornly by the doorway, craning her neck, standing tiptoe to peer through the crowd.

'Land sakes,' said 'Sheba, jerking at her crinoline, 'dinner's to be got! What's the matter with you?'

'Go ahead,' said Clory, pulling away, 'I'll be along ...'

Bathsheba and Willie strolled slowly out the street, Willie turning to gaze back at Clory now and then, but Abijah still stood about with the men, his hands clasped beneath his coattails, teetering on his heels.

'I suppose ye ken,' he said, drawing out his handkerchief from his coattail pocket to mop his face, 'that most o' the wheat's in the milk ... looks like a gude crop!'

'But the cotton,' said Brother Gardner, 'this year the cotton could be better.'

'I don't know,' Abijah said; 'we've got a hundred an' forty acres under-r cultivation and the President says it's reported tae be "equal in every way to that grown in Tennessee"!'

'I believe soil does better with change, just like humans ...'

'How are ye, Brother Trupp?'

'Oh, I cripple around! I cripple around!'

'... brush-and-earth dam'll never hold. No use fooling ourselves the floods are unusual any more, not after nearly four years.
Now a pile dam ... cut the big logs up in Pine Valley, use that old
cannon as a pile-driver ...'

'Ech, Bishop, the expense!'

'Country's no good without water, Brother Mac!'

'... Gude day to ye, Brother Eardley, gude day!... Did ye
notice Brother Eardley, Bishop? That mon has a stiff-necked
spir-rit!'

'Well, we'll have to have you two over to our house sometime
soon and have a hearing ...'

Here he came at last. 'Oh Free!' Clory cried, dancing about,
waving to attract his attention like any young girl. He was with
Miny Eardley and Gottlieb Uttley and Sis, and they were all
laughing and squealing as the boys yanked at the girls' sashes.
Miny, seeing Clory, tossed her head and touched Free quickly —
'Tag!' she cried, and gathered up her skirts and raced off up the
street, so that Free, the pursuing male, perforce raced after.

Those awful Eardley girls — Clory's thought leaped to his
defense — what was it about their bold, black eyes, and earthy
impudence that could so hold a man? Clory felt herself a blood-
less ghost beside them. Panic-stricken, she clutched Kissy's hand
until the baby cried out ... Was she, then, at twenty and a half,
on the shelf? ('Sheba speaking of girls who had let their time go
by, girls who were on the shelf!) For the first time in her life,
she, Clorinda, had deliberately gone out after a man and he had
turned her down. Was she truly become old, then, was her
beauty gone, her hot love time? Where was the girl who had
tantalized Free just to see him suffer, the coquette so sure of
her powers? ... That Eardley creature should not have him,
she should not! Her dear, boyish Free, with his bewildered eyes
and his shining head. She, Clory, would scratch out her eyes
first ... Oblivious to Kissy's cries, she grasped the child and
rushed over to Abijah, still chatting on the sidewalk ... To get

home and look in a mirror! To reassure herself ... She'd get
him back, she must! ... Forgetting that they were caught, and
she herself had prayed on her knees for Free to 'get over it.'

5

So she was jealous ... And I have no more right to be jealous
than the man in the moon, she said to herself, no matter how
many girls he goes with ... But David and Lucy had had their
party, and received their presents, and Lucy's father, Erastus,
had given them his blessing and a good cow. They were going
north in less than two weeks, now. Some strange urgency drove
her, so that when she took Kissy into the Tithing Office one afternoon for a dip of honey — bearing half a pound of cotton lint in
payment — she stood her ground even when the Eardley girls
tramped in, Bella Weeks in their wake, and went on reading the
sign-list above the counter —

Produce Accepted for Taxes		
Molasses	$2.00	gal.
Corn	1.50	bu.
Wheat	2.50	bu.
Cotton yarn	3.50	bunch
Cotton lint	30¢	lb.
Honey, dip	10¢	

There, that was it ... she had enough to pay for one dip, anyway — one couldn't donate *every* penny to the Tabernacle! ...
and nodded mechanically at Sis and Miny and smiled at shamefaced Bella, who would not look up, and gave her cotton lint to
Johnny Lowgie, who was the new T.O. clerk, and waited quietly
while he got a clean case knife and stuck it carefully through the
hole in the corner of the five-gallon can. This Santa Clara honey
was a clear light amber from the flowers of the white sage, and
very good, and she held the knife so that Kissy's tongue took it
off in little licks, making it last as long as possible. (How those

Eardley girls did fill up the little room, with their bold bosoms and eyes and monstrous crinolines!) Watching Kissy smack her lips, Clory's own mouth watered. So long since she'd tasted anything sweet but molasses. Ten cents a dip was a lot to pay for honey when you could remember your own bees. (Such loud voices! Ah ... what kind of honey was it that smeared these big girls to make the boys buzz around them so?) ... Here came Free and the strapping Gottlieb, with his red face, and Cecil Davis, slim and suave and elegant ... Free did not seem to notice her, there in the corner, nor even the baby gooing over the knife, but slapped a hand upon the counter.

'My treat!' he was insisting ... 'Have a dip on me!' and throwing down before the astonished clerk real money — some bishops' chips, the greenbacks he'd had hidden in Nellie's nosebag. Only Clory knew the significance of that money ... But your dreams, her heart cried out, the steamcars you were going to ride to freedom! What shoddy pleasure is this you are buying with your dreams? But he would not look at her, and he was so reckless, so fiercely gay that she could not bear it.

'Dips around again!' he cried, his head flashing-bright in the gloom — 'Spread 'er on!'

And the knife went in and came out, and tongues licked, and laughter spilled, and honey stuck to mustaches and hands, and the boys with threatening, sticky palms slapped at the squealing girls, chased them out into the sunlight ...

Clory was suddenly acutely conscious of the ringing silence. She was so still that the hand holding the knife for Kissy's licks had gone to sleep.

6

Pal got up the picnic herself. 'The town gave Lucy and David their party,' she said, 'but I want to give them a farewell treat ...' Good old Pal, thought Clory, lending me a hand.

Chores were looked after, and by mid-morning the young folks were walking and the old ones riding in the jolting wagons up Mount Hope and along the trail that spiraled to the Sugar Loaf. Great swings had been attached to iron pegs in the vaulted roof of the Light Cave, and there were quilts for the shady side of boulders. Abijah had his eye on a secluded corner just back of the Sugar Loaf, sheltered between it and another crag, where blossoming oose and green grass and squawberry bushes grew against the rock and there was much clean, soft sand for the children. But all the campfires for dinner were to be laid in the front, where the flat stones made a paved floor stretching to the lip of the chasm.

After dinner there were weight-lifting, and jumping-at-a-mark, and horseshoes for the men, hide-and-seek and run-sheepie-run for the children, and the supreme content of lounging, knitting, and idle talk for the women.

Watching, planning for her chance all day, Clory wondered if Free guessed at her desire and intentionally avoided her. He with whom she had once dreaded stolen intimacies!

She sat with Pal and Lucy, 'Sheba and Willie, and watched the children scatter over the tumultuous rocks, flit in and out of cave and cranny like sprites. Whoops and calls and snatches of song echoed among the cliffs; in front of her, worn by the gentle giants of erosion, the massive crag had split, and through the opening which thus focused the tossed sandstone world outside, she could see distant figures frolic up from the shadows, leap from point to point until they passed beyond the split. The hill swarmed with folks; to empty a few wagon-loads of people up here was like dumping a basket of apples in a haystack. No use to go hunting for him. But she was determined to have it out. There was still time ... a hurried announcement, last-minute preparations, and he and Bella riding off with David in the morning. She did not try to analyze the motive behind her driving determination — it was enough that he had shown a preference for a girl like Miny Eardley.

'D'you recollect,' said Willie, with her disconcerting intuition, 'that time hout at the Old Campground when you said as 'ow we 'adn't seen the last of our troubles yet?' She unpinned the fascinator from her hair, and smoothed her skirts over the swollen joints of her outstretched legs. (The decision not to wear crinolines had been unanimous.)

'I don't care,' said Clory, watching Kissy's chubby hands reaching for the dust-motes in the golden air. 'I don't care, if I help build a country where my child can sit at the rosewood desk.'

'Sheba, who would never slump even at a picnic, but sat stiffly erect, knitting — the only one whose hands had never stopped being busy — sniffed at such fancies. 'We must remember Brother Brigham's counsel about saving picnic leftovers for the widows and them poor folks at the Pig-Dirt Patch!' she shrilled. Pal, helping Patience Elizabeth build sand castles, smiled at Clory; and Lucy, playing a lonely game of jacks, stealing self-conscious glances at the engagement ring on her forefinger, remained prim and distant as became an unwedded female not yet inducted into the secret society of wives.

Clory shifted comfortably against the boulder at her back, her eyes on the garters forming under 'Sheba's flying fingers. You could sure tell a lady by her garters... Them Eardley girls always had wrinkled stockings... It would be fun when Kissy was old enough to knit and tat and wind bobbins... Clory smoothed the limp skirt of her old sheep's-gray linsey; she'd worn it to the picnic to save her other dress, but it was going in the rag-bag for sure this summer... she needed a new dress; she'd probably have to earn it some way, but they said the Social Hall would be ready for dedication this fall and that would mean a big splurge...

'I tell you, freight rates are too high at sixty dollars per ton!' — that would be Bishop Gardner on the other side of the boulder.

'Can't make it cheaper,' said David, who had only a small interest in Hunt, Wight, and Judd. 'In fact, we've talked of giving it up altogether, those desert Indians are so danged bad, unless we can hitch up with some big company like Wells-Fargo —— '

'The bottom's fell right out o' the hide market!' mourned
Abijah.

Through the crack in the wall in front of her Clory could see a
group of children holding hands, circling in some game ... their
voices came to her faintly, like fragments of a dream, 'King
William was King James's son —— ' Pouring through the crack,
the setting sun made a bar of gold out there, but on either side
was shadow, and as she watched, the dancing children passed
out of the shadow and into the light and back into the shadow
again, alternately transfigured and eclipsed. The gold light
quivered over the rocks and the colors seemed to melt and run
together, crimson to scarlet to orange ...

Bursting through the crack, Free and his crowd blotted out the
glory, raced over the sand, trampled the queenly yuccas, scattered Lucy's jacks, threw dust on 'Sheba's knitting — so suddenly that for once 'Sheba was too breathless to scold.

Steps and handholds had been scooped out of the towering,
perpendicular wall of the Sugar Loaf against which Willie leaned,
and Free, as sure-footed as a mountain goat, already had fitted
hands and feet and was spidering upward; but Cecil Davis, the
dandy, incongruous among the rocks in his store suit and fashionable stock and beaver hat, paused long enough to smile an
apology over his shoulder at the women. Gottlieb, puffing and
blowing and heavy-footed, with his big hands and his red face,
stood boosting up Bella from below, while Free, lying full-length
on the top, reached a long arm over the edge to catch her hand,
fluttering for the next hold. But Sis was more of a load.

'Looks like Sis's taken off her red flannel — them Eardley girls
never did wear enough petticoats,' said 'Sheba with interest,
watching the boys hoist up the girl's tall, solid body.

Such a shrill hullaballoo, such wriggling and grunting, such a
convulsion of starched underskirts and ruffled pantalettes!

'Why don't you join 'em, Clory?' suggested Willie, as usual
reading her mind. 'You ain't 'ad no hexercise all day — Oh,

Freeborn,' she called, settling the matter, 'look out for your
Aunt Clory!'

So there she was, her little foot in Gottlieb's hand that was the
size of a ham, and Cecil Davis, always with an eye cocked for a
pretty woman, shouting directions. She felt like a fly on a wall,
her hand, forsaking its hold, groping upward, grabbing air, and
Gottlieb's bellow down below and Cecil's refined inflections:
'The right foot...over another inch...no, up...there...
there!' — and Free's shout from above: 'The left hand, please...
more to the left...' (oh, his insufferable politeness!) and there
she was, her hand stretching to his (such a featherweight, he had
called her once), and her dark eyes questioning as he drew her
toward him, her eyes probing his that were so defiantly impersonal.

Racing along the top of the Sugar Loaf, jumping the deep
fissures in the giant rock, standing at the edge and looking out
at the panorama, the pastel mountains to the east and Steamboat
exalted in the sunset, the houses and square daubs of green in the
valley below, and the river like a shining worm, even a flick of
green in the sudden cleft of those blue mountains to the south,
those mountains that always seemed to move closer with the
twilight...

'Oh, Free!' Clory cried, on a rapturous breath, but only Bella
came to share with her the pulsations of light flooding the valley,
the baptism of the hills.

'I know some pretty new quicksteps,' Miny said hastily,
throwing herself in Free's arms, and Cecil took from his pocket a
jew's-harp, which he played after much arranging of his beautiful
mustache. 'Rooster, Cock-a-doodle,' sang Sis and Gottlieb and
Miny and Free, dancing on top of the world, while Clory and
Bella watched the light fade and the glory dim.

Clory turned and walked up to Free and put a hand on his
arm, unmindful that the others stared.

'I want to talk to you,' she said.

He flushed and ducked his head, but he walked with her over to where the steps led down, her shadow so tiny against the grotesque length of his own moving beside them over the rock.

At the brink she turned and faced him.

'Free,' she gulped, gathering her courage, 'David and Lucy are going north tomorrow and I thought ... that is, I wondered ... I — I thought you and Bella ... I — It seemed ...' Words bounced back from the stony barrier of his face.

He was very polite, very gentle, lowering himself over the edge. 'It's getting late, Clory. You'd better go home, now.' Only once did his control slip, and that was when he lost his grip and she heard the screak of tearing cloth. 'Judas priest!' he swore, and his voice was normal for the first time. But standing at the bottom, one leg of his buckskin trousers ripped from waist to hem, he was respectfully patient again, directing her descent. And when at last she jumped to the ground beside him, he bade her good evening as if she were a stranger, and prepared to clamber back up the cliff.

Clory stood staring up after him, frowning like a cockle burr.

7

Pal ran over to the wagon and put up her arms again to Lucy, looking like a clove pink in her new slatted sunbonnet and rose calico.

'Have a good time, you two,' she said, and kissed her once again, and smiled mistily at David and Brother Zebedee, a grinning, toothless gnome in the early light.

Back beside Clory, the two of them waving until all they could see of the wagon was its dust, she said brightly, 'I'm so glad you came with me to see them off.' But Clory, choking back her own anxiety and disappointment, could feel Pal willing not to cry.

'I should think it would break your heart.'

Pal's head came up.

'When my heart comes between me and my Father's work it will have to break,' she said.

8

The coming of the hot weather, with its worries over the dreaded summer-complaint, took the edge from Clory's premonitions of the spring. Especially as she seldom saw Free any more. He avoided everyone since he got his new buckskin pants which, Abijah chuckled, he'd have to wear or go without, and maybe they'd 'take him down a notch.' Getting a job hauling wood for Brother Snow, he'd rushed the order for his buckskins until Brother Peabody didn't have time to cure them properly, and of course it rained in Pine Valley, and of course the wet deerskin stretched until by the time he got home he was walking on the ends of the pants-legs. 'Sheba cut them off the right length and hemmed them up, and he drove off with Gottlieb Uttley the next morning on a freighting trip. Not that Gottlieb needed an extra man nor that Abijah wanted Free to go, but David's gentle persuasion had its way, and Free drove off behind the pounding hoofs of the twenty mules, happier than he had been for months. When he came back he looked, as 'Sheba said, like a 'whipped pup.' Not the Indians but the sun! His pants, dried at last with the desert heat, as stiff as two hollow tree-trunks, had shrunk until they came just below his bony, hairy knees. But 'Sheba, having made the cut-off buckskin into quirts, could not lengthen them, and Abijah, thinking this would keep him away from flighty girls, was deaf to his pleas. Free stalked about the yard and the barn, drove down to irrigate in a wounded silence.

Clory and Willie laughed tolerantly. He was so young and silly. And Clory, owning herself again, felt wise and strong, as if she were looking down upon his antics from Olympian heights.

Only once did he come out of his injured dignity. Digging post-holes for Abijah's new stake-and-rider fence, he beat a path to the drinking-barrel, and Kissy, playing by 'Sheba's wash-bench, chattered to him. Sloshing a dipperful of water over his face and head, he laughed at the child, but some animation in the little rosy face drove him toward her. A scorpion, orange body full two inches long, tail arched high, rested in the damp of an over-turned rock, and Kissy's chubby hand pointed with glee. 'Pitty, pitty!'

When Clory came running at Free's call, she snatched the child from his arms and shut her eyes against the fresh fierceness of her hate for such a country. He smiled at her gently. She reached out a hand and clung to him for a moment — oh, not that he meant anything to her! — and the touch of his skin completely stampeded her senses. Illogically, maddeningly. She could not speak at all, but only gaze at his burned face and neck, his brows and hair bleached tow-white by the sun, his light eyes all tenderness for her again.

'The desert,' he mumbled inarticulately, wetting his lips. 'It — it was even better'n we thought. The ground changes to orange out there, and the mountains are the color of — well, of fresh-killed beef. And then the ground is gray again and the wildflowers start — you'd love the wildflowers! — and Death Valley where the mountains are like purple grapes and the air is so clear you could reach out and pick them off with your hand ...'

'And the Joshua trees? Did you see the Giant Joshuas?' she asked faintly, lost in the shining of his eyes.

'Yes — whole forests, some young fellers with flowers at the ends of their arms, and others so old — so old and crippled, like giants with the rheumatiz ...'

'But still pointing toward the Promised Land,' she said, so softly he had to stoop to hear, her eyes so full of the vistas they had explored together that it did not matter she had never even been to Santa Clara.

But such moments were rare in a season that produced the first fair crops, crops exhausting all the man-power and most of the woman-power to harvest quickly against the possibility of drought or grasshoppers or flood.

Abijah was the best hand with a grain cradle in the whole country. He could do five or six acres of wheat in a day and was very proud of his skill.

Sometimes Clory helped him glean. A season's work meant a new dress, perhaps new shoes. She liked to watch him among the wheat, swinging the heavy awkward grain-cradle with unbelievable grace, the slide of his shoulder muscles smooth under the shirt. She liked to watch the rhythmic fall of the heavy-headed straws. And she liked to bundle the tipped-up grain after him, choosing the longest stalks for strings, tying on top and hurrying on to the next bundle. This year there was enough grain to stack, and one day she watched Abijah turn the crank of the fanning mill and the clean wheat pouring out of the spout on the quilt. She wanted to shout aloud at the sight of that wheat!

But with all the T.O. scrip for her gleanings, Clory was not able to get her new dress ready for the holidays. Nor was 'Sheba able to finish Free's new militia uniform. And all afternoon on the twenty-fourth, Free sat on the fence back of the barn making up his mind to go on a toot, while Abijah wrote in his diary —

Had court at Bishop Gardner's. Bro. E. confessed what he had said to me: Kiss my arse, damn you, damn you, turning his Buttocks to the brethren and slapping it with his hands and repeating above. But he was not truly repentant, for when asked not to hold Feelings he said to me — I'll Forgive and Forget all right, but damn you I'll always Remember this ——

So it was, that Sunday in August when Sis Eardley walked up the aisle at meeting and confessed her sin and asked forgiveness before the assembly, Abijah could not help feeling triumphant.

The town rocked. There had not been such a lovely scandal since Lars Hansen's pig got into 'Sheba Mac's garden and she said what she said. Clory, conscious of pleased rustlings all about her, found it hard to be properly sorry for Sis, whose downcast eyes, she felt, were still out for the main chance. Sis put on a good show with her tears and her broken words, and the congregation voted to readmit her to fellowship after the child was born and she was rebaptized. Married to Gottlieb, she — but by Monday morning everyone knew it wasn't Gottlieb. It was Cecil Davis.

The looseness of it all was what shocked Clory. Sis making such a to-do over her beau, Gottlieb, and all the while . . . Apprehension crawled along Clory's nerves like ants. Abijah declared he druther see a child of his dead, and 'Sheba, as usual barked about the younger generation — her bark the gruffer because it covered up fear, always strongest, like some misbegotten parasite, where love is strongest, too. But Clory could see Life smirking around a corner — this was a trick Life would go on repeating until the end of time with any material handy, hit or miss, Miny Eardley's calculating eyes . . .

The trial went on for weeks. Although it was conducted behind closed doors, with the utmost secrecy, everyone enjoyed the details. Sis and her father on one side, and Cecil and Gottlieb, who stood by him, on the other. Apostle Snow, who would be late for his own funeral, made it a point to be almost always on time. For there were accusations that had to be proved.

Every sordid detail was turned to the light, picked apart. A spade was called a spade. At what precise hour did the incident occur? Where? Were there other times? You're sure this was the only man? (Pause while Erastus quiets Sis.) Brother Eardley, testifying about the times he had gone down to the lucerne patch to rescue his daughter from the company of Mr. Davis, wrings his hands. Miny and Bella are called. Have they ever noticed anything out of the way about the behavior of the accused? Miny is explicit. Free is called and stands there in his sawed-off pants, blanched and quivering. No, no, he answers the question, oh, no. Bella gives him a long look. Abijah, a member of the Council, at the right hand of Apostle Snow, hawckks at his throat, cannot lift his eyes from his hands gripping the table.

It is rather generally conceded in the town that Cecil Davis, with his fancy 'seegars,' is as guilty as sin. Moreover, he is flippant about the whole affair, full of jests and quips and sallies at his own trial. Graceful as a cat and pleased with himself, he stands there jauntily twisting a point of his mustache, teeth glinting, eyes gleaming, alert and wary. No, he won't marry the girl, he says, nor even support her; it isn't his fault if she's a fool!... But he'll find out, threatens President Snow, it's as good as a man's life to pollute a daughter of Zion! Society has to be protected ... sinners have been sent to hell 'cross-lots before. Erastus, hating the whole sorry business, but hating more that sleek young dandy there without even the grace for shame, looks at Brother Eardley, too crushed to do his duty, puffs his lips in and out trying to control his temper ('Now, remember to control your temper, Papa,' his children were always saying), and pronounces judgment: 'Well, young man, *if no one else shoots you I guess I'll have to!*'

The whole town chuckles. And the boys, pitching horseshoes in the corral, are ribald. 'She's a bitch,' they agree, too young for pity. 'But Gad, he was travelin' like a bat out of hell — had fifty miles behind him by mornin', sure as preachin'!' But Free is suddenly nauseated, thinking how weak as water-gravy a man may be. If a girl accuses you — well, they rope you in, one way if not another. Here, they said, you must build up the Kingdom — any healthy girl will do ... But there was more to life than that. He had dreamed once of high pilgrimage, young passion brushing the stars ... and now they expected him to settle down with the taste of ashes in his mouth.

9

Not anything so romantic as ashes, it seemed; just Virgin bloat.

Erastus, standing on the bank of that deceitful stream as he had so often done before, studied the meandering length of it warily. You could not attack it openly, with a bull-rush, head-on; you could not wear your purpose on your sleeve. That river was too tricky — you had to fight with it, spar with it, wear it down. He had always known the usual brush-and-rock dam was too simple, too easy. Here was a stream you'd have to humor along and eventually whip with superior strategy.

It was always fooling him. All summer it dribbled thinly; one day the bed would be almost dry — and the next, a roaring cauldron. A thunderstorm in the canyons of Mukuntuweap could flood Pah Roosh when the skies above St. George were bluest. And there were beaver burrowing at the foundations of the dam — foundations which, to hold, had to be some way sunk below the quicksand of the river bed. There was the red clay, the gyp of the canal walls always softening. And there was the silt continually thwarting him — silt in the water itself, filling up the head-gates, blocking the canals... Problems for which someone had to figure the answers if the Dixie Mission was to survive.

No use lulling themselves with the thought that the Lord would do it all; no use going on patching up the canal. No use putting in new brush dams every year, damming the river a little farther up each time. Only reason they'd salvaged some of the crops this year was because the floods had come later than usual, after the grain and corn and hay were all in. You couldn't get around it: time to make another move. Those records up there in his desk spoke for themselves. Up to date they had spent the equivalent of twenty-six thousand dollars in repairs on the dam and ditches (last year they'd put the dam in nine different times trying to keep water out on the crops), making a tax on their farms of over sixty-three dollars per acre for water, alone.

And yet, how his counselors did object to his idea of a pile dam! ... With the Social Hall to be finished, the cotton factory going up at Washington, Erastus' own Big House, the county court-house, Brother Brigham's plan for the Great Tabernacle, not to mention hopes for their own homes, how *could* a man shoulder any more burdens!

So it happened that fall, Free wasn't the only one to rebel at having to stand waist-deep in Virgin bloat day after day . . . But a feller got paid twenty-five cents more a day for working in the water, and he needed new pants. He thought, standing sometimes up to his armpits in that cold water twelve hours at a stretch, helping to steady those mighty thirty-foot pine poles for the thundering onslaught of the pile-driver, that men with any gumption would never work that hard to make a living.

But Erastus puffed out his cheeks, smacked his lips, and planted his stocky body more firmly these days. At last he had that river with its tail between its legs. He directed the work hour after hour, his eyes not missing a sliding pebble, his spirit deep within him, patient, indomitable.

There were to be ten rows of poles, the rows about three feet apart and each row two feet shorter so that the river in flood-time could ease gently down in steps. Rocks and brush and more logs built up between the poles. The old cannon they'd brought with them from the city they'd rigged up in a frame, and hour after hour the horses on the bank hoisted it to the top and then let all those eight hundred iron pounds drop straight through on top of the steel-capped piles. Worked almost like a guillotine. An ingenious device, but even so, Erastus was afraid it would take most of his man-power the whole winter to finish the job. He could probably hire some of Tutsegabbett's Indians or some of the drifters down to the Pig-Dirt Patch below town, but they needed so much bossing, and he was so absent-minded about giving directions. People joked about having to ask him a question a day ahead in order to get an answer when they needed it, and he realized guiltily it was true.

10

In October, 1864, standing at the doorway of the new Social Hall that was two blocks north of the square and just across the street from his own Big House going up, Erastus welcomed his friends and neighbors. He was very jovial. He had not only got himself out on time for once, but he felt that they were dedicating a real accomplishment. More than a building: a milestone. Any other people would have said it couldn't be done. And they had done it. Taming the meanest country the Lord ever made. Brother Brigham himself had mentioned the fact during his visit in September, and Erastus still choked up at the memory. Having inspected the new dam, the Tabernacle foundations, and this new red-rock building with the inner room for private hearings and the like, and the basement kitchen for community suppers (there wasn't a roof on it as yet, but there was a real board floor), Brother Brigham had clapped a hand on his shoulder and said to him, 'Erastus, the Lord has been good to you, hasn't He?' Yes, sir, it made him choke up now to think about it. A word of praise from the Leader was worth all a man's efforts. Ptsahh!

Behind him, above the sound of the musicians tuning up, he could hear other men discussing Brother Brigham. But it was always the men who were silent he worried about. Brother Brigham was selling the surplus cotton over and above Deseret's own needs to eastern wholesale purchasers in Chicago at $1.25 per pound, and some of the brethren were disgruntled over the fact that the profit they toiled so hard to make should thus flow back into the coffers of the Church. These were the men who were silent, and Erastus thought how blind and foolish they were not to see that every nickel a man put into the Church came back to him fourfold.

He heard Bishop Gardner: ' ... you've got to give Kinney credit for trying. No other federal judge has ever been as fine to the Mormons.'

The men fell silent, remembering what Brother Brigham had told them of Judge Kinney's appeal for statehood. In the Congress a petition for the admission of Nebraska had recently been favorably considered and Nevada had been made a state — 'infants in age and population when compared to Utah, who has had a territorial existence for fourteen years, and at no time has she not had a larger resident population than either Nebraska or Colorado. . . . I ask for justice and equality . . . for one hundred thousand people who can with pride point you to their cities, their churches, their schoolhouses . . .'

But Congress did not want to look, no matter how many times Deseret pointed. 'They think they'll make us give up polygamy,' said Brother Brigham, 'but we won't till the Lord tells us to.'

'Aye,' said Abijah MacIntyre, 'the countr-ry's going to the dogs. Baptize an Indian and he turns around and scalps ye. Gold out of cir-rculation, and a silver dollar worth three dollars in greenbacks in the States . . .'

'In the City,' said David Wight, 'you can buy shelf-goods easier than cash-goods. I had no trouble at all trading wool for some laces for my wives, but I saw a storekeeper refuse fifty dollars in gold-dust for a bag of sugar because the feller wouldn't trade for some shelf-goods, too.'

'Oh, David,' called Pal. 'Oh, David, let's make a set; the music's starting up!'

And so it had, the strains of 'Money Musk' lilting out, teasing toes.

Peering down the street to make sure no more people were coming, Erastus emptied Brother Couzzens's molasses into the big barrel at the door (this barrel of molasses was going to Salt Lake to be traded in for books for the new library in the basement), linked arms with 'Old '46' and his lovely wife, and turned back into the room. Licking a bit of molasses from his thumb, he edged around the crowded floor, smiled at Marianne, Clorinda MacIntyre, Lucy, and Martha, and went on past them to Aunt

Ket, who never for a moment let him forget her position as first wife. While he was always having to reprove her salty tongue, he secretly enjoyed hearing it trained on others; and she was in fine fettle tonight, with her newly married daughter, her crimped gray hair, and the billowing folds of her new tan muslin. Erastus thought with affection that she looked like an animated haystack.

'I can't imagine,' she sputtered, clutching her reticule in the uncharted spaces of her lap, 'what the young ones are coming to. Look at that Bella Weeks — I'm surprised at Zebedee Trupp for dancing with her ——'

'Well, he won't . . . much longer,' soothed Erastus. 'This month Brother Brigham's sending him down . . . the new wife he picked out last spring.'

'But just look at her: only six widths in the skirt and hoops no bigger round than a thimble!'

'But Mamma,' called Lucy, leaning across Martha, 'that's the style! When David and I were in the north'— she paused to blush properly — 'we saw that hoops were getting ever so much smaller! They say ——'

'I don't care,' snapped Aunt Ket. 'It's indecent, girls showing their shapes like that!'

Marianne winked at Clorinda, who smoothed out her own new sprigged calico and tossed her head. It was better to be dead than out of fashion. She and Willie had spent hours poring over Belinda Hunt's *Godey's Lady's Book* and the *Harper's Monthly* David had brought from the City. But there was too much talk of Valenciennes frills and Madonna fichus and handkerchief sleeves — none of which would do for a daughter of Zion (which was a shame, she thought privately), and so she had to be content with gores and fluted flounces — borrowing Aunt Ket's fluter and spending days pressing the cloth between the hollow grooves — and the tatted-lace collar pinned with her mother's brooch, although she pretended to herself the yellow color of the dress was the stylish saffron shade. Her new shoes which Brother

Peabody had at last finished (and what a lot of joking from
Abijah about the thrill it must be to measure a lady's calf!)
were dyed black with soot, it is true, but tongueless and stiff
and four sizes too large. She wriggled her toes in the white stockings with the lovely pattern running slanch-wise across her legs
(white was more seedy-looking, but a good black almost impossible to dye), and reflected her feet were already so chafed from
the rubbing of the undressed leather that she'd have to take off
her shoes between every dance. But she was so proud of them
she didn't care; not many had new shoes for the Dedication!

The books had all said that 'a lady of taste consults that style
of coiffure which is individually most becoming to her countenance,' and so Clory had given some study to the matter. The
trouble was that her own hair was too wild to do up in a decent
waterfall. It seemed that the Lord had not meant her to be a
lady, after all, but she did what she could to remedy the Lord's
mistake, plastering down curly tendrils with 'Sheba's pilfered
lard until her hair gleamed on either side of the part like a blackbird's wings. She put up an anxious hand to the net — there
was still a daub of the lard in her handkerchief in case the wave
came back. She did hope the lard didn't smell. Abijah had
sniffed suspiciously when they first came, but he had to be floor
manager tonight, anyway, and it was to be presumed a younger
partner would put up with the lard for the sake of her stylish-
ness.

Free was such a goose. He wouldn't come because some of the
other boys were wearing parts of their new uniforms and 'Sheba
didn't have his finished. She watched enviously Mercy Wheelock
dancing with the Hunt boy, very grand in the only complete uniform in the room ... And then he was bowing before her, his
crimson sash swinging, and Abijah was calling for the assembling
figure of the Lancers. Proud that she had snatched him from
under the very eyes of an unmarried girl — she wasn't 'on the
shelf' yet, even if she was starting with her second baby — she

gave Abijah a gay little nod, flung up her head like a young filly, and swept by on the boy's arm to the waiting set.

Abijah, brushing browned flour over his hands — this water down here was so verra hard — reflected with satisfaction that she was making him an excellent little wife. Only on occasion, as tonight, did he feel the slightest misgiving. But tonight she was so very gay, laughter floating about her light as chaff — in spite of himself, his pulse quickened.

Clory, conscious of his gaze, blinked her lashes up at the Hunt boy until he missed a step, and when Abijah would have frowned, melted him with her smile. For a long time now she had been careful of Abijah, but the imp inside of her hammered at her will. It had been such fun to throw a slang word — to produce ripples in the pool of her elders' solemnity! . . . But what did one do when one became an elder oneself? . . . Except that of course she wasn't an elder, yet. She was still a girl who could skip and stamp and command men's eyes . . . She wanted Free to see her. She wanted to kiss her own firm flesh.

This was a ball to remember! Blindman's buff and charades and victuals! Ruffled and puffed berthas, flounced, gored, and ribboned skirts — there was Pal, five months along but in a new challis corsage with velvet passementerie. The smell of moth balls mingled in with the dust, and everywhere there was the shine of heirlooms at neck and wrist and ear.

> I could dance all night
> Till broad daylight,

hummed Clory, while Brother Hansen stroked deep beauty out of the homemade 'cello. Everyone was here. Folks from Washington and the Clara, Jacob Hamblin, Tutsegabbett, blanketed and curious in the doorway.

Abijah was at his best calling at a dance, timing his calls to the split second. His golden burr seemed an obbligato to the music bouncing back from walls whitewashed with the good slack-lime from 'Molly's Nipple,' rising like some jovial incense to the stars caught among the unfinished timbers of the roof.

Bathsheba, sitting by Hannah Merinda Lowgie, was very conscious of his good looks, his sturdy grace. His body was still firm-fleshed and vigorous, while Apostle Snow, for all the leanness of these four years, was growing a little paunch ... She was conscious, too, that Abijah's eyes had never left Clorinda all the evening. There had been a time in her own youth ... ah, what a lover he had been then! ... but now, she couldn't help it ... every night he spent with that girl was a stab. Willie, of course ... Willie, as straight up and down as a yard of pump-water ... If he had wanted Clorinda in eternity, which all the fuss seemed to be about, why didn't he just have her sealed to him? Men might claim this life was just a stepping-stone, but they seemed darned anxious to have pretty girls step with 'em!

'Come on,' said Hannah Merinda, scenting gossip, 'let's go sit by Ket.'

'— and she said,' continued Ket, happily huddled with Marianne and Martha and Willie and Lucy, who was big-eyed at being allowed to hear, at last, real female-talk, 'that he certainly told that woman where to get off! You know how slow and deliberate he is, and how he twiddles his thumbs. Well, here were all the Twelve and the First Presidency in that big room in the Lion House — 'twas their reg'lar meeting day, as all his wives knew — and in she busts with a bottle of patent medicine in her hand. 'Twas Lydia E. Pinkham's, and she paid no attention to the men, but asked him if she should buy it and began to tell him what it was good for' — here Aunt Ket's voice became so hushed the women had to bunch their heads closer to hear — 'and his face got redder and redder, and when she got through a-tellin' him all the things it would do, he said to her, real quiet, "Yes, I'd buy it if I were you, Harriet; go ahead and take it. Hellfire and brimstone couldn't hurt you!"'

Erastus, hearing the laughter, hastened over to get Aunt Ket in the next set and out of mischief. But just as they were asking Brother Mac to give them a Jenny Lind polka and Erastus was gesticulating to Young Miles to start the music, there was such a rumpus at the doorway that every head turned. Gottlieb Uttley and Freeborn MacIntyre stood there, quite obviously foolish with wine. Free's long legs were covered with mountaineer's leggings coming up to the knee and tied with a string over his short trousers, and his ankles jingled with spurs — guthooks, the boys called them; and Erastus, who hated spurs, thought that a very good name.

'Aye, it's a shebeen,' growled Abijah, his brows jutting — 'the Pig-Dirt Patch. I kenned they made spir-rits there, before ...'

He finally got the boys outside and the door shut, and with much 'hawckking' at his throat, went on with the dance. But he could not get back his good nature. He glowered. He was in a very paddywhack of a rage. And presently, above the din of the music and the dancing, there came a bawdy raucousness.

Four green bottles a-hangin' on the wall —

Clory, tripping by with Mr. Nelson, David Wight's new hired man, thought the whole thing very funny. Abijah looked as if he might explode. But when he went after the noise, he could not tug the door open. The music grew louder suddenly, and the lively polka continued to frisk about the room, but glances sidled toward the door. Erastus, feeling his own face reddening, went to help Abijah, but when finally, after much dignified grunting, they did jerk open the door, it promptly banged shut in their faces. And from without the bellow rose stentoriously:

Hoist yer leg up, hoist yer leg up ...

Mr. Nelson, swinging Clory, chortled with delight. The boys had a mule tied to the door, and every time the irate elders pulled it open, the mule reared backward from the sudden shaft of light and took the door with it.

Erastus, panting, wiped his hands on his trousers and his chin-beard jutted.

'Now this has gone far enough!' he said. 'I ——'

But that sentence was never finished.

Suddenly there was a hush outside, and then a yell and more yells and the wild pounding of hoofs. And dark and ominous above the faltering music the deep voice of the bass drum. Feet ceased shuffling, bare arms pricked with gooseflesh, people held their breaths. The silence throbbed with the thunder of the drum. Indians!

And then the door burst open and young Joseph MacIntyre staggered in, white-faced, black hair awry, muddy. That broke the spell and the dancers crowded around him.

'Navajos!' he gasped to Jacob Hamblin. 'I got away while they were after the sheep. They ——'

More pounding horses outside. The town guards ... 'stole all the cattle in the stray pen. Every bit of stock in outlying lots ... scalped a man in Washington ——'

There was purpose now in the hubbub. Jacob Hamblin and Shadrach Gaunt took charge. Pretty uniforms wouldn't matter now, but all the hours of drilling might. That stock had to be recovered. Its loss meant a famine. Any man who had a gun and a horse —— The women must prepare food, blankets. Jacob, after talking to Tutsegabbett, said he thought the Navajos must have gone out Pipe Springs way, toward the Colorado. Shadrach was all soldier now, and his eyes had the look of distance in them. 'Be ready to leave by daylight,' he ordered the men curtly.

A few of the men gathered in the Sibley tent to load shells, melting the lead, filling the molds, cooling the bullets, stuffing wadding and powder in the metallic cocoons and clamping in the bullets. They squatted by the fireplace talking in low tones. Abijah, sending two boys, would stay to guard at home. 'Sheba packed food for Joseph and Free, and the quilts which would have to serve as saddles, coats, and beds.

Free filled his powderhorn and slung it over his shoulder, buckled the bullet pouch at his belt, jammed the Colt six-shooter in its leather holster. There was nothing of the moon-calf about him now; he was masterful, alert, and, oddly, very happy, as he strode about in his old buckskin coat and short trousers, his guthooks jingling. Joseph, quiet, quizzical, got ready the double-barreled flintlock and Abijah's old cap-and-ball pistol.

And then there was nothing to do but go. Abijah, who never needed to worry about Joseph, sought out Free in the corral, where he was strapping the quilts on Nellie. He loved this wild towhead of his, but he was embarrassed and tongue-tied. The empty barns and corrals coming to life in the graying light seemed poor and sad and lonely. Clory with no milk for her child —— Fresh droppings from Nellie steamed upward in the frosty air, and Abijah hunched his shoulders and shivered a little.

'Well, my son,' he said, hawckking at his throat, 'I want ye to be humble and follow the Leaders o' this Church and ye will never go astray' — preach was not what he had meant to say at all, but he could not seem to stop — 'I have learned that if we do our duty the Lord will provide ... I hae not used coffee, tobacco, and strong drink, nor have I profaned the name of Deity ...' But Free was leaning down from Nellie, offering his hand to his father, who had wanted to hug him. The boy's eyes had that same crazy look they'd had that time of the flood ...

'Good-bye, Pa,' said Free, his voice gay and exuberant, and galloped out of the corral and across the yard, and threw himself down before Clory's dugout and strode in without knocking. Abijah stared helplessly.

For hours, it seemed, Clory had waited in the dugout, silent as death except for the soft breathing of her child — waited crouched beside the fireplace, still glowing like a single red eye in the darkness. And when Free came she had no qualms or doubts or hesitations, but let herself be swept up in his arms and kissed without preamble. O security, rightness, fulfillment! The smell of summer still clung to him.

'Darling,' he said with a rush, 'darling, do you remember last spring when I was so ornery with you? I knowed you wanted to marry me to Bella, and that was so silly. Judas priest, that was silly! You ought to of known there ain't anybody else for me — ever...'

The words were ringed round with a flame. He held her so fiercely for a moment he seemed to bruise her delicate flesh.

'And I've been afraid Kissy meant more to you 'n...anybody...'

Oh no, her heart was pounding wildly, *a child isn't enough. Dear God! a child isn't enough!*

But then Joseph was shouting outside, Joseph on the mule Free had tied to the Social Hall door.

There were sixty men in the little army. Sixty men and a packhorse. A nondescript army, soldiers in shirtsleeves. No fine cavalry horses, but the jackass, the mule, the spavined nag. Only Shadrach Gaunt was dressed for the snow they were sure to find at Pipe Springs, and he had on elkskin pants and buffalo-skin boots made with the hair inside. Having said good-bye to his womenfolk long ago, he waited patiently for the others, hands quiet on the reins, his eyes remote and concentrated, his jaw moving rhythmically, the coyote tail of his rabbit-fur cap ruffling in the breeze.

The women were brief and matter-of-fact about their farewells. 'Take care of Aunt Ket,' Erastus called to Marianne, and the Home Guard was off. Free stood up in his rope-stirrups and waved back at Clory until she was lost to sight, a little big-eyed ghost between Bathsheba and Abijah. 'Yippee!' he cried.

And it was that sound that echoed most often in her dreams

during the next two weeks. 'Yippee!' she would hear, and start up from sleep, rigid with fear. The same fear which paralyzed Bathsheba. A fear which drove the two women together for the first time in their lives. A tense companionship needing no words. Willie was excluded — Willie, who did not know this pain of loving a man — a sword you would not willingly withdraw. 'Sheba with her fierce mother-love, and Clory with this guilty hidden sweetness, oddly comforting each other.

The town huddled, shivering; each day that passed was one more day of safety. Abijah and Lars Hansen, who was sick, one old man, and some young boys cobbled up a roof for the Social Hall in case they had to fort in. Guns and ammunition were distributed to outlying families. A guard was kept, up on the Sugar Loaf where he could see a sudden diaper-on-the-post code. Women went to bed with a rifle on the pillow. People moved about with hushed voices. Fear like ice locked the settlement.

It was so easy to picture the Home Guard following in the deep snow a single track made by Indians walking carefully in the footstep ahead to fool the whites ... the whites who were so easy to fool ... The hand of a slain rancher sticking up out of the snow ... A horse rearing to catch the arrow in its forehead ... other arrows ...

And then there came a supper-time when Clory, feeding Kissy her mush, heard the first faint bawling of cattle — heard, and looked up to see by the faces of the others if she were dreaming.

She knew it, even as they hurried up to the square with the other hurrying families. Her heart had known it all along.

But she wasn't prepared for the limp way his body draped over Nellie. Somehow, she hadn't expected to find him so ... so *limp*. The chill air seemed to splinter around her and break into pieces at her feet. The hushed crowd, the blowing animals, the little packhorse whose hoofs had worn almost to the hide so that he left a circle of blood at every step, the Home Guard staring out of

hollow eyes, Joseph slumped over the neck of the limping mule,
the easy snuffles of those women whose men had returned to them
— all ceased to exist for her. There was nothing but the effort
not to give herself away. This was her fault, all of it — she had
brought him to this pass. But at least she must not shame
this last moment. Erastus' voice sounded remote, unreal...
'He just wouldn't obey counsel,' he said, his eyes on Nellie's torn
and bloody coat; 'he just wouldn't obey counsel.' Erastus was
suddenly an old man, hunched there over the pommel of his saddle, drenched and mudstained, half-frozen, shrunk into himself,
but Clory had no pity for him. 'A dozen arrows,' he kept repeating. 'We counted a dozen arrows.'... Why didn't they put
his head up? The blood would rush to his head hanging down
like that... he ought to get out of those wet clothes... Nowhere
was there comfort. What good was a testimony of the Gospel
beside that limp towhead? Nowhere did the darkness lift...
Clory's voice cracked on a high note — 'Oh, see,' she cried,
pointing. 'Oh, see, his pants have stretched again!'

THE voices seemed to come from an immeasurable distance, as timeless as the breeze on the Sugar Loaf. She thought at first it was still summer and the sound was the droning of bees in the hollyhocks outside the window. But she could not struggle up from the sea of lethargy long enough to distinguish words. It was as if she had been sucked dry and tossed, an empty husk, out into the void. But she liked being a husk, and when presently words forced themselves into the gray vagueness of her mind, she summoned all her will against comprehension. Some instinct warned her that outside her sanctuary were rending, tearing claws.

Then one word forced itself behind her guard, to blaze in characters three feet tall in front of her closed eyes.

'She's had a mis', a mis',' the whispers said, 'she's had a mis', a mis'.' Wondering drowsily whom they were talking about, she floated away again. But the insistent buzzing followed her, brought her back. Could they be discussing her? Cautiously she moved her body upon the bed. Yes, there could be no doubt about the lumps in her corn-husk mattress — since Kissy came she'd had no time to gather cat-tail fuzz. But at that thought her eyes flew open. She was Clory, who was to have another baby!

The furniture wore that unreal air objects assume just before daybreak. There sat Willie like a gaunt cockroach in her black Mother Hubbard, looking as if she had never been to bed at all. Her face was gray and lined beneath the uncompromising hair, and as she rocked and whispered, the squeak of the little chair and the gentle sibilance of her voice breathed a rhythm that seemed to have lived forever in that room. 'Sheba without corsets or hoops was as soggy as a rag doll with lumpy stuffing. As she hunched over the table, her strong, big-knuckled fingers busy, weariness lay upon her like a blight. It was as if a spring had snapped somewhere within her, and all her supports had buckled.

More than the hushed whispers, the wan light creeping over the ghostly walls, there was a gloom in the air like smoke. A pall clung to the two women; spent with their night-long vigil, they still had the funereal self-consciousness of those who sit up with a corpse.

Good heavens, Clory thought, do they think I'm dead? And then knowledge came to her, swiftly, blindingly, plunging through her like the beak of a hawk.

She twisted and gritted her teeth in an effort to escape, to evade, but her mind went on relentlessly picturing the thing at which 'Sheba's fingers picked and pulled — fringe upon a red sash, a sash that went with a uniform. A gay blue uniform. She screwed her eyes tight against the agony of remembrance. The baby brother, then, Kissy's baby brother, had been swept away on the flood of that grief — life running out of her as if she had been a shattered glass of water.

But life would not run out of the mind. For a moment the sense of being alone, lost, and forgotten was too much for her and she bit her lips to keep from crying aloud. Was all her life to be haunted with memories of that bright, living figure? Gusts of the burning sweetness, the pure radiance sweeping aside pain and longing and inner loneliness, sweeping on through, back into the past, only to leave the present blacker still?

A shiver of terror pierced her heart like an icicle. She had not meant to love him, but they had been in the clutch of something bigger than themselves. Some winged power over which they had had no control had swept them from the earth to the sky. She had said to him: 'All that counts is doing our jobs. We'll keep our love secret, where it won't hurt a soul in the world.' But words won't dout a flame. And she had not been able to stop loving him, no matter how hard she tried. Even after Kissy came, she could not destroy this burning essence that was the central core of her being. How was it wrong? It had seemed that a passion diffusing so much light and warmth could not be wrong. Where had been the first misstep? Over and over she recounted each pebble that had gone to make the avalanche.

Helplessly she writhed again under the despair when he had seemed indifferent; and then, even though he was dead, she found her spirit soaring on a sudden thrust of exultation — He did care! He did care! — only to sink away below the loneliness again. Hugging the times he had called her 'darling' as if they were hidden treasure, she fondled each memory over and over. Had he meant this? Had he meant that? Their last moment, when he had kissed her good-bye — she could still feel her whole body blushing, all her senses awake, her will blown out like the tallow slut.

Would that mood always lurk in the shadows of the dugout, waiting to recapture her? It seemed to her that all the old spoken words still trembled there — would they tremble there even when she was old, alternately bathing her in their beauty and drowning her again and again in that savage, recurrent loneliness as if it were an invisible sea? This torment springing out of the silence — you can never see him again, it mocked, oh, you can never see him again! When she had hands as withered and mottled as the claw of a hen, a cackle as querulous, the same demented enthusiasm for gossip as a hen for a new-laid egg, would the world still throb with this passionate longing?

Desire shuddered a remembered spasm along her nerves. Before she was born it must have been conceived, that hunger, as patient as the red rocks, waiting for the pattern of her life to wheel its preordained cycle. Ages ago among the rocks it must have lain, awaiting its cue to jump out at her. And now she would be forever at its mercy, buried forever under that weight of never-to-be-satisfied desire.

In her grief she glorified memory. They had said his death was a punishment for going against counsel, but if anyone had gone against counsel it was she. He was not to blame. Oh, no! It was all her fault from the beginning. She plucked guilt from him and hugged it to her breast and laved her hands in it. She would not have him sullied, she wanted him shrined, forever gay and innocent, forever young.

And he should be. Not by so much as the flicker of an eyelash would she betray him now. To wear gaiety like an armor all her life — but it would be so much easier to die oneself. How could she endure a lifetime, an eternity of exacting pretense, endless fatigue? But then her spirit fluttered upward again like some bright winged thing that had fallen to earth, and her will made itself into a fist.

Her lips were like boards as she moved them, forced them into the old, untroubled upward curve. For a moment her determination shook as a tired hand will shake, and her mouth drooped again. So easy to droop! But she forced the corners back up, bit by bit. This was something she would have to practice, the careless smile, the old gay challenge to life in her voice.

'Have I been a lot of trouble?' she finally said, shocked at the weakness of the sound.

Willie looked up from the chapped, red wrist she was rubbing, and smiled her deep, wise smile. Her glance in the mournful dawn was like a handclasp. But 'Sheba's eyes above her flying fingers were charged with undying enmity. Clory recoiled before the hate of that look. It was out in the open at last.

2

They had said she should not come to the funeral, but some bright flame of the will had upheld her. Sitting with the mourners on the front row, conscious of the rustling of humanity behind her, the craning of necks, she was grateful for this first public testing of her resolution. One did not have to practice smiles at a funeral, one had merely to temper one's grief to that felt by an aunt, a distant relative. One could dab discreetly at eyes burning with inward visions, and grit one's teeth against the sorrow that is so much harder to bear because it must be kept hidden.

'Sheba wore her grief proudly, like a crowning wreath, since it attested she had laid a son upon the altar, even as Abraham of old. When the dread of a lifetime is resolved at last, there is a truce with worry and a surrender to peace. And although 'Sheba's stern features were as white as the new lace collar on her black taffeta and as set in sorrow as a mask, she was erect; she would never bow her head publicly, even to tragedy. Pal, anxious eyes shifting from Clory's pallor, her little figure that seemed to have suddenly shrunk (how awful for her to have to wear the new yellow in which she had been so happy at the dedication!), thought that 'Sheba, having lost the battle, would wrest what pleasure she could from defeat — the funereal meats brought in by neighbors, the new importance at being the center of so much sympathetic attention, the subdued murmurs of admiration — 'How noble, how brave she is, not shedding a tear!'

The three women sat there: 'Sheba, stiff as marble; Clory, like a trodden dandelion; and Willie, serene as a nun with her gray dress, her neat hair, her colorless, untroubled eyes — for what was Death? 'He is better off,' said Willie, who would yawn in Death's face.

Beyond 'Sheba stretched the sober line of her sons: Joseph, chastened by remembered horrors, supporting his mother in her hour of grief; Samuel and Abraham, so clean they itched, and the twins and Isaiah, combed and brushed and big-eyed, frightened by a loss they could not comprehend.

Out of that row of eyes fixed upon Apostle Snow, struggling with the futility of language in the face of catastrophe, falling back upon commonplaces — he regretted that — 'ptsahh' — such occasion should mark the first public function in the new Social Hall — only one gaze flinched with torment. It is hard to force a lie to the eyes, and Clory, absorbed in the effort, following the proper flight of 'Sheba's handkerchief to her lips, could not keep the living anguish, the appeal for clemency, the bewilderment and the longing from her gaze. But 'Sheba had no more pity for that look than she would have had for the despair in the eyes of a trapped wild bird. She took the handkerchief from her mouth, and her thin lips pursed and tightened as if pulled by a drawstring. Her eyes, plunging into Clory's, were as hard as the points of knives. Squeezing her lids against that silent accusation, Clory thought again that 'Sheba could not really believe that Eardley girl's story. Again that feeling of hopelessness before the realization that Free could never come back to clear his name, himself . . .

Shivering, pressing her hands together as if she were pressing her thoughts into shape, forcing her gaze to dwell calmly upon the frock-coated dignitaries on the stand (the stand that was a stage with an arched backdrop concealing the thrilling fact of dressing-rooms — a stage where she would soon be supposed to strut as if nothing at all had ever happened), Clory found herself staring at Abijah's quivering lips. Naked lips surrounded by the brush of hair, a mouth as defenseless in its grief as a clearing in a jungle. Abijah had wanted his son dressed in garments; Free would have gone through the Endowment House if he could have got there, Abijah insisted stubbornly. But right was right, said Apostle Snow; you could not commit sacrilege even to console a father. Besides, he reminded Abijah, after the Temple was finished he could still do Free's work for him. And so, below the

stand, between it and the mourners' bench, Free lay in the plain
pine coffin Lars Hansen had made for him, valorous in the
uniform he had not been able to parade in life.

Clory had not once looked at that brave shell, empty of the
vital spark she had loved so much. Easier to keep one's eyes on
Abijah's quivering lips, even knowing that Abijah believed Miny's
story — believed it because he wanted to believe it, because it
piled up his score against Clory, because it gave him an added
weapon against his own desire for her. For a man can stand to
censure himself, but not to see his own son brought low. . . . Yes,
Clory's thought faced the fact with a sudden cool detachment,
'Sheba will forgive you sooner than Abijah. . . . Wear your gaiety
now, Clorinda Agatha . . . Wear your gaiety like a sword . . .

Why, thought David Wight, moving restlessly beside Pal, un-
impressed with the hush, the odor of sanctity, the solemnity of
Brother Wheelock's quartet singing 'Beautiful Isle of Somewhere,' why do people say such absurd things at a funeral?
Free wasn't a saint, he was a normal young man in love; but
they would make a saint out of him now he was dead, and make
a sinner out of Clory, who was still alive. David hardened his
heart against Abijah's obvious suffering. The fool, his mind
stormed in an unwonted rage, can't he see that he has brought
this all on himself by his own self-righteousness? . . . It's a terrible
thing to be so sure of the right!

Winter was coming early this year. The pine-nut baskets of
the Indians were full and brimming over, and the Lamanites
frantic to trade with the whites for any kind of food; for it will
be a long, hard winter, they said — much cold, much snow. Even
in October there were gray, leaden days.

Clory shivered in Apostle Snow's open buggy and hugged more
tightly into her old plush cape. She was sitting on the back seat
between Willie and Joseph, behind 'Sheba and Abijah riding in
front with Apostle Snow. 'Sheba's voice, going on and on, more
lifeless than the day, made the very air seem colder.

'He was so beautiful,' she said over and over, 'so beautiful!'

'Yes,' said Erastus, flicking the reins over the backs of the bays now they were out of the crowd. 'Yes...'

Clory, her eyes upon 'Sheba's black bob, which looked as if overnight it had been suddenly sprinkled with salt, kept seeing the coffin in the wagon box ahead — that long soldier's coffin draped with a flag made out of her old red skirt. (A flag for the Fourth of July! — Clory for stripes and Marianne for the field of blue and Pal for the stars...) Since there were no wildflowers out, Apostle Snow had cut the lucerne in the community field (for one must honor the dead), and the green leaves drooped along the flag...

Clory's very spirit seemed to strain at the confining flesh as the queue of wagons wound to the bleak little cemetery at the Old Campground, so desolate with alkali, so bitter in winter and so hot in summer that one wondered how its souls could find rest. Here was the outward sign of the price the land had exacted — a boy lost in a flood, a bouquet of tiny lives snatched before they had begun to live, Death's hard-won victories by flux, this last easy one by Indians...

The consciousness of people about her. Mixed tentacles of curiosity and sympathy reaching out. And then it was as if she were alone in a vast silence, alone with one unsupportable fact. Oblivious of veiled stares, obeying some instinct stronger than caution, she dug a handful of lucerne from the open sack and threw it after the lowering box as if she were throwing away all that remained of youth and hope. Once before the earth had lain pallid and shivering and listened to the bitter and final clunk of the clods, and once before 'Heaven' and 'angels' had been just words. She remembered, and all the hunger and fear and loneliness of her childhood rose up from the past as if to choke her. She wanted to scream aloud and batter with her fists at the patient faces about her. *It isn't worth it*, she wanted to cry. *Nothing on earth or in heaven is worth it! Can't you see that we're all just handfuls of dirt to be dumped in a box?*

And then suddenly, even as heads bowed and the last words fell into the silence, and the wind whipped out of the north to tear at her skirts, a warm light was blown into her mind, a luminous vibration, a surety greater than sorrow or privation or the fact of that new, red mound. Very still she held for that light to creep over the rim of the world, for that knowledge of laughter behind all the tears. So still that Willie's worried touch was as shocking as the prick of a needle, scattering the moment. Alone beside the grave, watching the backs of the crowd shuffling out through the gate, 'Sheba broken a little, leaning upon Abijah's arm, Clory sighed as if she were watching the flight of Something more buoyant than humanity.

But there was no peace. No decent interval for communing with one's soul. How strange that people should be so terrified of being alone! Even at dinner, with the neighbors bringing in cooked food, Abijah and 'Sheba, the Gardners and the Hansens, Joseph, shedding his drollery now that he was one with his elders — all must needs pick over the details of the tragedy as if they were sorting over beans for a pot.

'I ken Pipe Springs is about seventy miles east as the crow flies?' said Abijah, scooping up hot mouthfuls of Sister Hansen's precious baked potato as if he would satisfy his sense of loss with food.

'Yes,' said Bishop Gardner — 'Sheba had borrowed the Yeast Lady's table and the tent was crowded with diners — 'yes, and we made it in two days... Gathered men from Washington, Harrisburg, as far up as Mukuntuweap, spent the first night at Duncan's Retreat, crossed the mountain the next night, and got to Pipe Springs about twelve o'clock ... But there was no smoke coming out of the house, no men around the ranch at all ... Our scouts found Indian sign at Grand Gulch and the south end of Buckskin Mountains, all right, but ——'

'It was at Un-got-toh Canyon we first come on the trail of the stock,' interrupted Joseph with his mouth full. 'We clumb over a steep, hogsback trail, 'til we finally come to a high bluff, and from its edge we had our first sight of the Injuns. There they wuz, about a mile below us, a long line of 'em ridin' along on our ponies they'd stole, although they was mostly asleep a-horseback, and the rest of the cayuses and all the sheep and cattle millin' around and bellerin' to beat the band. We fired on 'em just as they passed the gap in the ledge, and you should have seen the blankets fly!'

Bishop Gardner put down his fork decisively. 'But we didn't whip 'em,' he said, 'and don't you think it. We only killed about seven, and the rest got away with most of the stock. The varmints dropped down behind the ledge, you see, and we couldn't reach 'em without going through the gap. You were mighty lucky, Brother Mac, to get back even them oxen.'

Abijah went on chewing and did not answer. He was thinking of the three oxen they had brought back, so thin he couldn't give them away, and his nice mules (the one Joseph had ridden home so wounded it had died) and all his sheep and his milch-cow gone, even his pig. He half-heard Bishop Gardner's story of finding the two Pipe Spring ranchers whose mutilated bodies had been preserved under the new eighteen-inch fall of snow, and how each Indian wore a stolen greenback plastered on his forehead ...

'Some of our men were foolhardy, though,' continued Bishop Gardner. Abijah looked up at that, and Clory caught the sunken fire of his eyes beneath the thick, overhanging brows. 'Colonel Gaunt dashed up the slope right into the line of fire. We could see an Injun plain as day, one knee on the ground, bow bent to the arrow-head, waiting coolly for the best shot. We yelled, and as the Colonel reined in, his horse reared and got the arrow in its forehead.'

He isn't saying so, thought Abijah, but he means my boy, too. My boy was foolhardy, going right out to meet them arrows. . Ech! Too late to threap on it now ...

Even after Clory got away, hurrying with Kissy over to the

dugout, she could hear the voices going on and on. The gray day was drawing to a close, but eddies of dust still ran before the wind. The neighbors had done the washing, but Abijah's garments were not yet dry, and they flapped on the clothesline like the caricature of a man, like Abijah deflated of vanity Clory shrank from the sight with a faint shiver of distaste and pulled at Kissy's hand.

In the blessed quiet of the dugout she sank to the little rocker, snuggled the child grown almost too large for her arms, and sang.

When Willie found her there, her voice had sunk to a whisper as intense as will power. The sound ran along Willie's nerves like a shriek.

'Oh Clory,' she cried, in a rush of pity, dumping her shovelful of coals in the dead fireplace, picking up the sleeping child, carrying her to the bed and tucking her in, 'don't sit 'ere like this!'

Stooping to the hearth, she piled brush on the coals, puffed a blow-horn, and watched the pattern of the branches leap into incandescence, blaze up the chimney with the fury and brevity of life itself.

'Come on,' she coaxed. 'Take off your 'oops and let me 'elp you into bed.'

But Clory smiled, her mouth twitching like a raw nerve, and her voice sprang up like a flute on a little note of apology. Her glance that would not meet Willie's flew about the room with its old capriciousness. It was as if her thought had determinedly pursed up its lips to whistle a tune.

Laws — Willie's heart was a quiver of pity — she's pretending to me, too.

But even as Willie watched, the girl's brilliance suddenly flickered out, her spirit flagged, seemed to give way at the waist and crumble into her hoops. With a gesture of agony she flung herself on Willie's flat breast and broke into long convulsions of weeping. Willie could only stroke the dark head, helplessly aware that she was watching a violation; it was as if Clory had suddenly stripped naked before her ... The hardest thing in life, she thought, is to watch suffering and feel helpless.

'There, there,' she crooned; 'sometimes the 'ardest thing in the world is to forgive yourself.'

Clory's drenched lashes struggled upward like wet moths.

'Oh, Willie,' she gasped. 'Oh, Willie — !'

'Nonsense,' said Willie, reading her mind, 'you'll never git rid of a skeleton by hiding it.'

Then Clory was smiling again, some subtle magic of personality defying tears, patting Willie's cheek and smiling her reluctantly right out the door.

Alone again, the girl went to the rag-bag in the corner, rummaged, pulled out the old linsey-woolsey. Unhooking her bodice, stepping out of hoops and dress, and letting them lie as they had fallen, still retaining their shape like some bright chrysalis, she pulled the limp gray garment over her head, and watched the folds of the skirt cling along her limbs, a desolate pattern of grief. Her heart knew some obscure satisfaction as if she had done penance, put on sackcloth. Only one impulse emerged clearly — to hide, to crawl off and lick her wounds.

Her body, weak from illness, exhausted from grief, protested at the climbing red road, but she forced her feet on up, step by step. Unconscious of lurking shadows, the hush brooding over the land with the twilight, she might have been hurrying through space, on some strange planet. Only with the looming presence of the Sugar Loaf behind her and the bite of the very chasm's edge beneath her feet, did her mad flight halt. All the twisted fibers of buried hopes and fears, all the longing and disappointment, pulled at her, propelling her over the edge ...

Erastus did not know she was there until a pebble slipped and bounded on the rocks below. She was poised like a small gray wraith not fifty feet from where he sat, as he so often did, dangling his legs over the rim. He kept his voice quiet.

'Clorinda,' he called. 'Clorinda.'

'Yes?' Her voice was smothered, the voice of one crying out in sleep.

He came to her then, his stocky body in its homespun like an embodiment of the gray twilight moving over the rocks, and stood looking quietly down at her. There was understanding in his eyes. Her violent trembling ceased. He pulled her down to the rocks and they sat there wordlessly, staring out across the valley, filling with night like a great bowl. The sky looked bruised, black and blue, and the wind came around the Sugar Loaf on its hunt. A pillar of red dust blew up from the rocks below them, wavered into the air, held together for an instant, and then sank down and whirled in broken eddies.

Presently Erastus began to talk. More to himself than the girl. Was a man a fool, then, to reach for the stars?

Beyond the darkened valley, mist shrouded the river like a dropped scarf and the yapping of the coyotes rose and fell, sad and haunting and strangely beautiful.

'Trying is all that counts,' whispered Clory, her voice so detached that she might have been listening for an echo. Twilight whispered slowly over her flesh. She would always be listening for Pan while she prayed to the angels...

And there shall be no more death, neither sorrow nor crying...

The voice seemed a part of the night and a wave of joy rose from her unconscious depths to answer it... That was it, she thought, that which would sustain her. Triumphant over a handful of dust. She was Clory who did not have a testimony of the Gospel, but the Light was still hers, growing brighter as one gained wisdom... The wave of joy broke, and the dazzling spray flooded her with love, faith, divine goodness. She was suddenly conscious of receding veils, the solid earth of maturity under her feet. Sorrow might come again, but it would find a tougher surface.

3

Snow fell by Thanksgiving-time that year, and neither the dugouts of the whites nor the coyote-hide wickiups of the Indians were proof against the cold. For the first time ice formed on the Virgin. Progress on the pile dam slowed until Erastus increased the pay of those willing to work in the water fifty cents a day. Even so, it seemed to him, inspecting the job, that the whole world was afflicted with colds in the head and chilblains on the feet and a light-minded attitude. Although, it was true, Abijah MacIntyre's exhortations against levity got under his own skin. But here came Zebedee Trupp bearing news that could not wait for him to go down to the crossing and be driven back across the river — waddling out onto the ice like an obstinate duck, sinking, swagger and all, into the icy water. 'Dod blast it, sonsawitchin'!' paraphrased Zebedee, gasping and thrashing at the thick slush churning about his armpits. Amusement ran from eye to eye, Shadrach Gaunt clucking to his mules on the bank, arresting the pile-driver in midair, shifting his quid to the other cheek and squinting at Zebedee solemnly.

'Be ye cold, Brother?'

Zebedee flipped mud from an indignant side whisker. His little pig-eyes glared.

'Wal, I ain't a damned bit sweaty!' he said.

Old 'Fifty-Cents-on-the-Dollar'!... Thank God for laughter, thought Erastus, watching young Miles throw a rope to Zebedee and the men go chuckling back to work... And thank God for levity, thought David Wight, who knew Zebedee carried a note — *Dear Sir*, it read, *You have asked me to become your wife. I accept, nothing further needs be said.* The elders had finally got the best of Bella Weeks. Well, David pondered, Zebedee would at last have his three wives, without which, advised the authorities, no man could amount to much in the Church. But still, even with Bella nearing twenty, practically an old maid, it didn't seem right to marry her to a man of seventy...

With so much of the stock gone, fewer men could afford to hire their share of work done on the dam and public buildings. Which was really a good thing, thought Erastus, chewing hard on his bitter cud of purple flagroot — that dang tooth was bothering him again — and snugging into the old shawl Aunt Ket had made him bring. He shivered, crunching over turpentine bushes, scrambling through mesquite and cat's-claw on his way to the crossing. Only Zadoc Hunt had failed personally to put in his turn at the dam.

4

There were times that winter when Clory was envious of Pal. David Wight with most of his sheep gone was still the same gentle, philosophical David — freighting himself, instead of hiring it done, working a team on shares and hauling rock for the cotton factory. Encouraging the *Cactus*, contributing his poems. Humorous, kindly, untroubled. He refused to allow himself or his family to be touched by the fear which haunted other homes. The loss of the stock was crippling, and although the harvest had been fair, even Erastus found it hard to keep up a pretense of cheer as the winter clamped down like a vise.

Abijah could not get over the loss of his mules. Shivering out of bed in the pre-dawn murk, coughing with the smoke the sleety wind chased back down the flue, he would stare from under his brows at Samuel slipping on his mother's shoes to go out and feed the stock, and end up by clumping across the frozen dooryard after him. Running a hand over the ridged, hairy hips of the three oxen, feeling Nellie's uneasiness through the currycomb, he longed with a bitter nostalgia for the old barnyard sounds and smells — Bessie's low mooing, the busy grunt of pigs, the shrill braying of his mules, and the fine, warm ammonia-sting of much fresh dung. No longer even a rooster to crow, what with Indians and cold and coyotes. And what good were three half-sick oxen to a man? That arrow-wound in Old Pete was still an open sore, in spite of creosote-bush poultices. Three oxen for a full tithe-payer and a Seventy! 'They rattle around out there,' he complained to 'Sheba, above the clang of the copper prayer-bell, 'like three beans in a tub!' And 'Sheba, who was having her own troubles, what with Isaiah still wetting the bed in spite of six whole years of marshmallow, reflected with weary tartness that Abijah probably missed his mules more than his son. For weeks at a time his red-backed ledger forgot to chastise the neighbors. Instead it grew very bold, and asserted that 'even a saint says "kusum" in times like these.' More and more it concerned itself with 'frugal repasts' and 'eatables hard to get hold of — not a bit of beef to be had. In the T.O. you can't buy a bit of butter, bacon, nor since last week, a can of lard...'

Then in shame he would gird up his loins as became a leader and gather his family about him for a fireplace sing, after which for a while the ledger would strut. 'I am of the royal descent of Ephraim,' it would proclaim, 'and a rightful heir to the priest-hood, which heritage is to be preferred to all the blood-stained nobility of Europe no matter how much roast beef they have! — I am a Saviour upon Mount Zion and my wives are Queens and Elect Ladies, and what care we for full bellies! My wife, Bath-sheba, should be ashamed of her whining for a Dobie house when she is preparing to dwell with the Royalty of Heaven!'

Nevertheless, he did start 'Sheba's house that winter, putting his boys to ricking the adobes on good days. He felt irrationally that he had to make it up to her for Free's death.

While he visited Clory regularly, the time was spent rather in duty than passion. There was more than constraint between them. As she dished up corn-meal mush from the spider, he would sit there like a whiskered bear, morosely gritting his teeth, staring at her under his lowering brows, more suspicious of this new humility, this new eagerness to please, than he had been of her old carelessness. He seldom spoke except to Kissy, who was

usually asleep by the time he came at night (even then sometimes
he would go over to the bed and wake the child with his fierce
caresses, drawing her into a charmed circle from the security of
which he regarded Clory as if she were an intruder), and Clory had
found that it did not pay to offer talk herself. Abijah's stern,
masculine dominance would allow her what he owed her and no
more, in spite of her efforts to tempt him with his favorite dishes,
even wishing aloud they could afford a sheep for the haggis
pudding he liked so well. To Clory, trying as never before to
win him, to be a good wife — she *would* understand 'Sheba, she
would learn tolerance and doing-unto-others . . . Duty was a
word as cold as a stone.

Abijah chose his Bible texts with care such evenings. 'These . . .
things doth the Lord hate: a proud look, a lying tongue, and hands
that shed innocent blood,' he would read to Clory as a prelude
to love.

Sometimes in the Sibley tent, before family prayers, he was
even more pointed. With the line of his dark sons there before
him as a reminder of the vague guilt in his own heart, he would
thunder, 'To keep thee from the evil woman, from the flattery of
the tongue of a strange woman; lust not after her beauty in thine
heart, neither let her take thee with her eyelids.' 'Sheba was like
a cat with a mouse under her paw, and Clory, sitting there,
white, the small trapped mouse — fully conscious of 'Sheba's
silent gloating, fully conscious of memory (taking Free with her
eyelids!) but staring valiantly ahead. When Willie could no
longer endure that mute, set smile she would hobble to Abijah
and wring her foolish hands, but his frown was so awesome that
it sent her scurrying back to Clory herself for comfort. Clory,
who had found, strangely enough, that she could laugh. 'Never
mind,' she calmed Willie's ruffled feathers. 'The Lord made us
all, 'Sheba and me, and Abijah, too, I guess . . .'

Pal was her refuge from the moodiness at home. Tucking Kissy
in bed, she would fly to Pal's quiet serenity. Watching her de-

voted, cat-like hovering over the high-chair where Patience-Elizabeth, flushed with night-time, absorbed in hunger, spooned bread-
and-milk, Clory would find peace flowing back. And after the
child was asleep, there was Pal at ease by the fire, compassion in
her brow, contentment on her hands and within her lap, as honest
as bread, as kind as the sun.

The two girls had long talks that winter. With the new puncheon floors David had put in, and the steady voice of the ormolu
clock exposing its insides on the mantel, the firelight winking on
china shepherdesses, on antimacassars and lambrequins and picture throws, on the fragment of cherubim from the Nauvoo Temple, daguerreotypes and spinning wheel, copper candle-sconces and
the blue-and-white checked bedspread Pal had dyed and woven
and lace-edged, the little house bucked the cold like a snug ship
in a choppy sea, and Pal knitted and laughed and shared with
Clory the fullness of her content.

'We aren't getting any younger,' said Pal, speaking with the
weight of twenty-two years, 'and we have to realize we're not
girls any longer, we're women with responsibilities. I was convinced when I married David that the doctrine of plurality of
wives was from the Lord, and now that I've given him Lucy I'm
more than ever convinced. We felt to embrace the whole Gospel,
David and I, that he might attain to kingdoms, thrones, princi-
palities, and powers, and although a woman can't hold the priesthood, David says I'll share with him in all these blessings.'

The freckles stood out earnestly on Pal's dish-face and her
glance was very blue at Clory, whose winged brows knitted, hands
pausing thoughtfully.

'I'm proud of my husband, Clory, and I love him very much,
but I'll gladly give him a dozen other wives if he wants them.
And I wouldn't expect him to love them less because he loves me
more for giving them to him, either. David's a man of God. . . .
We were both brought up in plural households, you know,
and to this day I love my half-sisters as well as I do my own. . . .

It was David who objected to plurality — he said it was too much responsibility and, anyway, he wouldn't ask me to share my affections with another woman' — Pal's smile was tender with reminiscence. 'Mother wrote me when he and Lucy were in the City that she was proud of me ... Here ——'

Pal got up and fumbled among David's books on the mantel.

'Here's her letter' — she leaned down to the fire to read the closely written foolscap. '"Your Aunt Mary and I used to visit, and plan our work together. I sewed for Auntie and she rendered my lard and made my head cheese at pig-killing time, and we quilted and put up fruit together. Your Dad spent a week with each of us, and much as I loved him, I used to be relieved when it was his turn to go to Auntie's, as it gave me time to get caught up on my work. ...."'

Pal looked up, but her gaze was absent. 'I remember, before Aunt Mary died, the well-worn path kittering between our two houses.' Again that little secret smile. 'Them were happy days! I remember when Father came the house had to be straightened and the best food prepared, and us children scrubbed and marshaled in to family prayers. There was a sort of council meeting at his arrival. If we'd been quarreling during the week he settled our difficulties and taught us about the Gospel. One of us brought him his slippers, another a drink, another a towel and basin of water. All week we saved our report cards to show him, and bits of candy or cake ... He held us all together and built up a sense of the *Family* ... You know, in all my childhood, I can't remember a single cross word between Father and either of his wives. He was a patriarch and they lived like the ancient leaders of Israel.'

Pal flipped the page and steadied her fingers on the last two lines:

'Listen: "Now, my dear child, I hope you will not question our sincerity nor regret your own action in following this doctrine. Through it and it alone, can we obtain celestial glory and live as fully as we should." That's it!' — Pal's eyes were bright.

'That's what we want to teach our children; *to live fully* ——'

'But ——' Clory bit her lip and then fell silent again. Her eyes, unseeing, brooding, were enormous in the firelight, brilliant with unspoken protest.

Pal leaned forward in a little gesture of sympathy.

'Of course it isn't easy,' she said. 'It's never easy to share your husband with another woman. Only now am I beginning to understand what a great person my mother was. Think of it, Clory! Think how it would be for a woman growing old, broken down with bearing babies, to have a lovely young girl come into the house ...'

Clory was seeing 'Sheba, her mole twitching aggressively — Could 'Sheba's bossiness be a defense for the effort it cost her to discipline the rebellious flesh — to turn her husband over to the child she had diapered? ...

'I have to keep telling myself it isn't easy for Lucy, either. I have to take myself in hand — to *make* myself be gentle and sweet and good. To watch every word, every thought ... But, you know, I've found out a funny thing. I've found out Lucy understands David better than I do. I guess I love him too much to understand him. And so when I'm hurt by anything he says or does I go to Lucy and we talk it over. ... I love Lucy, now. I love her better than a sister!'

Pal's clicking needles paused. When she looked up her eyes were a blue blaze.

'She's going to name her baby after me ...' Pal's voice softened, and she gazed into the fire where cottonwood embers burst apart and hissed upward. — Certainly no woman could pay another a subtler compliment, thought Clory. Would such a thing influence 'Sheba — Abijah? ...

'Of course, I know Abijah MacIntyre isn't David,' said Pal, as if reading her thoughts. 'But he's a wonderful man, Clory — it's just he's like 'Sheba, wants his own way — and it's been partly your fault. But I was thinking — you're sealed to him now, you'll be his for all eternity whether you like it or not. You and 'Sheba'd better start getting along 'cause you're sure as the dickens going to see an awful lot of each other! David says you can't run away from things by dying. We take all the things we've learned and all the things we've failed to learn, right along with us...'

Almost always when Clory called for Pal to go to Singing Practice (Willie was having liver trouble again, in spite of all her dosing with yellow dock), Lucy came with them. And when she wasn't visiting her mother in the evenings she made a third before the fireplace. Lucy with her lovely skin and her bent brown head saying softly: 'To think how I worried the entire eight hours we were getting our endowments! When the women anointed me with oil and gave me the garments with the promises about protecting from disease and an enemy's bullet if I'd be faithful, I kept thinking, "'t won't do any good to purify me! I can't live decent in plurality!" And when we saw the Creation, the Temptation, and the Fall, and we put on our fig-leaf aprons, I kept looking at David and thinking, "I'll fall, all right!" And then when it came time to "go behind the veil" I wanted to scream, I was so scared, because I knew I never could live up ——'

She stopped and smiled at Pal, and such a look of tenderness and mutual trust passed between the two that Clory felt shut out, a stranger.

But she began to spend more and more time at Pal's. Bundling Kissy up after the work was done, taking knitting or mending, going up for a whole afternoon.

This winter Apostle Snow got the brethren busy at making a sundial ('He would pick a time when we never see the sun!' grumbled Abijah), as a community time-regulator. There was no longer any excuse for a person overstaying her visit.

And yet occasionally Clory and Pal and Lucy were still happily gossiping when David and Mr. Nelson stomped in from the fields or the corral, boots streaming with muck, cheeks stung red with the cold. Of course, now that she was there, Clory must stay for supper. It was amazing, she thought, how much cheer could be crowded into clabber and soggum and corn dodgers. Kissy and Patience-Elizabeth, allowed to eat with the grown-ups, jabbered and banged with their spoons.

After the meal Pal and Clory must show off their children, before putting them to bed. Patience-Elizabeth, who lisped, blonde and chubby and twice as large. But always ailing. Always a sore throat forever having to be collared in fat-bacon; always red-rimmed eyes. 'I can't understand it,' worried Pal. 'I poulticed her all summer long with overripe cucumbers...' But Kissy, thought Clory proudly, was a wiry child — and then, brooding over the thin, bird-bones... how admit, even to yourself, that your child hadn't enough to eat? Kissy, the dark elfin thing, as slender and glancing as a fine steel blade. A chestnut wisp of a child with the eagerness that was her mother's own expression. Even in denim, with her stockings wrinkling on her legs and her straight hair tied with scraps from Clory's yellow dress, she was so starry-eyed, her cheeks so transparently flushed, that she seemed to be woven less of flesh and blood than of some delicate bloom of desire. There in the center of the grown-up circle she regarded the foolish faces calmly. Kneeling before the child, coaxing her with little cries and grimaces and gestures, Clory adored her until it was like a wound in the heart.

'Up — up in the sky...' prompted Clory, entreating Kissy with their own eye-language.

'A-pup in the sky,' piped Kissy dutifully, and stopped on a frown. 'That's a silly song,' she decided with royal imperiousness. Looking her disgust at Patience-Elizabeth, the lisper, hiding her head in her mother's skirts, she graciously offered a substitute. Even though grown-ups were silly, one couldn't hurt their feelings.

'Aunt 'Sheba taught me a song about a di'per ——'

'A — a diaper, darling?'

Nodding, she considered her feet for a moment and then raised her head and her reed-like voice:

'"Tom, Tom, the Di'per's son ——"'

At their hoots of delight she regarded her elders gravely. Grown-ups always laughed at things that were not really funny. But she gave it up and went over to her mother.

'Put me to bed with Patience-Elizabeth,' she said, turning around for her dress to be unbuttoned. 'I won't mind being wokened up.'

Clory caught her savagely and buried her face in the childish neck.

Since surrounding ridges were so drifted with snow that mail had been unable to get through to the valley, the men missed their news-clubs; and occasionally on such evenings at David's, other folks dropped in — Bishop Gardner, steady and dependable, with his intelligent forehead and friendly eyes; Abijah MacIntyre, crowding the room with his dark, overwhelming masculinity, his eyes shooting questions at Clory in the corner, the back of the hand he held out to David springing with hair below the knitted wristlet. Sometimes Apostle Snow stopped in on his way from a counseling (Young Miles was over-quick to take the rod to his children), always late but unhurried, his stocky body always weary, his kindly eyes preoccupied, the bald spot on his head, with its fringe of gray hair, red with cold.

Once around the table with its little hoard of old reading-matter, the men began to talk. Politics, the weather — cattle were freezing in Pine Valley, a man and his wife had perished in the snow on the road to Cedar Fort; the Indians — hundreds had recently died off in a measle epidemic, and the terrified white women, fortifying children with asafetida bags, and balsam and saffron teas to bring out a rash in case it was there, banged doors in the faces of starving, naked brown beggars who could not understand this sudden aloofness of the whites, and slunk away to crouch menacingly out in the brush.

'But we have to protect our-r own bairns first!' frowned Abijah whom the Indians loved.

Erastus nodded slowly, thinking he'd get Keturah to mix up a batch of turkey rhubarb or some such remedy and take it out to the camp.

'Brother Brigham says to — ptsahh! — "omit promises where you're not sure you can fulfill them — let all under your direction be united together in the holy bonds of love and unity — all is peace up here," but I ain't so sure he'd think it was so dang peaceful, with a mad Lamanite around.'

Mr. Nelson's brief smile flickered.

'But why do you stay?' he asked.

David slapped both hands on the table and leaned forward.

'I'll tell you why! Because we dreamed of a place of peace. We saw so much of bloodshed, so much of human beings like beasts. We're just common men, Mr. Nelson, tillers of the soil, hewers of wood and haulers of water. But we dreamed of brotherly love. Oh, not just the words... We wondered if human beings could do it, and that's why we're here.... No rich, no poor, and all things in common ——'

'Dang common, too,' said Bishop Gardner, idly picking his teeth with a broom straw.

'But our children won't be common! We'll educate our children, send 'em away and let 'em bring back the best there is!'

Apostle Snow's kindly drawl, Bishop Gardner's quiet humor, Abijah MacIntyre's rich burr, David's eager, excited voice, and Mr. Nelson's foreign speech with its 'idears' and soft *r*'s — they would spend hours discussing the state of the universe, wrangling over religion, debating dogma, as was the custom of the day. Conversation that veered and tacked, somersaulted and sizzled.

Clory listened and listened. Hunger for knowledge can be as real as hunger for meat. Hunger for knowledge and dreams of far places and shining cities.

But the argufying was what she liked best. David and Mr.

Nelson (it usually boiled down to these two) argufying on every subject under the sun. Clory thought Mr. Nelson seemed to have a lot of curiosity concerning the Mormons.

'An anthropocentric religion,' expounded David learnedly, 'with each man holding the priesthood instead of a few; an anthropomorphic God having body, parts, and passions ——'

Mr. Nelson swept aside the phrases.

'No; give it to me in a single word. No religion is worth its salt unless it can be made simple.'

'Well, then, Mormonism' — David looked at Apostle Snow as if for help, but Erastus only puffed his full lips in and out — 'Mormonism means — means *neighborliness.*'

'Hawckk!' applauded Abijah, and 'Ptsahh!' smacked Erastus, while Bishop Gardner picked his teeth delightedly.

But Mr. Nelson, waiting for David, merely nodded. He seemed possessed of a strange excitement. Clory thought he sometimes said things he didn't mean just so he could listen to David talk.

'Togetherness.' His voice was very soft. 'You were persecuted because you had *togetherness,* but it also gave you your strength.'

His eyes gleamed.

'*Togetherness!* The ability to sacrifice oneself for the Common Good — the Common Good, defined by all the people beforehand and then upheld by all the people. Our country was founded on that ideal, and we had it until we began to split apart into vested interests... If we can only keep Lincoln... That's what gave the early Christians their power: the ability to live *outside* themselves and *above* themselves for something greater than self.'

Clory thought his voice sounded like speaking-in-tongues, but he only waited a moment while the fire blazed high and the candles guttered in a sudden draft; then he was twinkling again.

'You, David Wight, couldn't live without your neighbor — he's your very life — and yet you'd sacrifice him if he were an apostate or an interfering gentile. People like you can be the

cruelest and yet the most soft-hearted in the world. You'd damn
a man and pray for him as you damned him!'

'Pts ——' began Erastus, breathing hard, chin-whiskers
jutting, but David cut him short.

'Not unless he deserved damning!' shouted David.

Clory wriggled with pleasure. Things began to get good when
voices were raised.

Before Abijah MacIntyre's growl could break into speech,
David held up a hand and began to count off points quickly on his
fingers.

'One: We believe that everything a man desires, all his urges
and feelings and passions, are inherently good in so far as the expression of them does not interfere with any other individual's
welfare — singing and dancing . . .

'Two: We believe that everything a man does is a form of
worship — pitching hay and scrubbing floors! That God was
never meant to belong to one day only out of seven.

'Three: We believe in happiness. "Man is that he might have
joy." *We believe in being honest, true, chaste, benevolent, and doing
good to all men.* Eternal progression — *As man is, God once was;
as God is, man may become.* Heaven isn't a place but a condition ——'

Mr. Nelson darted a sudden look toward Pal.

'And what do *you* believe, Sister Wight?'

Pal blinked startled eyes. 'Why — why,' she stuttered, overcome, 'David says I don't *have* to understand my religion, all I
have to do is obey it!'

The stranger threw back his head and laughed.

'Just what I've been saying, Mr. Wight! Obedience! Obedience
to the Group, without which the rest means nothing. But you
have to remember that some people are afraid of the Group —
some people think the Group means chains, whereas it's the only
real way of insuring liberty. That's why Mr. Lincoln is a great
man — because he tries to think in terms of the whole continent.

high and low. Brotherhood. It's the noblest concept in human experience!'

Mr. Nelson tipped back in his chair, his knees caught under the table-edge, his eyes again staring somewhere beyond the candle-light.

Erastus pursed his lips thoughtfully. In the moment of silence Clory could hear the frost outside crackle like brittle glass.

'To defeat the hate in the world and put love in its place . . . an idea, that. But you might do it, who knows? A despised and rejected people . . . Lord, Lord.' (He didn't *look* like a person praying, thought Clory, but ——) 'You've got a peculiarly American religion, growing out of a peculiarly American need. It's a democratic religion and it's new and fresh, not bloodstained and old like the others. Togetherness . . . The materialist says it can't be done, that human nature can't be like that, but if you people are ever let alone long enough to work out your destiny, who knows that you might not do it? But it is a big hunk you've bitten off ——'

Suddenly he was laughing at them all again.

'And by God (begging pardon to the ladies), I'd like to be there when you start to chew it!'

5

Damn-it-to-hell! thought Erastus, hoping the Lord was busy elsewhere at the moment. Flicking his mules with his reins he treated himself to a fit of temper. He was getting too old for this sort of thing, but with Gardner laid up and his two oldest boys on missions and Shadrach Gaunt up north fighting Indians and the brethren always grumbling. . . . Not blaming them, he had felt that he shouldn't ask another man to do that which he was un-willing to do, himself. Besides, there was only this last load to get out and then they could ship the order. Brother Brigham was in a hurry.

It did beat the dickens how Brother Brigham picked the very worst times to start some new project. At April Conference in the City the brethren had voted to erect a telegraph line through the territory. And now the lumber for this organ! Didn't Brother Brigham know the Dixie settlers were still getting out timber for their own Tabernacle? Didn't he know that the snows stayed late on the flanks of Pine Valley? But he must have for the organ's pipes the finest of jack pine free from knots and pitch!

It seemed that this pipe organ was to be the most magnificent in the world, an organ for Zion, forty feet high, to be built back of the pulpits in the new Tabernacle, to be flanked with hundreds of choir seats. . . .

Suddenly the old longing to be back in the City side by side with the leader was almost more than Erastus could bear.

Now that Lincoln was dead and the country in the hands of the Black Republicans he trembled afresh for Deseret. So few folks a man could trust. With the war over, David's Mr. Nelson had suddenly found the means to depart. But when David had insisted on outfitting him with extra money and provisions he'd broken down and confessed he had come as a spy to get information on the evils of polygamy for the *New York Tribune*. Erastus had thought all along there was something fishy about the fellow. If ever those Black Republicans got curious about polygamy —!

But meanwhile Brother Brigham would get his organ, though it might cost a man his life up among that tight-fisted timber. Just about used up Robert Gardner, already. Spring was late and he'd caught cold and was down in town now with Ket and 'Sheba MacIntyre cutting open live chickens and poulticing his lungs.

But with just the help of his boy he'd snaked out enough logs for this last job, ripped them up, and hauled them to St. George — all except this one last load.

Erastus reached Pine Valley by noon. He drove on past the meager log huts of the settlement, straight up the first canyon to

Gardner's sawmill among the pines. There was green grass in the valley, but a cold wind blew off the mist-shrouded flanks of the mountain.

There had been a recent snow. Erastus got out and began to lead the mules up the slope, his feet sinking through the crust halfway to the knee. But the animals tossed their heads until the harness rattled, bared their great yellow teeth, and balked.... Nothing so damned perverse as a balky mule. He gave it up and trudged on up alone. Probably save time by carrying the lumber down to the wagon.

The pines advanced like a dark army before him. There were old stumps in the roadway hidden by the snow, and now and then he stumbled over one. The crust was slick, melting underneath. Panting, he stopped and pushed his hat back from his forehead and squinted his eyes against the sun on the snow. Above him there was the mountain with gullies of oak sticking naked fingers into the air, and slopes of pine and balsam and cedar and fir leaning to the wind like young girls running; below him the valleys tumbled, faint with the first green distance of spring. He turned and plodded onward, savoring the clean, untouched smell of the air, the aromatic scents of leafy earth and quickening sap and resin.

Up at the mill the lumber had been carried out to the roadway and stacked, ready for loading. Erastus looked around the shanty for a moment, sniffing the good tang of gum and the piles of yellow sawdust. Out at the lumber again, he brushed away the loose snow — there was nothing so perfect as the veined, exquisite grain of yellow pine, and although it always hurt him to see a tree give up its life, he relished the fragrance of the wet boards. He picked up the board, getting a good grip on its wet edge, carrying it alongside his body, leaning aslant to its weight as he tramped carefully in his tracks back to the wagon. Soon the lengths of lumber lay golden on the running-gear; he puffed his lips in satisfaction — carrying two at once he could finish the job in a couple of trips. His body was flabby, unused to heavy labor, but he got the first two in his grasp, straightened, grunted, started back down the slope — and then it happened.

At first he thought his leg was broken. Overbalanced, he'd slipped and slid on the melting snow, the boards careening out of his hands, his arms flapping wildly; to save himself, he'd plunged into the deep drifts of the bank. The sudden sharp upthrust of a buried stump — the underneath, fleshy part of his right shin skewered like a forked piece of meat. He lay there a moment, dazed, and then pain bit through the fog. He sat up and took hold of his leg with both hands and pulled, clenching his teeth. The stump sucked loose and blood gushed through the tear in his soft boot. 'Like a stuck pig,' grunted Erastus, looking at the crimsoning snow. He flopped over on his stomach and began to crawl painfully back over to the trail. Ptsahh, a man might bleed to death . . . Erastus sat up and tugged futilely at his boot. If he could just make the wagon . . . Shaking with chill as his arms and knees crunched through the slush, he inched his way down the slope. Once or twice he lay back beaten in the snow, but some grim refusal to be downed drove him on. Then he was sitting up with the heel of his boot caught in the spokes of the wheel ('the farmer's bootjack,' sneered at by cowboys like Shadrach Gaunt), and the mules were pricking their ears and rolling their eyes at him. Erastus ground his teeth at them and wished the Scriptures hadn't made such an issue of profanity. But then he lay back and tugged, and the boot came off.

Below the back of the knee, flesh was peeled clear to the bone. 'A strip about four by ten,' he figured impersonally, twisting his leg around so that he could pull down into place the rumpled hunk of flesh, matted with blood and sock, hanging by the skin just below the knee-bend. He tied it there with his handkerchief and then pulled on the boot again, gritting his teeth. He was feeling faint, now, and very thirsty, and began to scoop up snow.

Not a chance in a hundred that anyone would hear him if he

yelled. But a man couldn't just give up. Soon he wouldn't have the strength to yell.

'Hulloa!' he shouted, cupping his mouth with his hands.

He could hear the sound bounce from canyon to canyon above him, and then the primal stillness settle down once more. For a moment he was panicky, and took out the small fear in the secret part of his mind and looked at it. He did not want to die.

'Help! Help!' he screamed, his voice made stronger with the fear. 'Help!'

Exhausted, he lay back in the snow and gave in to the pain and the cold and the fear.

It seemed to him that he must have dozed. But the sound came again. He opened his eyes wide. No mistaking it. There was a tremendous thrashing in the underbrush to his left and a man plunged through, crunched across the snow, and was standing over him. Erastus peered up through the waves of weakness. It was John D. Lee.

When Erastus opened his eyes again he was lying on a horse blanket before some glowing coals. Splashing along a dirt floor, sunlight poured beneath a hanging blanket that had been pulled aside an entrance poled and mudded up. The air had a dry, musty smell and looking upward, he could see the pocked, arched roof of a cave. John D.'s hideout at Further Waters. Yes, it was spring again and the Federals on the hunt. John D.! But he couldn't have John D. saving his life!

The irony of it brought Erastus upright. Pain jumped. He wriggled miserably. He was wet from the back of his neck to the seat of his pants. He put a hand inside his collar and brought out a half-melted gobbet. A shadow fell across the sunlight and John D. stooped under the opening.

'I'm afraid I had to drag you part of the way,' he explained apologetically, dumping in a corner his armful of wood and bringing to Erastus the saddle he carried in the other hand. 'Here, put your head on this.'

His face that had used to be hairless was unshaven, grizzled, and gaunt. Even his voice had lost its old hospitable booming. Erastus wondered irrelevantly if he'd ever again wear his red sash.

But John D. was bringing him something in a tin cup. 'Drink this,' he ordered, and Erastus shuddered and coughed as the hot whiskey and molasses burned his throat....

John D. pulled up the strip of flesh, packed pounded rock salt on the bone, and lapped the flesh back in place again. At the touch of the salt on the raw surface, Erastus forgot all about irony. John D. brought out silk thread and a needle. Erastus lay on his side, and the first stitch went in.

Suddenly the other man's hand faltered and his face went white beneath the beard.

'I can't do it,' he said, and got up and stood in the doorway, his back to Erastus.

Yaugauts, Erastus remembered; *yaugauts* — cry-baby — the Indians had named him.

John D. came back and held him up, supporting him with his arms.

'Do you think you can do it yourself?' he asked faintly.

Chicken-hearted, the Indians called him.

Erastus twisted his leg around, picked the needle up, and poked it through his skin, while sweat poured over him. Quivering, John D. sewed the parts Erastus could not reach, and when the job was done, tied the threads. Erastus lay back, panting.

'Now,' said John D., 'we'll bind it up tight in boiled-down chamber-lye.'

Erastus closed his eyes and let the pain seep through him.

Soon John D. was back with a soaked flannel bandage. When that was on, he stared at Erastus anxiously.

'I'd better go for help,' he said, 'and git you moved. You're apt to be a mighty sick man.' He hesitated, and there was pleading in his voice. 'The spirit of darkness which is the seed of apostasy in this settlement is appalling.'

Erastus' Conscience stood up, curled its lip, and sneered down at him. 'That,' spoke his Conscience, 'is because he hates to go down there. Many folks are inclined to inform on him. And yet he'd risk detection and even his life to save yours.'

'But he butchered!'

'Sure he butchered — because he was ordered to! Wouldn't you have obeyed orders?'

'But ——'

'Wouldn't you?' The voice was inexorable.

'But — but, Brother Brigham ——'

'It was all right with Brother Brigham until the gentiles started to make a fuss! Brother Brigham could have brought the guilty to justice long ago if he'd wanted to! John D.'s a sop thrown to the gentiles, a bone for them to worry over so they'll let the rest of the Church alone!'

'No sacrifice is too great for the Church. Better let one man take the blame than the whole Church.'

'Even if that man saves your life?'

'He's a murderer ——'

'*He's the only one who can be trusted unto death and still never tell!*'

'But he's safe enough — the Federals ——'

'You know they'll be after him again now the war's over!'

Erastus felt himself being covered, tucked in, cared for. He opened his eyes. John D. was standing in the doorway.

'John,' he said, moistening his lips, 'you never in your life turned away a man in need, did you?'

John D.'s eyes fell.

'Brother Snow,' he faltered, 'President Haight ordered me as my holy duty to inspire the Indians to that attack. He said the emigrants must be used up to save the Church...'

The silence closed in once more and Erastus was alone with his pain and his conscience.

He seemed to see the bell-post outside the driveway to John D.'s place at Harmony. He seemed to hear the bell ringing as it was always rung for dinner, and John D.'s blanket invitation to all within sound of that bell. An invitation taken advantage of even by the men who hunted him.

He seemed to see the fallen cairn and to hear the ghostly screams.

A certain Great Man pausing before the fallen cedar cross. 'Vengeance is Mine...' read the Great Man in his deliberate way, and then he added grimly, 'and I have had a little!'

Erastus tossed.

'Hard-gutted,' he muttered, 'for the common good. A man's got to be hard-gutted....'

But when the time came for him to leave, and David Wight and Abijah MacIntyre carried him out of the house in Pine Valley where he'd been for a week, out to a wagon loaded with straw and hot bricks and quilts, his voice was steady enough telling John D. good-bye, his hand steady enough shaking John D.'s hand.

'Good-bye, Brother Lee,' he said, hardening his heart against the appeal in the other man's eyes. 'Good-bye — and thank you. Ptsahh!'

David and Abijah brought him news. The pile dam had gone out in a flood that washed down the Virgin one night when every star shone in the sky. You could hear the river roar clear up in the town. They were afraid they couldn't get water out on the land in time for the crops...

'Hard-gutted,' said Erastus.

He was glad for the fine spring rain that covered up the tears on his cheeks. And his tears were not for the dam.

6

NOTICE!!

August 25, 1865

Mass-meeting to find out the amount of breadstuffs on hand in the City and to adopt some means of procuring more

Unexpectedly giddy from the potato smell that still clung to the dim interior of the T.O., Clory put the two earrings that had been her mother's down upon the counter. She looked up anxiously at the clerk — one of the Wheelock boys, since Johnny Lowgie had resigned to go on his mission.

Kissy clung tightly to her mother's hand. Feeling the tenseness in the little body, Clory smiled reassuringly down at her.

'No'm,' said the boy regretfully, handing the earrings back to her, 'it's still the same as I told you before; President Snow says we ain't to part with food even for money.'

Kissy tugged at her hand.

'Mamma, there's the honey-barrel!'

The boy shook his head at Clory's mute question.

'There ain't been any honey in it since last summer.'

'But why?' asked Kissy as they went out into the hot sunlight. 'Why ain't there any honey, Mamma?'

Clory stood a moment on the sidewalk, reluctantly screwing the earrings on again, staring absently at Pal's house across the street and the cottonwood sapling with its shriveled leaves. Yesterday she had walked the five scorching miles to Santa Clara to trade her earrings for a milk pan of flour, only to find that there was only one sack in the whole town.

Kissy began to whimper and diddle up and down with the burning of the sand through her thin moccasins.

'Come on, lamb,' said Clory. 'We'll hurry — it's cooler in the dugout.'

It was so hard to hurry with this all-gone feeling in the pit of one's stomach. Neither pigweed greens nor sego-root-and-rabbit stew seemed to satisfy when one was in the family way. All the old cravings were upon her. She was ashamed of herself, the way she sneaked over to the 'dobe stack where 'Sheba's house waited to be finished, and gorged herself on 'dobe dirt after the Sibley tent was dark; the way she broke off furtive bits of the twins' old school slates.

'Why,' asked Kissy out of her own small perplexities, 'why does Aunt 'Sheba keep her flour tied up to the rafters?'

'Because,' Clory made her voice gay, 'Aunt 'Sheba's big boys are not as good to mind as Mamma's lamb. They'd get into the flour and eat it raw, and then where would Papa's dough-gods be!' And, thought Clory, Kissy's just as well off without 'Sheba's flour — ground broom-corn seed looking more like the remains of sagebrush chewed between horse-teeth than human food. 'If we can't eat our seeds one way, we'll eat 'em another,' said Abijah, burned and bitter from the summer's endless repairing of ditches, and so there had been bread made from cane seed and flax seed and cotton seed.

'But why,' Kissy persisted, 'why did Patience-Elizabeth's mamma say she had so much to be thankful for when the cow died?'

Why, indeed? How explain the resistance of the spirit that could look at your children's tears of hunger ... The Eardley young-ones last night watching Kissy eat her greens-and-bacon grease. One child snatching a bacon-rind, scared eyes filling with tears over his sin, but his craving greater than his conscience. Clory couldn't bear it any longer and shooed them home ... At first there had been carrots ... carrots until Clory gagged, but Kissy munched them all day long. Now there were thistle roots and the scrawny bones of quail and blackbirds and chipmunks. Lon and Betsy Tuckett had had nothing but milk for six weeks — they'd let a portion thicken, mix with new milk, and eat it as if it were bread. Eliza and Charles Hichinoper had lived on beets for a whole month — they with a new baby. Lars Hansen's second wife had a new baby, too, and they had nothing but bran.

Kissy trotted along obediently, but her voice was wistful.

'Won't we *ever*,' she asked, 'Mamma, won't we *ever* have bread 'n' molasses again?'

'Why, of course, lamb, but right now we're going home to a nice supper of yant baked in the ashes ——'

'But I don't like squaw cabbage!' Kissy bawled, and just then spied something in the thick dust. She stooped down and scooped up her prize, eyes gloating, darting about to see if there were other claimants, her chapped mouth watering with delight. She opened her palm to her mother and danced up and down. It was surely the biggest kernel of corn Clory had ever seen.

Hunger was easy to bear for oneself. But that night when she had tucked in Kissy's scrawny little body, she walked across to the Sibley tent and stood irresolutely in the doorway. Willie, hobbling from crane to table with a dishtowel over her shoulder, threw her an anxious smile. 'Sheba was combing Isaiah's hair for lice. Always at sight of that fractious tow-shock Clory's heart squeezed. Long after one could no longer trace the outlines of a loved face in memory, the pain remained, buried but present, like a scabbed-over wound. But 'Sheba mistook the change in her expression.

'Just wait until *Kissy* goes to school!' she snorted, ducking Isaiah's head in the wash-basin. 'He's had 'em ever since last winter!'

She lathered vigorously and Isaiah squirmed and howled. He was big for seven years, brown and wiry and wild as an Indian, always shooting 'chinies' with the Peabody boys in the dooryard during Kissy's afternoon nap. ('Putcha on a pix!' — 'You fudged!' — 'I never!')

'Aw, Ma,' he yelled, pawing at his eyes, 'you got soap ——'

'Quit your faunchin' around, then!' shrilled 'Sheba, clouting him over the ear. 'This means a clean pair of overalls tomorrow. I declare' — she raised her eyes to Clory — 'Wait until you have to rub in red precipitate until you git all the skin off your hands, and your pillows all daubed up the next mornin' — after I git him dry I've got to spend an hour combin' out the carcasses! ... Well, come in! Come in! What y'u gawpin' out there for?'

Abijah, drinking Brigham tea as he always did when he felt low in the mind, lifted his eyes from his ledger to nod Clory a

perfunctory welcome. The summer had put gray in Abijah's
beard. His forehead and the back of his neck above the collarless
hickory shirt were burned red — his white skin had never been
the kind to tan. More than food for his belly did he miss the
browned flour for his big, well-shaped hands. The knuckles bent
above the quill pen were rough and leathery, the nails cracked —
more of a trial to him, Clory guessed, than the fact that he could
not get his boys to wear their vests these days. Writing, he
growled and slapped at the flies, gnats, and moths that circled
and buzzed around the candle flame.

Clory sat down in the little rocker near the door and fanned
herself with a rabbit-brush branch.

'What can we do? I — there's Kissy, and the new baby comin'!'

'Sheba pursed shocked lips above the bent head she pummeled.
'I-sai-ah' she mouthed. Clory shrugged irritably. A little plain
talk wouldn't hurt Isaiah. If 'Sheba knew what her precious
boys talked about behind barns!

'I don't know why you're such a fuss-budget,' 'Sheba said.
'You've had rabbit stew, and it's real strengthenin', too. You
don't need to wet your pants waitin' for the little flour I got,
because I ain't a-goin' to divide!'

Abijah looked up and bushed his brows.

'Does no gude to threap on it, Clorinda Agatha. As lang as
we don't gae daft aboot it, we're all richt. Some folks, now...
Aye, a mon shows what he is, times like these. That Sister Miles
is in a dreadfu' state, puir body...'

Another woman, losing so many children, going funny in the
same way as Eliza Hichinoper. Affectionate, romantic, sweet
women... Young Miles and his fiddle were in great demand; he
was handsome, often out at night, and his wife alone with the
hunger of the children and the crying of the coyotes, loving him
madly, constantly fighting the fear that he would take another
wife... But Young Miles, goaded by the accusing silences of his
wife, who never would adjust to a sagebrush country, tormented

by the complaints of his youngsters whom he could not feed, did not call on plurality to relieve his feelings — he whipped his children, instead.

'Ech, no gude to make a to-do,' repeated Abijah. 'The Lord won't let us starve.'

'Sheba, searching the scalp of a chastened and blubbering Isaiah, nodded virtuously.

'Besides,' continued Abijah, 'there's the meeting tomorrow — Apostle Snow ——'

'Oh, darn Apostle Snow!' burst Clory. 'I want *bread* — milk for my baby!'

Abijah twisted to glare at her, his chair scraping along the floor.

'I'll not have ye speerin' sic things o' the authorities!'

Where would they be without Brother Snow, he'd like to know! Held them all up this summer, he did — starting off the mule-races Fourth of July and him still on his crutches, pulling down a mule's ear to whisper, and bunting him in the rear to get him to race — life of the party, he was! Ech, they like to split their britches laughing! — Seemed like a man's wives needed counselling all the time . . .

There, I've messed things again, thought Clory miserably, as she and Willie went out into the airless night.

Abijah turned back to his ledger greatly refreshed. '" . . . that you can go and come back without swearing, Lon Tuckett?" He looked at me askance and said: "By Gorry, I don't know. This nigh horse is such a God damn balky fool I expect I shall swear some" . . .'

7

Erastus leaned his cane against the table, parted his coat-tails, sat down, humoring his bad leg, and watched the people drift in. He hoped all the heads of families came. They had never faced just this kind of emergency before. He already had all the names listed on the paper before him — 'Names' in the first column, 'No. in family' in the second, 'Amt. on hand' in the third, 'Articles to trade' in the fourth.

It was amazing how quickly those columns filled up. When the meeting was over Erastus sat alone on the stage of the Social Hall and stared at the new marbled wallpaper they'd put up in the heady enthusiasm of the spring.

Abijah MacIntyre. No. in family: 11. *Amt. on hand:* 10 lbs. *Articles to trade:* 3 ox, 1 mare (this very reluctantly, but he'd have to give up Nellie, decided Erastus, no matter what memories — the oxen weren't worth much. Abijah might hate it, but he'd tell the truth.)

Zadoc Hunt. No. in family: 8. *Amt. on hand:* 100 lbs. (He lies, thought Erastus. He's got some on hand — people say he takes his wheat to Washington in the night to have it ground so he won't have to divide!) *Articles to trade:* Saddle. (Another lie!)

Hannah Merinda Lowgie. No. in family: 7. *Amt. on hand:* None. *Articles to trade:* Coat; destitute.

Stiddy Weeks. No. in family: 6. *Amt. on hand:* None. *Articles to Trade:* Herbs.

David Wight. No. in family: 5. *Amt. on hand:* 50 lbs. *Articles to trade:* 4 sheep. (David would be honest, too.)

Ole Oleson. No. in family: 14. *Amt. on hand:* 4 lbs. *Articles to trade:* Two-year-old steer. (Being water-master is pretty poor pickings!)

Zebedee Trupp. No. in family: 4. (What! no children yet, Zebedee?) *Amt. on hand:* None. *Articles to trade:* Housecat.

Benjamin Jarvis. No. in family: 4. *Amt. on hand:* 4 lbs. *Articles to trade:* New issue of *Cactus.*

Ken Miles. No. in family: 7. (Your wife's buried five.) *Amt. on hand:* None. *Articles to trade:* Violin.

Shadrach Gaunt. No. in family: 4 (another coming up). *Amt. on hand:* 100 lbs. *Articles to trade:* Pistol. ('Why don't they eat Paiute biscuits?' you asked, but only a true mountain man could digest the staff of Paiute virility — squawberries, bullberries, sandgrass seed, sunflower seed, sprinkling of coarse corn meal

ground and baked two hours into reddish-brown cakes so hard
they would stun a rabbit at forty paces!)

*Orson Pratt, Jr. No. in family: 7. Amt. on hand: None. Articles
to trade: None.* ('You starve my kids,' you shouted, 'just because
I don't believe in Joseph Smith, but you keep a child-beater in
full fellowship! Go on, keep your damned wheat, I won't touch
it!'... Ptsahh, you're a crazy mut, Orson. Your lack of horse
sense is about as prominent as your Adam's apple, and you
always did have the biggest Adam's apple in the country!)

Erastus Snow. No. in famiiy: 33. Amt. on hand: 2500 lbs. (And
I'd better keep it on hand, too, in case we go on quarter rations....

There were seven families completely destitute and a great
many half-destitute. Men like Wheelock with thirty-five in the
family and only a hundred pounds of foodstuffs on hand, and
nothing to trade but the skill of his baton ...

Totaling the 'Amt. on hand' Erastus found a sum of 25¾
pounds per capita to last the winter until the next harvest. Of
course, there would be what the 'Articles to trade' brought back,
and possible help from Brother Brigham. But a mission should be
self-supporting. Erastus shook his head over that, as he did over
men like Zadoc Hunt who'd see a man starve before he'd divide.
Brother Brigham might bring help in September when he came
to dedicate the cotton factory. Meanwhile, Erastus had offered
to advance three hundred pounds of flour and some potatoes to
those most needy, and charge it against an account of livestock
put in by them. Livestock or public work. Danged if he'd give
any man charity! And Shadrach Gaunt and David Wight had
been appointed to take the articles to trade to northern settlements ... 'Elders to be allowed a reasonable compensation for
their service,' Erastus wrote at the bottom of the page.

8

'Shadrach Gaunt ain't a-gonna trade off *my* stock,' Abijah
had growled. If it must be done, he'd do it himself.

Even on the morning when he drove out of the corral gates, Clory didn't think he'd made up his mind. But he had the spare ox tied to the end-gate of the wagon and beside him Nellie — Nellie with her pride and her gallantry! His one good team of bulls pulled the wagon, the gaunt ridges of their hips swaying patiently. Clory held Kissy and sat firmly on the wagon seat, afraid that she would wake up and find the whole trip a dream.

She still didn't know how Abijah had come to let her go, but Willie couldn't, and 'Sheba had said the four days to Cedar Fort, with the sand and the heat — well ... So here was Clory, the very spit-'n-image of a proper wife, riding out beside her husband on an early morning. Of course, some folks might say the old red sunbonnet, limp enough in its own right, looked seedy with the yellow dress, but slatted sunbonnets were hard to get, and Clory could find no fault with anything. Not even with having to sit four days in hoops, which was the only way she could keep her figure from showing. Seemed like some women were just fattened up at five months, but she always got as big as the law allowed.

Kissy sat primly like a good little miss, her hands in her lap.

Wide eyes full of fancy beneath the pushed-back bonnet, her face looked like a flower. A very elfin flower with puckish tendencies. There were intriguing sprites behind all the brush. She lured them with little cozening songs that bloomed in her mind like puff-balls. Aunt 'Sheba had said this morning she was to mind her P's and Q's, but it made about as much sense as Mamma singing about the 'rabbit skin to wrap the baby bunting in,' when Kissy knew that if they ever got a rabbit they'd probably eat it, skin and all. But then, Mamma was always singing about 'Count your blessings,' too, and Kissy knew there weren't any blessings. Aunt 'Sheba said so. Not that Aunt 'Sheba told the truth, either. There was the day she got in the water-ditch and Aunt 'Sheba scolded Mamma about having 'time on your hands.'

Kissy had looked and looked but there wasn't anything there but a few blisters.

But the sprites under the bushes were real, and trying not to be a Trial like Isaiah, and the White Knight. The White Knight was really Uncle Free, who would come riding back some day from out of the bush where he had inexplicably gone, and she would love him with both arms and he would shine in the sun like the back of a lizard. Although she couldn't tell Papa because he bushed up like a porcupine, and she couldn't tell Mamma because the Look would come into her eyes, and Kissy's horizons trembled when Mamma got the Look.

'I'll be a lizard for Jesus,' sang Kissy tunelessly, 'and shine for Him each day ——'

'Oh, naughty,' said Mamma, and Papa frowned. Kissy couldn't see why, and lifted her wondering gaze, so like a fresh edition of Abijah's own. Of course the real song said a sunbeam, but it was just as easy to be a lizard as a sunbeam. And then Papa smiled and reached down to pat her head. 'She croods like a pigeon,' he said. That meant he was in a good humor, and the small icicle in Kissy's heart melted and ran out in little flashes of her hands in the sunlight, little aimless hummings.

Dry brush crumbled to powder under the wheels, sparrows drooped their heads under the mesquite trees, and the hills seemed to pale and shrink with the mounting heat. But it was a wonderful day. Clory began to sing.

My ain fireside, my ain fireside!

Abijah's rumble joined her, and when they had finished, his eyes were almost affectionate.

'I think,' he said, 'I can trade Old Pete, back there, for flour, and the mare' — he flinched — 'the mare for a good milch cow.'

He never would have believed he'd come to the trading of Nellie, but bygones were bygones, and a servant of the Lord had no time for regrets. If Free were only here today, he wouldn't

be making the trip. But none of the other boys had Free's de·
pendability. Abijah sighed, seeing the dead, as people will,
through an iridescent film. He missed Free with the nameless
throbbing of a severed limb, but life had to go on.

They stayed in Harrisburg that night and Abijah filled up all
the water-barrels. He had a barrel chained to the projecting cleats
on each side of the wagon and one tied on the back, and a gunny-
sack-wrapped canteen they carried in the front. 'Sheba had
finally parted with some of her flour, and the dark, coarse cakes,
together with what was left of the salt pork, Clory had packed in
the grub-box. The good bishop and his wives in Harrisburg gave
them a supper of beans and clabber which Abijah pronounced a
sumptuous repast, and they started on the next day, fortified, but
discommoded, as Abijah said, because of the unwonted fullness
in the stomach.

Abijah could not resist the comfort of a good meal, the release
from pressure, Clory's constant nearness, her determination to
please, and, with the stimulation of change, the flashing into life
of her old gay spirit; he thawed visibly and began to talk of little
things, odds and ends of gossip. It seemed good to hear his laugh
again. With the passing of the long, slow miles they drew together as they had not done for more than a year.

Impossible in this country for two people to travel long with
the unease of tension between them. Silences so vast, crowding
the edges of the world, that a man could not endure them and
resist human pressure, too. The trail lost itself in the red im-
mensities ahead, and there was only the sound of the oxen's
hooves sighing in and sucking out of the sand.

The country eased for a time into a vast plain. There were
glints of orange mountain behind the neutral ranges paralleling
the plain, and scattered flecks of orange in the dirt, but ahead of
them the parched earth with its squat gray brush ran on like a
dun-colored river.

Kissy slept, and Clory let herself sink into the timelessness.
Abijah's head nodded on his chest.

In the afternoon he halted the oxen to water them. It had to be done twice a day under that angry sun. He stood up in the wagon, stretching himself, and narrowed his eyes against a moving black speck in the distance. He tensed for a moment and peered. It might be anything, although it was unlikely an animal would be abroad in such heat. He did not like to think it might be an Indian.

After the wagon jolted on again they gained on the figure slowly. Presently he knew it for a man, but an hour had passed before he knew it for a white man. And then Clory recognized the shirt the man was wearing. Bed-curtain cloth with large red roses and blue birds flying among them. Traded from a California emigrant for garden stuff. It was Orson Pratt, Junior, and he was certainly under the influence of liquor. Abijah was puzzled, watching that figure, with its ridiculous shirt, stumble from side to side along the road. He had never known him for a tippler of wine.

When they neared Orson, he stood at the side of the road and silently watched them come.

'Whoa!' Abijah stopped the team.

'Where ye gaeing, Brother?'

Unsmiling, Orson gestured south along the road.

Abijah studied him a moment.

'Well, get in and spell yourself off,' he said, moving nearer Clory.

Orson put his foot (barefooted in that hot sand!) on the hub of the wheel and climbed in beside Abijah. Close up, Clory could see he was not drunk. He looked sick. His craggy face was pale beneath the tan, the furrows from his brow to his chin were deep as scars, even his brown beard was threadbare. His neck was stringy and blue with stubble. He swung the canteen from his shoulder and dumped it and the sack he was carrying on the floor, and sat hunched over, trembling, his hands hanging between his knees.

Abijah silently handed him his own canteen and Orson took a long, shuddering pull of the fresh water. Abijah waited a moment and reached behind in the grub-box for one of the cakes. Orson stared at it on Abijah's outstretched palm. 'Thanks,' he muttered, and began to eat it slowly.

'I been grabbling potatoes in Cedar Fort,' he said, chewing; 'fifteen cents apiece for spuds no bigger'n a hen's egg. My God, Brother Mac, my kids are starving! I seen their empty bellies swell!'

His mouth twisted suddenly and his Adam's apple shot upward. Kissy on her mother's lap stared in fascination.

'But I won't take any help from Erastus Snow! I'll die first!' His bloodshot eyes narrowed fiercely. 'You people don't care if a man rolls in a manure pile as long as he's one of you!'

Clory, her heart going out to him, held her breath for fear Abijah's temper would lash out. But Abijah merely sat and stared thoughtfully.

When Orson went to go, Abijah filled his canteen with fresh water, gave him the gunny sack from his own canteen to wrap his feet in, divided the cakes with him.

As they drove on, Abijah still did not speak, but there was perplexity in the sunken fires of his eyes.

'Ech,' he said deep in his chest, 'life's an ugsome circle. A mon hates ye, and ye hate the next mon because the first one hated ye...'

Clory did not believe her own ears. Could Abijah be growing old, that he would admit a doubt of himself or his place in the universe?

But it was on the trip home that the incident occurred which thinned all barriers between them. They were coming down the dugway into Washington, and suddenly there in the dust between the two oxen was a hairy tarantula as big as Abijah's spread hand. The off ox lurched, the bank crumbled, and the wagon tipped.

The nigh ox was the first to scramble to its feet, and then the other got up, bawling and pawing sand. By the time Abijah had crawled from under the wagon even the milch cow tied to the back was getting her legs under her again.

Abijah untied her, but he had no eyes for the animals. He looked wildly up and down the roadway, and then heaved at the wagon himself. With the four wheels sticking in the air it looked like an up-ended turtle. There was not a sound from underneath. He groaned, dashed away the blood from his cut cheek, and went at it again. He boosted it, supported it there, and called hoarsely to Clory. When she finally answered, the breath went out of him. 'Thank God,' he muttered, as she crawled from under, dazed, her dress torn and dusty, a bruise over her right temple and her hair loosened, but unharmed. She went at the lifting with Abijah, putting her strength into it. The wagon turned slowly over on its side.

Kissy lay where she had fallen, white as a dead child. The deep sand had cushioned the fall and saved the rest of them, but Clory doubted for a dreadful instant that anything could save Kissy. And then she was down in the sand beside her, forcing her own breath between the blue lips, rushing to the barrels spilling their water in maroon puddles, wetting her handkerchief, mopping the child's forehead.

But Abijah was like a madman. 'Help me, Mother,' he said, holding the child up, putting his ear against her chest, fanning her face. Not until after did Clory remember he had called her 'Mother.' 'I haven't any oil,' he said, 'but ——' He had always prayed as if God were there beside him, but now, placing his hands upon Kissy's head, he pleaded with such desperate eloquence that Clory leaned to kiss the horny knuckles. At that moment, with the blood of his wound, the dust of the accident, the sweat of his terror still upon him, stripping him of overlaid emotions, stripping him to the core, she loved him. All her life there would be instants, lost in memory, when the authentic passion for Free returned, when the glow, the warmth, even a breath of the old rapture brushed her and was gone like the falling of a leaf. But she could live with Abijah. She knew it now. She saw beneath the shell, and with what she saw, she could fashion a life. Even in the agony of suspense, even watching the stillness of that little body she adored beyond hope of heaven, something within her rose and sang.

Abijah stopped speaking; the sun poured down; a column of red ants portaged across one of the maroon water gullies. They waited. And then there was the flutter of movement in the throat. They waited, and Kissy opened her eyes and began to cry.

'Ech!' said Abijah, and blew his nose. It was a sacrament. The look he gave Clory absolved her of Free's death, even of the moment in Cedar Fort when he had given Nellie over to alien hands.

He talked feverishly on the way home, as if to make up for the months of neglect. Striding beside the near ox's head, he talked over his shoulder at Clory, asking questions, answering them himself, his big body vibrating with its own especial charm.

'I'll get wor-rk on the Tabernacle,' he promised. 'I'll start your house richt away. That ox was in its prime and I made a gude trade for it — couple hundredweight of flour and potatoes ain't so bad — and with the Jersey heifer Nellie brought ... Besides, when Brother Brigham comes things'll be better, you'll see.'

Brother Brigham, shrewd tactician that he was, met complaint with complaint. The Great Tabernacle was sheltering its first conference, and even with the larger space, crowds of visitors from as far north as Cedar Fort overflowed into the debris of the grounds.

> The basement now is laid, boys,
> We'll have a little fun.
> We've labored long and faithful
> Under the boiling sun ...

sang the Ladies' Chorus in David Wight's new song.

But Brother Brigham stared from the dirt floor at his feet and the rough boards hastily stretched across rocks for benches to the improvised willow roof that would someday be a main floor above his head, and jawed his people for grumbling in the midst of such blessings.

'I want you to speed this building up!' he said. 'What if the dam is out? Can't you put it back again? I promise, you'll look back and long for the peace of poverty, when the day comes for you to be tried with riches. . . .'

But with all the Leader's scoldings, Abijah remained unruffled. At dinner he regarded his three wives: 'Sheba, smacking her lips over her plate, Willie, gaunt and homely, bending over the crane, Clory, pouring him out his Brigham tea —— . . . Ech, she had always had a hand with Brigham Tea. Willie now . . . he turned from Willie with a faint sting of aversion. Always having miscarriages. A shilpit wife who made a shilpit drink. But Clory, still round with her pregnancy in spite of the accident — Clory, with her pretty gestures and yet with her gaiety subdued as became a wife in Israel — his eyes crinkled over the cup. Ech, he had made a proper pattern of a wife out of her, after all!

9

Clory supposed it was wrong of her to be so proud of her children that November morning in 1868 when she waited in the square with the townspeople to bid Abijah good-bye. But Kissy was such a little lady — six years old this fall and already a better hand with the baby than a grown-up. John himself, who was still babyish for going-on-three, clung quietly to Clory's hand, not bucking and squealing as he usually did. But 'Sheba's young ones! There went Isaiah, wild as a Navajo, riding a stick-horse through the brush of the square and back through the crowd, bunting people, kicking up dust with his feet and echoes with his mouth, while the twins, delighted at the opportunity, chased madly after him — 'Ma wants you! Ma wants you!' 'Sheba, her high-bosomed, tightly laced big figure still in old-fashioned full hoops, gasped and panted in the wake of her brood.

Clory was very proud of her own slim self (quite a feat to boast an eighteen-inch waist when you were twenty-four and had two children!) in the new pink calico with the draped skirt and real horsehair dress-improver. Abijah had even let her make the dress with a ribbon-edged peplum and a plaid ribbon at the neck to fasten with her cameo. There had been enough left over for Kissy to have a dress and pigtail bows out of the same material. Clory looked fondly down at the child, pantalettes ruffling on eager legs, clinging tightly to her mother's hand, drinking in the color and flash of the spectacle. Recently silver had been discovered in Pioche, Nevada, and a town had mushroomed overnight; here Clory had sold the pigweed greens — seventy-five cents for fifteen bunches — she and Kissy had gathered all spring, for the money to buy the bolt of calico from the factory.

Willie was the only human Clory had ever known who didn't seem to care for clothes. Where was Willie? Oh, yes — over there talking to Sister Joe Eardley and the Ferrano woman, as usual. Since Willie's rheumatics seemed to get so much worse every year, she could not do extra work to earn money, and rather than ask Abijah, she had stripped the ticking from her feather bed, re-covered it with the canvas of an old wagon cover, and made herself a dress out of the ticking. 'It covers me up,' said Willie absently; she would always be absent — probably go on asking, 'Do you want me tonight, Brother Mac?' even after he was in Scotland.

'Oh, Mamma —!' Kissy pointed. Her face beneath its sun-bonnet, hazel eyes long with dream, had an elfish fantasy.

Here came the bands. Staheli's Silver Band from Santa Clara, instruments flashing in the sun, the upthrust horns and clarinets and hautboys in the wagon box spangling the air like the music they made.

Next came the martial band, rootling and tootling, the sound
it made as solid as a drum.

The two bands drove on past the crowd, circled the square, and
came to rest in front of the Tabernacle.

The door opened and here came Abijah and Apostle Snow,
their talk finished. Clory could tell by the way Abijah's hand
lingered on Apostle Snow's shoulder how greatly moved he was.
Abijah was looking splendid, his beard and hair glinting copper,
his eyes dark with gusto and affection.

Suddenly the jostling feet quieted.

'My brethren,' began Abijah in his golden burr, 'it is with joy
and yet sadness that I part with ye all to do our Father's work.
A year ago in October Brother Brigham gave me the Call, when
I went up to attend conference and the dedication of the New
Tabernacle and pipe organ. Since then I hae studied ever-ry day
wi' bowed head. It is quite a thing to leave one's wives rustling
their own bannocks for two or three years, in times like these,
although my wives are gude women and have urged me to go. It
is also quite a thing to ken if I am worthy to preach the Gospel
in a foreign land. But finally the Spirit prompted, Go, and I . . .'

Clory was glad that she would still be young enough when
Abijah got back to have more children. In her secret heart she
was glad, not only because of the children, but because it would
make 'Sheba green-eyed. She couldn't say she was exactly Abijah's favorite wife, but still he brought her a nicer present from
Salt Lake that trip than he did 'Sheba. Of course the present
wasn't his exactly, since her mother had sent it as far as Salt
Lake, but Abijah needn't have brought it on down. Clory fingered the fringe on the edge of the shawl about her shoulders. In
the whole Dixie mission there was no finer Paisley shawl, the
fringe at the point of the triangle reaching almost to the hem of
her dress. No letter with the gift, as usual — just the shawl, like
the slippers, appearing out of nowhere, linking her with a long-
dead past, speaking to her with strange tongues of a love she had

never known. Her thoughts reached toward it delicately, won-
deringly, but she brought them back to Abijah. The circle comb
that anchored the drawn, silken strands of Kissy's hair was his
own present. And 'Sheba had got only fourteen ounces of mustard
and a few pepper corns. If only now she could get a string of real
gold beads for Kissy — not the amber kind that everyone wore,
but . . .

Abijah finished speaking and Clory listened critically. Yes, he
got more spats than most departing missionaries. Apostle Snow
prayed, and then it was time for Abijah to leave. He reached
inside the Tabernacle door for his carpetbag, and gave a last
glance up at the tapering red-rock tower within its timbered
sheath as if to remind himself that the Great Tabernacle would
be finished when he came home. The crowd began to break up
and move slowly to the sidewalk. 'Sheba and Willie were standing up at the front, near him, and Clory watched him kiss first
'Sheba and then Willie. She was glad she had stayed at the edge
of the crowd. She couldn't have borne to be third on the list before all those people. Abijah's eyes searched among the people,
lighted when he found her, and then he was threading his way
toward her.

'Ech,' he said, putting down his carpetbag and reaching for the
baby, 'the bairn-team — the thoct o' leaving them . . .' His voice
trembled.

He scooped up Kissy in the other arm and held them closely.
Kissy was a little frightened at the sudden nearness of his dark
bush, but John squealed and played with his beard.

'Take gude care o' them, Clor-rinda,' he said, kissing them both
and giving them back.

Eyes crinkling with tenderness, he enveloped her in a fierce
hug.

'Good-bye, lass.' His lips were hard on her own, his whiskers
pricking her face. One more second of love for Kissy, his especial
darling; he stooped to her, searching the golden depths of her eyes

for some assurance that she would not forget him; her little arms strained about his neck, and then he was gone, striding across the water-ditch to the mail-coach where the Peabody boy heckled his mules from the high seat like a professional skinner.

Suddenly some nameless fear clutched at Clory.

'Wait!' she called, oblivious of stares. 'Wait!' Grabbing up John, Kissy at her skirts, fleeing to Abijah on the sidewalk, she gazed up at him, her eyes smoky with feeling.

'Let us ride a block with you,' she begged. 'There's room!'

Abijah stared at her, grinned, glanced up at the driver on the seat, and shrugged.

Behind the mules prancing beyond the square, up to the Tabernacle corner and out the road that led to all the shining vistas she would never know, Clory felt like a princess. The pastel mountains behind the eastern Black Ridge swam in a dusky haze like the bloom on the grapes that had finally consented to grow over 'Sheba's wash-arbor. But somewhere out there a dust-devil spiraled like a sudden warning ...

10

Hurrah, hurrah, the Railroad's begun —
Three cheers for the contractor; his name's Brigham Young!

Clory sang, stirring the cows'-feet in the large brass kettle, poking the mess about with her stick, turning her head from the fumes of the glue. She would have her third baby next month, in June (how surprised Abijah would be!) and although the glue-making was growing more nauseating, it still brought good money. For missionaries' wives must support themselves. It had taken every shred of last year's crop, his mule-harness, and every cent he had saved to get Abijah off, for of course a missionary traveled without purse or scrip. All he had was his 'Letter of commendation: We, the undersigned, by the authority of the Church of Jesus Christ of Latter-Day Saints, recommend this our worthy brother and Elder, Abijah MacIntyre, to the fellowship of all Christians'; this, and his memorized introduction — as some irreverent wag garbled it, 'I am a Mission Mormonary without Body, Parts, or Passions!'

In his father's absence, Joseph worked as apprentice-mason on the Tabernacle, but of course the T.O. pay he received went to 'Sheba, who had herself put on the sheathing and shingled her two-room-and-lean-to 'dobe house, and moved in. She put the boys in the bedroom (thus blasting Willie's hopes), and in return they handed over to her every profit made in the fields or the lot.

Still, Clory and Willie hadn't done so badly — they had raised enough lettuce and radishes to peddle the surplus in Pioche, and next month there would be tomatoes to dry by the dozen. Tomatoes and peaches and plums, and squash to put down in molasses. Their homemade soap always sold well, and the beeswax they got from Lars Hansen was needed for the waxed threads useful in rug-, glove-, carpet-making. Almost every day Kissy carried a can of glue or a batch of soap or a cake of wax to the T.O. to trade for groceries. And then there were the combs — Lars Hansen had shown Clory how to make combs from the horns of cattle, and these Kissy traded all around the neighborhood for clabber. The only drawback to such work, thought Clory, was what it did to one's hands. She sighed, looking at the cracked knuckles grasping the stick, the scuffed red skin, the blisters, the gnarled joints. Still, with a new child to greet him, Abijah probably wouldn't notice hands.

Since leaving, he had written to his wives twice, both letters, as was proper, addressed to his first wife. But it seemed to Clory and Willie, hungrily waiting their turns at the letters, watching 'Sheba slowly turn the pages, that his first wife took an unconscionable time reading them. And it was only right, she said, that his boys have first chance after her.

When finally, after a week or more, Clory and Willie actually got their hands on the precious foolscap, they would shut themselves up in the dugout, Kissy's big eyes upon them, and pore over every word.

Abijah wrote once while still upon the plains, and sent his letter back with the P.E. emigrants at Florence, Nebraska.

> ... The more we travel together the more of the spirit of God rests down upon us, for He caused the Lamanites to follow us and give us good fat animals for our wore-out ones, and I can truly say that we feel to thank Him that we are counted worthy to be called on to go to the nations of the earth to bear our testimony — I rejoice that I heeded President Brigham's injunction to bring my Temple clothing with me, for it will ward off evil ...
>
> We have met once in a den of Methodists where I had much freedom of utterance, and once among some spiritual rappers who had not the power to perform while the Saints of the Lord were present.
>
> The Prophet has 'knocked out for himself a window in the wall of the nineteenth century,' and the Lord is knocking at the doors of the hearts of all men, and if they will only leave the latch-string outside, He will come in and bring peace to their souls. Indeed, I have already felt many times a foretaste of the millennium.

With this letter he sent home three vest patterns for his boys, and thirteen yards of muslin delaine — which 'Sheba will never divide,' said Willie, remembering Clory's longing eyes when the cloth was spread out; 'she'll make it up into shirts for her boys, first!'

The next letter was from Newcastle, on Abijah's way to Scotland, and it was concerned mainly with his voyage.

> The ship sprung a leak. It was loaded with wheat, and the water swelled the wheat, which got into the pipes and choked them. The carpenters dove to find the leak but could not.

The Presbyterian minister wrung his hands and cried, 'Mr. MacIntyre, what sort of comfort does Mormonism give you in times like these?' 'Every comfort in the world,' I replied, and I got the sailors to heat a heavy iron and run it down the pipes so the wheat could move and the pumps work. I started them singing the old songs we love so well, and we sang and we pumped, and we pumped and we sang, and here I am, hale and hearty, at an L.D.S. Camp meeting on Newcastle Green, exhorting a thousand people with my usual Freedom.

My Scotch blood loves the dialect here on the borders — the people talk with the Cumberland twang. The Spirit of the Gathering seems to be uppermost in their hearts over here, but I do not like the injunction of the authorities not to preach about Plurality, as the people want to know of it. I am full of light and testimony . . .

Abijah sent his love to his family, mentioning each child, and dividing himself meticulously among his three wives.

''Sheba would like to hog even our share of that,' said Willie.

But Clory smiled at Kissy and wondered how she could teach her to spell so that her father would be proud of her when he came home. She could not afford the tent-school Sister Couzzens had started up in the ward. And there were other things besides spelling. There were the things all the debating groups last winter had made her think about: education, beauty, c-culture — she groped for the words. Aunt Ket Snow had a new melodeon and her oldest girl had gone to the City to learn to play it. When she came back, Clory must find some way for Kissy to take lessons.

'Mamma,' said Kissy, staring out the window, her pointed chin on her brown fists, her eyes upon the twilight, 'what's a testimony?'

'Why — why — uh, it's knowing the Lord loves you . . .'

'But *how* do I know it, Mamma? I can't see Him.'

She turned great wondering eyes upon her mother, and Willie, covering her mouth to hide a smile, hobbled out to bed.

Clory, tucking Kissy in beside John, trying to find words for those rare moments when limitations thinned and the great Smile beckoned, trying to give her child the warmth of the love that rose up in her throat like tears, sometimes hated the Gospel that shut her children out from the gay things of life, shut them in with ignorance, poverty, and danger...

She moved the candle closer, dipped her pen and wrote:

Dear Companion:

Having a few retired moments this evening whilst all is hushed and still except our city guard, I improve same in writing to you. I feel lonely, therefore I prefer a lonely time to write to you. My family is all well, for which I feel to thank the Lord. I trust you are alive and well.

Great sorrow and trouble awaits us here as a people. All northern settlements are now ordered into forts. The President is now going into measures to wall in the City, and down here if the grasshoppers come again we may have to go on rations. I am doing well with my glue-making, but how do you think I feel with two children and Willie not able to help and not a man person about the house? We are counseled to keep our doors and windows well fastened in the nights and our guns well loaded by our bedside. Those that does not experience the like cannot tell my feelings, that is sure. My children is all my trouble at present. Property and riches in this life is nothing to me, for I find it is vain for the Saints to try to get rich. To live poor seems hard but the Lord is only giving us a scourging to make us mindful of him. The President says this Church never was in such danger as it is at the present time, but says if all will only obey his counsels he will take them safe through, but some are for rebelling.

I sleep with your Colt's pistol loaded on my pillow but know not whether I should have the courage to use it or not if the war whoop should be raised at my door, but I think I should be good for one Indian. Running would be useless, for I should never run and leave my children. If they died I would die too. Perhaps you think I am ascared. If I am ascared our leaders are also.

If the mail gets in I do not know that I can raise the means to pay for a letter from you. I had to run my credit and borrow this paper to write on, but I do not wish to trouble you with my poverty.

Brother is the most promising child you ever seen. He looks and looks as though he knew everything. He now begins to jabber like Kissy did at three and a half, and thanks to the mare's milk Sister Hansen gave me, he has got over whooping cough. He weighed twenty pounds when he was four months old. He now plays stick-horses with Kissy and pulls her hair. For certain he is a great fellow to play. Kissy is real pretty. She does all the dishes. She loves her singing school and grows more stiddy every day.

From your affect. companion forever

CLORINDA

P.S.: Oh! I wish —— (Clory changed her mind and crossed the rest of the sentence out.)

11

Not the Indians but the grasshoppers were the plague that summer. 'I feel like Job!' said Erastus, watching ten million starving demons fill the air with the mighty crunching of their jaws, strip the ripe wheat, the bark from the young trees, attack the corn that was just silking out, eat the silk and fall upon every green blade like a noisome blight. Men, women, and children beat them off with clubs, drove them into ditches and burned them, fought them until sleep came to be haunted with nightmares known as 'grasshopper dreams.' And there were no avenging sea gulls down here; there was nothing but a grim resistance of the will.

At last the *Cactus* proclaimed joyfully: 'The grasshoppers, after stopping with us four or five days, eating up our lucerne, corn, carrot-tops, and leaves from our fruit trees, hoisted sail and bid us good-bye. We wish them a very long and successful journey!'

All early crops, even beans and new potatoes, were ruined, but before the last grasshopper was gone, Erastus had the men in the fields, plowing up the ravaged land, replanting to fall corn, pumpkins, and squash. Corn won't turn into flour but it will make cakes and mush, and pumpkins can be sliced and the yellow rings hung on rafters to dry.

But the very next day a greater plague came. But on his knees in the light cave, he thought he knew how the Paiutes felt when they offered up a living sacrifice to those unknown angry gods. 'Oh, Lord,' he begged, 'no more, oh, Lord! In what way have Thy servants sinned?'

For there were plagues one could not beat off with a club.

Fly-time was always a time to be dreaded. The dog-days of August. There was something about the sultry heat that hatched flies in batches. Erastus, picking the buzzing, biting things off his skin, wondered why there were so many more flies in St. George than anywhere else in the world. In Salt Lake a man could sit outdoors in peace, but not down here. Not that it was any better in the houses, houses without screens. Fly-time grew so bad that summer that a man could not sit long enough to write a letter by candlelight, and a woman 'fanned her churn' at three o'clock in the morning.... Afterward, thinking it over, Erastus found it simpler to blame the flies than the Lord.

Lon Tuckett's boy, Millennium, was the first. A red humor appeared at the corner of the mouth, spread in a discolored blotch to the cheek, to the gums, to the palate, the lining of the mouth and the throat, until the flesh rotted and the teeth sloughed away.

Betsy, as women will, insisted on calling Stiddy Weeks in spite of Brother Brigham's counsel.

'It's black canker,' diagnosed Stiddy, peering through his spectacles at the flushed cheekbones, the quick, shallow breathing, the sloughing sores on the face. 'The beginning of an epidemic. Quarantine. Sulphured sheets over doorways. The child can't live...' (Black canker, the plague of Winter Quarters about which people still spoke in hushed whispers!)

Erastus was angry.

'The child doesn't need to die!' he scolded Lon, who frankly blubbered. 'The Lord is the one to decide and not the doctor. Don't admit the doctor because he leans toward death; admit only those who have faith!'

Erastus called his priesthood together. 'Ptsahh!' It was time the Lord gave them a Sign.

'Take word to all your children,' he counseled, 'that as soon as the boy gets well they shall have a party with candy and raisins!'

Parties — unheard of except on Christmas afternoon! So that all the week Betsy's boy tossed with fever, the children of the town, playing jacks and marbles in the dooryard, Injuns in the brush, paper dolls in the barn, gathered in knots to pray. Never was praying more fervent! Boys stopped in the middle of swimming to pray, girls slid down the haymow to prayer.

On Friday the fever broke and Millennium began to get well. Erastus, walking home from Lon's, was beside himself with joy. The Lord had given them a sign!

But the next day Marianne's baby had black canker. And before he had time to regret, it seemed to Erastus, the child was dead.

A pall hung over the town. People averted their faces and hurried on by a stricken household as if there were leprosy inside. If medicine or food had to be delivered, it was left at the gate. Human beings did not visit, but the flies winged busily from one sickbed to another.

There was dread in the air. Clory fought it, as well as the dread in her own heart, and the dread that seeped through to her children's faces. Life should never become less than buoyant for them! So it was that she let Kissy go to Sister Hansen's for yeast that afternoon. Surely an innocent enough thing to do. Although Serena, the second wife, had a three-year-old with the sniffles (Serena had named her baby Julia after the first wife), no one was really sick at the Yeast Lady's, and Kissy did love to listen to Lars pluck the bass fiddle, that only growled when a child touched it.

But twenty-four hours later Clory carried her babe out into the moonlight, that was brighter than a candle, to see if he still breathed. Regrets gnawed her. She had been careless during her pregnancy, gathering all those greens — She hadn't drunk enough milk . . .

'It's a punishment,' croaked 'Sheba, the moon-wash outlining her figure in the doorway.

'Nonsense!' Clory straightened from the crib. 'I ain't a-going to be a-scared about this, nor think it's spirits or — or things like that; something *natural* causes it, like flies, or lack of milk, and I keep telling myself that every baby that dies will some day make it easier for somebody to find out the truth . . .'

A shiver touched 'Sheba as if ghostly fingers played over her flesh.

Clory's voice, hardly more than a whisper, yet had the quality of light, as if she were pitting her soul against all the dark forces in life. She was like a flame. Her face in a luminous shaft from the window had an unearthly beauty; there was something undefeatable in the tilt of the chin, the sweet, full mouth, the proud sweep of hair back from the forehead. Age or grief would only accentuate these characteristics, high-lighting them with wrinkles and shadows, but nothing could destroy them. One hand on the cradle of the dead baby, Clory stared beyond the dugout out into the supernatural brilliance of the night as if listening for something, as if prepossessed with some nebulous destiny.

The next morning, when the wagon rolled away with the little body, she was leaning over Brother, soothing him, calling out encouragement to Kissy, whose peaked face seemed all eyes as she reached up to the dishpan. Willie was there to help early and late, but 'Sheba would not again venture beyond her own four walls. She shut her brood in with her, and only poked her head out of the doorway now and then, like a startled hen.

Clory worked with Brother. All the week of his illness she felt as if she were propping her own will-power against the sulphured sheet in the doorway, keeping death at bay. There should not be one flaw in her conduct, not one bad thought with which the Lord could find fault. And when the temptation to seek Stiddy overwhelmed her, she rummaged through his old Doctor Book, Doctor Chase's Prescription, and remembered that seeking him was going against counsel. She went through the days and nights like a person walking a tightrope over a chasm. Hannah Merinda Lowgie and Aunt Ket shouted remedies from the gate, 'Sheba from the doorway, and Clory tried them all. Gargles of rough elm bark, mesquite sap, poultices of soft pine gum, burned copperas put in soft grease and rubbed behind the turn of the jaws, behind the ears, on the throat and the top of the head.

But all the time she worked, there was a dread certainty in her heart, a conviction that this horror was as old as God, that it had lain in wait for millions of years, ready to jump out at her. The agonizing cycle, the fever and delirium, the yellow skin tightening across the nose, the soft cheek sloughed away, leaving a hole as big as a dollar, the mouth that twisted in agony. An eternity of days and nights without sleep until familiar objects swam before her eyes, changed and lost proportion. She was always having to touch a chair blocking her path to be sure it was a chair. Always having to pull herself up from her own dark inner chaos to reassure Kissy, shrinking in a corner like a little scared wraith.

'She's so quiet!' Willie wrung her hands to 'Sheba. 'It ain't natural! I could stand it better if she'd carry on!'

'Sheba's mole twitched in grudging admiration. 'She never will. She's the kind of a woman who'll be perfectly calm over double pneumonia and go all to pieces over a pain in the belly!'

When for the second time the death-wagon clattered up to her gate, Clory was waiting, dry-eyed, one hand pressing Kissy against her skirts. You lived, it seemed, only because you could not die. She turned from the sight of Ole Oleson hunched mournfully over the reins to stare at Willie and the Yeast Lady trudging across the dooryard. Sister Hansen was lugging Lars's big bass fiddle case, the polished wood reflecting gleams of the sun. She had it clasped by the neck with both hands, and when she reached Clory she shoved it toward her dumbly.

'Lars vanted I should,' she clacked, her upper plate slipping; 'Serena's baby iss on da mend. Da Lord, He giveth an' He taketh. — An' ve ban so sorry aboot Yohn ... the leedle fellow iss so very leedle, he will yoost fit — ...' There was never any time for coffins; people just wrapped the bodies in anything they had.

Afterward, when Ole had boosted the fiddle case with its burden into the wagon box among the others, the three women and the child stood at the gate and watched the rickety 'shandry-dan,' as Abijah would have called it, rumble away through the dust.

Kissy raised eyes so like Abijah's that Clory winced. She had failed him again.

'Mamma, have I got to die, too?'

And Clory, dragging words out of that desperate past built up by all the weak women gone before her, talked of Death. Words like 'heaven' and 'having a testimony' that, none of them, robbed her child's eyes of fear.

'Death means riding a comet!' said Clory. 'Think what fun it'll be to ride a comet! Brother and Baby playing hop-scotch with the angels. But you won't have to go — you won't have to go ...'

For Kissy was Free's, had always been Free's, belonged to Free. Kissy must live to fulfill his dream, wear the perfume, sit at the rosewood desk.

And yet when Kissy sickened, she had known all along it was inevitable.

Pal broke the quarantine and came to stand at the gate, her freckles emphatic against the pallor of her face. Children all over town had died. Lucy's baby, her own baby. It seemed easier to kill the babies than the flies. But Patience-Elizabeth still lived.

Clory stared at her friend as if she were a stranger. *Yours have been better fed . . .*

Willie fluttered her red wrists, but her pale eyes on Clory's anguished face were steady.

'Now, don't you fret,' she said. 'I just got through giving the Lord a good talking to . . .'

The sickness wore many faces, but the one Clory dreaded the most was the thirsty face. For everyone knew you must never give a drink to a child with a fever. Long after Kissy was too weak to talk she held the empty cup, seeming to beg for water, peering into its dry depths.

'She can't stand it!' Willie stood in the doorway of the 'dobe house and wrung her hands.

'She'll have to stand it,' said 'Sheba. 'She can't sit it and she's got to go through with it!'

The sound of singing drifted to the two women across the yard.

'Rock-a-by baby, in the tree-top . . .'

'Sheba shuddered.

'It gives me the creeps,' she said, thinking of Isaiah's rash. Of course, only a rash . . .

Clory leaned over the bed and smiled down at her child. There was a beauty in the quicksilver limbs; even her skeleton would have an elfin beauty. It was the seventh day and Kissy's eyes were rational. Clory crooned and wiped the damp forehead. So then she was going to be spared this much of her heart. She looked around and smiled in weary triumph at Willie and the Yeast Lady nodding in the gray dawn light. When she turned back to the bed the light had filtered there, too, for Kissy's skin was gray.

The two women got up and came over, standing behind her, looking down at the child. Willie put a hand on Clory's shoulder. She stared up at them until it seemed the dark expectancy in their faces brimmed over and flowed into her own, crowding out hope.

Already the change was dimming the brave shining of the childish eyes, pinching the features and making them, in some strange, taut way, lovelier still.

An idea stirred beneath the numbness of Clory's mind. For no reason she remembered Confederate America — 'Mec' — the little girl who had talked to her in Washington on that first eager trek — 'Pa would whup me.' What was there about Kissy's defenselessness to remind her of that child? She had been so confident then: 'It ain't necessary! Not if a body's able and willing to work!'

There was a movement on the bed, a grimace, a stillness beside which the rooster's crow was a puny sound. Clory turned to stone, thrusting that small grimace, that great stillness back into the nightmare of things that could not have happened. No — oh, no!

Willie took the Paisley shawl from its hook on the wall, draped the little body. Frankincense and myrrh.

Clory got up and walked out of the dugout, leaned against the dry wall, stared up at the sky. The fragrance of dew-drenched bergamot rose up from the earth at her feet. A jack rabbit pricked ridiculous ears and loped across the dooryard.

Her mind circled like an animal in a trap. She could not rid herself of the haunting, irrational belief that it was all a punishment. The thought rocked like a treadmill to which she was bound. What could a human creature know of comets? A human creature drugged with living until grief ripped apart the veil and you saw your naked, shivering self within, staring out at life like a river running swiftly down hill ...

Suddenly the last star in the gray glimmered brightly for a moment, and shot a trail of fire down the sky. 'A star dancing in the heavens,' Sheba would say, 'a child received with joy.'

A human creature *could* reach for comets. Your own up-reaching spark was real, and besides that, all you had was your pitiful human stubbornness, the embattled human will to survive. For why should you expect the world to pause in its mad spinning to listen to your cry — to solace you with its pausing — to console your grief, alone, one of so many griefs?

'Sheba would need spelling off with Isaiah. Clory turned and walked across the dooryard.

CHAPTER XI

ITWAS no time for sympathy, Erastus was sure of that.

One moment the town stagnated in the grip of the heat. Not a thing stirred but the flies and the red sand. Down at the river, patching up the dam (Erastus, coaxing water out on the fall corn, argued they had every chance to mature a crop if frost-time came as usual around Thanksgiving), the men worked stripped to the waist. Which laid them open to the buffetings of Satan, exploded Zebedee Trupp, the words whistling between his teeth — they must be disfected in their heads to go without their garments like that! Heat or no heat, he made out to wear hisn!

Lon Tuckett spat on his hands and heaved his end of the log to his shoulder and started sliding down the trampled mud of the bank. Brother Trupp could talk about being disfected in the head, him without no kids to worry about!

'I vum,' declared Lon, staring at the other man's squat upper trunk rising out of the roily water, the heavy home-bleach underwear, brown with dirt and matted to the skin with perspiration. 'I vum, I'd as soon go to the bad place, anyhow! Hell ain't got no terrors for me after Dixie!'

It seemed to Erastus that even the river shrank from the heat and scuttled under the shade of its banks. The leaves, filmed with dust, hung listless on the bushes. Up in town, in spite of having moved their beds out into the lucerne patches, folks woke in the night and gasped for breath. The feeling of death hung in the air.

All this one minute. And the next, it seemed to Erastus, thunderheads piling up over Pine Valley, and heat lightning at all the horizons. Then, one night, without warning, the charge of armies, the crash of artillery, the sky split apart with flashes of silver fire, rattle and bang and boom, blinding light stabbing the dark. Wind rushing at houses, flipping over clotheslines, uprooting bushes and sending them scooting across dooryards like fat demons; wind tearing at sheets and twitching away from reaching fingers pants and dresses draped on bedposts for the night. The first tentative drops of rain, and then a pelting, bursting torrent, and in the diminishing lightning flashes a mêlée of half-clothed people clutching sheets, pillows, mattresses, scrambling for shelter.

The epidemic was over. But it was still no time for sympathy. Already people were referring to the summer with lowered voices. Making a legend of it. The Year of the Plagues.

Erastus called a huge mass-meeting, squeezed everybody in town into the Social Hall. This was something that concerned them all. The body of the hall was jammed, so that the Pig-Dirt people and Old Tom the Negro had to sidle along the wall. At sight of that gray kinky head and black face against the light wallpaper, the MacIntyre twins pinched each other excitedly. Since Isaiah's death, 'Sheba's lips were pressed into a thinner line, the skin tighter over her high cheekbones, her nose more hawk-like, her eyes harder, but the twins rather enjoyed the sensation of being suddenly so fussed over. Besides, Isaiah had always lagged behind — he never could seem to keep up when they played Injun!

Willie, on the other side of 'Sheba, wiped her eyes in an excess of general pity, but Clory, beside her, was white and still. Beyond the twins, the older boys sat silent and awed.

Erastus got slowly to his feet, puffed his lips, fiddled with his hands beneath his coattails, and bowed his head.

After prayer he stood there a moment staring at the faces before him. Not many tears, mostly a set kind of bitterness, despair. He had the feeling that the faces were all set against him. But it was no time for sympathy. As soon as a man starts feeling sorry for himself, he's through.

'Well, folks,' he said quietly, 'this has been a dreadful business. Ptsahh! But we have to remember it's a natural business. The Lord is testing us. Plagues are no new thing to our people ... They happen all over the world, for that matter. Who remembers the green sickness at Nauvoo?'

Hannah Merinda Lowgie's hand, Aunt Ket's, Sister Mansfield's.

'Sister Lowgie?'

As she spoke, Hannah Merinda's chins waggled above her starched collar. Although her own brood had been spared, she had endured the suffering in every other home.

She shook her head, trying to find words to fit her memories.

'Babies dying like flies ...'

'Exactly,' said Erastus. 'Ptsahh! And there was the cholera ...'

'Da cholery, I vell r-remember him' — Ole Oleson was on his feet, his hands twisting his frayed straw hat, his huge red ears redder still with shyness and the effort of speech, his flattened nostrils black holes in the strained redness of his face. (But this was like testimony meeting and a man must do his part.) 'On da plains. Ve yust could not stop for da burying. My vife, she carry dead child three whole days. Vun morning ve miss my two leedle boys, find them twisted up under vagon vere dey crawl to die ...'

'And the blackleg scurvy at Winter Quarters' — Erastus took
it up mercilessly. 'I remember my wife, Keturah, getting into a
wagon with the flesh rotting off her' (he could see Ket sticking out
her jaw, mad because he'd recall that to harrow up all their feelings — but sometimes the only way you could make people appreciate the present was to compare it with the past), 'lying on
the floor of a jolting wagon all those months across the plains because she said it was better to die facing the West and Zion than
to stay alive and be among the gentiles. So you see' — Erastus
raised his voice and puffed his lips — 'We might be a lot worse off!
Can it be you've forgotten the mobocrats, that you lose your
courage over a few deaths? . . . I loved my two babies, too, but
just because they're gone doesn't mean we're going to give up.
We can raise more crops — yes, and we can even raise more
babies! Women can stand more than men . . . I want every woman here to quit her grieving and go to having another baby just
as soon as the Lord lets her!'

Lon Tuckett raised his hand, and at Erastus' nod jumped to
his feet. But he was ill at ease without his familiar cackle. He
gulped, looked down at Betsy, who prodded him with a frown.

'I gorry, I think we ought to quit,' he said, not looking up,
grasping the back of the bench in front. 'I'm tired a seeing my
wife and kids always sick and hungry. I'm tired a working my
fool head off for nothin'. It's ditch, ditch, ditch, dam, dam, dam,
till I'm sick of it!'

'*Ach, ja, ja!*' Betsy nodded vigorously, her eyes fixed defiantly
on Erastus.

'Brother Brigham wouldn't go through this for *us!* Besides, up
north there's good land, good water, a chance to make a decent
living, and — and *people . . .*'

For a moment Lon's voice held the terror of the land that assailed them all at times. The terror of the loneliness, the immensi-
ties, the spirit of fiendish perversity which seemed to ride the
silences, the fear that human strength never could conquer those

hills that stretched wave upon wave, hump upon hump, to the
south, those hills to the north like white battlements with winter
snow, like blue eternities with summer shade. Those hills that
reared their rocky heads, that crouched and sank like receding
waves beyond and beyond. Great barren hills that seemed to
have heaved themselves from the bowels of the earth... This
country was too big. A man couldn't get his teeth into it. Up
North where there were more people, a man felt safer, somehow ...

Erastus rallied his forces.

'Shame on you, Lon Tuckett! You, who didn't lose a chick nor
a child! Go and be damned, but it'll be just like apostatizing!
Ptsahh!... I tell you, this religion has no room for *skim-milk
saints!* A man goes where he is told and does his duty or he ain't
fit to be kept in fellowship!'

Erastus' chin-beard shot out.

Lon sat hastily down, his eyes upon his hands clutched in his
lap. But Betsy was not convinced. She returned Apostle Snow's
look, glare for glare. 'It's shust more'n a body can shtand,' she
whispered, her lips framing the words.

Erastus' voice rose to a quiet bellow.

'How do you *know* you can't stand it? There's no limit to what
a human being can do if he wants to!'

He got out his handkerchief, mopped his full, writhing lips,
and flung out his arm at them.

'You're all afraid,' he sneered. 'You're all cowards! No one
has actually starved yet, has he? The thing that makes you quit
is the *fear* that you'll starve! It's like a forced march, putting one
foot in front of the other ... The past is dead. Don't worry about
the future. All you have to do is live one day to the next. And I
promise you' — his voice rose again — 'I *promise* you in the name
of the Lord, things'll be better!'

He stopped, and his stocky body with its growing paunch
seemed to gather itself. Sweat beaded his full forehead to the

receding hairline. He mopped at his bald spot. His voice sank
to a quiet intensity. 'Do you remember what the Prophet said?
"If I were sunk in the lowest pit of Nova Scotia with the Rocky
Mountains piled on me, I would hang on, exercise faith, keep up
good courage, and *I would come out on top!*"

'I want to tell you, brethren and sisters, I've been proud of
you! Ptsahh! With folks like you I could settle fifty wildernesses,
and *come out on top, too!* ... You, Lon Tuckett, Jarvis, Miles!
Brother Brigham picked you because he could depend on you!
Cotton must be got out! And we're not licked yet. As long as a
man's on his feet and fighting, he's not licked! Hardships only
make us tough; they may bend us, but they'll never break us!'

He was leaning over the edge of the stand, now, and in truth
there seemed to shine from his steady gray eyes a spirit that was
invincible. Every face was lifted. New hope spread like a blaze
from eye to eye. He played upon them with his words as if their
faces were a keyboard. His voice softened, grew cajoling.

'We're going to need all the courage we've got. There's a worse
evil than sickness or dams or floods or grasshoppers. I've been
afraid of it for a long time, and it's almost here.... Let us ask the
Lord to forgive us for our grumblings. Let us sing, brethren and
sisters!'

At a signal Brother Wheelock stepped down to the edge of the
platform beside Erastus, raised those long, delicate hands of his,
and released the round, booming thunder of his voice.

> Why should we mourn or think our lot is hard?
> 'Tis not so, all is right!
> Why should we think to earn a great reward,
> If we now shun the fight?

Voices took it up. People were on their feet, faces transfixed.
The building rocked with the sound, that overflowed out into the
hot sunshine and rolled across the valley.

> Gird up your lo-oins, fresh courage ta-ake
> Our God will ne-ever us forsake;
> And soon we'll have this truth to tell —
> All is well! All is well!

2

'Sheba was always one to do her duty, and Clory had helped nurse Isaiah, hadn't she? Almost before her own child was cold. So 'Sheba, without inquiring too closely into such promptings of the spirit, decided to give Clory a birthday party.

'Sheba stood in the doorway of the 'dobe house and watched Clory stretch her mouth into a smile, tie the strings of the limp red sunbonnet under her chin, lift her blue denim skirts from the dust of the path, click the gate carefully behind her, and trudge slowly out to the sidewalk. She was going to help Pal with her carpet rags.

'I guess she thinks it's funny Pal asking her to come and help on her birthday ——'

'Well, there wasn't no h'other way we could su'prise 'er,' said Willie, pinning a towel on her head, coming to stand beside 'Sheba so she could bang the dust out of the broom against the step. Needed a new broom — they'd bought this three year ago come Hallowe'en from those folks down at Seldom Stop who went into the broom-corn business for a while.

'Sheba stared after that small figure, whose thinness was pathetic even to her.

'I've never saw her go even to Palmyra's without her hoops or at least a bustle before — She's changed.'

'H'of course she's changed!'

Willie banged the broom vigorously against the side of the house.

'Who wouldn't change? Look at all the things that's 'appened to her, and her only twenty-six! H'it's enough to make a body change!'

'Sheba's jaw tightened. Clory wasn't the only one who'd had things happen to her. No one knew what she, Bathsheba, had gone through. Losing her baby, whose towhead had helped to comfort, a little, the dull misery that had never healed over from her loss of Free. But she certainly wasn't going to let Willie go prying into that corner of her heart where she kept her memories.

Willie, glancing at the hard line of the other woman's jaw, the grim line of her lips, understood. Abijah had once said that 'women sit down to trouble like it was knitting,' and Willie thought he must have meant Bathsheba. There had been a time, right after Isaiah's death, when 'Sheba had wanted to bump her head on the floor, cut gashes in herself, and pull out handfuls of hair as the Indians do. She had made a dreadful to-do; there was something vulgar and indecent about such surrender to any emotion. Willie remembered a moment when 'Sheba had panted over to Clory's dugout wringing her hands. The girl had looked up from an empty crib and stared, dry-eyed. At that moment Clory had her chance at 'Sheba. She could have become the big woman's satellite, forever after basking in the sun of her intimacy, bound to her by the solemn league and covenant of women. It was true, 'Sheba had wanted someone to sit down with her to grief as if it were knitting — someone with whom she could dissect the details of the horror, someone who understood that talking about a thing makes it easier to bear, someone who'd wrangle with her over the weight of their respective burdens, someone to whom she could confide tragically, 'Even *you* will never know what I have gone through!'

Yes, 'Sheba had needed someone like that. Aunt Ket Snow had lost a little girl, it is true, but not a ten-year-old boy, not a full-grown son, nor had she had to hide any skeletons in her closet. And Hannah Merinda Lowgie's child had got well. So 'Sheba had wrung her hands to Clory and bleated: 'Oh, isn't this terrible? Why do you think the Lord picks on *us?*' And Willie, with a half-ashamed suspicion that 'Sheba's grief was partly put on, not entirely her own, but manufactured rather because she had thought it her duty to put herself in Clory's shoes — Willie, feeling that 'Sheba was therefore responding to suffering with Clory's own passionate temperament and not her own, had recoiled from all emotion and hurried the big woman out of the room.

Yes, that was the time Clory lost her chance at 'Sheba. But how could she have done differently? Some people took things harder than others, and the only way Clory could stand what she had to bear was to wall up her grief in a secret part of her heart, keep it private and sacred from alien eyes until it should become less sore and pulpy to the touch. Clory never talked about her trouble. Even with Willie she wore her armor of gaiety. But you knew it for an armor, thought Willie, when you looked at the girl's hair and eyes, blighted and faded as if a flame had burned its way through her flesh, as if she had thrown herself against life and been bruised. Yes, thought Willie, she could understand that defense of Clory's which never dared to let the polite pretense slip and expose the quivering, gray grief within, which never asked for sympathy. She could understand it even if 'Sheba couldn't.

'I keep wondering if she'll smile like that even after she's dead,' mused 'Sheba, half to herself, her eyes still on that blue figure turning the street corner. 'I guess nobody knows what she thinks.'

'Nobody,' agreed Willie softly.

'And nobody'll ever find out, not even if they take the trouble to unscrew the lid of her coffin!'

'Sheba's mole twitched resentfully as she turned back into the house.

The small 'dobe house had to be cleaned and aired from top to bottom. That was the trouble with a party — like as not folks would start playing some game like 'Teakettle' that 'ud send them scampering to every nook and cranny.

The floor had to be scrubbed, and if Willie, down on protesting knees with the mop-bucket, felt any spite toward 'Sheba for letting her redd up a house she was not permitted to live in, she did not show it. — In fact, she thought, groaning with the creak of

knotted muscles, she'd do more than scrub to bring back a look
of *life* to that gentle stare of Clory's.

'Sheba had a new rag rug bright with the red of madder and the
yellow of rabbit-brush blossoms for in front of the door, and the
smaller rugs to scatter on each side of the long table and in front
of the hearth and the bed. While Willie scrubbed, 'Sheba carried
the rugs out to shake them well. She supposed Abijah would
have a fit when he came back and found Willie still sleeping out
in the tent and the boys in the bedroom. But 'Sheba was tired
of seeing her boys sleep in wagon boxes. They were her own flesh
and blood, weren't they? That's more'n you could say for Willie.
Besides, Willie was used to the tent —— Besides that, what
mother wouldn't put her children first? And anyway, Joseph was
getting married soon. Now that the canal had reached Abijah's
strip of river land Joseph and his new bride were moving down
there to work it on shares. . . . 'Sheba, having been robbed of so
much, wanted the satisfaction of her other sons close as long as
possible. Clory said the long winters in the tent crippled Willie up
worse, but 'Sheba was convinced all that rheumatics-grunting
was just to get out of work. *She'd* been living in a tent right along
and it hadn't hurt her none! . . .

Willie was slow — she had only finished mopping under the
bed and around the squat black bricks of the hearth when 'Sheba
came back in. 'Sheba threw her rugs over a chair, glanced at the
drab bent head and bony shoulders seesawing above Willie's
rotating arm, and went to work herself on the ash-wood table,
folding the red cloth on a bench, sloshing soapy water over those
ingrained stains. This was where Isaiah had sat since he was a
baby, spilling his food. Pain clutched freshly at her heart and she
remembered all the times she had scolded and wondered why she
had been so blind. You thought about the freedom and peace
you'd have when they grew up, and when that time came, you
longed for them all to be young again. The twins were thirteen —
they wouldn't be kids much longer. The ruckus they made,

sweeter than music ... It was not *fair* — there ought to be some way for a woman to ree'lize how precious these harassed moments were when they were kids ... There! That grease-spot would not come out — she'd declare-to-goodness it was where Isy had spilled his lumpy-dick as he'd done every morning all his life long — things stayed the same, and only people changed. The stain was there, but Isy had gone ... 'Sheba wrung out her cloth in her bucket, tossed her head to flick a lock of hair out of her eyes, and turned to the benches. There were memories here, too; each one in his place — one moment having to reach up, the next, it seemed, so tall he had to bend over. One moment banging with a spoon until you wanted to slap him, the next so reserved, so withdrawn into his young-man thoughts that you wanted — well, you wanted to slap him then, too!

But Apostle Snow was right. You had to forget the past. There was work to be done in the here-and-now.

'Sheba was worried about the picnic. She stepped out of the way of Willie's encroaching mop-rag and walked across to the cupboard to give its dun-colored surface a lick and a promise. (How wonderful if they ever saw the day when paint would be closer than seven hundred miles!)

'D'yu think we'll have enough picnic?'

Willie straightened the kink in her back and puffed upward at the fly on her nose.

''d ought to be,' she said, kneading her fingers into her back. 'Salt-risin' bread and new-churned butter and Dutch cheese and dill pickles — it'll be a treat!'

'Sheba nodded. Any kind of bread would be a treat. They were lucky to have that bit of flour saved up, even if it was dark ''dobe-dirt' flour.

'The neighbors has been real good,' said Willie, mopping under the table.

'Sheba nodded again. Sister Hansen had offered to furnish the 'risin·' and bake the bread. 'Sheba wasn't one to neighbor much

and she didn't like to be beholdin' to nobody, but there were those
times last summer she'd sent over clabber to the Hansens, so she
guessed it was all right. Especially with the cow not givin' down
so much milk, what with the shortage of feed and all. 'Yulia'
Hansen did seem to have a knack with salt-risin', addin' saleratus
and ginger and sich. But Sister Joe Eardley was somethin' else
again. Who'd ever dream of Sister Joe savin' up a gourdful of
Indian corn a whole year? 'I save heem for special ti-ime,' she
had said, sneaking into Willie's tent last night. ''t will be goot for
youngvuns to parch.'

Dusting the Spode plates 'Sheba wondered if she'd better use
them for the dessert. But she guessed folks'ud be careful ...
Fresh California grapes for dessert should be good enough — of
course there'd only be a taste around, but there were the raisins
they'd dried last July. The grasshoppers had taken the peaches
and plums and almonds, but in another year ...

Lucky they'd saved the grapevines. She and Willie and Clory
and the boys working steady the three whole days and nights,
flapping at the green demons with sacks, scaring them into
trenches, piling on brush and setting fire to the brush. Singed
eyebrows and the feel of a hopper's legs clinging to your flesh.
But anyway, they'd saved the Californias, and for two weeks
now she'd been hanging up ripe bunches down cellar, their cut
stems nicely stoppered with wax so's they'd keep.

'Land sakes,' she said to Willie, over by the door now, 'Clorinda
does pick the unlikeliest time for her birthday. Can't make cake
because it's too late for the winter soggum and too early for the
fall, and right now we're short on grease — come hog-killin' time
in November, and I could fry her up some crullers or fritters or
doughnuts, and hot sausages. A'course, I suppose Ket and Hannah Merinda'll think we're pretty skimpy not to have chicken-'n'-
noodles, but I been years gittin' a good start on chickens and I
ain't a-goin' to kill my pullets ...'

Willie, grunting under the weight of the mop-bucket, hobbled down the steps and out the path to the street. She wouldn't dump the dirty water on the path for fear it might soften the hard-trodden pieces of tanned bark ('Sheba had at last got her walk paved with Brother Peabody's chips) nor on the two square plats on either side for fear the soapy stuff would kill the lucerne, just coming up green again after the grasshoppers — some day, Abijah said, he'd have lawn there, but until he could afford lawn seed, lucerne would do, with hollyhocks and sunflowers against the house and the fence ... Willie poured the water into the irri-gation ditch on the other side of the sidewalk and rested for a moment, scratching her back against the rough bark of a cotton-wood. The row of trees had shot up until they'd be shading the whole street now if it weren't for the 'hoppers ... the stark branches against the sun looked like bare bones.

Willie looked up at the little low house with its peaked, shingled roof, stout 'dobe walls, and pig-bladder-glassed windows. 'Sheba was certainly a rustler. She had a house to be proud of, with its two rooms and lean-to, even if she had made most of it herself.

'Sheba came to the door and put a hand to her mouth and called 'Le-hi-i! Ne-phi-i!' in a rising crescendo. 'I want 'em to come polish the copper candlesticks,' she said to Willie. 'I've got the vinegar-water all ready ...'

Inside the house the two women remade the bed built into the corner by the door leading into the other room — turning the straw tick on the bedcord springs, spreading on the home-bleach sheets and the bright patch-quilt. The antimacassars for the rockers, the picture throws for the picture of the Prophet and the 'Home Sweet Home' motto, the lambrequin for the mantel, were all freshly starched, newly hung.

'Next harvest,' said 'Sheba, dusting the Bible, the Book of Mormon, Doctrine and Covenants, and Pearl of Great Price to put back on the mantel, 'I'm a-goin' to have straw on my floor and an all-over rag carpet ...'

Willie went on cleaning the dulcimer, pulling her cloth carefully between the protesting strings.

The twins burst into the room, shouting at 'Sheba and pulling at each other.

'Sheba separated the wrangling boys, gave them the pan of vinegar-water and the candlesticks, and sent them out on the steps.

Lehi turned in the doorway, a lock of dark hair falling over his grimy face.

'Mamma, can I have a pickle?'

'No!' 'Sheba snapped, her mole twitching. 'You've et pickles all mornin'! Now git on out there before I tan your tehinders, both of you!'

There was a knock at the back door and 'Sheba went out into the lean-to.

The Yeast Lady stood there, her cheeks rosy from baking.

'The bread, he is r-ready,' she said, smiling, pushing her upper plate into place, 'shall I bring heem ofer?'

'Sheba shook her head. 'Would you mind keepin' it there, Sister Hansen? 'twill be more of a surprise.'

'*Ya, ya*, I keep him!'

She nodded brightly, her blue eyes gleeful as a bird's, and trotted down the path between the fig-tree and the wild-grape arbor that screened the washtubs. 'Sheba stood watching the plump little figure duck her head under the clotheslines, stoop under the stake-and-rider fence, and so cross the lane to her own lot. 'Sheba couldn't understand a person so innocently anxious to do anyone else a good turn.

'Mamma,' said Lehi, in the lean-to doorway, 'I'm all through, now, honest. Now kin I have a pickle?'

'I'll pickle you!' said 'Sheba, letting go her temper, dragging the squirming boy by the ear down the cellar steps.

Washing her hands at the bench in the lean-to, Willie was conscious of a significant silence. Then 'Sheba's furious voice.

'Another one! Hurry up! Before I get through with you, you'll be so sick of pickles . . .'

More silence. And then a protesting bellow.

'I *can't* eat no more, Mamma! I'll throw up!'

'You bet you'll throw up, but you won't do no more teasin'!'

A small boy catapulting up the cellar steps with both hands pressed tight around his stomach and his mouth wobbling against the rising tide within.

Willie grinned.

'Sheba strode in, spatting pickle-juice from her hands.

'Thank heavens! In another year they'll be old enough for girl-time and I'll have some peace!'

'I doubt it,' said Willie sagely.

3

'Mothers never do have any peace,' said Clory, watching Pal shake Patience-Elizabeth, pull the howling child into the other room to change her dress, bedraggled from many mud pies. Lucy spread a fresh piece of cloth on the table and scissored into it. 'Why not?' she said sharply. Snip, snip. Having lost her baby in the epidemic, she still thought hers the only tragedy in the world.

'Because,' said Clory, her eyes growing sooty with tenderness for that particular sharpness in Lucy's voice, 'because having a baby makes a hole in a woman that nothing ever again quite fills up, except having another baby.'

Lucy lowered her eyes quickly from that fixed, opaque gaze and concentrated on the strips forming beneath her scissors.

Clory stopped winding her ball of carpet rags and turned restlessly to stare out the window, across the road to the square where the shriveled old bowery drowsed in the sunlight. As she watched, a vagrant breeze stirred the dried overhanging branches of the roof and some leaves twirled slowly to the ground. They might have been hanging there for weeks, she thought, as brittle and fugitive as life itself, waiting the touch of the breeze ...

That was the trouble with her, always thinking. But telling yourself not to think about a thing only made you think about it the more. All you could do was to steep yourself up to the neck in other people's troubles, live each minute for itself, never look ahead. There was really a lot of comfort in taking turns with your friends, helping them clean house. A body never ran out of that kind of comfort, either, with all the fumigating going on since the epidemic. A lot of comfort doing things for others, but how they loved to let you do it!

Patience-Elizabeth's little kitten began to play with the carpet rags at her feet and jerk at the ball she held. Clory roused herself and picked the kitten up and snugged its softness against her cheek. The vibration of its purring tickled her hand. She rubbed her face against it and wanted to talk baby-talk to it, but she was afraid of Lucy. That was the worst — this feeling of moral nakedness that came to her when she ceased to pretend, ceased to fort in behind pride flaunting the colors of happiness. Yes, it was true, losing a baby made a hole that only another baby could ever fill up. That was something that men could never understand. They could shout words at you about God and religion, you could shout words at yourself, but the hole was still there. It was the smells you missed the most — that baby smell, all soft and fragrant from the bath. ...

Pal came in, buxom with a late pregnancy. She went to the cupboard to spread bread-'n'-molasses for Patience-Elizabeth, and then shooed the child out the door.

'Now see if you can keep clean five minutes!' she called after her, and turned her dish-face, anxiously as always, to Clory.

But you can't understand, thought Clory, rubbing the cat. You're too happy. Funny what happiness does to people — your hair used to be the ugliest drab, and happiness has made it fawn-colored ... But I wouldn't give up my six years of Kissy for a lifetime of Patience-Elizabeth!

Pal stood there, biting her lip. Clory was the hardest person in the world to do something for. A body could comfort tears, but what could you do with a smiling shell? All that day she had tried to get behind there where the real Clory lay prostrate and quivering. Sometimes she grew afraid that everything was dead behind that shell.

Without thinking she spoke directly out of her fear.

'God knows best,' she said, and heard herself with horror. It sounded like preach!

But Clory only smiled and went on rubbing the cat.

'At least He thinks He does' — Clory saying things like that was what frightened Pal the most. 'All men think they do — men have lorded it over women since time began, and polygamy hasn't helped them think any less of themselves. Give a man a little authority — see what happens to any man when he gets to be made bishop!'

She smiled into Pal's startled face as if she had suddenly become on most intimate terms with God. 'You certainly know God is a He, all right, from the way He made women!'

Flustered, Pal bustled over to the carpet rags at Clory's feet, bent her pendulous body to retrieve the ball that had fallen to the floor, and began winding vigorously.

'But you believe in the Hereafter, Clory!'

That great dark gaze of Clory's, deep with such communings of the spirit, charged with such inarticulate woe — even Pal shrank.

'Yes,' said Clory slowly, 'I believe in the Hereafter. Sometimes you have to believe in the Hereafter in order to endure the Here.'

And Pal gave it up.

Clory's eyes were still upon her face.

'I'm all right, Pal. I've noticed that with everything, some of us always live through it!'

And that was the trouble, she thought, but did not say — the living through it. The sun would soon be setting behind the

Black Ridge over there, the long shadows begin to creep across the valley, and she would have to go home to the dreadful peopled loneliness of the dugout. For night always came. She'd prayed and God hadn't answered. All you had was something inside of you, not something up there in the sky. You had to bite down hard on that tough core and remember that everyone's reaching for Something — don't think you're the only one who's reaching! And go on painting on a smile, even at home. No one in 'Sheba's house had ever wanted any weather of hers but sunshine ... But all the reasons in the world did not help the nights. When the sun began to set, she wanted to burrow her head in somebody's skirts. How like the coyotes ...

Pal caught a hint of that buried fear.

'Lucy and I will walk down with you when you go.'

Clory's face came alive for a moment. It would be a reprieve ...

'It's a birthday present,' said Pal, covering the dish with a napkin. 'You can't look in it until you get home.'

Clory smiled, pulled herself up from her chair in the corner, and reached for her sunbonnet on the table.

'What about David?' she asked, as the three of them went out the door.

Pal laughed indulgently.

'Oh, David never can be content with just his farm like other men. He's out to the sheep-wagon, now — they just moved down from Pine Valley Mountain last week.'

Clicking the gate behind her, she glanced out of the corner of her eye at Clory's unsmiling face and sighed.

Clory, with that unaware look about her, leaned upon the gatepost for a moment and gazed back at the wildflowers David had planted in Pal's front yard, the gold-hearted daisies lifting pale petals since the rain. The primroses were already asleep in the shadow of the step, but the little white daisies were still awake — awake and innocent-eyed, with the wondering, uplifted look of her own Kissy.

'My laws, Clory, you're thin!' Lucy gave Clory an affectionate squeeze. 'Pal would make four of you!'

'Has 'Sheba cleaned house yet?' asked Pal, puffing along.

Clory nodded absently.

'My, she's certainly a rustler!' Lucy was admiring.

Clory bridled a little at that. All those years Willie had kept house for 'Sheba, scrubbed and washed and baked and now 'Sheba kept Willie from sharing the house, just as she kept her from sharing Abijah's letters. And yet when he came home it 'ud be the same, 'Sheba getting all the credit for keeping a roof over the family's head when all she had to do was gobble up her boys' wages, while Willie and Clory spent all those hours stirring soap . . .

Clory looked at her hands, shapeless and red from dish-suds and wash-suds. She never got them healed up from one washday to the next.

'You know,' she said, 'I think there's just two kinds of people in the world, and they're both willing. One kind's willing to shoulder all the burdens and the other kind's willing to let 'em do it!'

And yet even as she said it, she wondered if maybe she hadn't always been too hard on 'Sheba. Maybe having a disposition like 'Sheba's was like having a wart on the nose, harder on you than on anybody else . . .

But nevertheless she couldn't understand Pal's and Lucy's rush to get her over to the 'dobe house. Nor could she understand all the light streaming from the windows. 'Sheba wasn't one to waste candles. But when she pulled at the latch and opened the door and all the voices shrieked 'Surprise!' in her face, she knew she should have smelled a rat.

She stood there a moment gasping and blinking. Pal and Lucy behind her, the circle of faces, all smiling, all intent upon her, trying to see whether the surprise had made her happy.

Shaking her head to rid her eyes of sudden foolish tears, she spread her hands in a little gesture of welcome and apology.

Willie, with 'Sheba over by the hearth, remembered Clory's old habit of clasping her hands under her cheek when excited, and swallowed hard.

'Thank you,' said Clory, catching her breath. 'Would you mind if I — I went over to clean myself up?'

They all laughed, and she clutched Pal's hand, ducked under the door, scudded straight across the tender, 'stooling out' lucerne to the dugout. And if, as she changed to the narrow hoops, the bustle, and the sprigged yellow calico of many memories, if an elfin, big-eyed ghost watched from every corner, Pal was there to chatter hard against that pain.

Crushing bergamot leaves in the palms of her hands, her skirts rustling among the sunflowers and hollyhocks around the step, she hurried with Pal back across the dooryard. Already shouts of laughter from some game were coming from the other house.

For a moment, highlighted in the open doorway, young Regular Wheelock's face bent tenderly toward Eppy Gardner. Then she took his arm, giggling, and they merged into the shadows at the side of the house.

'They're playing "Take a walk" already,' said Pal, lifting her skirts away from the stripped sunflower stalks, sad in the twilight. 'Here, take your present,' — she handed Clory the covered dish. 'It's only almonds, but I ——'

Clory lifted the napkin to gaze upon the little huddle of brown almond meats.

'Oh, Pal!' she said, choking. What pinching, bargaining, contriving!

Pal was brusque.

'Hurry! We'll miss all the fun!'

In the house Clory clasped outstretched hands, answered greetings gaily, pushed her way through the boisterous guests to 'Sheba and Willie by the hearth.

'For the picnic,' she said, handing 'Sheba the almonds.

For a moment 'Sheba's brown eyes were soft.

''Twill be just what we need with the raisins and parched corn.'

'Thank you, 'Sheba and Willie,' said Clory, looking from one to the other and swallowing. 'I didn't expect it ...'

Willie smiled and fluttered her hands at the cameo brooch fastening the plaid silk piece at her neck, and 'Sheba extracted her handkerchief from the bosom of her dress and blew her nose vigorously.

'Well, child, see you have a good time!'

Funny, thought Clory, turning back into the crowd, how suffering brings you closer to people. Part of herself seemed to have oozed out into 'Sheba so that she understood her better.

She went over to say hello to the Yeast Lady and the younger Sister Hansen and Sister Joe Eardley, gossiping busily on the bed in the corner.

It seemed that almost everybody was at the party. Johnnie Lowgie, home from his mission with a new, alert look about him and a new store suit; Mercy Wheelock gazing at him with her heart in her eyes. There was Susan, her sister, making sheep's eyes at young 'Rassy Snow, also home from his mission. Those couples 'ud be heading for the Endowment House soon ... Ole Oleson's two strapping girls, never seeming quite to know what to do with their hands. Miny and Sis Eardley ogling Gottlieb Uttley in a corner, and Gottlieb as indifferent as a tomcat. Everybody expected Gottlieb to marry Sis, or after Cecil Davis flew the coop and her baby was born, at least Miny. But Gottlieb seemed determined to be an old bachelor. With his cabin on Swiss Block over in Mineral Park he seemed to be doing all right, making wine — they said he had one keg he was storing for the second coming of Christ. Looked like both the Eardley girls 'ud have to enter plurality if they wanted husbands.

Clory went among them all, shaking hands, smiling, dodging the boys who wanted to spat her twenty-six times, and making her voice carelessly gay to the girls chaffing about approaching old age.

Here came 'Sheba's Samuel and Abraham, dark cowlicks slicked down, clumsy cowhide boots soot-blackened — sober, industrious, unimaginative. The two Oleson girls flapped their hands, squealed at them, drew them over into the corner, where one of the girls promptly tripped over the spinning wheel, hooped petticoats sprawling, sending the crowd into convulsions of laughter.

Clory went to the door to welcome Aunt Ket Snow and Hannah Merinda Lowgie, hooped and shawled and hearty. Even with all the neighbors' chairs it did not seem there'd be enough to seat the older folks. Lucy was already leaning against the bedroom door-jamb, and Pal got up and shoved her rocker toward Aunt Ket, and stood beside Clory, her eyes admiring 'Sheba's clocks and china figurines winking in the candlelight on the mantel.

Again Clory must go to the door to welcome Bella Trupp, she who had been Bella Weeks. Thank heavens, she thought, smiling into Bella's wizened gopher-face, 'Sheba didn't invite Zebedee or those other two wives of his. I couldn't have stood it.

'It's a long walk over here from Mineral Park,' whined Bella, her red-rimmed gopher-eyes ferreting about the room.

'I know,' Clory said, leading her over to Pal and Lucy, 'one of the boys will see you home. But I'm glad you could come.'

Bella's little eyes darted at Pal's cumbersome figure as she leaned there against the mantel.

'Oh, Pal,' she snuffled, going up to the other girl and staring hard. 'You're going to have another kid!'

Clory turned away with a quiver of distaste. Since her marriage Bella was exactly like a startled prairie dog forever darting down its hole. But Clory had never noticed her eyes being so runny before — whether she cried unconsciously all the time or whether her eyes just watered, it made you sick.

Bella's hot hand pulled Clory back; she leaned close, putting her snuffling lips at her ear.

'Oh, Clory,' she whispered agitatedly, 'don't tell nobody, but he's too old! I've been cheated! I'm as much a virgin as the day I married him!'

Clory flinched and went to start a game. *Oh, God,* she thought, clapping her hands to make her voice heard above the hubbub, *don't let me knuckle to life like the others — Bella Weeks, marrying for children and getting teched, Eliza Hichinoper losing her child to the Indians and getting teched, Sister Miles fleeing from the howls of her whipped children, forever trying to drown herself* ... Did people think of Clory the way Clory thought of Bella Weeks? Did people look at Clory and shake their heads — 'Poor thing, she's all right, but ...' Or did they say carelessly, off-hand, 'Oh, Clory's nice enough,' as that snooty Marianne Snow had once said about Pal, thus damning her with faint praise?

Help me to be strong, she prayed, laughing and clapping her hands for attention. 'We'll play "Pass the slipper"! Gottlieb, Abraham, Johnny, help move the table and benches over against the window! Who'll be It?' *Oh, help me to be strong.*

The scraping of furniture over the floor, the flopping of rugs out of the way, the scrambling for places in the circle, arms linked, backs inward, excited eager faces fronting outside. Gottlieb was It, his great red hands grabbing for the shoe traveling stealthily around the outside of the circle. And when he was too 'cool' and someone seized the shoe by its heel and whacked him on the rump to bring him back to the scent, his grimaces and contortions and clumsy swoopings and clutchings sent the crowd into spasms of mirth. Sharp smell of vinegar-and-soot shoe-blacking, smells of starch, cloth, heated human flesh, and the rising smells of dripping candle grease and dust.

'Oh, Aunt 'Sheba!' Young 'Rastus Snow spied her in the doorway. 'We want Clory to be Grandmother Graff — can't you make her?'

Clory shrugged, smiled at the laughing faces. And with the broom to lean upon, her body immediately took on the gnarled stoop of an old woman, her face the wrinkled quivering, her voice the whine.

(How that old mimic-sense of hers comes back, thought Willie, still rocking placidly by the hearth.)

Here comes Old Grandmother Graff!
You must neither smile nor laugh
But say right down, I will!

Clory intoned at the circle of solemn, held-in faces.

'Johnnie Lowgie, will you crawl like a cat on a tin roof?'

'I will!' prated Johnnie.

'Mercy Wheelock, will you sit on Johnny Lowgie's knee?'

Too much for Mercy, who loved to giggle anyway.

'A forfeit, a forfeit!' sang Clory, holding up the ribbon Mercy took from her hair.

Around and around the game went, while 'Sheba and Willie went out to prepare the picnic. . . .

'Heavy, heavy hangs over your poor head,' chanted Clory, redeeming the forfeits.

'Fine or superfine?' asked Joseph, sprawling in the chair in front of her, his black eyebrows quirking.

'Fine. What shall the owner do to redeem it?'

'Oh, go to Jerusalem with Glad Covington,' drawled Joseph.

And Clory, holding his tie aloft, danced hilariously while the crowd went quite mad with delight, watching Joseph and his Gladys chewing toward each other on the string. Would they *really* kiss when they met in the middle? For Mercy, Painting the Plow with Johnnie, showed no hesitation in plunking herself firmly on his knee and doing the kissing on both cheeks! But poor Samuel Mac, having to 'Kneel to the prettiest, bow to the wittiest, kiss the one you love the best,' stared about him with horror and finally ended by flopping desperately in front of his mother, whose mole twitched with pleasure.

Although even that, thought Willie, watching from the doorway, wasn't as funny as that great lummox of a Gottlieb having to Haul a Load of Wood and rubbing his forehead earnestly up and down the wall.

Yes, it was a good party. No matter what happens to us, Willie said to herself, we'll get by as long as we can laugh like this . . .

'We haven't found out about the marrying, yet!' simpered Sis Eardley, her big bosoms palpitating.

And Sis had to eat the thimbleful of salt, while a hush fell on the watching room.

'Don't drink no water!' cautioned Miny.

Sis standing before them all, her bold eyes flashing, her voice singsonging:

> With a hey nonny bright,
> And a second sight,
> Oh, Lover, show your face tonight!

Clory drifted to the rear of the room and sank down on the bed beside the Yeast Lady and Sister Joe Eardley, who were staying to help with the dishes.

'You haf goot time?' The Yeast Lady bubbled over like a hot apple dumpling.

Clory's answering smile was gay, even if her eyes were wistful. Trooping through the room, leaving the boys diffident and uneasy by the door, the girls called out to her.

'Come on,' shrieked Susan Wheelock, brandishing 'Sheba's mirror. 'They say if you go down cellar backward with the looking-glass over your left shoulder, you'll be sure to see his face!'

Clory grinned and shook her head.

'You forget I'm an old middle-aged woman.'

'"Star-light, star-bright, first star I've seen tonight"' — that would be Eppy Gardner's childish voice piping outside — '"I hope to see my true love by this time tomorrow night!"'

Clory smiled around upon Bella Weeks and Pal and Lucy. That was all over for her, that was all over for all of them. Only one face would ever haunt her dreams, only one dear face — and she hoped he was riding one of the stars the girls were petitioning. But what a fuss people made over all this marrying business! Just one human creature among all the teeming millions of the world for another human creature, and it thought it could not live without the other! But it could ... You thought you could not live beside an empty cradle, but you could. As long as the world had been, women had gone on losing and weeping but they lived through it!

Willie, still standing in the door, felt a stab of fierce affection ... Nothing could kill that girl on the bed. Her vitality was like a fine perfume clinging to the pieces of the vial long after it was broken and shattered.

4

Erastus did not see anything unusual in the fact that his people should so soon turn their backs on grief and plunge into merry-making. Always it had been thus. Blackleg scurvy, cholera, black canker taking their toll. A time of terror and prayer. As inevitable as the seasons that rolled around. As a young man in Nauvoo he could remember the Prophet Joseph comforting, heal-ing the sick. If the Lord sent a trial you accepted it and were grateful there were enough of the living to bury the dead.

Nevertheless, when the storm Erastus had been dreading so long howled closer to Deseret with the introduction in Congress of the Cullom antipolygamy bill, Erastus was almost glad. There was nothing better to unite a people, to make them stand firm against apostasy and plagues from within, than persecution from without. Excitement stole over the whole territory, a feeling of forces gathering.

The foe organizing themselves into the Liberal Party, Ulysses the Silent in the White House and his avowed campaign to 'wipe out the Mormons.' Civilize them — bring on whiskey shops for the men and whore houses for the women! Deseret futilely peti-tioning for statehood for the sixth time.

Men in the Dixie Mission were no longer satisfied with news-clubs that met in homes for leisurely discussions. They jammed the street corners, the T.O., the telegraph office, and on Fridays and Wednesdays, when the mail-coach came in, crowds waited for hours in the square.

('Men'll grab an excuse every time to get out of work!' Aunt Ket summed it up for the women.)

And Erastus would read carefully:

'Reverend Daniel S. Tuttle, Episcopal Bishop of Montana, Idaho, and Utah, makes the statement that "there seems to be less profanity, rowdyism, rampant and noisy wickedness among the young Mormons than among the youth of any other town or city where I've been."'

'Jiminy crickets!' Lon Tuckett slaps his thigh and throws his hat in the air. Johnny Lowgie, the new telegraph operator, keeps his fingers on the keys ten hours a day.

But the victories were few.

Pal and Clory sat on the steps of the Social Hall and stared across at it wistfully. Clory brooded, chin in hand. The sun made such a glory on the shingle roof, and it was as if part of the glory had spilled over and turned into dandelions on the ditch-bank. Folks were gathering now, and spurts of dust rose from the heels of racing boys and made a golden smoke in the air, a smoke that blurred even the outlines of the Big House. Something always came along to blur your castles in the air ... When the dust was gone, there was left only a ribbon of the gold trembling a moment on the roof; then that was gone, too, and the soft twilight grew and deepened until it had a bloom like the purple of figs. The murmur of the little irrigation ditch along the sidewalk was suddenly clear and sweet, even above the chatter of the crowd. There was the far-off tinkle of cowbells where young herders brought their charges home from the fields, the lonely mooing of a cow for her calf.

In the twilight the white door in the Big House opened, and Apostle Snow and his three wives plodded down the steps and across the road like figures out of a dream. David Wight and Benjamin Jarvis and some of the brethren went out to meet them.

Suddenly someone shouted: 'Hooray! There's the mail!'

Everyone pelted out into the street to peer south through the dusk. Clory roused herself and moved with the rest, feeling in the twilight that her feet never quite touched the ground.

The mule teams, avid for a warm stable, sprang into the home stretch, their harnesses jingling and the coach swaying. The driver glanced briefly at the empty square, sighted the crowd a block away, tossed his hat, and cracked down hard with the jerkline.

He always pants when he gets out, Clory thought abstractedly, watching him shake hands and guffaw and pop backs and slap at the dust on his britches; he pants and the mules pant and everybody else pants for the mail. All except me. It never does me any good to pant.

Then Erastus was taking the brown leather bags from the driver, who was still calling out messages and jocosely offering to deliver kisses for all the absent lovers. Color and flash, dust and stamping feet and laughter and excited voices, and then the mail-coach was clattering back down the road and Erastus was leading the way into the hall.

'No need for the post office tonight,' he said, 'I'll cry it off on the stand.'

Erastus' black, frock-coated body looked thinner in the candlelight from the wall sconces as he stood there puffing his lips and joking, fishing for each letter in the bag, frowning to make out the writing, calling out the names.

Clory huddled between Pal and David, the old hunger in her heart. A body wanted *folks*.

And then incredibly Erastus' slow, quiet voice pronounced her name. She was struck so dumb that she could not move, and he repeated it.

'Clorinda Agatha MacIntyre!'

'Go on,' nudged Pal. 'That's for you!'

There was the vague sensation of floating up the aisle and

folks twitting her. 'From your best beau!' cackled Lon Tuckett. She could feel 'Sheba's eyes boring a hole in her back. She would have to somehow get together the postage... When she edged between the benches back into her seat, Pal wanted to look, and necks craned around, but she stuffed the long envelope with its foreign stamps hastily into the bosom of her dress. Abijah had written to *her, to her alone,* not just a line enclosed in 'Sheba's letter, and such a message was never meant for outside eyes. But the envelope burned against her skin like a kiss... *You can tell it was a man invented polygamy,* she thought, *whether it was the Lord or Joseph Smith. Don't they know that women have to have love? That they tie up into hard little knots without it? But even a third of a man is better than none at all....*

Erastus was speaking in slow, deliberate tones.

'This Cullom bill means war — folks. We can't let it pass the Senate.'

He reached for the opened papers, read a word or two.

'The Mormons could give... two or three years' fighting at an annual expense to us of not less than two hundred million dollars ——'

He looked up, pulling at his beard, grinning.

'I ain't so sure about that, folks — but here's the *Millennial Star:* "'Fire and Sword' seem to be the favorite arguments of bigoted parsons, small-beer politicians, wiggling pettifoggers, and scheming speculators" — I guess we'd better realize we've got mobocrats in Zion.'

The audience stirred at this.

'Oh, not like Missouri! I think we can lick 'em, all right... ptsahh... but the gentiles have made themselves into a "Utah Ring," a "ring of hungry agitators knocking at the doors of Congress"... These carpetbaggers, folks, are mostly... lawyers who came in during the land-jumping times in '66 when we didn't have clear titles to our land, and they thought they could make a lot of money out of our troubles with the Government.... Now if

this bill passes, and Congress takes away all our right to boss ourselves, and appoints an outside governor who can put in his own
men, where'll we be? Brother Brigham says, "Like birds of prey,
they snuff the carcass from afar...."'

Shadrach Gaunt unfolded his long legs in the back of the room.

'I say *fight!*'

Erastus writhed his lips in amusement.

'We ain't all got hind legs to rear upon like you, Shadrach.
Wait....

'You see, folks,' — Erastus traced a forefinger under the headlines of the spread papers — 'not everybody's against us. Here's
the *New York Herald* saying this bill's a "cruel and tyrannous
measure," and the *Missouri Republican*: "It is nothing more or
less than persecution"... Too many are on our side. We won't
have to fight, but we will have to waylay this Cullom bill. Here
— even in the gentile *Tribune* from the city: "The proposed Cullom bill would let a male polygamist escape scot-free by simply
giving up his female companions, but the women and children are
reduced to pauperism and forced to beg or starve."'

Erastus pulled at his beard.

'How many of you "male polygamists" want to escape scot-
free?'

The audience chuckled.

'Ptsahh! We will now hear from the "female companions."'

Erastus sat down and Pal heaved to her feet.

'I will read you,' she announced, her voice shaky with stage-
fright but her dish-face earnest in the candlelight, 'I will read
you the Resolutions prepared by the Female Relief Societies in
the city.

'"Resolved: That we, the ladies of Salt Lake City in mass-
meeting assembled, do manifest our indignation and protest
against the bill before Congress..."'

'Bills' and 'Congress' were just words, but the letter beneath
Clory's heart was real. She crouched in her seat and pulled out

the letter and stared at it a long time. There was something so
final about slitting an envelope. Abijah's spidery handwriting:

My dear Wives: (Clory read it twice, her heart quivering
with disappointment — so he hadn't thought of just her,
after all.)

My dear Wives:

You seem to think we will be home next fall. I can only
say I came to do the Will of God. When he is satisfied and
willing for me to return home I shall esteem it a great blessing, one that I shall prize whether anyone else does or not ...

(He's mad because we don't write oftener; Abijah was always
one to take rather than to give ...)

I can truly say I did not know how the world lived before
I came here. I have seen poverty in all its forms and cor-
ruption out-of-doors and in the houses, which makes me
love my religion and mountain home more than ever.

As to the death of our children ...

(Here it came — Clory shut her eyes against it for a moment.)

As to the death of our children, you know that Death
continues his work, and will till he reaches the doom of us all;
I hope the fatal hour will not find you unprepared. I want to
ask you if you pray in your families and with your children.
Do you teach them to pray? This trouble is God's judgment
on you, Clorinda Agatha.

(Don't say it!)

I have sent by the hand of Oscar Shupe twenty-five dollars
to be divided amongst you; I hope you will receipt the
brethren for the same. I am in flesh ...

(She chewed desperately on a thumb-knuckle.)

You may think I have forgotten you, but never: the ties
and covenants that bind and unite us together are stronger
than Death and the powers of Satan. I have about filled
up my paper and must bring my letter to a close, ever praying the Lord to bless us in keeping his commandments and

living in purity before him and in laboring faithfully to
build up his kingdom ...

(She leaned her forehead on the back of the bench in front and
let pain twist her mouth. ... Of course, it was right that he should
not show partiality, but the letter had been addressed to her and
she had thought —— She had tried so hard to do the things a
missionary's wife should do, supporting herself, attending all her
meetings, preserving decorum. And the only line that was hers,
alone: 'This trouble is God's judgment.')

'"Resolved,"' concluded Pal triumphantly, '"Resolved, that
we acknowledge the institutions of the Church of Jesus Christ of
the Latter-Day Saints as the only reliable safeguard of female
virtue and innocence!"'

And then her skirts were rustling as she sat down, and she was
nudging Clory.

'Hurry up; it's your turn —— What on earth's the matter?
You look like a ghost!'

Clory patted her hair, hastily shoved the letter back into her
bodice, and stood up. The candlelight blurred before her eyes.

'Brethren and sisters, we women are ready to fight for our
rights! There is no spot on this wide earth where kindness and
affection are more bestowed upon women ...'

5

In later years, since the grapes had done so well and wine was
so plentiful, there had been drunkenness in the communities, and
Gottlieb always celebrated his days in town with a spree. What
with Virgin bloat and the mineral water of the Red Hill springs,
the wine they had been called to raise was a good thing for the
Dixie Mission (although folks did say there were those who attended meeting only to partake of that sip of wine in the Sacrament), but Erastus couldn't abide drunkenness. He had finally
persuaded the City Council to pass a law forbidding anyone to

purchase over five hundred gallons at a time, which stumped the casual drinker but gave plenty of leeway to those who wished to peddle wine in the North.

Linking arms with Gottlieb, puffing a little beside the other's easy stride over the harsh salt-grass hummocks, he writhed his lips and frowned.

'I trust,' he said tentatively, 'I trust, Brother Uttley, that — ptsahh! — that the new rule doesn't discommode you ——'

But Gottlieb wasn't at all disturbed. His red face broke into a grin.

'Vell,' he said, 'vife hundred gallon iss von pig trink,:Brother Snow!'

And Erastus had to be content with that. But he wasn't one to give up. He broached the matter to Brother Brigham, standing on the steps of the Social Hall, waiting for the Saints to assemble for April Conference.

But Brother Brigham twiddled his thumbs above the well-filled buttons of his waistcoat and regarded Erastus mildly. Since work on the Salt Lake Temple had been halted by all this governmental trouble he had for a time been afraid that his dream of a Temple for Latter-Day Israel — one that even Joseph would be proud of — was about to be shattered. He had at last decided to give that sacred responsibility to the Saints of Dixie. Here they were isolated enough to be unmolested and besides, Temple-building would mean he could throw the resources of the Church their way and so help save the Cotton Mission. He'd wondered how they'd receive the news — and here was Erastus being a fussbudget!

'You're a fussbudget, Brother Snow,' he said, taking in the wide, clean streets, the growing Tabernacle, the new gardens, the sober, industrious couples verging on the church. 'You fuss like an old hen.' And before Erastus could protest, the President had stepped down and was offering his hand to Clorinda Mac-Intyre, rounding the slope of the corner with Bathsheba and Willie.

Oblivious of Erastus' exasperation, 'Sheba's hard-eyed envy, the stares of the curious, he patted Clory's rough little hand, and his stern gaze that glittered so coldly behind the ramparts of his brows softened at sight of the small pointed face, the mouth that held its long chapped curve, the bewildered pain locked far back in the dark eyes.

'Clorinda Agatha MacIntyre!' he said, a smile teasing the corners of his set lips. 'Are you strong in the ways of the Lord?'

Clory's natural spontaneity rushed out to meet him and he was reminded of the child, Clory, a gay, dark-eyed sprite of a thing like his own flesh and blood, going to school with his own youngsters in the little stone schoolhouse back of the Beehive house. She had changed; sorrow and privation had laid cruel hands upon her, but the spirit he recognized still lived valiantly within the troubled flesh. He was not sorry he had given her over to adversity. Spirits like hers were what would keep the Dixie Mission on its feet long after a man's stout strength succumbed. Her unquenchable gaiety was good for a man like Erastus Snow, whose incessant fussing over details (as if one boy's tipsiness and one river's dam were all that plagued a Brigham Young!) almost drove him crazy at times.

But he squeezed her hand and murmured with distress over her pallor.

'You must not grieve, Clorinda Agatha; such long sorrow is unseemly. It was the Lord's business and therefore no cause for grief.'

Clory nodded humbly.

'I am trying, Brother Brigham. But it is so hard to make a living down here ...'

Brigham pursed his lips and stared down at her thoughtfully. Yes, he'd forgotten about Brother Mac's mission. 'Get the Indians to show you how to make buckskin gloves, Clorinda. There's always a good market for that kind of thing in the City, and you could command your own price from these silly gentiles pouring in.'

She thanked him, and he smiled so that his curly white beard spread like a fan, and offered her his arm. Her fingers touched the good black broadcloth of his sleeve and she swept by them all, 'Sheba and Willie, Apostle Snow and even that snooty Marianne, up the steps and into the building, prouder than she had ever been in her life.

Such a flurry of planting that spring! All the missionaries bringing home trees, the Lombardy poplar, the ailanthus, the mulberry for sericulture, Osage orange, honey locust, weeping willows and tamarisks. David Wight and Benjamin Jarvis organizing the Pomologist Club, inviting the town to Tree-Plantings.

> ... That be our aim and this our recompense,
> We'll dig and prune by science and by sense!

cackled Lon Tuckett.

> If you want fruit for your heirs,
> Plant pears!

concluded David in the *Utah Pomologist*, under which disguise the little *Cactus* strutted briefly.

Gottlieb Uttley, who had just bought from Tutsegabbett the Sonuvabitch Spring above the Upper Gap where the road wound between the Red Hill and the Black Ridge to Santa Clara, brought in peanuts, lemons, grapefruit, pomegranates from California to stock his ranch, with extra cuttings for the settlers, who enthusiastically carried water to the little plants, coaxing them to grow as one coaxes a baby to smile. Almost every home had its experimental plant to nurse. On the day that Gottlieb brought in his rose cuttings the whole town turned out to see. *Roses!*

Running all the way to Mineral Park, not noticing the searing thrusts of crusty alkali beneath her feet, Clory wet great plantain leaves to wrap about her cutting, which she carried home in her two hands, as if it might break. Following Gottlieb's instructions she put it under a glass jar, and gazed at the little wilted shoot and prayed.

Gottlieb had beamed at her fondly. Even unmarried she would have been beyond him, but he could still dumbly adore.

'Dis rose, he iss called Giant of Battles, he iss red und schweet, he climb all ofer your roof!'

And some day, thought Clory, I'll have him climbing all over the trunks of the cottonwoods in the street.

But 'Sheba sniffed at the little plant in its glass jar squatting among the hollyhocks lining the dugout path. She could understand taking pains with shade trees and vegetables and even sunflowers that grew without too much coddling. But all this to-do over roses. Humph!

She was still standing there, sniffing at Clory on her knees loosening the hard-packed soil at the roots of her flowers, when Buck Hairlip shuffled up to the gate. At sight of the Indian 'Sheba lifted her head contemptuously. This idea of Clory's, to learn squaw's work!

Clory took in his pot-belly, his dirty, civilized breeches, his broad swarthy face with its gathered upper lip, and remembered Tutsegabbett's hard, muscular leanness and dignity when she had first seen him on that long-ago trip to see the sego lilies. Already the Indian arts were vanishing. Squaws still tanned buckskin, but they preferred the white woman's skirts, layer piled upon layer with each succeeding season, until one could read a squaw's history through her skirts. There was even a difference in the old Indian-smell. Where before there had been a kind of wild honesty in that old odor compounded of sagebrush, unwashed brown skin, and years of campfire smoke, there now had come to be a taint that was peculiarly white.

Clory got to her feet and brushed the soil from her hands.

'Hello, Buck,' she said, smiling. 'They tell me your wife is a good hand at tanning buckskin.'

Buck understood English and could speak it after a fashion. He looked her over, taking in her littleness.

'That's a helluva squaw,' he muttered, shaking his head and stalking away.

'Sheba laughed, but Clory ran after him and grasped his bare arm.

'I know tanning buckskin takes work, but I'm stronger than you think. See?' She flexed her biceps to show him. 'Will you take me out to your camp to see your wife?'

The Indian grunted, nonplussed by such persistence in a female.

'Sheba was enjoying this. She strode up to Buck and peered down at him.

'Oh, Buck,' cooed 'Sheba in the tone of voice some women use to idiots and children, 'what pretty brown eyes you've got! Give me your eyes!'

'All right,' said Buck, his upper lip bunching back from his teeth, and his finger touching each eye in turn.

'Give me one tousand dollars I take this eye out; give me another tousand dollar I take other eye out. Good eyes. I only wear um one time.'

Clory had never seen 'Sheba so effectively silenced.

Clory turned back to the business in hand. The Indian was now ready to bargain.

Thus it was that while Pal and Lucy spent Sunday afternoons visiting the new trees being brought in, Clory spent every free hour of that spring among the mangy dogs and runny-nosed papooses of an Indian camp.

Never in all her history had Deseret been inflicted with a federal chief justice so boldly frank about his purposes as Mc-Kean. First of all he suggested that the guns of Camp Douglas be trained upon the new Tabernacle (preferably with its nine thousand seats filled up and all twenty of its nine-foot-wide doors

bolted to shut off escape, thought Erastus grimly); and he made
no bones about the nature of his judgeship in Utah — it was
simply a crusade.

'The mission which God has called upon me to perform in
Utah,' he announced bluntly, 'is as much above the duties of
other courts and judges as the heavens above the earth, and
whenever or wherever I may find the local or federal laws ob-
structing or interfering therewith, by God's blessing I shall
trample them under my feet.'

God must be at His wits' end sorting out prayers, decided
Erastus, sweating in the telegraph office that somnolent summer
Sunday before the Fourth, while the martial band and Staheli's
band took turns practicing in the hall above him.

Tomorrow the bands would serenade, and the cannon boom,
and gangs of youngsters on hayracks go melon-swiping, and
Benjamin Jarvis would read the Declaration of Independence,
and Erastus would give a speech about our 'Glorious country!'
with a small black imp of hate in his heart.

Yes, it looked as if the carpetbaggers had come. And though
Brother Brigham still refused to be agitated, even he must see
that they had but one purpose, to prevent any kind of local self-
government so that they might prey upon Utah and eat out her
substance.

You had to admit that McKean was thorough. Between that
Fourth and the next Fourth of July he managed to bring Utah
to the very verge of civil war.

In September the War Department issued a request for the
annual return of the militia of Utah Territory, and for this reason
Lieutenant-General Wells ordered out the Legion for a three days'
muster. Erastus could not leave, but sent Colonel Shadrach
Gaunt. And then, almost immediately, the first wire came.

Governor Shaffer had set aside General Wells's order, forbade
all gatherings of militia, and ordered all arms given up. So the

Legion went out: thirteen thousand men, efficiently armed, drilled, equipped, an organization dating back to Nauvoo days, an organization that had helped make possible the settling of the West. And it seemed to Erastus that the ink could scarcely have been dry before the United States soldiery took advantage of the helpless Saints.

At midnight on September 23, forty or fifty drunken men from Camp Rawlins entered Provo, armed with needle guns, bayonets, and revolvers. They dragged citizens from their bedrooms, demolished houses, scattered their contents in the street, paraded their victims, beating them with rifles and pricking them with bayonets.

'Come out, you God-damned Mormons and Mountain Meadow Massacreers!' they yelled. 'This has been Utah territory, but now it's Uncle Sam's territory, and we're going to run it, for we've got the men to back us!'

The devils can't even be tried, Erastus groaned, since Shaffer's destroyed the civil courts! And Shadrach Gaunt was up there. Knowing his nature, Erastus did not ever expect to see his lanky, taciturn colonel again.

But Shadrach galloped furiously in, one day; drew up his lathered cayuse alongside the Social Hall, where the usual spit-'n'-whittle gang and some Indians squatted in the shade.

'Where's Apostle Snow?' he demanded, venom in the cold squint of his blue eyes.

There had never been any love lost between Shadrach and the Indians he had fought all his life. They called him 'Me Make-Um Gaunt,' because Shadrach always wanted to fix everything himself, lick the world single-handed.

Buck Hairlip suddenly detached himself from the group and lumbered toward the startled pony, waving his hat in the air and shouting.

'Hello, you Gaunt! Hello, you Gaunt!'

The cayuse bucked. Shadrach, surprised for once, slipped off into the dirt

Instantly Buck was solicitous.

'Whatsa matter you, Gaunt, too much howdedo?'

But Shadrach was too full of his own anger to be even irritated.

He brushed off his buckskins, ignored the high laughter of the Indians, and strode into the telegraph office. Erastus had been there since noon. Shadrach's fingers played with the gun sticking out of its holster as if it were so much more sensible than these words he found so difficult.

'They ordered us to give our guns up,' he said grimly, 'but they'll git this un over my carcass.'

He spat with deadly accuracy at an ant on the wall.

'The God-dummed bastards! I caught two of 'em with a sister's spoons, and stomped 'm both down a gopher-hole!'

Shadrach expressed the sentiment of the community when he declared, 'By dang, I still say fight!'

'With wooden guns?' Erastus asked him one day in November, reading Brother Brigham's latest message.

'*Wooden gun rebellion!*' Brother Brigham headlined. The young Third Regiment Band held a drill in the Twentieth Ward schoolhouse to show off their new instruments, and the Federals rushed to the scene and arrested the principal leaders on charges of 'treason and rebellion.' ... 'They were just a lot of boys with wooden guns!' snorted Brother Brigham.

That winter Erastus began to think that all the years of famine and floods and plagues had actually been of a leisurely tempo. Shaffer died, but McKean was as lively and slippery as a lizard.

Erastus, even at entertainments, sitting in the Social Hall, immersed in 'East Lynne' with Clorinda MacIntyre as Isabella and David Wight as Carlyle, with Isabella on her prayer-bones begging, 'Oh, forgive me!' and Carlyle, that manly man, not able to see how he can, and Lon Tuckett choking from the audience, 'I can't stand this any more! For gosh' sakes, forgive her, man!' — with the audience convulsed, Erastus was still aware of that little warning gong in his heart: *Laugh while you can!*

On the Fourth of July, 1871, the Federals forbade the Saints to celebrate, forbade the appearance of the martial brass bands, and ordered out the United States troops to disperse the crowd at the point of the bayonet.

Erastus, tired of chewing his fingernails, decided that this was a *contretemps* deserving of some action at last, especially since the news had dampened the local doings.

'What do you want us to do?' he wired Brother Brigham.

The President's answer was characteristic. It came while the priesthood were assembled at a School of the Prophets in the basement of the Tabernacle. *The time has come,* wired Brother Brigham, *to build a Temple to the Most High in St. George!* A thrill of joy ran over the rows of elders. They were on their feet, cheering. Out of the whole of Deseret, *they* were to be given the privilege!

Erastus, contemplating the Tabernacle, its volcanic foundations and the walls of red sandstone in that corner of the square next to the bowery, loved them for the enthusiasm which could disregard empty bellies, finish a Tabernacle in one breath and start a Temple in another — plan for the dead one moment and plant trees for the living the next!

But that was before the arrests began.

That fall Thomas Hawkins was sentenced by Judge McKean to a fine and three years' imprisonment for adultery with his wives. Mayor Daniel H. Wells, Brother George Q. Cannon, Henry W. Lawrence, and Brigham Young were arrested and placed under bond for lascivious cohabitation.

'They make it such a nasty mouthful,' said Erastus, gagging over the words '*Lascivious cohabitation.*'

The crowd gathered there in the October twilight were stunned. Brother Brigham had once said, 'This is the Place — *because nobody else wants it!*' And now...

Erastus stood on the steps, his head sunk on his chest, one hand pulling at the gray fringe on his chin.

A murmur of protest arose and grew. The clots of people broke, re-formed, broke again. Red dust filtered upward into the blue October haze.

David Wight waited near the steps with his two wives, Pal and Lucy, whitely clinging to each other. Pal, frightened eyes on Erastus, was thinking that her father was in the city — her father with his three wives. Suddenly her little plump chin set. This was a land of religious liberty, was it not? She grasped Lucy and ran with her to the steps beside Erastus and held their joined hands aloft and cried in a firm, clear voice, 'Friends, this is my husband's wife!'

Startled faces stared at her. Erastus came out of his dark abstraction and grinned.

'That's just about it, folks,' he said. 'Ptsahh!'

6

The Lion of the Lord might scoff, but time and his enemies were beginning to tell on him. That November day in 1871 Erastus sat in his little office back of the stage in the Social Hall and watched Brother Brigham detach a geranium from the bouquet the Sunday-School children had given him, and fasten it in his buttonhole with fingers that were not as steady as they might have been. The President looked tired. There were new lines in his face, new shadows beneath gray eyes that seemed too weary to open fully. The hair still curled around the lobes of his ears but the brown had entirely faded to white there, now; and the beard that used to crisp with vitality almost to his high-buttoned waistcoat was white, too, and cut shorter, so that it did not quite cover his black cravat. Brother Brigham had never worn a mustache, but his beard had formerly grown thickly high upon his chin and cheeks around to his ears. The mouth was a hard, straight line.

But the thing that hurt Erastus the most was seeing Brother

Brigham lean upon a cane. His figure seemed to have grown pudgier in places and yet thinner all at once, and he had sighed, lowering himself into Erastus' big armchair, and confessed that he was having a little trouble with rheumatics in his legs.

And yet Erastus, almost twenty years younger, looked at the man across from him and was conscious of his own scanty chin-beard that had been gray-streaked for ten years, the growing bald spot on the top of his head, the sterile quality of his eyebrows, that in the last two or three years had practically vanished, so that when he observed himself in a mirror he seemed all forehead. And you couldn't account for the difference between them with the reflection that the Snows were not a hairy race. Even at seventy, Brigham Young had more spunk about him than any of his assistants. He was a great man. Erastus suddenly goose-pimpled with the abrupt awareness of the time, the place, the circumstances. He, Erastus Snow, was an apostle to the Prophet of God! How dreadful to have been born even a king at any other period in the world's history!

But Brother Brigham's temper had grown so short of late that one never knew quite what to say to him.

Erastus reached across to the desk and read again the scare headlines of the papers Brother Brigham had brought down with him.

'*Brigham Young has been indicted!*' blazed the *New York Herald*. '*The Mormons Arming! ...*'

His eyes upon Erastus, Brother Brigham smiled shortly.

'That paper came out a whole day before I was arrested!'

'Was there really any trouble?' asked Erastus.

Brother Brigham gestured vexedly.

'Oh, a few of the brethren with more zeal than horse-sense broke up a Liberal Party meeting ——'

'What about this fire in Chicago?'

Brother Brigham grunted and went on playing with the flower in his buttonhole.

Erastus read down the column sent in to the *New York Herald* by Mrs. Lippincott, the lady-lecturer.

> It was a strange thing to see these men standing at bay, with the people of the United States against them, giving generously to their enemies. About twenty-thousand dollars raised. It is Hagar ministering to Sarah ——

'Balderdash!' grunted Brigham, the old humor glinting for a moment in his eyes. Erastus read on.

San Francisco Examiner:

> The 'Mormon trouble' is instigated by a 'ring' of Republican politicians who...know they will have no show for promotion until the Mormon power is broken ... and so seek to create a civil war by means of packed juries, unprincipled judges, perjured witnesses...
>
> The packed grand jury found an indictment against Brigham Young for 'lewdly and lasciviously associating and cohabiting with women, not being married to them.'

'Find me that little booklet, "Footlights,"' said Brother Brigham. 'It's a program of entertainments in the Opera House.'

His left hand resting on the gold knob of his cane, he settled back in the armchair and closed his eyes.

Erastus was too engrossed to listen.

Here was the *Salt Lake Tribune*, bitter 'anti-Mormon':

> It was a decidedly novel spectacle yesterday afternoon to see the 'Lion of the Lord' sitting in the courtroom waiting for the coming of his earthly judge to try him.... The moral effect of Brigham's appearance and the conviction of innocence which it produced ... will bring many of the gentiles to the help of Israel, even as it has already brought two of their lawyers to the defense of the prophet. Perhaps there was more respect and sympathy felt for Brigham Young when he left the courtroom, feeble and tottering from his recent sickness. ...

Brigham's eyes were again upon his apostle.

'Some of 'em say I fled from justice,' he grunted.

Erastus shook his head over the stupidity of humanity and

gazed across at the tired old man sitting there, indifferent to both praise and blame, asking only to be left alone.

'Well, quit gawking at me!' Brother Brigham testily pounded his cane on the floor. 'It's time to go to the dedication, anyway.' He drew out his gold watch, whose chain gleamed across his vest. 'Eleven o'clock. Humph!'

The two men walked out into the mellow November sunlight.

'I told Amelia to meet me with the carriage by the Tabernacle corner,' said Brigham. 'I want to see what progress you've made.'

He pulled his frock coat straighter and sighed.

'You don't know how good this sun feels to me, Brother Snow. Now my house is finished I hope to stay all winter.'

Yes, he limped somewhat and used his cane noticeably, Erastus thought.

At the Tabernacle corner Brigham gazed thoughtfully at the large red-rock building, still encased in its pole-scaffolding, and at the miscellaneous clutter of stones around the yard.

'I don't know why you can't get ahead on this,' he said, his voice edgy. 'I pay the men in good scrip. With all this work, there shouldn't be a single loafer such as I see about the streets. That's what's the matter with this mission — loafers! Now, I want all this trash cleaned up from the yard and all the brush grubbed from the square — ten years, and you still have brush growing in the public square! And I want you to be ready to lay the Tabernacle capstone by December, at least . . .'

Suddenly he straightened and peered down the street. 'Isn't that Clorinda Agatha?' he asked, and when Erastus nodded, 'Well, call her! Call her!'

Erastus did as he was told, and Brother Brigham stood waiting for her, half-smiling, twiddling his thumbs.

'Clorinda Agatha!' he said, beaming down upon her. 'I brought you something . . . Where's that "Footlights" program, Brother Snow?'

Erastus, chagrined, feeling the color run into his skin that had
always been fair for a man, had to admit he'd forgotten it.

Brother Brigham's temper slipped.

'Go on home and hoe in your garden!' he thundered to Erastus.
'It's all you're good for!'

Brother Brigham sat in his barouche between Amelia and Emmeline and stared at the back of his coachman's shiny tall hat.
Where was Erastus? Why did the people keep him waiting? So
slow to gather! He liked punctuality!... The Temple site was
directly kitty-cornered from the MacIntyre block, and yet even
Clorinda was keeping him waiting.

'Now, Father, calm yourself,' said Emmeline Free.

Here came Clorinda, at last, lifting her skirts over the dust of
the road. She had something in her hand — a pair of buckskin
gloves. So she had taken his advice! He was pleased.

Clory rattled on about the gloves.

'No, I didn't make 'em,' she explained. 'They're Sally squaw's,
but I watched her and I'm going to make my own this
winter.'

Brother Brigham listened, interested, but he was impatient.

The wagons and people and carriages were gradually clotting
about the white hill he had selected — he counted forty carriages.
Even Staheli's band. But no Erastus.

'Where is Apostle Snow?' he asked Bishop Gardner, standing
by the barouche.

Bishop Gardner's mouth quirked.

'He said you told him to go on home.'

Brigham ground his cane on the floor of the carriage in exasperation.

He was getting hungry, and so were the horses, stamping and
rattling their tasseled harnesses.

But young Lehi MacIntyre galloped back on his pony, grinning
at his sudden self-importance.

'Apostle Snow said to "Tell Brother Young I'm hoeing in my garden!"'

And so, perforce, Mahomet had to go to the mountain.

The crowd, weary with waiting, cheered when they saw Brother Brigham's barouche rolling back down the long street, the white horses prancing.

Brother Brigham sat with a twinkle in his eye and an arm about Erastus' shoulders.

'You mustn't mind my tantrums,' he said.

When he finally stood up in the carriage to address the crowd, he had fully recovered his good nature. His forefinger came up in that old gesture and his words were quiet and deliberate.

'Brethren and sisters, when I got you all out to show me where to put the Temple' (there were grins at this; everybody knew what 'showing' Brother Brigham meant) 'you each had a different idea. Some of you favored the top of the Black Ridge because of the view, others Mount Hope because of the springs there. I said to you, "Brethren, none of you have seen the place to put the Temple. It's the white hill south of town."

'"But it's minerally down there, we can't make a garden down there!" you cried.

'And I said, "Yes, you can. The men with their teams can haul in good land out of the valley where the sagebrush is growing!"

'You thought you had me stumped when you offered me the objection of the bog, but I reminded you of the pile-driver which could pound rocks into the bog until the mud would ooze up on the sides and be hauled away, leaving the solid rock foundation.

'I said to you, "Brethren, you can see the Temple on this white hill from more points than any site you've shown me!" Now do you believe me?'

Shouts of 'Yes, Brother Brigham!'

'All right, then,' said Brigham, his eyes twinkling. 'Brother Wheelock, lead us in an anthem.'

After the song, Apostle George A. Smith knelt in the dust and bowed his head. Hats came off. There was no sound but the clear trill of a meadowlark out in the brush.

'Receive our thanks and the dedication of this land and our future work in rearing a Temple to Thy name . . .'

There was another anthem, and then Staheli's silver band played 'Onward, Christian Soldiers.'

Brother Brigham took the shovel, walked a pace or two, and uncovered his head.

'This is the spot where the foundation stone will be laid, and where the records will be placed. We will now proceed to break ground.'

Puffing a little, he dug a shovelful and then handed the shovel to Apostle Smith. When it came Erastus' turn, he was afraid he would wear blisters on his hands before he forced the blade through the baked, white ground.

The crowd was solemn and very still. Clory shivered.

And then the congregation sang, 'The spirit of God like a fire is burning; the Latter-Day glory begins to come forth,' after which Brother Brigham again stood up in his carriage.

'This is how you make the salutation,' he said. 'Raise the right hand to heaven and smite the left breast, exclaiming "Hosanna to God and the Lamb." Already, now, in chorus with me —!

> Hosanna to God and the Lamb!
> Hosanna to God and the Lamb!
> Hosanna to God and the Lamb!
> Amen! Amen! Amen!'

Brother Brigham raised his arms aloft to dismiss, but he never finished.

There was suddenly the sound of furious galloping.

The crowd murmured; Brother Brigham turned and scowled up the street at the churning dust of the rider. Johnny Lowgie burst out of the dust, drew rein until his pony's feet pawed the air.

'McKean,' Johnny gasped, waving a yellow slip. 'Brother Brigham, Judge McKean has charged you with murder!'

CHAPTER XII

E RASTUS stood on the steps of the Social Hall and tried to quiet the Saints. It looked as if every person at the dedication was following Brother Brigham, in spite of his express orders for them to go on home.

The crowd hushed, listening to Erastus' quiet drawl.

The defense, he said, had asked for a postponement of Brother Brigham's trial to the March term, 'according to previous expectation,' but McKean's court — catcalls and hisses at the hated name — had set the trial *one week from that day*, knowing the defendant could not possibly reach the city in that length of time.

The defense had explained that it was a three-hundred-and-fifty-mile trip, and that in many places the roads were not roads at all. But the court was obdurate. *Defendant must appear one week from today!*

Erastus held up a hand to soothe indignant snorts.

'It ain't the "lascivious cohabitation" — it's the murder charge. Brother Brigham and Mayor Wells have been accused of murdering somebody named Yates — during the Echo Cañon War...'

Zebedee Trupp, squatting on the ditch-bank, jumped up and waddled toward Erastus, his chin outthrust, his little eyes gleaming.

'My Gadfrey, man,' he yelped above the general outcry, 'that be fifteen year ago!'

'Where in the Sam-Hill's Shadrach Gaunt?' Hannah Merinda's chins wobbled belligerently. 'He'd show us how to fight!'

'Hush, Mother' — Johnny's new bride, Mercy, pulled her back in alarm.

Shadrach Gaunt had gone to Fort Defiance with Jacob Hamblin to attempt a treaty of peace with the Navajos. Erastus, remembering, was glad. All the Federals wanted was one show of resistance. One good excuse and they'd be upon the Saints like a pack of mad dogs. But Brother Brigham's people had given over one prophet into the hands of a treacherous mob — they were not going to be tricked into delivering another.

The door behind Erastus opened and Brother Brigham, George A. Smith, his first counselor, David Wight, Robert Gardner, and the rest of the St. George High Council crowded out upon the step.

A great shout went up.

Brother Brigham's lips were clamped shut in a hard line and his eyes were cold, but there was no sign of fear about him.

'I have sent word to them that if Brigham Young's guilty of any such crime let them trace it to me!'

He pounded on the step with his cane and his white beard trembled.

Remembering the accumulated insults of the years, Erastus looked at the old man standing there on the steps and marveled that bitterness did not turn him inside-out. But Brother Brigham's lips were already twisting with their old ironic humor.

'Don't worry,' he said, placid again. 'They can't do anything to me. It is as easy as an old shoe.'

But the next morning, when Pine Valley Mountain was white with snow, his brave words seemed like puffs of cottonwood down. If the weather had held ...

Work stopped in the Dixie Mission and men clung like flies to Johnny Lowgie and his telegraph key. After the fourth day the key refused to click: wires were down. Men talked in whispers, as people do in the presence of death or illness.

At Kanarra, on the second day out, the coach-train was met by the veteran lifeguard of the Prophet Joseph Smith. 'Brother John D. Parker wept like a child,' wired William Rossiter, official telegrapher of the party; 'he considers this going back an act of madness.'

But Brother Brigham went right on. All was well at Cedar Fort. In spite of snow on the ground, the weather still held. At Beaver, a hundred miles farther on, William Rossiter sent word: 'Tried to make Cove Fort this evening but blizzard came up just as we were hitching horses.' By the next evening he was wiring from Cove Fort: 'Foot of snow in Wildcat Pass, sometimes could not see our animals.'

Then after Cove Fort there was silence for four long days.

Erastus, knowing the roads, treacherous with chuckholes and thank-you-marms beneath fresh snow, twisting steeply and narrowly around the mountain-sides whose slippery edges rolled off into eternity, cursed his imagination. Brother Brigham's horses floundering in drifts. Cold that crept into an old man's bones in spite of hot bricks and buffalo robes. The grueling distances between settlements, notwithstanding the string Brother Brigham's foresight had planted between Salt Lake City and St. George.

Toward evening of the ninth day — still no news from the North — Shadrach Gaunt and Jacob Hamblin strode in upon the little group of dispirited men. There was something extra swashbuckling about Shadrach, stooping under the lintel, towering beside gentle Jacob with his 'straight-talking' eyes, clapping the Indian interpreter on his dusty, homespun back.

'Well, boys, you don't have to worry no more!' he yelped.
'We've got a treaty with them dirty Navajos at last!'

'*We?*' mimicked Lon Tuckett.

Shadrach narrowed his eyes at Jacob and laughed.

'Jake, here, goes into camp and parleys, but *I* hadta stay out
in the brush so the varmints couldn't smell me!'

Shadrach shifted his quid to the other cheek.

'Town looks like a graveyard — what's wrong?'

His keen, ugly face pointed into the gloom of the room like a
hunting-dog's in the wind.

Erastus told him.

Shadrach's squint lost its humor.

'Them bitchin' bastards!' he said slowly.

Jacob involuntarily lifted a hand in protest and Shadrach
swung on him vehemently.

'By gadder, Jake' — he looked earnestly at the others — 'he's
been a-croakin' to me about my swearin' and terbaccer (cripes, a
feller can't stummick that Injun crap forever!) all the way from
Pipe Springs, so I says to him' — he turned back to Jacob, his
guthooks jingling — 'By gadder, Jake, you do the prayin' and
I'll do the fightin'!

At that moment the telegraph instrument began to click.
Johnny Lowgie straightened, a smile on his face. Erastus grabbed
the paper.

'Arrived safely,' he read in a voice that shook a little. 'President tired but well. Brother Brigham left Nephi at 6.30 A.M. today, riding with Bishop John Sharp in an open buggy to catch
train at Draper. Horses had to be led. Arrived City midnight,
ready for trial.'

'Lots of snow up there,' said Shadrach Gaunt, looking for a
place to spit; 'seems like it's a different world when you drop
over the rim of the pocket — green grass here, an ...'

Erastus was too relieved to say a word.

2

The stitching was hard to see on the black velvet ribbon. Clory pulled at it with her pin, her eyes squinting. With thread so dear one could not afford to throw away an inch.

'I wish,' she said pensively, 'we weren't so darned far away from everything; I wonder if we'll ever see the day when things like pins and needles ain't — isn't — way out of sight!'

'Well,' said Willie, puffing over the churn dasher, 'be glad for Lucifer matches!' She looked curiously at the girl's bent head. 'Do they learn you not to say "ain't" at Sister Couzzens' school?'

Clory flushed.

'Oh, I just picked that up... I know that everybody thinks I'm crazy, to go to school with them kids just learning to read and write, but Willie, there's so much I don't *know*. And now's the only chance I'll git, before Abijah comes home.'

'Well, anyways, I think that woman charges too much!'

'No, she don't, Willie! Besides, since her husband's got himself another family to support, she has to earn a living same as us other women. Oh, Willie, Apostle Snow says that some day there'll be *free* schools! Think of it!'

Willie grunted, and churned vigorously, the cream sloshing as she pushed the dasher up and down.

'Mebbe — after we've grubbed brush for a generation! Look at you, stoop-shouldered at twenty-eight! And you never will have decent hands again!'

Clory's chin set. She knew her skin was like leather and her hair lusterless, but even a woman, if she slogged in the fields from dawn to dark, got four bushels an acre cutting and gleaning grain on shares. Every Saturday of the summer and fall she had had her gleaning of grain or cotton (twelve and a half cents per pound for cotton in the seed was not to be sneezed at with ordinary jeans at fifty cents a yard) for the factory at Washington. If you couldn't hitch a ride, you walked the full five miles; then, after you had dumped your bundle upon the counter, there was the wait while the clerk got around to weighing it.

But whether she came home with flour or thread or wool rolls or roughage or thrums or the harsh linsey woolsey, she had the means for trade that would finally end up in an Indian camp and another buckskin in her hands. Already, back of the dugout, she had three skins curing in their ten-foot-square hole in the ground. In another year she'd be a woman with a business of her own.

There was a knock at the door, and the Yeast Lady stood there in her Sunday poplin; beside her, Serena, the second Sister Hansen, with her little girl, Julia, at her skirts, hushed the new baby in her arms. (Lars was having his family at last.)

'You iss ready, no?' asked the Yeast Lady.

'Ready?' Clory and Willie chorused.

The pink wrinkled face looked perplexed. (I always expect her to curtsy, thought Clory irrelevantly.)

'Sister Mac, she ban leave long time ago ——'

'It's Abijah!' cried Clory, jumping up and letting the pink calico slide to the floor. 'I felt it in my bones! 'Sheba must've had that letter for months an' just forgot on purpose to mention it to us, so *she'd* be the only wife to go meet him in the welcoming parade!'

Willie put down the churn with a bang.

'An' me doin' her churnin' for her! It's like 'Sheba, to tell everybody h'else in town but us!'

Clory made a dive for the horsehair trunk next the cupboard.

There was the crocheted collar she could wear on the old black sateen ...

When her hair was freshly drawn and netted, her cheeks pinched to bring out the color, her hands rubbed with mutton tallow, and a sprig of dried bergamot inside her bodice, she stood in the doorway and flung the room a last-minute inspection. The dugout door had long since become a wooden one, but the floor was still hardpacked dirt (poor Free — Free who never had got around to laying those flat rocks he'd promised!) — cold underfoot in December in spite of the new braided rugs. The geranium on the cupboard, and inside, the gourd-bowl filled with the herbs she'd raised last summer, anise seeds and powdered sweet marjoram, and bunches of spearmint and peppermint dangling like bats from the ceiling, but not much improvement to show for ten years of living, not much for a wife to show to a homecoming husband!...

An excitement clamored in her veins, stronger than her exasperation over 'Sheba. She wanted to diddle up and down as Kissy used to do. Abijah was coming home! There would be *life* about the place once more! Maybe Abijah would see the improvement inside of her. For there was improvement. She was able at last to take out the memory of her children and look at it without tears. And Free's corner of her heart had long since been sealed for all eternity. The past lay with God. She held out her arms to the future.

The welcoming parade had already gone when the four women reached the square. The townspeople stared at Clory and Willie curiously. Imagine wives not caring enough to go out to meet their husband!

The old bowery had long since been torn down, but the 'dobe T.O. still squatted sturdily in the half-hearted sunshine. Against its southern wall Pal detached herself from a tangle of women and waved to Clory, and made her way toward her through the chatting, laughing crowd. Clory's smile was reluctant. Pal was too obviously the happy matron with Patience-Elizabeth, a long-legged nine-year-old, on one side, her little boy on the other, and the new baby in her arms.

'Ain't you excited?' called Pal, hurrying toward her. 'Do you think it will rain before they get back?'

Clory took her eye from the ditch-banks, where the grass was as green as remembered grass in that first December of '61, and scanned the sky with its dark rolling cargo. She thought, *I don't care if it rains all the rest of my life if I can just have another baby. I've got a lot of time to make up!*

'David went out in Apostle Snow's buggy,' the other girl prattled, 'but I didn't get up here until the last minute. This morning Lucy had such a bad turn with her youngest! Aunt Ket says the cat sucked its breath —— '

Clory went on cooing to the baby and did not answer. But Pal was full of talk.

'I suppose they'll take their time. Men almost always do. Apostle Snow'll want to show Brother Mac how far along they've built the canal and how they've patched up the dam and how much better the grain crop is, since they've learned to change off with the lucerne —— '

Young 'Rastus Snow gave a sudden shout from the road.

'They're coming!' he cried, throwing his hat in the air.

Clory began to tremble violently. *My hair*, she thought, panic-stricken, *my fingernails! Why didn't I borrow a dress from Pal?* She turned wildly to Willie for reassurance. Willie smiled down at her.

'A woman with eyes like yourn,' she whispered, 'don't never need to worry about the rest of her.'

The crowd surged out of the square, across the sidewalk and the ditch into the road. Suddenly longing to run and hide, pressing her hands upon her heart to still its thumping, conscious of the crush of bodies behind her, grunts and laughter and bits of disjointed speech, Clory stood in the front ranks and waited with Willie. There was the far-off thumping of the martial band, the squeal of the fife, and then, overlaying the bread-and-butter music like a silver frosting, Staheli's band from the Clara.

The sky hung like a saturated gray blanket, from which presently snow began to fall.

The nostalgia of these aliens for a white Christmas! Clory
thought how gray had been all her holidays since Abijah's going;
of course, the first Christmas when the children were . . . but since
then, eating her heart out at 'Sheba's rowdy Christmas mornings,
she had hated the day. Remembering childhood Christmases
when she and Free had haggled equally over a homemade rag
doll, she wondered if another Christmas would find her with life
at her breast and in her heart.

Far down the street the two bands turned a corner (*always*
playing different tunes at the same time!), and bugled and
drummed in their wagon boxes behind the tasseled, prancing
teams. Behind them the mail-coach with its driver on the high
seat, his feet on the treasure-box, and beside him the Wells-Fargo
messenger with a sawed-off shotgun on his lap. And within the
coach . . . clear red ran in Clory's cheeks as she peered through
the curtain of snow.

And then the line of buggies and wagons and riders a-horseback
were following the bands and the mail-coach into the square, and
the music blared and the horses whinnied and snorted, and the
crowd jostled and holloed.

It seemed to Clory that her cheek was so hot the snowflakes
sizzled against it, but she shivered in her shawl as she watched
Abijah step out of the coach, and with him Apostle Snow and
David Wight and Robert Gardner. While the driver went around
to the boot to get his carpetbag, Abijah stood there among the
men, pumping hands, looking up at the new Tabernacle, his
great laugh rumbling, his burr running like a rich thread among
the other voices.

Joseph was helping his mother down over the wheel of the
buckboard, and then his new wife and child. Samuel and Abraham vaulted over the tail-gate. The twins reined in the mustang
until its forefeet pawed the air. 'Sheba strode instantly to Abijah's side, as if she would annex it by squatter's rights.

'"The h'early bird catches the worm,"' said Willie.

'"Finders keepers,"' agreed Clory.

She stared hungrily. There was a vaguely foreign air about him — probably the bowler hat and the white low-cut waistcoat he wore — but he had not changed much in three years. He had put on weight, but his body was still straight and firm-fleshed. His deep, full beard, newly parted in the middle and brushed back on each side, shot ruddy glints even in the wan light, but she could not see that the years had added much gray. His hair still held its shining curl back from the part, and his brown eyes sang with the old enthusiasm. His big body still radiated its old vitality and verve, its old overwhelming masculine charm. He still wore the same broadcloth suit, the pants wrinkled from long sitting. Clory longed suddenly to brush and scrub and press him back to his normal immaculateness.

'Come h'on,' whispered Willie, tugging at her sleeve. 'We'd better go h'on up — people'll think it's funny!'

Clory drew back in a sudden fright.

And then Abijah's eyes had found them and he was leaving the dignitaries, good-naturedly shouldering too-eager fellow citizens, briefly clasping outstretched hands, his white teeth flashing here and there; was making his way toward her; was there.

Clory's hand was at her throat, her eyes like saucers. She forgot to smile.

His greeting for Willie was generous and affectionate. But then Clory was in his arms, drowned in his kiss, the good man-smell about her once more. The wet brush of the snowflakes, the jocose jollying of friends and neighbors, the prickle of his whiskers on her face, all merged together in a great delight at having him home. One got tired of the constant society of women. Female society grew to be insipid, like sleazy silk; only man-goods had 'body' and pith when you whanged it. Three years was a long time to be separated from one's man. Now she could better understand the elders' constant insistence on young missionaries' wiving as soon as they got home. She could even understand how

a polygamist wife with an absent husband might be tempted to
run off with a too-persuasive gentile. Maybe the terrible threat
of blood atonement was the only way some women could be
hobbled!

Abijah held her at arm's length and inspected her.

'Clorinda Agathy!' he murmured, oblivious of the people
around him. 'Clorinda Agathy!'

He saw a small girl in an unfashionable black sateen dress with
a plain white collar. A small, big-eyed girl with the clear red
running in her brown cheeks, a girl whose body seemed to shrink
with shyness. A small girl without a bustle or bangs. Even the
rebellious hair was netted.

Abijah was pleased. Here was a wife who had done considerable retrenchment, a wife more to his liking. 'Hawckk!' A wife
worthy of a High Priest and Seventy.

He could feel her trembling and his smile was tender, a little
amused. He had forgotten the clean smell of bergamot about her,
the blue hollow where her dark hair swept back from her temple,
the curve of her brows, the way her lashes brushed her cheek.
He had especially forgotten her wholesomeness, clean-limbed like
a sunflower putting up from the ground. Ech, he was fairly
droukan in her sweetness!

She raised her eyes, and suddenly there was a look away back
in their sooty depths he had never seen before. A wincing, a hint
of buried anguish. He sobered, then, and leaned and kissed her
on the forehead.

'Aigh,' he mourned, 'puir little mither. The bairn-team . . .

> But oh! fell Death's untimely frost
> That nipt my flower sae early . . .'

But he was not before a congregation now, he was before his
own wife whose face was as sad as a stone.

There had always been something not quite saddle-broken in
Clory, something that was one with all gay, roguish creatures,

young calves and colts kicking up long legs, elves and sprites. This habit of laughing at herself and life, this elusive mischievousness, was what he had most distrusted. Now he praised God she was growing out of her kittenhood, but he had not wanted her to lose her gaiety! He realized suddenly that all those years in a strange land, all those hours of preaching on street corners, of tracting from house to house, all those bleak days on the ocean and afterward crossing the plains — even beneath the thrill of riding the new steam cars — through all the times of danger (for most of the world showed Mormonism a mailed fist), through it all he had longed with all the passionate intensity of his being for the sound of Clory's little laugh. The laughter with the ring of bells in it. Still holding her and studying her, he sighed unconsciously. To have to exile yourself for three years in order to appreciate what you had left at home! Ech, what a blastie coof was man!

The bands were rattling out of the square. Wagons and buggies churned new slush, were homeward bound. Snow-dappled twilight filtered down with a swirl of wind, a mounting chill.

'Sheba could stand it no longer. She forsook the bulwark of her sons and flounced toward Abijah and his two other wives.

'Well!' she squawked above the home-going sounds, 'mebbe I'm a freeze-cat, but *I'm going home! I* want some supper!'

His families and his children about him once more, Abijah beamed. Even while his voice rumbled on at prayers, he could not resist peeping at the goodly circle, each kneeling before the bench, heads lowered decently. Joseph, his eldest, waywardness brought to heel with marriage, and beside him his wife and child (Ech! Abijah stopped right in the middle of assigning the gentiles to hell-fire to realize that he had become a grandfather!); Samuel and Abraham, slow and easy-going, great strapping youths ready for wiving themselves; the twins, poking each other furtively, still scalawags for all their lank long-leggedness.

Abijah's 'Amen!' was loud to drown the ache in his heart for the two towheads that were gone, for his little maid with the wondering, golden eyes. Strange that you could shove others over on a bench and fill up vacant spaces, but the heart went right on seeing the ones that were missing. But in the Lord's work there was no time for repining.

'Aigh,' sighed Abijah contentedly, picking up his fork and looking down the long length of the pleasant table ('Sheba had put on her Spode, and produced, as if by magic, a new white tablecloth), the real rag carpet stretched over straw that rustled when you walked upon it ... 'Aigh! There's nought like a mon's ain hearth-stane!'

His smile drew them all together; 'Sheba at the foot of the table, Clory at his right and Willie at his left, and the boys in between. 'Sheba's mole twitched with pleasure and her eyes were soft when she looked at him, but her smile was knowing and secret.

Over Abijah's shoulder Clory caught Willie's eye and winked. 'Sheba must have been stealthily planning this supper for weeks. Haggis pudding and fried chitlins that were supposed to have been used up a month ago! Grapes pickled in molasses, their purple jackets sleek and bursting with juice, when 'Sheba had said there wasn't enough of a crop to pickle! And spuds — 'Sheba must have done a lot of bargaining in Pine Valley or Cedar Fort!

'Pa,' said 'Sheba, gazing at him across the table, her strong cheekbones pink — heaven's sakes, thought Clory, that look of a female to her mate — I guess no woman ever gets too old for it! — 'Pa, these apricots come off'v your own lot. That tree in front of the house ——'

Clory glared at 'Sheba.

Fibber! Those apricots came from the trees along the fence in front of the dugout! Those were the only trees on the lot that did well, and that was because I manured 'm and packed water to 'm myself, all summer long!

Abijah smacked his lips and forked preserve on his piece of johnnycake for another bite. A reminiscent look came into his eyes. He wiped his whiskers with his handkerchief and leaned back in his chair. The boys chewed silently so as not to miss a word.

'Reminds me o' our first meal in the Highlands. A real Scotch dinner with turnip broth, leeks, a boiled mutton joint, oaten bread and scones . . .'

Willie caught a glimpse of Clory's eyes on Abijah. Eyes like great pools of ink, she thought; easy to see how a man might lose himself in such eyes.

' . . . held forth in Tamworth, in the Arcade. I paid a man to sweep the place, and then engaged the town crier to go through every street and notify the people. "In the Arcade this evening at seven o'clock Divine Service will be held by Elder MacIntyre from America!"'

For a moment, his voice roaring up from his chest, Abijah *was* the town crier. Clory sat enthralled. This was better than when he'd open his carpetbag and give out the presents!

'The audience stood stock still, their attention riveted upon me. But I had better audiences even than that in London! . . . Ech, London! A wonderful place. Rusty-lookin' old Newgate . . . London Bridge, where I leaned against the iron balustrade on top that was put there to prevent suicides . . . Black Friars Bridge, Westminster — they've got the Thames tunnel lighted with gas. Mummies in the British Museum — coats of mail, the last beheading block. I stopped at 35 Jewin Street and had dinner with several of the American brethren . . .'

Clory tore her gaze away to stare questioningly at Willie. Wasn't London Willie's old stamping ground? But Willie shook her head at her ever so slightly. Even in the midst of her fascination Clory's heart rebelled at Abijah's indifference. It would never occur to him even to remember that Willie was from London. His affection for Willie was like a man's affection for a stray dog — he wasn't curious about her antecedents.

'Well,' said 'Sheba, jumping up, her broad bosom jiggling, 'I hate to interrupt all this, but if we're goin' to get this mess cleared before folks starts a-comin', *I've* got to get busy! Willie, you're on the end o' the bench — will you open the door so's it won't smell s'much like a pup's nest in here?'

As she slid out from the bench the corner of Willie's mouth quirked and her gaze widened briefly at Clory. 'Sheba had even planned a Welcome Home without telling them! Clory set her little jaw.

'I'll be right back to help, Aunt 'Sheba,' she said dutifully. At least fix her hair . . .

As the boys got up, pushed back benches, and 'Sheba stirred the room into its accustomed activity, Clory walked to the door with Willie, who was quivering with suppressed laughter.

'Don't hit beat all,' she whispered to Clory, 'how 'Sheba likes to catch us with our pants down?'

But in spite of 'Sheba's haste, Clory and Willie were still doing dishes and Joseph's wife was in the other room singing the baby to sleep when company started to arrive.

Bishop Gardner and his two wives, such genteel folks that 'Sheba was somewhat flustered at not being quite ready. But then in a twinkling, it seemed to Clory, the room was crowded. The Tucketts, the Jarvises, the Hichinopers (three young men who flatly refused to enter plurality, much to Abijah's concern), the Hansens, the Wheelocks, Shadrach Gaunt and his wives, Zebedee Trupp and his wives, 'Old 46' and his two wives, the newly acquired Sister Couzzens trailing dismally in the wake of the first, who automatically entered a room as if it were a royal court.

More voices, laughter outside, and here were Pal and Lucy and David, stamping snow from their feet. Pal, taking in Clory's black sateen, her vexed expression, confided under cover of the shouted good evenings, "'Sheba said it was a su'prise, made us promise not to tell! We thought of course *you* knew!'

Some of the men were squatting on 'Sheba's rag carpet, backs
to the wall; others leaned an idle elbow on the mantelpiece, the
women clustered around upon the chairs and the bed, Lars Hansen bent over the giggling Yeast Lady sitting with Serena by the
hearth ——

'Vhere did I get you, Yulia?'

'Oh, vell, what were you doin' dere, Lars!'

There was a knock at the door and Erastus and his three wives
bundled in out of the storm.

'The cow's tail!' someone greeted him, and Erastus grinned
good-naturedly and mopped the snow frosting his beard.

Now that everyone was here, the real purpose of the evening
could be taken up and Abijah get at the telling of his experiences.

Handsome Mac. Clory watched him standing there against
the firelight, reveling in his rôle of story-teller, the joy lines
crinkling his tawny eyes, his big-knuckled, well-shaped hands emphasizing a point, his voice softening and burring to suit the tale.
He had such a way with an audience, holding them spellbound
while the fire roared up the chimney and the snow pattered softly
against the pane. Come Sunday, he would be given the time in
meeting, but tonight his talk was intimate talk for his friends.

' ... I had one full house mostly Methodist, their local preacher
with them. When I got through I asked them what they thought
of such doctrine, but not one of them would say a word but walked
silently away. I felt that I was sowing seed but the reaping time
was out of sight. And I found the supposed Saints without faith
enough to purchase one penny's worth of Gospel light or give a
night's lodging to an elder. One gentile drew a bucket of muddy
water from the well and yelled at me, "So you believe in baptism
by immersion?" and doused me with the water. "Yessireebob,"
says I, pulling off my coat, "and we believe in the laying on of
hands, too!"'

Guffaws, while Abijah's brown bush curved in a grin.

'But I got 'em! I got the whole bunch o' them according to

logic and dogma, and not a one had a leg to stand on! Says I,
"Premise: Be ye perfect and be ye one" — Abijah tabulated his
points on his fingers. 'First I tackled the Catholic: "When your
church reigned supreme it was the Dark Ages! You didn't do
anything in Mexico in four hundred years — why, the Incas had
a better government than Cortez! I'd be afraid of your Kingdom Come!"

'Second, the Protestants: "You've established tolerance but
had no unity!"

'Third, the Heathen: "Who would you select among your
heathen philosophers — Plato, Aristotle, Socrates — as a standard, an ideal, who could stand before his wife and say, 'I am the
Way and the Truth and the Life'?"'

Abijah shook his magnificent bronze-colored head.

'Only Jesus can do that! And so I picked apart every religion,
folks, until there was only Mormonism left. "And here," I says,
"*you have everything. We recognize a Supreme Authority, we have
cohesion and unity, we've made progress out of the weak and un-
learned of the earth!*"'

Others of the brethren had been on missions, and as the evening grew stories grew with it, topping Abijah's.

When the wine and cake had been served and the last guest had
gone, 'Sheba plopped with abandon across the bed.

'I'm plumb tuckered,' she sighed.

Abijah came in from seeing Joseph and his wife and child off in
the buckboard — such a long cold drive down to the farm in this
storm! — and shook the snow from his shoulders and stretched
his big body like a lazy cougar.

'Aigh,' he yawned, 'a guid party. But the trip an' a' —'

The boys having long since gone to bed, Clory and Willie
lugged at benches, putting the room to rights. Abijah, coming to
give them a hand, suddenly straightened, his face quickening.

'The presents,' he boomed. 'Ech, I maist forgot the presents!'

Beaming mysteriously on the three women, Clory and Willie by the table, 'Sheba on the bed near the hearth, Abijah strode through the door into the bedroom, where he had put his carpet-bag and bundles. He was back in a moment, his eyes half-angry, half-puzzled upon 'Sheba.

'Mother,' he said from the doorway where he stood with his arms full, 'the new house is just richt, but the bedroom — why are the boys in the bedroom? Ain't that Willie's room?'

'Sheba said nothing but stared defiantly back at him.

Clory stole a glance at Willie's flushing sallow face.

Abijah dumped the bundles on the floor and the little vein began to beat in his forehead.

'Ech,' he began, his eyes graying with anger, but 'Sheba stared him down. He gritted his teeth at her. Aigh, a mon's wives! He had thoct to come home to peace, but...

'Go to bed,' he ordered Clory and Willie curtly. 'Guid nicht.'

In spite of his anger he'd give 'Sheba his first night, as was proper. But his contentment was torn. 'Sheba sat up and began to unbutton her shoes, but he stooped to the carpetbag at his feet and extricated a red-backed ledger which he carried to the table where the candles burned low. Ink, his old feathered pen in the cupboard... A measure of calmness returned to him as he turned the pages of the ledger. Aigh, a mon's wives... He dipped his pen.

'I return like the sow to the wallow,' he wrote with under-scorings.

3

Before noon the next day, Abijah had Willie installed in her rightful place in the bedroom. 'Sheba, accepting defeat, said not a word, but stood silently in the doorway between the two rooms and watched Clory and Willie carry the latter's meager posses-sions around the back, through the lean-to, drop them on the bed, and trudge out for another load.

'Sheba's eyes glittered with malice. Clory, hurrying away from that gaze, wondered again why the coming of a man should make such a change in a woman. While Abijah was gone 'Sheba had been almost like a friend.

If the gentiles think polygamy is any fun, I'd like to see one of their women try it!

Clory scuffed at the snow still crisping the path.

'Sheba's brief truce was over, she had taken up her cudgels again.

'But worth the unpleasantness,' thought Clory, 'to see Willie's joy at having a room of her own. So little to ask for so many years of slogging!'

Time was bending her gaunt body as a sapling is bent by the wind, and Clory, watching the gnarled knuckles clutching prayer book and Bible, ached with pity. But Willie's hare eyes were shining at the moment and the liver spots almost hidden in the faint flush on her cheeks.

She really hasn't changed much in ten years, thought Clory. *... I'm the one who's changed!*

'Cheenge is the law o' life,' sighed Abijah that evening as he dried his wet feet before the fire. 'My feet have cheenged in three years to nought but corns and chilblains. But up in town I see new houses, new faces — aye, and I miss some old faces, too.'

During the morning he had investigated every frozen furrow of the lot, planning spring gardens, and that afternoon Apostle Snow had driven him around the mission, through the slush of the fields where the canal crept forward inch by inch.

'Tae think,' he said, studying the patient effort with which Joseph teased water on his farm, 'that I figgered when we first came, tae have water on that strip in a couple o' year!'

'It's a hard country,' said Erastus.

'Aye ...' But there was progress.

Clory brought him the flour she had remembered to brown and he filled his tin box, massaged the rest on hands and wrists, and smiled slowly up at her.

'Sheba, setting the supper-table, caught that smile.

Abijah finally got around to giving out the presents. In Newport, where he changed for Birmingham, he had bought himself a solid gold hunting-case English lever watch, and this he had to remove from its chain, and first pass around among the family. It was his dream, he said, to buy each of his boys a similar watch some day, and meanwhile he had brought them home each a vest pattern. Figured navy alpaca for 'Sheba, brown checked Mozambique for Willie, and ten yards of 'grass' cloth for Clory, who fingered the bright material lovingly — she thought it just the color of young lucerne with the dew on it. And very stylish, since the fashions nowadays called for materials that 'would stand alone.' Maybe Abijah would let her have a fichu . . .

Swamped in the gratitude of his family, Abijah was suddenly wistful.

'They've got trinket-peddlers in stalls all along the sides o' the Thames tunnel. I would hae liked . . .'

Clory, caressing the cloth against her cheek, finished his sentence to herself. He'd have liked to bring home trinkets, but trinkets were foolish unless there were children.

'Aigh,' sighed Abijah, seeing something other than the candle-lit table.

'Someone else sent ye a present, too, Clorinda.'

Clory's heart began to pound.

He twinkled at her and got up from the table and fumbled under the bed for the largest package of all. He'd hidden it there, saving it until the last.

A caster. Shorn of its trappings it stood there before them all, glittering in its pride of solid engraved silver — a tray complete with vinaigrette and cut-glass containers for pepper, salt, and mustard, and a tall handle to carry it by. No one in all the Dixie Mission had anything to compare with this. One more treasure to add to the rosewood desk, the perfume bottle. Once again that voice had spoken to Clory out of the dim past where her memory groped so vainly. What fancy did her mother have of this heathen wilderness where she had consigned her small daughter? Sending her Paisley shawls and silver casters when mostly she hungered for bread. Did she say, 'With a Paisley shawl and a silver caster she'll be a Social Leader'? *The Paisley shawl made a shroud for my child*, thought Clory. If she passed her mother on the street, she wouldn't know her ... But the caster and the rosewood desk and the perfume bottle could be handed down. For there would be other children. And for them a society ready-made, a society that would not shift with every passing breeze ...

Abijah understood how she felt about the children. And she had never thought he would. As life went on — rising at daybreak, family prayers, the chapter from the Bible, the twins cleaning out the stable, cleaning down the mustang and feeding it and the cattle, Abraham or Samuel milking, and then the day's work commencing after breakfast — as life went on, joy upsurged in Clory's heart. She found herself singing again, her voice sounding in her own ears like the screak of an unused rusty gate. There was a new warmth in Abijah's brown gaze that was all hers. It was as if by steeling her will against despair, by keeping herself gay and valiant for his coming, she had attained a new stature in his eyes. He had fought his love for her before, he had mistrusted it, but now he was like a boy with his first sweetheart. And for Clory life once again had meaning; she could quit excusing God.

A week with 'Sheba, a week with Willie, and then he would be all hers for a week. Sometimes at the table his eyes anticipated, made her promises. She strung the days together on a steelstrong thread of energy. The dugout floor cleaned with sand from the river, sagebrush burned on the hearth to give the room a smell of wind and stars, the old pink calico (now that she had a new dress) starched and cut up into curtains, the bedclothing laundered, sheets and pillowcases put away in bergamot. She climbed the Red Hill one cold day and dug oose root with which to bring a new luster to her long black hair. Her step grew light, her eyes confident and joyous. Massaging butter into the tanned, roughened skin of her face, rubbing mutton tallow on her hands (that stubborn humor in the tender crevices between her fingers!), she thought: *Now I know how a tree feels in the spring when the sap starts up in its branches.* Pal, helping her make the new dress (plain, since Abijah preferred it that way) with a simple polonaise and train, ruching-edged, a coatee bodice whose tails supported a great bow over petticoated crinoline ruffles in the back — Pal marveled at the change in her. 'You're prettier than you ever were in your life, Clory!' And Clory's answering laughter was as unbidden as the song of the meadowlarks in the valley. For the whole of the two-weeks wait she went on knitting Abijah's wristlets under 'Sheba's very nose.

And when their moment came and he shut the dugout door behind him and took her in his arms, she clung to him in a very luxury of content. But even as he kissed her, murmuring endearments, she struggled for words. She looked up at his flushed face, at his eyes swimming with golden lights, at the little vein beating on his forehead, and tried to tell him that she had suffered, that she had learned from suffering.

'I have grown up to fit you, now; I have made myself into a wife.'

But Abijah merely gritted his teeth, groaned at her lovingly, and picked her up and carried her to the bed. And in her utter surrender there were new heights, new vistas only guessed at before. A sweet sensuousness possessed her, a lethargy drugged her limbs. But as he kissed her temples she pushed him away long enough to make him listen.

'You may not like me when you find I've been bad. I loved Kissy more than my God and I know it ain't right the way I've mourned for her. Seemed like I had Brother and the baby so short a time I hardly knew them . . . I could forgive the Lord for Brother and the baby. But Kissy — oh, you can't know what it was like to lose them *all — all together* . . . Pal was spared *her*

little girl! And then Isaiah — we'd thought we'd save Isaiah. I
was so tired, I hadn't taken my clothes off for weeks, I'd run over
here to grab a bite and I went to sleep with my head in my bread-
'n'-milk. An' then the twins a-shaking me, their eyes as big as
saucers, an' them a-saying, "Aunt Clory! Aunt Clory! Isy's
dead as a doorknob!"'

All the defenseless nights when the horror had escaped the
locks and bolts of her will to haunt her dreams, rushed at her
now, and she wept. Luxurious tears that did not have to be
denied. What relief to take off the mask she had worn so long, to
be her shivering, fearful, grieving self!

Abijah rocked her as if she were a child and let her cry herself
empty against his shoulder.

'There, there,' he crooned, 'puir lass ... We maun remember
'tis the Lord's will. Kissy, aye, Kissy was a bonny thing. We
won't see the likes o' my wee maid again. But she was an "old
spirit," Clor-rinda. She didn't need this life.'

You men, her heart cried even as she clung to him, *you men with
your politics and your business and religion, don't you know a
woman can't put grief aside so easily!*

For she knew that other children might come, happiness might
come, old age and death, but never so long as she lived would the
beauty of that little face be dimmed in her memory.

'The link is not broken,' murmured Abijah, hushing her long
shuddering sobs, 'the weld is sur-re and strong and it draws us
upward and urges us onward and prepares us for a stronger union.
a greater joy.'

But there was such peace in baring her heart of all its hoarded
worries, washing her memory clean of self-accusings. She wanted
to tell him that the greatest pain lay in the knowledge that Kissy
had grown beyond her. One moment she is just a child pestering
you with questions — 'Mamma, what's a testimony?' — a child
you survey with sweet scorn from the height of your larger wisdom; the next, you can teach her nothing else. She knows all the

secrets the wind whispers on the Sugar Loaf. And you find your-
self praying to her instead of God, just as you used to pray to
Free. Do all bereft women pray to their loved ones instead of to
God?

And that was the sin of it, putting your child before your God.
She tried to tell Abijah how all the hours of lonely brooding had
magnified her shortcomings in her own eyes until she believed
she had sinned beyond redemption.

But Abijah kissed her lips and drew out his handkerchief to
wipe her eyes, held it to her nose and made her blow as if she
were a child.

'Clor-rinda,' he murmured, holding her close, his voice hoarsen-
ing, 'Clor-rinda, I hae wanted to tell ye for a long time aboot
the letter. I was wrang to tell ye Kissy's death was a punishment.
It...'

Then, indeed, she lifted her head to stare at him. Stared in the
dim firelight until he dropped his eyes. Could it be that Abijah
was humbling himself? All her heart rushed out in a flood of tenderness for him — a child who'd confessed and was sorry.

'Things are gawin' tae be better,' he said. 'There will be more
bairns. Ye hae made yersel' into a fine woman, Clor-rinda.
Soon's I get things straightened around I'll build ye a house...'

And by the last day of December there were 'dobes ricked up
back of the dugout. Clory was beside herself with delight. A
house, after ten years of the damp and smoke of a dugout!

When Abijah came home from working on the dam or the
canal, his hands blistered and cracked from unaccustomed friction with the shovel-handle, she would be waiting for him, standing patiently in the corral while he climbed stiffly down from the
buckboard, taking him into the house, where she had ready tallow
salve and a basin of warm water for his feet. He must listen to
tales of his children, how smart was Brother, how sweet the baby
whom his father never saw. And Clory must show him her
treasured keepsakes — a wooden teething ring of Brother's,
Kissy's circle comb.

Every wife had something to show Abijah. 'Sheba could show him how she had finished the house, but with the first January thaw Clory took him to the pit out back of the dugout and showed him her buckskins.

'But,' he said, helping her shake the putrid-smelling hide free of dirt and hang it over a post, 'God willing, Clor-rinda, ye will never have to earn your own living again.'

She smiled at him and went on scraping the skin with her sharp stick. All polygamist wives had to earn their own living sooner or later. Never again would she be caught unprepared. And so he grinned tolerantly at her independence and helped her scrape off all the hair, flesh, and dirt from the hide, even helped her wash the heavy thing in soapy water and hang it up for its ten-day stretch in the sun.

4

It was hard to find any fault with life that spring even though one scolded about the G.L.U.'s, the Gentile League of Utah, and its avowed purpose to break up 'Mormon Theocracy.' Even though for the seventh time Deseret was refused admission as a state.

On the whole, Erastus felt that the Dixie Mission was running as smoothly as a well-greased pig. This insistence of the authorities on taking more wives — even Young Miles had finally acquired a couple of likely-looking females on a freighting trip up north. Shadrach Gaunt running the pile-driver at the Temple site, Zadoc Hunt getting out those mammoth hunks of rock without dynamite. The capstone being laid on the Tabernacle spire.

Erastus stared at the red-stone building, four-square and enduring and arrogant. Robert Gardner had hand-hewn with a broadaxe the poles for the roof, balancing it in spite of using only wooden wedges and iron braces hammered out on an anvil — shingle nails were a hundred dollars a keg. The turn flights of

front stairways, the great hand-carved front doors, the windows
— they had freighted in almost two thousand panes of glass at
eighty cents a pane. On the Tabernacle's forehead, below the
little fan-shaped center window, appeared the scrolled white
slab:

Holiness to the Lord
Commenced A.D. 1863
Completed A.D. 1871

The Temple would belong to the Church, but the Tabernacle
was theirs. They had built it during the hardest years a people
ever endured.

May peace abound within thy walls
And glory round thee shine...

sang the choir in David Wight's anthem, and Clorinda Mac-
Intyre's soprano soared above all the rest. Even Abijah was finding less fault with his neighbors.

When the High Council met for the March term of court, first
voting in Zadoc Hunt as the new mayor, there were only two
cases on the trial docket.

Tutsegabbett felt that although the horse, the rifle, and the
saddle blanket Gottlieb Uttley had paid him for the Sonuvabitch
Spring were long since used up, the spring was still as good as new
and he should be paid more horse, more rifle, and more saddle
blanket!

Shadrach Gaunt, whose first wife (the mother of the two sisters) had died some time before with flux, wanted a divorce from
Sarah. But Erastus said divorce was a serious business and they'd
better consult the Lord. However, two weeks later the midwives
were of the unanimous opinion that Sarah was dead from 'bleeding of the lungs induced by too much talking in the open air.'
Shadrach was jubilant.

'By gadder,' he said to Erastus after the funeral, 'I'm the only feller in the hull Territory who married his cake and et it, too!'

Star-struck with happiness, Clory laughed at Abijah's dark-browed gravity and darted among the hollyhocks where peach blossoms petaled her dark hair, out into the street where the cottonwoods were shedding fluff, and grass pollen and green locusts and tiny gray-veined moths rose up about her skirts.

It was almost as if life were beginning all over again!

Nevertheless, in spite of contentment, it did not seem right to Erastus to hold conference while Brother Brigham was kept prisoner. But appealing to McKean was a waste of time. Failing to bring Brother Brigham to trial on a charge of murder, he still refused to let him go, feeling, no doubt, that the very act of detaining such a famous prisoner upheld his contention that 'common-law bigamy and polygamy were one and the same thing.' But the Saints could be as stubborn as McKean. The forty-second annual conference of the Church convened in Salt Lake City on April 6 and was dismissed — hopefully — until the 9th.

Erastus, feeling that the least the Dixie Mission could do was to follow suit, read aloud the telegram to his assembled townsfolk and sent them all home.

'Ptsahh! We won't have conference until the Lord sees fit to take Brother Brigham out of jail. When you hear the Martial Band you'll know it's time for conference.'

'But my heavens,' chattered Clory, frolicking homeward beside Abijah, 'Brother Brigham's been in there for three months! They can't keep him locked up *forever*, can they?'

'Sheba snorted at such driveling and sailed ahead down the street in all her new majesty of figured navy alpaca, looking, with her large bustle, like a respectable navy-blue camel.

Abijah was setting his new watch by the sundial in the square the next day, when the news came. In spite of 'Sheba's sour looks, Clory was cutting out her first pair of gloves on 'Sheba's smooth table, her mouth twisting painstakingly to follow the

snapping of the shears, when they heard the Martial Band.
Willie dropped her knitting and hobbled to the open door. There
was no mistaking that strong, triumphant drumbeat. The three
women picked up their skirts and ran.

But when they panted into the square Erastus ruffled his chin-
beard and grinned at them. No, no conference yet. But a telegram from Washington. Erastus stood on the steps of the T.O.,
flanked by the Martial Band in its wagon box.

'Ptsahh! This is from the United States Supreme Court:
"Jury unlawfully drawn. All indictments quashed."'

A roar of joy drowned Erastus. The first real gesture of justice
from Washington in all these years. Elders forgetting their dignity and jumping into the air and the women laughing, crying,
hugging each other.

Finally he signaled Brother Wheelock, and the long boom of
the brass drum rolled out into the sunlight. When he had attention again, he held up a fistful of telegrams.

'The New York *Tribune* says: "Effect of this decision is to
make void all criminal proceedings in the territorial courts of
Utah during the past eighteen months and render necessary the
immediate discharge of one hundred and thirty-eight prisoners
who have been illegally held at the expense of from forty thousand
dollars to fifty thousand dollars which there is no law to provide
the payment of;... decision is considered as very damaging to
the National Administration, as Judge McKean was supported
in the course he took by the President..."' But in spite of con-
gressional orders McKean held on to Brother Brigham for almost
another month.

5

The Sabbath always had a special feeling all its own. A peace
about it, special sounds and smells. The fresh smell of newly
scrubbed skin and clothes, of starch, flower-sachets, vinegar shoe-

blacking, the sound of rustling petticoats and stiff shirts, genteel conversation, the refined jingling of harness on a newly curried team. Even the chickens in the barnyard clucked on a quieter note. But a late-April Sabbath in Dixie had a still more precious quality. Bees bumbling among the sunflowers, an oriole pluming his feathers in the green, sun-dancing world of the apricot and peach trees where the fruit hung like marbles, a robin teaching his young to fly over in the milkweeds along the ditchbank; with his well-filled waistcoat, a very bishop of a robin, and quite out of patience with life for pestering him with this parenthood business. And the youngster trying wings all fuzzy with youth, anxious to take off but not quite daring, looking piteously back at the grown-ups in such a hurry to thrust him out where cats with green eyes lurk. There! The father is on the gatepost soiling his immaculate bill with worm juice to bribe his child.

How are you going to *know*, thought Clory, wandering along the lane by the plum trees, out to the back where the grapevines spread like lace above the washtubs; how are you going to *know* what is best for a child? How to protect it from cats with green eyes?

Such things didn't seem to worry Abijah who had to walk the length of the new Tabernacle aisle (such a distance after the cramped Social Hall!) to take his place on the stand with its three pulpits along with Bishop Gardner, David Wight, Brother Wheelock, the visiting brethren from Santa Clara and Washington.

People rustled into benches, nodded, smiled, greeted one another, gazed around with awe at the vaulted roof, the aisles, the pillars of this meetinghouse they had built. It didn't seem possible they had got together a hundred and ten thousand dollars. . . .

There was Zebedee Trupp three-deep in wives, and Shadrach Gaunt's one and only wife baring her breast to nurse her new baby, and Bella Weeks staring at the woman with obsessed eyes. There was Pal with her three children and getting ready to have another — she'll be sick before me, thought Clory, who couldn't seem to keep up with Pal even in this — and Lucy with her two. Feathered fans and boas, aigrettes and beribboned lace-covered pancake hats. But then David was never as strict as Abijah. Marianne Snow up there in her plum-colored silk, just pinning up her matching dotted face-veil, folding her matching, lace-edged sun-parasol.

Meeting was usually a drowsy place, in spite of the excitement of the new surroundings. Clory watched a fly crawl over the windowpanes that had been brought across an ocean, across Death Valley where giant Joshuas thrust upward like beacon lights; stared beyond the stand at the ominous, All-Seeing Eye Brother Milne had painted above the organ loft to remind worshipers that they should live with an eye single to the glory of God, at the shield below the eye — 'Holiness to the Lord,' a pair of clasped hands, and then 'Faith and Union'; at the plaster rosettes curling along the ceiling; at the elaborate bronze plating on the three mighty chandeliers — twenty-four oil lamps in each chandelier, they said; at the stand-lights for the rostrum, the carving on each upreaching iron arm delicate enough for a sultan's harem; at the lights on the pillars, and the pillars themselves, ten feet high to support the gallery, turned out of pine logs on Bishop Covington's water-lathe at Washington; at the motto hanging below the right gallery: 'After clouds, sunshine,' furnishing an encouraging text to a speaker as well as hope to a weary congregation ...

Bishop Gardner, having learned from experience, decided not to wait for Erastus but stood up, called the meeting to order with his eyes, and bowed his head. Clory thought how much better she liked Abijah's sonorous praying — it had meat to it, while Bishop Gardner's was simple and matter-of-fact like Erastus' own. Even with her eyes shut she was conscious of the flowers on bosoms and in buttonholes, clove pinks and bachelor buttons and hollyhocks, and the jugs of wildflowers on the stand.

Amen!... A stir, Brother Wheelock lifting his hand, the congregation singing. Clory always too small to see over intervening heads where Abijah's eyes would be seeking her own.

The bishop from Washington arising to say a few words that everyone feared would multiply like the sands of the desert before he finished.... He hoped he might have the spirit of the Lord to be with him that his few words might be of value to the brethren and sistern. He thought what we need worse than Gospel doctring is a few words about weeds in our front yards, Washington worse than St. George, and weeds in our water-ditches. After the fine storms of the winter, weeds were bound to grow, but so would good things if given a chance. He thought every man ought to use up every inch of his lot; manuring it well would keep his corrals cleaned out, too. Now that the South was producing again, cotton wouldn't be worth while much longer, and he figgered we should raise more sugar cane, soggum was a product that would always sell in the North...

A little bustle of interest, eyes turning away from the speaker to stare at Erastus coming up the aisle, carrying papers in the hand that did not hold his silk hat.

The speaker hastily concluded his sermon and sat down.

Erastus was here, at last.

'Brothers and sisters,' he said, writhing his lips and taking his time about it, 'I bring you greetings... from Brother Brigham who — I am glad to report — was free to attend conference in the City this morning!'

A wave of relief.

'I guess nine thousand people must have been in the Tabernacle just as we are in ours... Of course... you can hear a pin drop as Brother Brigham and his counselors walk slowly up that long aisle to the front rostrum. All those folks hardly daring to breathe, for there he is, the Leader, leaning on his cane but alive and well.'

'"A word to the Latter-Day Saints," he says, his voice rather weak at first. "Good morning!"'

'"Good morning!" responds the congregation with one voice.
'"How do you do?"
'"Very well!"
'"How is your faith this morning?" — raising that forefinger.
'"*Strong in the Lord!*" roars the congregation.
'I think,' proceeded Erastus, 'that will be my text today —
"*Strong in the Lord...*"'

Clory and Pal must sing their duet David had made up, Clory
slender as a grass-blade in that shiny green cloth with the draped
overdress, Pal whose rolls of well-corseted fat quivered as she
sang:

> A queer old chap is this Judge McKean,
> A curious chap, I vow...

The meeting was long. The afternoon was hot. Before all the
visiting brethren had arisen to say a few words, heads were
nodding.

It was time to attend to the business of the Conference. Brigham Young, Prophet of God in this last dispensation of the Fullness of Times, must be sustained as President of the Church of
Jesus Christ of Latter-Day Saints; his counselors, the Twelve
Apostles, the Presiding Bishopric, the Seven Presidents of the
Seventies, Church Patriarch — Erastus read off the long list of
names.

'All those who feel to sustain these brethren in their offices
with your faith and prayers, will make it manifest by the usual
sign.'

Right hands went up briefly.

Now for the local business. Heads chopped off, new heads
crowned ... Keturah Snow was sustained as Stake President of
the Relief Society, Bathsheba MacIntyre as her first counselor ...
'Sheba's mole twitched with disappointment. It was hard always
having to play second fiddle to Ket.

Sister Clorinda MacIntyre sustained as Stake President of
the Young . .'ies' Retrenchment Society ...

But — Clory jerked to shocked attention, sat up straight on the bench, her black eyes dismayed — *I don't know enough! Anyway, don't they understand I'm going to have a baby?*

'Never mind,' whispered Willie, reading her mind. 'You'll be h'all over it by the time winter classes really start.'

Working in the Church Auxiliaries will be good for her, thought Willie fondly.

I'm going to name Willie as one of my counselors, decided Clory, tingling with surprise and the sense of new importance. *Sister Couzzens as another, and see that Pal's a teacher* ... There was Pal signaling congratulations a bench ahead ...

Because of his duties in the stake, Brother Robert Gardner is being released from the bishopric of the Fourth Ward and Brother Abijah MacIntyre named in his place. All who feel to sustain ...

Abijah, Bishop! 'Sheba was strutting inwardly, and Clory could see Abijah putting a hand to his mouth to cover the impulse to hawckk, as he always did when he was emotionally stirred. Abijah, Bishop! His eyes were slits of pleasure....

People sang lustily, much refreshed with naps and good exhortation.

'I feel,' said Erastus, 'that I could not do better than to conclude with Brother Brigham's prayer of this morning, a prayer he made after three months in the hands of his enemies.

'" ... and I bless you strangers, and say to you, peace be unto you ..."'

6

In spite of being bishop, Abijah still hated unpleasantness, but he was very tender with the little graves that May day. This was new to him, but Clory came out here so often that the children were not dead to her. Except — she found herself thinking as she gave Brother a bouquet of blue larkspur, he had always looked so sweet in blue — except that they should have grown *larger*. Impossible to think of Kissy as a long-legged ten-year-old learning to make bread. Brother six and the baby four. And Isy a big boy, and Free... that meadowlark singing his heart out over there on the mesquite branch, singing his song 'twice over...'

She lifted her skirts and went over to join Abijah and they walked arm-in-arm among the graves, picking their way among the crumbling headstones.

Hosea Eardley who lay into the collar

This recent mound that was Shadrach Gaunt's Sarah —

I called upon the Lord and he heard me and delivered me out of all my troubles

Abijah chuckled. 'I'm gawin' tae be guid to you,' he said, and picked Clorinda up and carried her over the rough ground to the buckboard.

'But you can't expect a man to carry you in his arms *all* the time!' Clory scolded Pal, whose pains began on a hot evening in August. 'David leaving you have Stiddy Weeks for your birthings and waiting on you hand and foot! You're a lucky woman, Pal! Here, drink this, and Lucy'll have the doctor here soon.... My laws, you can't blame David for not wanting to miss his newsclub with the news so excitin' nowadays!'

She spooned lobelia between Pal's chattering teeth and thought about the summer's events crowding one another's heels.

'Abijah says we don't reelize how lucky we are to be in Dixie. He says human life ain't safe in the States nor in Salt Lake either, for that matter. He says Grant's turned the country over to the swindlers and no God-fearing man ever will be safe until that fool's out of the White House!'

She thought of the trouble between the Mormons and the G.L.U.'s raging all summer through the streets of Salt Lake, which, Federal Judge Haydon prophesied, rubbing his hands, 'would soon run blood.'

'It's hot,' Pal moaned. 'I wish I could have my baby out in that bed in the lucerne patch!'

Clory fed her more lobelia.

'Sure it's nasty, but think how lucky you are to have such good deliveries. Poor Willie, having nothing but miscarriages all her life. She can hardly cripple around now, and she's puked up her food every morning of the whole nine months, but she's so happy she can hardly contain herself because she's carryin' this'n its full time.

'I've learned that Abijah *means* well,' she laughed, to divert Pal's mind from its preoccupation with pain. 'And he'd certainly like to be good to me if it wasn't too much bother!'

A man with three wives, two of them having babies, with crops to harvest, and this new job of bishop on his hands, a job that meant real labor caring for the tangible needs of the people in his ward, a man with all this and politics-worry besides — what can a woman expect? asked Clory.

And yet, with the help of the neighbors, Abijah got her house finished before her own travail began the next month. A black-rock foundation laid up with sand and clay mortar. Adobe walls laid up with the same plaster, two 'dobes deep, making a substantial wall a foot thick. Wooden rafters covered with sheathing and shingles hauled from Pine Valley. A rough 'dobe house, the inside walls left unfinished, unwhitewashed, just the gray, pockmarked 'dobe dirt, a floor of rough wood — and yet a wonderful house! Imagine not having the cold and damp of a dirt floor seeping up your legs when you rocked a child! Clory thought of her resolution to have a house of her own that first spring of '61, a resolution that had not faltered for ten years. Well, the hands that had helped her build that house and the little feet that had played in it were stilled. Houses lasted so much longer than the people who lived in them. There was a wrench when the dugout, with its memories, came down.

But here she was, on a gauzy day in September, beginning

labor on her cattail-fluff mattress, listening to the noise of the
Temple pile-driver, drinking in the snug contours of her room.
There was something voluptuous about lying between harsh unbleach sheets in her own house and remembering all those pioneer
women who had huddled under willow wigwams and borne their
children in rain and sleet and snow; remembering herself bearing
Kissy in the dugout with rain and gobs of mud plopping through
the roof on the bed.

'You do think,' she begged, tensing under pain, 'you do think,
don't you, Sister Lowgie, that you git what you pay for? That if
you give Life enough, it gives you something back?'

'There, there,' said Hannah Merinda, spooning out hot camomile tea. 'Don't fret ... It ain't as simple as that, but there is a
Pattern. Life has learned me that much ... We'll see that you git
this baby, and then I don't think you should have no more,
Clorinda. You ain't husky enough. Drat the men! Somebody
ought to tell Abijah ——'

Willie stood in the doorway, her body bloated beyond all recognition, the liver spots livid as birthmarks against her pasty skin.
She clung to the doorway for support, her eyes anxiously questioning the midwife.

'Clory'll be all right,' promised Hannah Merinda, thinking,
Willie'll never go another month — My laws, what a rash o' birthin's!
'Utah's best crop' is right!

But when midnight came and Clory's pains had 'flatted out'
and the anxious sisters burned feathers to coax her back to fight,
she demanded something else. She remembered the drowning
kittens that had obsessed her at Kissy's birth, the kittens that
fought on blindly ... but that kind of fighting wasn't enough.
There came a time when a person reached out for something
greater than human will, for something beyond implacable Nature.

Abijah and Lars Hansen anointed her with the beania oil, laid
hands upon her damp forehead.

'We unitedly lay our hands upon thy head — this oil which has been dedicated and consecrated and set apar-rt for the healing of the sick in the household of faith . . .'

Where had she heard those exact words before? And then the moment came back to her — Abijah leading his followers to the 'Land of the Unlocked Door,' building a dugway to conquer a mountain of lava rock, administering to an ox so that it might pull another woman in labor to safety . . . And Abijah's faith had been triumphant. She had seen the ox clamber to its feet with her own eyes.

' . . . We seal upon thee and the child in thy womb blessings of life, health, strength, and vigor . . . We do this by virtue of the holy priesthood in us vested . . .'

But Abijah had had that mysterious thing called a Testimony about which people talked so glibly. They said you had a conviction like a burning of the heart. She held herself so still that not a muscle moved and willed the conviction to come, but nothing happened. And then as she lay there, hardly daring to breathe, denying the flesh and the material walls about her, invoking the Spirit thing, there came one of those rare instances that had sustained her all her life. Horizons parted — laughter lived.

'Hurry!' smiled Clory, opening her eyes at the anxious faces bending over her.

7

It was going to be a wonderful winter with Apostle Snow entertaining in the Big House and Brother Brigham spending the season in St. George. Brother Brigham in the White House two blocks north and one block west from the Tabernacle corner. Here was where Amelia lived with her hired girls and her retinue and her punctilious ways.

On another corner lot two blocks down the street lived Lucy B., the other wife whom Brother Brigham brought to live in Dixie and whom Clory came to love.

A wonderful winter with greater prosperity now that Brother
Brigham had come to live among them, with parties, dances, balls,
with Clory arranging dramas and tableaus and persuading Sister
Couzzens to teach The Poetry of Wordsworth in the Young
Ladies' Retrenchment Society.

A wonderful winter with Abijah in fast-day meeting so proud
of his new son, whom Clory was christening James, after her
father. Pal had named her boy Frank after *her* father. And now
Willie...

'Isn't it funny,' rejoiced Clory, 'that us three women should
have sewed on our layettes together all spring and all summer, and
now the months of preparation bear fruit together? 'Sheba would
say there's some meaning to it, that they'll all be together when
they grow up — but then, 'Sheba —!'

Willie was forty-six years old.

'I dunno,' acknowledged Hannah Merinda, thumbing the pages
of *Doctor Chase's Prescription*, ordering cayenne pepper stimulants and dandelion tea for water around the heart, seeing 'that
she first of all gits a good cleaning out ——

'For swelled joints,' read Hannah Merinda, 'two hens' eggs
beat fine, add one tablespoon of salt and black pepper in a pint of
vinegar. Mix well and rub the parts downward...'

And it was Clory's turn to brew teas, send Lehi up to Aunt
Ket's to borrow the piece of Castile soap she loaned out for birthings, prepare the scorched linen cloth dipped in hot beania oil, cut
open the dried Malaga grape-raisin for the baby's navel.

It was a girl child, and Willie, weak and spent, smiled thankfully at the tiny red creature wailing in Clory's arms. Abijah
did not have a girl. He would be pleased. A girl to take the place
of Clory's little maid.

'Didn't I tell you,' crowed Clory, 'we're gettin' a new start in
life?'

Willie smiled and slept.

Abijah, tiptoeing in, gazing in awkward man-fashion at the

child, poking his big brown forefinger within its curled red fist, was delighted. Willie wasn't so shilpit after all! His great beard jutting, he strutted and hawckked at his throat until the midwives had to shoo him out of the room.

Clory was in the living-room bathing the baby with warm beania oil when the three midwives finished with Willie and came in, Aunt Ket closing the door carefully behind her.

Hannah Merinda looked at the child on Clory's lap, at the girl palming oil over the spindling limbs, at Clory's ripe figure where the life coursed richly. Well, the child wouldn't lack for a wet-nurse if anything should happen ...

'I think we'd best tell you,' said Hannah Merinda, her plump face worried, 'the afterbirth didn't come.'

Clory's eyes above the baby's head were wide with sudden fright. Abijah looked up from his ledger on the table.

'We can't get it out ourselves. But don't fuss, yet; sometimes it comes even twelve hours after.'

But the next day when Hannah Merinda called again, the afterbirth still hadn't come.

'Willie complains she's got cramps in her belly and limbs,' the midwife frowned to Clory, hanging diapers on the line. 'She can't keep nothing on her stummick, neither, nor nurse the babe ...'

Clory turned and removed the clothespin from her mouth, her lips setting in a hard line.

'Stiddy Weeks could git it out, couldn't he?'

Hannah Merinda nodded, her pink dewlaps quivering.

'But you know what Brother Mac'd say ... Let's wait and see.' She trotted worriedly around the house.

Clory walked thoughtfully in to Willie, defiance gathering in her breast.

Willie smiled whitely up from the pillow where her gray hair straggled. Her cheeks were yellow and sunken. She moved her tongue distastefully around her teeth and pulled a wry face.

'My mouth tastes like a birdcage,' she said weakly, 'but I've got a fine girl, hain't I?' She turned to look down at the babe in the crook of her arm.

Suddenly Clory couldn't keep her chin from trembling. Willie saw it.

'Somethin's wrong! Tell me! I got a right to know!'

Clory was all instant contrition, pushing the bony shoulders back upon the pillow.

'It's nothing. Just the afterbirth. Sister Lowgie ——'

'Clory, Clory,' Willie's hoarse voice fluttered, 'I'll die if h'it don't come out. Clory, I don't want to die. I've just started to live. Clory...'

'Sheba was kneading bread, the table quaking as her strong forearms dug into the dough.

'If Willie's going to have a long sick spell,' she said, looking up from her thumping, her small eyes hard and bright, 'I ain't a-gonna have her around here to wait on!'

Clory eyed her coldly.

'Where's Abijah?'

'Takin' a load of cane to the soggum mill.'

Stopping at her house, peering at her own sleeping babe, she shrugged into a shawl and hurried up the street, her skirts whipping about her legs. She met Abijah at the corner. He reached out a hand and pulled her up beside him on the seat of the buckboard.

'Abijah,' she said, clasping her hands to still their trembling, 'you'll have to get a doctor. Willie ——'

Abijah took his eyes from the swaying rumps of the oxen and frowned at her.

'You know what the prophet says, "Trust ——"'

'But Willie's dying!'

'Well,' he pursed his lips, 'I think you're a mite excited, Clorrinda, but...'

When he came out of Willie's room later, he wasted no time taking his hat from its peg.

'I don't know sickom about this business, myself. I'll go counsel with Brother Brigham, lay the case before him.'

Clory stopped biting her fingernails and sighed with relief.
In the other room she smiled reassurance at Willie, tossing and
picking at the covers. Already there was a faint foul smell about
her.

'If h'anything 'appens,' whispered Willie, 'don't let 'Sheba
raise my baby, Clory.'

'Pooh,' derided Clory. 'Nothing's goin' to ——'

'Promise!'

Willie's eyes were relentless, and Clory's dropped before them.
'Of course.'

The sick woman seemed to be sleeping when Clory heard Abijah come.

He was taking off his coat when she opened the door. He looked
at her but said nothing.

'Well?'

He went on draping his coat over the back of the armchair,
cleared his throat, sat down, crossed his knees, pressed the tips
of his spread fingers together.

'Brother Brigham said,' he announced, not meeting her eyes,
'to "let Nature have its course, that if we would obey his counsel
the afterbirth will come away of its own accord and she will get
better and all will be well."'

'But ——'

He glanced at her sharply from under his brows.

'If I went contr-rary to that counsel, Clor-rinda, I'd be considered weak in the faith in the authority of the Holy Priesthood!'

Abijah meant well. He had faith. The next day he had the sisters wash Willie and anoint her with the consecrated oil from the
crown of her head to the soles of her feet and dress her in clean
linen. Laid back on her bed, she seemed more cheerful. Abijah
himself put his hands upon her head and blessed her by the
authority of the Holy Priesthood in him vested. When he had

finished Willie smiled up at him, so big and vital in the little room.

'Willie,' he said, 'ye ken I want to do the best for your welfare, don't ye?'

Her lips formed 'yes.'

'The Prophet, Joseph, said to "trust in God when sick..."'

Willie's mouth still held its faint curve, but her eyes on his were dark with the resigned wisdom of women.

The next morning she woke up screaming with pain. There was a swelling starting up in her belly and the room reeked with her stench. 'Sheba backed out, holding her nose, and thereafter flatly refused to go in. Clory removed the baby to her own house and the Yeast Lady came to watch the two children.

It took Willie two weeks to die. There were times when she was stronger than Clory, who walked the floor and beat her hands together.

'Don't take on so, child,' whispered Willie. 'None of us are livin' for h'ourselves, anyways; we're h'all livin' for the future. Starvin' or dyin' or fightin' with the gentiles, none of it matters. We're buildin' something precious to 'and on, and some day when we look down from 'eaven there won't be any cold, any 'unger, any 'ardness like Abijah's, any meanness like 'Sheba's.'

'Oh, Willie!' Clory wailed, throwing herself on her knees by the bed, 'don't leave me! You're all the mother I've had...'

'Don't 'old on to me, Clory. My time's come and I'm ready.'

There were days when Willie gave way to the fever and babbled incessantly. Other days when she was gripped with strange obsessions. The day when she craved Casaba melon.

Abijah hunted all over the mission and finally found one that had been picked and ripened in the house.

When he brought the slices into the room, flinching under the stench, he was hesitant.

'Ain't you afeard it'll be too cold for your stummick, Wilhelmina?'

'It can't 'urt me where I'm goin', Abijah.'

So few things one could do for her. Rubbing her legs with hot vinegar water, feeding her half a teaspoon of wine now and then.

One morning her teeth were set, her skin the color of white of egg. Abijah laid his hands upon her and prayed with all his power, reasoning with the Lord.

'Abijah, I 'ope nobody ever blames you for my death,' whispered Willie.

But he only looked pitiful and bewildered at that.

Then fresh agony gripped her so that she could not talk, and Abijah sternly rebuked the pain.

Clory, crying quietly in the corner, could stand it no longer but flung herself upon Abijah, beating at him with her fists, railing at him as he stood staring down at the bed.

'It's your fault! You're killing her!'

Willie struggled to rise, held up a shaking hand, and Abijah got himself out of the room.

'Hush, child. Nothing great was ever accomplished without sacrifice and sufferin' and loss. I'm part of the loss. An' what do *I* matter?'

But Clory ran across the dooryard to fetch the girl child. Maybe Willie's baby would spur her to fight.

Willie's eyes were tender and wet for the first time.

'Do you think I'll 'urt her, huggin' her too 'ard? Ain't it funny, I planned on *her* comin' so long an' now *I* won't be here. Take good care of her, Clory.'

Her eyes were suddenly diffident.

'I'd like her named Tempelina after the Temple I won't never see. Will you do my Temple work, Clory?'

Clory nodded dumbly.

'I want you should see I'm sealed to Joe ———'

Bit by bit during those long night reaches, the story of Willie's past came out, that past so dreadful that she had kept it hidden all her life. And bathing her pain-wracked limbs Clory saw deep, embedded scars along her elbows, her knees, the bottoms of her feet. And in an anguish of contrition Clory understood that queer hobble, like a jointed, mechanized doll.

'... so happy,' muttered Willie, her eyes staring vacantly at the ceiling, 'Joe and me and the two kids on the ocean. 'ow good the chicken bones tasted after the sailors had thrown them away! ... They said it was too late to start but the men was anxious. And we women didn't know nothin' except we 'ad to push them 'eavy carts a thousand miles.'

It seemed to do her good to talk. The night listened outside the walls. Clory leaned her forehead on the hot hand.

'I remember one elder says we should trust in common sense as well as in the Lord. ...'

Greasing axles with bacon and even soap. Chewing a crumb of buffalo meat until it got white and tasteless. Rationed to less than half a pound of flour a day. Feet festered, wrapped in rags. Remnants of human bodies eaten by wolves. Five hundred head of cattle stiff amid the snowbanks. Tents and wagon-tops blown away and wagons buried up to the tops of the wheels. Men pulling their handcarts up to the moment they died. Wading a river and cutting shins against the blocks of ice. Joe eating a dead horse in the moonlight, mistaken for a wild animal, shot. Ground too frozen to dig graves. Sixteen die in one night, bodies piled up. Not enough men with sufficient strength to pitch tents. Sat on a rock until morning with dying children on my lap. Feet frozen, bare upon the snow, I crawled forward on hands and knees, then on elbows and knees. 'Sister, the martyrdom of Joseph and Hyrum was nothing compared to this!'

Willie's faint voice singing, 'For some must push and some must pull ...'

She never could carry a tune, thought Clory pitifully. But maybe the Lord'll let her be in His choir anyway.

Willie's gaunt face had a glory. Suffering had carved deeper the wrinkles at the side of her mouth and extending down her chin. There was always saliva in those wrinkles. Clory remembered her gesture of wiping it off with the back of her hand ... Lips sharply outlined — a mouth patient, not drawn down at the corners with self-pity, but set in lines of patient endurance. She had always been so patient with Abijah. Clory wondered if that query of hers would go wailing down eternity: 'Do you want me tonight, Brother Mac?'

There was nothing left in Clory's heart but a great pity. Nothing but the will to keep cheerful until the thing was over. Cheerful, with Willie saying wistfully, 'I needn't of died!' With Abijah asking her, 'Do you feel happy in your mind concerning the work of God?' Willie distributing her keepsakes — Clory must have the life-preserver she'd worn across the ocean, the life-preserver with the little nozzle under the right arm where you blew in your breath to inflate it.

Clory was alone with her when she died. It was one of those clear autumn nights of unearthly beauty, so still that, sitting there while Willie fitfully dozed, she could hear the faint rustle of the dried skeletons out in the corn-rows.

Willie's voice had faded to an echo.

'*There's not enough love in the world*,' she said once. 'You're needed, Clory, because you *love*.'

She became very apologetic after a paroxysm of pain.

'I'm sorry to 'ave such a 'ard time dyin' ... Don't let 'Sheba lay me h'out. I'll be just another dead body to 'Sheba!'

And then when Clory had promised, and the pale eyes had lost their look of desperation:

'A voice, not a whisper, but still and low said to me: "If you will leave your 'ome, father and mother, you shall have Eternal Life." I 'ave 'eard the same voice since, not in dreams but in daylight, when in trouble and uncertain which way to go; and I *know God lives* and guides this people called Mormons. ...'

Her eyes, already filled with the mystery of the last long trek, were dark with faith.

'Don't never knuckle under to life, Clory. Don't never knuckle under, if you 'ave to crawl — all — the — way!'

Parting the gray hair, drawing the middle section straight back, the two sides down over the ears, braiding and coiling the braids behind, Clory was conscious only of a gentle sadness. No overwhelming grief, for Willie had been too strong, too undefeated by life for that. And the funeral must be fraught with that same serenity.

Everybody was there. Willie would not have believed she had so many friends. Clory looked at the faces about her, wondering at the changes the years had made. Sometimes one never took the time to see the woods for the trees. 'Sheba's face had folded in on itself, her nose become more hawklike, her chin sharper, her mouth thinner, her voice shriller. While Abijah seemed to have expanded, become heartier, more cheerful. There was David Wight — a hint of premature gray the whole length of his sideburns, from the streak on his temples to the bunch on his jaw. There was Pal, almost middle-aged. Here was Clory herself changed more than any of the others. And Willie? Willie was done with change.

'Handle her gently!' she wanted to cry out to the pallbearers, to the men at the cemetery. One more mound. Quite a little family out here now. She could almost hear 'Sheba thinking, *real sociable.* . . . Death and birth, and life going on . . .

CHAPTER XIII

BROTHER BRIGHAM could always be depended upon to do the unexpected. Into this new spirit of the Dixie Colony, which now that it was sheltering the Prophet of God on Earth was become very self-assured and cocky, into this new urge of liveliness and youth, Brother Brigham introduced the silkworm.

Brigham's wife, Amelia, in the White House with her husband's secretaries, stray cousins, several coachmen, assorted servants — Amelia, with her fruit comport and old long-stemmed wineglasses on the table (she always had a standing order for the best wine made in the county); Amelia, with her queenly figure, her watered silks, rings on both her forefingers, pearl beads wound high around her throat and a locket pendant, and the little sunparasols she affected when riding in an open carriage; Amelia, with her real side-saddle, with her bright blue brass-buttoned habit whose skirts even when she rode just missed the ground (nor could you criticize her, for the Mansfield girl who worked there counted the petticoats!). Amelia introduced the making of flowers from milkweeds, the Union Club, the Young Historical Club, the new corset, boned and curved to fit the fashionable figure with its full bust, narrow waist, curved hips, and arched stomacher, and the steel backboards to train women in the correct carriage necessary for the Grecian bend.

To Amelia belongs credit for the new note of nicety, but to Lucy B., whose house had no especial name, who, herself, had no regal airs to separate her from her sisters (but whose slavish devotion to Brother Brigham was a household word) — to Lucy B., the second wife whom Brother Brigham installed in the Dixie Mission, belongs credit for the silkworm.

Lucy B. was the bold-breasted fine figure of a woman whom men's eyes instinctively follow down the street. She had blonde wavy hair that was the despair of other women and she dressed as stylishly as Amelia, but she was a democratic neighbor and citizen. Also she was every bit as much a lady. Even Bathsheba MacIntyre, who courted her to her face and talked about her behind her back, had to admit that. Coming to buy a pig from Lon Tuckett she completely routed the little man by insisting on a lady pig. She felt it unseemly for a gentlewoman to own a pig of the sterner sex. Her imported black-and-white chickens that were prone to fight womenfolks she called 'abacaterian' chickens, both preserving decorum and relieving her feelings.

Lucy B. started giving music lessons that fall on the organette in her nice house with its real store carpets.

Clory studied along with the groups of children and took in washings and made dresses by hand for fifty cents apiece to pay for the lessons. All this, besides raising two babies and preparing for Abijah's visits, which now were every other week.

And there were the gloves which soon now she hoped to have ready to ship to the Z. C. M. I. in the North. She was learning to have a squaw's feeling for buckskin, declared Sister Joe Eardley, who knew about leather and 'sewing up the boot, the sole to make r-ready.' A beaded pair of gauntlets should bring at least three dollars, counseled Lucy B., who told Clory of the pair Brother Brigham had owned and worn for thirty-five years. And so Clory pushed in the awl, developed flexible fingers that could turn the heavy buckskin, trim and press with the smoothing iron which required two hands to heft, and hummed scales and nursed this flowering of her old dream of beauty.

Often after an hour of wheezing on the organ 'Tell me the tales that to me were so dear,' she stopped to rest in Lucy B.'s rocking-chair, with its quilted back-rest of elegant brocaded States carpet, and nurse Tempie or Jimmie, who slept on Lucy B.'s big bed during the lesson. Such an elegant living-room, with its Seth Thomas clock and hand-painted kerosene lamps. Clory greedily gazed and could not tear herself away. Here was a woman who knew some of those lovely secrets hidden behind the horizon, tucked away in the past.

'Yes, indeed,' said Lucy B., sitting very straight in her chair, opening her mouth just wide enough to say each word. 'We wives never allowed any dissension in my husband's household: A stranger entering the room where we were assembled could not have told which children belonged to which.'

Clory had a sudden memory of what happened if she dared to reprove the twins. 'Sheba swooped down like a mother-bear. In her jealousy of the babies, 'Sheba was more subtle, and Abijah seldom caught her at it. When he did become aware of hidden friction, he would bellow impartially, as if he could reform human nature with noise.

'There are no half-brothers or half-sisters in this family! They're *all one!* If you plant carrots in one garden and carrots in another, they're all carrots regardless of the garden!'

But Clory, consumed with a vast need to transform all her carrots into orchids, could not be bothered with 'Sheba.

Shamelessly she would memorize another woman's customs. Lucy B.'s individual lamps on the hall lowboy so that each member of the family would have his own to light his way to bed; the kitchen table always with its white cloth and caster in the center — Clory would memorize and trudge home, a child on each hip, but determination in her heart to at last shape life. What was done, was done, and Abijah was a man you had to forgive if you lived with him. Moreover, he was her man. At least half of him.

But even after all these years she still hoped for too much from 'Sheba, who only laughed at her enthusiasm for Lucy B.

Through the socials, theatricals, Sunday-School picnics, and the Young Ladies' Retrenchment meetings ran an endless current of speculation concerning these two wives of Brother Brigham.

'Sheba and Aunt Ket made a cud out of Lucy B.'s idiosyncrasies and chewed it over and over; and 'Sheba had her own private tales, which she rehearsed at every excuse with uplifted brows and hands and zestful eyes.

But the 'pot-o-mush' story was the choice one, and it belonged equally to the entire Relief Society, congregated that day in the Silkworm Room in the basement of the Social Hall.

There was the rich brown smell of the cocoons in the hot water over the kerosene burner. And when the glue had melted, there was Lucy B. daubing at the cocoons with a whisk broom to get up the silk ends, and explaining to the fascinated women as she demonstrated, wrapped the threads around the pulleys and bobbin of the silk reel, and turned the wheel. In that room were a thousand silkworms Lucy B. had raised from butterflies imported from Japan, and for the six weeks previous to the cocoon stage the Relief Society sisters had taken turns feeding the wriggling white things crawling about over the mulberry leaves and crunching until the air in the room crackled. The cocoons had taken possession of the room, the worms having spun behind the pictures of both the Prophet and Brigham.

Lucy B. with pardonable pride must hold up her beautiful twill pieces woven 'in the gum.'

' ... several kinds of worms, some of them extracting from the mulberry leaves an orange glue, others pale yellow or pale green. Now I will teach as many ladies as like the process. A good reeler can reel a pound a day. How many —?'

Every hand in the room was up, and Lucy B.'s ordered tones were lost amid the shrill feminine clatter.

Into this female absorption strode Brother Brigham's dignified, high-hatted coachman with a note. Lucy B., reading it under the barrage of curious eyes, wrinkled her brow.

'"Will be at your place at four P.M." P.M., P.M.... what does he mean? Oh, pot-o-mush, pot-o-mush. I'll go home and put it right on!'

She smiled at the astonished ladies and in her stately manner prepared to gather up her reticule, her dolman, her bonnet.

What Brother Brigham thought of all this no one ever knew. He kept his own tight-lipped counsel and went about with his head above such things as ladies' rag-bees, went about with one eye on the slowness of Temple-building at home and the other on Washington where Cannon was being accused of taking an 'oath in the Endowment House of disloyalty to the United States Government.'

2

The President's Thanksgiving Proclamation should be read to the entire family, Abijah decided, as he stooped under the lintel of Clory's door. But it seemed a shame to waken her, except that the babies would get her up soon, anyway. She was overdoing this business of the gloves, he thought, peering down in the early morning gloom at the white neck with its ruffle of unbleach nightgown, the long braids tumbled over the pillow, the lashes a dark crescent on cheeks that had not yet got over pallor from Jimmie's birth and the shock of Willie's death. He was more grateful than he could make his stubborn lips confess that she was taking Willie's death so serenely; he could well remember the day when she would have nursed her bitterness until it smashed this new joy they were building together. But she had forgiven him — not that he considered he needed forgiving. The Lord took Willie because it was her time to go, and Abijah hoped if he had it to do over again he would still have the strength to remember he was only a private in the ranks, whose job it was to obey.

Nevertheless there were occasions when he felt humble before this slip of a girl whose eyes seemed so much older than the rest of her. More ambition than a man would think her slender flesh could contain, so that in spite of his scoldings and in spite of raw, cracked hands she sat up night after night beading gloves by the blue flicker of a tin lamp. And yet, before she went to bed — the table cleared, the white cloth, the silver caster. The gracious living she craved for herself and her children! Even in her sleep one arm was flung along the quilt toward them, sleeping there in the double cradle Lars Hansen had made. Remembering that next week he could come back to her, Abijah choked with a sudden rush of love and bent his bearded face to hers. . . .

Clory twisted her hair in the new English chignon, pinched her cheeks before the cracked mirror above the cupboard. Amelia Young, according to the Mansfield girl, used prepared chalk and carmine. But one must keep one's looks as long as possible. Don't knuckle under, Willie had said, Willie who would never be dead to her, but was still there in the room with her red wrists and patient smile. . . . Kissy stretching up to reach the dishpan, and sometimes in the cradle Baby and Brother were more real than flesh and blood. Today Tempie was even wearing Kissy's christening gown, for a pioneer mother could not afford to be sentimental. And, thought Clory, I can't afford to waste Willie's brown Mozambique, either . . . The Tabernacle bell began to ring its half-hour prompting for the meeting, and Clory forgot even the querulous babies. Clasping her chapped hands beneath her cheek, she listened to its loud-throated silver clangor and thrilled to her shoe-tops. Civilization was after all just a matter of sounds: first the coyote and the tom-tom, then the cowbell and the bass drum, the bands, and now this last triumphant token, the Tabernacle bell that Abijah said you could hear clear down in the fields.

Abijah carried Jimmie, his unblinking stare upon his father's great brown beard, and walked beside Clory, who held Tempie; 'Sheba and the boys, splendid in new tight homespun jeans, smartly brought up the rear. Although 'Sheba had her head high, her nose was undoubtedly out of joint by this arrangement, but for once she was helpless, since after all one could not really find a new baby under a cabbage leaf.

At the square they met Pal and David and Lucy, Bishop Gardner and his three wives and their families. Abijah nodded and beamed.

'Weel,' he boomed, 'we're getting to be quite a town! Outgrowin' the bowery and the Social Hall...'

They walked past the old bowery, not yet torn down but taken over by mesquite and salt grass, past the little T.O. and post office, closed and shuttered today, on up to the sandstone building on the corner. The spire was at last completed and the meeting-house a reality in almost its entire magnificence.

'We'll never outgrow the Tabernacle!' chuckled Bishop Gardner.

Since there were some finishing touches left on the decorations and the town clock not yet arrived from London, there was still débris in the yards (in spite of Brother Brigham), and ladies lifted their trains and gentlemen their polished boots to stroll about among the rocks and visit. Abijah and 'Sheba went on through the gates with the others, but Clory stood on the sidewalk, shushing Tempie and straining her neck to gaze up and up at the mounting red flanks and the steeple with its white-picketed deck and the golden weathervane, that had cost so much to build.

One more treasure to be handed on with the rosewood desk, she thought, as Bella Trupp darted out of the crowd, her red-rimmed eyes beseeching, her hot hand clutching, 'I'm still as much a Virgin!'... Sister Miles throwing herself into all the ponds at the foot of the Red Hill, Eliza Hichinoper with her whine, her eyes burned out with a deeper melancholy...

'It's the finest building of its type west of the Mississippi,' pronounced a voice, and Clory turned to see the famous Thomas L. Kane, who had championed the Mormons throughout their long history. A present visitor at the White House, he stood with Brother Brigham and a group of men peering up at the shining spire. Jacob Hamblin and Miles P. Romney, the architect, and others of the Tabernacle artisans were there. Lon Tuckett who had perched on the golden ball at the foot of the weathervane and crowed the noon hour every day while the spire was being finished. Brother Burt who had made a plaster out of boiled-up gypsum for the lacy cornice-medallions, the molds for which Brother Milne whittled out of wood.... Gray-headed Tutsegabbett was there, too, in his inevitable hunting shirt, leggings, and blanket. Fixing his dark, unsmiling gaze upon the Leader, he listened to him as he told the men that it was an immortal distinction to have worked upon the Tabernacle.

'What did you use for mortar?' asked General Kane, shielding his eyes against the sun and gazing up at the precise checkerboarding of all those square red units.

'Blood and guts!' cackled Lon Tuckett.

Inside, the main floor seemed crowded (people hugging the real coal-heaters along the aisles) and Clory climbed the self-supporting circular stairway that spiraled to the gallery which semicircled the building toward the choir seats, empty today, and the organ loft with its tall new organ where the Snow girl sat. Below the choir seats, the rostrums sloping gently down in terraces appeared to be filled with dignitaries. Brother Brigham, General Kane, and all the men who had worked upon the Tabernacle, Erastus' counselors, Abijah and the rest of the bishops, Brother Hamblin, even Tutsegabbett.

Clory's worried eye located 'Sheba holding Jimmie as if it pained her....

Prayer had already been offered, and as she slid into a seat Brother Wheelock tapped with his baton, the Snow girl's feet squeezed the treadles, and the organ's plaintive rumble summoned the audience to rustle to its feet.

'We thank thee, O God, for a Prophet,' voices sang lustily, eyes affectionately upon Brother Brigham. During the hymn Erastus and Aunt Ket came in, Aunt Ket finding a seat beside 'Sheba and Erastus proceeding unhurriedly up to the stand, where Brother Brigham welcomed him with a shared hymn book.

Erastus brought the meeting to order. This is the day on which we thank our Father for all His blessings, not the least of which is the fact that we have with us President Young making his first appearance in this Great Tabernacle . . .

There was a stir, and Erastus sat down and Tutsegabbett got deliberately to his moccasined feet. He gathered his blanket more tightly about him, stared unwinkingly at the people, and began to talk in his version of the English speech he had learned with such effort.

'My people have at last got eyes open. I am like the sun just rising in the East, and so with my people. For long time we in the night. Our hearts could not understand. All that Brigham and Jacob and Erastus have said is straight; but when I talk to Mericats, their talk is not straight. And so with all the white people until I saw the Mormonies.'

Tutsegabbett paused dramatically and drew his aged body up to its full height.

'Today I meet with Brigham and Erastus and Jacob to worship with them white man's big On-Top God and to give the hand of my people in forever peace!'

Tutsegabbett sat back down amid a buzz of appreciation. The muscles of his wrinkled face did not move but his eyes were alive with pride.

When Brother Brigham stood up, advanced to the tribune, laid his hands upon it, fixed his steady gray eyes upon all those uplifted faces, and then began to speak slowly, as always, and then growing more impassioned so that his white beard trembled and his forefinger came up in its old emphasizing gesture, a sigh of satisfaction swept the people and they relaxed against the benches. This was what they had come for.

'The Saints don't think much of your cotton mission up North,' began Brother Brigham, and amusement rippled. 'But I believe we can never go beyond the duty of Saul, son of Kish, who went forth to seek his father's asses and found a kingdom.' Twiddling his thumbs, he waited for the laughter. 'And it is indeed a kingdom, when you can build with your own efforts a Tabernacle second to only one in the whole of Zion. For this reason I want you to have the distinction of completing the first Temple in the Lord's vineyard, so you can after this life walk back to the presence of God and give the sentinel angels the key words, and thus earn eternal exaltation. I see by your faces that some of you think this is a hard assignment, but you will not have to leave *this* Temple. And I promise you' — Brother Brigham raised his forefinger and leaned across the tribune and the audience held its breath, savoring the moment as one of those strange electric instances when the Lord's Spirit rested down upon the Leader. — 'and I promise you, in the name of the Lord, that new riches will flow into this country, that the way will open up for you to build this Temple in a manner you least expect!

'But first, you must retrench, you must make yourselves worthy. We shall take the old broadsword and ask, "Are you for God?" And if you are not heartily on the Lord's side you will be hewn down.

'We will start with the men. Some of them here in this audience are not fit to hold the priesthood! Some of them are lazy. Why cannot a girl work the telegraph? You'll see a great big six-footer, who'll eat as much as three or four women, stuffing himself until he is almost too lazy to touch the wire! Now let the girls work the telegraph and the men on the Temple!'

From where she sat, looking down upon the congregation, Clory could see folks begin to squirm. Johnny Lowgie, who worked the telegraph . . .

' ... I will speak my mind to the young men on the subject of their tight trousers,' continued Brother Brigham. 'There is a style of pantaloons very generally worn, about which I would say something if there were no ladies here. *My* pantaloons button up here' (he indicated the ridge of his hips) 'where they belong, that my secrets, that God has given me, should not be exposed. If it were the fashion to go with pantaloons unbuttoned I expect you would see plenty of our elders wearing them unbuttoned. This shows the power that fashion exerts over the majority of minds.'

Clory's roving eye discovered Abraham and Samuel sitting beside Abijah, well up near the front, and studiously regarding their laps. She snickered.... And remembered with a pang Free's struggle to get any pants at all ...

' ... anything that will tend to destroy the lives of my sisters I despise, but I do not believe in making my authority as a husband or a father known by brute force, but by superior intelligence. I can show you, wife, where to put everything in your house. But if you will put the swill-pail where the water-pail should be, I must go somewhere else to drink water, and not run the risk of drinking out of the swill-pail in the night.'

Lucy B. looked somewhat flustered, thought Clory, but there sat Amelia as stiff as a ramrod.

' ... I have offered to give my wives bills of divorcement if they do not stop yielding to the foolish demands of fashion. I asked some of my wives the other evening, "What is the use of all this velvet ribbon — perhaps ten to thirty yards on a linsey dress?" And I was asked very spiritedly in return, "What use are those buttons on the back of your coat?" ... Now, if the size of this Grecian bend continues to increase you will soon not be able for the life of you to tell at a distance a lady from a camel!'

Brother Brigham suddenly struck a pose, flexing his little finger and erecting his buttocks to imitate a fashionably dressed female with tilting hoops and Grecian bend until even the women roared.

Clory squeezed her bustle so hard against the bench that Tempie woke up and began to root around for food.

'... this Grecian bend will result in deformed children! Personally, I'd much prefer to see a Mormon bend!... It is the custom of some sisters to have a long trail of cloth dragging after them through the dirt; and still others at dinner parties in the height of gentile fashion have their necks so low that their — well, I suppose that they wear a band over the shoulders to the waist, but I feel like the gentleman who was asked if he had ever seen such elegance before.

'"Is not this beautiful?" he was asked. "Did you ever see the likes of this?"

'"No, sir," said the party questioned. "Never since I was weaned!"'

Sly smiles on the faces of all the men, and the ladies' turn to stare at their laps.

'... Break off your sins by righteousness! This is the word of the Almighty to you, through his servant Brigham. Keep your secrets secret, and your homes so neat and nice that a female angel will feel like coming there to visit.'

Brother Brigham paused, drank from the glass of water at his hand, and people relaxed against the benches.

'Now,' said the Leader, bringing up that forefinger, 'I have on my mind one more thing: the United Order of Enoch!'

The Saints again sat upright. Why, that was the law the Prophet had introduced whereby a man consecrated all his property to the Church!

Watching Brother Brigham, Clory thought, it won't work. Too many called him hard, even among his own people. But she remembered Lucy B.'s story of the servant-girl with child, the footman-seducer who escaped, and Brother Brigham coming to the rescue, hushing the scandal, adopting the child.

'We will name her after her birth month,' said Brother Brigham. 'July Adopt-to Young!'

'How was it in the time of Enoch? Had they some rich and some poor then? No. A society like that would never have to buy anything; they would make and raise all they would eat, drink, and wear, and always have something to sell and bring money, to help increase their comfort and independence. Of course, some would not be contented ... I see a great many who profess to be Latter-Day Saints who would not be contented in heaven! But we want to see nothing of that in this little society. It is time for the Saints to be One! Now, brethren and sisters, forsake fashion, join the United Order of Enoch, and the Lord will show you how to build your Temple!'

3

'If he doesn't hurry up and decide we'll all go crazy.' For three nights now, waiting for Abijah to get undressed, she had lain and watched him stare at the shoe in his hand, his mind making itself up about the Order. It was not an easy decision, since a man turned the fruits of his labors into a common storehouse and received therefrom according to his needs. Lars Hansen had entered an inventory of his possessions even to a change of raiment. And there were the rules a man and his family must covenant by baptism to obey: never to take the name of Deity in vain nor speak lightly of sacred things; never to miss family or secret prayer; never to break the word of Wisdom; never to speak or think evil of one another or find fault; always to keep the Sabbath holy; always to return that which one borrows; always to observe chastity and personal cleanliness; always to pay tithing; to cancel all individual indebtedness contracted prior to uniting with the Order, and to contract no debts afterward contrary to the wishes of the Board of Directors; to labor honestly and diligently and devote oneself and all one has to the Order and to the building up of the Kingdom of God.

'It will be verra hard,' sighed Abijah, still staring at the shoe.

'Ye can no longer make money on the side for schooling and such, Clorinda. It will be share and share alike.'

He looked so much like a troubled little boy. Clory choked down a torrent of rebellion.

'If you think it's right for you to join, Abijah, I'll not stand in your way.'

He made a little sound of affection in his throat and leaned over and kissed her. . . . Ech, 'Sheba wasna like that. 'Sheba was as balky as the mules he'd again have to forego.

Somehow Clory felt sorry for him there in the dim lamp-glow, kneeling in his night garments, his bushy head in his hands, praying in a muted whisper that went on and on. Men were such babies, always revolting against reality . . . Suddenly she awoke with a start, jerked erect to see Abijah sitting up in bed, peering wild-eyed around the room, its white walls eerie in the haggard moonlight from the window.

'I've had a vision!' he ejaculated, his disheveled beard grotesque. 'I saw as plainly as wi' the naked eye that the Father and the Son were enthroned on high and angels ministered before them. Indeed, so glorious was the scene that I longed to leave this sublunary sphere.'

At the sonorous phrases Clory's mouth twitched with its secret woman's smile.

'I heard a voice in a tongue unknown to me, apparently in poetry. When I asked the interpretation it came instantly: "Without the United Order we canna become one. Angels canna hold communion with us. The dead canna be raised nor Jesus come to dwell." And I said, "It is enough! I am prepared to join!"'

And yet, when the fire and the fervor had faded, Abijah found the Order as irksome as anybody. He had just harvested the best stand of fall corn in the valley, and it was hard to turn that in and receive as his share no larger a portion than that given shiftless Zebedee Trupp. And it was hard to restrict all his fault-finding to the red-backed ledger. 'Sheba was always having to be hauled before the Board of Directors for playing euchre and drinking tea. His boys were always having to be reprimanded for speaking lightly of sacred things. Even Clorinda refused to 'devote oneself' and furtively went on making buckskin gloves that she hid so that he could not turn them in. He himself sometimes forgot to return that which he borrowed. Never before had he realized that his family fell so far short of the ideal. Only in the matter of secret and family prayers could he be sure, and then he had no way of checking the secret.

From the very first day there had been grumbling, when they all went down to the river to be baptized and Nephi had come shivering out of the water and chattered, 'Judas priest!' And 'Sheba flatly refused to let him make a deed of gift of her house and its possessions.

But as the days wore on and officers were elected, Abijah being made a vice-president, and they canvassed the town to see who were *bona fide* members and how much grain there was in the place, a man came to have a genuine satisfaction in the idea that he was loving his neighbor as himself. Only eighteen persons over the age of fourteen declined membership. And out of the ones who joined, committees were appointed, one to determine how many acres should be planted to each kind of seed, another to determine exactly what the valley could produce, another to apportion the 'store goods' from the Co-op. To each man a like credit was given for work, whether old or young, able-bodied or infirm, tradesmen or common laborers.

All the departments of work were overhauled: Peabody's tannery and shoe shop, Ferrano's cooper shop, Mansfield's blacksmith shop, Eardley's pottery and tinshop, Lars Hansen's carpenter shop, Benjamin Jarvis's and Sister Couzzens' schoolrooms, Hichinoper's dye-and-oil shop, Lon Tuckett's tailor shop. Gradually order began to come out of the original disruption, and the various craftsmen, gladly giving up farming, found that they could make a living at their trades again. Lars Hansen was frankly overjoyed that at last he could clear out some of the bed-spreads, tables, chairs, lounges, cupboards, picture frames, and chests that had accumulated through the years. Within a month his turning-lathe was put to making Christmas toys.

The women were organized and pooled their knowledge. Bro-ther Burt, the plaster man, carved a wooden mold and showed them how to make plaster-of-Paris dolls' heads, arms, and legs. Lucy B. Young was in charge of this division. Old Sister Burt suggested collars of wolf and coyote skins for overcoats.

Aunt Kate Eardley, much to her delight, was made forewoman of the town dairies; she must patrol the homes to check on the meticulous scalding of milk buckets, pans, and churns, to see they were set to air in the sunlight.

Aunt Keturah Snow had charge of midwifery, with Bathsheba and Hannah Merinda under her.

Everything was exceedingly systematic. Sister Amelia Young taught the ladies to knit and color wool flowers for table decora-tions. Reform was instituted even in table manners: plates must be turned over the knife and fork and not turned right side up until after prayer. And no longer was a boy whose voice had fully changed allowed to procrastinate about choosing a vocation and looking around for a wife.

'Get married!' Abijah would trumpet in Sunday meeting, his face as imperious as a bearded eagle's. 'Boys, get married! If you've only a straw tick, get *married!* And if you've only the tick without the straw, *Get Married!*'

For Zion's strength lay in numbers. An army in righteousness.

Samuel and Abraham began to take turns borrowing Abijah's best suit in order to court up an Eardley and a Ferrano girl, respectively.

The arising hour was 5 A.M., when Brother Wheelock bugled 'Oh Ye Mountains High' from the deck on the spire of the Tab-ernacle. At 8 A.M. the Tabernacle bell assembled all hands at the

square for the orders of the day. And at sundown Brother Wheelock bugled 'Do What Is Right, Let the Consequence Follow' as a
signal to quit work. On Sundays the summons to meeting was
'Come, Come, Ye Saints.'

Once a week the cooper, the carpenter, the shoemaker, the
chair-maker, the potter, the blacksmith, the midwife, the overseer
of the Co-op visited each home to ascertain the family's needs.
Once a day Ole Oleson came to the back door to collect the swill,
which he hauled off in a big barrel on a 'lizard.' Stiddy Weeks at
last came into his own with his drugstore, his composition pow-
ders, his boneset pills, and he was immediately put at the head of
a committee to investigate all cases of sickness and discover
which men were shamming.

Here was Gottlieb Uttley turning the land watered by his
Sonuvabitch Spring into a garden spot with roses and oleander
bushes. Gottlieb had 'green fingers' with growing things. He'd
been put in charge of the Order's acres of tomato vines and he
bragged that when he went out to weed in the early morning he
could hear them say, 'Lay over boys, lay over!'

Every Friday night there was a free theatrical or dance.
Brother Brigham introduced the Scotch reel or polygamy dance
wherein each man required two partners. 'First with yer right,
then with yer left,' called Brother Wheelock to the piping of the
music. And there was no need for any woman to sit out.

The head of each family owned his home, only as part of his
'stewardship'; and Brother Brigham ordained, 'All that any man
can get is a living: "Thou shalt not be idle, for he that is idle shall
not eat of the bread nor wear the garments of the laborer!"'

Not even Gottlieb's bachelorhood, about which he was as
stubborn as salt grass, could dampen Erastus' ardor, and Abijah
wrote very proudly in his journal: 'Our idea is home-making, and
not skimming the cream of the country with a six-shooter and a
whiskey bottle...'

And yet, now that the Temple hands had nothing to do but

their specific job, the building did not grow fast enough to suit Brother Brigham.

4

Meeting with the men in their news-clubs that spring, reading the gloomy news from the East, Erastus was so grateful for temporary peace that he would not tolerate one discordant thought. Zion might not yet have achieved the ideal, but when you balanced her record against the national public scandals rocking the States, you were pretty proud. There was Vice-President Colfax, who had been so critical of Mormon policy, being impeached for bribery in connection with the new railroad; there were the postal-contract frauds, Indian-service frauds. The financial pirates had so bled the country that business crashed with a boom, silver was demonetized, and the nation scraped the bottom of the meal barrel.

But there was no panic in Deseret. In fact, there was greater prosperity, since for the moment her enemies were too busy to notice her.

'But they'll be back,' cautioned Erastus. 'We'd better be happy while we can.'

Every day he drove down Temple Street to watch the upward progress of the old pile-driver, encased in the entire bark of a cottonwood tree, and its thunderous descent on the piled black rocks in the cavernous trench below.

On March 10, 1873, the first of the giant foundation rocks, some weighing seventy-five hundred pounds, was laid on the black volcanic footing, a redwood box filled with records and plates of silver, T.O. and factory scrip and bishops' chips, a copy of the little *Cactus*, and a bottle of consecrated Dixie wine sealed into the rock; and the building was officially begun.

In April the Tabernacle clock arrived from its long journey over oceans and plains and mountains and one morning many eyes gazed upward to the space above the little deck on the spire where Lon Tuckett miraculously balanced himself and tinkered with the fourth face of the monster-clock. And then into the silence, stamped with the authority of a voice that means to go on forever, bong ten deliberate strokes. As the silver bonging dies away among the hills where the coyotes howled, the crowd huzzahs.

'Don't be too cocky,' warns Orson Pratt, the apostate, who walks the streets these days convulsed with a vast mirth. Brother Brigham had promised the Temple workers that if they would labor faithfully not one should be hurt, and Orson buttonholes Erastus, who has just got rid of another trouble-maker — Brother Brigham having at last excommunicated John D. Lee.

'If your God is so all-powerful,' croaks Orson, his hairy Adam's apple lurching, 'let's see him make a ten-year-old steer in two minutes!'

But Erastus reminds the Relief Society to keep Orson and the Pig-Dirt people supplied with the necessities...

Clory was happy that summer in spite of Abijah's frequent absences fund-gathering for the Temple. Being Goddess of Liberty in bunting and cheesecloth, watching the Sugar Loaf fireworks from the deck of the Big House. Bribing the twins to gather the long top joint of the straw, soaking it in alum-water to make it pliable and glossy, coloring some strands and bleaching the rest with sulphur smoke, shaping the crown over a quart lard-bucket and pressing the top, sides, and brim with Lon Tuckett's tailor's iron, she made herself a stylish, flat-weave Sunday hat that quite took her breath away when she tied the calico streamers under her chin and stared at herself in the cracked mirror over the cupboard.

'You're happy, Clorinda Agatha MacIntyre,' she said aloud to the browned, pointed little face distorted there in the imperfect glass. 'You've learned to love your husband and to get along with his wife — well, almost, except when she tries to boss you too much about the babies.'... They said Polygamy was a principle for refining the spirit. If you could live in it gracefully you had conquered the flesh and your own soul, and one who had conquered his own soul had just about conquered life. Clory thought about 'Sheba. To live in plurality with 'Sheba you had to be as slippery as an eel, as harmless as a dove, and as wise as a serpent. You conquered your soul, all right!... 'Well, Clory,' she said to the mirror, 'even if your breasts do sag from too much nursing and you've got a little tummy so that no amount of corseting can bring your figure back, you're happy! You've licked the thing that tried to lick you!'

Like Clorinda, Erastus was to look back on that year of the Order with its epidemic of straw hats — bleached and upturned headgear startling above bearded masculine faces, but nevertheless protection from the sun — and call it the happiest year he had known....

On the records of the United Order of Enoch of the St. George Stake of Zion for the end of the year 1873, we find this entry:

> Whereas Henry Miles has seen fit to sever his connections with the United Order and upon settlement it is found he is in debt to the Order to the sum of $665.95, and whereas he has been unfaithful in his labors, loitering and trifling his time away and otherwise breaking the covenants he made when he united with us, therefore be it resolved that it is just in every way to hold him to the full and complete payment of the above-named indebtedness. Nevertheless, as he has a large family to support, be it further resolved that as an act of charity to his little children, the above indebtedness be canceled by the entry on the ledger of this resolution.

The original plan had been to cancel both debts and credits at the beginning of each year and for all to begin anew on an equal basis, but there were too many members like young Miles.

'There is only five cents' difference between the man who works and the man who idles,' complained Abijah MacIntyre, 'and the man who idles gets the five cents, for he is always at home and

can get first choice when anything is brought into the T.O.!'
Abijah was sour, having put into the Order a harvest of barley
and corn, his own and his boys' labor, a buckboard and wagon,
and two ox teams, and one year later drawn out only the wagons
and teams. Too many men found themselves losers, and yet the
oldsters would have been willing to continue.

'Give us a change, a change!' the young people cried, as youth
always cries.

But perhaps the greatest blow to the Order was the discovery,
when the books were finally balanced, that Mayor Zadoc Hunt
had more days of work to his credit than there were days in the
year!

The noble experiment had failed. But all was not lost. That
Christmas — assembly in the basement of the Tabernacle: Indian
club exercise and tableau with red fire and magnesium illumina-
tion — Erastus surveyed his community and was not ashamed to
uphold its accomplishments even to Brigham, whose face these
days seemed more than ever like parchment, whose eyes could
not hide their longing for proof that this work of his lifetime would
stand.

'Enoch hats, a half-finished Temple, brush grubbed from the
sidewalks and the square,' inventoried Erastus, 'and above all,
something you can't see but is worth much more to a man — a
sense of responsibility toward his neighbor, an armor against
selfishness and greed...'

5

In spite of his enemies, Brother Brigham found time to present
to the Dixie Mission the Temple's baptismal font, which he had
cast at the Salt Lake foundry at a cost of five thousand dollars.
Apostle Snow put Bishop Abijah MacIntyre in charge of hauling
it down from the City, but at the time John D. Lee was being
tried for murder in the federal courts at Beaver, and Erastus was

worried. The armed troops that had converged upon Utah at the time of the massacre were now firmly entrenched — Camp Douglas near Salt Lake City, Fort Crittenden near Provo, Fort Cameron near Beaver. And the same spirit of hostility swept Deseret, the same wild rumors.

From Cedar City Abijah telegraphed the probable hour of his arrival and Erastus took the MacIntyre ladies and drove to the point of the mountain to meet him. He had a new light buggy without a top, and he drove with the two women and Clorinda's babies in the seat beside him. The team kept up a spanking trot even over the brushy road beyond the Temple, its sprawling boulders and timbered skeleton capping the limestone knoll. If they could just get it finished before the government opened up full blast on polygamy it would stand as a sort of citadel. Morale was what counted during a siege.

But this job of getting out the lumber! Brother Angel, the Church architect, estimated a million feet, all to be hauled from Mount Trumbull, nearly eighty miles away. For a year the roads had rumbled to the monster wagon-trains of Shadrach Gaunt and his men, six ox or mule teams and five thousand feet of lumber to a wagon. Robert Gardner was making a masterful undertaking out of his Trumbull mission, running the sawmill and camp under the old Order, allowing Hannah Merinda Lowgie six dollars a week for cooking and washing for the twenty-five steady hands and keeping the dairy. But Erastus thought of the boys working half the night, loading lumber out of those heavy snowbanks on the upper slopes of the Colorado, struggling for four days to drive three miles out of that black mud and slush.

The whole of Deseret contributed to the Temple. One man in the City handed over eight hundred dollars in gold. Even Bathsheba MacIntyre had washed for sixteen of the workers for over a year.

Erastus glanced at the big woman beside him now, her face proud and strong beneath its veil and straw hat. She could be charming when she wished, but he had an idea her charm was mainly for public consumption. Neither of the babies would be good with her, and Clorinda was having to hold them both, coaxing them to play 'Bean porridge hot.'

Erastus made conversation.

'The country surely needs rain, doesn't it?'

Hair flying in the spring air, cheeks flushed, Clorinda sparkled at him over the heads of the romping youngsters. . . . Easy to see how that color and flash could get under a man's skin. Erastus wanted desperately for her to be happy, but Brother Mac should be taking another wife, and some women couldn't stand it. Sister Miles, now, had gone to bed for three weeks with the vapors.

Of course Clory was different. . . . Those were two nice youngsters, the boy heavy-browed like his father, same dimple in the fleshy bulge of his stubborn chin, same sensitive mouth. Even now you could see he'd be always a little slow, a little quiet, doing a deal of thinking that never showed through on the outside. The girl was mousy like Willie, square and chubby, a home-body at two and a half. None of the wild grace of Kissy. The Lord never repeated himself, and it seemed that Clorinda was not to have another elfin child, what with all these miscarriages Keturah told him about. Remembering the softness and bloom that was Kissy, remembering the price they had paid to colonize, Erastus sighed.

In spite of fatigue, Abijah's brawny vitality subdued all his sons. Samuel and Abraham and the twins were lined up in the roadway behind him now, each trudging beside his roped and tarpaulin-covered wagon. Pulling up his team, Erastus called out, and Abijah, blinking into the brilliant sunshine, took his hand from his eyes, slipped the yoke-ring from the pole so that his oxen could stand to cool, and walked up to the buggy.

'Things are verra tense up North,' said Abijah, pushing back his hat and mopping his forehead. Dust and sweat had caked its wrinkles and the joy-lines of his eyes. 'Folks are all excited

over John D.'s trial. I guess you kenned the deputy marshal's
arrested George Adair and put him in irons — they've had him
up there in jail for months trying to bribe him into testifying
falsely against Brother Brigham. The gentiles don't want
John D., they want the Pr-resident. We had orders not to show
our cargoes to anyone except bishops, but all down the line soldiers tagged us and tried to peek. They thought we were haulin'
cannon, but not a one got to look!'

Needing a breather before the long pull up to town, he got in
beside Erastus. There were matters on Abijah's mind. Recurrent
fear of another drought, bran-mush and lucerne greens; when
Samuel left for the New Zealand mission field in a couple of weeks
his new wife would expect her share of loaves and fishes.... In-
creasing polygamy arrests, and the brethren having to pay such
high bail, appealing and appealing the cases. So many of the
leaders dying — Apostle George A. Smith now gone. And Brother Brigham being released again barely in time for President
Grant's visit. Not that it did any good. That devilish McKean
got booted out, and folks said that Grant cried, 'I've been de-
ceived!' after being driven through the lines of Sunday-School
children, but he still refused Mormon hospitality.

'I don't know what else we can expect from a nation stampeded
with plutocrats and tax-graft,' said Erastus.

'At least we hae no a panic on!' Abijah grinned at David's
latest effort in the *Cactus.*

> They should do as we do, let their 'silver god' slumber,
> Take checks on the T.O. and peaches for lumber!

By six o'clock that night the massive iron font was resting on
the backs of its iron oxen in the Temple basement. As fast as the
boys unloaded the wagons the pieces were put in place and bolted
together. Apostle Orson Hyde, who was visiting at the Big
House, wept for joy.

'Thank God,' he said, 'I've lived to see another font in place in

the Temple of our Lord. This people will never be driven from
the Rocky Mountains!'

By six-thirty Erastus was baptizing his counselors and the
bishops and ward teachers for the remission of their sins and a
renewal of their covenants.

After the font was in, Temple-building seemed to gain a new
spurt of ambition, but Erastus was not appeased.

He formed the habit of driving daily to the fields and studying
the diminishing river, the wheat that sun-parched before it was
ripe. There had not been such a drought since '62. It was as if
the land were making one last stand before capitulating.

Once again people moved their beds out to the lucerne patches
and sweltered through the long, close nights. The very moonlight was hot. Mothers remembered with a sick dread the Year
of the Plagues, and Erastus had a hard time averting panic. As
the summer wore on, Temple-building lessened until he himself
almost gave way to despair.

On the Twenty-Fourth the citizens celebrated as usual with
a parade and program and races for the children in the afternoon.
Abijah was away on a trip, but Joseph brought his family up from
the field in the morning and Clory took the children and they all
went. But now during the long, smothering hush of the day she
sat without bustle or corsets in her doorway, fanned listlessly, and
watched the babies make mud pies in the bergamot. In her heart
was the old wild longing to escape. The children had passed their
dreaded second summer, but they were still vulnerable to plagues
and scorpions and prickly heat and the whims of this land. For
fifteen years Clory had tried to root herself in this hot red earth.
There were even moments when she loved it. But it seemed impossible to tear out of her soul the ancient yearning for the cool
valleys of the North. Children could be raised in peace and safety
there. With a passionate intensity she hated raising them around
that domineering woman next door, stretched full-length on her
rag carpet trying to nap.

Clory sat and fanned and dozed, and young Julia Hansen,
daughter of her who had been Serena Lee, passed by on her way
to the doings in town. An affected child (how could she be otherwise with all that spoiling by Lars and the Yeast Lady?), she
minced along in her new white dress made out of the last of the
Yeast Lady's good linen sheets from the 'old country,' stockings
knit in the modish shell pattern, and cloth shoes Lars had contrived from a pair of his old trousers. She was very grand, even
to the dandelion in her belt.

Clory smiled at the vain little face.

'You sure look pretty!'

'Thank you, ma'am.'

Condescending to smirk, young Julia went back to her self-
absorption.

Half-asleep, gazing at the south mountains floating on the
horizon like a mirage, at the rose bush Gottlieb had given her
curled with decay, Clory had a sense of listening to something
very far off, something older than memory. Alien music, sheen of
gauzy silks, potpourri and sandalwood. Peacocks and asphodels!
Her heart strayed in such meadows, but her feet were caught in
cockleburs.

She awoke to a feeling of rain on her face. The sky was a queer
turgid yellow and the air was full of sulphur smell. She hurried
the children into the house and stood in the doorway, watching
the reluctant great drops plop.

'Sheba called from across the yard, 'Smells good, don't it?'

The rain sluiced down in earnest now, and the parched earth
drank and wriggled and steamed.

Young Julia Hansen ran sloshing by like a picked chicken, her
pants-cloth shoes squelching water and mud.

Clory hid a smile.

'Me wet!' cried Tempie, pulling at Clory's hand, and 'Wet!
Wet!' echoed Jimmie, wide-eyed with the fathomless wonder of
children.

There was the staccato bark of hoofs on the road, and Joseph galloped up on his mule. His black head ran water and his eyes were wild.

'River's flooding!' he gasped. 'Get word!'

Clory stared foolishly after his flying figure. Why, it wasn't possible! How could there be a flood? Even now the storm was abating.

'Sheba came splashing under the eaves of the house.

'Let's go down,' she said. 'The twins can drive the buckboard.'

The roads were filled with wagons and buggies and boys on horseback. Frantic people gesticulating, yelling. Abraham, who had been at the doings, clattered by with the Peabodys.

Nephi goaded the creaking old oxen and muttered bad words under his breath, but even so the river's bank was lined with women and children when they got there.

The men were all shoveling dirt or hauling brush and rock or just futilely racing up and down. Zebedee Trupp waddled around like an angry duck, his yellow tooth gleaming as he bawled out orders. Clory could see David Wight out in the stream, ramming sandbags against the barrier, the murky water churning above his waist. Hard to believe that only yesterday she could have waded across without getting wet above the ankles.

The pile dam's ten-line fortifications of which the men had been so proud were still holding, but water was cutting between and undermining the thirty-foot pine poles. Ole Oleson bossed the gang of men reinforcing the leaks with mud and stones and brush relayed from the shore. The 'easy steps' by which the settlers had hoped to drain in gentle succession the worst anger of an embattled Pah Roosh were proving not much more effective than the old earth dam thirteen years before. The main body of the flood was still held at bay, but the water rose momentarily. The roar was terrifying, and Tempie hid her face in her Uncle Nephi's neck and began to cry.

Apostle Snow came stumbling along the bank, his face as white

as the crusted alkali, his Sunday suit mud-splashed, and dirt
streaking his bald spot where he had rubbed a distracted hand.

'Come on!' he yelled to the twins. 'We'll need all our man-
power if we hold 'er!'

'Where's it *coming* from?' Clory called after him.

'Cloudburst up in Mukuntuweap!' he bawled over his shoulder,
his middle-aged body staggering clumsily over the uneven ground.

'I wish Shadrach would come!' Clory heard him mutter as he
hurried away. 'Shadrach and Gardner at Trumbull...'

Listening to the frenzied river, Clory remembered another
time of terror, another flood. Another night when the Virgin's
bellow carried all the way to town.

Joseph panted up to them, his black eyes anguished.

'We're sunk if it goes out,' he gasped, gesturing with his shovel.
'Look at it! All my fruit trees —!'

'It's gone out before,' said 'Sheba, who was enjoying the spectacle.

He turned on her furiously.

'D'you realize how many miles of public ditches that river
feeds? Thirty-four! And seventy-four private ones! And with
all the patching we've done, the damn thing has cost us nearly
eighty thousand dollars to date! It *can't* go out, I tell you!'

But it could. Clory thought as she had on that other night
long ago: There are some things ordained to be.

The men working in the water hesitated, listened to the accelerated boom above them, tossed away their shovels, and made for
the shore. Clory thought it must feel like running in a nightmare
to try to wallow through that whirling current.

'Go on back!' the men yelled to the watching women. 'Get out
of the way! She's a-comin'!'

Lon Tuckett was the last one out, and as friendly hands
tugged at him, sobbing exhaustedly, there suddenly appeared upstream a monster onrush of water as dark and thick as lumpy
dick made with 'dobe-dirt flour. Driftwood and haystacks and

dead animals rode on its bosom. The human beings stood stock still, not breathing, as the flood struck the dam with a reverberating impact that shot boulders into the air and snapped the thirty-foot poles as if they were pipestems. That jade, Pah Roosh, fled wantonly along to freedom and the sea.

Clory, reliving the past, was scarcely conscious of the children gleefully dancing beside her, the broken voices of their elders.

'I'm through,' blubbered Lon Tuckett, drawing a hasty sleeve across his eyes. 'For fourteen years I've bucked this damn bitchin' river, and I'm through! I'm sick a-seein' my kids die off and Betsy goin' hungry! Betsy's always hated it here! By gorry, a man's a fool —!'

'Nobody quits in the Dixie Mission,' Erastus told him dully. 'You can't quit.'

'Like hell I can't!'

For once the little red-headed man left behind him more tears than laughter as he turned and fought his way up through muck and cat's-claw to where his team and Betsy waited.

Erastus' eyes still followed the mad flight of the river. His lips writhed.

'There goes more than cotton and cane. There goes more than food. There goes our blood and tears and sinew. There goes the Temple.'

'No.' David shook his tired head, gazed beyond the river and the burning flats. 'Brother Brigham promised us the way would open up, and it will. And we won't starve, either. Do you remember? "New riches will flow into this country..."'

'It would have to be a miracle,' Erastus sighed. 'And miracles don't happen nowadays.'

But they do. Two days later at Leeds, twenty miles east of St. George, silver was discovered in sandstone where silver had never been known to exist before in all the history of minerals. A town of rickety tin buildings and wooden huts and upturned powder casks, a town of five thousand people, boomed over night. Prosperity for the Dixie Mission. Quail dropping out of nowhere into the camps of the starving Nauvoo refugees. Manna from heaven for the Israelites.

6

At 2 P.M. the Temple hands in their working clothes marched double file up the street to the courthouse to welcome Brigham Young and his retinue. The men carried two banners, one inscribed with 'Holiness to the Lord,' and the other with 'Zion's Workmen' and an All-Seeing Eye. Behind these, stretching across both lines was a third banner, 'Welcome to Brigham Young, Our Chief Builder.'

The men's faces were creased with smiles, but they were orderly. They debouched on the south side of the new adobe courthouse, with its stone stairs and pillars and arched colonial doorway and hangman's trap in the spire. Far down the road they could see rising dust and the approaching company of carriages and scouts on horseback.

Struggling with suppressed elation, the men whispered among themselves. Uncanny how the woodwork inside the courthouse resembled birdseye maple, and those columns in the Tabernacle resembled marble. And now Brother Milne, the Scotch artist, had painted the Garden of Eden room in the Temple until you felt you were wrapped in the greenness of a tropical forest.

Looked like the weather would be perfect for the dedication tomorrow. Dixie Aprils were enchanting, with the oose and cactus in bloom on the hills and the roses climbing the poplar trees.

And now the President's party is turning the corner.

The Temple hands, stretched in a single line, are very still. The scouts, the coaches, and finally Brother Brigham himself pass slowly in review. The workmen take off their hats and bow low to the ground. Brother Brigham returns the salute. The coaches roll on by, and the Temple hands two abreast march back down to the shoveling, plowing, and scraping yet to do on the white-capped knoll.

There was a thrill in the very air, Clory thought, as she stooped to let Tempie hook up the back of the emerald green moiré. Studying her bangs, to which Abjiah had at last consented, the crisp ruching beneath her chin, the scalloped tops of her fine leather shoes, she knew that not even in her teens had she been so good-looking as she was now in her thirties. And the children were entrancing. Jimmie with his black curls and Kate Green-away jacket and pleated skirt. Tempie in her Swiss bodice and pantalettes. Clory tilted the new pillbox toque over her eyes and went out to join 'Sheba and Abijah. Even if the Temple was only a block away, they were going to ride in the white-topped buggy with the matched mules.

The building arose from the barren ground like a great white wedding cake. It was eighty-four feet high to the top of the para-pet, battlemented like an old castle, and there was a hundred-and-thirty-five-foot tower on top of that. There were twelve Gothic buttresses along each side and five along each end, and the three-tiered spire had panels to balance the line of the buttresses. Inside, there were two spiral staircases winding upward the entire height of the building, eleven rooms in the basement and one main room above, with eight smaller rooms around it.

Long before the ceremonies were to start, a vast throng of people wandered around the block, squinted upward from the roadway, felt of the solid rock walls with their hands as if to bol-ster the evidence of their eyes. A Temple that would cost a million dollars. The world would have said it couldn't be done, and so they did it.

'Do you remember the angels in the sky when we dedicated the Nauvoo Temple?'

Keturah Snow sat in her husband's coach and studied the chaste white walls through half-closed eyes.

'And the rushing sound,' said Martha in an awed voice, 'the "spirit of God like a mighty rushing wind."'

'I remember the tiled floors and the Bible scenes painted on the plastered walls, and the font that they said was a copy of the baptistry in King Solomon's Temple,' said Hannah Merinda, 'but it wasn't as grand as this.'

'No,' sighed Aunt Ket. 'Nothing could be as grand as this!'

Around the immense upper hall the throng assembled. Silk ribbons, fringe, tassels, jet, bugles, and embroidery, but uncovered heads and stockinged feet, for this was the House of the Lord. Taffeta sound of many skirts. Lavender and bergamot and lye soap. Half-audible beating of many hearts. The twelve Apostles were there, the Presidents of Stakes, dignitaries from all of Zion. But the Lion of the Lord had to be carried from room to room in a chair.

'Redeemer of Israel,' sang the choir, and Clory was conscious of a sheen, a mellowness in the air.

Awe deepened her voice as veils fluttered and Glory stood revealed.

Erastus bowed his head and called forth blessings upon the surroundings, the Garden of Eden, rooms celestial, terrestrial, telestial.

The Twelve, the Presidents of Stakes, the High Council, and Brother Brigham carried by Erastus and Bishop Gardner went into the sealing rooms.

When they returned, the meeting was Brother Brigham's, and a sigh of anticipation rustled the throng. As the President got painfully to his feet and began to speak hesitantly, his voice gathering strength and resonance, Erastus squeezed back the foolish tears and reflected that this moment was worth all that had gone before.

One morning the brethren had brought him word that Sister Miles had at last found a pond big enough. Another morning he had watched Lon Tuckett and Betsy rumble away. The first of them all to quit. Before he left, Lon had shamefacedly given him a scrawled sheet of foolscap. His last piece.

There's nothing here to cheer, except prophetic sermons...

There had been still another morning when the good Catholic fathers of Silver Reef had offered their first Mass in this new country in the St. George Tabernacle. As the mighty Te Deums rolled out over a Mormon congregation, the Tabernacle clock had struck ten, inexorable as Fate above the solemn chanting. Erastus on the stand had watched his people look at one another, a silent cheer spreading from face to face. But on that March day of 1877 as John D. Lee toppled into his coffin at Mountain Meadows, Erastus saluted him.

Of such, the price a people paid.

'This is the greatest time since Adam,' preached Brother Brigham. 'Solomon had a temple, but as far as I can learn little or no endowments were given. The Jews killed the priest between the altar and door because he would not divulge the secrets of the holy priesthood.'

A sudden gust of wind rattled the windows and Brigham pointed with his cane. 'The Devil's mad right now!...

'I tell you we have no business here other than to build up and establish the Zion of our Lord, who holds the hearts of the living in His hands and turns them as the rivers are turned. But the negligence, the folly of the Saints!... Some, if they had the power, would build a railroad to the bottomless pit. People act like fools, and I will never cease to strive until Satan is overcome and driven from the earth. There are men here who are no more fit to be here than the Devil from hell!'

His eyes glinted beneath their brows, his white beard trembled, and in his earnestness he smote the pulpit with his cane until the room rang. He looked down at the marks on the polished wood.

'You can putty this up, smooth it over, paint it, or leave it here as a testimony.'

The forefinger came up in its old gesture...

The President reorganized Stakes, set the priesthood in order, defined the duties of the apostles, Seventies, high priests, elders, and lesser priesthood, and set apart Abijah MacIntyre to be first president of the first Temple in the new Zion.

Even after the meeting was over the people would not let the Leader go. They waited for him outside on the grounds, beyond the fence, in the road, and as he appeared in his chair in the doorway and Apostle Snow and Bishop Gardner carried him on out, a cheer burst forth that echoed from the Sugar Loaf to the pastel mountains.

Brigham held up his hand to the cheering, clapping multitude. The skin of his cheeks stretched tightly over the bones, his stocky body appeared to have crumbled within and settled down upon itself as an ancient mound settles.

'There are those now living who will see this valley thickly populated from ridge to ridge and from the red hill to the river.'

He spoke meditatively and yet with conviction. The crowd quieted, leaned closer to hear.

'I see spires pointing heavenward and the Temple standing in the center of the valley, Utah's Dixie at the head of the State instead of the foot...'

His voice lagged as if he were very weary, sunk to almost a whisper.

'"What doth the Lord require of thee but to do justice and to love mercy and to walk humbly with thy God?

'"For behold, this is my work and my glory, to bring to pass the immortality and eternal life of man."'

The banked fires of his eyes swept these Saints he had nourished so long.

'I would say to you... "Do not betray your heritage." There are some here who will bring it glory... but to you all I would say, "Love God and each other. Love laughter."'

His puckish humor played upon them for a moment.

'I calculate to die in the harness!'

A strange stillness fell upon the sober old ones with their burdens of floods and governments and polygamy, upon the laughing young ones with their heads full of kisses and the ancient mystery of lying together. Wonder touched their faces as the hushed lines parted to let Brother Brigham's chair go through. More than a tired old man had passed. An epoch had passed.

CHAPTER XIV

CLAIMS

Come! All you long-legged, gan-
der-shanked, bowlegged, sway-
backed, brush-headed pieces of humanity, and buy what you can
never get rid of — a good mining
claim at Silver Reef. Molasses
wanted in exchange. Go in lemons
and come out squeezed!

DAVID read and chuckled and handed the *Cactus*
around the breakfast table.

'It looks like the local boys're all determined to be "squeezed,"'
said Pal, comfortably sugaring her mush and steering her fat
flesh into billowing middle age. When a woman was the mother
of six children and still managed to come first with her husband
and yet be adored by his pretty second wife, she had no fear of
middle age.

'Timmie Gardner ith going!' lisped Patience-Elizabeth, a chubby fifteen-year-old who was already coaxing to put up her hair and wear a bustle.

The family laughed at the blush dyeing her freckles.

'This is once it's going to be hard to traffic with Babylon and yet "handle not of her unclean things,"' said David. 'But nothing can stem the tide. That strike's too rich.'

He beamed upon his noisy family, Pal with her six, Lucy with her three, and was glad nothing could 'stem the tide.' As early as last August the 'Reefers' were paying seventy-five cents a dozen for peaches, twenty-five cents a pound for fresh grapes, a dollar and a half for one watermelon, two dollars for a gallon of wine that they bought in five-hundred-gallon lots. A wonderful market for mutton, thought David. Comforts and even luxuries for his loved ones.

Other men read Benjamin's announcement with conflicting emotions. Brother Brigham had exhorted against a mining-camp civilization and a 'golden god' since the days of '49, but when the precious ore meant bread, a Temple, new blood in flagging arteries, even Brother Brigham had to capitulate.

Abijah MacIntyre wrote in his red-backed ledger: 'If the time has come to try us with riches, all right. Some of us have passed through poverty, and if we cannot stand the opposite, we are poor things.'

And yet Abijah regarded the evidences of his prosperity dubiously — the matched mule team, the schooling he planned for Jimmie and Tempie. Every day now he came home to some new rug or window curtain or personal fol-de-rol — 'Sheba selling crocheted picture throws to the miners, Clorinda her buckskin gloves. He had at last been able to equip Clorinda's house with real table, chairs, and cupboard from Brother Hansen's shop, and a trundle bed for the youngsters. And this past winter no one had enjoyed more than he the comfort of 'Sheba's new Charter Oak stove. But in the midst of his physical pleasure there was the

chill of doubt. Brother Brigham had fought mining, and these
things were the result of mining. A man who had been chosen
to fill the high office of President of the St. George Temple had no
room in his life for doubt or imperfection. Feeling like a no-
vitiate on probation, he instituted a reform throughout his family,
a soul purge that should fit him to undertake his duties. 'The
time was come in which to unsheathe the sword like Moroni
of old and to cleanse the inside of the platter!'

But Abijah's family did not seem to share his own enthusiasm
for all this spiritual catharsis. In fact, there were times, he
thought, when they deliberately flouted their shortcomings in his
face. It appeared that everything had its price, and the price of
cleansing the 'inside of the platter' was eternal vigilance.

Erastus, also, was finding this spring of '77 that everything had
its price. The price of the new rock dam they were hopefully
building was the saloon near the Big House, the pool table that
created loafers, the drunken miners that occasionally slept in St.
George gutters, the new sheriff in a community that had never
needed a sheriff before, the new jail in the basement of the courthouse, doors that were having for the first time to be
locked.

But the biggest price was the young-man-power that drifted to
the mines in spite of all its elders could do, in spite of inducements
at home such as the Young Men's Mutual Improvement Association, which had just been organized throughout the Territory.

Apparently, decided Erastus, all a man could do was to caution
the boys not to visit saloons or gambling halls, to attend to
prayers. That, and to take full advantage of this miracle, this
Bonanza City — silver chlorides and horn-silver lying exposed in
shining sheets all over the reefs — as he himself intended to do.

On May Day Erastus met with his people — in time to get
water on the crops! — and dedicated the new rock structure bar-
ricading Pah Roosh. This dam was several feet higher than the
other, it was built at a cost of four thousand dollars, and David

Wight had discovered a bed of impregnable blue clay which they
had puddled all over the face of it.

Erastus studied the hopeful faces of his long-suffering people
lined on each side of that mild and innocent-looking stream, and
his voice shook.

'Oh, Lord, we pray Thee that this dam may stand — if it be
Thy will . . .'

He paused in spite of himself. Mines never lasted, Brother
Brigham was right . . . This dam *had* to stand. If it *didn't* — if it
didn't . . .

'If not, let Thy will be done.'

Erastus was filled with a grim presentiment. Keturah laughed
at him, said he got crankier as he got older, but he could not help
it. He did not believe their period of probation was over. He
knew with a sick unease that there was an ordeal ahead more terrible than even Missouri and Nauvoo.

Occasionally, worried about changing conditions, he called for
Abijah after his daily session at the Temple and walked home with
him. It seemed to them both that there had been something final
and foreboding about this last departure of Brother Brigham's
after the dedication in April (although the President often declared these last few years had been full of joy); something
ominous about the way he was putting his house in order, re-
signing minor official positions, choosing five additional counselors, reorganizing the various Stakes of Zion. In the sealing-room
Brother Brigham had denounced the 'iniquity that exists in high
places,' accused the seven presidents of the Seventies of being
'dead to their duties and of staying in their quorums when they
weren't fit to live.' Brother Brigham had demanded Retrenchment, a tightening of moral fiber all over Zion, and Erastus and
his counselors, already aware of a vague sense of loss, a sense of
their own inadequacy when there should be no Brother Brigham,
felt that the least they could do was to follow his example.

2

As usual, Abijah's zeal ran away with him. His affection for
'Sheba had long been as matter-of-fact as an old shoe, but his love
for Clory still retained the alarums and confusions of ecstasy.
Now in her thirties she had taken on a second blooming that left
Abijah, trying to make his nights with her dull fulfillments of
duty, weak-kneed with passion and torn with a thousand remembered intimacies. To pacify his conscience he reverted to the old
resentment against her attraction for him, telling himself that her
eternal feminine sorcery was really what stood between his soul
and God, rather than his own nature.

He became dreadfully hard to live with. But this time Clory
was armed with understanding. As soon as he again got used to
being merely a man, he'd get over it.

Meanwhile, he kept his family in a turmoil. One night at supper
'Sheba served him with pithy radishes and he bluntly told her that
they 'clunked' down his throat like 'croaking frogs'; afterward,
tossing beside Clory, he could not sleep until he had got out of
bed and walked across the dooryard to wake 'Sheba and apolo-
gize, which so amazed that acid-eyed female that she forgot to
find fault with Clory for a whole day.

On another evening when the ambient air was full of moonlight and wayward scents and the liquid whistle of mocking birds,
Abijah so far forgot himself as to gather his family around the
doorstep for a 'sing.' While Clory's fingers plucked an undercurrent of enchantment out of the dulcimer, the boys sprawled in the
lucerne and made harmony for her shining soprano, Abijah's velvet bass.

> Ye'll take the high road,
> And I'll take the low road,
> And I'll be in Scotland afo-ore ye...

Tempie and Jimmie, his arm about her neck, their little ghost-
like bodies in the gloom locked together in the charmed world of

childhood, sang tuneless scraps, simple and sweet as clover, that eddied and were drowned in the larger flow of sound. Jimmie's gaze upon his mother's thrown-back head, half-closed eyes, was all unstinted adoration, but his gaze upon his father was puzzled. This was one of those rare moments when something stripped Abijah of his mask, when his earthy lust for life nakedly flew its flags and beat its drums. It seemed to young Jimmie that his father's laughing face, suddenly focused in the moonlight, suddenly springing out of the nothingness of the dark, had shaken off secrecy for a moment and made them a gift of his soul.

But then Jimmie's mother began a song that for some strange reason made him want to cry.

> I dream of Jeanie with the light brown hair
> Borne like a vision on the summer air...
> Oh-h-h! I long for Jeanie and my heart bows low...

And his father, no longer the brawny Apollo, faltered, retreated into his own private world of frowns, stamped into the house, where he snatched his journal and accused himself hastily, lest temptation again overcome him, of a 'levity not consistent with that character which ought to be maintained by one who was called of God as I had been'...

In all the grown-up world of pretense, this dual nature of his father's was what most bewildered young Jimmie. Sometimes he was nice and kind and funny, playing horse or outlaw with a child, sleeking his great brown beard into points to look more frightening. Jimmie had never forgotten last Halloween, just after he had turned five years old. His father was a special favorite with junior goblins, ghosts, and witches. They chased him about, thinking him to be really scared, until on his hands and knees he fled through the house, under the furniture and out-of-doors. That had been a memorable time. Since then his father had been mostly his fierce and terrible other self, shouting about hell and heaven and sin and secret prayer. Jimmie and Tempie tried secret prayer, praying all night for some ice cream, but the next day there had been the same old bread-'n'-milk. So, thinking that even if God didn't like them they could still please their father, they outdid each other making up sins, since sins seemed to be what he was mostly concerned about.

But apparently even sinning didn't please him.

3

That spring it often seemed to Clory that just because Abijah was so merciless about small misdemeanors, young Jimmie deliberately provoked him. It was hard to be fair. She was so inordinately proud of Tempie knitting Abijah's bed slippers at five and a half, and Jimmie weeding the garden better than either of the twins. But here was Abijah like a little boy, too. Trying to be perfect, and bewildered because life so often slapped him down for his pains. All her mother-instinct rushed out to him, and she fondled his shaggy head and tried to make up for life's indifference.

Now in the colony there was at last time for love-making. Silver money (only yesterday Jimmie had run home crying over a quarter some miner had given him — disgusted with a 'piece of tin' when he had hoped for an apple!), a growing sense of security, Abijah freed from onerous hours in a boiling sun.

Clory wheedled him, coaxed at the abysmal, innate sweetness she loved and that he could never quite hide.

Well fed, Tempie bringing him the basin of warm water for his feet, Jimmie the brush for his hair that was silvering now, he stretched out in Clory's rocker, beamed around the pretty, fragrant room, and sighed with content. Aye, she had always been able to give him that!

Long after the children were in bed and the night came through the open door whispering about the chaste fire of the Sugar Loaf, the coyote cry still trembling like a lost echo far back in the hills, nearer scents of phlox and verbena and bergamot, he drew her down to his lap and let her gentle fingers smooth out the creases in his forehead.

'Darling, why do you fret so?' she murmured, careful not to awaken his defenses. 'We can't be any more than human, and I reckon we're no worse than most. You know, the Lord said, "Man is that he might have joy!"'

For the moment Abijah succumbed completely to her spell and kissed her laughing lips and the shadowed crescent of long eyelashes that had always so delighted him. All the artist in him was fascinated by the satin flesh of her neck, the curve of her breast that had never lost its beauty.

The old earth turned voluptuously and groped for the nearest planet, and Abijah's hot, dark personality kept its tryst with this wife he had alternately hated and loved for sixteen years. The night swept in around them and carried away on its pagan tide their human sighings and breathings and gropings.

Young Jimmie, half-asleep in his trundle bed, listened to the amorous night and in some infantile and primitive way guessed at the human sighings and breathings and was bitterly jealous. He would find some way to bring his mother's attention back where it belonged.

The next day he and Tempie crept down to the cellar, where they were expressly forbidden to go, and Clory was suddenly startled by a scream which brought her running. Jimmie was up to his armpits in one of the twenty-gallon barrels of peach preserve 'Sheba had put up last summer.

Tempie clapped her hands and danced up and down, and Clory wanted to laugh at the sight of her son greedily licking at his sleeves, but 'Sheba found nothing funny in the situation.

She stood there, stooping under the low roof, head thrust forward, the ugly red climbing her cheekbones and her mole twitching violently.

'If you can't control your brats,' she squawked, 'I will! Or better still, I'll see that Abijah does!'

Sympathizing with dead Sister Miles, Clory sat in her pretty room, stuffed her fingers in her ears, and shrank from the bellow-ings in the woodshed. Tempie got off easily, since she was a husky little girl and Abijah was tired and she resisted with bitings and kickings and scratchings. But Jimmie accepted the blows stol-idly, only whimpering a little, knowing that afterward his mother would be all his own again, not even a bit his father's, and that such a reward would be worth many whippings.

Hating Abijah, Clory soothed and comforted the children, knowing it was wrong. And that night she was as cold toward him as the moonlight, knowing helplessly that that was wrong, too.

She could have handled herself and the children and Abijah, could have handled her own small family, bringing it honesty and affection and dignity. But 'Sheba with her jealousy of the two youngsters was the problem. 'Sheba going about her household tasks with a jaundiced eye on them playing in the yard. 'Sheba always expecting trouble. Jimmie and Tempie seldom disap-pointing her, sneaking dead mice into her bureau drawers...

'Sheba's own babies had suddenly become tongue-tied dark giants with an obsession for haircuts and the latest slang. One night Clory heard them return late from a dance, very dignified and glassy-eyed, bullying all the pugnacious shadows, baying the moon like maudlin puppies.

Abijah, too, heard them — Abijah who only yesterday had it in writing from one of the Twelve Apostles that St. George young men used tobacco and wine — in fact, said the Apostle, he would predict that 'within five years there will be such a scarcity of young men to marry the girls that it will amount almost to a calamity!'

'When a man ish of age,' Nephi expounded to his outraged parent — 'When a man ish off fage and a voting chitizen...'

By noon the next day the twins were gone, bag and baggage, to Silver Reef, and now that Abraham was working Abijah's other farm, 'Sheba was alone...

Mixed in with Clory's awareness of her son's childish hate for the big woman was a dull apprehension. She looked around her on the polygamous families she knew. Many 'other mothers' raised a dead wife's children as if they were their own, but some were not mothers at all.

Clory thought of all the women who had 'knuckled under,' and shuddered. But then the *Me* within her rose up with such glorious shouts of triumph that she was strong again. Stronger than life. Stronger even than 'Sheba. It was because of that strength that she finally quarreled with Abijah.

4

In June Samuel came home from his mission amid celebration and fanfare, his dark good looks buttoned up to the chin in a short checked coat, a derby hat, and a splendid drooping mustache. He was full of the wonders he had seen, England languishing over Oscar Wilde's luscious clothes and the new Empress of India, and New York a-dither over a building to be ten stories high, and a man named Damrosch who was doing musical things on Fourteenth Street in the finest opera house in the world. The city had a higher skyline, but instead of the old lovely outline of masts on the rivers, there was the smoke of many steamships.

In Salt Lake women were putting wool flowers under glass shades and photographs in fretwork brackets and china plates on drawing-room walls, and there were horse-cars on the streets, a new Doctor Thompson's ginger beer shop, and much talk of these new electric lights. Professor George Careless was organizing the Handel and Haydn Society and putting on the *Messiah*, and the Cathedral in the Desert was being host to all the finest traveling opera companies in the country. Ilma de Murska in *Lucia di Lammermoor* and *Il Trovatore*, and Amy Sherwin in *Pinafore* and *Martha*.

Long after Samuel had married and gone to manage his father-in-law's vineyards in Santa Clara, the winged words echoed in Clory's heart. All the gay inheritance that now never could be hers. She wondered if all pioneering women had such a ceaseless struggle to adjust, to deny the lusts of the flesh. There were times when her being rose up in a dark tide of rebellion that threatened to overwhelm her, and then again, ashamed of herself, she looked into Jimmie's eyes and saw there his children who would sit at the rosewood desk . . .

She had just plunged her hands into the dishwater when she became aware of an ominous silence. She ran outside, but 'Sheba was ahead of her. There stood the two children, hand in hand, their eyes fixed guiltily upon the water-barrel, where floated the limp body of one of 'Sheba's chickens. One of her 'abacaterian' chickens she had got from Lucy B. Young.

'Who did it?' shrieked 'Sheba, rescuing the chicken and brandishing its dripping feathers before the terrified youngsters. 'Who did it?'

At the touch of Clory's comforting arms they burst into tears.

'Jimmie didn't mean nothing,' sobbed Tempie from the refuge of Clory's skirts. 'He flipped the chicken with a rock and it looked so deaded we put it in the water-barrel to bring it to!' Life was so very sa-ad.

If Abijah hadn't come around the house at just that moment and if 'Sheba hadn't pounced on him like a fury . . . If he hadn't been dispirited and irritable . . .

'Of course they maun be punished,' he said to Clory, the little vein in his forehead beginning to throb. 'If ye can't control yer bairns ye'll have to take the consequences!'

A long-pent something snapped within her.

'*My* bairns!' she screamed, her black eyes blazing. 'Jim's always *your* child when he's good, and *my* child when he's bad, and I'm sick of it!'

Tears forgotten, the children stared with awe at this grown-up maelstrom they had precipitated.

'That woman's to blame!'

Clory's voice cracked and she pointed a shaking finger at 'Sheba.

'Always picking on the kids! Always egging them into mischief! Always ——'

'Stop it!' thundered Abijah. 'Ye know I'll have no fault-findin' one wife to anither!'

He glared. He could not understand this quarreling among his wives. Having himself for a husband should make up for a lot of things. Besides — she was weaning the boy entirely away from him. They had private jokes with each other over which they laughed uproariously. They had a code of winks and grimaces that shut him out. Once before Clory had done that with a son of his, estranging him from his father.

'Ye think he's *your-r* child, alone!' raged Abijah. 'Look what ye're makin' out of him! A sissy! "Cat's got his tongue," folks are always sayin'. "Cat's got his tongue!"'

Clory stopped short, appalled. That's right, she had been thinking of him as her child, alone.

'You — you never loved him,' she subsided weakly, 'never like you loved K-Kissy.' Stumbling over the name.

But she had to relinquish Tempie and Jimmie for punishment. Abijah locked them in the dark cellar, from which presently the sound of weeping grew louder, became hysterical.

Clory sat on the cellar steps and watched the heavy purpled twilight gather in the valley and in her heart. When Abijah came to unlock the culprits, she was grimly controlled.

'There's just one thing I want to say to you,' she said, standing up to him, daunting him with her eyes. 'Reform me if you like, but not Jimmie. If you ever touch these babies again, I'll leave you, if we all go to hell! I'd rather see Jimmie in hell than like 'Sheba's boys!'

He stared at her in amazement.

5

But of course he did punish Jimmie again, while Clory smoldered helplessly. Smoldered, and always managed to take out the sting afterward: 'You know how boys *are!*' Even when the children deserved punishment, she imperceptibly leagued with them against their father.

Abijah put the youngsters to herding the cows, down to the field in the morning and back at night. And because he said that Jimmie with his curls looked more like a girl than a boy, he one day got the scissors and cut them off. Clory cried and put the severed ringlets away with Kissy's circle comb, Brother's teething ring, and a piece of Free's old buckskin pants.

Life was a queer contradiction to Jimmie. His mother mourned over him. He felt obliged to correct the situation which made her mourn. His father punished him for correcting the situation.

His mother mourned because he was always so late coming home with the cows. He made a whizzer, a flat paddle attached to one end of a stick, which made a loud screech when whirled around one's head and was designed to hurry up the stock, but instead, it stampeded them like wild deer, and Papa had to hire men to round them up again. The resultant punishment forced Jim, at five and a half, to an inescapable conclusion: Papa was on Aunt 'Sheba's side and was not really his friend. Life was a man-sized job. But one must not weaken, because of Mamma. All the beauty in the world lived with Mamma. Aunt 'Sheba had only lucerne and lye soap, but Mamma had flowers and sweet smells.

Once again Clory began to toy vaguely with the old recurrent longing to escape.

'You've got kidney trouble,' Stiddy Weeks told her on a hot afternoon in June. 'Most women around here have kidney trouble from the bad water. I wouldn't advise you to have any more children.'

His long-suffering eyes were kind.

'"The back is suited to the burden," Sister Mac!'

Willie's old refrain!

He picked up her hands, that by now were almost entirely covered with itching, watery, blistered sores.

'H'm. Salt rheum. You'll have to keep these bound up and do no more hard work!'

Clory crept home from his dim shop with its queer harsh smells, and thought she felt just like one of those big brown bottles with her heart for the label: Deadly Poison.

When she nerved herself to tell Abijah — who so hated unpleasantness — he stared at her, his brown eyes puzzled.

'But Clor-rinda,' he burred. 'All those waiting tabernacles!'

She gave a little grunt of vexation at his misunderstanding.

'I tell you ——'

He picked up her bandaged hands, caressed them tenderly.

'Ther-re, ther-re,' he said. 'Get Bathsheba to give you something for your paddies, and don't fret about the comin' of the bairns. That's the Lord's affair!'

Clory had to be content with that, concluding privately the Lord wasn't very efficient about his affairs.

Life went on according to its habit, and if Clory continued to grow thinner and more hollow-eyed, if her old vivacity occasionally was forced, Life seemed no more concerned than anybody else. There were always a few sheep who never survived the shearing! . . .

As usual it was Pal's keen eyes that spotted trouble.

Of late years an estrangement had grown up between the two girls. Clory told herself it wasn't because she was jealous of Pal's happiness, her fine, growing family, but something within her winced at the sight of those six bouncing children. Here was Patience-Elizabeth, a plump, dish-faced young lady with a hearty giggle who was already talking about beaux. Whenever

Clory looked at her she saw instead a dark-eyed ghost, the half-glimpsed outline of an elfin sweetness, a vanished grace trembling on the edge of expression. Some things hurt too much to be borne. Were better avoided. She had learned long ago that the world is impatient with memories.

It was Pal who bridged the coolness between them. Pal, and her boy, Frankie, a lad full of bucolic mischief, equipped with an inventive mind and fleet legs that carried him away from an escapade while the slower Jimmie was left behind to take the blame.

Whenever Frankie came to play Clory sat on the doorstep and watched, no matter how hot the hour. Frankie putting a bat on his dog's head and the hysterical shrieks of the children at the antics of the dog trying to paw it off. Shrieks that might disturb that woman across the way, that woman who always told. Frankie, with his uncomplicated life, never could understand why Jimmie's mother was always hushing them up. And then there came the smothering afternoon when he had the wonderful idea of tying a tin can to his cat's tail and then setting fire to the cat. Dozing, Clory jerked erect at the cat's yowlings, the terrific din of the can, the shrill glee of the youngsters. All that was left of the cat was a trail of smoke as it streaked across the yard, but 'Sheba gloated from her doorway. Alarmed by grown-up emotions he sensed but could not understand, Frankie scooted for home, and Pal came to Clory that night.

She was diffident about coming. After all, now that her husband was the President, Clory was the rightful leader of St. George Society, and if she didn't take full advantage of her position 'Sheba certainly did, being as uppish as might be expected at wool-pickings and the like. Now was Clory's big chance to snub that snooty Marianne Snow, but when Pal found her sitting alone on the step, chin on bandaged fists, woebegone in the dark, she forgot all about Society.

'I come to tell you that I spanked Frankie good and put him

to bed and that you must tell President Mac it was not Jimmie's
fault.'

Suddenly Pal's good heart got the best of her and she was beside Clory, her arm around the drooping shoulders, her bulk
overflowing the step. Here was something worse the matter than
the peccadilloes of kids.

And then Clory spilled it all — the trouble with 'Sheba, her
fears for the youngsters.

'I could manage Abijah if I had him alone,' she cried bitterly.
'Oh — this way of living, two women to one man!'

'Sometimes it ain't so bad,' said Pal thoughtfully.

'Yes, but David Wight's a different kind of man than Abijah
MacIntyre!... Oh, Pal, what a fool I've been! Do you remember
when we were girls I was always the little ninny who was going
to reform the world? Well, plurality's a trap you can't get out
of, and our world never will be reformed!'

The years dropped away and the two women were girls again,
arguing about polygamy, picking it to pieces and putting it back
together, trying it here and trying it there, seeing if it really
fitted anywhere.

'Do you remember what Lucy B. said in last Relief Society
conference? David made me memorize it: "I believe those who
choose celestial marriage and do right therein, casting out all
selfishness, have attained a mental power, a spiritual plane
above those who have not."'

Clory's voice was frankly skeptical: 'Do you *like* polygamy?'

'We-ell, it's hard. There's no denying that. But a lot of
women would have been old maids without it, and it's building
up the kingdom.'

'Darn the kingdom! Oh, Pal, I had dreams. I used to think
that giving up the folks we love, colonizing where a town had no
right to *be*, eating lucerne greens and everything, not to speak of
Missouri and Nauvoo — I used to think by suffering so much
we'd gain the wisdom to build something lovely ——'

'We will!'

'No. We'd ought've run away that time when David caught us and showed us the sego lilies! Run so far and so fast ——'

'Nuhuh,' said Pal, shaking her head. 'You ain't that kind, Clorinda MacIntyre. You wouldn't run if you had the chance. You'd see it through.'

6

All during the corn-huskings, the peach-cuttings, the watermelon busts of August, Clory pondered the situation. A divorced woman was outside the pale, her chances for salvation extremely slim, since a man could enter heaven in style, with trumpeting and fanfare, but the only way a woman could get in was by clinging to some man's coat-tails. Even Brother Brigham, who performed marriages free, charged ten dollars for a divorce!

Sometimes Clory would catch 'Sheba's eye upon her and break into goosebumps at the thought of Abijah's first wife reading her mind. 'Sheba, with her boys all gone and only an occasional letter from the twins to break her empty days. How, wondered Clory, would a woman go about telling Abijah she wanted to leave him? That was the problem, for even with bandaged hands there must be some way up North for a lone woman to make a living for two children . . .

The Trupp divorce case was to Clory a test case. The stolid German girl was flesh and blood, not a timid ghost like Bella. For once a plural wife had her courage screwed to the point of truth-telling.

The embittered, hatchet-faced old first wife locks the cupboard doors against her; the neighbors find her without food, groaning with flux in a hut no better than a chicken coop; the first wife refuses to let Brother Trupp visit her; he sneaks out one night and the old woman follows him, finds him in bed with the girl, breaks the window-pane over their heads, and amid a rumpus that alarms

the neighbors for blocks around, jerks him home by his elegant
mutton-chop whiskers . . .

'The Prophet Malachi says he hates separation and divorcing!'
counseled Erastus.

Berated by him, the bishops, and the ward teachers, the girl
shrank like a great pallid owl when Clory went to see her.

'Dey tell me nuttings,' she confided in a whisper which grew to
a scared bellow. 'DEY TELL ME NUTTINGS!'

But one morning Clory saw her off on the stage . . .

It was about this time that Gottlieb Uttley came home from
the City with a new plaid suit and an obsession about the Iron
Horse and the look of a hungry dog toward Clory. Like the first
lucerne patch in the days when it was the only green thing in the
valley, Gottlieb's Sonuvabitch Ranch near the Upper Gap with
its roses and real lawn-grass had become a rendezvous, and Gottlieb promptly set about using it as a base for fruit busts in the
hope of enticing a thin girl with a pointed face and great dark
eyes.

Late one afternoon when Abijah was at the Temple and the
whole earth drowsed with heat and petunia scent, Clory boosted
the two squealing children up to the hands reaching down from
the hayrack and let Gottlieb himself pull her up over the fragrant,
dangling hay. Red paws hanging like hams below his wrists, he
grinned at her foolishly as he straddled there like a Colossus
outlined against the heavens. From where she had flopped beside Pal, Clory smiled lazily up at him, and well rewarded, he
blundered over the sprawled and shrieking merrymakers and
went back to his driving. The topheavy load lumbered out the
street like a gigantic thatched turtle. David's lusty baritone
began 'Wait for the Wagon,' while down at the other end Johnny
Lowgie started up 'Three Blind Mice,' and the two schools dissolved in a mania of sound. Clory relaxed against the hay, and
twinkled at Tempie and Jimmie and Frankie Wight and the
other youngsters trying their valiant best to outscream their
elders.

'I'm glad you could come,' whispered Pal under cover of the noise.

'I'm glad the kids could come,' said Clory, squeezing Pal's hand. 'They don't get a treat very often.'

She let her body crunch deep into the faintly perfumed cushion, chewed on a dry, sweet stalk, and gazed up at the sky, just recovering its color after the onslaught of the sunset. The unhurried roll of the earth and the mystery of all its trysts. What secrets it could tell! She wondered, as she had so often done before, if you gazed with all your might into the depths of those high blue heavens, would veils part like mist and your tired heart learn some of the Answers? So often she had felt herself on the verge of the complete and final Beauty, aware of a queer, compelling rhythm, of a conviction that one more moment of stillness and you could break through into that phantom-world edging reality. Isolated in the crystal chalice of her thoughts, she shut her eyes and willed to invoke one of those mystic, mighty moments when the Smile came through. But nothing happened except the raucous singing of the crowd. Hers was too earthy a perplexity, and her mind went back to its circling. Would she be a quitter to leave with the job half done? Would Abijah really care? Would the children be better off without a father than with an unwelcome 'other mother'? How would it feel to grow old without a man, the fires of life dried up, wasted? She chewed on her bit of hay and savored the secret, fecund taste it had. Did your body grow old like the hay, dry and brittle to the touch, but all the remembered sweetness of life still running in your veins? And the hay, its tender youth now spent, was just beginning to serve. You would not mind so much if you could grow old like the hay. Or perhaps if you ran away from your destiny, you dried up on the inside, too. . . . You did not worry so much about salvation as of loneliness like a mildew, like a rust . . .

'Gottlieb's place is really grand, ain't it?' said Pal.

Clory nodded absently and watched the children dart like hummingbirds among the sleepy flowers.

Gottlieb came up with two dripping slices of watermelon.

'Howya lika dat?' he cried proudly.

Clory munched the juicy flesh, spat out seeds, and smiled at him and inwardly shrank from his hearty bucolic odors.

Gottlieb must entertain them with his all-consuming passion, the train. The crowd whooped and the boys slyly goaded him on.

'I vont to tell you,' he shouted earnestly, 'haf you heard D.R.G. Western Railroad and Santa Fe connecting togetter in Saint George? Dat makes you smiles, but pretty soon railroad will be here in a year.'

And to the hysterical delight of his audience his thick lips began to puff, 'Sho-o-o, sho-o-o,' his feet to shuffle slowly, then faster, faster, while his clenched fists and stiff arms jerked like pistons. The crowd squalled and rolled on the lawn when he threw back his head and bayed the stars in a whistle. Then, while his feet shuffled and his arms pumped, his stentorian roar called out the stations at strategic intervals: 'Br-rovo City! Chunction City! (Ged oud of da r-roat, you cow, you, or else I keeck you mit my cow-catcher!) Peaver City...'

'Howya lika dat?' he asked Clory anxiously. 'I, Gottlieb, condooc-tor-r! Shut-the-door-opener!'

'Don't mind her — she's teched,' called Joseph Mac. 'Come on over and be the train again!'

On the way home Clory made up her mind. The darkness hung soft and close, and Tempie and Jimmie snuggled against her like two puppies, half asleep with the gentle sway of the hayrack and the singing. The hardest thing would be to make them understand.

'Sometimes it is better to go away even though it hurts,' she began, and the children pricked up their ears. 'Not that you are mad at the folks you leave behind, but just that you belong somewhere else. And if it is right for you to go, there will always be Something to show you the way... A long, long time ago when Mamma was a little girl, some bad soldiers came to steal the peoples' homes, and Brother Brigham called in all the Saints to help fight. Far beyond the Black Ridge near the ocean, which you'll both someday see but Mamma never will, a group of Saints started out to cross a desert where men died of thirst and Indians and burning sands. They were very scared, as you sometimes are when you go to Sister Hansen's for yeast, but they trusted in the Lord and prayed for a Sign. And sure enough, just as they came down out of the mountains to the edge of the desert, there before them was a vast forest of strange trees. Gnarled trees thousands of years old, but very straight and tall, with branches only at the top. "Here," said the Saints, "these trees are like Joshua leading the Israelites"; and so they traveled in the direction the strange trees pointed and at last came to the Promised Land . . .'

She was so anxious to have it out with Abijah that she did not stop to wonder why lamps should be burning in both her house and 'Sheba's. She rushed the two sleepy, whimpering children in through the door, and did not even think it strange that he should be waiting there in the little rocker.

'Oh, Abijah,' she cried, blind to his ravaged face, the tears trickling into his beard. 'I've come to tell you ——'

'Clor-rinda!' His voice was lost and helpless. 'Brother Brigham is dead!'

He needed her. She went to him without a word.

CHAPTER XV

ERASTUS SNOW, Brother Brigham's Apostle, and Abijah MacIntyre, President of his first Temple in the new Zion, climbed the steps of the Lion House. Eliza R. Snow, Presidentess of all the Relief Societies and a nominal wife to Brother Brigham since '49, awaited them at the top. This commanding, white-haired former wife of Joseph Smith quietly shook hands with the two men. Erastus tried to speak but was stopped by the look on her face. Silently she led the way out of the hall, and up the stairway to the room overlooking the street where the Leader lay in state. During his illness he had been moved from his canopied bed in the alcove to a couch before the open window, and here he still was, but pain had left his face and only grandeur remained.

Kneeling by the bed, gazing at the Lion of the Lord brought low in death, Erastus thought he could see upon those stilled features some of the inward glory people said had lighted them toward the end: Brigham Young was indomitable, and not all the mourners around the bed, not all the murmuring sighs of grief from the multitudes outside the window, could dampen the triumph of his passing.

'You are all so good,' murmured Brother Brigham, and after the elders had prayed for him, 'Amen!' in a clear, distinct voice as if confirming the faith of a lifetime. And then, with his last breath, 'Joseph! Joseph!' as if that faith had suddenly been rewarded.

If, thought Erastus during the days that followed, if the greatness of a man is measured by the number of people who love him, then Brigham Young was truly a great man.

All day on Saturday, September 1, in spite of the steady rain, Zion thronged to the Great Tabernacle for a last look at the Leader. Long lines of people of all classes, ages, and degrees. People in special trains, in carriages, wagons, on foot. More than twenty-five thousand people visited the Tabernacle that day.

Amid a flood of newspaper and magazine comments, all the world paused to say something of the man who had led twenty thousand exiles on a march of thirteen hundred miles through a wilderness, and in thirty years planted colonies from the Salmon River in Idaho on the north to the Colorado River in Arizona on the south, and yet who spurned all titles but one, the one that 'read, right sprucely: "Brigham Young, Painter and Glazier."'

Sunday, September 2, was a perfect early-fall day. The rain had scrubbed and polished the sky and the mountain air had a luster like the inside of a sea shell. Until noon, the hour of the funeral, crowds continued to file by the plain pine coffin on its plain flower-covered catafalque. Wreaths and garlands of flowers also decorated the Tabernacle — no dismal practices for him who believed that death is but a birth into a larger sphere.

I, Brigham Young — the Leader had said — wish my body put in a 'clean and wholesome state,' my coffin made of 'plain one-and-a-quarter redwood boards' and having the 'appearance that if I wanted to turn a little to the right or left I should have plenty of room'; at the services all my family present that 'can be conveniently' but to 'wear no crape ... nor make any parade....'

But you cannot prevent the grief of the heart, thought Erastus, however much you destroy the outward signs. 'Hark from afar a funeral knell,' sang the Tabernacle choir of almost three hundred voices, and Erastus gazed at the thousands and thousands of Saints overflowing from the benches into the aisles, the galleries, the doorways, the grounds, and remembered all the times Brother Brigham had jawed them into order, how he had never been afraid to call a spade a spade, how this man with his love for the downtrodden, the weak, and the helpless, his innate tenderheartedness and kindness toward his family, could in public transform himself into a raging prophet who by the very brutality of his language shocked his people into goodness. '*My name shall be had for good and for evil...*' But few among all those faces stretching away into the dim corridors of that silent, flower-filled place had his name 'for evil.' It was only outside of Brother Brigham's vast egg-shaped building 'built like a bridge' that hatred lay. Outside the City itself, outside the encircling mountains, little men crouched like vultures to feast upon the fallen great, to fasten their claws on the spoils. All the world waited to see if Mormonism would survive.

'...It seemed to me that he was indispensable,' said Apostle George Q. Cannon, and Brother Brigham would have been pleased to know that the quiet tones carried to the farthest nook and cranny. 'What could we do without him? He has been the brain, the eye, the ear, the mouth, and the hand for the entire people of the Church of Jesus Christ of Latter-Day-Saints...'

But Erastus knew as he sat there that nothing, neither plagues nor mobbings nor the death of its prophets, could destroy the thing for which the Leader had lived.

'Brigham Young's Funeral March' burst from the mighty organ in a golden wave of sound, and the procession began, four thousand people marching eight abreast east along South Temple Street to the Leader's little private cemetery on the hill....

The last words of the prayer hung in the mellow air, and Erastus thought he could hear the Leader's own voice, beginning hesitantly as always, gaining fluency, the raised forefinger of his emphasizing:

'Give me a good place where my bones can rest that have been weary for many years...then go home about your business.'

A great sigh broke from the hearts of the multitude and seemed to roll across the city.

Erastus gazed beyond the blue upthrust peaks hemming in this sanctuary. 'Mind your own business' had been the Leader's motto all his life, but Erastus gazed beyond the peaks toward those cities where lived men who would not let a Mormon mind his own business.

2

It was ironic, he thought, that they should be preparing for Gethsemane just as prosperity had unmistakably descended upon Zion. In the Dixie Mission the new rock dam seemed to hold, and the people, forgetting their troubles, sang and danced and engaged in home theatricals. And Erastus went on tightening his defenses.

Yes, times were changing...

Erastus was heavy of heart the day Amelia moved out of the White House on Diagonal Street, two blocks north of the Tabernacle — the White House on its corner lot with the little 'dobe office building, from which the President had administered the affairs of the Church for so many winters.

Amelia was going back to the City for good, and Erastus walked up to the White House on the day that John Webster Watson, her English butler, locked the carved doors and clicked shut the green gate Brigham Young himself had made.

'He wanted you to have these,' said the butler, and handed Erastus two cut-glass wine decanters, ruby-red with a pattern of white grapes. Airtight, with numbered glass stoppers, they were expertly fashioned, as were all Brother Brigham's possessions. Erastus turned them over in his hands, and his eyes filled with tears as he thought of the man who had fused two cultures, New England and Great Britain, into a distinct whole that absorbed every nationality under the sun, the man who had taught that recreation itself should be learning. Life would never be the same without him.

How his old ironic humor would have flashed on the day that Lucy B.'s daughter, Susy, defied the majesty of the law!

'You can't make me sign that thing!' she sputtered to the judge of district court in St. George. '*I'm* a daughter of Brigham Young!'

'I don't care whose daughter you are!' roared the judge. 'You'll either sign this deed or go to jail for contempt of court!'

And go to jail she did, for one whole day in the basement of the courthouse.

The town chuckled, but Erastus shook his head. Such a thing would not have happened if the Leader had been living.

The children scattered, as they were bound to do, one daughter going on the stage in New York, whence she sent trunkfuls of expensive costumes for the plays in the basement of the Tabernacle.

The children scattered, and the White House stood closed and shuttered and only Lucy B. remained.

Sometimes Erastus watched her in Sunday meeting in her buff-colored lawn dress, her pork-pie hat with blue ribbon strings, her black grenadine shawl folded cornerwise over her shoulder, her lace mitts and fan with pearl handles that she would slowly open out to its full circle with the swansdown edge. Erastus would look into her calm brown eyes and long to pillow his head on her bosom, she seemed to carry about her so much of the Leader's spirit.

Times were changing, and no longer was there one to whom he could take his perplexities. He stood alone, and no longer were law and order conditions to be brought about with words.

There were times when the Devil triumphed in spite of all Erastus could do. Take Benjamin Jarvis and the small matter of pied type. When winter came and Benjamin had his hands full teaching school, he found it more difficult to see that the little *Cactus* went on faithfully recording births and deaths. Perhaps that was why one day there appeared an issue with the proud announcement: 'Born, to Mayor and Mrs. Zadox Hunt, a ten-pound sow.'

Even Erastus could not soothe Zadoc. The upshot of the rumpus was that Benjamin threw up the paper and the pupils and decided to go to school himself, in the East.

Half the town saw them off the morning they left — Benjamin and his wife and their five handsome youngsters. David Wight was sick at heart. Benjamin, his literary crony.

'Who'll print my po'try now?' asked David, trying to laugh.

Benjamin's white teeth gleamed briefly beneath his black mustache.

'Start a paper of your own!' he cried, clapping David on the back. 'I'll miss you all,' he sobered, 'but I'm not sorry things worked out this way. I've dreamed of Harvard for a long time——'

'When he gets through,' piped his pretty wife, 'he's going to teach in the University in the City!'

'Take good care of the Mayor!' grinned Benjamin as the mail-coach drove off.

David stood in the road gazing after it until there was nothing to see but dust.

There, he thought, almost bitterly, there's what a man can make of himself who isn't saddled with polygamy! And yet they say we enter plurality because we like it!

Lucy gazed up at him anxiously, but it was Pal who read his mind.

'Never mind, Father,' she comforted. 'Schoolin' isn't everything!'

David came out of his abstraction and smiled down at his wives.

'No, I guess not,' he said. 'Some people have to fight the battles!'

By Christmas the new St. George Stake Academy was opened
in the basement of the Tabernacle. As teacher, Erastus hired
⸻ng Guglielmo Giosue Rosette San Giovanni, son of Sister
Couzzens, he with the black eyes and black hair and flashing smile
and the eastern schooling, bought with the money she had smuggled in her apron from the castle vaults. In no time at all his
vivacity and charming ways had earned him the nickname of
'Sanjo,' and before the month was up, Sanjo and David and Charley
Hichinoper had started a new town paper. It was to be semi-
monthly, hand-written in the finest Spencerian script — *The
Vepricula* (Sumus Discipuli) by *Cerus, Signor,* and *Mark Whiz.*
By spring it had claimed the attention of even the *Deseret News.*

'Listen to this!' David read aloud one night to his family
gathered around the table: 'Guglielmo Giosue Rosette San Giovanni conducts an Academy, teaches a business college in the
evening in the basement of the St. George Hall, runs one newspaper and outruns several others...'

Pal was indignant.

'The paper's *yours!* I don't think it's right for you to do all the
work and Sanjo to get all the credit!'

But David only laughed. He was himself again.

Kaleidoscopic years. Throughout all their swirling phantasms
Erastus tried to remember one thing, Brother Brigham's counsel:
Deliberation. Common sense.

With Hayes in the Presidency, anti-Mormon measures tread on
one another's heels. During the Miles polygamy trial Mayor
Daniel H. Wells, called as a witness, refuses to describe the ceremonies in the Endowment House, and is imprisoned in the penitentiary. A great celebration greets his release. 'When Free-
masons and Oddfellows are compelled to make their secrets public, it will be time enough to practice on the Mormons!' Once
again Mormondom has defied the might of the land.

But defiance means little against the fact that Mormon mis-

sionaries are being mobbed and murdered in the States. Against
the fact that eastern churches are unanimous in declaring that
any minister to 'barbarous Utah' is compelled to preach with a
'Bible in one hand and a pistol in the other!' The Presbyterians
even suggesting that Congress send in 'civilized young men ... to
fumigate the Territory and finish up the pest!'

Garfield shot, the entire country rocks with the story that
Utah is holding 'prayer circles' for his death, that the assassin is a
paid member of the Mormon Church, that 'old hag of hell.'

Judge Black pleads before the House, 'You are urged to govern
them as an overseer might govern slaves, but polygamist Cannon
is denied his seat in Congress after nine years of faithful service.'

President Arthur signs the Edmunds bill in spite of three peti-
tions endorsed by seventy-five thousand people pleading for a
fair investigation. The Edmunds bill — up to five hundred dollars in fines or five years in prison for any man who will not desert
his plural families.

Truly, Erastus' Devil would not be scotched. The ordeal was
upon them, the ordeal whose heralding smoke he had seen from
afar, the ordeal that was to climax Nauvoo and Misery Bottoms
and the Year of the Plagues.

3

Abijah's presence always carried a lusty flavor. Clory thought
that only a moment ago the room had not looked crowded, even
with the table set for supper in the center and Tempie's paper
dolls littering the carpet in front of the bed and Jimmie's bridle
and spurs thrown carelessly over the rocking-chair. She noticed
these last with a guilty start, remembering all the times Abijah
had reminded Jimmie and his mother, too, that the barn was the
place for such things.

Putting down a dish and nervously wiping her hands on her

apron, she turned back to the Charter Oak range Abijah had put up where the fireplace used to be.

Blinking a little from the September sunlight, he stood in front of the door yawning and stretching his big body with the lazy grace of a cat, but any minute now he'd burr at her about 'spoiling the boy,' and there would ensue one of those pointless wrangles she had come to dread.

Instead, she heard him grunt, push the spurs to the floor with an irritated jangle, sink into the rocker, and slap open the *Deseret News* in his hand.

'Mother, did you read this?' he roared, just as she started toward the table with a plate of hot green corn. Clory blenched and her bandaged hands trembled and the corn rolled in its golden grease off onto the carpet.

Abijah bushed his gray brows at her.

'What's the matter with you? You acted scared out of your-r wits!'

His eyes narrowed with suspicion, and Clory, picking up the corn, helplessly read his thoughts. He was so touchy as he got older ... all this trouble over Jim. Even that day at the Temple 'Sheba snorting, 'H'm! Young one cries during baptism means the Devil's a-going out of him!' And her own too-persistent efforts to get away. He was sulking now, his mouth in such a hard line that his beard quivered ... he'd be wondering if she really appreciated his visits — time was when he'd thought she could hardly wait for her turn to come around ...

'I *am* scared,' she acknowledged when she got her voice steady. 'Don't you think we ought to be more cautious, Abijah? After all, the Deps were here only last week ... they got that Olsen woman up for contempt of court ...'

Abijah continued to frown at her over the outspread paper.

'She didna have her wits aboot her!'

'But ...'

Clory stared unseeingly at the sunlight striking through the

window on her silver caster. Even 'Sheba was scared, keeping a
snake's rattles over the lintel of her door to charm the Deps away.
How, Clory wondered, could any woman keep her wits about her
with strange men flinging questions:

'Do you go to bed with this man?'

'Have you ever had children by him?'

Her mouth grew dry with terror at the very thought. What
could a decent woman do but refuse to answer? Betray all
standards of reticence and honor or go to jail. And it wasn't the
insulting questions, nor the ignominy of being carted off to prison
— for prison in this case was a personal victory and the town
bands and the authorities cheered you on — nor was it even the
marshals handcuffing you and dragging you to Salt Lake as if
you were a common strumpet or a — a — prize sow. What hurt
was the thought of your children. At the thought of 'Sheba
doing for your children you clutched the back of the chair to
keep from screaming.

'Well, why don't we eat?' demanded Abijah grumpily, already
ashamed of his truculence. Lately it was getting so he could
scarcely think of Jimmie without truculence. Bathsheba's sons
were good boys, but not even Samuel seemed to care much about
religion, and Abijah had prayed that this one son, who bade fair
to be his last unless he married again ('Sheba dried up like a far-
row cow and Clory shilpit as a kitten!), should make a career ot
the Gospel.

'What's holding us? Where're the bairns?'

Clory sighed and went to the bedroom door to call Tempie,
who was getting dressed up for her father's coming, and to the
stairway to call Jimmie, who was still asleep. He had just got
back that afternoon from the Arizona Strip, where he'd been
working with Shadrach Gaunt's cattle, cutting out yearlin's.
Abijah would see only that he was grimy and disheveled and still
half asleep — he'd never notice that at ten Jimmie was doing the
work of a man. Abijah, who wanted his son to be a scholar in a

boiled shirt, and Jimmie, whose books would always be the rocks and streams and stars.

Just as she thought, the boy stumbled down, rubbing his eyes, and Abijah scowled at him. Tempie came in, fresh in brushed pigtails and a clean pinafore. Her father kissed her perfunctorily, and Clory observed the ceremony with rancor. It was true Abijah would never love another girl-child as he had loved Kissy, but he shouldn't let Tempie know it. That was another trouble with polygamy — the children of wives taken only in duty sometimes felt that they never had a father.

Plying herself between table and stove, getting them all seated, Clory sighed again as she bowed her head and waited for Abijah's blessing.

Abijah mumbled, raised his head, picked up his fork, and wondered why the joy he and Clorinda had had together should have been so fleeting. Nothing that he did seemed to please her. Ech, he could curse a fyllie. She was really a very lucky woman. Not every wife had a husband up in the Church, a good provider without any bad habits. He had fixed up her house with the attic room for the boy, the back room for the girl, even a lean-to. He'd planted her a good vegetable garden — why, this ear of corn came out of her own garden! He'd bought fig and pomegranate seedlings from that Uttley fellow, he'd even sowed her a square of lawn-grass in the front . . .

Not until Jimmie had gone up to bed and Tempie had filled her father's browned-flour box did peace come once more to the room.

Clory relaxed in the rocker and fumbled with her bandaged hands at the bed-shoes she was trying to knit for Abijah. He stared at her over the edge of his paper. He resented the signs of illness in her face; they seemed to be an imputation against himself as a husband. Nor did it seem quite modest that illness should lend her beauty an added integrity; it wasna fitting for a daughter of Zion to go on being lovely at thirty-eight, especially a daughter of Zion who could not even bear her husband children. All these miscarriages ... but neither illness nor maturity could destroy the beauty in her bones. Dark-circled eyes and hollow cheeks only lent her face an added mystery. He'd have felt somehow more compensated for her deficiencies if the miscarriages had left her scrawny and ugly.

Feeling his eyes upon her, Clory made an effort.

'What does it say in the paper, Father?'

For a moment the girl he had known flashed out at him from the woman she had become. Her smile recovered its old warmth, her voice its note of little silver bells ... She could always do that to him. Feeling his loins go boneless with the old desire, Abijah read from the *News*:

The P.E.F. dissolved so that converts may no longer be helped to Zion, a man supporting or even visiting his plural family held to be guilty ...

Clory reflected that the new law would please 'Sheba. At last 'Sheba's position as first wife would be impregnable, her lifetime of tyranny vindicated before the whole world. 'Sheba, whom the years had drawn with still a harsher outline ...

I guess the years aren't too kind to any of us, thought Clory, giving up the knitting and clasping her itching, burning hands ... But she couldn't prevent a twinge of satisfaction over 'Sheba's loneliness.

Of course there were times when Abraham with his little ones and Joseph with his two wives and their families all came up from the field, and Samuel over from the Clara, and the twins from Silver Reef, Nephi with his new bride — times when 'Sheba's old house rocked like a ship on a sprightly sea; but mostly she was alone, except for Abijah's visits, and it did seem too bad he had to keep up the two households.

Although he seldom mentioned the fact any more, Clory knew what he thought — knew how 'Sheba insinuated little wedges of mistrust here and there. 'Clory has never been willing to give and take,' 'Sheba would sigh, and Abijah would remember Clory's obstinacy over a house of her own that first winter twenty-one years ago, would remember her youthful tactlessness and forget all the placating years since ...

4

The Reign of Terror. Fourteen thousand people disfranchised. Thousands of women and children made homeless. Prices on the heads of all the Apostles. An expurgatory test oath made to cover a man's whole past life. Fathers fleeing to Mexico, where they have to register the children of their loins as *bastards*. Going on the Underground.

'*I married my wives in good faith. We have lived together for years, believing it was the will of God. Before I will abandon my wives as concubines, and cast off my children as bastards, I will fight the United States down to my boots. What would you do?*'

The Saints in the Dixie Mission keep Johnnie Lowgie at Silver Reef, where travelers from the North must always stop before going on into St. George. When the United States deputies are coming, Johnny telegraphs 'Send me two chairs,' or three chairs, according to the number of deputies.

President MacIntyre and Apostle Snow call all the priesthood to the Temple. Here, to try to avert the threatening evil, they remember their enemies in the ceremony of the washing of feet. Erastus flees to Silver Reef.

Zebedee Trupp, still optimistic about his childless state, adds Sis and Miny Eardley to Bella and his old first wife and builds himself a house on the Utah-Arizona line, so that when the raiding officers come he and his wives can step into the next room and be safely in Arizona.

Zadoc Hunt betrays his Church and deserts his plural wives in order to escape the penitentiary. Zadoc Hunt becomes a 'cohab,' that word to be spat out among God-fearing men as if it were a piece of filth.

Shadrach Gaunt organizes a Rifle Club — oh, very peaceful, just a little practice shooting. David Wight and Charley Hichinoper and Peabody and Joseph Mac are all armed with Ballard britchloaders; it is 'counsel' to be armed.

As for Shadrach himself, he courts the Deps, he stalks them as he would Navajos. And when he catches up with them, they lick their chops in glee. They had heard of this bad man, they did not expect to trap him so easily.

'How many wives you got?' demands the Law.

'Three,' replies Shadrach meekly.

'Where are they?'

Shadrach's lips draw back from his yellow teeth.

'One alive and two in the cemetery!'

Young Jimmie comes home to Clory, his eyes that have always been so clear and innocent prematurely clouded with a man's dark knowledge.

'Mother, Ralphie Gardner says that they took him to the court at Beaver and asked him — and asked him' — his voice sinks to a shuddering whisper ...

Clory drops to her knees and clasps her son and stares up into his piteous young face.

Oh, God, her heart cries. *Oh, God!*

'Darling,' she says, 'this time will pass. It is bad, I know, but you are not to be afraid. Just remember the Lord is in your heart ...'

She hesitates, wondering what she can do to wipe out this stain, to keep intact his fair, boyish vision of life.

'You are not to be afraid. The Deps are bad men but you are not to fear them, only keep out of their way. And if they do catch you and ask you who your father is, you must say *you don't know*. Do you understand, darling? *You don't know!*'

'But why, Mother?'

Bewildered at the inexplicable dishonesty of this grown-up world, the boy is yet doubling his fists over the nameless hobgoblins menacing his mother.

'But why?'

And Clory struggles in a morass of ugly facts and uglier words. How can she keep unsullied her child's young and lovely dreams?

It seems only a moment ago that she was teaching Kissy how to die. Now she must teach Jimmie how to live.

Death means laving your hands in star dust. Life means — well, what does life mean but a hellish horror?

5

The worst thing about living on the Underground, thought Clory, was getting food. All you could do was wait until it got dark and sneak through the streets like a fugitive.

'Mamma!' chattered Tempie, 'I'm cold!'

'I know. Huddle down in bed a minute longer and we'll run right fast...'

Ever since Marianne Snow's boy had routed them out before daylight this morning with word that the Deps were on the prowl, Clory had not dared light a fire. She and the two children shivering behind shuttered windows and locked doors all day long...

Jim came clattering down the stairs in his mittens and cap and Clory whirled fiercely upon him, finger at her lips.

Out the back way, tiptoeing down the path, under the almond trees spreading naked branches against the sky, through the grapevines whose dead leaves hung like shriveled brown flesh, starting in a sweat of terror at the crackle of a twig underfoot.

Up in town, where there were lights from the houses and people on the streets, you slunk as close to the fences as you could, three waifs amorphous as the night.

But when you reached the T.O. with the light from its windows streaming into the darkness, with the chatter of voices inside, there was no use skulking any longer. You grasped the latch boldly and walked in.

Clory kept her eyes strictly upon the matter in hand, averted from the group of men spitting and gossiping by the stove. Terror lurched in her breast like a live thing.

'A box of matches, a sack of flour,' she said hurriedly to the clerk.

Clory had never seen Armstrong and McGeary, but she knew instinctively that they were in the group around the stove. The apostate, Orson Pratt, was there, Adam's apple working with his ribald sniggers, and Zadoc Hunt, the renegade 'Cohab,' all sly insinuations and pompous belly. There were a few of the men from the Pig-Dirt Patch, squatting and whittling and chewing, sociably swelling the laughter.

But the witlings of the bunch were those two swaggering there in the popular conception of western dress — Levis tucked into boots, studded belt sagging with pistols in each holster, leather jackets over open vests, ten-gallon hats. Armstrong was a surly rawboned giant with cold eyes and a Texas longhorn's mustache, but McGeary was a preponderous stomach of a man with eyes like a startled frog's and a chest like a pouter pigeon's. Obviously fashioned by Nature to be one of the jolly, Santa Claus type of men, McGeary had soured in the making into something faintly reptilian. The two made a strange pair, but to the people they hounded they represented the kind of Menace the primitives might have known, bodiless, unescapable.

'Snow, now,' said Armstrong in what he fondly imagined was a western twang, 'Snow won't be hard to get. They tell me he has a little memorandum book in which he keeps track of his wives. Swipe the book, by God, and we'll know where to raid!'

'Better watch out, you'll ...' the rest was whispered, but the ensuing guffaws drove the blood to Clory's cheeks.

'We ain't found David Wight at home, neither' — that would be McGeary's high-pitched bleat — 'but he won't be hard! If he don't change his Goddam habits he'll get his mileage paid to Beaver, yet!'

Clory handed the packages to Jim, retreated into her shawls, and darted with the two children out of the room. The Deps did not yet know her by sight, but they were after Abijah, and some day ... The only reason Abijah had escaped so far was that they could not get into the Temple.

She thought wildly of what they had said about David. How could they expect a man with limited means to maintain a separate establishment for every plural wife!

'We'll just stop in at Aunt Pal's,' she said to the children. Warn her ...

The merest thread of light outlined the window. Clory knocked, and called softly, 'It's me, Aunt Clory!' The door opened a crack and she and the children slipped into the room, that room where there had been so much happiness.

Patience-Elizabeth was huddled with the children near the stove, coaching them furtively in that ritual now become so monstrously familiar to every plural mother. The older boys and girls were as boneless with weariness as a bundle of rags, but the littlest ones, Pal's Lucy just turned four and Lucy's five-year-old, were held at strained attention by Patience-Elizabeth until they were stiff as statues.

'Now, what do you say when a strange man asks you where your Daddy ith?'

And the concerted childish treble: 'For all you know, *you* might be my Daddy!'

Looking at their innocent faces like upturned flower-faces, Clory thought they might be reciting a memory-gem in Sunday School.

At her question Patience-Elizabeth looked up, took away from her mouth the hand she was tremulously chewing, and gestured silently toward the inner room.

Leaving Jimmie and Tempie with the others, Clory opened the bedroom door, and as she closed it behind her again, shut out that childish parroting as one shuts out the memory of a nightmare.

'For all you know, *you* might be my Daddy!'

She found Pal bending over Lucy on the bed. There was a basin of water on the chair near-by and Pal was bathing her. Lucy glanced up with her soft brown gaze.

'I would have to be in hands at a time like this!'

'She's been hidin' out in her mother's cellar all day,' whispered Pal indignantly. 'Mud and cobwebs — 't's a wonder she didn't catch her death of cold!'

'They raided up there once today,' moaned Lucy. 'Marianne hid in the linen closet and Martha out in the privy!'

In the midst of her anxiety Pal had to laugh.

'Have you seen the Big House lately? It's fairly honeycombed with secret passages and trap doors and hidden stairways!'

Clory shook her head, thinking of the Underground Abijah had built in her own house — a set of hinged steps covered with rag carpet and opening under the floor into a dark, damp little hole scooped out of the earth.

Lucy moaned again, and Pal fed her peppermint and horehound tea.

'That ought to backen 'em. It's a shame her mother or Sister Lowgie can't be here, but I don't dare call them ... David ought to be here anyway! He attended every one of my birthin's, and I think he ought to come see Lucy even if it does mean the pen!'

'Oh, no, no!'

Lucy struggled to sit up, and Pal crooned to her and smoothed the damp hair back from her forehead.

'There, there! I didn't mean it...'

Clory was suddenly struck with how old Pal looked, and then the thought made her remember that she was forty, too; forty years old, and all their bright young dreams had ended in this shameful vigilance. Pal's square body still seemed to be made up of fat pincushions, but her dish-face was more than ever sunken with wrinkles, her blue eyes were harried.

Clory told her what she had overheard the man say about David.

Pal nodded.

'I know they're after him. David's been hidin' out in the brush for a week. Sometimes I nearly go crazy worryin' about whether he's cold or gets enough to eat. This food problem! What do the Feds expect us women and kids to do? Whether our husbands are on the Underground or in jail, we'll still starve!'

Pal's eyes grew hard at some memory.

'Last week I went up to Belinda Hunt's to buy some of that flour she's got socked away.

'"How much a pound will I have to pay you?"' I asked.

'And she says offhand, "Oh, about ten cents."

'So then I says, "Well, I'm willing to pay that much."

'Whereupon she frowns with them genteel eye-brows of hern; "Upon further consideration I think the flour should be twelve and a half cents, seeing's it's so scarce."

'So I bit my lip and thought of how hard it is to git to Washington now, an' I says, "All right, I'll pay it."

'When darned if she didn't up and say she oughta have fifteen cents! So I told her to keep her old flour and I hope it rots!'

Pal spooned Lucy's tea with a hand that shook a little.

'It ain't enough to have a husband in polygamy but the dirty Cohabs have to pick on you, too!'

Clory shivered suddenly in her shawls.

'I've been scared to have much of a fire,' Pal said. 'Oh, dang the men and their itch for wives!... But, there, it's counsel to go on with life as if nothin' had happened. All the men are takin' more wives. I suppose you heard about that man in Washington who went up to the City and took four at once? Never laid eyes on 'em, but he knew 'em at once, he said. Saw 'em beforehand in a revelation.'

'But there are men being sent up, too' — Clory came out of her preoccupation with chill. 'Brother Wheelock for three years and Bishop Covington for three years and six months.'

Pal sighed and went to get a hot brick for Lucy.

'I know,' she said when she got back, 'I dream of how it would seem to be *free* again, and us visitin' the City and maybe settin' eyes on them new-fangled electric lights and ridin' to the train in that new "thorough-brace" stagecoach that they say is put on rockers so it sways just like a rockin'-chair, a *Jerky* they call it, and it makes the hundred miles to Milford in a day and a night...'

She broke off to giggle at Clory.

'D'yu think we'll ever grow up? Here we are, building castles at forty years old!'

Clory laughed and went to the window.

'Well, the lights in the T.O. are out and I've got to scoot home. I ——'

But that sentence was never finished.

There was a scratching on the pane and Pal's hand went to her throat.

'David!' she whispered. 'Oh, he shouldn't have come!'

David it was, saddened and older, his eyes haunted, his unshaven cheeks thinned until his face had a withdrawn, brooding asceticism, its humor blown out like a light. But his smile was tender as he tiptoed about, fondling his children, snatching Pal's soft bulk in a big hug, bending over Lucy with tenderness and pity.

He kissed her and turned to Pal, his bristled chin quivering.

'Damn their black hearts,' he cried. 'By God, I'll ——'

The children stood in the open door, their eyes wide upon Father, who never swore, and Pal gestured warningly.

David subsided weakly upon the foot of the bed, his head in his hands, his body shaken with hunger and cold and despair.

'Don't take it like that!' whispered Pal. 'Remember it was Brother Brigham who said to put a woman out under a sagebrush and see if she couldn't have a baby without a doctor! If we got Aunt Ket here now we'd have McGeary and Armstrong upon us like a bunch of hornets! Lucy'll be all right... What we've got to do now is tend to you.... Patience-Elizabeth, Hannah, Palmyra...'

Stealthy rushings about to get hot water for Father, his razor, hot soup, while the little ones stared in sleepy amaze at this insane grown-up activity in the middle of the night.

'I can wecite my piece,' piped little Lucy, twisting her apron bashfully. '"For all you know you might be my Daddy!"'

David choked and Pal joked about the bones in his soup and bustled the children out to bed. 'Daddy will kiss you good night later...'

Clory gathered up her two and started for the door. It was safe enough now...

Then the sound came. The eerie squawk of a child's tick-tack on the windowpane. That sound echoing down all those sleepless years through the darkened streets of Zion. That warning as bloodcurdling as a Navajo war whoop, as full of raucous menace as the whirr of a rattlesnake.

David started up, spilling his soup, and Pal was instantly there taking charge, capable, unhurried.

'Hand Father those sandwiches, Patience. Here's your coat, David. Slip out the back way. Here, kiss me — come back when you can... Let's see, Clory. I know, crawl under Lucy's bed. I'll pretend your kids are mine, along with Lucy's. We'll put the slopjar in front of you, they won't look beyond that. Let's see, Lucy...'

Lucy's face was glistening with terror, her distorted body trembling under the bedclothes.

'Don't let 'em in here, Pal!'

'There, there,' said Pal. 'I won't...I know, Patience-Elizabeth, you can be takin' a bath, right there by Lucy's bed. They won't come in then!'

'But, Mamma —!'

'That will do!' said Pal firmly. 'Get your clothes off!'

It seemed to Clory, entombed under the dust of the bed, there could not possibly have been time to set the stage before she heard the tramping of men's heavy boots, muttered oaths as they crashed into the naked thorns of Pal's yellow rosebush, stumbled over the tubs of water settling for the morning's wash.

'Open in the name of the law! We are United States deputies!'

Silence for a moment, and then the squeak of the bed in the other room, the patter of Pal's bare feet across the floor.

Clory could see her, shapeless in her nightgown, facing them in the doorway.

'What do you mean, breaking into decent people's homes in the middle of the night?'

'Aw, don't give us that, sister.' (That would be Armstrong's nasal twang.) 'We know Wight's been here. We just about caught him, too.'

'If we kin lay our hands on that plural wife a his, we ketch him anyway!' (McGeary's whinny.)

'Well, there's nobody here, so go on about your business!'

'Shall we search the house, Mac?'

'Yeh, might as well...'

Silence again except for the trample of feet, Pal's own patter resolutely following. The crack Clory could see under the door grew dark as the lamp went into the other rooms; then it grew light again.

'What is this, a game?' Armstrong sounded annoyed. 'These damn Mormon bastards are all alike! Ask a kid who he belongs to and he says, "*You* might be my Daddy, for all you know!"'

McGeary sniggered at the other's mincing falsetto, and then Clory heard whispers, Pal's voice suddenly sharp.

'There's no one *in* there, I tell you!'

The bedroom door burst open, and in walked Armstrong like an evil genie suddenly materializing from the smoking lamp in his hand.

Patience-Elizabeth cowered and screamed, and the deputy stopped, momentarily frustrated.

'Huh!' His voice sounded puzzled. 'There's a dame takin' a bath in here, Mac.' And then as the light struck full on the bed and Lucy's frightened face — 'But by God, there's another havin' a kid, and I'll bet my guthooks she's the one we want!... I'll give you five minutes to git your duds on, sister.'

Sound of Patience-Elizabeth fumbling, blubbering; Lucy's long hushed gasp as though some spell worked in her and she could not throw it off.

There are moments too dreadful to be borne, times when the human will seems too flimsy a thing to be pitted against all the evil in the world.

They sat there, throughout the rest of that long night, two women and two men. Pal sent Patience-Elizabeth to bed, and Clory endured an agony of self-control until her feet and legs and finally her whole body numbed from tension.

Pal made the best of the situation, coaxing Lucy to relax even in the brutish horror of such a vigil, to drink the horehound tea.

'It will backen the pains,' she urged.

The men enjoyed themselves.

'Why should she "break the pains"? I've never seen a kid born!' whooped Armstrong. And then, turning quickly back to Lucy as if to catch her off her guard, 'Whose kid is it?'

'I tell you I don't know!' gasped Lucy, hysterically tossing. 'I don't know!'

'She don't know,' mimicked Armstrong. 'She don't know!'

'I guess she's the Virgin Mary!' — McGeary's obscene bleat.

Armstrong slapped his thigh.

'That's good! All we've got to do is stick around till the second comin' of Christ!'

It went on and on. Clory lay like a dead woman on her back, seeing all the long travail of her people and the women who had borne the brunt of it... as if all those women were reaching out their burden of wrongs to her, she was filled with so black a hate that she wanted to scream aloud.

And Lucy's pains crowded in spite of Pal's warnings to 'flat out.'

The men smoked, the odor of their pipes drifting through the stuffy room like incense from some foul shrine.

Lucy sickened, nauseated, and Pal held her while the terrible strain of her vomiting rocked the bed.

'Phew!' tittered McGeary.

Pal flew at him like a snarling cat.

'You curs! You're not men, you low-down spawn of Satan! Is there nothing sacred to you ...'

'Now, sister.' Armstrong took the pipe from his mouth and stared at Lucy curiously. 'We'd go if the Virgin Mary would tell us whose kid it is.' And then savagely, as if to trap her with the ferocity of his attack: '*Whose kid is it?*'

On and on.

'*Whose kid is it?*'

'*Whose kid is it?*'

The strain was intolerable. Clory's lips were bleeding where she had bitten them.

Armstrong went over and sat on the foot of Lucy's bed, playing jocularly with her toes.

'Come on, sister. *Whose kid is it?*'

Lucy's outraged, shuddering sobs.

Pal shoved her chair back decisively and Clory heard her go into the other room. Then there was silence ...

Silence during which Clory felt as if she were standing on the edge of an abyss screaming at the world stretched smugly on the plain below. Beating her breast and screaming at the mocking lips, the shrugging shoulders, the deaf ears. *Can't you see we're human beings like yourselves? Can't you see we eat and sleep and suffer like you? Only in our praying do we differ ... and if the same God listens to us all, why do you hate us because the words we use are not like yours? ...*

'Put that down, sister.' Armstrong's snarl was quietly ominous.

'No' — Pal's voice was like iron. 'I've stood all I'm goin' to. If you don't get out of my house and get out quick I'll kill you both where you stand! I'm prepared to do it and I'll take the consequences of the act!'

Another silence in which thoughts, hesitations, denials, a lifetime seemed to hang.

And then the heavy scraping of a chair, yawns, Armstrong's twang.

'Hell, McGeary, come on. There's a lot of time to get Wight.'

When daylight filtered over the land like a clammy gray ghost it found Pal in hysterics; Lucy in a faint, and Clory distraught between the two, trying to bring some semblance of calm to that tormented household before the children awoke.

Shadrach Gaunt strode in, his eyes narrowed, his jaws moving balefully, his body a coiled threat even at fifty-odd.

'I been watchin' from acrost the street by the T.O. I told the dummed god-darned bastards if I ever heerd of either of 'em pesterin' you folks agin I'd stomp both of em into a gopher hole!'

It was the same dawn that found David burrowing into the earth, afraid that the pounding of his heart would betray him, crouching under a mesquite bush so close to Armstrong's booted feet he could have touched him as he passed.

It was the same dawn that found Clory and the two children scudding home through the chill streets like frightened rabbits. *I can't stand it!* she cried with all of her being. *I can't stand it!*

6

But it seemed that one had to stand it. Once again she found herself starting up in the night, the old torment springing out of the silences, stinging her flesh. Again the shadows of the dugout were about her and Free and Kissy and Willie were not hurts she had suffered and overcome, sorrows that had faded to the faint sweet nostalgia of dried rose leaves; Free and Kissy were real, and the lessons were all to be learned over again.

No longer was she strong, mistress of life and her own soul. Sometimes polygamy seemed more than a condition, it was a Thing and she had thrown herself against it and been bruised. Abijah could come seldom, and she tossed through the long sleep· less nights listening for the sound of the tick-tack, dreading the Loneliness that lurked in the shadows waiting to recapture her, to engulf her again in its dark tides.

But there were the children, whom most of the time she didn't dare send to school, and she found herself once again having to practice the careless smile, the old untroubled upward curve of her mouth. Forcing the old vividness to glow for the children.

It seemed to her that winter that the wind blew more than it had ever done before, that all the sere, stiff salt grasses were running before it, and that all the world joined in the race. She often found herself panting as if she had been running and could not seem to stop. A whole winter of running. *I can't stand it,* she thought, and knew that she could, because other women all over Zion were enduring the same thing.

Plural wives with new babies sleeping in fields, on the ground, under bushes. Other plural wives fleeing to Pipe Springs in Arizona, seven pregnant women there at one time. Fleeing into St. George to visit families, eluding the marshals by an hour or a moment, fleeing back out to safety with the aid of friends along the line. Drumming of a horse's hoofs like rapid gunfire in the silent night, tick-tack on the windowpane. Muffled jangle of harness, soft blowing of a horse, muffled hurrying figure glimpsed in the starlight, vanished. Hasty kiss of farewell — Take care of yourself, tears ...

Joseph Mac's young second wife dragged with her child before the judge at Beaver, swearing the child is a foundling and then going home to beg the Lord to forgive her for lying.

'Do you mean to tell me that isn't MacIntyre's baby?'

'No' (desperately pleading with those unknown gods not to take the child because she denied it). 'No, only that it isn't my baby!'

Hiding for months in 'Sheba's cellar, coming out only after dark like some strange nocturnal prowler.

Sometimes 'Sheba joked about it — 'Our neighborhood is popular with the Deps!'

Clory and Joseph's wife and Serena Lee Hansen all in a row. Three women on the Underground.

Sometimes Serena Hansen, that tall woman with the haunted dark eyes, who had already gone through marriage with one man wanted by the law, would slink out of the Yeast Lady's cellar and creep like a shadow along the street to Clory's. And the two fugitives would sit in the dark and whisper and sing together, and the muted notes of the dulcimer wove a lament that was the same for every song.

> McGeary would do well
> To engage a place in hell;
> For the road he's on
> Will take him there, I know.

But behind the defiant words (it was counsel to be cheerful!) lay heartbreak. And Clory never guessed that sometimes her son lay listening to that muted humming, listened and remembered his mother's clear song that he used to fancy shot up to the stars ... and spent the whole night slaying dragons ...

'I haven't been in the sunshine for eighteen months,' whispers Serena, holding tight to Clory's hand. 'Lars says we'll go to Mexico when he gets enough money, and I keep dreaming of the time when we'll climb every hill to shout and sing! My children are farmed out among strangers, I haven't seen them for months. But Lars *can't* go to prison. He's an old man, Sister Mac, and it would kill him. Lars says they won't take him alive, he says he'll not desert me for any law. We've got a big watchdog on the place now, in case the Deps ... Oh, it seems so silly to call it *lascivious cohabitation*' (mouthing the words as if they tasted nasty). 'Aunt Julia couldn't have children and she worships mine as if they were her own and we've been so happy . . .'

A wail that is cut short by the omnipotent tick-tack, and in a moment the women, clutching quilts and pillows, and the two children stumble into the darkness, are swallowed up by the night, the swaying corn-specters whipping against their white faces as they flee between the rows. A moment — and the Deps have lurched cursing on out the street. Then it is time to duck and scuttle again, out beyond the Temple where the children scoot into the deeper, safer brush like quail, hugging the earth as if they had been lost and come home. Nature gathers them to her breast, making them anonymous with all the mysterious goings-on of the night, giving them comfort at last. For it is always an all-night vigil when the Deps come, and scorpions and centipedes and even snakes are kinder.

7

It was ironic, thought Clory, that in spite of all the messages she had lately sent to Abijah that she must see him, his first visit in months should be prompted not by love but by anger (that righteous anger of his!).

It seemed that with all the other hurryings in the Dixie Mission, life itself was speeding up. Strange and wonderful promises gleamed upon the horizons, and among them was electricity, that flaming sword that might turn to a searing death in a boy's hands or merely a tiger's tail which one could neither hold on to nor let go. At least, that is how the conference visitors found it that April of '85 when they went to lift the tin cup attached to the public drinking-barrel on the Tabernacle grounds. And Jim and Frankie Wight maneuvered the various magnets and wires and peered around the corner in silent convulsions at the spectacle of a staid frock-coated dignitary shaking off the cup as if it had stung him.

But inevitably repercussions of this peccadillo in the very shadow of the House of the Lord reached Abijah in the fastnesses of his Temple retreat, and he exercised his royal will and sent word to Clory when to expect the Presence.

Oh, my! Clory regarded tenderly this hulking dark giant who was her son sulkily braiding a quirt in the corner, thought of his questing mind probing among all the curiosities of this so-curious world, and wished there were some way to give youth the wisdom of experience without young feet having to climb the same old rocky paths.

'Darling,' she said, 'you mustn't provoke your father. You know how he is.' And had the elusive feeling that the words echoed, as if she had said them once before. Was it to another sulky giant with ripe-wheat hair? She sighed, thinking of men with their uncouth mouthings and clumsy clutchings elbowing through life, women eternally stretching forth weak arms to curb their headlong blunderings and eternally sweeping up the wreckage afterward.

'My gosh, I can't be like he wants me to be,' mumbled Jim, taking the end of the quirt in his strong white teeth and beginning to plait with his square-tipped pliant fingers.

Waiting for Abijah was always a time of tension. Waiting in the darkened house, shushing the children, starting up in a spasm of terror at the yowling of a cat, even the scamper of mice in the rafters. Protest of straining senses, compulsion to be on the move, from door to window and back to chair. Peering out at the blowzy day, all wet and bedraggled, slopping behind the hill in a melancholy mist of drizzle and mud.

And then the sound of a stealthy footfall running on the path, a panting behind the closed door like rapid heart-beats. The hasty kiss, the whispered greeting. The making certain through crack of door and twitched windowblind that all is well.

Then Abijah must be fed his supper, must hold court, give counsel . . .

Jim was getting older, Clory thought. He did not take Abijah's reprimands with the old docility. But sitting there sullenly, with Abijah shooting wrath at him from under his brows, Clory thought her son in his dark temper more beautiful than a celestial spirit.

'Your Aunt 'Sheba has told me about you,' scowled Abijah, his hands beneath his coattails. He turned accusingly to Clory. 'Did ye know that yesterday when he was helping Mokiac Indian grub that brush for Joseph, getting that new strip ready for cane and corn, the Lamanite went to sleep under a bush and Jim dr-ropped red ants on his britch clout to wake him up?'

At the memory Jim's lips twitched in spite of earth-shaking proximities, and Clory threw back her head and laughed until her eyes were wet. It was the first time in months she had laughed aloud — that delicious husky laughter of hers — and Abijah was not pleased.

'Ye humor him in his wrong-doing,' he flared. 'Ech, such behavior is not fitting in the son of the Temple's President! It is just as 'Sheba says: ye spoil him until he'll be no gude to himself nor anybody else!'

Striding about the room, Abijah came back to point an imperious finger.

'Will you behave, lad, if I let ye off this time?'

But with the perversity of the young in every generation, Jimmie refused to answer. He did not want to be a leader, a high priest, a Seventy, or even an apostle, he only wanted to ride horses and ... and ... Besides, away back in his mind there was a vague unconscious resentment against his father that had nothing to do with the whippings. A fellow did what it seemed he could not help doing at the time, and if it was wrong, he got punished for it. That was the law of life. But his mother's bandaged hands and these miscarriages — sometimes he and Tempie had been alone with her and helped with the blood and the horror — this quenching of the gaiety within her, he had watched it struggle up like a moth with bruised wings — these were the things that rankled until his mind doubled up its fists, and he'd never yield to his father's wishes if it killed him, by gosh! He saw the moment as his tragedy, alone; he was too young to pity Abijah with his longing to found a dynasty in this Church he loved; too young to pity Abijah's hurt disappointment at God for giving His Servant such a son as this.

And so Abijah buttoned up his dreams and his coat — for one must not lose one's dignity even when doing what one could to rectify God's mistakes — and merged his paternal anxiety and his strong right arm in one of those cataclysmic relapses that Clory thought must afford considerable amusement to the beasts of the field. Not that he enjoyed doing it; he was bitterly annoyed over the necessity, since he was not as young as he had been and it was hard, sweaty work, rumpling him up both inside and out. But it was plainly Duty and he would not shirk, though Duty might gobble up moments snatched from the Deps and designed for the family he had not seen in weeks, and even besmirch the rest of his visit.

Clory waited with Tempie, who sat there in her young-girl aloofness, all prim and controlled and distressed, and found herself wishing that the Deps *would* get Abijah. Certainly no mood in which to broach the tugging desire in her heart. But Samuel and his wife were going, and Marianne Snow and Bishop Gardner and his first wife — it was a chance to get away — and she was sure if she and the children ever got away she'd never come back.

Her very need made her diffident. Music, gaiety of the city. Adelina Patti giving her concert there: the great Adelina Patti ... When the cataclysm was over and the universe had settled into place once more, she held out the name to Abijah as if she were coaxing a hostile dog to eat. All winter she had been running. Dear God, if she could just run this once more — far enough ...

But Abijah straightened his coat and washed his hands, obscurely sore inside somewhere, himself, and 'hawckked' in

irritation. It was no th' time to be gallivantin' off. She had
muckle need tae stay home and mind her bairns, now that he
couldna see t' them himself. Counsel was tae go on with life as if
nothing had happened, and was he, Abijah MacIntyre, tae be the
first tae disobey counsel? At least she got tae see him now and
then. What if she was like Apostle Snow's wives with a husband
on the Underground at Silver Reef? Aye, *they* never were the-
gither, and yet no one ever heard of those women kickin' up a
broil!

Clory found herself down on her knees to him (something she
had never thought to do with any man), pleading as if for a stay
of execution. The great Tabernacle, the wonderful Playhouse,
all those things she had never seen. A glimpse of those radiant
and lovely visions that all her life had waited just beyond the
horizon. One little boost was all she needed, one little boost beyond these imprisoning hills and she'd fly her own wings, even at
forty.

Abijah strengthened his tender spot against Clory's tears and,
a little embarrassed, shrugged her away.

8

Thinking he was sick of the place, the smokestacks, tipples
against the sky, the very argot, 'ore' and 'raster' and 'retort,'
Erastus turned his back on Silver Reef's flamboyant Main Street
and plodded on out to the quiet sagebrush where a man could
invite his soul.

He had been among strange people and strange ways for almost three years now ... And this place was a vulgar wench with
challenging eyes and spangled skirts. He longed with all his heart
for the demure gentility of his own town.

It was dreadful to find yourself floundering in the desolation of
age when ruin stared your people in the face. The Pioneers were
old. Erastus writhed his lips in anger, thinking of the way he

fumbled for things when he should be grasping Fate by the horns and bulldogging it to victory.

The Pioneers had taken this land with the beauty of its hills and its opalescent valleys, with its saintly yuccas and gaudy cacti-blooms, with its gila monsters and rattlesnakes — they had taken this land and wooed and won it, and in return it had brought forth homes and gardens. A land of infinite promise. What couldn't they make of it if the States would leave them alone!

But the first fine frenzy of youth had passed and the Pioneers were old. He sat on a rock and chewed a twig of bitter sage and wondered if this land to which they had given their lives was to pass at last into the hands of thieves and carpetbaggers. Wondered if men were fools to cherish the Dream against such odds. For they were the weak and the humble, those whom the centuries had always denied the right to dream. Was there, then, something inherently stronger in a lie than in the truth? In wickedness than good? In ugliness than beauty?

The hail was repeated before Erastus heard and lifted his head.

Johnny Lowgie galloped over the clumps of sagebrush, waving a yellow telegram as Erastus had seen him do on so many other occasions.

'The dam's out!' shouted Johnny, panting up. 'Hay and grain just ready to cut — Brother MacIntyre says not to come if you think there's danger of the Deps, but ——'

Suddenly Erastus was not old any more. His gray eyes gleamed; even his stocky body that had been so palsied and finished a moment ago seemed to fill with strength. He had a job to do. His people needed him.

'An earth dam, a brush dam, a pile dam, a rock dam, twenty-three years of it. I'm about through.'

'Crops unwatered, our means all used up, and most of us hiding out and unable to get any more...'

'You shouldn't be here, should you, Brother Wight? I hear the
Deps are hot on your trail — you and Apostle Snow . . .'

'He would come, Bishop Gardner. Lucy and I tried to persuade
him not to, but he said the dam was more important than the
Deps!'

Erastus listened to the voices shout above the brattling flood
and was almost happy. Here was an adversary who might be
treacherous but whom he could understand and respect . . .

'We'll have to scoop out all the quicksand and put in an entire
new bed ——'

'Oh, that would be an awful job!'

'Well, if we can't do it, I don't want no more. I don't want no
more brush dam and no more Dixie Mission.'

It was true, thought Erastus; unless they could find a way to
dam the river permanently, the Cotton Mission was finished.
All that they had built through hunger and Indians, plagues and
persecutions. But his shoulders were once again strong to the
burden. He was oddly confident.

'David . . . d'yu think you can forget the Deps long enough
to write something funny in the *Vepricula*? We've got to —
make the people laugh . . . Ptsahh!'

Not since the days of Brother Brigham had the Tabernacle
been so thronged. People jammed the galleries, stood up along
the aisles.

Erastus sat on the stand in his old place and ran a finger over
the brown painted surface of the pulpit as a man touches the face
of his beloved. There was a thrill of pleasure in the very touch of
familiar things. These buildings, the Social Hall, the Temple, the
Tabernacle, were like bone of his bone and flesh of his flesh.

He was in no hurry to start the meeting. He relaxed on the
cushioned seat and watched laughter live on the faces of his people as the little *Vepricula* crackled on every bench.

' . . . It was decided upon by a body of stalwart water doctors to take the Virgin out of her bed to see if she could be confined. But upon undertaking labor with her they found that besides being far too shallow for intelligent advice, she had strong symptoms of the gravel in her bottom and had developed a large rupture in her side through which her water was ebbing very fast...'

There was almost a holiday spirit over the audience. Small gossipings, greetings, Fear banished for the moment.

'I am — reminded — of — Abraham Lincoln,' drawled Erastus, the old humor around his eyes, his white fringe of beard jutting with the old challenge. 'Lincoln *knew*. "We have grown in numbers, wealth, and power as no other nation has ever grown," he said in '63, "*but we have forgotten God.*"

'That is what we must do, my brethren. Go back to God.'

Erastus leaned over the pulpit, and for a moment his kindly face flashed with such power that Clory could see Brother Brigham standing there, the forefinger of his emphasizing...

'Remember, folks,' said Erastus, and his voice was proud. 'Remember *this is still America*. She may make mistakes and our people may be the victim of those mistakes, but *she's still America*. Zion will not die, persecution will only strengthen her, and some day she will take her place in American life. For she has a place, folks!... Government of the people, by the people, with brotherly love: this is the rock our country was founded on. ...To us has been given the vision beyond what any other people ever had before. That every man should be *free* — free to worship God according to the dictates of his own *conscience*. ...America has forgotten her vision for the moment. Everywhere I look I see men fighting only for themselves, greedy, selfish, fattening on the toil of others. But this time will pass, folks. America has forgotten her vision, but *the day will come when Zion will remind her!*

'And for the coming of that day we can afford to sacrifice and suffer. "And what seems to be a loosing of present comforts that we have gathered around us will be like bread cast upon the waters." ...'

It was then that Erastus saw them, Armstrong and McGeary, down the length of the aisle, framed in the Tabernacle doorway. He was almost glad. The long strain was over. And the All-Seeing Eye on the wall back of him was still counting the sparrows' fall. He had faltered for just a moment, but his eyes came back to his people, humorous, kindly, unafraid, and he finished his sentence.

' ... will be like bread cast upon the waters, which after many days shall be gathered like seed that brings forth much fruit.'

Banks and bosses of bloom. Bare shoulders and curls and scents, even some of the carmine and rice powder which rumor said Stiddy Weeks sold along with his boneset pills. The gayest motley St. George had ever worn, for David Wight and Dixie's beloved Apostle were going to jail and this was their farewell party.

Abijah MacIntyre is master of ceremonies (McGeary and Armstrong are always drunk after a big haul), and he rumples his shock of gray hair and calls for the program.

'Cheer up, folks! This isn't a wake!'

Clorinda in white, her little pointed face all eyes above the boned net collar, leans over the dulcimer, plucks tentatively at the song she had prepared — a Madonna with bandaged hands.

'I can't sing it,' she falters — 'that rollicking tune...'

She lifts her head as if she were listening to something very far off. Then her voice culls a melody out of the past, muted with tears, freighted with the long passionate lament of her people. Nauvoo, Winter Quarters, the years of heartbreak in Deseret, the undying hope for a better day...

> 'By the rivers of Babylon we sat down and wept—
> We wept when we remembered Zion.'

CHAPTER XVI

THE Year of the Plagues. The Reign of Terror. But the one ended in time, thought Clory, while the other bade fair to go on forever.

Tempie was a clever little seamstress for being only fourteen, but Clory's own fingers twitched for the feel of the needle. Watching Tempie patch Jim's overalls, she sat there nursing her bandaged hands, thinking of the advantages the buckskin gloves could have brought these children she loved. Perversely, now that she could not fill any of them, orders were pouring in by the dozen.

Watching Tempie sew, her pale eyes intent on the stitching, watching her mix bread-dough, her mild-colored braids jerking to the rhythm of her plunging, still childish arms (already she was a young lady begging for long skirts and her hair up, rightfully demanding of life all the tributes due young-ladyhood), Clory felt about as necesssary as a gutted pine-nut bur tossed up by the Virgin.

The Church was so disorganized that Abijah did not get his salary for months on end, and when it came, 'Sheba got away with most of it — 'Sheba, who had things all her own way now that Abijah was so seldom home.

Sometimes Clory found herself dreaming of 'Sheba, all Brob-
dingnagian bosom and nose and twitching mole, leaping across
the sky, blotting out the sun — a housewife who had drunk of
dragon's broth. Sometimes Abijah came to her in those dreams,
stripped of his motley, a lusty lover with tender eyes and a song
on his lips, the next moment an accusing archangel whose wings
had draggled in the fleshpots.

'Mother!' Jimmie said for the second time. 'Mother! If
Tempie doesn't hurry with those pants, Mr. Gaunt'll go off and
leave me!'

Clory smiled at her brawny son, who had only one pair of overalls to his name and had to go to bed while those were patched.
When he got back from the round-up . . .

Jimmie watched his mother struggle up from that dark world
of her own where he could never follow and hated the thing that
took her there, hated the dark mood that caught her away in its
claws. There was nothing about life that a boy had a right to
expect, nothing about life that was normal and decent. For
three years he had watched his world shiver into bits about him,
all the normal pursuits of boyhood denied him. Not that he cared
so much about school, but a fellow had a right to security. What
had he done that all his horizons should be stabbed with this
mad and jangled lightning? What had he done that strangers
from the States — men who can see that he is, after all, a human
being like themselves — should regard him as if he were a monster
and inquire where were his horns?

People said the trouble was polygamy, but Jim thought that
was silly. Polygamy was simply one of those inexplicable ills of
life like having that Young Julia Hansen for a sister, having the
big neck like that Sis Eardley or a corn on your toe like Father.
All marriage was senseless to Jimmie, but surely if a man multi-
plied his own miseries he didn't need any outside punishment . . .

There was something wrong somewhere. Especially the something that let his mother cry so often, which choked up her song.

It was a brute of a world, merciless and unmeaning, and all he could count on were the hills and his horse.

2

The Reign of Terror ... Often, as soon as a prisoner's term was up, he would be rearrested at the penitentiary door. He was help-less, since he was being punished for a crime he had committed years before it became a crime. As if a man were suddenly jailed for having worn a mustache in his youth. Thirteen hundred pris-oners upheld by the conviction that there among the bedbugs and the beans they ate of sacred bread. Apostle Snow dreaming of miracles, David Wight drawing maps and sending in his contribu-tions to the *Vepricula* ——

> '... While the marshals are slumming
> There's no thought of succumbing,
> For The Babies Keep Coming, in Utah!'

Eighteen eighty-six, and on the one hand Zion begs Washington for help, pleading for statehood for the twelfth time, while on the other hand Professor Careless gives a grand musical concert in the Opera House. As if that indestructible something which is the essence of Deseret would not be cowed. A spirit that is light, free, volatile, no sooner is it crushed in one place than it springs forth with renewed shouts in another.

Abijah fortifying himself behind the great white walls of the Temple reading Apostle Snow's letter.

> David's map is drawn of an imaginary spot, of course, but unless we can find a place like it on the Virgin the Mission is sunk. This looks to me like the final test. If the Idea we've spent half our lifetimes to establish is a good sound principle of human life the Lord won't let it die. ...
>
> David's idea is a sort of diversion works or 'spillway.' Hunt for a hogsback or stratum of rock jutting out into the river bed. The scheme is to cut a section of rock from the

hogsback to make the 'spill' and then dam the channel of the river so as to throw the stream over the 'spill,' thus leaving full play for the floods, while the dry dam across the original channel would turn the water into the head of the canal. In other words, we'd have a diversion works which would split the river into two different streams. David estimates we can irrigate three thousand acres instead of the thousand we've been doing with the ditch alone.

I realize this scheme will mean a dredger, men to drill and blast, steel equipment — I haven't any more idea than the man in the moon where we'll get such expensive machinery, but I firmly believe the way will open up, and I want you . . .

Abijah stood at one of the tall many-paned windows looking out over the fall lucerne greening the white-capped hill and felt Erastus' spirit about him so compellingly that it was like a hand laid on his shoulder. All his life he had towered a head above Erastus, and yet there was such quiet authority in the other's gray gaze that it had been like looking up at him. Now Erastus seemed to be there beside him, writhing his lips, waiting for Abijah to get busy about this commission . . . 'ptsahh!'

But already Abijah felt himself an alien in the spirit of struggle that had always been the Dixie Mission. Logan was one of those green northern valleys, plenty of food, no Virgin bloat, one of those easy northern valleys Clorinda was always prating aboot . . . Already, thinking of it, Abijah felt himself engulfed in a wave of homesickness. Nevermore to undertake a commission for Erastus Snow . . . And yet, there was a quick new flutter in his blood as if something alive were trying to escape, and even as he suffered with prophetic nostalgia there was a never-to-be-vanquished part of him that stepped out upon its front porch, stretched to test the vigor of its muscles, and shuddered in a delicious excitement at the thought of those neat ankles twinkling just next door . . . Abijah recognized the sensation. He had felt the same way just be-

fore he took Clory. His heart beat high with animation. Ech, a
MacIntyre dynasty at last!

Suddenly troubled, he passed a reassuring hand up over his
beard. But it was still glossy and full, crisp to the touch, the
white in it only accenting the power of his manhood. His hair —
still thick and curly, no loss of virility there; even at sixty-six
women still loved to run their fingers through his hair.

With a sudden spurt of energy, feeling very youthful and lusty,
he sprinted down the red-carpeted hall, the stairs, into the wash-
room, where he instantly became absorbed in the mirror, pushing
back his lip to peer at his strong white teeth, pulling down the
underskin of his eye to see if the whites were bloodshot, smoothing
the bit of cheek above the beard — those tiny criss-crossed veins
— but — 'hawckk' — no worse than mony a young man had!
Ech, a MacIntyre dynasty!... But even as he panted with the
unaccustomed exertion and scowled at his aging heart for leaping
around like a fish out of water, he came up with a jerk, remembered
that he was a servant of God, and whirled about to glower back
down the hall as if he could still see his treacherous self gamboling
there.

Aye, this was going to be a verra sad business, he reminded
himself as he decorously retraced his footsteps, but Zion's endurance was coming to an end (President Cleveland had just refused
to sign, because of its unconstitutional measures, the new Ed-
munds-Tucker bill confiscating all Church property), Zion was
giving concessions to the enemy, and the President of the whole
Church had just written Abijah MacIntyre that he was appointed
to be the first president of the Logan Temple, but that he must
take with him only one wife...

3

It was 'Sheba who told her, striding across the dooryard,
stooping under the lintel, standing there with her arms akimbo

watching Clory put up her hair with something that was almost like humor glinting in her eyes. As if they had battled about the thing for so many years it had finally become funny.

This new way of piling the hair on top of the head, thought Clory; so hard to do decently with bandaged hands. She gave a little grunt of exasperation and rewound one of the shining coils. ... Her hair was still black and glossy, had very little frost in it for being forty-two years old. But the eyes that stared back at her from the mirror were ringed with lines and sad. Too-big eyes, they had the dark settled melancholy of a mountain lake at dusk. The day had been long — and whipped with wind and waves. For a swift moment Clory longed for evening, too, and an end to this aimless bustle of living. Age did more to a woman than to a man, no matter how much she softened with mutton tallow or bleached with buttermilk. The face in the mirror bore the unmistakable imprint of the years — as if you rubbed the down from a peach or the bloom from a rose petal. The days passed and you were never quite the same again. Youth was all the treasure a woman had, and it behooved her to spend it well, for it never came again ...

'Abijah has just been appointed first President of the Logan Temple.'

'Sheba tasted the words, savoring their effect on the other woman.

But it was Tempie, quietly piecing quilt blocks on the bed, who showed the most reaction.

Clory's hand faltered until the hairpin fell from her grasp, and for just a moment something tumultuous leaped up from the prison of her will, but she downed it sternly. People who looked upon too-sudden hope were sometimes blinded.

'But the authorities say he can take only one wife.'

'Sheba's dry voice was grimly amused.

Now, indeed, the hand holding the tortoise-shell comb pushed it home until it drew blood. In the mirror Clory watched her own face pale, and then that wild free something beat at her cheeks, flame up in her eyes, knock at her heart until the breath between her lips came warm and fast. She waited until the first shock had passed before turning around. 'Sheba must not see the hope that was like a reprieve . . .

There was a knock at the door, and Clory went to open it like a woman in a dream.

'Aunt Julia says, may she borrow some flour?'

That was the excuse on the girl's lips but her eyes were as brazen with curiosity as a bird's. She did not bother even to nod at 'Sheba and Tempie.

Mechanically repeating the amenities, Clory was puzzled. She was not used to receiving visits from Young Julia Hansen. The Yeast Lady, yes, but not this pert minx with her bold rib-boned bustle . . . Clory, who seldom disliked anyone, had always felt a half-admitted antagonism for Young Julia. The girl had nothing whatever but youth.

While Clory went into the lean-to for the flour, 'Sheba watched the visitor take in the room, her stare become possessive in the manner of any female regarding objects with which she intends to become intimate. From Will's paper wreath to the scrim motto and the rawhide-bottomed chair with its tatted antimacassar, the rosewood desk, the silver caster on the table, the bright acquisitive glance came briskly back to 'Sheba as if she were a cracked teapot that could be thrown in with the other things, if necessary.

'Sheba made conversation politely and fists out of the hands in her apron pockets. The hussy! . . . But the thing was not declared yet. It was too soon to fight . . . But she, Bathsheba, intended to triumph if she had to fight half a dozen women.

Clory gave Young Julia her flour, and Jimmie came in from irrigating just as she minced out the door. Sweat-streaked, his overalls grimy, he thrust his hands in his pockets and glowered at the figure retreating down the walk, its bustle twitching.

'What she want?' he growled, beetling his brows like his father.

The dark uncouth youth of him, little boy sometimes lost in that big man's body — Clory brushed aside the girl's visit, her own bandaged hands, the miscarriages, and dimpled at her son. The old sign language. 'I've something nice to tell you,' it said.

But Jimmie still had his eyes on the girl.

'Mother, I don't like that person!' he said. 'D'yu know that the boys make fun of her and her bustle? They call her the — the gopher's hind end!'

Clory laughed at the distaste that sat upon his youthful countenance.

'Never mind! We don't have to have anything to do with her!'

Her voice was gay, full of little flute-notes and excitement.

'Sheba snorted contemptuously and took herself home. *A lot you know*, she said to herself, *but you'll learn! It's as plain as the nose on your face! But I mean to be the one to go in spite of hell and high water.*

4

'Sheba's too old, Clory assured herself again and again while Abijah sneaked in the rest of the week's visits with his first wife. *'Sheba's too old to run a big household and entertain for him, she's too old to have any more children, while I — well, there's always the chance that I can carry one through the full time again.*

This was Abijah's opportunity to make up to her for all her years of unhappiness. Maybe up North away from 'Sheba she might get to know him as a real husband and young Jim come to care for him as a real father, someone to love instead of fear. A boy needed a father... Decent clothes, plenty to eat for Jimmie and Tempie, a chance for their education — and for herself, to fulfill at last her old dream of the beauty in life.

Hope was like a spur, goading her. She planned with a frantic absorption. This was it, this had to be it. A woman who had been third wife for twenty-six years had a right at last to be first.

To declare before all the world: 'This is my husband. Not just a third my husband, but all of him.' Peace and security, the long strain over. Her need was so savage she could scarcely contain it.

The hands, the salt-rheum ... back to Stiddy Weeks for salve, up to Hannah Merinda for poultices. This miscarriage business ... she thought of her body with contempt, her body that could not even go about its woman's business without making a fuss. What was Abijah's word — *shilpit?* That was it, she was a weakling and *shilpit.* ... The old Thompsonian course of medicines — 'Cayenne pepper to give power to the blood, lobelia to physic and relax the system'... Clory found herself chewing desperately on bitter root and wild milkweed and prickly pear. ...

She prepared for Abijah's coming like a bride. The good food he loved, the haggis pudding. Fresh browned flour for his hands. The children sensed her strategy, entered into her mood of gentle beguilement, treading softly through the days so that there should be no preliminary jar or discord, so that the way should be smooth for his coming ...

If it hadn't been for the joyous cheeing of blackbirds, a phalanx against the blue November sky. If the air hadn't been as soft against the face as a young girl's cheek. If a more luminous autumn hadn't gilded the cottonwoods, fired the trumpet-vine and the peach leaves and the pomegranates until they hung like crimson balls. If the air hadn't been rain-washed and sweet with the scent of the fall roses, profligate blooms spilling themselves over all the fences.

Abijah had not meant to deceive her, to let her build up false hopes. He had meant to be very businesslike, to make the visit curt and decisive. But she was so unexpectedly lovely waiting for him there in the doorway, framed against firelight. There was a helplessness about her that robbed him of all his arguments. He forgot that he was a servant of God and remembered only that he was a man and she was very much a woman.

To Clory, watching him come up the path, the world was sud-

denly filled with the pink radiance of apple blossoms. The waiting
had been so long and so hard. The patient waiting through all
the years. A young-girl tremulousness seized her. A little pulse
beat in her throat: *This is it. This is it. This is the consumma-
tion of all these years.*

Abijah's kiss was fervent, and he put an arm about her and led
her into the room where the children waited.

He'll tell me after supper, thought Clory. There were the
'How are you's' to be got through with; he would have to listen
to the children's joys and griefs, give them counsel.

She watched him smack his lips over the haggis pudding; the
lamb was young and tender, the seasoning just right. Did she
know the Deps had got Brother Mansfield? Aye. 'Twas the
apostate, Pratt, gave him away — told 'em he came home at
dawn every morning to water his mules ...

I can bide my time, thought Clory. *Keep him in a good humor. . . .*

But then, supper was over, and the children were in bed, and
Abijah still said words as if he were talking against time, as if
he were talking against that look of sweet expectancy in her little
pointed face, that look like an echo from her girlhood. It used to
enrage him so, that questioning tilt to her head as if she were
listening for something too refined for his ears.

Bedtime, and Clory was thinking, *He's been saving it to tell me
now.* But when Abijah had put on his night shoes and, still
wallowing in unaccustomed loquacity, performed his nightly
ritual of fifty strokes of the brush to his beard, fifty strokes of the
brush to his hair, Clory gritted her teeth. *A woman has ways to
persuade a man* ... And so there was Abijah, abandoning himself to her charm, drowning in sweet lust ... but finding no use
for words at all. Long after he snored beside her, Clory lay
awake staring at the dark, willing him to tell her when morning
came ... That was it. Why hadn't she thought of it before? He
had been waiting all along for the calm light of morning when
they could make plans dispassionately.

At breakfast they spoke of inconsequential things. Abijah was as chipper as a colt.

'Jimmie, look out and see if the coast is clear-r. Aye, your mither's sic a sleepyhead'(jocularly) 'she forgot to call me!...'

Clory could stand it no longer. Something within her snapped like a spring that has been wound too tightly.

He stood there in the doorway, tall against the dawn light on the south mountains, shouldering into his coat, wrapping his muffler around his throat; and suddenly in the passionate intensity of her need she flung herself upon him, clinging to him, straining up at him, staring up into his face with its sweetness and tender mouth all hidden by the beard. For a moment, before the naked appeal in her eyes, his own tumultuously answered, widened and flooded with golden light until they were like the sunrise, but then, as if struggling with resolve, grayed and dropped.

'You are going to take me with you, aren't you, Abijah?' She tried to keep the desperation out of her voice. ''Sheba's too old, and I can work, I' — she remembered her bandaged hands white against the black of his coat and hastily thrust them behind her — 'I can keep a big house, preside at socials. You used to say all I was good at was parties. Well, now...I can have more babies....'

Her voice trailed off at the irritation in his face.

'We'll see, Clor-rinda, we'll see,' he said impatiently, in a hurry to be off.

He picked up her bandaged hands and looked at them, and for a moment Clory thought something like pity lived far back in his eyes. Some hard barrier melted. But then they glazed over again, lighted with the restless eagerness that had nothing to do with her.

'We'll see,' he said, kissing her brusquely on the forehead, plunging down the step, pulling on his gloves, sniffing the air as does a male of any species who is on his way to newer pastures.

Expecting him momentarily to kick up his heels, Clory watched him stride out between the dew-wet rosebushes with a hand at her throat. He *had* loved her, he loved her now, at least as long as he was with her. And last night he had really seemed all hers, so tender, so . . . so . . .

Fear like a weasel sucked at her courage. The primal fear of every woman that something longed for and just possessed will be snatched from her.

5

Christmas, and the Deps even more alert to catch a homecoming polygamist. A dreary Christmas. The Dixie Mission with its murky nights, its shuttered windows and stealthy footfalls like some somber ship laboring uncertainly in dark uncharted seas. Nothing of the oldtime spunk about it, even the Paiutes grown fat and slothful intoning from door to door: 'Chrismas geef! Chrismas geef!' The sound seemed to worm like a maggot through Clory's thoughts. 'Chrismas geef!' Not much Christmas gift for any of them. Abijah still putting her off.

Valentine's Day — and for once the dreaded sound of the tick-tack turned prankish and innocent. Not even the Deps could kill the innocent habits of childhood. Through all the dark lanes of the Dixie Mission, across all the dark back-door-yards young figures scudding, sly missives dropped. The cowering town echoing to the shrill childish call: 'Valentine night tonight!' And still Abijah was evasive.

Easter, and the world washed with lilac-smell. Clory stood in the doorway, watched the children with their painted eggs trudge off to the Black Hill, and realized that all winter long Abijah had eluded her grasp. Always moody, sometimes he came home and did not speak at all, and other times he wore the self-satisfied smirk of a cat that has just swallowed the mouse. At such times he was very solicitous, bringing her little gifts, getting up in the night to fetch her a drink of water — he was always nicest to her when his conscience bothered him. That he might be courting up another wife she dismissed as unworthy of even Abijah. Besides, he would announce the fact ... there was no one. That Young Julia Hansen — but no man in his right senses could see anything in that wench. 'Sheba had acted mysteriously all winter, but then, 'Sheba ... Oh, no, no. Abijah simply would not, could not do such a thing. She would not believe it. He was simply keeping her in suspense as long as possible. He had always been a tease ...

The Yeast Lady clicked the gate behind her and trotted briskly up the path. Clory smiled a welcome, but there was no answering smile on the other's wrinkled pink old face.

'It is yoost that you must come quickly. Dis t'ing, he is not right. Ve haf told her ofer and ofer but she vill not listen. Now you must come. *Ja, ja.*'

Without a word Clory went with her down the path, her heart pounding, wishing herself still back in the limbo of uncertainty where there was still hope. She thought she knew how a prisoner must feel going to his execution. The high-held head, the expression of serenity to mask from a curious world the shrinking gray fear within.

They picked up 'Sheba at her gate, and the three women marched on the Yeast Lady's house like an avenging army.

The girl upon his knee, Abijah did not even have the grace to get up when they walked in. There was a fatuous grin over his face, and Young Julia was being very kittenish stroking his beard. *The gopher's hind end*, thought Clory irrelevantly.

'Well!' said 'Sheba, arms akimbo, 'this *is* a pretty kettle of fish!'

Since his wives would not allow him to ignore them, Abijah decided to become thunderous and defy them.

'Ech! This is a blastie note! Is a mon to have no privacy?'

'Sheba snorted.

'You'll think privacy when I get through with you!... And

that shameless hussy there, why, I ought to snatch her bald-
headed!'

Young Julia shrugged and curled her lip.

'It's a free world!' she said in her hard young voice, looking
'Sheba up and down. 'If you're such an old hag you can't hold
your husband ——'

'Why, you little bitch!'

Shrill with wrath, 'Sheba started for the girl, but Clory put
out a restraining arm.

'No, 'Sheba, not that way!'

She went to Abijah, who was fulminating at the whole room,
and stood there silently staring up at him, a small person laced
with unexpected steel.

'You can't do this, you know,' she said quietly. 'It isn't fair
to either 'Sheba or me.'

'Clor-rinda should be the von to go!' indignantly interposed
the Yeast Lady from out of a past filled with cradles Lars had
made, the innumerable little kindnesses Clory had given, a big
bass-fiddle case that had coffined a baby.

Abijah's eyes dropped before Clory's wordless gaze, but he
pouted like a child that sees his candy threatened.

There was a rumpus at the back of the house and Serena bolted
in from the kitchen, blinking like an owl suddenly awakened in
the daytime.

'You shouldn't haf come!' gasped the Yeast Lady, wringing
her hands. 'The Deps!'

Serena was grim. 'I had to come. There are some things even
worse'n Lars going to jail.'

Her breast heaving, she stood in the doorway and eyed her
errant daughter. Young Julia hastily grasped Abijah's arm.

'That won't do you any good,' said Serena, marching up to the
girl, taking her by the shoulders, and shaking her until her teeth
rattled. 'You oughta be spanked within an inch of your life!
What do you mean, busting up a home? It ain't decent! That

man's got a grand-kid almost as old as you!' Punctuating each sentence with a shake.

Julia began to whimper but clung tighter than ever to Abijah, who went on shooting sparks indiscriminately.

'It — it ain't decent,' repeated Serena, at a loss for words. 'Think of your husband sleeping with another woman!'

But at that, Young Julia tossed her head and became very arch.

'It ain't the sleeping I worry about,' she said, smirking up at Abijah. 'It's the staying awake!'

Clory was suddenly nauseated. Staring at 'Sheba as if she had never seen her before, remembering the chit of a girl she herself had been, she was gripped with an acute and unexpected sympathy. Why, this was how 'Sheba must have felt! There was understanding in 'Sheba's own eyes and something like dour humor. And between the two women a queer and instantaneous bond.

'If only Lars vas here,' moaned the Yeast Lady in her cracked old voice, that somehow reminded Clory of a withered and faintly musty flower...

Defeat. That was the reason for the bond. Clory walked to the window and stared blindly out at the yellow sunlight. It was then she saw Lars, plunging out of the brush below the Temple, plunging across the deep sandy ruts of the road, glancing anxiously about as he ran, an old man harassed like a hunted fox but impelled at the moment by something stronger than fear.

'Here he comes,' said Clory dully, and the Yeast Lady trotted up to her, twittering like a perturbed mother-bird.

They heard the shot before they saw Lars fall — curiously, in segments...

'By God,' said Armstrong. 'You didn't cry "Halt."'

'Yes, I did, too. I said it the same time I fired!'

As dangerous as a rattler but not as generous, McGeary cackled nervously and frogged his eyes at the figure lying in the dust of the roadwav.

'Well, hell,' yawned Armstrong, weary of running down recalcitrant fugitives. 'It don't matter. One less to worry over.'

Still sitting their horses on the MacIntyre corner from where they had first seen Lars, the two men shaded their eyes against the sun and peered at the dust yet rising from the spot where he lay like a bundle of old rags.

'Yep, he's a goner,' said Armstrong. 'Damn fine shot, by God!'

He clapped McGeary on the back, and the two men clucked to their horses and wheeled about up the street, reeling slightly in their saddles from last night's hangover . . .

Such a withered old human creature. Too many years of unremitting toil, none of the softening comforts. He was as dry and brittle and brown as a chip. Abijah put him down on the couch and Lars looked up at them, his white mustache all rumpled and pink from the dust of the road, his eyes dark with the knowledge that his moments were numbered. Only time for a word, but he would not waste it on Young Julia, even though he had risked his life to do just that. Instead, his eyes silently beseeched her, eloquent with the counsel he had planned. But Young Julia, in spite of frightened tears, stared back with the hard, bright stubbornness of youth, until finally even she could bear that appeal no longer and buried her head on Abijah's shoulder. Abijah promptly patted her and became very manly and comforting.

This has done it, thought Clory, even as she hurried to and fro with wash-basin and warm water for the oozing red on Lars's blue jumper. *All it needed was a bit of grief to waken Abijah's pity. He'll never give her up now. She makes him feel too young and protective . . .*

Lars's eyes traveled on past Young Julia—what was done, was done, and he could teach her no more — stopped at Serena's face, and softened —*ja,* she had been a good wife, he had loved the children — came to rest at last on the Yeast Lady's. Comfort at

last. Love that was like a kiss given and taken trembled in the air
between them, and Clory thought of the long road Lars had traveled, to go down at last before an assassin's bullet. The long road
away from another, older world, across an ocean, across a continent, to meet at last in a bawdyhouse in a little frontier town a
girl with the Madonna look that Lars believed never quite dies in
any woman, no matter how fallen.

But it had been worth the price. His eyes promised the Yeast
Lady that. He had no regrets. He had staked his hope on her
and she had not failed him. He had staked his hope on the Church
and it had not failed him.

Belatedly remembering that he was a servant of God, Abijah
knelt by the bed.

'Would ye like to be administer-red to, Brother Hansen?'

But Lars shook his head. His smile was already like a memory.

'Celestial Glory, Brother Hansen. Ye'll go to meet Abraham,
Isaac, and Jacob...'

Again that faint shake of the head. 'I — don't care anything
aboot — Abraham, Isaac, and Jacob' — the labored whisper
suddenly strengthened — 'but if I don't find the Dixieites in
heaven I'll ask for a transfer!'

Clory thought of the cookies her children had eaten in this
house with its huge stone chimney and faintly old-world air.
Wooden sabots still on the mantel — smögasbord — and years of
happiness. There was something infinitely reassuring to her in
the tenderness that pulsed like a warm glow between the little
old man on the bed and the little old lady sitting beside him,
holding his hand. If out of the stuff of life human beings could
create such goodness, such trust and devotion, what did it matter,
a failure or two?

'...as a shock of corn fully ripe,' summed up Abijah, thinking
the end had come, but Lars's eyes fluttered open, there was one
last breath left —

'Vhere did I find you, Yulia?'

The Yeast Lady's smile was strong and confident.
'Vhat were you doin' there, Lars?'

6

Abijah's children came to her. Joseph, his mischief buried beneath layers of maturity, beetling his dark brows, pulling his superb black whiskers, looking so much like his father twenty-six years ago that Clory caught her breath. Samuel, still talking about his mission — 'Now, when I was in the States...' — Abraham, the slow plodding farmer, the twins from Silver Reef, Nephi sobered with the cares of married life, Lehi with flowing tie and drooping mustache, still very much the young buck. Clory watched them filing in, crowding the room, and could have sworn she saw the shadow of a towheaded one, taller than all the rest. 'Good riddance to bad rubbish,' he would have said.

But the others crossed their knees, held their hats, and cleared their throats. A solemn conclave of sons.

'Ma says she's done all she can,' said Joseph, the spokesman, 'and so we've come to you. In the first place, what we can't understand is why he *wants* this — this girl. At his age. He's already got two wives, and one still young' — his eyes added, 'and still pretty.' ... 'We can't understand it!'

Lehi retained enough youth to see humor in the situation.

'Well, you know Ma's old saying — "A new broom sweeps clean!"'

Samuel uncrossed and recrossed his legs angrily.

'He must be out of his mind — or in his second childhood! Why, he's old enough to be her grandfather!'

Lehi chuckled.

'There's no fool like an old fool!'

Joseph pressed his fingertips together and brought them back to the point.

'Aunt Clory, even if he can't take Ma, he owes it to you and your children' (Jimmie and Tempie stared wide-eyed from the corner) 'to give you what care and attention he can instead of marrying and rearing another family. It doesn't show respect to either Ma or you, and we want you to stop it.'

Stop it. Clory smiled at him sadly.

'Your father has every right in the matter, you know. Your mother might have stopped my marriage . . . but she didn't. We all believe the principle ——'

'Ye-es,' Joseph grudgingly admitted, thinking of the risk he had run coming here, his own plural wife on the Underground. 'Yes, we all believe the principle, but we don't want this marriage, and I'll bet your own children don't want it, either!'

He turned demandingly on Jimmie and Tempie. But Jimmie could find no words. All he could do was to scowl and make fists of his hands. As for Tempie — she was sorely bewildered trying to imagine her father even liking Young Julia, since she herself had heard him say a thousand times that anyone who wore bangs and a bustle would go to hell.

Joseph came desperately back to Clory.

'This marriage ain't right!'

But Clory smiled at his vehemence and spread wide her hands as if she were emptying them of something . . .

And I am emptying them, she thought, listening to Abijah's farewell speech in Sunday meeting. *I am emptying them, my hands and my heart.*

'Ech, it's like tearing the hear-rt out of my bosom!' thundered Abijah, thumping his chest. (And he really does look as if he meant it, decided Clory, with his beard all trembly . . .) 'Aigh, the sacrifices we make in the name of religion! It ain't only the women who suffer in plurality . . . when I think of Bathsheba, the love of my youth and the wife of my heart, and how I am having tae hur-rt her' — there were tears now, on his cheeks and in his voice, that voice that could charm a stone image — 'and when I think of my third in the Covenant, my young lass left alane, and my twa young bairns — *I* am the one to suffer-r!'

He had to stop to unfurl his handkerchief from his tail-coat pocket and blow his nose, and Clory wanted to applaud. *Well done!* she thought. *Now he can go off with the sympathy of the community. Handsome Mac, the martyr and hero* . . .

He was magnificent at his sing, that final evening sing with his sons all about him (Clory had coaxed them to be there), and Young Julia (after all, Lars had wanted no mourning) looking like Lady Astor with Devonshire ruffles below elbow sleeves, kilted skirt, and the worsted jersey that clung to her figure with such obvious devotion.

All the old songs — 'Kathleen Mavourneen, the gray dawn is breaking' — you had to hand it to Abijah. He was invincible. There was something about the proud tilt of the leonine gray head, something about his unquenchable enthusiasm for living, his amazing vitality, something about the swing of the melodies, some subtle defiance for hardship and heartbreak . . .

It may be for years and it may be forever . . .

Clory could not bear it, and, pleading a headache, left them singing there on 'Sheba's doorstep, singing to the stars, and crossed the dooryard to the sanctuary of her own house and let the tears come.

But when Abijah came to tell her good-bye she was collected again, armored in pride, going casually about the business of preparing for bed, and when he stooped under the lintel the glance she managed to fling him was indifferent.

Abijah was at a loss . . . Curse a fyllie, she had always left him at a loss. He had thought of himself as going off in a blaze of glory, kissing Clor-rinda's tears, this hurts me more than it does you, but the work in Logan will be hard and you need a rest, I shall think of you down here as resting — a few sentimental reveries over the past, aigh, the past, the past, we've had a good time, my lass, but what will be, will be, and we maun think of us all as meeting on the Other Side . . .

Instead, she was actually flippant. She made him feel like a foolish boy ... And then unexpectedly all their years together did overwhelm him. His voice trembled, he forgot everything except her nearness, and went to take her in his arms, but Clory was too quick for him.

She held out a polite hand, and her smile in the shadows of the lamp was hard and bright.

'Good-bye!' Flippancy to cover up hurt, never to let him know. 'Good-bye while you're handy!'

Good-bye. The word seemed to spurt from under his feet as he walked away from her down the path. *Good-bye.* The word lay heavily on the air. *Good-bye.* She was limp for a moment, thinking how it would feel to be old, to be finished, alone and lonely, with life still unappeased in her heart ...

7

Pal was as indignant as she could make herself be with the thought of David coming home in the fall.

'I think you should've told him!'

But Clory shook her head, sinking down for a moment on the nearest rock.

'No, if he didn't want to take me for myself, I wouldn't let him take me just because I'm pregnant again! Besides, who knows, I'll probably lose this one, too.'

Pal's kind eyes were anxious. There was a look of evanescence about Clory.

'This polygamy business' — Pal sighed and dug her heels into the black rubble and began to climb. 'I tell you, a woman has to be *hard-gutted* ...' She thought with sudden amazement of all these months she had lived on debts owing her husband. She, Pal, going out after debts long outlawed, and getting 'em, too. Astonishing how many debts easy-going David had let pile up!

Clory said nothing and the two silently went on with the climb,

Pal panting and puffing, her rolls of flesh jouncing as she dragged her bulk up the face of the hill, and Clory little and wiry. Two middle-aged figures outlined against the lemon-yellow sky of sunset.

It had been Pal's idea — to get away from the care of the house and the children for an hour, the worry about husbands. 'We used to climb these hills all the time when we were girls,' said Pal. 'It'll be good for us to get away from *people* for a while!' As Pal's amiable chatter bounced back from the imperturbable lava boulders, Clory quietly gathered the candytuft springing between the stones.

'You're takin' it too hard!' 'Sheba had scolded ('Sheba with her beaked nose, her defiant shoebutton eyes, her indomitable body that seemed to toughen as it grew older. Death would never come after 'Sheba — she herself would just decide it was time some day and lift the latch... 'But no monkey-business!' Clory thought she could hear her say). 'You're takin' it too hard!' 'Sheba had scolded. 'Land's sakes, what's a man more or less? "A wooden mother's better than a golden father!"' 'Sheba, who had suddenly become her friend, just as she had been when Abijah was on his mission. 'Sheba, her ally.

Clory began to laugh hysterically and sat down upon a boulder, the weak tears rolling over her cheeks. Pal stared in affright.

'Yesterday,' gasped Clory, 'yesterday she brought me a lot of old beer bottles she'd found behind the saloon — "Have to make *some* use of the danged place!" she said, and began to stick 'em in the ground and make a border for my path — *my* path!'

Life and its muddles... You started out with your toys all shiny and new, and one by one they got broken and scattered. ... Suddenly she hated Abijah so bitterly that she resented even the part of him that was Jimmie — and so much of him *was* Jimmie, his shock of hair, his fierce masculinity. But he should not be like his father!... And her mind was off on its old hunt down the years, ferreting out mistakes, subtracting her excuses. In what way had she failed? How could she have done differently? And always the recurrent torment — would the shadow of her failure rest upon the children?

In spite of her resolve to be sensible, not to get emotional about this thing, her mind went on playing 'Sheba's game. 'Sheba, who so loved the old person's pastime of shuffling and re-dealing the lives of her friends. This one should have married that one, 'Sheba would say, tracing all the ills that had happened since to that single omission. 'Sheba shaking her head darkly — 'She married the wrong man in a fit of pique and look what the kids turned out to be!' But, protested Clory, if she'd married the other man they'd be different kids! They wouldn't be the same humans or . . . maybe they wouldn't be here at all! And so it's a circle and you finally conclude it's an insane scramble — either that, or else it's all planned for some Purpose bigger than you or anybody else and you couldn't change any of it if you tried.

Religion teaches about free will, but Clory couldn't see that. It wasn't free will that made her marry Abijah or love Free or lose the babies. Mostly the last certainly wasn't free will. Maybe Someone Else's will, but not hers. . . . And her circling thoughts bumped up against the same stone wall: The lack was hers, the fault was hers. There was no doubt about it. Abijah said when people were in tune with God they got a testimony as a sort of natural consequence. Therefore if you didn't have a testimony it meant you were too full of faults to find God. . . . But you couldn't be less than honest with yourself, could you? She had fooled herself a lot, but lately she'd been getting her thinking straightened out, and no matter how it hurt to face facts she wasn't going back to the old blind state — she *was* a failure, and that's why all her toys had turned to dust in her hands.

Or it might be that a testimony was like other escapes — like thinking you were beautiful and good when you really weren't . . . people covering up their little shivering souls with a lot of fancy thoughts because they couldn't bear the truth. Clory didn't believe a lot of people had a testimony who were surest of it. If God was the kind of Person who paid much attention to the people who shouted, 'Look at me, how good I am!' then she didn't want to know Him, anyway. 'Sheba thought she was Beautiful and Good, but she wasn't. Abijah thought he was Always Right, and he wasn't.... But maybe — Clory's mind bumped again at the stone wall — *maybe thinking they're so full of faults and I'm not makes me just as smug as they are....* So all you can do is face the fact of your failure and try to strip the treacherous mind of excuses ...

Staring blindly out over the town, already scorched with the dragon's breath of summer, chewing a stalk of candytuft, she said to Pal, 'I'm going crazy.'

Pal laughed and shook her and pointed excitedly.

'Look, Clory! Look! There is the cave and here are the sego lilies Tutsegabbett showed us, remember? When we wanted to run away. What little fools we were! Look — look down there at the homes and the stores and the Tabernacle and Temple, all the things we've helped to build!'

But all Clory could see were the sego lilies at her feet, the sego lilies that had no right to be as lovely and unchanged when she herself had grown so old and finished — and unwanted ...

One night when summer lay like a hot hand over the earth, Gottlieb Uttley brought her a tub of grapes — great black grapes bursting their jackets with juice. He stood there in her stifling little room, huge and red-faced and kind, wreathed in his familiar hearty odors of garlic and sweat and the barnyard.

Heat had sucked her dry and she felt like a lifeless husk as she welcomed him, found voice enough to offer him a chair. But Gottlieb did not want to sit. She could see his slow brain working in his little eyes. Her pregnancy ... Abijah's going ... the Deps ... His great hands opened and closed with futile rage, and she noted impersonally the sweat oozing from his heaving chest,

soaking the already wet blue shirt, dripping onto the leather
trouser-belt.

'I shed blood on 'em mit the axe!' bellowed Gottlieb, thrusting
his head forward, glaring about the room as if Clory's tormentors
might be lurking in the corners.

She could see him groping frantically for words.

'My Sonuvabitch Spring she do bretty vell now, garten stuffs,
blenty water, melons, blenty grass und flowers. I give you all
of him, I give you my Rose Cow — uh, I give you anyting! I
give you anyting! If you marry me!'

Her refusal was so gentle and yet so absent — as if she could
not quite bring her spirit back from where it had gone — that
he turned upon himself and began to slap his own ears until
they puffed out like red sausages.

'*You*, Gottlieb! You pig tamn fool!'

And then, stealing a glance at her as if he would surprise into
being the Clory he had once known: 'How you lika dat?'...

She could not help it. She felt as if she were weighted down
with the woe of all the women of Deseret — all those thousands
of women caught in the snare of polygamy. She could not shake
off the feeling of failure. She had cheated Jimmie and Tempie out
of their birthright. None of the sunlit peaks of life for them —
nothing but the shadowed valleys of poverty. During the long
sleepless nights all the phantom figures of the past came trooping
around her, pointing accusing fingers. Free — 'A world where
men can marry the girls they love?' Kissy — 'Mamma, what is
dying?' Willie — 'We are living not for ourselves but for our
children.'... She had failed, the Pioneers had failed, Zion had
failed. And the splendid dreams that had brought them across a
continent to settle at last on the sands of the desert ('because
nobody else wants it') were idiot-babblings, signifying nothing...

'You should go to the Temple,' they told her, Pal and even
'Sheba (who had lately annexed religion and held it like a sword
against life) — 'Go and be baptized for your brother, your father

and mother' (her mother, who was probably dead by now).
'Go and have them sealed to you so you can be with them on the
Other Side and you'll feel better!'

And so she went to the Temple.... 'Hot as Tophet, isn't it?'
said Charley Hichinoper, the new President. And then for a time
there was peace and the soothing details of the ceremony, her
feet taking steps, her voice mechanically repeating formulas, her
mind gratefully suspended in that gray limbo where there were no
thoughts ... It was 'Old Fifty-Cents-on-the-Dollar' who shocked
her into wakefulness again. Brother Zebedee Trupp up for a
Temple session from his hideout on the Arizona Strip. Zebedee
with Sis and Miny, his sour old first wife and Bella, more wizened and gopher-like than ever ('I'm as much a virgin — !')
— Zebedee with his one tooth gleaming unctuously and the familiar acquisitive gleam in his little pig-eyes — the wife-gather-
ing gleam.

Zebedee clutching her hand moistly and trying to look holy
in his Temple robes.

'My own dear sister whom I have not seen since leaving the
celestial halls of heaven' — a moist squeeze — 'my very own
dear sister in the spirit world. The Lord has just revealed it
to me ...'

Clory fled in horror, ran all the way home, and even in the
stifling dusk, banged the door tight against all the nameless horrors of widowhood.

8

They were coming home, those heroes of the Cotton Mission,
Erastus Snow and David Wight. Each with the State's ubiquitous
blessing, five-dollar bill, and fifteen-dollar store order for a suit
of clothes.

Not since Brother Brigham's day had such an air of festivity
pervaded the town. Bands and flying flags. A sumptuous fruit

feast in the basement of the Tabernacle. Fall grapes brushed
with the bloom of the shadows on the pastel mountains, melons
like the new green springing up in the hedgerows after the rains,
quinces as golden as the autumn sunshine. And flowers — those
wide windowsills of the Tabernacle dripping zinnias, tawny tiger
lilies, fringed and spicy pinks, Sweet William clusters, and yellow
pools of golden rod.

Pal and Lucy in a very mania of activity... please, Clory,
may Patience-Elizabeth borrow your tortoise-shell combs for the
welcoming parade? David must not know we've gone hungry,
he must not know we've lacked a thing — not a thing!...
Marianne and Aunt Ket and Martha are all dolled up, but Lucy
and I will smile so hard David'll never notice we're wearing the
same dresses as when he left!

Clory gave of her few gewgaws, the flowers in her garden, the
fruit Gottlieb still insisted on bringing her. And when the children had gone and the neighbors had gone, 'Sheba and the Yeast
Lady and Serena, when she could no longer hear even the tender
shrilling of the fife, she went, herself, out between the up-ended
beer bottles of the path, out between the roses distilling themselves into the dusk, up through the quiet streets, diagonally
across to the square where the old bowery had stood, up past the
T.O. to the Tabernacle, puffing somewhat now because the street
began to climb.... On this corner the Social Hall she had once
thought so grand and now seemed such a meager old maid of a
building. Was it Free in his buckskins she could see standing
there in the doorway?... And then Main Street was through
with and Mount Hope began. A road that spiraled and elbowed
and presently dropped you off with the soaring red flanks of the
Sugar Loaf at your back and the world spread out down
below...

The Welcoming Parade. Clory watched it, dwarfed with distance, the Martial Band and the Silver Band, instruments catching the last gleam of the sun, Brother Wheelock, home from

prison, again ignoring the Deps and the Underground, being very youthful on the drums whose gay tattoo echoed among hills that such a short time ago had known only the coyote chorus.

Time had no meaning up here. She sat there watching the carriages and wagons spill their little ant-like people into the Tabernacle, itself ant-like from here. Watching them spill out again, the bands roll tootling home. . . . The twilight lay in crimson pools among the boulders, stroked the Black Ridge with a mist of lavender, a singularly clear mist that left the valleys in shadow and rode only the slopes with a nebulous softness. You could drown yourself in that mist . . .

Erastus found her there, an older Erastus with flabby paunch and the skin of his cheeks hanging in folds. He came toward her over the rocks, and his shaved head and face gave him a queerly innocent expression like a baby who has leaped suddenly into maturity. He did not seem at all surprised to see her there.

He sank down beside her with a sigh of utter content ('I'll steal only a moment,' he'd promised Ket. 'I've got to get the feel of the whole valley before I know I'm really home'), dangled his legs over the edge, and bent his gaze upon Clory. Apostle Snow — who had always swung off on a side road because of a red flag sticking up and a silent call for help, leaving his council stewing in its own juice the whole evening. Apostle Snow, with his eyes full of compassion and understanding. He studied Clory's swollen figure. Her lips twisted.

'Abijah's last gift to me. It would be the only one to carry the whole way.'

Suddenly she began to talk as she had not talked in months.

' . . . so you see I'm a failure. I'm like Free — I didn't obey counsel either. Why, I haven't even got a testimony!'

Erastus writhed his lips. 'Ptsahh!'

A testimony. 'I know that Joseph Smith was a prophet of God. I know that the Gospel is true.' — the old phrases he had heard all his life.

'Prison has taught me many things, Clorinda Agatha ... But I'll tell you — I'm not sure what a testimony is, myself.'

He laughed a little. Heresy!

'The way I look at it, the thing we've got that's immortal is an Idea. And maybe that's why we've been persecuted. ... Maybe, human nature being what it is, the world will always stamp upon that Idea ... But you can't kill it, Clorinda Agatha — it's older than the world.'

His words seemed to come from out of the past, as if they had lived forever, as old as time, as old as the rocks.

'*Thou shalt love thy neighbor* ... Everybody's reaching for it, only some religions are going 'cross-lots, some kitty-cornered ... None of us have yet come within a million miles of it, but the big thing is that we try. And as long as we try and admit we're trying, there's hope. A mosque or a pagoda or a Tabernacle ... and maybe we're a little closer to it in the Tabernacle because we've gone out for it deliberately, colonized for it. I believe that to be Zion's mission to mankind, Clorinda Agatha — to create among these barren hills a little inviolate world, a little sanctuary where the Brotherhood of Man and the Fatherhood of God are not just words but living, breathing realities ...'

He came back to Clory then, to her own personal problem, and reached over and patted her hand.

Dusk was seeping from the floor of the valley like a wave that would engulf them, but for the moment they were caught up into light.

'Some of us may lose, Clorinda Agatha. There are bound to be mistakes, and we've made our share, and right now Zion is reeling from body-blows ...'

He reached into his pocket and brought out the Church's last *Epistle*.

'President Taylor dying in exile ... our leaders hunted like rabbits ... "The war is openly and undisguisedly made upon our religion," he read. "To induce men to repudiate that, every en-

couragement is given.... The man who agrees to discard his
wives, escapes imprisonment and is applauded; while the man
who will not — admit his past life has been a fraud and a lie, who
will not say to the world, 'I intended to deceive my God, my
brethren, and my wives by making covenants I did not expect to
keep' — is besides being punished to the full extent of the law,
compelled to endure the reproaches, taunts, and insults of a
brutal judge.... Whether it be life or death, freedom, or imprisonment, prosperity or adversity ..."'

Erastus shook his bald head.

'No man knows ...'

And then his voice grew impassioned again, his worried old eyes
bright with the Dream:

'You may lose, Clorinda Agatha. I may lose. *Zion* may lose,
for the time. But the Idea' — he saw all those myriads, the op-
pressed and downtrodden, marching hand in hand straight into
the dawn of a better world — 'the Idea *can't* lose.'

The shadows of the twilight gave his tired old face turned up
to the stars the stern tenderness of an archangel.

9

The day was cold and drizzly — not a very good day, Erastus
decided, on which to go looking for miracles. Which also seemed
to be the thought uppermost in the minds of the people trudging
along in the mud behind him, if he were to judge by facial expressions. But his conviction had been with him so long that it had
taken root and become part of him, like a leg or an arm. What
must look to the others like the silly whim of two not-quite-bright
people still suffering from the hallucinations of prison was to him
and David an accomplished fact — all they had to do was to con-
vince the rest of the community. The Idea was immortal, and
therefore the physical means of realizing it must be immortal.
Twenty-six years of praying (which was what it had amounted

to), and the answer was at hand. As simple as that. Like a mathematical formula ... x plus y equals z, world without end. ...

Everybody was there to see this legerdemain. All the colonists. Even Tutsegabbett, old and shriveled but still faithful. Some strangers in the group, hangers-on from the saloons, mining men from Silver Reef. Even the women, shepherding youngsters, slogged through the mud after the men.

And then the river doubled, as if a giant hand had shoved it in the ribs. David, striding ahead of the others, in his eagerness fairly skimming over the ground, rounded a corner, climbed a rise, pebbles and mud skidding from under his feet ... swung about to face them, his eyes alight.

'This is it!' he shouted. 'I knew I'd recognize the spot!'

The others stared up at him until he yelled at the stupidity in their faces.

'Why, the hogsback, of course! I'm standing on it! See?' He pointed a shaking arm toward the rocky finger poking out into the stream. 'We'll cut a section from right under where I'm standing to make the "spill" — dry-dam the river over there, throw part of it over the "spill" and part of it through the canal on the other side — don't you see?'

He flung up his arm like a — a triumphant gladiator, Erastus thought. That was it. Straddling his legs against a background of meandering Virgin and tumbled mesa and black hill and ... and nothing, with a foot on the prostrate figure of his enemy — Pah Roosh, fallen at last.

But the others were still skeptical. Bishop Gardner, Brother Peabody, Young Miles, Eardley, Ferrano, 'Old '46,' even gentle Jacob Hamblin. Pratt, the apostate, was suddenly all engineer again.

'My Lord, look at the country your canal 'ud go through! Why, you'd have to hold a man out over the point of that cliff even to put in your surveying peg! This is one job you'll have to turn over to the Three Nephites!'

He guffawed.

'By gadder, Wight,' said Shadrach, chewing speculatively, 'if you dam her from the spill to the left bank she'll take a plug twenty, twenty-five foot high and at least six hundred foot acrost!'

'Of course!' crowed David, 'of rock cemented with mud and at least fifteen feet wide on the top . . . Did you find the blue clay?'

Shadrach nodded slowly.

'But ——'

'Then don't you see?' David's words tumbled. 'Diversion works — sand gate — iron gate and windlass to regulate spillway . . .'

Erastus heard him like a man in a dream. The miracle had happened. Only faith to begin with. No factories nor industries, even very little farming . . . and then Silver Reef. And now that the Reef was petering out . . . a dam at last. A dam after twenty-six years of dams and floods and pigweed greens and Virgin bloat. But a miracle should be accompanied with trumpet blasts and earthquakes. The thing was . . . was too easy.

'But a job like this'll take a lot of money!' Charley Hichinoper went on arguing.

Ole Oleson nodded, his big ears flapping at the stream he had wrestled with most of his life.

David looked enthusiastically about as if he expected greenbacks to sprout out of bushes.

'Wells-Fargo? . . . What about it, Brother Hunt?'

Zadoc Hunt frowned and let them hang on his words a moment.

'We-e-ell, land's no good without water and my company's got as much staked in this country as you have, Dave!'

Shadrach Gaunt spat and dug a meditative forefinger under his still black braids.

'But still . . . just plain sensible, Brother Wight — how in hell are you going to git all that big machinery you wrote home about?'

David was still the undaunted schoolmaster, looking over his class for some bright pupil to supply the answer.

A man stepped out of the crowd, a short, commonplace man, smiling a little at his part in the unconscious drama.

'My name's Greg,' he said, holding out his hand to Erastus. 'James Greg. I had a contract with the railroad to bring it from Milford to Modena and we got held up because of the snow. Maybe you don't know it, but the roads on all sides of you folks are blocked. Well, I'm held up here with a lot of teams on my hands and a gang of Irishmen eating their heads off in Silver Reef now. I'm interested in getting feed for my stock and my men until spring — I got all the equipment, and rock men and powder men — I'll take my pay in land, and I reckon the men'll take theirs in water scrip — do the job for practically nothing just to git 'em fed ...'

Pal and Lucy came running and stumbling over the rocks and hummocks of mud.

'Clory!' gasped Pal. 'Clory! Listen to the men yell! Hear 'em? Do you know what they're cheerin' for? The Mission's saved! Oh, Clory, think what that means! *We've done it!* The Mission ...'

'Land's sakes,' said 'Sheba. 'She ain't interested in missions! Can't you see she's about to have a baby?'

CHAPTER XVII

I dreamed as I lay on my bed of sweet slumber
That Saint Peter, who bosses the gate and the keys,
Refused to admit quite an army in number
Because of their lives of most indolent ease.

An old Dixie Pilgrim next made his appearance.
With rag-tattered jeans and a broken straw hat;
Meekly bowing, he asked for a ticket of clearance,
Said Peter, 'You need no such ticket as that.'

Said Peter, 'Good friend, we are all well acquainted
With all Dixie Pilgrims and loved 'Rastus Snow —
They are worthy to enter and will surely be sainted' —
As he passed through the gate, Peter bowed very low.
                    Requiem
He rests from his labors, from dread chills and fever,
His long-handled shovel he left down at Price;
He heeds not the roaring of old Virgin River...
He's fumbling his grub-sack 'neath tree Paradise.

ANOTHER Clory MacIntyre recently found this final effort of David's in the elegant scrawl of the old *Vepricula*, yellowed and rat-eaten and belatedly put under glass by the Daughters of the Utah Pioneers. The last issue of the *Vepricula*, a copy or two of the little *Cactus*, one of Brother Wheelock's dog-eared hymn books, Abijah's old red-backed ledger — 'I exhorted

with him about living with a woman alone as housekeeper ...' —
The militant righteousness of seventy years ago pops out at her
from the dust of the pages.

Here they are, all about her, the precious household gods preserved with such infinite care through flights and mobbings and
Indian battles. An Enoch straw hat, frayed around the edge, a
pair of the barrel staves Ole Oleson's wives used for hoops, spinning wheels, and the hanks of cotton and silk, dyed indigo-blue
and madder-red, yellow from rabbit-brush blossoms, green from
creosote leaves, shit-brindle from wild sage. Colors outlasting
time ... see this cheerful strip of rag carpet beside Aunt Ket
Snow's old loom.

Here an orchestrone from the glamorous days of Silver Reef,
Abijah's prayer bell, 'Sheba's cathedral clock with its hoarse
old-man's voice silenced forever, Clory's dulcimer with one paddle gone and the wires all bent and twisted. Here are the dishes,
'Sheba's Spode pieces, the iron spiders and patty pans, the tea-
caddies, the gourd bowls, Abijah's mustache cup, Clory's Nauvoo
Temple plate ('Holiness to the Lord, House of the Lord') given
to her by her father in Winter Quarters, the Utah Pioneer Jubilee
mug (1847), with its scroll of oxen and handcarts and Indians.
And here on the wall are the picture throws, the lambrequins and,
antimacassars, Clory's gilt framed motto in cross-stitch scrim
('Welcome to all' in shaded pink and green), Will's brown-paper
wreath (clasped hands and gilt doves). In this glass showcase
Willie's life-preserver she brought from England in '57, all mildewed and rotting, a baby's nainsook christening gown that might
have been Kissy's, and the schoolbooks. On the fly leaf of Abijah's
Book of Mormon we find inscribed in the round graceful letters
of mid-Victorian penmanship:

> The books we think we ought to read
> Are poky, dull, and dry.
> The books that we should like to read
> We are afraid to buy.

The flourish following these lines was long and curling, and then the book had been shut hastily while the ink was still wet because it was all blotted and blurred. We can only guess at the identity of the rebel. Perhaps it was Clory herself, whose spirit so beat against the bars... Time-eaten schoolbooks, and *Little Lily's Travels*. Shake the last, and dried rose petals drift out of the pages — surely from Clory's Giant of Battles which Gottlieb brought back from one of his freighting trips (roses that were so hard to raise!), and which has now grown taller than Clory herself, and quite mad with crimson-hearted blooms.

Here are the guns and bullet-molds, stuffed now with the brittle half-cured leaves of the Paiute tobacco Shadrach Gaunt raised; the sword that fought in Carthage Jail for the Prophet, Free's double-barreled flintlock that went after Navajos, his brass powder pouch with a dried bergamot leaf in the very bottom of it.

Here is even *Dr. Chase's Prescription*, the old Doctor Book that belonged to Stiddy Weeks, and along with dust a younger Clory finds among its yellowed leaves an old tithing receipt of Abijah's dated 'City of Joseph, 1845' (entitling the bearer to the Privilege of the Baptismal Font), a piece of T.O. scrip, and one of the tin Bishop's Chips that paid for goods in 'Chips and Whetstones,' a whetstone being a 'thing you sharpen an axe with when you haven't got an axe.'

And here in this corner is Clory's rosewood desk, grown too old-fashioned for her children's children, after all, and beside it, her old hair trunk. Within the trunk, among the cobwebs and the faint odor of bergamot, lie a hooped-skirt frame of almost eighty years ago, a little boned bodice with demure round collar, a silver caster, a bottle of consecrated beania oil, and her old red sunbonnet, threadbare and shapeless but still defiantly gay. And down in the very bottom a cigar box containing a doll's patch-quilt (a square of the old red cassimere, one of the sheep's-gray linsey-woolsey, another of the 'grass' cloth dress Abijah brought back from his mission). Next to the patch-quilt is something tied up in a bit of buckskin that might have been an unfinished glove or even a piece of the pants over which Free suffered . . . loosen the knots and nestled there are a cut-glass perfume bottle, one of Jim's baby-curls, Brother's wooden teething ring, Kissy's circle comb, and the large star-ringed copper penny Free wore next his heart. On the floor of the trunk is a layer of bergamot leaves and among them a random bit of prickly pear Clory chewed so desperately . . . a handful of bergamot leaves that crumble to dust when touched, keepsakes . . . and memories.

Inanimate things, speaking with a thousand voices out of the past. What do they say to that younger Clory musing upon the Temple as beautiful in that desert country as an iceberg, upon the Tabernacle, symbol of a people's self-discipline, upon the courthouse, so purely New England that one expects to see at any sunrise some hard-gutted battler for individual liberty standing upon the portico reading the Bill of Rights? What do they say to that younger Clory musing out the window upon the ailanthus trees planted by the Pomologist Club, and now grown so tall to sprinkle tawny seeds upon the roof?

Only the young and fragrant ghosts can tell, hurrying out of the old daguerreotypes that have to be turned into the light just so to catch a glimpse of laughing eyes and tinted cheeks and clove pinks in shining hair — only the young and fragrant ghosts hurrying out of the portraits on the walls, scurrying along the polished hallways, drawn together with hushed laughter and whispered consultations. The dewy-eyed young ghosts in sunbonnets and ribbon-plumed calicoes . . . Eliza, who lost her child and her reason; lovely Sister Miles, who lost her life; Bella Trupp, still 'as much a virgin' — all the valiant tribe, forever young, forever anticipating the whole incredible adventure. And they put ringleted heads together and advance upon that younger Clory and hold out their arms to her. For a moment a shadow falls across their smiling faces, their eager eyes grow beseeching, their soft pink palms calloused and blistered. 'We hand it across the years,' they say to her. 'Your heritage. What have you made of it? Where is the brave new world?'

2

Perhaps she had cried 'Wolf! Wolf!' once too often, thought Clory, and the children could not get 'Sheba to come. But it was certain, this time — the pains were unmistakable. Where *were* the children? She wanted them here — to hold their sane youth against the dreadful shadows that advanced toward her beyond the fringe of lamplight. Shadows that spoke in the gruff old voice of Stiddy Weeks — 'You must not ever have any more children ... you must not ever have any more children ...' Shadows that howled at her with mocking, goatish glee. Shadows that saw Loneliness swoop down upon her in the long black nights when her hands groped for an empty pillow, and sometimes it was Free who should have been there and sometimes Abijah, but the groping hands fell away again and the unkissed lips closed over little sighs.

'You must not have any more children ...' But she *was* having a baby — to please Abijah, who was building up his dynasty with another woman.

The pains knifed into her again. Brainless, brutish terror drove her up out of the bed, into the Mother Hubbard, along the black street like a small lost gnome.... There, that pain was gone; hurry between the pains, a matter of putting one foot in front of the other, never looking behind you to see how scared you are. There ... that must be 'Sheba's house now. And that figure looming up out of the darkness one of the children ... but it's on all fours. Why would Jimmie be on all fours? ... That old dog of Hansen's? ... Make the stiff lips close over the words, 'Here, Shep' — then it jumped.

A wrenching and tearing. The smell of blood. Clory stooped

and picked the dead baby up in her apron and turned and walked back home.

This business of dying was just as Willie said, not half so bad as living. If only the voices wouldn't keep calling her back from the softness, the peace . . . At first she thought she must be sinking into that first early bed of cat-tail fuzz, but then her hands explored the mattress and she knew. Her house and its memories rose all about her, the house that had once been a dugout, and she knew the place of rest toward which she was drifting was really death. But it was glorious and she felt a vague resentment toward the voices, like timeless buzzing bees, that kept calling her back.

'Clory never crosses anybody . . .' (That would be Pal.) 'She's like a well. No matter how long you tell her your troubles she's still up to the brim with sympathy . . .'

That's kind of you, Pal. She wanted to say it, but the effort was too great.

'I've buried my whole neighborhood and laid them out.' (That would be 'Sheba's comfortable voice — 'Sheba was always comfortable around deaths.) 'I hope she goes in her sleep — it's a nice way to go as long as it has to be done. I don't think a person ought to have to *know* about it!' (Let's see. . . . what was 'Sheba's record now? A thousand bodies?) It was queer to think of herself as a body — queer and not true. For the part of her that counted would be gathering little wild-stars along the Milky Way. . . .

On and on. Days merging into other days. Already the footprints of Indian summer blotted out by the first autumn rains, sliding down invisible gray ribbons, thrumming gently on the roof. Until she grew impatient with life and its clutching hands. Why wouldn't they let her go?

She lay suspended in a dream of peace. For the first time in her life no decisions to make, no counsel to obey . . . It was

ridiculously easy. All you had to do was let go and the tide
carried you out ... She was vaguely aware now and then that
grief lay beyond the fringe of her dream, but the thought only
made her impatient — yes, and pitying for the poor blind fools
who lived beyond the fringe.

Only once did reality stab through her dream. 'Sheba — with
her ideas of comfort — came whispering: 'Clory, can you hear
me? Do you understand what I'm saying? I thought you'd like
to know — I've just had a letter from Abijah and he says Young
Julia's had a miscarriage ...'

And suddenly that indestructible something that had always
been Clory began to bubble and laugh until it routed even the
dream.

'She's losing her mind!' gasped 'Sheba.

A soundless howl broke from her lips. She panted, and was
lost again in another convulsion of mirth.

The distressed faces around the bed swam toward her and she
tried to reassure them.

'Clory! Clory! What's the matter?' That would be Hannah
Merinda.

But all she could do was to shake her head and laugh up at them
with her eyes.

What an awful thing to happen to Abijah!

And then the faces swam away again and the dream returned.

Sometimes she sang, little catches of the songs that had defied
a wilderness. 'Come, come, ye saints ...' Singing as if she wrote
in her heart's blood her own wistful cadenza, singing as if to seal
with her blood the final resolving chords. And sometimes in the
long hush of the night, when the watchers around her bed dozed
sprawling in stark unlovely attitudes, she would hear the Tabernacle town clock striking and know with a sort of detached om-
niscience that it was a senseless sound, because nothing ever really
dies. Even those toil-stooped 'Clary Dutchmen' would be ped-

dling at the gates of heaven: 'Peaches for lumber, two bits for a few. Come out to de wagon, I taste-ee for you!'

Time marching on, but the dreams of the past going with it. Some day the pioneers who had lived and loved and fought would all be nothing more than names carved on stones for curious children to read, sprinkle idly with flowers ... and dash shouting on by. Someday her house would be dust ... but she knew with a sureness like a loved handclasp that above the dust there would still be a pulsing in the air on bright moonlit nights — the remembered throb of a heart.

Erastus came, with his kind old eyes and little familiar grimace ... and suddenly his quiet voice rang with a queer prophetic power. He was not Erastus any longer, he was Brother Brigham, catching her up in his strange and mystic spell.

All the rivers run into the sea: yet the sea is not full.

Our generation passeth away and another generation cometh: but the earth abideth forever.

The torch was lit, even if it were only a tallow slut. Life would go on ... She saw them, the whole heroic cavalcade, marching toward more deathless stars. And she knew with an ancient exultation (she who had never been farther than Cedar Fort, to be in all the history books!) that she would not have changed a moment of it. Tomahawk and war whoop, bran mush and lucerne greens, Virgin bloat, the Year of the Plagues, the Reign of Terror. She felt a detached pity for the generations yet to come who couldn't plan and build a world. *Here*, she cried, reaching her bandaged hands across the years, *here it is: the Land of the Unlocked Door* ...

But here was Jimmie, with his eyes full of tears (such silly things, tears!) — her hostage to the future. She saw him strong and unafraid, wide-shouldered to carry the Dream. Each generation with its desert to cross ... but one must make an effort to tell them that there are always the Joshua trees, if poor stumbling humans will but lift up their eyes ... Always the Joshua trees, pointing toward the Promised Land.

Shake off the encompassing mists, make the voice gay (Jimmie always loved gaiety!) ... 'You know how boys *are!* ... This I would say to you, my children: "Love much and laugh more, at yourselves if nothing better ..."'

And now there is no more time. Already the radiance is trembling on the horizon, the flushed light leans down from the west, the Great Smile beckons. And suddenly, with the shock of a thousand exploding light-balls, she recognizes the Great Smile at last. That which she had searched for all her life had been right there in her heart all the time. She, Clorinda MacIntyre, had a testimony! ...

'Jimmie,' she said very clearly and distinctly, 'will you see that my fingernails look nice? Sometimes the women neglect fingernails.'

THE END

BIBLIOGRAPHY

Deseret News. Two bound volumes, 1856 and 1858, and other issues.

The Tribune. Miscellaneous issues.

Washington County News: June 25, July 16, September 3, 1936; July 2, 23, 30, 1936; August 6, 1936; July 8, December 2, 1937; January 6, 1938.

Reminiscences of Early Utah, by R. N. Bascomb.

Historic Dress in America, by Elizabeth McCallan.

John D. Lee, by Charles Kelly.

Zealots of Zion, by Hoffman Birney.

History of Utah, by Hubert H. Bancroft.

The Early Far West, by W. J. Ghent.

Story of the Mormons, by William Alexander Lynn.

Pioneers and Prominent Men of Utah, by Frank Esshom.

Utah State Historical Quarterlies.

Utah, the Land of Blossoming Valleys, by George W. James.

A Comprehensive History of the Church, by B. H. Roberts.

The Fourth Reader. Salem Town, 1842.

Fourth Grade Reader, by Mark H. Newman, 1845.

Davies' Intellectual Arithmetic, by A. S. Barnes, 1863.

Pinneo's Analytical Grammar, 1859.

Prose and Poetry, by Emily B. Spencer, 1880.

History of the Church, Period One, by Joseph Smith.

Concordance of the Book of Mormon.

Wilford Woodruff, by Mathias W. Cowley.

Narrative of the Exploring Expedition to the Rocky Mountains in the Year 1842, by Captain J. C. Fremont.

The Prairie Traveller, by Captain Marcy, 1859.

The Tragic Era, by Claude Bowers.

Thomas Paine, by Elbert Hubbard.

New American History, by W. E. Woodward.

Brigham Young, by M. R. Werner.

Brigham Young and His Mormon Empire, by Frank J. Cannon and George L. Knapp.

Age of Reason, by Thomas Paine.

Day by Day with the Utah Pioneers of 1847.

Book of Mormon.

The Bible.

The Doctrine and Covenants.

The Pearl of Great Price.

Journal of Discourses, by Brigham Young.

Church Chronology, by Andrew Jenson.

Articles of Faith, by James E. Talmage.

Medical Aspects of the L.D.S. Word of Wisdom, by L. Weston Oaks.

Scrap Book of Mormon Literature, published by Ben E. Rich.

Joseph Smith, An American Prophet, by John Henry Evans.

March of the Mormon Battalion, by Frank Alfred Golder.

Memoirs of John R. Young, Utah Pioneer of 1847.

The Wonderlands of the Wild West, by A. B. Carlton.

Mormon Settlement in Arizona, by James H. McClintock.

Life and Travels of Parley P. Pratt.

The Women of Mormondom, by Edward W. Tullidge.

Poems, by E. R. Snow.

Case Against Mormonism, by Robert C. Webb.

Various volumes of the *Progressive Reference Library, The New Universal Encyclopedia, The New International Encyclopedia.*

History of the Utah Volunteers in the Spanish American War, by A. Prentiss, editor.

Knowing Yourself and Others, by Donald McLean.

Utah and the Nation, by Leland Creer.

Joseph Smith and His Mormon Empire, by Harry M. Beardsley.

An Expedition to the Valley of the Great Salt Lake, 1849, by Captain H. Stansbury.

Life Story of Brigham Young, by Susa Y. Gates and Leah D. Widtsoe.

William Clayton's Journal.

The Utah Expedition. Letters of Captain Jesse A. Gove, edited by New Hampshire Historical Society.

Indian Studies, by Albert Reagan. Utah Academy of Sciences, vol. 12.

Natural History of the Great Basin, by Vasco M. Tanner, vol. 1, 1940.

Representative Women of Deseret, by Augusta Joyce Crocheron.

Dressing the Part, by F. P. Walkup.

Costume Throughout the Ages, by Mary Evans.

Western Wild Flowers, by Charles Francis Saunders.

PAMPHLETS AND MAGAZINES

Bound volumes of *Harper's Magazine* for 1860.

United States Department of Agriculture, Bulletin No. 124.

About one hundred diaries and biographies of the WPA Federal Writers' Project.

Women's Style Catalogue of the year 1800.
Woman's Exponent, 1896.
The Ladies' Standard Magazine, June, 1897.
Relief Society Magazine. Several bound volumes.
Improvement Era. Miscellaneous volumes.
Numerous early records of the city of St. George.